WHISPERS
FROM THE
CARIBBEAN

Afro-American Culture and Society Series
Volume 11

WHISPERS
FROM THE
CARIBBEAN

I Going Away, I Going Home

WILFRED
CARTEY

Center for Afro-American Studies, University of California, Los Angeles

Library of Congress Cataloging in Publication Data

Cartey, Wilfred G., 1931–
    Whispers from the Caribbean: I going away, I going home / by Wilfred Cartey.
        p. cm. [Afro-American culture and society, ISSN 0882–5297; v. 11]
    Includes bibliographical references and index.
    ISBN 0–934934–35–5; ISBN 0–934934–36–3 (pbk.)
    1. Caribbean fiction (English)—History and criticism. I. Title.
PR9205.4.C38 1991   91–15641
813.009′9729—dc20

Center for Afro-American Studies
University of California, Los Angeles

Library of Congress Catalog Card Number: 91–15641
ISBN: 0–934934–35–5
    0–934934–36–3 (pbk)
ISSN: 0882–5297
Printed in the United States of America

Cover art by Carlos Spivey
Text typography by Malcolm Litchfield

That night when I left you on the bridge
I bent down
kneeling on my knee
and pressed my ear to listen to the land.

I bent down
listening to the land
but all I heard was tongueless whispering.

On my right hand was the sea behind the wall
the sea that has no business in the forest
and I bent down
listening to the land
and all I heard was tongueless whispering
as if some buried slave wanted to speak again.

Martin Carter, "Listening to the Land,"
Poems of Succession

CONTENTS

And what is of the world
is of ours
to draw on
to build from
and no one has the patrimony
of the power of the world
we are not artifacts
of mastodons
and never must be
we must root ourselves
within the singing blue mists
of our mountains
indigenizing
all our waters
we must flow within the amber crystals
of our dreams
we must sing
beholden to the singing
of our lands
our rivers

beholden to our flowing dreams
beholden not to mastodons
and finding our way
to cross the rivers
we must find
that ultimate geology
within the mist of blue
within the hills of Mona
and find our dreams
within ourselves
together
and

to the sea
will flow
eight rivers
pure and free
and our children
sommersault
into their dreams

Wilfred Cartey, *Embryos*

.

ACKNOWLEDGMENTS

To the Center for Afro-American Studies for coordinating the project, with special reference to Claudia Mitchell-Kernan, who was the Center's director when the work was initiated. To the Center's Mona Dallas Merideth and Jacqueline Tasch for their continuing efforts to achieve editorial perfection. To the Research Institute for the Study of Man for its ever-generous assistance over many years, and especially to Professor Lambros Comitas, Judith Selakoff, June Anderson, and Yvonne Jilkes. To the Research Foundation of the City University of New York for its PSC/CUNY Research Award, and above all to Brenda Newman for her ready and able facilitation of that grant's administration. To the Trinidad and Tobago Public Library with special reference to Lynette Comissiong.

To generous research assistants Jennifer Radtke, Jennifer Beaumont, Michelle Fried, Linda Jean, Rosita Sands, Edissa Weekes. To Professor Jerome Brooks for his scholarly foresight and vision, and for his meticulous attention to the text. To my brother, Sam Cartey, for his unswerving support and encouragement. To Anna Winand for her continuing facility in capturing me in my many moods. To the many authors who, with spontaneous generosity, granted me permission to use quoted material from their work. To Toyomi Igus, without whose help this manuscript may have remained but a whisper.

The Caribbean has its own spirit force and energy, rich with its own problematic possibilities and dreams, intoning ever its own singing presence and marvel—there, where there is bitter fruit and sweetness, space that's ever evolving, fragmenting, cohering, but moving always toward its own ritual, dynamic unfolding, I say thanks.

INTRODUCTION

As in *Whispers from a Continent*, published by Random House in 1968, the purpose of *Whispers from the Caribbean* is to design an esthetic paradigm within which to study Caribbean novels written in English, and by extension to locate Caribbean consciousness. The book's objectives are:

to explore and mold a socio-esthetic analysis of the writings of English-speaking novelists in the Caribbean by the study and analysis of approximately seventy novels.

to investigate the interrelationships, the correspondences and parallels, both thematic and stylistic, among Caribbean novels.

to search for the individual essence of each of the writings.

to establish a political, historical, and cultural continuity.

to note and to signify images that are characteristic not only of the Caribbean area, but that are also related to the African images in *Whispers from a Continent*.

The larger intention is to depict through the analysis of character and image the consciousness that is manifested in the novels and that is particular to the Caribbean area.

In a special way the world intersects at these islands, for one cannot speak of them meaningfully without speaking at once of Africa, Asia, Europe, and America. At this point of intersection, Caribbean personality has derived from the symbiotic intermingling of all of these cultural rootings, from the history of servitude and freedom, of domination and the quest for self.

Whispers from the Caribbean is divided into two parts, "*I Going Away:* The Shaping of the Caribbean Personality," and "*I Going Home:* The Evolution of the Caribbean Presence." The paradigmatic construct, then, is the movement from personality to the attainment of presence. *Personality* as used here is a historical term; it evokes the person as affected by the combined forces of colonialism, of economics, of historical imperialism and Great Power rivalry. *Presence* is a cultural or spiritual term; it suggests the person in his own spiritual interiority, his selfhood as bestowed on him by his own people, their values, their worldview, their mores. Both *personality* and *presence* are in a constant state of tension and interaction.

Our premise is that through a transformative vision, the personality will fragment itself, discarding any of the oppressive historical conditions which have negated the possibility that the individual or the people might achieve a holistic presence and society. Thus in Part One, the constant preoccupation is to locate and discuss these negating conditions. In Part Two, the focus shifts to those images, those circumstances, which bring about the necessary transformation from Caribbean personality to Caribbean presence.

The study, then, is a search for cultural patterns in literature: the folk evolving into a socially cohesive community through a pattern of fragmentation, a "going away"; a breaking away from disjunctional sociopolitical forces; then a "going home" to a possible new fusion of elements. In this fusion we seek prescriptions for a cohering social reality, unified by a dynamic indigenizing of social, cultural, and political elements, an indigenizing with its prognosis of a holistic Caribbean society.

As in *Whispers from a Continent*, in which the larger structural design was built on two countermotions—the movement away and the movement back—so, too, in *Whispers from the Caribbean* the larger structural formulation incorporates and suggests two movements patterned on the evolution of a Caribbean social consciousness. How the novelists see this social consciousness, how they perceive its evolution, supports this countermotion, giving rise to the formulation, "I going away, I going home."

The novelistic images central to Chapter 1, "Rhythm of Man and Landscape: The Mixings," show the parallel vibrations of landscape and history, of phenomena and passions, of atmosphere and emotion. The physical phenomena of the Caribbean area—the sea islands and the mainland of Guyana; the waters of the sea, the rivers, the creeks; the jungles and forests, the insects and animals, the heat and the storms—form the backdrop upon which the history of the Caribbean area plays itself out.

The harmonious rhythm of the land of the Amerindians was acted upon by various European colonizers, who introduced the plantation system and the use of Africans as slaves. Violence, racial admixture, and the development of class and caste distinctions were the results of this foreign imposition. This was heightened by the later import of Asians and East Indians as laborers, bringing two more peoples to the chronology of blood of Caribbean society.

Yet the land is alive and takes on psychic qualities. The land affects and is affected by the various peoples and admixtures of blood of the countries of the Caribbean. All of these elements fuse to provide theme and motif for Chapter 1.

Chapter 2 describes "The Rituals of the Folk: The Crossing of Rhythms." The style of village life which has evolved since the end of slavery and indentured labor in many instances reflects what has been retained by African and Asian peoples of their previous cultures. The ritualism and communality of life, the amalgam of beliefs among the back-yard folk—*obeah*, Hindu practices, and revivalism—coupled with the bittersweet quality of rural folk living, the tragicomedy, are captured in the novels of this chapter. Here we witness the growth of some writers from childhood to adulthood, their retention of colonial values, and their subsequent rejection of the imposed value system.

In the movement away from the village, its bittersweet life and the certainty of ritual growth, everyone undergoes changes as they encounter the evolving urban reality. The results of this encounter are explored in Chapter 3, entitled "Entrapment and Flight" to designate its predominant metaphors.

The gentle harmonies and strident cacophonies of urban life—the dance and laughter of the poor struggling for existence, yet with an intrinsic sense of belonging to the squalor of their cities—are played out in these novels, which capture the harshness of slum living, of overcrowded urban areas, which tell of the hopes and fears and joys, which narrate the shifting amorphous living.

The novels of Chapter 4, "The Fragmented Reality: The Separated People," analyze the social fragmentation consequent on the effects of race, class, color, and sex differentiations—differentiations that make for fragmented personalities, often leading to a feeling of alienation, aloneness, and discontinuous living. Here, as characters grope for the meaning of their lives, the central images are of barriers, separation, and alienation.

Layers of Caribbean society are painted in their varying colors. These novels show evidence of the values of a middle class still saturated with prevailing European value systems, the social hierarchy of color and class, and the intricately textured movements of a multiracial society. The novels depict a system of education which leads to estrangement from the ritual of the folk and the rhythm of the land, yet provides an impetus for the eventual movement to independence through the politics of the middle class.

Many leave; the less educated, unskilled, the semiskilled, even professionals—writers, teachers, nurses—flee in numbers. Paradoxically many flee to their erstwhile mother country, England, in search of work, glamor (of which they have been told), success, and adventure. Some go to the United States and Canada for similar reasons, while a few search for their roots in Africa. In Chapter 5, "I Going Away: The Exiled Ones," the novels tell of the flight of those self-exiled to the cold northern areas where they live among alien whites, their awareness awakened to the meaning of living in the Caribbean lands, and their nostalgic recalling of that living. Yet the characters here experience the tragedy of their inability to return to that Caribbean living without having "succeeded."

As we move into Part Two, "*I Going Home:* An Evolution of the Caribbean Presence," the notion of "away" and images of movement out are replaced by images of return to an indigenous culture. The novels of Chapter 6, "The Search for Polity: The Fashioning of Dream," treat the search for new political realities within the Caribbean—the coming of independence and the problems attendant on that. It is a time of excitement, of hope, yet a time of groping and of doubt.

The characters are shaping their own indigenous polity. Perhaps the fragmentation of the personality has taken place. The characters are more Caribbean, with all of its problematic possibilities, with all of its prognosis for dream. The shift here is from the miscegenation of Part One to suggest a creolization of peoples, an indigenization of their culture.

No longer being acted upon by history and no longer entrapped within the confinements of layered society, certain individuals act out of their heritage and are capable of responsible, positive action whereby they create their own essence, forge a new communality. The novels of Chapter 7, "The Rootings of Self: The Adventure of Communality, The Shape of Myth," show how, by so doing, they attempt to make the Caribbean a truly free and vibrant land, where man is in tune with landscape, where landscape is no longer simply historical but takes on the qualities of the extra-historical, the mythic.

Yet so recent is the season of adventure of Caribbean peoples that the promise of coherence and the hope of wholeness will only respond to a transformative vision.

PART ONE

I Going Away:
The Shaping of the Caribbean Personality

CHAPTER 1

Rhythm of Man and Landscape:
The Mixings

Lands open
To sunshine and sky
And to the endless winds
Passing their eternal rounds.
Lands that hold in their bosom
Space like a benediction.
Lands smoky with their dreams
That drift across the world
Like memories of ancient beauty dimly recalled
Lands full of the music of birds
Crying softly a vague and formless meditation . . .

Wilson Harris, "Savannah Lands,"
Kyk-Over-Al Anthology of Guianese Poetry

In a half-twilight world, the already mixed-caste woman, Kaywana, Old Water, is bedded by a Dutch adventurer:

> It was about an hour past noon when he followed her into the jungle. The sky did not have a cloud, but no sunshine penetrated the tangled foliage overhead. The air stood still amid the tree-trunks and the vines and the fallen palms; you could feel it like a humid cobweb around you. A brown twilight pervaded everything, and the silence pressed down, warm and damp and alive; now and then it seemed to lick your cheek.
>
> Their feet made no sound, for the ground was covered with thick layers of moist leaves—decades, perhaps a century, of fallen leaves. A yielding, spongy carpet. (Mittelholzer, *Children of Kaywana*, 11)

And so, landscape, man, and history, from the very beginning of the Kaywana trilogy, merge together, a creative act on an axis, both horizontal and vertical, gazed on by a reptile which is of time present, time past, and time to come:

> A lizard made a dry rustling as it wriggled from one twig to another, moving over the dry fronds on which they lay. They watched the twig, silent, and after a moment saw it appear again, black and shiny . . . . A suspension of time linked it with them and with the silence around them and with time travelling over the earth; time gone and time to come. (14)

The earth there with its strata of fallen leaves is of no time, but of all time— damp and alive, secure from the heat of the sun, receptive to human forms. Thus from the very beginning Edgar Mittelholzer sets up the interplay between landscape and human form, the connecting vibrations between biology and biography, which form the essence of the Kaywana trilogy.

But the sense of landscape and landscaped history does not ordain only Mittelholzer's writing; since Caribbean man is affected by the force of the elements and the power of his surroundings, landscape enters the writings of all Caribbean authors. Thus often images are earth images, redolent with smell and heavy with sap. Time, which hangs suspended, is cut, and the earth on which Old Water lies with her lover quivers. For a historical interruption—so much a part of the settlement of the Caribbean by European powers, in this case, the Spanish—even as it makes Kaywana for the first time doubt the power of her earth and her instinctive relationship with her landscape, destroys her Dutch adventurer-lover:

> He put on his clothes in a hurry and said that he must go. "I've got to go now, Kaywana. Now. I can't wait."
> He squeezed her arm briefly and hurried off.
> She moved after him—but slowly, not trying to overtake him.

The jungle quivered again. She could feel the sound deep in the earth—beneath the thick, moist layers of leaves under her feet. It gave her a feeling of insecurity. She distrusted the earth; for the first time in her life she felt that the ground on which she walked might betray her. (14–15)

Precise historical data fuse with landscaped history and together they control and direct the course of the van Groenwegel family, whose emotional and spiritual genealogy, crisscrossing, branches out to form the Kaywana trilogy. Like the fallen leaves of the jungle the trilogy enumerates a layered piling-up of the lives of this family, stretches across decades, perhaps centuries, and portrays the family's arching rise, its growth, and its ultimate decay. Each age reveals a distinct, at times dual personality: the fire-blood actor or the painter-dreamer; contrasting tugs which pull the family across centuries to a re-creation of permanent human history. A second coming takes place with the union of Adriansen and Kaywana; Adriansen, strong, commanding, cunning Dutch adventurer, and Old Water, the first-blood. The union does not take place in the jungle as did that between August and Kaywana. Yet, the jungle, as it does throughout the trilogy, pervades the atmosphere. The union takes place within a house, not outside, for it is the beginning of the household of Kaywana's descendants. Here there is no "humid cobweb" (11), no dampness, no heat; only cool, mild, water vapor. Yet the union is passionate, and the jungle is ever present:

> The air this afternoon was mild and water-vapourish, and the trade-wind could be heard humming around the building, cool and evening-chilled with the scent of the jungle in it. The tobacco plants kept rustling with a far-off, mysterious peace . . . .
> He moved in the chair, and his grip on her arm tightened. He pressed his face against her belly and began to caress her breasts—with urgency, his face in a glow of blood and his limbs in a tremor. He took her desperately, the sunshine scarlet on their struggles. (22–23)

And so begin the children of Kaywana, whose six generations sweep across the first book of the trilogy.

The second book of Mittelholzer's trilogy, *The Harrowing of Hubertus*, opens with the imminence of slave rebellions. It is the "era which began with thunder" (131); it is the time of Hubertus's harrowing, heralded by insect noises and conjured up by the ever-pervading jungle smell. As so often in the Kaywana trilogy, consummation of love, of desire, is set against, and indeed often arises from, a densely landscaped backdrop, evocative with sounds, heavy with sensuousness: a lush landscape which conjures up mystery or magic and goading instinct, rips bare a residue of repressed desire. And in the insect night, with desire uncovered, Hubertus's harrowing begins. Subverted by desire, his controlled conjugal fidelity to Rosalind breaks down and he yields to the more passionate Faustina:

> The night-time insects had commenced their shrill fluting, and the air seemed to quiver around them as though the several screeching choruses were intricate veils, each interweaving with the other in a delicate, invisible dance—a dance executed against the low, richer background of frog noises; the croaking of big ugly males and the tinkling chirrup of the tiny tree-frogs. The damp, leafy smell of the jungle seeped into their senses, and of a sudden the first questioning cry of a goatsucker sounded far away amidst the trees, a lonely magical call. Time-destroying. This might have been an evening on the Berbice—or on the Essequibo. (*Hubertus*, 61)

Of paramount importance here is the symbolic content of the act, an act which shows that a battle between desire and will and an eventual triumph of the former over the latter is of no specific time—is, in fact, "time-destroying"—nor is it circumscribed by any particular region. Yet, ubiquitous as it seems (it "might have been an evening on the Berbice—or on the Essequibo") the act contained within the riverwater image takes place as before on "the soppy carpet of century-piled leaves" (95). It is a single act but one heavy with dramatic overtones, fraught with doubts and the questioning cry of a lonely goatsucker (perhaps that of Rosalind), an act charged with tensions. The landscape is no passive observer, but forewarns them of the problematic entanglements and ensuing internal conflict:

> The heat swirled across her thoughts like purposeful tentacles determined to put doubt upon any attempt at mental activity. It seemed to twine up from the path with the sole intent to entangle, confute, and then strangle whatever came within its sphere of intense endeavor. Each tick and crackle of a dry-leaf under their feet might have been the birth of a new tentacle that in a minute would burn upward to twirl some unknown tension about them. (70)

And so the members of the van Groenwegel family move through the trilogy, alternating strong-weak figures, actor-dreamer people, instinct-guided or will-directed characters. Bequeathed with one or another of these alternating character traits, often torn by their conflicting pulls, but always conscious of their fire-blood and the necessity to preserve its power, the van Groenwegel family runs its way to ruin. All the descendants of the children of Kaywana are dispersed; the call of the Kaywana blood stifled and drowned. From the hot-sun twilight world of Kaywana's first bedding to the falling dusk and gathering twilight, across the history of plantation slavery, the van

Groenwegel family runs its own history, its own course. Even as slave plantations decline and the history of slavery comes to a close, so too the history of this family, masters of many slave plantations, ends. And as the tale of this family is ended in the third book of the trilogy, *Kaywana Blood*, the line of Old Water runs out in the creek and flows away:

> The tide was on the point of turning, and the water was wrinkled with little whirlpools. Leaves kept moving in circles here and there, and *missouri* grass had grown stationary in midstream, like little islands awaiting orders from some unseen geographer. Dusk was falling rapidly, and along the banks fire-flies winked palely amidst the *mucca-mucca* stalks. . . . they seemed evil eyes . . . panicked messages—messages of death and the crumbling of the world. (Mittelholzer, *Kaywana Blood*, 466).

And though Mittelholzer, the unseen geographer, has signaled the twilight of the van Groenwegel family and brought its line to an end, yet, through an evocative telescoping of the landscape, the same geographer gives a sense of duration to the family's history and a permanence, indeed, an immediacy to the past. The family disintegrates, but, in fact, cannot die because the landscape lives on and continues. Time, space, history link together and stretch out, establishing continuity, creating traditions and links in the Guyana landscape. Leaves fall and die and pile up; characters pass away and the dead pile up. Yet, the geographer makes the cycle of birth and death continuous, both in landscape and family:

> Around them rose the scent of dried leaves and rank herbs—leaves that had fallen and dried and rotted during the past decades. Leaves on which rain had been dripping since the time of Kaywana and Adriansen. But the shrubs were new—of the past year or two, or less. By next year they would be dead and others would have sprung up. The leaves remained, however, piling thicker and thicker, the new dead ones pressing down the old dead ones. . . . (*Children*, 146)

The unseen geographer imbues all elements, all phenomena—their corresponding colors, their particular smells—with the power of recall: the rain, the leaves, the moonlight, the wild flowers, and the river:

> [Laurens] saw the river, choppy and shimmering in the bright mid-morning sunshine—the river, his grandmother Kaywana, had heard whispering in hushed monotony on many a night when she lay alone in the big four-poster in a room in the old house on the mainland.
>
> A soft land-breeze came in. It smelt of the jungle, chilly and with a suggestion of old leaves in it. A suggestion of wild flowers, too—perhaps the large purplish ones on the mainland that bloomed on the tangled

vines which covered the patch of earth under which the bones of Kaywana and her children lay. (58)

Here Mittelholzer gives deep signification to his cyclical interpretation of
history, for the children of Kaywana are all the peoples of Guyana, a mixed
race of Amerindian and European, of African and Asiatic. Like the leaves,
which die and press down on older dead leaves but sprout again in a
continuous cycle, so too the children of Kaywana continue through space and
time; their acts of love unfold in places which re-create the past and recall
the beginnings of the many different children of Kaywana. Here, descendant
of slave, Katrina, and descendant of slave owner, Laurens, continue the
miscegenation begun with Kaywana and Adriansen:

> Katrina bent over him and kissed his forehead and his hair and then
> his lips. There was moonlight on his face. A waning half-moon had risen
> over Kyk-over-al. The same half-moon Kaywana had seen. In this same
> room. (128)

The visual permanence with which Mittelholzer imbues his landscape
creates a genealogical link binding together the children of Kaywana. And
though each descendant is particularized, his actions and gestures, placed
within oft-repeated and similar contexts, become carriers of the family
traditions, as permanent as the earth. The moonlight over Kyk-over-al pulls
the past into the present, giving an immediacy to Kaywana's past actions and
immortalizing her presence. She is the mother of the line of children. And
all things flowing backward through memory and springing from an identical
force are unchanging, appearing always the same. Thus, through landscape,
whether it be peaceful or violent, Kaywana can never be forgotten for she
lives in the memory of her children:

> Some days there would be a gale on the Essequibo. High wind with
> slanting rain rushing over the bush and the choppy water. It would go
> swooping up the Mazaruni, and when Laurens looked across at Kyk-over-
> al he would see it like a frayed monster sleeping mysteriously in the river,
> hazed but unheedful of the pelting moisture . . . . Grandmother, thought
> Laurens, must have seen it often like this. Perhaps she used to stand at
> this very window looking out, as I am doing now, and feeling lonely. (97)

However, paradoxically, landscape—the rhythm of the seasons—tells of the
passage of time, a recurrent motif which runs through most of Mittelholzer's
writings. Through this motif all phenomena become cyclical; space is
unending, and the elements of Kyk-over-al timeless:

> It clouded over and rain began to fall, then it cleared and sunshine
> glittered on the greens of the jungle. Last year, the year before, and the

year before, the rain and the sun had done just the same as they were doing to-day. And next year, and the year after, and the year after, it would be the same with the rain and the sun. And the trees. (*Hubertus*, 57)

Yet, an ever-changing social order evolves against this backdrop of the continuous cycle of elements and phenomena. Natural phenomena, land-scape, provide the essential backdrop to the evolution of the social order. Indeed, when contrasted with the evolving social order, landscape actually becomes the essential foreground, its permanence heightened by its juxtapo-sition to the impermanence and flux of that social order. Further, the history Mittelholzer treats, which is the accumulation of that social order in its totality—in this instance, the rise and fall of a plantocracy, the course of slavery, and the decline of the plantation system—has duration. And the sense of historical duration is highlighted by the transitory nature of its single events. Like landscape and history, the tradition of the van Groen-wegel family—that is, the accumulation of the biographies and lives of that family—also has its own abiding influence, an influence which may be destructive to individual members of that family, but in itself seems indestructible. Reaction to family tradition becomes the catalytic agent for actions and dreams of most of the characters of the trilogy. For instance, here, late in the family history, a descendant of Kaywana, Dirk,

grunted and kicked a dry *awara* seed that happened in his path at the moment. An *awara* seed sucked and scraped clean of the bright yellow pulp, sticky and stringy, that had once covered it. He grinned briefly, remembering the many *awara* and *cookerit* palms Jacob and himself had raided, and the many feasts they had had sitting on the bank of the canal aback . . . . But this is August, 1816. I'm a married man, and Jacob is getting married in November. Time, by God! Time hacks away at the past, chops down all your green and cherished escapades. But it builds up, too. Yes, Time builds up. There's the sawmill. There's the plantation I mean to turn into the most compact and most profitable sugar-plantation in Berbice. There's the timber grant upriver. And there's, last but most vital and cherished, my dear beloved. My tall, sturdy, mysterious wife. And soon there'll be our sons. The new van Groenwegels to take the Old Blood to the pinnacles! (*Blood*, 218–219)

And so, across the chronology of Guyanese history, the Kaywana trilogy pivots on tradition, as the goad to character action, and on landscape, as the reflector of emotions and sensibilities. For all Mittelholzer's characters, landscape is vital, almost becoming their pulsebeat. Jacques, the grandson of Kaywana, says:

"Do you hear that? A goatsucker. Amelia, you won't ever know how much
that bird means to me. This is my terrain. The bird sounds and the
smells of the shrubs and the grass and the earth." (*Children*, 494)

And:

in Hubertus, there was a great love of trees. Of trees and of all things that
grew from the soil. (*Hubertus*, 15)

Not only are characters infused with rhythms of the earth, but all things
are charged with its sights, sounds, and smells. And thus Mittelholzer, the
novelistic geographer of Guyana, of necessity paints, in his impressionistic
strokes, the landscape of Guyana in its many varying moods, for the moods
of the Caribbean area are so varied, so changing, and often so emotionally
volatile. Mittelholzer, the landscape artist, quickly captures the fullness of
a soft day, gently brush-strokes the cool, damp coming of a rainy season, and
in the multidimensional canvas evokes sights and sounds, smells and colors.

And in the composite of man and landscape which is the Kaywana trilogy,
even as the characters vary between weak-strong, so, too, landscape alter-
nates between soft-hard, gentle-threatening. In Mittelholzer's composite, the
strong characters prevail and control. Similarly, the landscape possesses a
dramatic strength, a power, at times, even a threat:

Lightning still flashed in the south. She heard thunder—low, faint, a
portentous mumbling over the mysterious distant jungle. The jungle
through which snakes and strange wild creatures moved. The rain must
be hurling itself down in savage drops through the trees, and the lightning must be slicing giant *mora* trees in half, or splitting them down the
middle. The thunder must be one continuous clatter of noise. (*Children*,
48).

Here, Kaywana, pure-water, fire-water, half-caste Indian woman, steeped in
the law of her land, does not run, a quality—that of not running—which
becomes the strong point and the motto of the van Groenwegel family
tradition. In cutting images, the unleashed violence of the jungle, indeed at
times of much of the Caribbean landscape, makes Kaywana recall the
beginnings of her many children. Rain, lightning, thunder, creek water,
jungle—all the lushness of the landscape in which Mittelholzer revels—often
become representative of the members of that family, often mirror the states
of mind of that family and at times reflect the death of its members.
Kaywana's death struggle is crisscrossed by the interplay of moonlight and
blood:

Kaywana was fighting savagely. Once the moonlight struck full on her
face, and her eyes glinted with a terrible hate . . .

> . . . Kaywana bled from her nose and from her mouth. The moonlight
> kept flashing on and off her face. (54–55)

And the river's hush tells of the passage of pure Old Water.

And so, in a scene as savage as that of the violent jungle thunderstorm
with its slashing, crashing, hurling, and splitting, Kaywana is killed, as she
and her children fight ferociously against attacking members of her very own
Indian peoples. It is her Indian blood, however, her fire-blood, which has
injected courage and fierceness into her children. And even though the
source of her Indian blood has been steadily drained—as her ancestors and
family were sold into slavery and destroyed by the exploitation of cunning,
scheming European settlers such as Kaywana's common-law husband,
Adriansen—her blood will continue to flow in the veins of her children and
her children's children. In fact, Kaywana herself is not really a character, for
we know little about her. She is rather a symbolic continuity, blood persistence, the engenderer of natural passion and strength. Thus many of her
children become executors of the family tradition and actors of its motto:
"No van Groenwegel must ever run from an enemy" (72). And so begins the
whole genetic interplay of the pull of the blood.

In the trilogy, Mittelholzer seems to ascribe certain definite characteristics
to differing national, racial stocks. And Kaywana's Indian fire-blood, nurturing fierce strength and natural passions in those of her children where it is
dominant, becomes an all-controlling force. Indeed, in such characters, the
fire-blood becomes the single, pervasive, dominant force which controls all
their actions and reactions, emotions and ideas. For weakness is to be
shunned and strength admired and preserved.

Willem, one of the sons of Kaywana and Adriansen, preserving the
strength of both his passionate, fierce mother and of his cunning, scheming
father, instills the tradition in his children, Kaywana's grandchildren:

> "It's blood that counts. . . . Blood. Men can say that we're van Groen-
> wegels with the bar sinister. Let them say it. Not a mortal can drain the
> blood of that old man from my veins—or the veins of my children. What
> was in my father is in me and in mine. Ha! And my mother! Who can
> take her blood from me? Who can rob me of the fire she put into me? My
> mother was a fighter. Do you know what it is to have a mother who can
> stand up with her sons and fight to the death?" (61)

Indeed Willem's character, like many another protagonist in the trilogy,
receives a sculpted definition from his insistence on strength, force, and
power. His gestures and his actions are fired by one thought, that of the
dynamic strength of his mother's blood; his ideas are willed by Kaywana's
dramatic resistance and death. It is obvious, then, that the past becomes an

insistent gong, extolling and reverberating with Kaywana's heroic defense. And for Willem, any situation which calls for physical courage, taking him back to his own childhood, demands the show of a courage equal to that of his mother, Kaywana:

> "Fire!" called Willem, "Fire on them!" His voice shook with excitement, and a vivid picture of himself in a nightshirt arose in his fancy. It was as though the past had miraculously surged into being once again. He was ten, and his mother was directing operations. (81)

Thus it is that Mittelholzer carries the history of the van Groenwegel family along a vertical axis whose pendulum moves from present to past, from past to future. Willem's urging his children to fight takes place in 1666. In the second decade of the nineteenth century, Dirk, one of Kaywana's great-great-grandchildren in *Kaywana Blood*, accepting the family history, swings back to the earliest beginnings of the van Groenwegel family tradition to shape his actions and beliefs:

> "They all say I'm obsessed with this family pride of mine. But I can't help dreaming of the future—I can't help remembering the past." (*Blood*, 132)

And since again in Mittelholzer there is an insistent dialogue of biography and the elements, of man and landscape, so the sandbox tree resurrects a sense of Kaywana's strength, the single most important catalytic goad to Willem's character:

> Willem looked at the sandbox trees again. A deep calm came upon him. He felt big and confident and stable; unshakable. He felt like his mother. He tried to throw his mind back to that night when he was ten, and the blood began to move up through his chest as though it were a scarf reaching for his head. He felt suddenly dizzy with pride at the memory of the past. (*Children*, 77)

For Willem, family pride and the strength of the fire-blood must never be lost; indeed it should always be drummed into the minds, into the very bloodstreams, of his children, and of all the children of Adriansen and Kaywana. Here Mittelholzer seems almost to postulate a sense of genetic breeding: Willem attempts to inculcate his own passion, his idea of honor and power, his pride in the van Groenwegel family tradition, into Laurens, the son who seems to have inherited the fire-blood:

> ".... there's Laurens. I have hope for that boy. . . . I must consolidate him. He won't let me down. He'll take our name far, and take it with

honour and power. I'll keep on drumming that into them. Honour and power. Fire-blood." (96)

At times, then, the desire to perpetuate the fire-blood and its attendant qualities becomes obsessive, and sequentially the attempt to curtail another inherited genetic trait, painter-dreamer-weakness, not only becomes obsessive but provides for the essential problematic tension of many of Mittelholzer's characters in the trilogy. For Mittelholzer constructs his characters along weak-strong lines, along faults which reveal rifts and uncontrollable explosive emotions. Indeed, in *Children of Kaywana*, Hendrickje, one of Mittelholzer's strong female characters, pushes the question of strong-weak into the realm of ethics and morality:

> "I dread to think what these children are going to be like when they grow up . . . . Oh, well. Better dissolute animals than high-thinking dreamers. We've had too many soft-brained van Groenwegels in the past. It's kept down the fire. I want these children to have guts. I want them to live like men and women of iron. They must be ruthless and unscrupulous. They must have no foolish notions about pity and nobility—" (329)

In *Kaywana Blood*, toward the very end of the trilogy, Mary, who has accepted her great-grandmother Hendrickje's ethic of not differentiating between cruelty and strength, between ruthlessness and pity, almost physically and incestuously attempts to keep the van Groenwegel family tradition from dying, to keep the children of Kaywana's fire-blood alive:

> "Grandma Hendri was . . . very cruel . . . . but she was a great old lady in other ways. She was one of the Hard Ones, Adrian—strong like Papa, dear. You must love her."
>
> "Even though she was so cruel?"
>
> "Don't think of her cruelty. Think of her strength. Love her as you love Papa, and think of her as a great van Groenwegel . . . ."
>
> "You love Papa very much, don't you?"
>
> "Yes, yes. The same as you do." She shifted nervously, and began to tie the letters together again, her hands shaking slightly. "And the same as I love you, you pestering little boy." She put aside the letters and, with a squealing gasp, caught him to her and hugged him close. "I want you to grow into a fine, strong man like Papa, do you hear me Adrian? Strong, strong. You must never yield to weak, fleshly temptations, my darling brother. Oh, God! Oh, God!" She released him as abruptly as she had gripped him, and began to pace about the room, and he watched her curiously, not surprised for she often behaved in this way. After a while, his eyes narrowed in admiration, and he smiled, and said: "I'll be strong when I grow up, Mary—strong like Papa—and you." (*Blood*, 403)

Mary and her brother, Adrian, are the last generation of the line whose strength of tradition Mary thinks must be perpetuated at all costs. Yet from the very first generation a weak streak has appeared in the character of Aert, which acts as a contrast, a foil, to his brother Willem's strength. Mittelholzer seems to ascribe strength to the characters who act upon or create a situation and weakness to the thinker-dreamers who often are acted upon or who react to the driving force of strong characters. Aert, although he fights courageously against the invading Carib troups, dies clutching books to his bosom, symbolically wounded in his groin and therefore impotent to create the family tradition:

> "The Captain died the following morning of a severe wound in the groin
> . . . . clutching two haversacks of books to his bosom as though they were
> beloved creatures to whom he was greatly attached." (*Children*, 96)

Ultimately, then, Aert's weakness is twofold: his avocation, his love of books, and the physical destruction of his procreative organs.

Yet, for Mittelholzer certain avocations are in themselves a proof of inheritable weakness. One of Willem's sons, Reinald, a dreamer somewhat like Aert, does not, like Sussanah and Laurens, inherit the strength of his paternal grandmother, Kaywana:

> Reinald, at eighteen, was tall and physically not unlike what the dying
> man had been fifty years ago. But the curve of his mouth was weak, and
> his blue eyes were the dreamy, nervous eyes of his mother and his
> maternal grandfather who had been an artist-musician in Hamburg. (57)

Such weakness is scoffed at not only by Willem but by Hendrickje, the single character who seems to have inherited all the forms of strength of her forebears. Hendrickje, the daughter of the union between Laurens and Katrina, a former slave, inherits the cruelty of Kaywana's first son, August, the cunning shrewdness of her great-grandfather Adriansen, and the fire-blood of her Indian great-grandmother, Kaywana. Hendrickje, who is perhaps the central character of the *Children of Kaywana*, not only reflects the passions fused together by the mingling of all these character-blood types, but becomes the refractor of the passions of almost all the other characters in the novel. Conceived in rain and born during a torrential rain, Hendrickje inherits her great-grandmother Kaywana's gray-green eyes, and from the cradle gives off a sense of physical strength:

> Rain was falling when Hendrickje was born . . . . "See that forehead!
> She's got character, Laurens. She's going to be a remarkable woman." He

insisted they should name her after him. Her eyes were blue when she was born, but, eventually, turned gray-green. (138)

Even as a child she jeers at her Uncle Reinald's weakness:

> "I can see it . . . . Uncle Reinald is a lost man."
> "Don't be disrespectful," said Laurens, frowning at her.
> "But it's true, Father. Uncle Reinald isn't alive. He won't bring any glory and honour to the family. That's why he's a lost man." (143)

From her, vitality emanates. Not only has she inherited the personality characteristics of Adriansen and Kaywana, but the maleness and the femaleness of her great-grandparents, as well:

> "You should have been a man, Hendrickje. Yes, by God! You're the personification of old Adriansen and Kaywana. But man or woman, I believe you're going to do big things for us. You have the right spirit." (159)

Hendrickje, Mittelholzer's he-woman, has one driving purpose, that of continuing the family name and the tradition of strength. So compelling is this purpose, that though her various passions are distinctive, though they shift and change, yet in her very stature she seems hewn in one-dimensional strokes. Both the strength of her body and of her spirit are used to perpetuate the family tradition, to carve out a family dynasty:

> "The family, Father. The family, for me, will always come before everything else. I know it's a risk marrying Ignatius. I know there are good chances that we may produce a few weaklings here and there. But I keep trying to convince myself that there will be enough strong ones like me—and yourself and Grandfather and Great-grandfather and Kaywana—to see us through, to take the name down with honour and power, to keep up our motto. I have faith in myself. My spirit is strong, and my body is strong." (178)

For Hendrickje, there is no middle ground: she will create a dynasty or, in the attempt, destroy the family line. Ruthlessly, relentlessly, she pursues her goal; and everyone, anything, may be sacrificed in its attainment:

> "Even now I will not admit defeat. Even now I will not give up my ambitions. I have these two boys, and I shall make them, mould them, into what I want them to be—or break them. I will never surrender . . . ." (228)

And indeed Hendrickje in the unnaturalness of her passion, even as she extends the family dynasty, destroys her own immediate family and her home. The interplay between herself and her son Adrian as she attempts to mold him—her incestuous relationship with him, the fierce passions, quarrels, and fights which at times explode in brutal scenes, her manipulating him into a marriage with someone of fire-blood—becomes one of the pivotal points of the novel, providing it with much of its dramatic tension. The development and course of Adrian's madness is hammered out and traced by Mittelholzer through many scenes, and like Hendrickje, who is dominated by one passion, Adrian, too, becomes obsessed by an equally strong passion, an all-consuming hatred of his mother. Adrian's mental disorder begins in the unnaturalness of his home:

> Something must be the matter with my mind. It isn't natural. But, of course, nothing has been natural in this house. We haven't grown up like other children. (242)

For him, the unnatural home has been created by an unnatural mother: "an absolutely inhuman fiend, a being without tenderness or regard for any living creature, child, slave or acquaintance" (228). And in order to counter the strength of this unnaturalness, the ferocity of his mother, her animality, Adrian reacts equally brutally. And fire-blood turns on itself: "I have fire in me, and it's going to be used against her" (237).

Adrian has seen his brother, Cornelis, driven to homosexuality by Hendrickje; he has seen his father, Ignatius, become a pervert, a masochist, in her brutal sadistic clutches. And determined not to be destroyed, he in turn vows destruction. Adrian's brother, Cornelis, who has been "like a hunted beast" (291), turns against the family and fights on the side of his French lover against the Dutch. Adrian's reaction is more personal. For him, Hendrickje evokes wariness: "Treat her as you would a dangerous snake. That's what she is—a snake. Venomous" (294).

And just as fire-blood breeds fire-blood and violence breeds violence, so too the reptilian qualities which Adrian ascribes to his mother make him equally venomous and reptilian:

> "We've been smiling at each other like that for the past fourteen or fifteen years, but behind our affability we hate and distrust each other like serpents of different varieties . . . ."
> ". . . Since that day when I made her small before the soldier in our ruined house at Fort Nassau we have been like two reptiles waiting to pounce and destroy each other." (290)

Eventually Adrian falls prey to this lurking hatred; his obsession leads to his derangement, which finally ends in madness:

"When I remember what she did to Father, how she made him drown himself—and all she's done to both of us—I tell you, I'm going to be revenged on her. One day I'm going to torture her to death. One day I'm going to stand by and watch her die in a slow-fire. And I'll chop her up piece by piece. I'm going to be a murderer." He began to stammer incoherently. He made choking sounds, trembling.

After a moment, he told himself: I'm sure now I'm not sane. She's made me into a mad beast like her. All I want to do is kill—hurt and kill. (232)

It is not by accident that reptilian images are ascribed to Hendrickje, or that Adrian refers to his struggle with his mother in such images, for Mittelholzer, the unseen geographer, commingles the passions and emotions of his characters with the qualities and moods of the Guyanese landscape. The contours of the characters' personalities merge with the geography of their birthplace, as when Hendrickje, "the reptile," indirectly announces to her mother her first pregnancy. Her scheme has brought forth the desired result: "Kyk-over-al looked like a black reptile sleeping out on the shimmering water" (173).

Landscape not only provides images, lending itself to character depiction, but at times gives structure to series of episodes in which the characters are involved. Thus landscape can be an image, a representative symbol, a portent or commentator. Here, love play, too, is captured in reptilian images:

They spent a long time together, and she was like a wriggling snake of charm that had lured him into a magic valley. He kept breathing in her cinnamon fragrance. It eclipsed the smell of the earth under them; the smell of the dry leaves and the leafy-chill in the air when twilight began to close around them. (282)

The lovemaking of Rosario and Jabez always takes place on coffee plantations, not in the jungle, marking the cultivation of the land. But even the cultivated coffee plantations provide a warning, for the coffee trees rustle when Jabez's former friend, Samuel de Haart, now a rival for Rosario's snakely charm, approaches. Thus, landscape not only warns of violence, but often, invading the consciousness of characters, portends death. When the mulatto, Hannah, jealously drowns herself after her former lover, Laurens, turns his attentions to her sister, Katrina, all the elements of the earth seem to participate in the telling of her drowning. The hushed landscape of Kyk-over-al broods. In a play of reds and blacks, black clouds take on Hannah's shape and the dark water, reflecting red, announces her death:

No breeze blew. Once he woke and heard the river's hushed sounds. He thought: The river sounds secretive and ominous, as though a terrible event were about to happen . . . .
. . . (the air is still—and hot.)
He fell asleep again, but woke before dawn. Beside him, Katrina sighed and tossed in her sleep. He looked out and saw Kyk-over-al, a dark, long shadow in the river. . . .
The river kept on whispering. . . .
As he looked he saw the gray water, daubed with red reflected from the sky, pattern itself with ripples. After a moment, however, the ripples began to fade, and suddenly the water smoothed itself out and recovered its glassy calm. (134–135)

Landscape is sensitive to action and seems so aware of changes which characters are undergoing that it becomes moodscape.

One of the principal elements of the landscape is river water. For Guyana is a land of creeks and canals, of great waterfalls and vast rivers. Kaywana was called Old Water; Hendrickje could be called Black Water. For Hendrickje's lovemaking, her conceptions, her pregnancies and miscarriages, her secretive seductions of Ignatius, her incest toward Adrian, are played out against the backdrop of black water, accompanied by the sounds of its whispering, sucking, or sighing: "Outside, the black water kept sucking at the bank, making a low, sensuous sound" (190–191). Here the water is injected with Hendrickje's passion; black water and Hendrickje merge, giving off the same sensuous sounds. The sluggishness which accompanies one of her early pregnancies, the tenuousness of the embryo, the newness and the thrill of the beginnings of motherhood which offers a possibility of continuing the van Groenwegel family line—with all of these, the landscape is tremulous:

> A sluggish mist was drifting in wisps over the surface of the black water. The morning air felt chilly and water-vapourish but exhilarating, fresh and leafy. (214)

But this watery promise is not fulfilled, for the child from this pregnancy is stillborn. So the wispiness of the scene, its tremulousness, changes. And Hendrickje's second pregnancy, lit up by moonlight and flashes of fireflies, is touched by the chill of evening. Always the sound of the water recalls past evenings, past lovemakings, passionate landscapes:

> She watched the moonlight on the river. They could hear the water sucking at the bank. The water in the little creek on the Essequibo often made similar sounds in the quiet of the afternoon. The little creek up which the two of them used to go secretly to make love. The moonlight

looked silver-chilly. Fireflies flashed in white bright blobs amid the low-hanging foliage of the trees on the opposite bank. (221)

Mittelholzer, unseen geographer, often uses the sounds and colors and sights of various elements as structural motifs; indeed at times he over-saturates many scenes with these motifs, lessening the effectiveness of his landscaping by over-repetition. Everywhere, at all times, at all turns, there is water, rain, river, creek, thunder, lightning, fireflies, moonlight: a baroque, somewhat cluttered canvas on which Mittelholzer attempts to capture the very lushness of the Guyanese landscape.

As generations of the van Groenwegel family progress, Mittelholzer's landscape changes; jungle area blends into cultivated plantation. Now many acts play themselves out against the background of plantation life rather than only within a jungle framework. Generational progression is marked by a parallel progression in the landscape. And at times, as in the scene which follows, when Hendrickje's grandchildren, Pedro, Lumea, David, and Jacques are on the way to kill their mother, Rosario, social chronology (the development of plantation landscape) is marked in the process of a single day; Mittelholzer, moving the scene from jungle to coffee fields, to cassava and eddoe, in telescoping style, links social change, time and action. As the group moves through the jungle to the cultivated lands, day turns to dusk, dusk to night. It is in the darkness of the night that the violent killing of their mother takes place. The shifting scene progresses to its violent end in the play of sunlight and darkness, glimmer and gloom. The jungle with its screeching, hissing sounds is watchful, seems to be looking on:

The jungle met overhead, and the sunlight penetrated only in slim odd shafts slanting in through the bamboos and tall *mucca-mucca* shrubs with their arrow-shaped leaves that watched them in dark-green solemnity from the banks in unending rows. They could hear the low croaking of an alligator, and David was eager to search for it, but Pedro said they had no time to spare. Floating clumps of *missouri* grass hindered their progress now and then, but they had anticipated this and had brought cutlass-es. . . .

. . . The sunshine came redly through the bush, and tree-frogs had begun their night-time fluting amid the undergrowth. The air was chilly and rank with the scent of leaves and wild flowers. Overhead, they heard the churlish screech of a hawk and a fluttering amongst the foliage of a tall *courida* tree . . . .

When they reached the cane-fields the sun had not yet disappeared, but by the time they had begun to creep through the coffee fields dusk had set in in earnest. Fire-flies flashed in the gloom under the trees, and

insects made a high-pitched cheeping. Pedro called a halt once to listen.
He thought he had heard the hiss of a *labaria* . . . .

Darkness had come down when they were crawling through the
provision patches, but a four-day-old moon crescent in the west threw a
soft, pale radiance over everything, making the cassava leaves glimmer
dully atop the slim, knotted stalks. The eddoe leaves, too, glimmered
. . . .

They saw the jamoon tree, slim and tall and twisted, its trunk
ascending in three main columns that branched outward horizontally and
then became lost amid the thick foliage higher up. (355–356)

The spreading jamoon tree will ever hang over, will ever recall the violent
murder, and man will transfer his passions and emotions to phenomena:

Jacques felt his heart beating as though it were contained in the core
of the tree. Within his own body there was only the echo of it. (358)

Here, a phenomenon is not merely used decoratively, but it begins to
assume more and more the anthropomorphic quality common to many of
Mittelholzer's later landscape images.

The movement toward the anthropomorphic image takes place through
the identification of landscape with a past action. The whole replay,
perpetuating action, cuts across time and fixes landscape in that time. Thus
scenes and actions are twice-told, a kind of symbolic repetition of motifs
which provides that density, the weightiness of Mittelholzer's style. Landscape triggers off the memory of characters who relive past actions, and the
author recounts the scene in almost the same words as before. Jacques, who
is perhaps one of the characters most affected by landscape, who identifies
with and reacts to landscape, recalls:

The long, slim, bare stems of the *mucca-muccas* were in dense shadow, but
here and there the moonlight glimmered on the shiny, arrow-shaped
leaves. Secretive and intelligent the leaves looked. And old. As though
these might have been the very same shrubs his boy's eyes had gazed
upon that afternoon when he and Pedro and David and Lumea had
landed here on their way to the Laplace plantation. The *missouri* grass
looked the same, too, as though these might have been the very clumps
that he had seen floating in the black water that afternoon. The alligator
might be no sentimental conjecture, for alligators lived for centuries. It
could be the identical one croaking there now. (497)

Here landscape, still watchful, charged with the past, spans the life of a
single character from boyhood to manhood and takes on a different mood.
Though conjuring up the same scene, Mittelholzer, even as he cuts across

time, injects various moods into that scene. In his landscaping, although motifs are often repetitious, the mood is constantly altered, the tone is modulated. For landscape is acted upon; and even the sensibilities of the characters impinge on the landscape, contouring it. The animated landscape injects itself into the senses of the characters; the dialogue of man and landscape continues:

A raucous laugh came ribboning through the dark. The insects churred tirelessly. They could smell the jungle and the river—a wet, vegetable scent, dark and heavy in the night air, but refreshing.

"You sense the wetness in the air?" he said. "I can smell wild flowers. I'm on the Canje, Amelia. The Siki Creek. We're hunting alligators, and it's getting on for seven o'clock, though there's moonlight and we can hear a goatsucker hoo-yoo-ing in the bamboo thicket. The *mucca-mucca* shrubs are watching us from the edge of the water like thin men nodding in the dark." (434–435)

Anthropomorphic transference begins and things take on human qualities and human form. It is not surprising, therefore, that Jacques' character is almost defined in an elemental framework. In earlier generations of the van Groenwegel family, the members were characterized by either the weak or strong strain; the opposition between these conflicting strains and variations provided the generational interplay. Though from very early, slave-blood entered the veins and line of the van Groenwegel family, strength character-ized by one's determination to continue the family tradition was often demonstrated by one's treatment of slaves. Jacques, the first character to feel the pull of *both* weak and strong strains, reveals the tug in his actions during a historical slave uprising, mirroring the effects of the two strains in his reactions to landscape, to either the dank penetrating wetness or the dry-weather earth. Jacques has not demonstrated the strength, ruthlessness, or cruelty of many of the other van Groenwegels, or the historic cruelty of masters to slaves:

"We treat them so cruelly—apart from branding them and beating them, some planters have introduced such tortures as making them lie naked on broken bottles and tying them down over a nest of stinging ants. Pedro had invented one of his own. He told Grandma and Grandma thought it so good an idea that she adopted it. A smooth, flattish stone is put over a fire to get hot, and the slave to be punished is made to stand and watch it getting hot, knowing that he is going to be made to sit on it with his trousers off. I hate seeing acts of cruelty like this, but the others glory in them. I suppose I must be made differently." (366–367)

At first when dealing with the slave leader, Cuffy, Jacques proves himself tractable and weak, allowing himself to become Cuffy's official secretary and letter writer, allowing his own mistress to be confiscated and abused by Cuffy. The first real sign of his self-assertion comes with his flight from captivity and his escape, while still haunted by the presence of his slave captors, who symbolically loom out of the landscape:

> Rabby urged Jacques into a clump of ferns and creepers, and the voices went past within a few feet of them. . . . The swizzlestick trees gave place to wild pines and wild cacao, with a clump of manicole palms here and there like slim black ghosts looming up before them . . . .
> . . . Through the trees ahead they could see the sky. It was streaked with carmine and purple. Jacques listened to the soft, sensual sucking of water amid vegetation.
> They came to a tiny clearing on the bank of the river, and Rabby said that this was their destination for the time being. Long ago this clearing must have been a regular landing-place for *corials*, but the jungle now hung well out over the water and ferns and dragon's blood fringed the bank. The ground was not so sandy here—it was a crumbly loam—and in the grey light of dawn they could see innumerable *aeta* palm seeds strewn about amid the short grass and low herbs and ferns. Frogs were fluting, and the night-time churr of insects had not yet ceased. The dank, wet odour of the black water came up to their senses, and Jacques found himself smiling reminiscently. (472–473)

Yet Jacques persists, for the van Groenwegel tradition seems to reassert itself, and the pull of the past is reawakened in him:

> "If you want to know the truth, Rabby, I'm itching to get back to the old house on the Canje. I want to be with my brothers and grandmother. I'd have given anything to have been there with them when they were attacked. I want to get to them, Rabby . . . Yes, that's my one aim now. To get into the old house and help them defend it if necessity arises again." (474)

The escape is marked by fluctuation of character, movement between weak-strong strains, reflected by either dank, penetrating wetness or dry-weather earth. Landscape cuts across both character and action, uniting them through continually changing scenic patterns. As Jacques stands guard during the escape, the whole scene is saturated with water images:

> The rain held off, but water made a swift gurgling on every hand. The dam was muddy and treacherous . . . .

A few minutes later, crouching among the coffee trees, they looked out upon the rebel camp in the pasture. Fires, as usual, were burning, but the wood seemed wet from the rain and smoked profusely . . . .

Overhead it was starry, but the stars had a watery look, and there would be more rain before dawn. Perhaps before midnight. They could hear the sound of water gurgling in trenches about the plantation. Tree frogs fluted cheerfully, revelling in the wet. (482–484).

Yet he would wish it were otherwise, for though beginning to feel the pull of his family tradition, basically he yearns for quieter times, and feels nostalgia for more fragrant, softer landscapes.

And as Jacques becomes proud of his growing strength, as his self-reliance deepens, and as he becomes more at peace with himself, resolving the tug of strong-weak, a calm strength from the landscape flows into him:

There was a moon in the east, and the sky was cloudless. A true October night. The ground was parched and cracked, and the air sweet with the scent of dry twigs and dry-weather earth . . . .

. . . The canes waved gently, pale-green and fairy-like in the bright moonlight. Insects churred in a high-pitched chorus, and one could smell the dry-weather aroma of grass and starved herbs and shrubs, strong and spicy in the fresh, dew-laden air. . . .

. . . Jacques began to crawl forward toward the drain that separated the dam from the cane-field, silently and with the stealth of a salamander. He signalled to the others to remain where they were.

The canes made a faint lisping in the cool, soft drive of breeze that came from the south-east—a land breeze, heavy with the scent of the jungle. (489, 492)

This conjunction of man and landscape and history in Mittelholzer's *Children of Kaywana* is by no means fortuitous. For the evolution of Caribbean society and its foundations derives from the land itself, from the implantation of slavery throughout the Caribbean. The sea was the conduit; the land, the receptor. It is there that the Black slave from Africa toiled and labored; it is there that he suffered and died. It is for the sowing and harvesting of the land that the slave suffered physical as well as mental cruelty. And so often the land, the receptor, through the psychic interplay of man-spirit and earth, is made to give off its own signals, warning that unnatural, excessive cruelty of man to man does not pass unheeded. At the moment of death of Kaywana's son, August:

"there was a raging . . . a violent thunderstorm. A few minutes before he breathed his last a mango tree not very far from the house . . . was cut in two by the lightning, and the few slaves in the room cried out and chanted a foreign dirge which . . . must be African in origin, though there were several words of Dutch to be heard in between. They were frightened, and one of them muttered audibly that this storm was with a purpose. The spirits of the sky were angry with their master for his cruelty toward them." (65)

Mittelholzer, the unseen geographer, makes his landscape react to the death of a cruel slave owner. Yet, he never delves deeply into the phenomenon of slavery, never analyzes its morality. Nor, except for a passing reference to Africa, does he really attempt to recount residual African culture. To be sure, there are bizarre references to "occult powers" of the African, as he touches on the motif of *obeah*, one which is recurrent in Caribbean literature. Jabez poisons himself with a green African potion. During Cuffy's slave insurrection, his rival, Atta, resorts to *obeah* to predict the downfall of Cuffy:

> Near the stable, Atta and his cronies, Accabre and Goussari, were discussing the situation and working *obeah*. Accabre smiled slyly and rolled palm seeds along the ground. A black candle was burning in the shade of a calabash with a vent at the top. Accabre muttered a few words in an African dialect, and sprinkled a little greenish powder from the bill of a toucan on each of the palm seeds.
>
> "Watch how the powder settle," said Accabre, lifting the seeds with care. "I read plenty in this powder, Atta."
>
> "What it say, Accabre?" asked Atta.
>
> "It say a big man among us going to dead soon." (461–462)

And more closely deriving from African ontology, but already influenced by the implications of race, the mulatto lover of Hendrickje attempts to placate bush-deities:

> On the floor, under the table, lay the head of the rooster. This was the work of Hoobak, one of Hendrickje's leader-bullies. Hoobak was an *obeah* man, and his mistress allowed him these liberties because it flattered his vanity and, incidentally, satisfied the wishes of Bangara, who was superstitious and believed that unless these rites were performed at least once a week the bush-dogs would wreak evil on him for being sexually intimate with a white woman. (310)

Indeed, the history that Mittelholzer presents in his trilogy begins in Guyana and hardly touches on previous times, or elaborates on the original cultures of the races of the Caribbean. He does not weave into his novels any history of the Amerindians, but only presents them as they interact with the European settlers. His history is actual; his historical novels principally depict the white settlement and the interaction of Europeans with other races. Mittelholzer chooses as his historical perspective the master class and its relationship to other groups, their images reflected in that of the master, controlled, changed, or distorted by his actions. Their picture is presented by the master, their action controlled by the master, their reaction derived from the action of that master. And on so many days the van Groenwegel children

> stood and watched them sweating in the fields. Black bodies with muscles that rippled. Close-cropped kinky-haired heads—heads bent with the apathy of enslavement. The sun beat on them, and sometimes rain came and dribbled on their tough shapes. Men of Africa, thick-lipped and thick-skulled. They looked oft-times like beasts out there, toiling in the noon. But when you looked closer you were startled, for you could glimpse the flame of humanity like magnificent lightning in their bloodshot eyes. (32–33)

This picture, one of the few in which Mittelholzer portrays people of pure African stock, is a composite of brutishness, physical strength, and resignation. But in Mittelholzer's larger canvas, resignation changes into rebellion, and the physical quality of the Blacks is used not only to plant seed but also to populate the land of Guyana. The blood of the Black men mingles not only with the soil as they toil and labor for the master, but mingles with the blood of other races: Amerindian and European.

But often this mingling did not take place willingly; miscegenation, a corollary to plantation slavery, often stemmed from brutal possession of Black slaves by white masters, making studs of Black males and raping Black females. To possess Black slaves often was a pastime for the master class, who indiscriminately sired mulatto children. Jabez van Groenwegel and Samuel de Haart "were notorious. There was not a young female slave on the two plantations with whom they had not been intimate" (281). This indiscriminate breeding gave rise to the mulatto class and initiated the whole, complex hierarchy of color and complexion that still plagues all Caribbean society. Here lies the beginning of the pyramidical value system that did not question the humanity of whites but was startled by the "flame of humanity" in Blacks, which ascribed value and honor to whiteness and stigmatized Blackness. Thus it is that the only detracting element in the make-up of a young mulatto member of the van Groenwegel family, though he possesses some white features and Indian fire-blood, is his Black blood:

> He was eight, and gave promise of growing into a huge specimen like his father. He had his Grandfather Adrian's forehead. Hendrickje patted his shoulder and smiled down affectionately upon him. "So much spirit,

eh? So much spirit. The old blood. It must come out. Never mind the black taint." (393)

Thus it is, too, that Hendrickje, from her dominant matriarchal position within the van Groenwegel family despite her mixed blood, can arrogantly scorn Rosario's Indian-Spanish parentage: "You half-breed bitches always bring a lot of rottenness into a family" (329). Miscegenation produced the whole, complex hierarchy of skin shading in the Caribbean, creating a class gradation of superior-inferior based solely on complexion.

Mittelholzer, in his treatment of the social history of the Caribbean, not only presents the method by which slaves were divided and ruled, but analyzes the way in which the slave was inoculated with a sense of inferiority. Hendrickje, in attempting to create the van Groenwegel dynasty, sets purposefully about her method of divide and rule, of bribery and preferment to those who carry out her designs, of punishment and debasement to those who attempt to resist her system of "slave-socialization." This is how she creates the Black leader-bully:

> "I've got to see about the slaves. I'm going to pick out the best fellows and see if I can train them into leaders for the weaker ones. I must have a few upon whom I can depend absolutely. I'll give these chosen ones special quarters and special rations. I'll flatter them and keep them keen and eager to lord it over the slack and the idle." (184)

Through this calculated design she makes slaves suspicious of one another, and teaches the leader-bullies to value cruelty by equating it with power. This purposeful distortion of values, with its consequent reward to the slave, also brings its own reward for the master: a distorted sense of loyalty, veneration, and adulation of Black slave to mistress:

> "Look at the system I've created among the slaves. You see how successfully it's working! I encourage them to tell tales on each other, and I give the tale-bearers extra rations and reduced tasks as a reward, and the malefactors get less rations and more work as well as punishment. My three lieutenants, Rabonne and Pardoom and Henwah, look upon me as a great queen or empress. I can see it in their eyes how they venerate me. And why? Because I've lifted them into a stratum of dignity by giving them whips and investing them with the authority to mete out punishment. I've flattered their vanity, and they would die rather than betray me." (190)

Not only does the slave master attempt to introduce a distorted sense of allegiances of slave to slave and of slave to master, but the slave master also calculatedly attempts to break, through physical torture, the will of any slave who shows a rebellious spirit. Hendrickje instructs Jabez in a few of the physical methods used in maintaining plantation control:

> ". . . where the slaves are concerned we've instituted such a system of punishments that they don't dare to try on any organized slacking when picking time comes around. We don't hesitate to have them tarred and feathered."
> "Tarred and feathered! Literally?"
> "Literally. You seem shocked." She wagged her head slightly, smiling. "We have to be severe, Jabez. It's the only way. The other planters do it, too. The stocks, also, are proving very effective. For serious offences we have them put in the stocks for days, administering a daily dose of lashes. That always breaks their rebelliousness." (294–295)

But tarring and feathering, and the cruelty of the stocks, did not completely break the will of the slaves, nor did the severity of punishment entirely crush their rebellious spirits. For slave uprisings, which provide Mittelholzer with an opportunity to dramatize history, come stealthily with cadenced rhythms through the twilight gloom:

> The wailing could be heard again in the distance. A ghost-noise that grew louder as the sun sank in the west and the day faded. Soon they could hear it coming like a rhythmical chant out of the twilight that was settling over the fields and the mysterious jungle beyond the fields. (412–413)

And Mittelholzer, as he integrates history and landscape, paces Cuffy's rebellion—one of the fiercest of all slave uprisings—with jungle noises, and in a morally symbolic statement mocks it with the parrot-snake's indifference to the fate of the masters:

> So Fort Nassau passed the nights of the twenty-first and the twenty-second and the twenty-third hearing only the buzz and churr of insects and the bubbling of fallen palm-berries in the black river—the sucking sound of the water on the banks. Those who happened to be awake heard those sounds . . . . The others . . . slept soundly—with a soundness none of them deserved . . . .
> All slept peacefully. Only one leisurely parrot-snake, twining its way amid the fronds of a tall *paraipee* palm which had pushed its plume above the other jungle trees, watched the reddish glow in the distance over the jungle—far in the east and in the south where houses and sheds, sugar-mills and store-houses were on fire. But that was a long way off, and the parrot-snake was too indifferent over the fate of men to sound an alarm. (425)

The master class, though speculating on the possibility of such uprisings and living in fear of them, felt so secure in its rigid control of the slave class that it was virtually unprepared for the rebellious action of its slaves. When these uprisings came, they were accompanied by the destruction of many plantations, and were guided not only by desire for revenge, but also by deep-rooted psychological need to debase the master class. Mittelholzer, as he depicts the character of the slave leader Cuffy, attempting to rid his Black followers of feelings of inferiority toward their former masters, probes into the inner dynamics of attitudes of superiority and inferiority and sexual possession. To be sure, Mittelholzer's description of Cuffy is somewhat cavalier—"A medium-sized fellow, very tough-looking. He walked with a slight limp. When he smiled he showed perfect teeth" (444)—yet Mittelholzer ascribes shrewd psychological insights to the slave leader:

> Cuffy looked at the guard, "Peddy, this is my woman. You see her here? This is my slave—my white slave. See her here naked? Look at her good. Look at her all over and shame her. Go on. Put your eyes on her. All over her. All over! She not your missy no more! Look at her and shame her till she can't shame!"
> "Yes, Governor, I looking." Peddy grinned self-consciously.
> "Slap her behind."
> Peddy shuffled his feet about.
> Cuffy scowled. "I gives you an order Peddy. What you frighten of? She is my slave. You black but you as good as her. Do what I say!"
> Peddy did it—half-heartedly, showing his teeth all the while.
> Jacques kept a stolid face. Amelia winced, but nothing more.
> "Peddy," said Cuffy, "you still a slave."
> Peddy giggled.
> "Yes, Peddy, you still feel she too good for you to touch because she white and you black." (454–455)

Slapping Amelia's behind is no simple act, but one fraught with deep psychological overtones; this scene is no flat scene, but one which has many hidden resonances. A Black slave is ordered to slap not the face but the behind of a white woman of the master class. She, symbolically, has been stripped of her clothes, of her outer trappings. In her white nakedness, she stands, the possession of a Black man, but even more, she is now white slave, he, Black master. This dramatic psychological reversal of roles is aimed at totally liquidating the inferiority complex by which Peddy's mind is paralyzed. The reverse leap from being dominated to dominating is too wide for Peddy, whose slave mentality boggles at the thought of an action so audacious as slapping Amelia's behind. In Cuffy's thinking, to slap her face would be merely to insult her; slapping her behind, to shame her. All the interplay of white-skin/black-mask, all the complex hierarchy of West Indian attitudes to pigmentation, are present in that scene; all of these elements are reflected in the physical changes of the participants.

Yet, Mittelholzer, caught in his own paradoxical attitude toward color, deftly shows us the inability of even the slave leader Cuffy to break down his own complexes, for the one-time slave trembles uncontrollably with anticipation of possessing a white woman, and gulps with deeply concealed desire. To be sure, Mittelholzer is showing how deeply stamped on the slave mind is his feeling of inferiority, and consequently how great is the need to remove this feeling by shaming a former slave mistress. Here Cuffy by his action shames not only Amelia, but, by symbolic extension, the entire van Groenwegel dynasty:

> "You never think one day come when you got to lie in bed with black man, eh, Georgie? But that what you got to do now." He moved toward her and halted. "I got no mercy on you. I is Governor now. Yes, me Cuffy standing here. I is Governor, and you is my woman. You hear that, van Groenwegel? From now she is my woman. And not just for lust I want her. I want her so I can shame her—and shame her! Every day I going to shame her like how you white people shame our black women." He put out his hand and fondled her breasts. His head trembled. He gulped. "Yes, Georgie, I got to shame you. I got to make you so shame you never want to look black man in the face again and think yourself better than him." (449)

Now Cuffy in his assumed role of Governor, in his designs to denigrate the white Amelia by demanding a kiss "in white-man fashion," jarringly pokes into her ingrained prejudice:

> "Get up from there and come here to me."
> She rose from the floor and came.
> "Hold my face and kiss me."
> She made no move to obey.
> "That is always the hardest thing for you to bring yourself to do, but you got to do it. You got to kiss me good-bye in white-man fashion. You got to know I is Governor. Your boss. You is my woman. Hold my face and kiss me, Georgie. On my lips." (464)

All of this social history—the foundation of many Caribbean social attitudes—moves against a background of specific historical events and developments which show the evolution from European conquest and settlement to development of plantations, to establishment and maintenance of a system of slavery. For it is evident that Mittelholzer, in the Kaywana

trilogy—*Children of Kaywana, The Harrowing of Hubertus,* and *Kaywana Blood*—
is attempting to create a vast multilayered canvas on which unfolds the
colonial history of Guyana, and by extension, of the Caribbean.

Children of Kaywana tells of the relationship between the Dutch West
India Company and the private planters, of the use of monopolies restricting
the wholesale enslavement of Amerindians to encourage the enslavement of
Africans. Mittelholzer also describes how Black slaves were treated differently by the Company than by private planters—the Company feeding the
slaves more poorly, yet treating them with less "savage methods of cruelty"
(387) than the private planters. The unseen geographer not only presents the
arguments of coastal-versus-interior development, and sugar-versus-coffee-
versus-indigo cultivation, but he often paints the physical evolution of the
plantations themselves. The earlier landscape of jungle and piled-up leaves
has in many areas undergone changes, has been cleared and cultivated.

> The compound, the water-tanks, the slaves' logies; beyond the indigo
> fields, the canefields—[Adrian's] eyes took them in and roved round
> toward the edge of the up-river jungle. Beyond this jungle there were
> more fields—fields of another plantation. Then more jungle. More fields
> . . . more residences, water-tanks, slaves' logies . . . . (242)

Personal and social intercourse between members of the plantations—
sketchings of plantation society—becomes the center of social history as *The
Harrowing of Hubertus* unfolds.

Since the social history in *Children of Kaywana* is played out against the
background of slavery, it is not surprising that the relationship between
violence and morality, cruelty and expediency, between bestiality and
humanity, weakness and strength, should be debated in *Children of Kaywana.*
Since, too, the measure of one's strength or weakness is related to one's
treatment of and actions toward slaves, the whole question of the coercive
use of strength and its brutal application is linked to the struggle for survival:
"This is a country and an age in which we have to live desperately if we're
to survive. Only violence can suffice" (353). Even as "the van Groenwegels
never run" becomes a motto of the family, and passing into a tradition
becomes almost an inherited characteristic, so, too, the brutishness, the
cruelty which was often necessary to maintain this tradition, is thought not
only to be innate, but indeed a prerequisite to the maintenance of the
established social order:

> This is a brutal world. Life is cold and heartless. Among the plants,
> among the beasts, among men—yes, among men, too—it is the strongest
> that survive. The weak go under . . . . Life is struggle, struggle—all the
> time struggle. You can only get what you want by fighting for it. Be meek

and surrendering and you're lost . . . . Never surrender! Never retreat! (363)

Conversely, the quality of animal savagery which may result from an embattled social order can only be kept in check by physical strength applied with reason and restraint. Strength is differentiated from cruelty by its method of application. Often, therefore, an action is judged not by the intensity of force involved, but by the method of application of that force. Indeed, the rightness or wrongness of an action is in direct relationship, not to the brutishness of the action, but to the degree of control exercised in its application:

> "And in order that savagery might be kept in check we must be strong— physically strong. Physical strength results in moral strength. Strength respects strength, and peace follows. Strength despises weakness and strife follows . . . . it is instinctive for all creatures to despise weakness; weak people secretly despise themselves for their weakness. Even those who may say they abhor a show of force in their deep selves admire strength and are contemptuous of weakness. Strength, I have discovered, to be effective, should be employed in a reasoned and unemotional manner." (496)

Although the philosophical debate between the rightness and wrongness of an action or emotion concerns Mittelholzer in *Children in Kaywana*, this debate does not preoccupy him as it does in *The Harrowing of Hubertus*, where, in fact, it becomes the single issue, the focal point of Hubertus's harrowing, the central and oft-repeated motif of the novel. In *The Harrowing of Hubertus*, the debate takes the form of an interior monologue, through which Hubertus's character unfolds. The novel thus becomes an elaborate character study of Hubertus, whose every action is scrutinized, whose every passion is analyzed. Scrutiny and analysis—recurrent reflection upon motive, cause, and impulse—all tend to slow down the pace of the novel, and though robbing it of narrative speed and of the dramatic quality of *Children of Kaywana*, make it denser, indeed, more tightly wedged together.

Hubertus's character is built up on a series of parallels and oppositions, a constant pendulation between natural and unnatural, feeling and principle, action and word, an ever-present fluctuation between instinct and control, passion and restraint. These continual oppositions gradually turn inward; the dualisms in his character progressively weigh on his introspective nature until his initial strength of character declines into an early senility which droops and stares into vacancy. Quite early Hubertus echoes those flaws in his character that will lead to his decline, when to his daughter Luise he says: "You're harrowed, my girl. Perpetually harrowed. It's from me you have inherited the capacity . . ." describing himself as "a wicked, unpredictable man. A self-torturer" (*Hubertus*, 159–160). But this statement is immediately countered by Faustina, who pinpoints the essential contradiction in his character, between the action itself and his analysis of that action:

> Faustina gave Luise a hug. "Take no notice of him, my dear child. His words mean nothing. It is always his actions you must judge him by. Remember that, and you will understand him: forget it, and you will deem him a despicable soul." (160)

To act without restraint, to yield to desire, is not only weak but is considered, by him, unprincipled. Thus he must attempt to excuse the weakness of the flesh. Speaking to his former mistress, Faustina, who has just announced her impending marriage:

> "I'm human, and I could not say something to you which would have meant the loss of your nearness. I have my weak spots despite my principles." His eyes were half-shut, and she could hear the breath like an agonized wind inside him. (94)

The beginnings of his harrowing come from the containing of passion within him. For he has inherited Kaywana's passionate fire-blood which he is unable to quiet, which he tries unsuccessfully to restrain. He is aware of the pull of his blood and thus consciously attempts to restrain that pull by seeking out and eventually marrying a woman who exercises control and restraint.

> "I'm a passionate man. You know that, Rosalind. It's in my blood. We are a passionate family."
> "I wouldn't have married you if you weren't. But you know how to control your passion—that was what I liked most about you."
> "Yes . . . . Always control. Always restraint." (29)

His decision to marry Rosalind is therefore consciously linked to his attempt to dominate his passionate nature, to cool his fire-blood. Consequently, their marriage is not a passionate one, and in their *ange-bête* relationship, he equates passion with bestiality, purity with restraint:

> "That's why I revere my Rosalind. So pure, so restrained. My dear wife. English, a little cold and withdrawn in company and to casual acquaintances, but warm with a pure warmth at her core . . . she loves me and knows that I have a strength that God has given me to stamp upon the beast." (71)

In his youth, Hubertus, as many slave masters, has with abandon possessed many Black slaves, has without thought enjoyed the pleasures of the flesh, indeed, has been surfeited by his constant pursuit of pleasure. Thus it is not only God who helps "stamp upon the beast," but also overindulgence and a feeling of satiety. Memory of his many experiences with slave women now takes the place of actual experiencing; thought replaces action:

> As he approached the logies he experienced a twinge of regret . . . .
> Regrets, when they came, seemed borne on a soothing breeze from the
> satisfying past. He had had his pleasures; the memory of them was
> enough for his imagination now that he had matured; he could taste them
> in retrospect and be quietened. (43)

Thus, in reliving past pleasures, he continues to experience them vicariously. He is gratified by the thought that although he has access to many slave women, he now refrains from further intercourse with them. His knowledge of his power over the slaves and his self-indulgent magnanimity in refraining from using that power supplant his urges, his desires:

> He kept remembering the shapely black breasts he had gazed upon, and
> the knowledge of the pleasure he could have derived from them saturated
> him and heightened the ecstacy of triumph he felt . . . . Triumph over
> the flesh. Only the years, he thought, taught one how to score such
> victories. (44–45)

Yet he is not always able to "stamp upon the beast," to rein in his passions, and it is his inability to do so which eventually leads to his harrowing. He hoped that marriage to Rosalind would still the beast, that he would derive a measure of restraint equal to hers. Thus to feel desire for a former mistress and to yield to that desire undermine his self-controlled rigidity. His natural-self triumphs over his shadow-self: "He kissed her again, slightly mesmerized, hearing dimly the admonishing voice of a shadow-self, but not lost. Tottering but intact" (48). His inability to resist the passionate Faustina when married to Rosalind becomes one of the principal recurrent motifs in *The Harrowing of Hubertus*, in fact, the central plot of the novel. Rosalind knows of the pull Faustina exercises over him; Faustina senses that Rosalind has never really experienced a deep passion with Hubertus. And since passion is often recalled in landscape, Faustina, using water images, tells of her fulfillment with Hubertus:

> And I wonder if she has even once tasted with Hubertus such bliss as I
> have done. I do hope she has—once, twice, innumerable times. . . . In a
> dry, soft bed and on damp leaves under rain-dripping trees. Poor creature
> . . . . Oh, sweet wet leaves! Lovely damp rain . . . . (97)

Rain and water, wet, piled-up leaves—which at the beginning of the trilogy were the natural love bed for Kaywana—exercise their own control, and releasing natural urges free Hubertus and Faustina from any societal ethics. For Faustina, to act freely, to accept the pull of landscape, is to act morally:

> Oh, make her understand how the scent of wet leaves will ever be with
> us so long as we live, and that it couldn't be wrong. Only evil people
> could think it wrong. By every rule it was right. (96)

Though the landscape sanctions their act, the result of the act—a son, Graeme, borne to Faustina early in her marriage to Cranley—increases Hubertus's tottering and becomes another element in his harrowing. He is not unaware that Faustina has borne his son nor is he really harrowed with having yielded to his instincts. But since he is not sure whether Rosalind, restrained as she is, either senses or knows about Graeme's paternity, Hubertus's harrowing stems not only from this uncertainty, but also from the very clear discrepancy between his professed principles and his unrestrained actions. In his mind, the question of his paternity is not an issue, nor is deception a factor in his harrowing. He is anxious that the act remain hidden; he is intent that Graeme's illegitimacy remain concealed.

This question of concealed parentage and illegitimacy, with its corollary, bastardization, becomes a recurrent motif in Caribbean life, and consequently in much Caribbean literature. Duplicity, which so often accompanies the question of bastardization, is rationalized by Hubertus, who is constantly driven to analysis of his actions, whose assumed shadow-self continually hovers over his natural-self:

> "I do not subscribe to the view . . . that the fleshly in us can only be
> related to evil . . . . It is contrary to all one's instincts . . . . If the flesh is
> abused the result is evil, but if the flesh is respected and treated with
> reverence and restraint only good can come from such an attitude." (118)

Thus his growing self-deception draws no distinction between his having deceived Rosalind and his revering her.

For Hubertus judges not the action but the attitude. The ramifications of this idea extend far outward into much of Caribbean life, pervading its society, affecting many of its values. In the Caribbean, importance is placed not upon what is done, but upon how it is done, a factor which controls the actions of many protagonists in Caribbean novels, an element which influences the behavior of many Caribbean types. Thus Hubertus's pose can easily obscure, and his sham piety explain away, any uncontrolled behavior, any "corrupt" action:

"Unprincipled in men's eyes, my dear—but not in God's. God can see into our hearts, and He knows when we act in a spirit of corruption and when we act because of urgent necessity." (93)

It is obvious that Hubertus is concerned with the relationship between action and responsibility, and analyzing the impulse of an action often attributes it to a force—landscape, God, blood—over which he has no direct control. He refuses to accept personal responsibility for an action, but by introducing explanatory factors rooted in the larger society, drawn from the outer reality, he basically remains societal man and does not become existential man. To be sure, in a rare statement which contradicts his philosophical basis, he accepts the possibility of one's freedom to choose: "Everyone has it in him to be good. You are no exception. If you are bad it is because you choose to be so" (37). Yet, for him, actions are often willed by a power outside himself, God and passions, directed by family tradition and the tug of blood. Essentially then, his dialogue is with society. He has not entered into the dialogue of self-in-action, of man acting and accepting the responsibility of his actions, thereby creating his selfhood. Perhaps his harrowing stems from his inability to free himself from the pull of blood, to enter the dialogue of self-in-action.

In addition to his all-consuming interior dialogue, he is in dialogue, too, with the society, participating both in the affairs of the plantocracy, as an officer of the Burghur Militia, and in the functioning of his own plantation, Good Heart. So that Good Heart might not fall into a decrepit state, Hubertus, acting out of "urgent necessity" (93), finds that he must engage in illicit trade with countries other than Holland. And consequently, as the dualism of his character prevents him from participating in the rule of his colony, he finds that he must resign from the Militia position. Personal behavior and historical activity intertwine again; personality plays itself out against an historical backdrop. Hubertus and other Dutch plantation owners, along with neighboring English plantation owners, are shown in social interplay at weddings, christenings, and Sunday breakfasts, where discussion often centers upon affairs of the colony—fear of raids by privateers, immigration policies, the many change-overs of colonial rule—so characteristic of that time in the Caribbean—all forming the background upon which Hubertus moves.

Yet, although Hubertus participates in the developing social history of the colony, in fact he is influenced not by social, but by personal—that is, family—history and ties. Indeed his harrowing, his ambiguous adventure, derives in part from a dualistic reaction to the blood of Kaywana's children: veneration and repulsion. He, the principal carrier of family blood and tradition, simultaneously questions and worships his inheritance. It is not surprising that a man in quest of his own morality and freedom should attempt to scrutinize anything which controls his freedom and prescribes his morality. Thus on the occasion of his choosing an English-born colonist, Rosalind, for wife, and his consequent alliance to the English plantocracy, his analysis is that:

> "However much I may want to I cannot forget the blood in my veins. Van Groenwegel blood. Blood that part of me venerates, though the other part may despise it. Faustina and I are the only two van Groenwegels who know the Tales of Old. The tales of our family's heroic deeds. We have never repeated those tales to our children, because we do not wish to keep an overweening pride in family. That is wrong. Grandma Henrickje went too far. But those tales are a vital part of me. Their impression will never be wiped out until I die . . . . The van Groenwegels never surrender. They die rather than surrender. But there it is—the other half of me rejects this principle." (227)

But he is the carrier of the van Groenwegel blood, and though he might doubt the pull of his blood ties, his daughter, Luise, does not doubt this force, indeed is quite affected by it. However, she is not only affected by the pull of Kaywana blood, but like the Kaywana stock seems sensitized by landscape. Indeed, in *The Harrowing of Hubertus*, Luise is the conjunction of history—through blood ties and landscape—through her psychic reaction to it. As Hubertus's harrowing deepens, he repeatedly ponders on his own sanity and wonders about the nature of his blood inheritance. Have the van Groenwegels, through their insistence on their family motto which demands total allegiance, become obsessed by tradition, possessed by a family mania? Thus after Luise, unclad and armed with two muskets, attempts, like her grandmother Hendrickje, to thwart a slave attack, Hubertus remarks:

> There is something of Grandma Hendrickje in you. Despicable woman, from all reports. A monster. Yet, she was a van Groenwegel. She died in battle. Mad. Mad like yourself. Mad like me. (154)

Here Mittelholzer is already projecting the decline of the van Groenwegel family, as it journeys toward obsessions and madness. Luise has seen signs of madness in her father, a condition which he in turn ascribes to her:

> "You're mad . . . . But how can you help it? It's the blood in you. There is madness in the van Groenwegels, I'm convinced of it as I was never before. Yet it's a madness I admire and revel in." (154)

Luise has already seen the incipient madness in her father, whose ambivalences and ambiguities not only warp her father's reactions, but, in fact, disjoint them.

His eyes had lost their wildly desperate look. Now they were the shifty, tortured eyes of old. Often, as a girl, Luise had wondered why they had looked like that. For the first time she thought she understood. It was his look of suffering. He never knew whether to be proud of their blood or ashamed of it. (149)

Here he is fully aware that Luise, like him—perhaps indeed like all of the van Groenwegels—cannot escape the pull of their blood, which in its transmuted state now injects a degree of madness into the family line.

The subplot of *The Harrowing of Hubertus*—the relationship between Luise and her cousin Edward, the continual family inbreeding—accentuates rather than alleviates the van Groenwegel malady. Luise accepts a mad congenital streak yet wonders about the control exercised on her by her blood inheritance. And, as Mittelholzer further picks up the dialogue of behavior and landscape he makes Luise state:

Why must some people be born with a mad streak! I'm mad. I know I'm mad, yet I can do nothing to help myself. Nothing. Nothing at all. I'm like a dry leaf that must always be blown wherever the breeze wills . . . . She laughed. That is a bad analogy. I cannot see Edward as a breeze. A breeze is soft, kind. It would blow a leaf into cool, shady places . . . . Oh, this heat. (175)

Edward reemphasizes this new element which now transfuses the family inheritance. Now to make love in the rain seems not natural, not sanctioned, but rather a sign of madness:

"You're obsessed. Mad. You're mad like me. Like your father—and mother. Out there making love in the rain. We're a mad family."

She laughed. "Very well. We're all mad. Come and make love to me—in the bed. Not in the rain." (199)

Luise's character provides Mittelholzer with a mirror for the psychic shiverings of Olivia in *Shadows Move Among Them* and the mercurial reactions to changes of atmosphere which become the dominant tonalities of *The Weather Family* and *Of Trees and the Sea*. But as yet Luise's sensitivity is not as finely attuned to psychic shadows and landscaped shimmerings as is Olivia's in *Shadows Move Among Them*. Indeed Mittelholzer, as he so often does, sketches the outline of Luise's character:

Small things that might have left no impression on her sisters made a lasting impression on Luise. She had been born with a sensitive, easily impressionable nature. And she was mercurial; even the sudden rustling of the trees in a soft wind might affect her mood—cause her to fidget and glance about her with an abrupt longing for something she could not define. (*Hubertus*, 139)

And thus, living between shadow and light and sensitive to their interplay, Luise is not only volatile and temperamental, but, touched by the family blood, is often eccentric and erratic. Landscape is not necessarily, then, a love cushion as with Kaywana, but entering into it can bring a relief from oversensitivity, in fact presages the eventual fading out of the family line, the suicide of Mary and Adrian in a creek. Luise searches for solace as the bickering world of grownups impinges upon her. Her reactions are instinctive and emotional; her desire to lose herself in nature, to be liberated by it, immediate and compelling:

> She continued to grip the rail and stare down at the rivulets of water in the compound. A desperate longing to be free of living showered through her spirit like a spray of rain from some other world—a world in which there was no resentment, no anger, no itching urge of passion. (159)

The gurgling, the trickle, the rivulets, the showering—all oft-repeated water sounds and contours of Mittelholzer's landscape—are usually used not to prohibit and stifle but to arouse and accompany passions. In Mittelholzer's Kaywana trilogy, much sex takes place in watery dampness and falling rain. Indeed, in the trilogy Mittelholzer's scenes of love are saturated with rain and water. It is not surprising, therefore, that Luise and Edward, like Kaywana and Adriansen, Katrina and Laurens, Hubertus and Faustina, as if reenacting tradition, first make love to the sound of rain:

> He laughed, and she laughed, and then they lay still and listened to the rain . . . . The gurgle of water in the compound seemed to come from years ago . . . .
> . . . she began to hear the rain again. It emerged out of the mist of blue whorls and the singing echoes that sagged criss-cross through the vast space being gradually emptied of feeling.
> . . . She touched his cheek, hearing the lovely rain. And the gurgle of water in the compound. (200–201)

Luise, like all the characters of the Kaywana trilogy, is caught in the pull of the distant past, touched by the echoes resounding from many years ago. The van Groenwegels are all deeply affected by the course of family history and by the larger movements of social history. In *Children of Kaywana*, we noted the establishment and inculcation of family tradition, the development of plantation slavery, and the acquisition of territory by the European colonists. Across the biography of a single man, *The Harrowing of Hubertus*,

Mittelholzer stresses the process of the family tradition and its incipient disintegration, the ambiguities attendant on this disintegration. In this novel, slavery has become a way of life; the plantocracy, a controlling force. In *Kaywana Blood*, the central van Groenwegel characters, Dirk and Mary, attempt not only to restore the family tradition but also to withstand the dissolution of that tradition, and by perpetuating slavery to preserve the old way of life, the plantocracy. But their attempts are in vain, because Mittelholzer relentlessly pursues the dissolution of the family, whose decline parallels the decline of slavery as an institution. The nexus of the family not only collapses but the family itself becomes so extended, so spread out, that it seems to fade away. And even the name of van Groenwegel slowly disappears, for the products of miscegenation between master and slave are often denied the family name and forced to adopt different ones. Indeed, Graham, a van Groenwegel, must change his name in order to marry a mulatto woman.

Not only family history, but the whole social history treated in the Kaywana trilogy, hinges on slavery as an institution. The decline of slavery brought with it the visible decline of the plantocracy. The disappearance of many slave plantations led to the beginnings of freed villages; the fading away of the plantocracy saw the rise of colored, free society. The trilogy is thus linked together not only by the history of the children of Kaywana, by the biography of the van Groenwegel family, but by the question of slavery, its moral consequences, miscegenation and bastardization, the disintegration of the slave system and the rise of freed men of color. All these become a vast elaborate canvas, a collage of the social history of Guyana.

Often in *The Harrowing of Hubertus*, as in *Kaywana Blood*, Mittelholzer, the historiographer, does not integrate many historical details into the fabric of the novel, nor does he intertwine history with the biography of his characters. And thus, elaboration rather than the drama of history works to slow the novel's pace, with historical exposition often replacing novelistic re-creations. Yet, so insistent is Mittelholzer in his historical detail, so elaborate and sweeping the strokes with which he depicts history, so massive the contourings of that history, that history is not only a dominant theme, but, possessing its own character, indeed becomes an essential statement of the novels, giving them a certain weightiness and density. To be sure, Mittelholzer piles up and accumulates many historical details, but his documentation of these details gives an authenticity to his narration, a veracity to his fiction. Further, this constant juxtaposition of historical fact and fiction achieves a contrasting effect which, by placing fiction in relief, heightens its imaginative quality. History, too, on one level gives to the story line a straight, uninterrupted chronology, a structural sequence, which, when alternating with recall and flashback, lends a fluctuating quality to the story line, an inner mobility to plot development.

Thus we follow historical phenomena which have affected the making of the Caribbean area. Slavery, as an institution, is not simply presented, but all of its multiple ramifications and future social consequences are revealed throughout the trilogy. Even Hubertus, guided as he is by personal ethical considerations, does not question the morality of slavery or its evil consequences.

> The negro slaves . . . he considered as beings in an entirely separate category. [They] . . . came from the jungles of Africa; they were heathens who had been intended by God to be the servants of the white Christians. (20)

He, like so many slave masters could only ascribe brutishness and savagery to a slave, could only be guided by a paternalistic attitude in dealing with those he felt to be naturally inferior, "his serfs" (144). In this instance, his habitual analysis of actions is completely suspended, his constant moralizing set aside.

> Sunday was the one free day allowed to the slaves. On this day they tended the provision patches alloted to them, and sang and beat their tom-toms. It did not matter to them that they were desecrating the sabbath, heathens that they were. Heathens, thought Hubertus, . . . were not accountable to the Almighty for their actions. God pardoned them from the outset, for they knew no better. For them there existed no harrowing problems of right and wrong. (43)

Indeed, Hubertus is the epitome of the white slave owner who not only patronizes the slaves and justifies their servitude, but, in fact, attempts to stifle and destroy their heritage. He, in his superior judgment, knows what is best for "his people."

> The slaves that night would hold a dance. Such occasions of merry-making took place about twice a year on most plantations, and planters, as a rule, allowed a whole-day holiday in order to give their people time to cook and make the necessary preparations. Some planters even shared out extra rations—though these were few. Hubertus was one of the few, but he saw to it that strict rules in respect to the conduct of the festivities were observed. (69)

Thus progressively Mittelholzer shows how deep feelings of white superiority were inculcated and how they took root in the minds of the white plantocracy of the Caribbean. To Hubertus, as to so many masters, slaves are so infantile that when rumors of a possible slave insurrection reach him, he cannot truly conceive of its taking place. His feeling of superiority is indisputable; his condescension evident. Thus he addresses the slaves as if they are children, indeed, simpletons:

> "I know that you can be good people when you want to be. You can work hard and obey orders. I wish you well, as I have always done, but when you disobey my orders and the orders of the overseers, then I shall not wish you well. I wish only to be kind and humane toward you, but if you . . . persist in not obeying the orders of the overseers, then I shall be angry and I shall not be kind to you. I shall be harsh. I shall punish you." (144)

Mittelholzer shows that the still-persistent attitudes of white superiority plaguing the Caribbean stretch far backward in time, with their roots in the history of plantation slavery. To many of the planters it was inconceivable, not only that slaves could rebel to achieve their freedom, but even more so, that freedom would be given to slaves by colonial powers. Mittelholzer, as he touches on the phenomenon of slavery, realizes the close correlation between capitalism and slavery. And many planters argued that since abolition would mean a tremendous loss of revenue to any colonial power, the slaves would never be granted their freedom by the metropolitan powers.

> "Such a measure could never be passed. England depends upon her West Indian colonies for the bulk of her wealth. What would happen to the merchants in Bristol if the slave trade were abandoned? Parliament would never be so idiotic as to let a thing like this go through." (*Blood*, 60)

In *Kaywana Blood*, the plantocracy is more concerned with its continuing loss of capital, the evident infeasibility of continuing the slave system, and the enroaching decline of its status and power.

But abolition did take place, and with it the decline in prosperity of the plantocracy. Mittelholzer seems principally concerned with the fortunes of the planters; he neither deals with the reaction of the slave class to abolition nor does he treat affairs of the slaves after abolition. He does sketch the fortunes of those slaves who were products of miscegenation, who were directly related in one way or another to the van Groenwegel dynasty, either as mistresses or as legitimate and illegitimate colored family, and through them he shows the beginnings of free colored society. Yet, he omits any detailed references to free slaves as a social group. Nowhere in the trilogy do we see the development of this group or its social evolution. Indeed Mittelholzer in his preoccupation with one class, the plantocracy, to the exclusion of another class, the vast body of slaves, does not portray the grand drama of abolition. Nowhere do we feel the vast social churnings consequent on abolition; nowhere do we see the uprootings and movements of vast numbers of slaves attendant on this social upheaval. Mittelholzer's failure to deal with this large social group in the historical development of Guyana makes his portrayal of Guyanese history lopsided, his treatment one-dimensional. However, Mittelholzer does present the decline, the dissolution of a family line and bankruptcy of the plantocracy and the decay of many plantations. But decay and decline began to set in even before abolition, and the fortune of many families, including the van Groenwegels, were on the wane. The last generation of the van Groenwegel family fights to hold onto its fortunes, and to retain at least a semblance of "master-distinction."

> "Times are not as good as they used to be, Dirk my lad. Slaves are expensive, so economy must be our watchword, mustn't it?" . . .
>
> "Quite so, Uncle Raphael, but surely there are appearances, if I may say so, which should by all means be kept up. With a name like ours in the colonies . . . ." (165)

In terms of Caribbean social attitudes, the keeping up of appearances is no simple illusion, but rather is fraught with many social consequences and complexities. For it is not merely the desire to keep up a front which is at stake here; it is the desire to keep the van Groenwegel blood pure, that is, to conceal any of the mixtures of miscegenation, the brown and Black offspring, and further to shun the "second cousins" of the family, to reject any illegitimate relationship of a van Groenwegel of the master class with a member of the slave class, to deny the master's name to the bastard. Thus it is that the ball is passed to Frick, the slave overseer, who is ordered to assume fatherhood for Jacob, the bastard son of Nibia and Storm, a late member of the van Groenwegel line.

In *Kaywana Blood*, Black concubinage becomes instutionalized to such an extent that Storm and both his sons are all unable to resist the physical attraction of Black women. Storm is bound to his English wife, Elizabeth, by duty, to his Black servant, Nibia, by passion. His son, Graham, having fondled Nibia's breast while suckling as a child, now in his manhood is aroused by a Black woman. So strong is his fixation, so deep is his yearning for the Black woman, Rose, that when she abandons him after their marriage, he not only becomes a homosexual but, furthering the decline of the van Groenwegel line, becomes impotent. However, in the complex sexual relations between races which provide the basis for interlocking plots and subplots of *Kaywana Blood*, we discover that Rose, though not carrying the van Groenwegel name, is indeed the daughter of Hubertus by the mulatto woman, Sarah Hubert, whom subsequently Hubertus respectfully sets up as a provision shop keeper. But before Rose's cousin Graham can marry her, he is forced by his brother Dirk, who is striving to keep the van Groenwegel blood pure, to adopt another surname. Thus it is that the marriage of

Graham and Rose hurries the decline of the van Groenwegel destiny on two levels, in reproductive powers and in name. At the same time that Dirk forces Graham to adopt another name, Dirk is passionately involved with Rose, an involvement which continues after his marriage to Cornelia. Like Hubertus, Dirk is torn by contradictory passions, in his case, the cult of van Groenwegel tradition and passion for the Black woman, Rose. In the tradition of many of the children of Kaywana, his passion vibrates with the landscape, is echoed in the elements.

> The trembling in him now was like a cloud of fulfillment settling through his loins—a thunder-cloud wreathing with heat and murmurous with soothing noise. (272)

Indeed *Kaywana Blood* revolves around sex and passion, miscegenation and bastardization. In this, the last of the trilogy, Mittelholzer accelerates the decline of the van Groenwegel family, quickens the dispersion of the blood, and often, in recapitulation, tries to emphasize the cause of the dispersion and decline.

> "The sexual urge. That is the driving force, my child, behind all our actions and our destinies. It colours our lives from birth to grave. Only blinkered fools like the fools we see about us these days are unaware of it. The sexual urge. Yes. It can make or break a family. Mary, Adrian. They would have been alive today but for the madness of the urge that drove them to what they did. Francis. Pelham. Uncle Edward and Aunt Luise. Cousin Hubertus. It was the sexual urge that fashioned their destinies." (498)

Kaywana Blood thus becomes a tracing and retracing of parentage through family letters and documents. Multiple questions make for numerous intertwining situations and crisscrossing conflicts. Thus *Kaywana Blood* is not tightly-knit together, but spread out and diffuse; the lines of development often blurred and indistinct.

The fire-blood of Kaywana no longer dominates the passions of her children. Thinned by time and diluted by adulteration, it has lost its potency. Now the children of Kaywana have merged with many peoples and have spread out across the land. And their family line is no longer sharply defined but obscure, its descendants indistinguishable. Mittelholzer, as he attempts to bridge the past with the present, leaping across years and giving contemporaneity to his trilogy, rapidly sketches the social evolution of Guyanese society. Many of the members of the van Groenwegel family, especially brown- and Black-complexioned ones whose names have been altered, go abroad to pursue the professions so typical of colonial peoples: law, medicine, engineering; some become political leaders. Perhaps Mittelholzer's novelistic premise is that though the fire-blood of Kaywana is adulterated and seemingly lost, it never really disappears but lives on. However, the later descendants of Kaywana abandon the life of the plantation, can no longer, as did Kaywana, feel the deep pull of the landscape. They have begun the movement toward the urban areas, and have already begun their long exile to study in the European cities.

In the Kaywana trilogy, history is used as a backdrop that gives structural chronology to the novels; the plot is an elaboration of the events that went into the development of Guyana. In Mittelholzer's *My Bones and My Flute*, history is injected with a sense of mystery, becomes the total mood background, an evocation shrouding the past. In the Kaywana trilogy, the characters are primarily controlled by the pull of blood; in *My Bones and My Flute* and in *Shadows Move Among Them* the characters are affected by emanations from the spirit world, by psychic tremorings of the historical past. In the trilogy, the principal characters, whether slave owner or slave, are makers of history. In both *My Bones and My Flute* and *Shadows Move Among Them*, the characters are engaged in either an adventure or experiment based on that history. In fact, history is not only mood or atmosphere but becomes the principal motif against which the story unfolds. Now the ruins of the former plantations haunt the memories of characters and evoke wonder. The sense of wonder lends to history a new reality and, sensitizing it, imbues it with a new image. Mittelholzer's principal narrator in *My Bones and My Flute*, Milton Woodsley, ponders on the nature of plantation life and resurrects its historical setting:

> I found myself smiling as I tried to imagine what Goed de Vries must have looked like two centuries ago when it was a flourishing sugar or cotton plantation under the Dutch. All that jungle that loomed beyond the clearing must have been cultivated terrain . . . . Perhaps at this very hour a bell would be clanging stridently or a horn cooing to call in the gangs from the fields—or, if they had already come in to summon them to evening repast under the soughing branches of a sandbox tree; or for the day's punishments which the overseer or his assistant had to superintend. This same reddish sunshine must have shone on many a naked black body secured in the stocks, and the casual overseer, puffing at his long thin-stemmed pipe, must have stood and watched these bodies on many a day turn a richer red than even sunshine can distill. (Mittelholzer, *My Bones and My Flute*, 48–49)

As in the Kaywana trilogy, natural phenomena evoke past occurrences: the red sky of the setting sun mirrors the blood-red scenes of punishment cruelly administered in the past to slaves. In *My Bones and My Flute* and in *Shadows*

Move Among Them, history is thus charged with sensations, landscape resonates with psychic emotion. For instance, the bones of the slave master can find rest only after they are buried in a Christian ceremony under the very stone on which the slave stocks of old stood. And ironically again, it is the Bible belonging to Rayburn, a descendant of slaves, which is used in the atonement rites for the burial of the bones of the Dutch plantation master.

Many of the principal characters in *My Bones and My Flute* and *Shadows Move Among Them*, springing from ancestors whose bones are buried in the earth of Guyana, seem to be physically attuned to the landscape, to receive its vibrations and to react to its moods. In *Shadows Move Among Them*, Mittelholzer shapes his novel around the harmonious interplay between natural phenomena and human emotion; in *My Bones and My Flute*, between historical landscape and emotional states.

The characters in *My Bones and My Flute* enter and inhabit a deeply psychic atmosphere, where not only do they receive psychic tremors, but also seem to give them off. In both novels, landscape is all-important. *My Bones and My Flute* centers upon the psychic reactions to the touching of a historical parchment and the consequent fluctuating emotional states of the Nevinson family and Milton Woodsley, the principal characters whose old creole ancestry goes back to the late eighteenth century. It is clear Mittelholzer has opened his lenses even wider not simply to explore the visual landscape, merely natural phenomena, but to embrace the larger cosmos, the unnatural of the cosmos. Now his lenses delve behind the real, and grasping at the surreal, attempt to capture its unknown dimensions. Mittelholzer digs into these dimensions and imbuing them with a macabre quality, pushes his characters into a perilous encounter with them. The further the Nevinsons and Milton penetrate into the psychic cosmos which Mittelholzer is unfolding, the more heightened are their sensibilities, the more emotional their reactions, in fact, the more physically tuned-in they become to the unfamiliar, the unnatural, to those regions beyond man's comprehension.

> It was no ordinary peril . . . but one that was warped and unnatural and sickeningly horrible—a peril from which we seemed to know with a peculiar certainty there would be no slipping out of once we had been overpowered and entrammelled . . . .
>
> We "perceived" that there was this fearful and stinking pocket of nether-life awaiting us. With probably the same psychic power that creates a series of retrospective pictures in the mind of a drowning man we "knew" what menaced us. And we could sense, too, that unless we fought with all the fury and bitterness and impassioned determination human will could generate, we might as well consider ourselves already as lost creatures . . . we had moved within range of forces that had

nothing to do with the forces with which men are familiar, and we were about to dodge out of reach of normal laws and be gone forever into a new and slithering revolting sphere of intelligence. (*My Bones*, 193–194)

In his claim that a chance shifting of events initiates the action of the novel, Mittelholzer is moving away from the explicable into the realm of the accidental, from the natural to the supernatural. Mittelholzer, who states that the only responsibility of the author is to dovetail events, seems to accept the existence of a "nether-life" and of new spheres of intelligence.

The characters, once they are under the influence of these psychic forces, are unable to resist their pull, and slide irrevocably into them. The psychic landscape seems to become both insubstantial and oppressive, and the direct correspondence between the characters' nervous reactions (not, as in the trilogy, their emotional states) and the psychic changes in the landscape becomes increasingly more apparent. Now both the senses and the sensory world, even as time becomes a transformer of landscape, disintegrate and dissolve. Indeed, the concept of landscape that Mittelholzer developed in the Kaywana trilogy undergoes change, for here the vitality of elements, of green leaves, of sunlight, of pregnant sound, diminishes; now they seem to lose their potency and creative force. Landscape has almost become a mirage, an illusion.

> I am aware of . . . a shadow-voice which assures me that there is no substance in the scene I am beholding, that everything I discern is simply a grand imposture thrust upon me through the artifices of my functioning nervous system . . . —all the mobility, all the aliveness, all the pregnant vigour, of this array of symbols that shimmers in my awareness—is, in reality, death. Death in the guise of movement and sunshine, death in the guise of green leaves and a pattern of sounds. (43–44)

Damp, high-piled leaves were the procreative bed for Kaywana's children, symbolizing continuity and timelessness, the merging of space and time. Now in *My Bones and My Flute* and in *Shadows Move Among Them*, the original regenerative force and revitalizing energy have been lost through the violent history of plantation slavery; the spongy carpet, layers of leaves, have become piles of human bones. These bones do not seem at rest, do not constitute the ontological link which the earth provides between the living and the dead ancestors. Indeed, the history of plantation slavery has imbued the once-vital, lush landscape with a quality of death, with

> a musty, sweetish rankness that at one instant would seem very refreshing and make you want to breathe deeply, then would suddenly awaken your distrust, for there would seem to enter it an earthy dankness as of

centuries of rotting leaves and the bones of long-buried corpses. (*My Bones*, 53)

Yet the link between history and landscape is established, and that spirit world which heightens the sensibilities of many Caribbean peoples and breeds superstitions is created. In *My Bones and My Flute*, the characters eventually seem embalmed in a spirit world where rot and putrefaction prevail. They move beyond the boundaries of actuality, enter a nonmaterial, unmeasurable time, a time which is inimical and threatening.

It is not surprising that in such a landscape, in such a setting, superstition and magic become some of the principal motifs of *My Bones and My Flute* and guide the development of the plot. The tension of the novel comes about through psychic confrontations, and the emotions of the characters are directed by these confrontations; yet the plot is simple. Mynheer Voorman, a Dutch plantation owner, died along with his family in the slave rebellion of 1763. His experiments on the flute and his dabbling in black magic had brought him into conflict with the dark powers of the world, so that his spirit was in danger of falling into their grasp. Before he died, he wrote a parchment and cast a spell on it, condemning anyone who handled the document to be empowered by the piercing call of the flute until the document's instructions were carried out. The action is generated by the attempts of the characters of the novel to free themselves from the curse of the parchment. The plot is developed in a series of melodramatic scenes, all of which present the varying reactions of the characters to the call of the flute. At first Mrs. Nevison cannot hear it, but slowly after nightmarish sequences in a dream, she, too, comes under its spell:

> I heard a flute playing ahead of me, and I had a terribly strong inclination to follow the music. I just felt I *had* to find out who was playing the flute. I ran on along the path. And then the most horrible thing of all happened. I felt a bony hand grip my arm from behind, and a voice whispered in my ear. I can remember the words distinctly. 'No farther to-day.' I felt I was going to faint—and then I woke up. (110)

Though the dream is narrated in flat tones which hardly grip the senses, its effects heighten the tension and in the subsequent crisis break down previous social distinctions and barriers. Although Mrs. Nevison claims to have "never hobnobbed with niggers" (96), as her fear of the furry demons increases, she appeals to Rayburn, the Black servant, to still her shaking spirit. At first his presence wards off her fears, but eventually, they both experience the pull of the flute. Now all the characters plunge further and further into the nightmarish adventure:

> We found ourselves moving—stumbling like drunk people along the
> track, it seemed to us, though afterwards we discovered it was deeper into
> the jungle itself, into the very bushes themselves and quite off the track.
> How long this journey lasted we were unable to calculate. Time
> seemed a myth, a meaningless symbol. We lurched on, driven by an
> incomprehensible compulsion. We had no will in the matter. Our mouths
> opened and shut as we attempted to yell at each other, but there was no
> sound. Evanescent twigs and leaves and branches brushed past us, grey
> and insubstantial; furry softnesses charged into our rushing bodies without
> injury or pain. (214)

Perhaps they have become so attuned to the inimical landscape that they
are oblivious to its threats, are dizzied by their nearness to the psychic call
of the flute, and unheedingly stumble through the undergrowth to the place
where the Dutchman's bones lie. Thus undergrowth becomes both barrier
and conductor. Space and time fuse and both, now charged with tension,
become more extensive yet less immediate. It is not until the final climax
that immediate local influences dominate the characters.

The landscape, charged with slave history, is all-compelling, all-controlling, and yet it is not as compelling or as influential as in *Shadows Move
Among Them*. In *Shadows Move Among Them*, from the very beginning, the
tremors of the landscape, its shadowiness, envelop the lives of all the
characters. Landscape becomes vital, sensuous and vibrant, seems curative
and kindly. Thus it is that characters do not stumble under its pull; dreams
are not unusual, but are accepted as the natural state of being. And even
though the system set up by the plantation owner Harmston hardly differs
from plantation autocracy, even though slave chains are used to frighten
servants, yet here there are no unburied bones of slave masters seeking rest
within the landscape. What is presented in *Shadows Move Among Them* is a
modern counterpart of the plantation system ruled over by a benign, yet
autocratic "plantation master." The established order seems harmonious:
Reverend Harmston is not harrowed, nor does he indulge in overt concubinage, for the local influences can induce a state of sleep-walking during
which one's urges and desires can be satisfied. But in this modern plantation
structure created by Mittelholzer, not only the master and his immediate
family sleep-walk. Even Gregory, the newcomer from England, succumbs to
the local influences, sleep-walks and does his thing.

The young, sensitive, paranoid Englishman, Gregory, who felt threatened
by his wife's accomplishments and menaced by her presence, comes to his
Guyana cousins, the Harmstons, on his discharge from a mental institution
to recuperate from his illness. It is hoped that the local influences will be not

only restorative but also therapeutic. At first the landscape of Guyana seems, to this high-strung and nervous young man, as threatening as his wife's accomplishments, as menacing as her presence. The alive, watchful natural phenomena vibrate with presences behind which shadows lurk; the whole atmosphere is oppressive; the spirit world, ominous.

> As the stream narrowed and the jungle reared silently higher and higher and denser on either bank the blacker and more evil a smile the water appeared to brew. The shadowed spaces made by the low-hanging foliage momently seemed to gather a deeper gloom and to glower with the sullen menace of many watching eyes: eyes concealed amid poison-berries and slow-drifting blossoms. The trade wind, which had made the heat in the little town at the mouth of the river so bearable as not to be heeded, no more could be felt; gradually it had withdrawn as though sensing in this savagely vigorous verdure spirits alien to its cool, ocean-free careering. And as it had fallen back the heat, poised and silky, entwined itself with stifling power around the steamer. (Mittelholzer, *Shadows Move Among Them*, 10)

Here even the elements seem to be in contention: the earth at odds with the water and the wind. The dense jungle foliage not only rears up over the river, bringing out its more evil qualities, but it also stifles the freedom of the wind.

The narrow river takes Gregory further and further into his own shadowy interior as well as the gloomy recesses of the region. Already the shadows are beginning to "move among them," protecting Gregory from the probing gaze of the other passengers, but not from the scrutiny of the jungle, which watches "back at him with malicious glitterings in the scorching sun" (12), or even from his own objective self-scrutiny: "In these moments he saw himself outside his body, viewing his body" (12). Gregory is as tremulous as the landscape, living two lives separated by shadows. As Gregory approaches Berkelhoost his auto-scrutiny deepens, his disembodiment brings about that two-ness which leads to a breakup, a fragmentation:

> Innumerable times he had pictured himself breaking up into so many pitiable bits . . . . In such instants he cringed outside himself and whimpered in spirit-silence, sorry for his plight and in need of companionship—and the pity and love of his fellow-men. (13)

This search for pity and love takes him to the Harmston family, to Olivia, and to the eventual conjugal love of Mabel (where the shadows become increasingly more benign). Soon his anxieties, his nervous bouts of trembling, his quickening fears and rapid emotional changes come under the therapeutic, soothing influences of the landscape.

> Intangible like the warm wind that flooded in through the window
> unhurried like a funeral, night moved within the arc of time, and the
> jungle waited, brewing imperturbably, out of the dew and dead leaf and
> mould, the aroma of dawn. The river flowed in the moonlight, and the
> moonlight dimmed and went out, but the river flowed on without a grunt
> of comment. When early morning fog began to wreathe and turn the air
> grey and honey in the light that grew like a cloud over the jungle the
> river kept on flowing, never for a moment moved to cry out yea or nay.
> And not a leaf or limb in the whole jungle winked or nodded in recogni-
> tion of the event. (224)

The relentless cycle of time, the calm, measured passage from night to day,
color tones that modulate from gray to honey, and an ever-flowing river,
unhurried in its certainty, not fearful of its continuity, all induce a calming
reflection, making Gregory wish hypothetically to live "without fear of
tomorrow's thunder" (226).

Now the whole landscape seems clearer and brighter to Gregory,
matching his own increasing loss of anxiety, his growing lucidity. Changes
have taken place. Before, "anxiety . . . closed in around him . . . like the
neutral walls of a terrifying limbo" (13); now he is smiling. The jungle then
"reared silently higher and higher and denser on either bank" (10), reflecting
black and evil in the water; now the jungle is fresh and is "reflected with
leaf-detailed clarity" (227). Before, he was scrutinized by the jungle's probing
eyes; now he calmly looks at the jungle and reflects:

> It seemed very safe in its inarticulation. No matter how long he watched
> it it would never talk back at him or advise him how to keep sane. He
> remembered how long he lay in bed this morning and watched it growing
> clearer in the mist and brightening daylight, how he wished he could
> have been it instead of himself. (231–232)

It is evident that for Mittelholzer a vital and animate spirit force exists
within the vegetable world; the spirit-world is real. It would not be difficult,
then, to achieve the merging of man's spirit with the spirit of the trees and
the river, for Gregory to absorb the mood of the foliage and of the river.

> Such a plurality of greens, Gregory thought, watching the jungle from his
> window . . . . Shadows were lengthening . . . . If I could probe into the
> green it's possible I'd find reality glinting like a jewel within the chloro-
> phyll. Crystalline rivers of living spirit in leaves and branches . . . . (169)
>
> . . . if I joined my spirit to the passivity of this water and the trees I
> would achieve the peace I want. (201)

Withal Gregory is a neurotic Englishman, a foreigner who, by achieving a correspondence with the landscape, succeeds in quieting his anxieties and allaying his fears.

Olivia, however, is not a foreigner. She does not have to achieve correspondence with the landscape; rather she vibrates at its center. So much in harmony is she with the world around her that she seems to be the spirit and essence of that world. Olivia, probably one of Mittelholzer's most winsome characters, slips and slides and frolics through the shadows until she herself seems to become a shadow. She is a child of the landscape, an impish spirit-creature of Berkelhoost, sensitive to all its movements, its every mood. "The sunshine was on her back—not hot noon sunshine but cool, wine-coloured and mixed with long tree-branch shadows" (18). She lives the shadows, seeing everything and everyone as embodying shadows: "I wonder . . . what new shadows . . . [Gregory's] bringing with him" (9), she queries. She lives in a spirit world, in her world of shadows, soothed by its melancholy, a chameleon of its twilight colors. She is in total communion with shadows that move through the church, her favorite haunt.

> And now her blood rose in mist above the pew; in a minute the whole church would be filled with a sunset glow . . . . In the jungle, far away, a bird began to sing. It was a sad song, but it soothed her, for the magic-swan was singing it. Her swan-song . . . . (6)

For her all the sights and sounds of her region are interwoven; all is evocative, everything is mood. Hers is a world of whispers, of muted tones, of cool recesses. It is a spun cob-webbed world, a world of creatures, of insects.

> [Olivia] hugged her knees tighter, and giggled, feeling cosy and full of secrets. . . .
> She turned on to her stomach and leant over and peered under the seat. When her eyes got accustomed to the dark she made out a milk-white web at the back. . . . In this web lived a blue-black hairy bush-spider. No one but she knew that it lived here. (7)

This is not the demon world of *My Bones and My Flute;* here the landscape is animate, alive with eyes and evocative of history and ruins. Some of these ruins recall the days of slavery, of torture, of chained bodies and manacles. Such manacles, which now are the playthings of Olivia, still are the instruments of punishment for the half-Indian, half-Black groveling Logan. Indeed, Berkelhoost in its social hierarchy is quite reminiscent of a slave plantation, albeit a benign one. At the bottom of the heap is Logan; just a shade above him is the sadistic Ellen, who from time to time revels in beating the somewhat masochistic Olivia. Above Ellen are the socialized and Christianized Amerindians, the Buckmasters, who are the objects of the plantation master's "sleep-walkings," and so on to the neurotic English foreigner, Gregory, who is yet for Ellen and Logan a bossman. And at the top moves the benignly cruel, austere, pompous Reverend Harmston, Olivia's father, spinning his own social philosophies. "He's everything in one up here" (193), says Olivia of her father, even though he repeatedly chastizes and slaps her for her impudence.

Olivia lives the world of shadows, deeply feeling them; her father intones the world of shadows, verbalizing them. For Olivia, the shadows are subjective reality; for her father they are an objective, externalized reality, but a reality on which the senses play, actualized by the senses, fantasied by dream. To be sure, given his social philosophy, Reverend Harmston will not undergo the harrowing of Hubertus, torn between his "shadow-self" and his real self, between the word and the act, the outward show and the inner sensory perception. Reverend Harmston accepts the existence of the sensory world, realizes the pull of the senses, and believes in psychic shadows. Such is his religion:

> "I believe . . ."
>
> "In what I can sense," the congregation responded . . .
>
> "And I believe . . ."
>
> "In the reality beyond the shadows . . ."
>
> "The shadows that move among us," intoned Mr. Harmston. . . .
>
> "Verily, I believe . . ."
>
> "In God the Father of all Myth . . ."
>
> "Himself," intoned the reverend gentleman, "the most wonderful Myth."
>
> "And in Jesus Christ," chanted the congregation.
>
> "Born of Joseph and Mary," continued Mr. Harmston, "in natural union."
>
> "In natural union," confirmed the congregation.
>
> "Jesus, among men, the King of Dreamers . . ." (137–138)

For him the shadows that move among them are the tenuous, sliding dividers between the visible real world and the insubstantial world of dreams. Indeed, perhaps here lies the pulsebeat of Mittelholzer's creations, as he novelizes the real, and actualizes the imagined. So tenuous is the line for him between the world of spirit and of matter, of illusion and reality, of fantasy and actuality:

> "We ourselves, unwittingly, have created reality, my boy, and we have created it out of the dream-stuff of our own fancies. . . . We can exist in harmony with reality—which is to say we can be happy—only if we admit

the tenuous quality of reality; if we perceive the close affinity between actuality and dream." (198)

Olivia puts it much more simply:

> Day-dreams and sleep-dreams, thought Olivia . . . . I wish I knew what's the difference between them. I've had as many nightmares imagining things during the day as I've had at night in bed when I'm asleep. (224)

And even Gregory, who gradually has come under the influence of the shadows and has started to move among them, finally slides easily between illusion and reality, and now moves in tune to the rhythms of the landscape around him. Now the water is cool and real, and the darkness, which "entwined itself with stifling power around the steamer" (10) on his first journey to Berkelhoost, has disappeared:

> The sky, he saw, had not yet lost its light . . . . Every detail of the sky lay reflected in a cool river . . . . it was in the water the actual existed and in the sky the make-believe. (327)

In *My Bones and My Flute* and *Shadows Move Among Them*, the landscape, infused with the quality of the past, with history, shivers, becomes psychic, and often seems to be spirit-world. Characters are caught in and ruled by phenomena that slip between reality and illusion, move from the natural to the unnatural. The whole mood is shadowy, often insubstantial; the atmosphere, surreal.

In *The Wild Coast* and *Black Midas* by Jan Carew, the characters, vibrating to the secret rhythms of their birthplace, are affected by their relationships to their geographic environment, by their nearness to their roots. In Carew the fate of the characters is determined completely by their relationship to their natural environment. Indeed, Carew is a novelist of a different order than Mittelholzer. Through a picaresque presentation he delineates various regions of Guyana, yet his novels operate not, as in Mittelholzer, on many levels, but rather on a single plane. Carew, a good storyteller, lays out the tensions and problems of his characters without probing, like Mittelholzer, deeply into the emotional consequences of these tensions. He is more a novelist of movement and action than of emotional analysis.

Carew's characters live closer to the earth in freedmen's villages along the coast or in the interior of Guyana. And since their language is also consonant with their environment, their dialogue is earth-palaver; their descriptions of one another, earth-metaphor. Unlike Mittelholzer, who in the Kaywana trilogy records the history of Guyana particularly through the biographies of the plantocracy, history in Carew is recorded by the old folk, carriers of the old tradition of the villages. An old man of the village, Grandpa, tells Aron:

> "Boy, the white man does write down all they story in black and white, but we does keep we own lock up in we belly. Time will come when we got to write we story too 'cause if we don't write it down it going to get lost. Now all the young people going 'way from the land. In long time past days we used to tell we story with drum, but soon even the drum won't talk no more." (Carew, *Black Midas*, 22)

Perhaps soon, the type of villages which Carew presents in his novels will disappear; but before that time, Carew in *Black Midas* and *The Wild Coast* sets out to capture the secret rhythms of these villages strewn along the coast of Guyana and the vibrations of the peoples of these villages. For Carew, each landscape, each region, possesses its own particular rhythm, its own pulse-beat; "the sounds of wind and surf were like heartbeats in Tarlogie" (*The Wild Coast*, 181–182). To be attuned to that landscape is to receive strength from it; to be in harmony with a region is to be fortified by it. Since a person's strength and weakness, his tranquility or anxiety, his entire mood or being, are in direct correlation to his proximity to his roots, character development is directly related to the character's movements from one region of Guyana to another. Thus it is that Carew ascribes distinctive moods to various landscapes of Guyana, which in turn create their own distinctive emotional reactions and sensory responses in his characters. This relationship between man and landscape is accepted by the principal character in *Black Midas*, Aron, or Shark as he is called, who touches many people, who traverses many regions.

> I had persuaded Santos to leave the small enclosure of his easy-going life, and once he left it the secret rhythms which reach from the earth, on which a village child is born, to his heart had jangled themselves out of harmony. (*Black Midas*, 165)

Through the descriptions of various types of people, pictures are presented of that element in the landscape akin to their personalities. In this way, Carew establishes correspondence between man and landscape. Thus there are river people and town people; forest people and village people.

> The moment we had left Bartica [a town] I had noticed a change come over [Pancho]; he became at once more relaxed and more alive. The rhythm of life in the forest was one that he could respond to like a dancer to a drum . . . . he was a river-man endowed with all the tension and the ease, the speed and the power of water running down from the mountains
> . . . .

He knew the language of the forest creatures, and would talk to them as if they were human. (259, 262)

But even as man appropriates specific regions to himself, each region, too, can exert its own particular pull on a person, inject its own particular quality into his movements. So even though the protagonist of *The Wild Coast*, Hector, was born in the city and lived there till the age of nine, the development of his character, his sensibilities, are completely molded through the earth of Tarlogie.

And since many of the characters in Carew's novels are traveling men, their wanderings and their travel sweep them through the vast spreading land of Guyana. Their lifestyle, an adventure, is as grand as the landscape through which they move. They are "giants subduing a wide world . . . heroes of big spaces" (*Black Midas*, 160). But the landscape, though grand and vast, is often dangerous, inimical, threatening: a land of vast savannahs and waterfalls, yes; but one also of savage animals and reptiles: "This bush does make you like a wild beast, and then you does got to fight you way back to prove you is a man" (160). Spontaneous violence is endemic to the forest interior, and as the heroes go forth their actions refracting from that landscape are often volatile, imbued with an instinctive passion and charged with reactive violence.

At the high point of Hector's initiation under the tutelage and guidance of the old master bushman, Doorne, and the giant of a son, Tenga, he makes his way across the swamplands and goes into the dense forest on a dangerous wild hog hunt. At that time he reacts impetuously and with reckless spontaneity to a bloody and violent battle between a jaguar and a pack of wild hogs:

> The fight sickened, and at the same time, fascinated Hector. His sympathies were all with the jaguar and up to the end he wanted him to escape. He found himself shouting encouragement, and when the jaguar was defeated fury took hold of him. He sprang down from the platform and rushed at the hogs. (*Coast*, 115)

No less impetuous, no less recklessly spontaneous is Aron's rescue of a man drowning in a treacherous river deep in the heart of the interior. Both of these reactions may be characterized as innocent, albeit ignorant of the dangers of a violence inherent in the landscape. For Carew's landscape explodes with the primeval violence of the creatures inhabiting the wild coast, its swamps, its vast forests. The elements, too, unleashing their inner power, threaten and brutalize, furiously ripping away any element of nature that stands in their way.

The wind gathered strength and suddenly it was ripping and roaring through the forest, scything down giant moras, greenhearts, aramatas. There was a crashing and a thundering and the earth trembled under us. (*Black Midas*, 264)

In this interplay of man and landscape, Carew is exploring the essential nature of the wild coast of Guyana, perhaps attempting to show the origins of any violence which lurks in the landscape, which lies in the shadowy history of Guyana. The question posed is whether violence, so much part of the historical development of settlement and plantation slavery, has become endemic to the landscape where, to some of the descendants of slaves, the history of violence still seems to live on, a residual, lurking patrimony: "The long nights of dungeoned darkness [were] too full of the voices of dead slaves calling out for vengeance, not to breed terror." (*Coast*, 208)

Clearly, as in Mittelholzer, landscape becomes the carrier of history. Yet in Carew, it is not documented but oral history, reenacted and recounted in the mouths of old folk, like Sister, Hector's guardian:

Why you think that [piper owl] does always sing sad songs? I will tell you why, it's because the souls of dead planters does live inside them . . . .
. . . Them old planters was greedy men, mean with stony hearts where pity never had a place to lay its head. On nights like this when the wind is high you can hear the slaves crying out over the swamp and the piper owl does sing songs over them to mock them. (130, 131))

Thus in Carew landscape is not only co-extensive with man's sensibilities, but also with his traditions.

The central protagonist of *The Wild Coast*, Hector, is the descendant of a Black mother and a man who paraded as a Dutch master. After living for nine years in Georgetown, he is sent back to Tarlogie, where his father has an estate, to be cured of his city ways—in fact to learn there that part of his family history, which is known only to the old Black woman, Sister, who "was working for the family before your papa born" (17). In Tarlogie, where the sun "gets in your blood and the wind starts to cool the marrow of your bones," Hector begins to feel the secret rhythms of the area where many of his family before him lived. Thus Hector's return to Tarlogie is a return through landscape to his history, to be initiated into the lifestyle of the coast, there to be taught the secrets of the bush by the old man Doorne and the secrets of passion by the Black woman, Elsa. European and African ancestry is unable to resist the call of the drums, to repel the root call of his African blood. Here, man, race, and landscape cohere.

The wind-dance was a link with Africa. His ancestors had been hauled out of this continent and scattered over the hemisphere . . . . The wind was a symbol of absolute freedom, it was invisible, amorphous, imbued with titanic energies, no stockades could contain it nor could whips and chains humble it. (*Coast*, 95)

His fragmentation from an imposed European foreign tutelage leads to a vitalistic linkage. As if impotent to resist a compelling sexual urge and passion, he violently seeks to possess the samba woman, Elsa, who energized his father's virility and now initiates Hector into sex, taking his virginity. All is generational interplay, precedence, all landscaped history. The passion, the turbulence inherent to the landscape, not the ethical principles enshrined in foreign books, prevail. Hector, too, it seems, follows the flute of his bones. Similarly, Aron, no longer innocent, and forgetful of his earlier bookishness, is affected by the passion and brutal greed with which the mining interior seems fraught:

I couldn't help thinking that if I killed Santos and threw his body into the river I could say that I saw the cannibal fish destroy both he and my uncle. (*Black Midas*, 164)

Later as a diamond king, he falls prey to its violence.

Here, too, all is generational interplay; the curse handed down by Aron's grandmother on the head of Richard, Aron's uncle, is played out. All is historical precedence. The omnipresent landscape seems to demand its sacrifice and, more so in *Black Midas*, its retribution. Thus it is that, often in Carew, landscape is not simply the stage where passions and violence are enacted; rather it is participant, often a symbolic presence heralding misfortune, a spirit-animate force demanding its sacrifice, its atonement.

As Elsa is a figure of generational interplay, both Sister and the old man Doorne are the carriers of Hector's family history and the history of the village; Doorne has mastered the lore of the coast. Hector is told by Doorne that he should not forget his slave ancestry, nor reject the fact that he has come from the womb of a Black woman:

"You got the blood of the master and the slave in you' veins. You' papa trying to forget it and acting like he is a white man but you mustn't never forget it, boy." (*Coast*, 47)

Had he, like his father, continued living in the city, he, too, would have forgotten the rhythms of the earth. Thus his initiation into manhood through the Black woman, Elsa, is not simply seduction, but rather a reentry into the womb of the earth. To learn the ways of the forest is to enter the womb: he undergoes the ordeal, the trial by water, the crossing of the swamp. In a supine position, as though a supplicant, Hector crosses from one space to another, from swamp to forest. Thus through symbolic correspondence Black woman has become earth mother. The awakening of Hector's senses and the regaining of his strength, which he would have lost in the city, is depicted in a series of phallic images:

> Life in the forest was geared either to stillness or lightning movement—the stillness of a tall tree or the speed of a snake striking. The forest is a womb in which life is lived in an eternal, dark gestation, only the undulating belly of treetops is exposed . . . . While [Hector] walked under them, the trees breathed their stillness and their strength into him. (112)

But into that forest womb, symbolic of continuity and timelessness, expressive of creativity and regeneration, "sunlight and wind had not reached down to the forest floor for a long time and the air was heavy with the smell of decay" (112). These are the swamps and the forests that can only be mastered through God-given strength, and not through inherited privilege. And strength and stamina are not taken for granted by the descendants of slaves. Whenever they succeed in crossing the swamp they chant their thanks "celebrating another victory" (118). It is from such a landscape, where the ancestors of Aron Smart had long gestated and sent their roots deep down, that he flees, in search of more passionate movement.

> They were children of slaves . . . . They felt time like a river running in their blood, but I wanted to feel it like passion flaring up swiftly and dying away. (*Black Midas*, 10)

Thus it is that *Black Midas* initially describes a countermovement from *The Wild Coast:* Aron Smart leaves his village to go vagabonding and to be initiated into manhood by adventuring through different environments in Guyana; Hector's initiation into manhood takes place in the village on the wild coast. To those with adventure in their blood, the pork-knockers who go seeking quick adventure and wealth in the gold mines, life in the village on the wild coast seems too sedentary, and though possessing its own drama and violence, is still not exciting enough to satisfy their restlessness.

> They had a lust for gold and diamonds, because in searching for them, they could cut loose from everything that tied men down to life on the coast. (*Black Midas*, 114)

Aron refuses to be tied down to life on the coast until he has given full play to his restless spirit, until he has experienced, through movement, the rhythms of many regions, of many landscapes. His initiation is not, like Hector's, a deepening of roots in one area, but rather a transitory passing through several areas. Like elements which in themselves are in constant motion, Aron's initiation is through perpetual movement. He achieves a symbiosis with the landscape, becomes at one with the environment:

> The sun was in my blood, the swamp and river, my mother, the amber sea, the savannahs, the memory of surf and wind closer to me than the smell of my sweat. (42)

But since all elements of the landscape and all environments possess their own particular tone, their own color quality, one can only be at home in them by learning their accents and sensing their expressions; not through theory but through lived experience. Later when Aron goes into the city, he never truly learns the accent or expression of the city; he remains ill at ease there. His dialogue is really with the rivers and the interior landscape. He returns to his village, his senses shaped by having traversed many landscapes in all their varying moods and differing atmospheres; his sensibilities turned to the secret rhythms of the earth, to its creative forces, or jangled by the inimical power and fury of the elements. He ends his exploration by restating the many landscapes through which he has journeyed, landscapes which have invested him with his essential being. Thus the dialogue of man and landscape has momentarily ended:

> Since I left Mahaica my life had run like a liana through forests of time without beginning or end, . . . at nights I used to lie in bed for hours thinking about my boyhood in Mahaica, my days with Dr. Ram, my first trip to Perenong with Santos, the interlude with Belle. . . . The people who had featured in these experiences talked to me and walked beside me, tutored me and laughed at me all over again, and their laughter echoed down all the rivers I had travelled. (274)

In Mittelholzer's *Of Trees and the Sea,* the mood is sensuous, the atmosphere more physical and immediate, the characters dominated by natural phenomena rather than by the spirit-world. They vibrate to the sensual quality of the Caribbean landscape: the essential presence of the trees, the pull of the sea, the power of the hurricane. This is not surprising, for the foliage of the Caribbean is so vibrant and so varied are its trees. The Caribbean islands themselves move to the rhythm of the sea, stumble under the hurricane's power.

Thus, in *Of Trees and the Sea,* the whole novel is pervaded by these natural features. The essence of the novel is the interplay of the characters' emotional states with vibrant forces emanating from the Barbadian landscape. From the very beginning, trees and sea interact with moods of characters, are not background, are not merely setting for the novel, but a foreground which tugs on the characters' sensibilities and paces and directs the development of the novel.

> They could hear the wind making a quiet swishing amidst the leaves of the big manchineel tree outside their windows, a subtle and rather solemn sound in the early morning, but not surprising, for manchineels are solemn trees, huge and filled with deep frowns within their dense foliage. The wind brought a sea-weed smell from the beach, for the sea was only two hundred yards from their cottage, though invisible because of the intervening screen of other manchineel trees. (Mittelholzer, *Of Trees and the Sea*, 7)

The cottage of Roger Wort—an Englishman who has recently arrived to take up the position of Comptroller of Beaches and Sea Defenses with his wife, Pat, a journalist—lies close to the sea and is shaded by manchineel trees. It is these manchineel trees with which Pat becomes passionately obsessed; the sea near which her husband indulges in his first unfaithful act of passion with Daphne Sedge, a poor *bacra*.

The young Englishwoman's growing obsession with the manchineels parallels her increasing involvement with an old, licentious light-brown colored man, Mr. Drencher. Indeed, the development and tempo of perhaps the main plot of *Of Trees and the Sea*, the deepening affair between Pat and Mr. Drencher, is reflected in Pat's sensitive reaction to the manchineel trees: she comes under the sensual influence of Drencher and under the sensory power of the manchineels. The more pervasive the manchineel trees become, the closer their leaves move into Pat and Roger's bedroom, the more the trees seem to encroach on their newly married life. And soon the position of the berries poisons their marriage:

> She took deep breaths of the morning air sensing now the faintly sour aroma of the manchineel berries. Her married home scent. A scent she had come to associate with Barbados—with this comfortable bungalow-cottage, her new home in this lovely island—and with her life with Roger. (96)

It is not surprising that the encroachment of the manchineels serves a dual function, for *Of Trees and the Sea* abounds with parallel developments, symbolic references and correspondences. The trees become more laden with berries, their foliage extends under and into the bedroom and in an obvious anthropomorphic transference two branches take on the form of the protective, yet seductive gnarled hands of Pat's admirer, Mr. Drencher.

> Their foliage seemed to have drawn closer to the cottage—more screening and protective. Two berry-laden branches had actually stretched them-

selves in under the veranda roof, and hung now like hands, warted and multi-finger-nailed, casting shadows, not too obtrusive though warped, on the grey floor-boards. (96)

And as Pat comes more and more under the protective custody of Drencher and undertakes, at his suggestion, a more thorough study of the trees of the island, she is pulled by them, fully absorbed by them; the seduction is complete.

"He's suggested I should write articles on the trees of Barbados, Roger—detailed descriptions of all the trees here. So I'm going to be busy not only writing but studying the leaves and berries and trunks and flowers of all the lovely trees we see about us. Cordias, manchineels, casuarinas, mahoganies, flamboyants! Oh, Roger darling, there's something vital in me now—"

"Well, I should hope—"

"Yes, I know what you mean, dear!" she laughed. "There's life in my womb—wonderful life. Oh darling, if you only knew the things that old man did to me this evening after seven o'clock!" (115)

And in a baroque, overornate poetic prose, Mittelholzer presents a dense picture of the consummation of their affair. The final extension occurs, trees are her love; all is transposed image, breasts to breakers:

Her dear manchineels, like her dear old man, would lean lovingly over her sleeping form without dagger or stake—with finger of fulsome joy and caressive comfort . . . .

In the coppery crepuscle she could watch the rise and fall of her breasts, brown-eyed breakers that could peer into unknown depths of the dark as they rose and fell in thunder . . . . And nippled slippery slumber. . . . (187)

As in *My Bones and My Flute*, where the initially pragmatic Mrs. Nevison, by burning the parchment, attempts to destroy its psychic emanations, so, too, in *Of Trees and the Sea* Roger attempts to destroy the pull of the manchineel trees upon his wife by frenziedly cutting them down. Both attempts expose the characters to the hidden power of the objects: the devilish, furry hand of the parchment and the poison of the manchineel berries.

Further Roger, the scientific man, cannot resist the affect of the local influences on him, and is eventually seduced by them. In a movement parallel to Pat's seduction, he is overcome by the charms of Susan, a poor *bacra*. But she is more than that, she is casuarina tree. In her depiction, human forms and vegetable shapes become completely interchangeable: Mittelholzer's landscape is here totally anthropomorphic.

Casuarinas are very different from manchineels. Tall and slim and always moaning softly, even in the faintest drift of breeze, they are wraith-like but unfrightening, furry but never fierce, fumbling at the sky but with a secret purpose rather than with futility.

Susan Sedge looked like one herself—slim, tall, her hair fuzzy as it usually was early in the morning. (10)

Not only does Mittelholzer depict her as a casuarina tree, but she, too, identifies with it: "If only I didn't tremble like this! Now and then I even feel I'm going to sway as the casuarinas are swaying in the wind outside now" (67). Not only her physical characteristics but her reactions, her total personality, correspond to the essential qualities of casuarina trees. Like Milton in *My Bones and My Flute*, Roger slowly begins to lose his scientific and pragmatic approach under the influences of local forces; the intangible force of the atmosphere begins to assault his confident certainty. Thus it is that he wonders at the charm of the casuarinas, becomes baffled when he is unable to grasp their illusory nature, and under their charms almost suspends his rational faculties. For the landscape of the Caribbean affects the sensibility of all people, and Roger is no exception.

He listened to the casuarinas sobbing their subdued tale of furry deeds enacted secretly in the teeth of the sea-scented trade-winds, and such a bouyancy enfolded him that he might have been about to drift off into some shady gap where swaying nymphs with tearful eyes implored men to do things they would never, in a rational moment, have thought of doing . . . . He had to chuckle to himself. Such odd fancies had been coming to him of late. It must be something in the air of this island. (57–58)

These local influences which elude Roger's rational analysis are a compound of emanations from the past, perpetually stored in the landscape, charging it with psychic, irresistible power. The seashore and the bordering clumps of trees where during the days of slavery the slave masters raped their female slaves, sating their appetites and lust, seem to have absorbed the countless played-out passions and now in themselves are fertile with passion. The old, licentious Mr. Drencher tells Pat of the inescapable seduction of the woods and the beach which have been so long saturated with passion:

"One might even excuse the superstitious fools who say that a strong spirit of earthy love pervades those woods. I have felt the influence myself on many an occasion. It reaches this cottage sometimes, as my servant girl can testify. And the beach—the beach is drenched with it . . . . It's particularly strong there. It has been said that no couple who have sat or reclined on the beach, near the edge of the woods, have ever

risen without indulging in some conclusive gesture of love. In the evening
dusk it's fatal. No possibility of escape." (139)

Thus it is that Roger, though charmed by the casuarina trees and Susan,
cannot escape the passionate pull of the beach or the seductions of Susan's
sister Daphne. As in the past, in times of slavery, the tale of miscegenation
continues: Daphne becomes pregnant from Roger; Pat from Drencher.

For not only are the woods and beaches saturated with passion, but the
cordia trees, with their "red and bell-like blooms and untidy, floppy leaves"
(13), add yet another quality of passion to the surrounding landscape of trees:
they turn the landscape from merely sensuous to neurotic; it takes on a
lurking, sinister quality:

> Sea-weed . . . sinister clumps of it, purple and grey-green or sienna and
> dark-green, would clutter up the water near the edge of the beach, so
> that, in wading out, one felt one might be threshing through the defences
> of an uncertain enemy. At any instant some itchy garland of sickly berries,
> dirty ochre in hue, a parody of mistletoe, might coil itself about one's
> neck either to suck or to strangle, or perhaps to leave a fatal streak of
> some iodiferous jelly that would corrode a channel through the flesh to
> the warm river of the jugular. (81–82)

> . . . the breakers—so insistently sinister, so sisterly in their soothing
> summons as I move on to the beach to prove the certainties of their
> schemings . . . . (186)

Indeed, the breakers with their changing color patterns of "bottle-green,"
"pale-green," "shadowy-green," "sky-blue," "dark-blue," brew dreams, and
toss up on the land untangled clumps of threatening seaweed. (81)

All is entanglement, built around the scheming of characters to fulfill
their desires, indulge their passions, in a landscape which exudes sensuousness, in an atmosphere which is at times as tangled as the plot:

> The air was like a mesh of cobweb electrically charged, taut and mam-
> mal-warm, ready to crackle and spark if one became too agile in attempt-
> ing to rip aside the trapping strands. (190)

To unravel the tangled web of relationships and cross-relationships, to bring
the merry-go-round of scheming and counterscheming to an end (for such
is the plot of *Trees*), Mittelholzer injects yet another tangle to the denouement (for family trees which sprout out of slavery are as entangled as the
foliage of so much of the Caribbean area). The relationship between
landscape, history, and man in the Caribbean provides Mittelholzer with yet
another twist, indeed, quite a surprising one: the discovery that the English-

man Roger is related to colored Drencher. And like his character Drencher, who in the novel is the creator of the web of entanglements, Mittelholzer can say, "I'm only doing my best to disentangle the entangled foliage of our family trees" (247).

Indeed, few of the plots in Mittelholzer's novels are unentangled: family trees intertwine; landscape and history weave together, crisscrossing; relationships are mirrored and knotted together, a mess of passions, feelings and emotions, winding and spooling out. But not only within a single novel is the plot a series of threads, raveling and unraveling, but across novels, as in the Kaywana trilogy, threads link together, a thread from one being carried over and taken up in another. Thus certain motifs, hinted at in one novel, are at times picked up and expanded in a subsequent novel. The electrically charged atmosphere hinted at in *Of Trees and the Sea* becomes the total background-mood and atmosphere of *The Weather Family*. The incipient threat of the sea to the trees, merely touched on in *Trees*, is recurrent and elaborated on in *The Weather Family*. The landscape does not simply stimulate passion, evoking it, the elements do not merely arouse emotions; rather in *The Weather Family*, the elements are made to control all feelings, dominate all passions, in fact the whole novel is punctuated by weather. The characters—the Larches, Mr. Harbin, and others—not only see their every emotional state in terms of weather changes, but also are totally influenced by the weather. Consciously or unconsciously all these characters begin to anticipate the build-up of the hurricane. The movement toward a climax in relationships among the various characters is paralleled by the build-up of hurricane Janet. Weather does not control the presentation of character, but, guiding the novelistic theme, it provides the very structure around which the novel is built. This group of sensitive people is further sensitized by the weather and ultimately the characters become as high-strung and as charged with tension as the electric current of the hurricane. In all instances, the outer reality of weather is not merely a gauge, a barometer of mood of the characters, but is in direct correspondence with the inner realities, the characteristics of the protagonists. And so constant is the correspondence between the outer and inner realities that often they seem to flow together and become indivisible, a single reality.

> "Sometimes I can see us all, the whole family, as if we were shapeless masses (cloud masses?). I see us without faces—only with moods. We drift about in the sky and sometimes we look shiny white with sunlight and sometimes we look grey and slow-moving . . . . Then sometimes we skud about in tiny flecks . . . . Then we can get thundery, and a quarrel breaks out, me generally on Daddy's side and Aubrey too. Peter and

Leila on Mother's and Aunt C's side (cold and warm air-currents?)"
(Mittelholzer, *The Weather Family*, 18)

All is anthropomorphic correspondence. With the coming of a hurricane,
not only are clouds and cold and warm air currents affected by the electricity
in the air, blood is affected by the weather. Here Aunt Clarice accepts
without questioning the pull of blood and of weather: "Well, he's a Larch,
my dear. The weather is in his blood" (33). Thus many characters in the
family, themselves unable to unravel the complicated web of social entanglements and emotional ties, almost yearn for the hurricane to free them from
those entanglements, to resolve their emotional ties.

> To us in this house . . . a hurricane seems an exciting event to be wel-
> comed so that it can be studied through all our various instruments, and
> recorded and written about. But to other people it's a frightening thing—a
> disaster to be feared and prayed against before they go to bed. (223)

The former are the Weather people who move to the rhythm of weather,
come under its pull, are influenced directly by it and react to it.

Already, before the approach of the hurricane, thunder, and rain, and
lightning are used as a stage music, to rock the course of an intrigue,
clarifying or making it more explicit. Eve has dissolved her marriage because
it lacks dramatic tension for her, it does not have the flux, the ever-changing
inner-dynamic movement of weather, especially of hurricane weather. She
needs "a certain resistance" in her relationship:

> Not quite like the sea and the rocks. Not an obvious shoving and hitting
> against each other.
>   . . . What I mean, darling, is a sort of undercurrent of opposition. A
> positive and negative interplay. (112)

Aunt Clarice's resentment of Eve, whom she has suspected of being her
rival for Harbin's affections, passes as quickly as a thunderclap when she
learns that Eve is only seeking advice and consolation in a platonic relationship.

The hurricane's coming exposes the true feelings of the intellectualizing
of Harbin about Caroline. In his diary, Caroline, who has disturbed his
intellectual composure, his rational approach to their friendship, seems to
him "too fresh, too real, too sincere. Too much of the sun and the wind . . . .
The clean smell of limestone and seaweed" (183). As the hurricane approaches, cutting more and more into Harbin's intellectual composure, in a
dream state, "the drizzle" becomes "bullets" for him, and his cynical
laughter takes on the quality of a "harpoon."

And as the hurricane builds up in ferocity it does not simply threaten physical exteriors but now assaults the inner human emotions and wages war on the whole physical reality: the trees and sea and houses all come under its raging power.

> The cordia and oleander trees outside the block of flats hissed animately, their slim flexible limbs bending as if under the lash of an inquisitor. The sea, far across the road, uttered a coughing roar, not fearsome but hollow as if sucked from a cave howling with menace. A canvas awning at the back of the building kept flapping like a spectral wing half-materialised out of the Astral World, waiting for the specific gust to tear it forth into the rain-lashed tennis-lawns bordered by flimsy young casuarinas . . . . (291–292)

In a series of verbs denoting quick, fierce movements, Mittelholzer, accelerating his pace, depicts the increasing, savage momentum of the hurricane which penetrates each member of the Larch family.

> Peter, from upstairs, shouted down: "Billows' roof! Billows' roof has just been ripped off!" Leila squealed and jostled him to see out of the bathroom window . . . .
> Caroline, standing on a chair and peering through a small space between the paper pasted on the panes, saw the sails of the Dunkleys' fan-mill twirling round and round in a dizzy, erratic dance . . . . The house vibrated right in the middle of its marrow—up in the roof the wind thumped and bumped. Down under the floor it darted earthquake shudders that came up through the soles of her feet. Outside, it was a panther panting past, lithe and ruthless, pawing and savaging everything in its path. (317)

Through a series of alliterations, Mittelholzer skillfully uses onomatopoeia to create the sound effects of the hurricane, which now resounds in drums and bassoons and flutes. The barometers and instruments which formerly measured and gauged weather, have been transformed, and now musical instruments orchestrate the weather. The insect world of the Kaywana trilogy is here restated, but not merely as accompanists to passion:

> The percussions began to foreshadow their coming predominance. Now and then a faint drumming interrupted the shriek of the woodwinds . . . . The fiery flutes continued to frolic. The passionate piccoloes peep-peeped their chicken-tunes in high-powered peppery squeaks, shaming the shivering buzz of the bassoons with their background shush-shush policy . . . . the whirr and hum and chur of crickets and mosquitoes, the

miniscule thunder, the thimble rumble, of millions of tiny drumming creatures with wings of thinnest gossamer. (306)

Clarice, unable to secure the affection of Harbin and alone in a house nearby, "[whines] like the wind, [whimpers] like the background oboes, [sighs] once or twice like the wheezing bassoons" (93). High-strung, she gives herself up to the hurricane's destructive power and to the elements which seem locked in struggle. She is saved from her sought-for destruction by Mr. Cromwell, and accepts his proposal of marriage. And at the climax of the hurricane, Harbin, stripped of intellectual strains, asks to marry Caroline, who has braved the hurricane to look after his safety.

Thus in the Kaywana trilogy, the basic determinant of character development is blood, with landscape providing a vitalizing background, becoming a conjurer, invoking previous corresponding events. In *My Bones and My Flute* and *Shadows Move Among Them*, the characters are already affected by landscape, which, sensitized by historical events, becomes psychic, a spirit world of local influences. In *Of Trees and the Sea* and *The Weather Family*, the characters are directly influenced by phenomena: their emotions dictated by a quality inherent in landscape; their passions spurred on by a force within the elements; their actions by the weather. In *The Weather Family*, the hurricane, the whole landscape, is conductor, calling into play all the instruments: the passions, emotions, and feelings of the characters. All is movement and sound, and the hurricane in a vast symphonic explosion rises to a crescendo. Man is caught in the revolving center of warring elements: of trees and the sea, of earth against wind and water.

Whether from the vast landscapes of Caribbean lands or the equally vast expanses of the sea, all these environments hold in them "space like a benediction," space which is creative and psychic, destructive or restorative.

CHAPTER 2

The Rituals of the Folk:
The Crossing of Rhythms

I am the archipelago hope
Would mould into dominion; each hot green island
Buffetted, broken by the press of tides
And all the tales come mocking me
Out of the slave plantations where I grubbed
Yam and cane; where heat and hate sprawled down
Among the cane—my sister sired without
Love or law . . .

E. M. Roach, "I Am the Archipelago,"
Anthology of Guianese Poetry

Stone upon stone
Boulder upon boulder
Whipped by the wind
And beaten by the sea
Crag upon crag
They rise
Cracked by the scorching
Sun
Rock upon rock
Hewn by the hammering
Waters
Pitted by the swirling sand
They stand
Time's sculptured handicrafts

. . . .

Stone upon stone
Boulder upon towering
Boulder
Rock upon rock
Crag upon majestic
Crag
They stand
Our island women
Rise
And glisten
In the morning sun.

Wilfred Cartey, *Waters of My Soul*

The sea, or the ocean, washes the land; and riding high, washes away some of the coastline; or receding, leaves at times a swampy littoral. High-crested rivers run, overflowing their banks when swollen from the heavy rains, or sometimes smelly riverbeds run dry trickles of yellow water, for the winds then are not moist with watery vapors, but dry, and with the sun, bake and crack the land, and drought grips the earth. The wind blows an incantation to the lives of those who live in the rural areas of the Caribbean, lives governed by the cycle of the weather and the satisfying of basic needs, lives ordained by ritual.

> Caya was beating out a fast one-three rhythm on his drum . . . . The wind-dance was a link with Africa. His ancestors . . . had arrived naked and empty-handed, bringing nothing with them but their memories. But wherever a man wanders he will find the neighbour-wind, the companion-wind, the messenger-wind . . . rolling on the grass and reeds . . . a symbol of absolute freedom . . . invisible, amorphous, imbued with titanic energies, no stockades could contain it nor could whips and chains humble it. For the descendants of the slaves the meaning and the message of the wind-dance had not changed. (Carew, *The Wild Coast*, 94–95)

Villages like Mahaica, "a bowl axed out of swamps and forests on a river bank" (Carew, *Black Midas*, 9), often spawned without design or plan, lie trapped between swampland and forest, or sprawl between small, winding roads and bushlands that push into the interior. Some villages straddle hills and climb upward, a cluster of precariously hanging houses; others lie isolated, deep within valleys ringed by hills which cut them off from the outside world. In such villages live clusters of people of African descent or East Indian origin—or a polyglot of African, East Indian, Chinese, Spanish, French, and Dutch peoples. In these isolated and unexposed villages, African or East Indian customs, festivals, and beliefs persist, or, merging with those of other peoples, become syncretic. It is here that is enacted the ritualistic dialogue of men with rural society—the central metaphor of these novels. The rituals of birth and death, of initiation and growth, of hate and love, of doubt and belief, all derive from the natural, the fundamental dialogue of man with the land. For in these basically agricultural communities, the inhabitants, attuned to the rhythms of the seasons, caught in the cycle of the weather, attempt to satisfy their essential needs, to fulfill their basic desires:

> Time in Tarlogie was a river trapped at an ox-bow and flowing round and round in circles. The seasons of sunshine and rain were too disorderly for them to be forecast on a calendar . . . . The long intractable seasons—the

rainy season and the dry season—had brought disaster so often that they were forgotten as soon as they had passed. (Carew, *Coast*, 68)

The laughter that follows calamity is one of irony and forbearance; the silence, one of patient acceptance. But in the community of village living there is often not silence, but loud laughter, drunkenness, explosive quarrels and fights, and eruptive violence, shattering the monotony of the routine living. In these villages, however, all is not simple reaction to calamity, for calamity is often followed by periods of transition, prosperity. And in the communality and village living, there are simple pleasures too: easy laughter, a running of children in the wind, the mating of lovers, and a folk wisdom of the old.

Indeed, emotions and passions, as of the characters in these novels, often seem to take on the fluctuating rhythmic patterns of the weather and the seasons. Whereas in the novels of Chapter 1, most of the elements are background influences to the psychic conditions of single individuals, here the elements are actualized, become vital foreground, affecting the collective consciousness of the whole communities. Landscape acts as a determinant of lifestyle, an agitation-initiating ritual, forming and exposing the essential nature of specific village communities. Drought and rain, river and sea, and the wind around them cast their influence into the very core of village living, summoning violence, arousing love—in all instances, heightening reactions.

Thus, in *A Quality of Violence*, the protracted drought unleashes predatory violence lurking in the ritualistic soul of the village community in St. Thomas. In the prologue, author Andrew Salkey states how violence is triggered when drought attacks the land:

When the drought comes to the land, it comes like a carrion-crow, circling at first, circling slowly and far above the water on the land, then it descends frantically at an angle, diving for bounty which is never earned
. . . .
    And those whose lives are nearest to it sometimes resent it with a strange violence in the blood . . . .
    The drought brings a touch of madness to the land, a kind of rebellion. (Salkey, *A Quality of Violence*, 19)

The novel describes the build-up of passions, the rhythmical climactic movement toward a final violent act; build-up and movement which match the increasing chaos brought on by the drought.

Drought is also the catalytic force in the short story, "A Drink of Water" by Samuel Selvon, in the collection, *Ways of Sunlight*. Here, too, the continuing lack of water unlocks in both father and son daring, passionate actions.

From the very beginning, Selvon, like Salkey, describes the ravages wrought by drought on the land, on beast, and on man:

> The time when the rains didn't come for three months and the sun was a yellow furnace in the sky was known as The Great Drought in Trinidad. It happened when everyone was expecting the sky to burst open with rain to fill the dry streams and water the parched earth . . . .
>
> . . . Somewhere in the field a cow mooed mournfully, sniffing around for a bit of green in the cracked earth. The field was a desolation of drought. The trees were naked and barks peeled off trunks as if they were diseased. When the wind blew, it was heavy and unrelieving, as if the heat had taken all the spirit out of it. (Selvon, *Ways of Sunlight*, 112)

The drought thus brings to agricultural village folk, who live close to the earth and whose livelihood is so dependent on water, burning fevers and blazing passions. In *A Quality of Violence*, blazing passions are channeled into sacrificial rituals, aimed at bringing an end to the drought which lies heavy on the land. Even as appeals are made through ritualistic offerings for the satisfying of desires, ritual becomes a substitute for such desires. In fact, ritual becomes hypnosis, eventually seeming to cast a spell over those who observe it; the reason for the ritualistic offering is lost in the hypnotic spell of the ritual. Everything loses its clarity, its focus, becomes unreal: cause and effect merge, their differences blurring. Even as the cycle of the weather is interrupted, the common sense of the village folk is suspended. Irrationalism takes the place of sound judgment, of folk wisdom; and as the pattern of the weather is changed, ritual, which has formerly ordained hope and belief and has informed folk tradition, becomes as destructive as the weather:

> The procession had its own rhythm. It was always difficult to break it. It was an old love, an old reverence, an old dependence on routine, rhythm, and ritual . . . the drought was no ordinary thing. It was the meaning behind the procession. It was the "conqueror" of the meeting-yard. (Salkey, *Quality*, 163)

But even as the dry wind scorches the animals and the sun cracks the land, even as drought destroys and conquers, driving villages to violence and to frenzy, the coming of rain which has so long been prayed for unleashes equally frenzied reactions, not of doubt and insanity, but of hope and hysterical joy. For water cools the burning fever of the sick villager and thanksgivings merge in tears and raindrops:

> And then it came sweeping in from the north-east, with a rising wind. Not very heavy at first, but in thrusts, coming and going. They opened

their mouths and laughed, and water fell in. They shouted and cried and laughed again . . . .

[Manko] picked up the cup and ran out into the lashing rain. Sunny, watching from the poui tree, was astonished to see his father standing motionless in the downpour. He had taken off his shirt, and his bare back and chest were shining with water. His face uplifted to the sky, was the face of a man half-crazy with joy. He might be laughing or crying, Sunny could not tell; and his cheeks were streaming, perhaps with tears, perhaps with . . . rain. (Selvon, *Sunlight*, 120–121)

So similiar in shape are a raindrop and a tear, falling like beads from the eye of man and the eye of the sky. And when the rain falls, it brings such freshness to the sun-baked, parched land that no longer are the "trunks of trees peeling, as if diseased" (112). Now for Ian McDonald, trees are sculptured by the raindrops, which make them glitter and glow with newness.

In his *The Humming-Bird Tree*, McDonald evokes all the shimmer and tremor of the new raindrops banging on a tree, all the laughter and frolic of playing in the warm Caribbean way. After quick tropical showers, everything seems so precious, for the rain has caressed the land; the sun, the waters, the wind, the trees—and the new rain-dripped world, vitalized by water, seems so alive:

It was only a lash of rain; it didn't last long. When it stopped we squatted on the wet black root again, exhausted with our fun. The sun now came through the trees in places strongly and made wide marks of gold on the rock where we sat breathing hard. It was a new world. (McDonald, *The Humming-Bird Tree*, 4)

Rain, drenching the land, vitalizes it and leads to new beginnings; so in these novels, water becomes a ritual conductor, too, leading to new relationships among many of the characters. On the banks of rivers, in the flow of river water, on the seashore, in so many other settings, water becomes initiator, baptizing new birth and consecrating new loves. In Samuel Selvon's *Turn Again Tiger*, the limpid water illumines Tiger's first true encounter with Mrs. Robinson, his white employer, in which Tiger seems for the first time stripped and made aware of his own body:

The woman on the rock was stretching her foot out and playing with the fall of water on her toes. Reasoning his fear, Tiger watched her turn sideways and cup her hands in the fall . . . .

The woman, when she saw him, plunged into the pool, and though it was not deep the water was up to her neck, for she bent her knees to cover her nakedness . . . .

He heard the splash when she dived and he turned his head, trying to do it casually. The water was as clear as crystal and the sun was pouring on it . . . .

Then he flicked his eyes away, suddenly embarrassed that she was looking at him, as if he were the naked one in the water. (Selvon, *Turn Again Tiger*, 62–63)

Here, water, although unable to conceal the white woman's body, at the same time distorts it. In a scene in Michael Anthony's *Green Days by the River*, where the motif of water and recognition occurs again, the water is not clear and limpid; rather it conceals the body of the young protagonist from the laughingly probing eyes of an East Indian woman laborer to whom he is attracted.

In both scenes the interplay of water and nakedness, of modesty and concealed desire, hints at the emotional developments of the characters and throws light on that sense of "shame" which is so much a part of Caribbean behavioral patterns. Yet that sense of shame never prevents but rather triggers a low-key ribald humor suggestively charged with sexual implications. In both of the scenes, it is the male who is embarrassed, who feels a sense of shame at the "part [of him] below the water." However, in the polyphonic, polyrhythmic *Song for Mumu*, by Lindsay Barrett, where river water often strengthens and purifies and cleanses, there is no sense of shame and no prohibitive behavioral modesty when the young Mumu, standing in the water, is the beckoning point, the still, desiring center for her lover, Joker. In a ritualistic ceremony of incantation and ascensional, so unlike that of the realistic drama of procession to violence in *A Quality of Violence*, water is conductor, unifier of father and sons, as when father initiates son into manhood; water is the consecrator of love between son and woman. It is not surprising that the avowal of love between Mumu and Joker should take place in the water, for though Mumu roamed and ran the hills, she's been dipped in the water by her grandfather in baptism, in a votive act which reassures the whole community that Papa Peda has not, with the loss of his sight, lost the feeling for life and love:

Standing, bouncing the child expertly on to his shoulder Papa Peda stretches a hand for Lazzirus to take. Take me to the river Lazzirus. So old Lazzirus saw him blind as he was dip the child head first into the river three times and kiss . . . [the] sole of the left foot. But Mumu didn't even cry, soaking wet, didn't utter a simple child's squeal of horror or delight even, just clung to Papa Peda's head all the way back home. And Lazzirus wondered. Then he didn't care any more, for he knew now old Peda had not lost life or love with his sight and the village knew too. (Barrett, *Song for Mumu*, 36)

In the flow of water, the essential link between grandfather and grandchild, the continuity of the family is preserved; the ontological link between water and blood is affirmed. The vitalizing force of water is confirmed in the chant of the River Woman:

> Water is my blood
> Water is my life
> Where the sun flows
> Where heat is a flower running
> Water is my blood. (41)

For the white-skinned lad, Alan, and the East Indian girl, Jaillin, in *The Humming-Bird Tree*, water becomes the unifier which strips them both of increasing societal restraints against their association, and for a moment gently rocks them together, naked and free, but hidden from the gaze of those who would interrupt their love. For the first time in the novel, water liquidates the barrier of skin complexion and of station which has continually barred them from freely expressing a pure and youthful love. All is buoyant, free-feeling; everything is pure liquid motion inducing longing for an eternal possession of the moment:

> I held her hand again. Her wet hair gleamed. It was darker than the night yet it was more full of brightness. I began to feel a complete peace coming into me. . . .
> . . . The sea slid by, cold-stained by a million octopus. No fear though. Above everything the sense almost of desolation, the world all gone away to die, leaving us alone, secure, the only children in the world. (McDonald, *Humming-Bird*, 137–138)

But the ocean only brings temporary peace and quiet to them, and for a short while belies the harsh reality of a society still plagued by race, caste, and class. And thus even as the water unifies, it quickly leads to the severance of their relationship as the full force of societal stigma crashes down on them. For, to the Caribbean peoples, the water of the ocean both unifies and divides, takes on symbolic meaning as the Middle Passage across which the rape of Africa took place; it is both carrier and destroyer, a legend to those island people who continue to live only off the land. So sings the River Woman as she spins to Mumu the folk tale of the ocean:

> . . . the king cast camp upon the ocean shores and massed his men to attack the roaring thing on the following day, but in the night the white men sailed up to the shores and found the camp.

Over the years they stole humanity from that world to fulfil hungers of
this world, dragging us across the evil river.
The evil river claims its toll . . . .
Yes yes Mumu we are the descendants of the Evil River's victims.
Only the rivers in the land have we mastered.
The ocean is not our friend. (Barrett, *Mumu*, 66–67)

The peoples of the Caribbean have not as yet mastered the ocean, but live
dependent so often on returns from the limited areas of land. Even in
Guyana, where the land is vast and rich, the interior lies as yet unopened
and the majority of the inhabitants live crowded in towns and small villages
which cling to the banks of rivers, shoulders of roads, or to the shores of the
sea. The constant struggle to live on small plots of land, so often overbur-
dened by continuous planting, becomes a recurrent motif, a touchstone of
conflict in many of these novels. And because the ancestors of the majority
of the peoples of the Caribbean once lived bound in slavery to the land, to
work the land is often despised, or becomes a ritualistic statement of
complete dependency, of an unbroken slave cycle. It is this interlocking
dialogue between man and land, and man's continuing dependency on and
knowledge of the elements, which particularizes the people, lending their
speech a very distinctive and indigenous vocabulary:

They knew the rains that fed the yam mounds, the banana shoots, the
mango walks. They had names for all the winds that blew over the
canefields. (Salkey, *Quality*, 22)

Even those, especially the young, who attempt to leave the land, linger, their
senses still pervaded by it:

He kept telling himself that he would go away and never return, but
bonds he had refused to think about surrounded him. The smell of burnt
cane was strong on the wind. (Selvon, *Sunlight*, 71)

At times the land seems to demand its own allegiance, the village, its own
love.
Thus it is that the dialogue of man and land is reestablished, and the
contrast of mutual give and take, of dependency, reaffirmed. And now the
vital necessary relationship between the land and those who live close to the
earth is clearly restated; the regenerative power of that land, simply accepted:

The vibrations were positive and overtly compelling. They had the
power of the pull of the land on those who drew their strength from it.
It was the power of a two-way attraction. It wasn't parasitic. The land

tugged and the peasant tugged in return. Each was satisfied. The two-way pull was symbiosis. Each fed the other. (Salkey, *Quality*, 160)

This symbiotic relationship that Salkey ascribes to the peasants of St. Thomas and Jamaica is more firmly entered into by the peasantry of Haiti, where the African ontological relationship of man to earth is more firmly rooted, and, still surviving, remains a source of history and belief.

In that cycle, indentured laborer, now villager, so often lives completely dependent upon ex-slave master, now estate owner or estate manager. The poverty of his own life, wedded to the prosperity of the estate and its lushness, is a union not of equals, but of inferior to superior; his life, obscure; his dwelling merging with the land, but not reaping its bounty; his living, a continuation of decades of exploitation.

> The few scattered huts of the village were tiny when he could discover them, for they were built of clay and thatched with palm leaves and blended into the scenery as if they were deliberately camouflaged . . . .
>
> . . . Cane had brought them all from the banks of the Ganges as indentured labourers to toil in the burning sun. And even when those days were over, most of them stayed shackled to the estates. (Selvon, *Tiger*, 5)

Thus shackled to the land, many of the villagers attempt to flee an overcrowded village to begin anew elsewhere—a perpetual quest for the necessities of life, for self-sufficiency—an elusive, often unattainable quest:

> The huts were quite new, for the first villagers had only come there about three years back. These had broken off from a much larger village and come to this place where the Government had let them have enough land to graze cows, keep donkeys and goats and fowls, grow rice and ground provisions. The first-comers had been joined by others. They all complained that there was no opportunity in the big village they had come from . . . . Old Boss of the village, had negotiated with the Government for the small piece of land. Not very many others had been as lucky. (McDonald, *Humming-Bird*, 56)

Yet for some of these very villagers, perhaps for the older ones, the life of the village has its own particular rhythm, its own irresistible pull, its own language. All of this they have captured in a continuous dialogue whose shifting metaphor provides them with an inner dynamic perception of their own reality:

> The land and its mysterious gifts and wealth is the life of the people. Try to take it from them—even try to tell them that it might be taken away—and you start a revolution. Impose laws and taxes on the Haitian

peasant and he'll meet them because he won't part with the land. The
land is his religion and his security. It is his own way of claiming to have
a history which includes past and present and insures the future. (Salkey,
Quality, 35)

It is not surprising then, in *Song for Mumu*, where Lindsay Barrett
attempts a symbiosis of African oral idiom with Caribbean rhythmical
formulations, that the basic relationship betwen Papa Peda and his fields is
clearly articulated; man must work the fields, plant the land, to feed his wife
and children. This is a natural compact where earth produces, and man
provides.

> Papa Peda, a farmer himself, was always there in his fields come hot sun
> rain too, breaking the hard dry earth with his axe and hoe and watering
> it . . . .
>   . . . To feed two lovely mouths, he used to say, when The Farmers
> wailed keen laughter from Fat Polly's dark bar at him beating a path to
> his field in the bright hot sun, to feed two such lovely mouths a man
> must break the soil and ply his axe and hoe all year in rain or in sunshine.
> (Barrett, *Mumu*, 6)

Perhaps if the symbiotic ontological relationship and the sympathetic
compact between man and land were really accepted in the Caribbean, the
hoped-for success in agricultural ventures, such as the one forced upon
Shellie in *Green Days by the River*, might be realized. But the still persistent
slave mentality continues to grip the minds of the descendants of slaves,
preventing them from entering into that compact.

> *For I'd never be in want again . . .*
>   . . . with all that land on Cedar Grove, rich with fruit and rice and
> ground provisions, and with cocoa stretching far alongside the river, there
> could be nothing but success. (Anthony, *Green Days by the River*, 188)

So many of the hopes of the Caribbean lie in the acceptance of the compact
between man and his sea, man and his land. But seldom, given the still-
prevalent class hierachy, do successes occur. Many villages seem trapped in
a pre-emancipation hierachy, where the large estates are owned by expatriate
whites but under the local control of white estate managers. So often even
the attempt to establish the sympathetic compact of villager controlling the
land is thwarted by the avarice of many local whites. It is not surprising,
therefore, that within the village ethos presented in these novels, the white
estate manager or owner is a recurrent figure, indirectly controlling the lives
of many of the villagers.

In *Song for Mumu*, one such figure, the Rich Man, is presented in all his sexual aberrations, his greed, his dominance. Though rich, he is a figure to be pitied, unlovely and grotesque, "a tiny red blustering old man twisted and grinning" (Barrett, *Mumu*, 29). Yet it is this ridiculous figure who exploits The Farmers and steadily dispossesses them of their land. Similarly, in *Turn Again Tiger*, the white supervisor, Mr. Robinson, a grotesque, decadent figure, seedy and sexually aberrant, is not a landowner but a white bossman upon whom many farmers depend for their livelihood. Symbolically he remains untouched by the tropical sun and like the Rich Man is blotched and red:

> Robinson hadn't tanned in the tropics, he had reddened, and there was a clear arc above his chest dividing suntouched skin from covered. (Selvon, *Tiger*, 74)

Both of these men, in their impotence, exploiting not only the land but the sexual powers of The Farmers, connive in the studding of their wives by their hired laborers. For in many instances the white female figures in these novels are as decadent as the white owners and white managers; at times, as sexually aberrant; at times, simply lascivious.

Perhaps one of the more sympathetically drawn white supervisors is Alan's father in *The Humming-Bird Tree*. He is forthright and honest, egalitarian and benevolent. Yet so aware is he of his station, his class, and his color that his relationship with the laborers is never softened by truly warm, human gestures—never truly friendly. Like his wife, though attentive to the needs of those removed from them by class, he remains cool and aloof, bent on preserving class distinctions.

Given their exploitation of the villagers, their decadence, or their aloofness, these men and women, though often controlling the economic livelihood of the village, never really become an integral part of its life, but live isolated from it, remain on its perimeters, for their roots do not really go deep into the earth, nor do they really feel the secret rhythms of the land. The villagers have their own secret rhythms, essential hierarchy, their own communality of shared suffering and pleasure, their own deeply enriching, yet at times, retarding folk quality.

This folk quality seems subsumed in the lives of the elders of the village, who like Grandpa, in Carew's *Black Midas*, attempt to keep the young from abandoning the village; the elders are the true preservers of folk tradition, the carriers of folk wisdom. Revered, respected, or even at times regarded with an indulgent affection, they attempt to pass on to the young their own acquired wisdom, and through moral and maxim, to show them the true and right path. Old Boss in *The Humming-Bird Tree* is also such a figure. And in *Song for Mumu*, the Old River Woman is imbued with memories of Africa and a wisdom of the rivers: "The eyes of this Old River Woman were like dark lakes in whose depths all knowledge was hidden and from whose secrets new secrets could be birthed" (Barrett, *Mumu*, 64). Just as Kaiser and Jaillin even unwittingly absorb the sayings and wisdom of Old Boss and hear from him about their Hindu customs, so too, Mumu learns of her African heritage from the Old River Woman. So much of the wisdom comes to these older folk from the instinctive, yet vital memories of Africa and Asia from which their ancestors came. These memories, still fecund with strong folk tradition, make for endurance and perseverance whose imprints have molded the old folks' features.

> It was a strong black face with the lineaments of age and suffering marked clearly on it. The opaque parchment skin with its deep grooves and its convolutions emphasized the qualities of patience and endurance her slave ancestors had handed down to her. (Carew, *Coast*, 32–33)

But at times the descendants of slaves inherit not only patience and endurance, but as their memories grasp after ritualisitic links with Africa, they also acquire many beliefs, many observances which apprehend a spirit world. Thus it is that the spirit world is actualized in many of these novels, and a folk belief derived from living close to the land further heightens that very spirit world. But since that world is not clearly defined, it is perceived and interpreted in a variety of ways, some of which border on the superstitious. The existence of the spirit world is not questioned by the old man, Doorne; nor is it questioned by many of the village folk. Rather, so completely has it been integrated within the lives of the villagers, that it forms a natural and instinctive point of reference.

> "Every word I tell you is true, Master Hector, if you come down here on a moonlight night and put you ears to the ground you can hear people groaning worse than a po-boy tree in the high wind." (Carew, *Coast*, 46)

At times, however, in the villages, indeed throughout the Caribbean, an acceptance of a spirit world, and a credence given to those who are believed to be in touch with it, can lead to unscrupulous and destructive behavior. Thus it is with Ma Procop who

> had scattered her plot with a weird miscellany of broken bottles, old tin pans, dirty coloured rags, animal bones, barrel hoops and various constructions of the sign of the cross . . . . the scene served to scare away thieves, who thought the old woman was dealing in obeah. (Selvon, *Sunlight*, 95–96)

Obeah becomes a constant motif within this literature: a method of assuaging or relieving pressing needs, a panacea, or an instrument of coercion and control. The drummer man, Caya, preys on the credulity of his prying fellow villagers and is able not only to ward them off but also to surround himself with an air of mystery:

> Caya lazed away most of his days on the rum-shop bridge and at night he retreated to his hut on the edge of the swamps. His hut was avoided by all, because his neighbour was Batista, the obeia-man and he had spread the word that Batista had drawn a ring of fire around his dwelling and to come too close was to call down disaster. Those in trouble and seeking advice could consult him during his drinking hours but once he had retired for the night, only his women friends (of whom he had many) were permitted to slip across Batista's obeia ring. (Carew, *Coast*, 92–93)

Such figures as Batista, who are not simply novelistic creations but who actually exist throughout the Caribbean, flit in and out of novelistic situations, or at times, as in *A Quality of Violence*, control and create situations. With deep and penetrating insight, Dada Johnson deliberates on the dynamic relationship between the existence of basic needs and the necessity to satisfy those needs even for a moment. The unanswered question here is whether he is a charlatan or a shrewd observer who, intuitively sensing the basis of the needs, satisfies them through skillful manipulation. He is at once a consequence and product of a society where any form of worship, any ritual practice, becomes a prop, an aid to survival, a partial substitute for sufficiency, a compensation for want. Through such a man as Dada Johnson—*obeah* men, *shango* men, shepherd men—release from material deprivation often comes through cathartic participation in rituals which, touching an ever-present spiritualistic nerve center of so many Caribbean peoples, proffer a possibility of hope, a point of faith:

> "I give those people plenty to believe in. I give them cause to have a faith. I know that you think it is just a lot of foolishness and all that. But, you have other things to hold on to. Those people you hear outside depend on me and what I can give them. I telling you that, now. I am not just one day of the week to them. I am all seven—morning, noon, and night . . . . All I do that is bad, is collect a little 'dues' off them, and that is my living. And for that collection, I give them hope and faith. I give them what the big decorated church door can't satisfy, no how."
> (Salkey, *Quality*, 47–48)

His claim to give "what the big decorated church door can't satisfy, no how" is no idle boast, since through ritual he provides an arena for a deep immediate emotional participation. Yet in his ritual he utilizes many religious artifacts particular to that big decorated church, perhaps unconsciously legitimizing his own form of worship. For in the minds of so many, rituals which are not European are questioned and doubted, evil superstitions practiced by the wicked, indulged in by the ignorant:

> "Voodoo and Pocomania can't be explained as no search for nothing like a Christian Lord or anything like that. You just in one of your fool-fool moods. Voodoo and Pocomania have their own set of gods. They have a different code of worship and the people who worship them ask for different things. They ask for evil things like death for their enemy, and things like forgiveness and brotherly love are never contemplated, no how." (37)

Yet this spell is induced by symbols deriving both from the "Voodoo and Pocomania" and from the "Christian Lord," from a syncretic conglomeration of sacrificial hardware:

> thirteen candles, two "yabahs," two Bibles, a bamboo crucifix, a couple of medallions, three saucers of logwood honey, two loaves of unsliced bread, and a small bowl of rooster's blood. (44)

The social and historical circumstances of the Caribbean derive from, at once, a merging and separating of many various peoples and cultures producing a syncretic conglomerate of beliefs which are sensed but not understood, practiced but not clearly perceived. Any sudden deed, any ailment, any unexpected occurrence, is ascribed to an inexplicable, malignant force over which an individual has little control, unless he calls to his aid potently supernatural objects and artifacts. And since responsibility for "trouble" is rarely ascribed to the malfunctioning of the society, remedies are not sought in the immediate society, but rather in an otherness. Alice, an old, lonely, worn-out domestic servant, does not ascribe her fatigue and sleeplessness or her pains to long years of benevolent drudgery in the household of Alan's parents, but rather to

> a host of jumbies with fire-eyes and forked tails like the devil; they had hammered on her door, spat curses at her. The whole time, she told us, she lay in bed, kissing her ring and saying her chaplet over and over. (McDonald, *Humming-Bird*, 34)

The ring and the chaplet, *obeah* and Christianity, combine to cushion Alice's poverty and suffering, and allow her to endure; perhaps they stifle the harsh corrosive reality in which she lives and over which she has no control. Like rum they are opiates, narcotics which, even while dulling the senses, provide easy stimulation, quick relief from the problematic, and induce a release from the monotonous routine and boredom of so much of village life.

Thus it is that Christian worship, Hindu ceremonies, Pocomania, and all other rituals become a balm, a salve, to continuous deprivation—as well as "feting," bachanal, and rum drinking, a mode of expression open to those whose creative potential remains untapped and goes to waste. The village rum shop often becomes the only true stage where the village men enact the drama of their lives, with all its bitterness, pain, laughter and joy.

In *Song for Mumu*, the men of the village, bought out of their lands by the old white Rich Man and now laborers on an estate instead of farmers on their own plot, spend most of their free time in the rum shop, attempting, it seems, to dispel from their minds, through drink, their dispossession, their loss. Caya, who is a master drummer, fritters away his time at the rum shop, "eating, drinking and gaffing" (Carew, *Coast*, 92). Indeed, the rum shop is often the true communal center, the hangout for the village men, its provisions as disparate as the lives of its frequenters. Under one roof would stand rum shop, shop, and parlor, catering to men, women and children—in fact, to almost the whole community. But in these communities men are dominant, so the rum shop is the most frequented part of the establishment, the principal area where they spend much of their nonworking, nonsleeping time.

Such village establishments, supplying all the immediate necessities of the people on credit or on trust, sometimes make money, depending on the shrewd business sense, industriousness, and personality of their owners. The parlor shop of Tall Boy prospers not simply because he is industrious, but because he is a "creolise Chinee" who "people would think . . . is born Trinidadian" (Selvon, *Tiger*, 22). But not so Otto's Parlour, for he is typed as being lazy and unconcerned, as almost having succumbed to the langour and heat of the village:

> He ignored customers when he saw them with a glass or jug—he knew they wanted snowball—and rolled over, turning his back to the door and pretending to be fast asleep. (Selvon, *A Brighter Sun*, 57–58)

Thus in this fiction of the rural folk life, the shop, rum-shop, or parlor owner is a conspicuous character, his establishment a frequent setting for many village scenes. Indeed, since rum drinking, the ability to hold one's liquor, to "fire one," is often a proof of one's manhood, it is not surprising that many young village men frequent rum shops, for the rum shop provides the villagers with a place to boast about their exploits, their successes, their affairs—whether real or fictitious. In these rum shops, so many experience vicarious manhood:

> [Kaiser] ordered a half-tot of rum for himself.
> "You too young to drink so," Ramlal said.
> "Min' you' business. I'se a customer, ent I?" Kaiser snapped. "I'se paying good money." In the corner old Jess grunted sourly:

"Gawd, but young people rude rude dese days," she said. "But I
know what it is, you trying to play big man . . . ."

"You hear what she say?" Ramlal took up the tale. "Little boy, don'
play man befo' you is one." (McDonald, *Humming-Bird,* 66)

Kaiser's tossing off the rum is not merely boasting or showing off but clearly
shows that he is fully aware of the intrinsic value given to one's ability to
drink rum. For the offering of a drink of rum to a young person, the request
for rum by a young person and further, the drinking of rum, all clearly attest
to one's entry into manhood, revealing that one has ceased to be a boy and
has ritualistically crossed into manhood. Rum drinking thus takes on an
elevated status, not only as indicator of manhood, but as initiator into
manhood.

Only men got drunk, not boys . . . .
    . . . He wanted to buck up his courage and say something to show
them he was a man, that could swallow rum just as they did. (Selvon,
Brighter Sun, 17)

Clearly, here attitudes of characters are affected by communal and
societal perceptions about behavior. Given, too, the close interdependence
of characters with their immediate surroundings and with the elements upon
which so much of their livelihood depends, the surroundings, the elements,
play an intrinsic part in the shaping and molding of attitudes. Thus, not only
are the lives and habits of the villagers charted by societal attitudes, but they
are affected also by particular qualities reflected in the landscape. The
elements and the landscape play a significant role in choreographing
emotions and attitudes of protagonists, locating man in his essential contacting with his ecological condition.

A river flows in the valley of *Turn Again Tiger,* where sugar cane ordains
the lives of the villages and becomes the central metaphor of their
existence. For here man still receives, still seeks, answers in the vibrations
of the land. Hills and valleys, mountains and sky, rivers witness the unfolding of emotions, reveal the possibilities inherent in work, make man wonder
and seek answers about the nature of living.

From the very beginning of *Turn Again Tiger,* the possible relationship
between man and land, a rhythmical interplay between them, is suggested:
"He looked down into the valley from a hill, as if he expected a message to
be written there telling him what to do" (Selvon, *Tiger,* 5). It is in this valley
that the main protagonist of the novel, Tiger, as he works the cane, attempts
to apprehend the nature of his existence; seeks the reasons for action;
ultimately stumbles on the purpose of his life.

Sugar cane, the central metaphor, is the social backdrop, revealing a plantation structure and system; it is, too, the model and modal center of the day-to-day living of the rural folk. Indeed, it provides the cyclical configurations of their existence. It gives the structural direction to the unfolding of the action and plot of the novel. Thus from looking down at the valley from the hilltop seeking answers, Tiger arcs toward the realization of the cyclical patterns which qualify the parallel movements, the essential progressions, of man's life and earth's flow.

> And the very earth had done a job, bearing the cane that made the harvest possible.
>
> And I? [Tiger] thought, hacking his way towards the last of the standing cane . . . I don't know, but as if I learn a lot in this year that gone by, nothing exact that I could put my finger on, but is almost as if I didn't take no step backward, and it was forward all the time . . . .
>
> Tiger looked around him—not at the workers, but at the land, which would sprout green things when the rains came and washed away the burns of the harvest.
>
> "The old land never have a rest, Tiger . . . . Soon something else going to grow here."
>
> "It just like we," Tiger said. "We finish one job, and we got to get ready to start another." (218–219)

Before arriving at this simple yet profound realization of the inherent relationship between man and land, Tiger comes close to bumping himself off before his harvest time. He is scorched by the intensity and heat of an unfulfilled lust and passion for a white woman, the supervisor's wife. He becomes peevish with an undirected and persistent questioning into the nature of his own being. He not only burns the books in which he sought answers, but is almost consumed by continual fits of drunkenness. And even as Tiger attempts to escape, to quench by moralizing and philosophizing the passions for the white woman, Doreen, he understands the visceral link between him and cane. He ponders:

> Who in the whole world know that Tiger existed? Who would care if he died? A man could fling out his arms and circle the globe, or with his mind's eye look into every corner of the earth, but what was the use of that? . . .
>
> . . . he reached for the top of the mountain while his feet were trapped in the canefields. (135)

In this spatial, vertical relationship, cane symbolizes entrapment, that initial inability of the rural folk to break out of its hold. Later when Tiger resolves his dilemma and receives regeneration through a liberating act, cane becomes a symbol of flow rather than one of entrapment. And not only does the cane symbolically reflect Tiger's growth; the hill surrounding the valley often becomes an indication of Tiger's condition. "All his life led to . . . indecision on the hill, looking down into a dark valley" (107). Yet the valley has its own peace, its own harmony, marking passage of time. Selvon, in *Turn Again Tiger*, captures the flow of the lives of the villagers, the coherence of the elements, the interplay of sun, moon, sky and stars:

> Time went by leisurely in the valley, and Tiger watched the physical manifestations of it—the sun in the sky, the wind across the cane, the fading light in the evening, the villagers doing their work. Come night, the sky sombre-blue, stars fighting for spots in which to shine, the moon throwing gold carelessly against the sides of the hills. (111)

And again, at times, the physical phenomena not only reflect but actually fuse with and shape man; a total special conjoining between man and phenomena results.

> Soylo walked across the ridge above Five Rivers leading his donkey, and the two of them made a remarkable picture against the evening of the sky, it was as if the fading light was giving them a glory, carving them in motion, each small detail recorded and etched for all time. (30)

Even as human form and physical phenomena blend and merge together to offer a feeling of timelessness, so too do social function and physical phenomena blend to produce a correspondence that denotes the unending interdependence between cane and the villager, locking them in a symbiotic time and space. Here, all is color, fusion marking the end of a season, telling the end of a day.

> After the after-glow of the sunset in the west, another part of the sky glowed with a pale red light as they fired the trash in the canefields of Five Rivers, burning away all the dry leaves so that only the stalks of cane would remain and make the reaping easier. (197)

We have noted the metaphoric and symbolic use of cane in the mood form of the novel, yet cane becomes more than a symbol, more than a figural representation of the lives of the villagers. When actualized, cane represents all the lingering, residual effects of plantation slavery and of white domination in the early part of the twentieth century in the Caribbean. Cane and working the cane are etched in the very skin of the laborer, now foreman, Babolal. Working the cane is all that he has known, all that his son, Tiger, sees stamped on his body.

He watched his father closely, seeing the lines which furrowed his forehead, the tan of the fierce sun visible even on the dark skin. His father smelled of work. The wild, sweet smell of sugar-cane was part of him. His body exuded this smell. (8–9)

And even though Babolal is so totally linked, fused with cane, he gains in stature; he is completely at home in the sugar cane field, indeed achieves dignity there.

> Tiger wondered if he should go with them. But he knew Babolal could be trusted once he got into the open, among the cane. There wouldn't be anything in the fields he didn't know about. He would gain confidence and hold his own. (77)

Even so, Tiger resents the hold which cane has had over the lives of his people, the servitude which they underwent, the persistent exploitation they suffered. Intrinsic to the leisurely development of the plot, essential to the narrative unfoldings, indeed, vital to Tiger's groping toward his realization of self, are his attempts to break the unremitting cycle of servitude to cane. Thus Tiger flees the endemic servitude of the cane plantations of Chaguanas to settle in the half-rural, partly urban Barataria, becoming more self-reliant, less governed by the whims of white plantation domination, by the ritual of East Indian subservience. Barataria offers Tiger the beginnings of economic independence, limited as that is, from his initial living in a state-hut to occupation of his own house built with his own hands and with the aid of his friend and neighbor buddy, Joe Martin. From laboring on a large plantation, Tiger, like his friend, Dean, becomes a small proprietor-farmer, filling his own small plot, harvesting his fruit, his vegetables. Barataria, too, affords the promise of an embryonic social cohesion, knitting a close friendship among Joe Martin, Dean, Tall Boy and Urmilla—peoples of African, East Indian and Chinese descent, thereby creating the social ingredient so necessary, so vital for the Caribbean—the creolization of the races. Selvon represents them locked in basically stereotypic functions and attitudes. Tiger's father, Babolal, comments on Tiger's material progress in Barataria.

> "You have electric light," Babolal went on, looking about the room, "and these chairs," he pressed down on the soft cushion, "and you have water in the kitchen, you don't have to go by the stand-pipe in the road." (7)

Joe Martin, Tiger's surrogate father in Barataria, notes with pride Tiger's social and mental growth since his arrival in Barataria.

Joe looked at Tiger like a father watching his son, thinking how he had known him from the early days in Barataria when he wanted so much to prove that he was a man . . . . For Tiger had set out to be a man living next door to him, and he had watched him week after week, month after month, year after year, and he felt a kind of responsiblity towards Tiger . . . . (193)

Why, then, does Tiger leave this self-rooting in Barataria and take what could be viewed as a backward step by returning to a sugar plantation deep in the country? Clearly, even though physically distant from a cyclical pattern of cane servitude, he seems still psychologically shackled by a long tradition of such servitude. Perhaps he hopes becoming the bookkeeper, a job demanding a minimum of literacy, will differentiate him from the unlettered villagers of Five Rivers, and bring him closer to the erstwhile dominant white supervisory status. His father, Babolal, had similar secret yearnings, and interpreted his new position in Five Rivers not as that of laborer, but as that of estate supervisor.

Indecisive at first, Tiger finally comes to a decision to leave Barataria when the gossip and rumors of others take on a quality of fact:

And so it happened, in conversation with friends, I hear you going away, when you going? What you go do with the garden? and suddenly there was no more problem, he felt a great relief, and could have laughed at all his bother. (16)

Perhaps Tiger's return to the source of his former servitude can be interpreted as a descent into the valley, into a pit, in order to reemerge cleansed and liberated. This reentry or reemergence becomes the central plot of the novel. Tiger's realization that although his father was a foreman, supervising a new cane experiment in Five Rivers, the estate and plantation were actually controlled, directed, and ruled by a white supervisor, produces the first traumatic challenge to his sense of freedom. Tiger's encounter with the white supervisor's wife, his flight when greeted by her, brings about a deep emotional turmoil and thus Tiger seems to be controlled by all the residual psychological dominance released by white presences.

So much of the action, then, involves the play of memory affecting the present; recalling a cycle of subservience leads to Tiger's indecisive stumbling, a seemingly reactive rebellion, but it is through this stumbling rebellion that Tiger arrives at a point of freedom.

On realizing that he has come to work on an estate controlled by a white overseer, all of his youthful experiences come screaming back. Recalling the stories of the old East Indian laborers produces mental turmoil in the present. Memory of the white man, the white overseer, wells up in Tiger.

So persistent are these memories that recalling them becomes a constant motif of *Turn Again Tiger*, indeed in many of Selvon's Trinidadian stories. The theme recurs in perhaps one of his finest stories, "Cane is Bitter," in *Ways of Sunlight*. So endemic, so recurrent are the memories, the tales of the white overseer, that they seem to become part of the folklore of the rural Indian in Selvon.

Tiger's return to Five Rivers not only provides Selvon with an opportunity to explore the psychological effects of plantation servitude, but affords him the chance to devise parallel novelistic structures contrasting a purely rural village, Five Rivers, with the marginal urban village, Barataria; to present comparative statements about the nature of generational differences, about age, and about the nature of action and decision-making. Five Rivers is still caught in all the folklore and rurality of the village, of people segregated in distant villages and cut off from constant traffic and communication. It is a refuge for some. Soylo, the Hindu, has lost a son in the harvest of canes and comes to lick his wounds in Five Rivers and to feed on his tragedy. The oversized More Lazy just waddles without purpose or intention to Five Rivers after losing his house and sheep by gambling. Selvon presents these characters with all of his storytelling skill and craft. They are essential to Selvon's depiction of the folklore of Five Rivers and later to his notion of the liberating action. These characters clearly contrast with Joe Martin, Dean, and Tall Boy, their counterparts in Barataria, who seem to possess a clear notion of their identity and functions.

In Five Rivers, Tiger, in his constant pondering, attempting to grasp the meaning of work and life, arrives at such conclusions.

> A baby had soft hands and soft skin on its body, but it grew up and the sun and the rain hardened that skin, and the struggle to live made the eyes sink in the head and the skin grew coarse and wrinkled. That was something, just being, and maintaining an equilibrium in a place where nothing seemed worth living for. (*Tiger*, 46)

Often Selvon interjects his own moralizings, his own philosophy, into the thought processes of his characters, making them the carriers of his ideas. For instance, the novelist makes his characters wonder, is there a purpose to life, or is there merely a drifting along, controlled or undirected? Further, is man essentially doomed to arrive at decisions in aloneness without being able to call on others for assistance? Tiger grapples with his own dilemma, his own need to break the cycle, to reject the white presence reiterated by Soylo and others:

> "I can't help you at all at all at all." Soylo stopped sharpening his hoe and looked across the valley to the mountain, and his voice was animated

now. "Every man have their own life to live. You best had find something quick, Tiger." (158)

Tiger begins to break the cycle of the white presence with a gratuitous self-liberating act, fraught with all the residuals, the psychological entanglements, deriving from plantation servitude and colonial domination. To Tiger it is a necessary, urgent, liberating act—one in which he is truly a participant, caught up in a historical happening, rather than an initiator of that happening.

A year has gone around since Tiger and Urmilla and their daughter, Chandra, came to the Valley of Five Rivers, and a cycle has seemingly been broken—Tiger will return purged to Barataria to engage in a form of social, political action, to till his own fields, to await the birth of his second child.

Selvon ascribes a measure of causation to Tiger's act—he has become, during the year, not a field laborer, but in fact, a house attendant, indeed a house slave to a white overseer and his wife. But we attribute no causation, no psychological reason for the action of the white overseer's wife. Was it curiosity? Clearly, the questions which we are left with are: Was Tiger purged of his deep-seated inferiority complex by one single sexual encounter with the white woman, Doreen? Could Doreen's lust or her curiosity be satisfied by that sexual act? If so, then could it be that the deep-seated and complex racial overtones were lacking in resonance, nothing but a novelistic interruption of a historical reality?

To answer yes to these questions would be to overlook the linkages existing between *Turn Again Tiger* and the short stories set in Trinidad in *Ways of Sunlight*. For *Ways of Sunlight* contains not only the germs and embryo of *Turn Again Tiger*, but in fact, there is clear evidence in one or two of the stories of certain themes and motifs which contour the novel. The characters More Lazy and Soylo appear with slight deviations in the story "Holidays in Five Rivers." Not only do some of the same personages appear, but also motifs and themes, social realities and economic configurations, recur in both *Turn Again Tiger* and *Ways of Sunlight*. Two of the stories, "Cane is Bitter" and "A Drop of Rain," indicate the integral relationship of an East Indian laborer of the period to land—his dependence on the weather, his dependence on cane, both of which make for an endemic and continuous form of indenture and servitude.

In "Cane is Bitter," the narrative conflict revolves around a young man's desire to break away from the recurrent cycle of laboring in the field, a cycle of poverty and ignorance. His education in the city leads to his estrangement from his family, or rather his family's inability to cope with his need to break the cycle of ignorance and poverty, and though he is still skilled in the reaping of cane—as skilled as his brother, Harry, or any of the other laborers—his refusal to enter into the traditionally arranged marriage contract with Dulce is viewed as defying tradition, indeed as a kind of rebellion; so closely interwoven were the traditions and the culture with the cycle of work, with the socioeconomic configurations of the estate. Education is viewed as both a boon and a threat.

The thrust toward education, the pushing of their children to obtain education, and thereby mobility, often comes from East Indian women in Selvon's writing. Urmilla, Tiger's wife, keeps the idea of Chandra's education constantly in Tiger's consciousness. It is the mother in "Cane is Bitter" who instigates her son's going to the city to be educated. Selvon seems to propose that the only way to break the cycle is through education, perhaps with its attendant departure from the village and its extension, the estate.

In "A Drop of Rain," the young son, Sunny, has not as yet left the country, the land; he still lives close to his father and mother, whose lives are totally dependent on, tied to, the cycle of the weather. In this potently narrated story, we note the ritual ordinance of rain and drought in the lives of the rural villages. Here the village folk, as in Salkey's A Quality of Violence, have their emotions, their fortunes, their very existence affected by the cyclical changes of weather, a new drought, and at times excessive rain. In "A Drop of Rain," as in so much of Selvon's writing, the elements often mark or emphasize conflict and its resolution, indicate both the problematic and the resolved.

In "A Play of Light and Dark," the coming of the rain cloud obscures the moon but brings light and luminosity to the characters. When the prayers of the villagers to the rain god are followed by rain, their tenacity, the deep belief of the village fold, is confirmed; after the drought the corn would grow so much greener.

In three stories, "Johnson and the Cascadura," "The Washerwoman," and "The Mango Tree," folk belief and faith, folk sayings and superstition, are the conditions, the motifs, leading to the denouement, the plot resolution of the stories.

In both "The Washerwoman" and "The Mango Tree," the central figure, Ma Procop, somewhat glibly plays on the superstitious beliefs of the villagers. In the former story, against the backdrop of village superstition, Ma Procop, as in a Brer Nancy folk tale, outwits the scheming and covetous Ma Lambi, takes over her business, that of washerwoman for the small village, and sends her packing, and so seems to verify the superstitious belief that a *soucoyant*, a devil woman, cannot look at her own image in a mirror.

In "The Mango Tree," a loosely constructed story, the folk statement and belief—that if girls climb trees the fruits of the trees get sour—is so often repeated and, finally, borne out. In these stories, as in "Johnson and the Cascadura," the catalytic ingredient is the acceptance of folk beliefs.

In "Johnson and the Cascadura," Urmilla, the beautiful East Indian girl, knows and believes that any foreigner to the island who eats the fish, the cascadura, will have to return to the island. Although this belief is central in bringing the story to a happy conclusion, it is this very conclusion that evades the deep and essential social problem of the white foreigner coming with all the colonial trappings to a plantation, and making love in the fields to the most attractive native woman, who has refused the best of the native suitors.

Here is acted out a basic plantation relationship which the old man so frustratingly discussed in *Turn Again Tiger*. The white overseer's copulation with the Indian woman in the fields in this story has no deep resonance, no true social signification. To be sure, Selvon attempts to make the colonizing figures—Franklin and Johnson—benign, generous and egalitarian. Yet, the basic plantation structure ordains their attitude. The white plantation owner, Franklin, can easily say to the Indian middle-man, Sam (with whom he maintains somewhat cordial relations), that he should stifle the rumors about the white visitor, Johnson, and the native woman, Urmilla, even though Johnson himself, careless of Sam's feelings—rather, not even speculating about his feelings—dramatically states, "I love her, Sam."

But Sam's reaction is not social and moral indignation, but personal, emotional peeve. Indeed, this benign, "cute" story portrays a plantation relationship without noting all the deep problematic circumstances of such a reality. Rather, Selvon coats it with sugar and seasons it with the cascadura.

In "Gussy and the Boss," another problematic racial encounter involving a foreign white company that has fired all but one of the native employees, Gussy, is presented by Selvon without any of the deep subsurface scrutinizing demanded of him. Selvon posits a colonial situation without analyzing its consequences. Even though the firing of all its native employees, the benign yet supercilious attitudes of the white foreigners, the grovelling subservience of Gussy, are the external contours of the story, yet its texture derives from Selvon's caricaturing (a device seldom employed by Selvon) of Gussy, the victim. That the emphasis is placed on ridiculing this character, rather than delving into the social and political ramifications of relationships between white foreigners and poor natives, is to present a serious social reality with a calypso technique. Old Sookdeo, the East Indian laborer, a farmer, locates the unending cycle of labor in an office of white people, of growing old in a leaking hut, of relaxing with rum and only watching the young girls, a cycle that ordains his life pattern and that of so many other villagers. But when that relentless cycle is broken by the uprooting of many villagers from their little plots of land for the building of a highway by the Americans, Sookdeo laments its loss. He, too, like the cycle, is broken: "Everything gone and done for dis old man now. Time for Sookdeo to dead. Garden gone, nutting to do" (151).

Other villagers, like Sookdeo, initially curtail their work, abandon the care of the land, which leads to a kind of incipient death of the land. Gone is the sense of purpose; even the sun cannot bring light into the villagers' feeling of loss: "It was like a loss of sunny, seed-bursting days, for no one bothered now with the farming of the land" (72).

Whereas Sookdeo's life seems to spin downward into a space unaffected by energy of sun, in *A Brighter Sun*, as the title suggests, the central character's life arches upward into space, energized by light and sun. For *A Brighter Sun* describes the spinning, the circling toward manhood of Tiger, who will move jerkily to a dawning comprehension of the flow and nature of life.

> "You don't start over things in life . . . you just have to go on from where you stop. It is not as if you born all over again. Is the same life."
> (*Brighter Sun*, 209)

It is this movement toward maturation, toward comprehension, which shapes Tiger's characterization and becomes the central motif, the essential plot structure, of the novel. Indeed, Tiger moves out of the narrow social confines of the rural, out of the closed racial reality of his village, to be initiated into a larger social fabric whose threads are still not woven together. In this social reality, the rural is still differentiated from the loosely spun urban condition. The races are still rooted in stereotyped reactions or perceptions, the sexes set in their own roles, the classes still set in their notions of superiority and inferiority. The young children reinforce, by their repetition, ethnic stereotypes. They taunt one another with such sterotypic joking:

> "Chinee, Chinee, never die,
> Flat nose and chinky eye!"
> But Ling was no coward, even though Henry was bigger than him. He put his hands to his ears to shut out their voices and he sang:—
> "Nigger is ah nation,
> Dey full of bodderation.
> Meet dem by de station,
> Dey stink wid perspiration!"
> . . . A white-skinned girl, dressed neatly with a blue ribbon in her hair was called, "Whitey cockroach!"
> She retorted, "Black tar-baby!" (55–56)

Even as the children, unwittingly perhaps, repeat such jingles, some members of the older generation, too, are fixed within narrow ethnic confines. As Tiger and Urmilla move toward a measure of ethnic neighborliness with Joe Martin and his wife, Rita, Tiger's father and mother remonstrate:

> "Is only nigger friend you makeam since you come?" his *bap* asked. "Plenty Indians liveam dis side. Is true them is good neighbour, but you must look for Indian friend, like you and you wife. Indian must keep together." (47)

Such a rigid ethnic position observed by the older generation also operates at the level of interracial relationships. An East Indian, Boysie, and his creole girlfriend, Stella, are confronted by its incidence not in the rural sectors, but in the urban area. Perhaps the assertive reactions of Boysie and Stella point toward the possibility of eventual ethnic coherence and cohesion, from which the creolization of groups of people would derive, yet this creolization is but embryonic; reactions to cross-racial relationships are still fixed, still rigid.

Tiger, the initiate, does not have the somewhat carefree attitude displayed by the more worldly Boysie. Newly arrived in Barataria, he is still wrestling with the problems of relationships between races and between sexes. His wife, Urmilla, also attempts to make such relationships more elastic but initially at least, she is confronted by their fixedness. As Tiger wrestles with his father's admonition that he should stick to Indians and search out Indian neighbors, Urmilla, caught in a racial and sexual bond, tentatively stretches out.

> The big thought [Tiger] had postponed came back . . . . Why I should only look for Indian friend? What wrong with Joe and Rita? . . .
>
> [Urmilla] would have liked to talk it over with him, but she knew that Indian women just kept the house and saw after the children and didn't worry their men. But she wanted it to be different with them, that they could talk and laugh together, and share worries. Would Tiger stop her from talking to Rita? If he did, she would have to obey. It would be lonely with no one to share gossip. (48–49)

Here, both Tiger and Urmilla are caught in the untextured, the unresolved nature of the social fabric, reflectors of a community still lacking communal cohesion, yet still groping toward this group consciousness. Three problematic social conditions, those of race, the positions of the sexes, the playing of rural and urban circumstances, affect their behavior and direct the growth of both society and the characters. Thus to share, even by a gesture, the unasked, unanswered problematic questions of race, of sex, brings momentary feelings of well-being to Urmilla, to Tiger.

It was as if he drew power from the darkness, as if in the struggle
itself there was understanding and truth, if he could only find them. He
pulled Urmilla's hand to him. The girl was glad. She held on tightly.

He thought, This must be growing up. I must be really coming man
now. (49)

The darkness, the wind, the elements always seem to blend with Tiger's
emotions, to indicate directions. For clearly Selvon, by the very name of the
novel *A Brighter Sun,* has clarified the relationship between elements and
people, between his central character's growth, his stumbling toward that
growth, and the earth, the elements.

Between Tiger and the earth, the elements, there is flow, there is
harmony. They co-penetrate; there exists all the coherence of rhythmical
interplay. When close to the elements, Tiger has none of the unease, none
of the uncertainty which beset him when confronted by the fragmented
social reality, by problematic racial and social undercurrents. Confronted by
a galling social and class prejudice when he is slighted by a colored attendant, who rushes away from him to serve an old white woman, his reactions,
though assertive, are but tentative, lacking in assurance, weak. Disregarded
and slighted by the old white woman, too, who "sniffed the air and cast a
surprised look at the Indian" (92), he backs away with uncertainty, indeed
with a feeling of shame. The scene is paced, the episode charged, with all
the tensions endemic to a colonial situation, fraught with all the complexities, all the problematic undercurrents of race and class.

Later Tiger views the situation as portraying the colonial difference
between rich whites and poor natives—East Indians and Blacks—as depicting an inherent, material inequality. From a hill overlooking Port of Spain,
in a scene which will be repeated in Earl Lovelace's *While Gods Are Falling,*
Tiger remarks on the material inequality between the dwellings of those who
live in the rich suburbs and others, perhaps like Joe Martin, who grow up
and live in the poor slum neighborhoods. Even so, even when struck by this
awareness of the basic inequality in the social fabric of Trinidad at that time,
Tiger on the hilltop feels life and its growth possibilities flow through him,
and he is vitalized by a knowledge of an uninterrupted ordained life flow.
Indeed, in the midst of his tentative searchings, his initiation into the social
dimensions of Trinidad, on the hill all is assurance, all is empowerment.

The wind came down from the hills behind St. Anns in thrusts of
sweet, wild smells, and again he felt a power in it he would have liked to
possess; he sat under a cashew tree and fell back on the grass, becoming
aware of a hundred insect noises in the bush, the movement of leaf, and
a throb in the earth itself, as if life buried there was pushing to come to

the surface. It must be trees growing, it must be roots delving for food. (99)

Evidently Tiger's perception of the landscape and his awareness of its life force make his own growth consonant with the growth potential of the trees around him. His character at this level is emanating assurance for he is linked in an almost pantheistic relationship to the elements. From them he receives directives for growth and at times enlightenment. At such times Selvon imbues the landscape with mobile colors, projecting vital forces and possibility, indicating the symbiotic relationship of man and the elements:

> It was getting dark; he must have been in the gardens longer than he thought, for the sun was sinking. He watched it with deep feeling, not giving of himself so much as drawing from it what he could . . . . Deep purple merged in red and yellow, outlining the clouds . . . . A blue evening haze settled on the hills. A twilight descended on the city. (101)

This symbiotic relationship between Tiger and the elements often not only directs growth, but leads from speculation to introspection, like change that comes about through nature, the natural cycles of night and day, sunset and sunrise, measuring the changes which affect Tiger's shuttling movements from boyhood to manhood.

> But this one was different. It was for him the sun set . . . . He thought that when it rose in the morning things would change. For changes were sudden with him, one day he was a little boy and the next day he was a man, one day he didn't have to worry about anything and the next he had a wife and a child and the shop to pay. (101–102)

It is not surprising that the birth of his child, Chandra, is mirrored in the landscape, heralded by the elements. The night is lit up even as Chandra brings light to Tiger—led by the light of the moon brightening the night.

> Tiger left Joe and walked outside in the street. Tonight was a big night. It was like the time Chandra was born. The moon was full, lighting up the village. Trees cast shadows. A late goods train rumbled and belched black smoke. It slowed as it travelled through the village, then surged on, and he could hear the grinding sound of the wheels grow fainter. He just felt like walking and letting the night wind hit him in the face. (112)

Tiger's highest point of assurance, his moments of clarification as to how to grow, how to proceed, are all marked by or receive their illumination from the elemental reality. Here the dialogue of man and land is intense, charged with a grandeur, with its own compelling power; then all is certainty, all

surging confidence: "the power was all around him, he could feel it throbbing in the earth, humming in the air, riding the night wind, stealing through
the swamp" (113).

However, his relationship with the social reality does not evince that
certainty and confidence which are so evident in his relationship with the
natural order. He doubts his intelligence; he criticizes himself for being
unlettered; he questions the validity of being both a father and husband.
Chandra, the very child who once brought illumination to him, now seems
to imprison him, denying him the possibility of another form of illumination,
education.

> When Urmilla and the baby were asleep he looked up at the roof and felt
> revulsion for his wife and child. They were to blame for all his worry. If
> he were alone he could be like Boysie, not caring a damn. He would go
> to the city and get a job—not an ordinary job, like how Boysie used to
> work in a grocery, but something bigger. He would even go to school in
> the night and learn to read and write. Right here in Barataria he could
> have gone to school, but everybody would laugh at a big married man like
> him going to class with a slate and pencil. (81–82)

Thus, fatherhood, even while liberating and pointing to natural growth from
boy into man, brings with it a contrapuntal reaction, that of being man-father
while still being man-child. How, then, to break out of this illiteracy
becomes a recurrent question controlling Tiger's actions and thoughts. He
berates himself, linking illiteracy to his racial origin.

Yet Tiger's attempt to acquire education, as well as his desire to emulate
Boysie and acquire knowledge of the city, bring their own complications,
leading to other unanswered questions. Movement toward the acquisition of
education brings with it a countermovement, a further feeling of inadequacy.

> "But look at me. A stupid coolie boy from the country, can't even read
> and write. That is what people say about me. They does call me a force-
> ripe man. You think I like to remain ignorant?" (109)

The delineation of Tiger's character is marked by simplistic and often
repeated conjectures as to the nature of things, the meaning of being, the
purpose of life. Clearly, Selvon has entered into a sympathetic contact with
his character, for the simplistic nature of questions which Tiger repeatedly
asks is not underscored. Tiger is not presented by Selvon as a figure of
ridicule; his questing is not parodied or held up to scorn. It is not incorrect
to say author V. S. Naipaul would have made Tiger into a figure of ridicule,
would have satirized his simplistic philosophizing. Selvon attempts to make
Tiger's questions and statements ingenuous, so that the repetition of

questions such as the following, though at times tiresome, is never comical, indeed never even sneered at nor "pappyshowed" by Tiger's friend.

> But what I want to find out most is about things in general, about people, and how I does feel funny sometimes. Man, if I tell you 'bout things I want to find out! What I doing here now? Why I living? What all we doing here? (100)

Even when Tiger's neighbor and friend, Joe Martin, tells Tiger that "all of that old talk is a lot of balls," it is said not with malice nor with condemnation. Indeed Tiger's experience, his simplistic questioning, stand in sharp contrast with the experiences and lifestyle of his neighbor, Joe Martin, who seems to be a character foil for Tiger. Selvon depicts Tiger's character in a spiraling fashion. Tiger's repetitions of questions are circular, his relationship to the elements deriving from a cyclical order. The depiction of Joe Martin, on the other hand, is linear, affording Selvon an opportunity to describe the barrack-yard living of central Port of Spain with its fights, its prostitution, its robust camaraderie, the street-corner preachers, the evolving music of the street band. But further, Joe Martin's character, in its linear presentation, is devoid of the complexities and doubts which assail Tiger. Joe Martin's experiences are redolent with the sense and smell of the city; Tiger's with the wind and smell of cane burning at harvest time. Clearly here, Selvon is using his characters to achieve a contrapuntal play between the rhythm of ways in the rural areas and the pulsations of life in the city during the war years. Selvon presents Joe Martin to us through his recollections:

> "Boy, listen. It had a time when I did small, dey send me to school in Nelson Street. All right. I learned a, b, c, and how to count. By de time dey ready to put me in first standard, I decide long time it ain't have no future in dat. I used to break *buisse* . . . ."
> ". . . Ah grow up big, having experience. Ah screw so much woman dat I can't even remember dem. Ah tief. Ah go hungry. Ah drink rum. Ah smoke. Ah play cards—Ah was a rummy test in me days, and don't talk 'bout wappee! Yuh cud play cards?" (110–111)

Joe Martin is a representational character, typifying the West Indian Sagaboy. The friendship between Tiger and Joe Martin is Selvon's way of pushing the two distinctive characters, a rural East Indian type and a Black city dweller, toward a creolization, a possible communal coherence, the merging of races, the approximating of environments.

In Naipaul's *A House for Mr. Biswas*, Mr. Biswas pursues his dreams of acquiring and owning a house which he can call his own, a pursuit which is radial and totally central to the action of the novel. He lives in many areas, occupies many spaces, inhabits many interiors, so that the conglomeration of areas, spaces, interiors and his inhabiting of them perhaps represent not only the myriad circumstances of his life, but also the true acquiring of his house. Indeed each interior—and there are so many interiors—daubed and delineated by Naipaul in this novel with its own particular biology, its own chemistry, each interior becomes celled and germed where the novel *A House for Mr. Biswas* undergoes its principal spawning. At the intersection of interiors, at the conjunction of dream house, at the point of search for ownership, at cardinal and interlocking areas, Mr. Biswas attempts to locate his sphere of influence, in many instances, of noninfluence, of invisibility. But the central area where his dreams interlock, from which his emotion or lack of emotion derives its timbre, its echo, is the house of the Tulsi. This house seems to ordain his every action, his every dream, to signify his every defeat, any minimal victory. The house of the Tulsi is the sounding board of Mr. Biswas's future, the echo chamber of his past, a past which is forever present, inescapable.

> The future he feared was upon him. He was falling into the void, and that terror, known only in dreams, was within him as he lay awake at nights . . . . He was always tired, always restless. (Naipaul, *A House for Mr. Biswas*, 204)

And indeed many of the interiors through which Mr. Biswas passes are makeshift, gloomy reflections of his own gray life. His movements from dark interior to dark interior trace the trajectory of a life lit by momentary hope, brightened by few successes. His characterization, a linear progression along that surface, is peripatetic, a series of jerky movements from interior to interior; the contours of the novel run ramshackling through many episodes, taking Mr. Biswas from his ill-fated birth to an unromantic death in a house symptomatic of a final failure. Almost all of the interiors are redolent with decay, devoid of life and air, shuttered and musty enclosures filled with broken objects, evidence of broken dreams, of unfilled lives.

In Bhandhat's house, where Mr. Biswas lives and works for a while, "The room in which Mr. Biswas slept [has] no window and [is] perpetually dark" (56). In the rum shop adjoining the room, so many anguished lives are drugged by alcohol. The shop, "a long, straggling settlement of mud huts in the heart of the sugarcane area (the Chase)" (127), is where Mr. Biswas spends six years of his life always waiting, thinking it will be but a transient halt. Here, too, the interior is dark: "a short, narrow room with a rusty galvanized iron roof," with walls that "leaned and sagged" (127), with cobwebs portraying abandonment, revealing the unraveling of dreams.

Mr. Biswas's life is as ramshackle as the shop and, as if to stress the hopelessness of his dreams, the shop goes up in smoke, is burnt. The Tulsi shop, however, remains a permanent fixture, a fixed point of reference in the lives of the swarming Tulsi family: the myriad children, the many wives and husbands and in-laws; a fixed point of reference, too, for Mr. Biswas. Yet, even in its fixedness, in its seeming permanence, behind its "facade that promised such an amplitude of space," there is gloom, clutter, diminished space.

> There were no windows and light came only from the two narrow doors at the front and the single door at the back, which opened on to a covered courtyard. (74)

The house where his mother, Beptil, lives in her own reduced way is constricting, too, in its musty gloom and smallness. Mr. Biswas leaves this reduced space. In his imagination and through his readings of "Samuel Smiles," Mr. Biswas escapes to an "intoxicating" dream world which is so different from his mother's cluttered room, to landscapes of dream, romance. But the interior to which he goes, the romance that takes him away from his mother's house, runs him not into dreams—but into the crowded, gloomy interior of the Tulsi house, where his living is amorphous, controlled and undifferentiated. He is literally led into the household to become one of the many occupants of the Hanuman House.

> He followed Seth through the back door to the damp, gloomy courtyard, where he had never been. Here the Tulsi Store felt even smaller; looking back, he saw life-size carvings of Hanuman, grotesquely coloured, on either side of the shop doorway. . . .
> They climbed a short flight of cracked concrete steps into the hall of the wooden house. It was deserted. Seth left Mr. Biswas, saying he had to go and wash. It was a spacious hall, smelling of smoke and old wood. The pale green paint had grown dim and dingy and the timbers revealed the ravages of woodlice which left wood looking so new where it was rotten. Then Mr. Biswas had another surprise. Through the doorway at the far end he saw the kitchen. And the kitchen had mud walls. It was lower than the hall and appeared to be completely without light. The doorway gaped black; soot stained the wall about it and the ceiling just above; so that blackness seemed to fill the kitchen like a solid substance. (78–79)

Naipaul seems to have filled most of his description of interiors, indeed of exteriors as well, with dimness, gloom and decay. The external reality pasted in by Naipaul is devoid of light, heavy with small reflecting figures equally lackluster and dull, their skins stamped with the smell of their trade. In Awacas the stores are described by Naipaul with quick rapid slashes. There are little rooms bulging with dry goods and "grocer's shops, smelling damply of oil, sugar and salted fish" (62). The assistants stand with

> pencils tapping bill-pads with the funerally-coloured carbon paper . . . .
> Grocers' wives and children stood oily and confident behind counters.
> The women behind the vegetable stalls were old and correct with thin
> mournful faces. (62)

Naipaul invests the places of commerce along the Eastern Main Road, the houses, their inhabitants, with a quality of hopelessness, of incompleteness, of haphazardness. His vision of rural reality as depicted in *A House for Mr. Biswas* is totally different from that of Samuel Selvon, whose canvas gives off rays of light even in the midst of hopelessness. Naipaul imbues the rural landscape not with sunlight but with darkness; revels in indicating the bareness, the incipient, the incessant, movement of phenomena or people toward decay, to dying. In Green Vale, another rural area to which Mr. Biswas travels in his unending movement, "dead trees ringed the barracks, a wall of flawless black" (102).

> Half the leaves were dead; the others, at the top, were dead green. It was
> as if all the trees had, at the same moment, been blighted in luxuriance,
> and death was spreading at the same place from all the roots. (185)

Even when the landscape may have evinced possibility, even when Naipaul is at his most lush in describing the flora and fauna, in presenting evidence of growth and cultivation at that intersection of man—in this instance, the Tulsi brood—with such a landscape, there follows blight, destruction and the tiring of dreaming. In describing Mr. Biswas's first coming to the estate just beyond Maraval Road, Naipaul tinges the landscape with all the vibrancy of colors, of yellows and reds and purples, imbues it with all the vitality of growth, the freshness of fruit in bloom; there is the flowering of the landscape, here where perhaps Naipaul is at his most lyrical, at this interlude he showers his two main characters, Mr. Biswas and Mrs. Tulsi, with flowers.

> Below the overarching trees the road was in soft shadow . . . . Mr. Biswas
> began seeing the fruit trees. Avocado pear trees grew at the side of the
> road as casually as any bush; their fruit, only just out of flower, were tiny
> but already perfectly shaped, with a shine they would soon lose. The land
> between the road and the gully widened; the gully grew shallower.
> Beyond it Mr. Biswas saw the tall immortelles and their red and yellow
> flowers. (358)

After this momentary lyrical interlude, so rare in *A House for Mr. Biswas*, Naipaul hones the landscape to a wanton and mindless destruction, demolishes the lyricism of growth, exposes the barrenness of insensitivity and perhaps of greed. The Tulsi brood, symbolically unable to appreciate the beautiful landscape, defoliates and lays it waste. A possible source of dream for Mr. Biswas dries up; he is seized by a feeling of entrapment, staggered by feelings of insignificance.

Not realizing the romance which his reading of "Samuel Smiles" has conjured up, Mr. Biswas turns to other sources of escape, to other readings: "Though he never ceased to feel that some nobler purpose awaited him, even in this limiting society, he gave up reading Samuel Smiles" (164). He turns to religion and philosophy, but he is unable to escape the reality of his own circumstances or of his own immediate living conditions. A feeling of entrapment, then, of an inability to escape the immediate threatening reality, becomes another factor, another element shaping Mr. Biswas's actions and character.

The motif of entrapment becomes recurrent, indicating a weakness, an inability to be decisive, which at times affects the whole course of his life's history. After being snared into his marriage with Shama by Mr. Tulsi and Seth, Mr. Biswas reflects sadly that "the world was too small, the Tulsi family too large. He felt trapped" (82–83). He is entrapped by Mrs. Tulsi as well, by her "mood" (149).

It is in the Hanuman House, among its many inhabitants, that Mr. Biswas evinces a deep sense of uselessness, ponders his insignificance, indeed the futility of his being in the world. All the interiors through which he has bungled, all the occupants whom he has encountered, and his own seeming purposelessness, flash before his eyes, through an enumeration of his dysfunctional living. Small wonder, then, that Mr. Biswas suffers a deep sense of loneliness, is constantly gripped by fear, experiences anguished disappointments, to such a degree that his characterization assumes a repetitiveness, becomes a series of anticlimactic or, rather, totally predictable anticipatory reactions.

Here, then, Naipaul attempts to ascribe a negativity, a sense of nothingness, to his character, to his so anti-heroic character. The author pushes Mr. Biswas, it seems, not irrevocably but intentionally toward the void, assuring his fall into that void, clothing him in a decided nothingness. With an existential articulation, the void opens for Mr. Biswas:

> The future he feared was upon him. He was falling into the void, and that terror, known only in dreams, was with him as he lay awake at nights . . . . He was always tired, always restless. (204)

I n *The Mystic Masseur*, the mood is not one of unending gloom and darkness; Naipaul does not push his central character into a void; the claustrophobia that encircles the dreams and the very life of Mr. Biswas is not present here. The tone of this novel is wry. The central character is lampooned, his pretentiousness satirized.

The trajectory of this easy-paced narrative, with its full externalization of social attitudes and foibles, describes the growth of Ganesh Ramsumair from shy, unassured adolescent to successful, pompous legislator. It is this growth which gives to the narrative its action, its plot—it is the externalization of detail which lends it a comic circumstance, informing its social reality. As in Selvon's *Turn Again Tiger* and *A Brighter Sun*, the novelistic time is the war years, 1939–1945, when the Trinidadian society was undergoing its own social, political, cultural transformation. Naipaul in his delineation of Ganesh's character ascribes to that period a circumstantial quality, assuring the providential nature of Ganesh's growth and material success. Naipaul's characters are thrown by chance into the milieu in which they find themselves—chance becomes the given for them. Mr. Biswas is born with a negative sign, born "in the wrong way" (12), six-fingered and at midnight, destined to "eat up his own father and mother" (13). Ganesh Ramsumair, though, has been born with a gift, what in the novel is called a "hand" for healing the sick. Ganesh and many others firmly believe that in spite of the difficulties of any moment, great things were going to happen. But Ganesh must function in the larger society, and he does so by acquiring the external tools of survival—books, education. His character describes an arc from unself-consciousness and vague feelings of hidden talents to a point of being pushed to the exercise of these given talents by chance circumstances; from a badly dressed schoolboy, who never stopped being a country boy, through Pundit Ganesh Ramsumair, to the final glory of G. Ramsay Muir, Esq., M.B.E. He reaches his high point of creativity as a mystic masseur:

> No one could lay evil spirits better, even in Trinidad . . . . No one could tie a house better, bind it, that is, in spiritual bonds proof against the most resolute spirit. (Naipaul, *The Mystic Masseur*, 133)

He could master any ball-of-fire, *soucouyant*, or *loup-garou*.

Even though he achieves material success and through this, a degree of social mobility, yet, in fact, his character circumscribes a downward arc. There is moral degeneration and an acceptance of glamorous mediocrity. Even though Ganesh, the mystic masseur, mediates, his character is neither introspective nor guided by psychological considerations; rather this is a manifestation emerging from the social reality. Naipaul's presentation of that social reality affords him full scope for his comic satirical eye. He unerringly pinpoints pretence, shame, affectation, fraudulence, which underlie the religious, educational, cultural attitudes of that period. It is affectation which qualifies the presentation of Leela's growth and affords Naipaul, as in so many other instances, full range for his satirical skill. Before her marriage to Ganesh, and in her own way attempting to impress him, she constructs a sign that stirs the admiration of both her father and Ganesh, thereby underscoring its pretentiousness.

NOTICE

NOTICE, IS. HEREBY; PROVIDED: THAT, SEATS! ARE, PROVIDED.
FOR; FEMALE: SHOP, ASSISTANTS

Ganesh said, "Leela know a lot of punctuation marks."
"That is it, sahib. All day the girl just sitting down and talking about these punctuation marks. She is like that, sahib." (39)

Later on as the wife of the politician, Leela's language becomes even more pretentious and affords Naipaul even more play for his romping humor.

She told Suruj Mooma, "This house I are building, I doesn't want it to come like any erther Indian house. I wants it to have good furnitures and I wants everything to remain prutty prutty. I are thinking about getting a refrigerator and a few erther things like that . . . and all that people says about Indians not being able to keep their house properly is true true. But I are going to get ours painted prutty prutty—" (150)

As in the above quotations, many of the motifs which recur in Naipaul's elaborations of Trinidadian—to be more precise Hindu—society are manifested through essentially comic formulations. For the painting of signs, the making of pamphlets, the broadcasting on loudspeakers of slogans, offer Naipaul countless opportunities for satire, for irony, in *The Mystic Masseur, The Suffrage of Elvira, Miguel Street,* and *A House for Mr. Biswas.* The slogan, "Vote Harbans or Die," spurs on the action of *The Suffrage of Elvira.* Ramlogan requests "nice wordings" for the marriage invitations.

"But you can't have nice wordings on a thing like a invitation."
"You is the educated man, sahib. You could think of some."
"R.S.V.P.?"
"What does it mean?"
"It don't mean nothing, but it nice to have it." (*Masseur*, 44)

Here education is equated with display, even as success is equated with overuse of the language, as the attainment of a house with "good furnitures . . . new refrigerator and a few erther things like that" (150).

When Suruj Mooma talks about a proper shop like those in foreign books, when Leela attempts to speak "good English," there is an unerring comic intent in the portrayal of their acquisitive ambitions. However, these characters also show evidence of an incipient social breakup of traditional Hindu culture and society in Trinidad during the 1940s. The author's surface humor, his intended levity, do not bring out those inner nuances which mark the onset of shifting social conditions, their attendant uncertainty of behavior, of ambition. Leela is caught between two idioms, her own Hindu and her newly acquired education, her sari and her bodice and long skirt. Indarsingh uses two names, one East Indian and one creole, depending on the area in which he is campaigning. The switch is weighted down with all the incipient movement toward the creolization of Hindu culture that affects so many other Naipaul characters, especially in *A House of Mr. Biswas*. When introduced,

> Indarsingh came in an Oxford blazer and Swami, as an organiser of the *Bhagwat*, introduced him to the audience. "I got to talk English to introduce this man to you, because I don't think he could talk any Hindi. But I think all of you go agree with me that he does English like a pukka Englishman. That is because he have a foreign education and he only *just* come back to try and help out the poor Trinidad people. Ladies and gentlemen—Mr. Indarsingh, Bachelor of Arts of Oxford University, London England."
>
> Indarsingh gave a little hop, fingered his tie, and, stupidly, talked about politics. (*Masseur*, 199)

In spite of the evident pretentiousness of the gesture, it is but reflective of the much-repeated questioning of such moves, indeed at times, the belittling by the characters of their own Hindu and East Indian attitudes.

Clearly the high point of the parody of Hindu custom takes place during Ganesh's wedding to Leela where the custom of the kedgree is comically portrayed. Ramlogan's attempt to escape the payment of the dowry by stressing Ganesh's attitudes, Ramlogan's connivance and greed, are humorously foiled in a scene that manifests all of Naipaul's comic bent.

> Ramlogan gave a short forced laugh, and lost his temper. "If he think he going to get any more money from me he damn well mistaken. Let him don't eat. Think I care if he starve? Think I care?"
>
> He walked away.
>
> The crowd grew bigger, the laughter grew louder.
>
> Ramlogan came back and the crowd cheered him.
>
> He put down two hundred dollars on the brass plate and before he rose, whispered to Ganesh, "Remember your promise, sahib. Eat, boy, eat son; eat, sahib; eat pundit sahib, I beg you eat." (50–51)

In spite of such a parody of Hindu custom, Ganesh derives his political strength from Hindu voting power gained through the formation of branches of the Hindu association.

Ganesh's character thus receives its shaping, its contours from two realms, a traditional Hindu sphere and the external influences brought about by his reading of many books, by his "book-learning." His characterization is charted along occupational lines: student, teacher, masseur, pundit, author, politician. He chances into them, and into various social circumstances deriving from these occupations. Indeed, Ganesh does not grow by some tortuous, or as he prefers to call it, ordained happening; he stumbles through the process in a derivative fashion, shoved along by external forces, not guided by inner organic certainties, certainly not by dynamic inner urgings. Without really intending to, he acts on an impulse to which later he will ascribe ordinance. He enters, rather, falls into, marriage and this, too, he later posits as ordained.

> "I suppose," Ganesh wrote in *The Years of Guilt*, "I had always, from the first day I stepped into Shri Ramlogan's shop, considered it as settled that I was going to marry his daughter. I never questioned it. It all seemed preordained." (41)

He enters into reading and writing, the acquisition of books; he enters politics, all of these haphazardly, by the merest of chance, and Naipaul repeatedly holds up to scorn and ridicule Ganesh's accomplishments: the acquiring and reading of books.

Thus Ganesh's development, indeed his characterization, is a series of chance stumblings upon previously unperceived, unintentional courses of action. The many people who interact with Ganesh, the other protagonists of the narrative, are portrayed in all their idiosyncratic attitudes, filled in through the repetition of creatural or absurd gestures and actions. The Great Belcher repeatedly belches; Beharry constantly mumbles; Ramlogan slaps his thigh and looks at the thick black hair on his hands; Leela weeps. And all of these actions punctuate the dialogue with which Naipaul flavors his narrative, their repetition adding and further accentuating any humor inherent in a situation.

The use of the gestural to aid characterization, to offer possibilities for the humorous portrayal of personages, becomes an oft-repeated technique in *The Suffrage of Elvira*. The setting for Naipaul's parody of political enfranchisement and suffrage is a somewhat picturesque landscape, trespassed on by two external forces: Harbans, a Hindu from the city who is campaigning in Elvira, and two American-born Jehovah's Witnesses who are proseletizing in Cordova. At the very beginning of *The Suffrage of Elvira*, as if by sign, the two external forces collide:

> The bumper covered with two *Vote Harbans for Elvira* posters hit the
> back mudguard of one cycle and sent the cyclist stumbling forward, her
> hands still on the handlebars. But she didn't fall. (Naipaul, *The Suffrage
> of Elvira*, 8)

The bumper is the harbinger of the entry of democracy into Elvira; the
carriage of the bicycle contains Jehovah's Witnesses' pamphlets crying out
AWAKE! Clearly the two external forces bring with them all the problematic
processes which will infect the village rituals and the practitioners of these
rituals, dislocating both rituals and rhythms.

The novel becomes the unfolding of plots and subplots which comically
reiterate Mrs. Baksh's statement about democracy, that "Everybody just
washing their foot and jumping in this democracy business. But I promise
you, for all the sweet it begin sweet, it going to end damn sour" (28).
Further lampooned is the whole idea of politics and the political awakening
of Elvira. The bringing of suffrage to Elvira finds a fertile field for political
corruption and bribery, and the novel is shot through with scheming and
chicanery. That Harbans, the candidate, is already corrupt before his entry
into politics highlights the recurring motif of corruption. The road to Elvira
is full of ruts and holes, maintained in that state by Harbans's scheming.

Thus it is not surprising that the campaign Harbans runs in Elvira has
many pitfalls and ruts brought on by the materialistic scheming of the central
characters of the novel. This scheming, plotting and counterplotting by
Hindu, Muslims, Christians offer Naipaul full range for his wickedly farcical
humor. Each character is endowed with a physical characteristic which, when
emphasized and repeated, lampoons and caricatures that personage.

Most of the characters in *The Suffrage of Elvira* are stamped with unattractive physical features. Dhaniram is described as "a big exuberant man with
a big belly that looked unnecessary and almost detachable." Chittaranjan, on
the contrary, is small and skinny with a permanent smile on his face.
Ramlogan, the rum-shop owner, is fat and greasy, his hands covered with
thick black hair. Not only are the characters unseemly, but most of the
interiors that they inhabit are dark and cluttered. Not only are the characters
presented in all their physical unwholesomeness, not only do they inhabit
dim, shabby interiors, but their lives appear equally unwholesome, equally
devoid of light.

The coming of suffrage to such an area could have been depicted as
pathetic; rather, Naipaul underscores the comic, highlights the absurdity of
the process. By punctuating the dialogue with gestures, by offsetting the
serious with the absurd, by underscoring the inherent quality of greed with
which he imbues his characters, Naipaul creates an explosively humorous
canvas, which, however, is lacking in deep subsurface political causation. All

is fully evident, devoid of inner mobility, lacking in larger sociopolitical ramifications.

Quarrels between the neighbors Ramlogan and Chittaranjan are made into conflict situations; the rivalry between the two young men, the Hindu Lorkhoor and Foam, provides the novel with much of its central action. The presence and many appearances of the wasted mongrel dog, Tiger, lend the novel its mood, its intrigue, oftentimes its quality of the unknown. Ramlogan and Chittaranjan's quarrel stems from the intertwining of their trees.

> "And look at the Bleeding Heart," Foam went on. "Root in Ramlogan yard, but the flowers crawling all up by Chittaranjan bedroom window. And look at the breadfruit tree. Whole thing in Ramlogan yard, but all the breadfruit only falling in Chittaranjan yard. And look at the zaboca tree. Same thing. It look like *obeah* and magic, eh?" (28)

Their quarrels are replete with pathetic humor, with comic interplay. In many scenes, emotional outbursts, weeping, other signs of anguish, are superficial and quickly changing. Naipaul uses this surface transitoriness, the quick shifts of humor and emotion, to full effect in his comic depiction of the political process, of political meetings, of elections.

From the very beginning of the novel in a linear progression, Naipaul introduces all of his central characters, Harbans, Baksh, Foam, Chittaranjan, Ramlogan, Preacher, the Witnesses. Each person's physical, external characteristics are presented, their dress, their mannerisms, their foibles. Personages are also set in their own particular interior, their own space, the description of which merges and blends with their physical form. Then the novelist brings many of them together, interaction giving the novel its shifting narrative structure, its peripatetic, episodic movement, which yet achieves interconnectedness.

So much of *The Suffrage of Elvira* revolves around the figure of Harbans. It is from him that bribes and payoffs are requested, it is from him that many payoffs are received. Further, his emotional outbursts refract and reflect the predatory, grasping materialism of other characters, who revolve around him to such a degree that "spending on them," that is, the buying of votes, offers the committee an opportunity to develop a social welfare scheme, which becomes the nexus of one of the principal novelistic plots. The scheme, its origin and its execution are at one and the same time comic, yet charged with pathetic undercurrents.

In a discussion which is weighty with comic undertones, Naipaul deftly pushes the buying of votes to its most ludicrous, indeed its most insensitive end. Throughout, then, is an underlying note of the grotesque, indeed of the brutal:

Chittaranjan sucked his teeth . . . . "Dhaniram, you talking like if you
ain't know how hard these negroes is in Elvira. You ever see any negro
fall sick? They just does drop down and dead . . . ."

"All right. They don't get sick. . . . [But] two or three bound to dead
before elections."

"You going to kill some of them?" Baksh asked.

"Well, if even *one* dead, *we* go bury him. *We* go hold the wake. *We* go
take *we* coffee and *we* biscuits." (57)

Throughout *The Suffrage of Elvira* the maudlin, the grotesque, is subsumed in the comic, enveloped by it or enshrouding it.

Again, the superstitious beliefs of many Elvira residents act as a vehicle
for humor, at times grotesque. Thus it is that characterization of the mongrel,
Tiger, ordains the evolution of the novel, becoming one of the principal
catalytic agents of action. Harbans superstitiously senses that the appearance
of the Black Bitch and the Witnesses is a sign. Later the appearance of the
dog or of its progeny is not only a sign but becomes a representation of evil,
of *obeah*. The dog grows in stature: "Ten die. Big dog in the night turning
tiny tiny in the morning. Send him away and he came back. A lot of good!"
(138).

The many dimensions ascribed to the dog, its many random appearances,
often give to the novel a creatural reality which subsumes prediction; that
Mr. Cawfee will pay for kicking Tiger with his life takes on all the quality
of omen.

Mr. Cuffy raised his boot and kicked Tiger away. And for a kick on
a thin dog it made a lot of noise. A hollow noise, a *dup!* the noise you
would expect from a slack drum. Tiger ran off whining . . . .

"God go pay you for that, Mr. Cawfee," Herbert said. "He go make
you dead like a cockroach, throwing up your foot straight and stiff in the
air. God go pay you" (173).

Thus this novel is often tinged with an extramaterial dimension, bordering
on the extrasensory, devoid of that immediate realism in which Naipaul
situates his satire.

In *The Suffrage of Elvira*, the social reality is depicted by Naipaul with a
jaundiced eye, mirroring the comical beginning of the political process in the
village of Elvira. Parodied as it is, its depiction is myopic, lacking in a
fundamental depth perception which would ascribe historical causation to the
social reality. Yet both *The Mystic Masseur* and *The Suffrage of Elvira* present
the shifting and evolving configurations evident in the social order, in the
fabric of tradition and in the rural ethos of Trinidad and Tobago with the
coming of electoral politics. Even though the historical causation is lacking,

suffrage, a political emancipatory process, is posited, a process which eventually may offer young Foam, Lorkhoor, and perhaps Nelly, opportunities for a measure of social mobility, of political maturation.

No such possibility, however, is open to the East Indian village protagonists, Kaiser and Jaillin, in Ian McDonald's *The Humming-Bird Tree*. These two young East Indians remain caught in a web of fixed racial and social entanglements deriving from the clash of cultures, the clash of races. The novel, set in the early 1940s, depicts the essential separation between white landed gentry and the East Indian working class, so that even though the essential reality presented by McDonald seems idealized, indeed at times, idyllic, this idealization is charged with, indeed, negated by a deep problematic social reality. The attempted idealization of the friendship between the young white boy, Alan, and the East Indian, Kaiser, comes into constant conflict with the social reality dominated by an unswerving discrimination, by a constantly reinforced classism and elitism. Thus, throughout *Humming-Bird* there recur dual clashing perceptions of the same ritual rhythms, of the same circumstance.

> All of a sudden I saw our position more clearly than I had ever seen it. The force called prejudice had spilled out in front of my eyes. What was I to think? It had come out of me naturally as a sneeze so I knew that it was not something I could easily get control of by conscious thought . . . . I felt now a little of the power that was wrenching our friendship apart . . . . Society was closing around me with its masks, distinctions, special instincts and cunning. (McDonald, *Humming-Bird*, 113)

This statement analyzing the continuous conflict which besets the main protagonist and narrator, Alan, in itself underscores the basic ambivalence and the ambiguity not simply of a behavior, but of the rendition of that behavior. Alan is but a young boy, and such a clear analysis of his dilemma derives from an introspection which, in truth, is McDonald's. The novel often operates on two levels, two voices: the young voice relating an event, the other older voice analyzing the reaction: a process which at times robs the event of its immediacy.

> A child is as unsentimental as a cynic. Nostalgia for him is just the insistent mental demand for a previous pleasure . . . . At the window I was overwhelmed by the hurt and beauty of the past just because it was the past and would not come again in that way. (143)

This statement accurately, if not intentionally, represents the outcome of the idealized and idyllic relationship between Alan, the representative of the dominant white class, and Kaiser and Jaillin, the rural natives. Kaiser and

Jaillin have trespassed on Alan's privileged reserves. The penalty for this trespass is their dismissal. The objective statement stressing "hurt and beauty," nostalgia and the past, removes Alan from the immediacy of the dismissal, offering him the secure vantage point of nonparticipant observer, of nonvictim. The outcome of the friendship of the two boys, Alan and Kaiser, is laden with all the contempt of a supercillious, superior attitude.

> Kaiser carried his red sack of belongings in complete dejection; it looked heavy as if it was full of stones and tears. He was abject and defeated to an extent I had never imagined he could come. His clothes were unkempt like a clown's. His whole body trailed like a wounded, weak animal. I found that I despised him. (142)

The village reality described by McDonald—or by Alan—stands in direct contrast to the true effective reality in which Kaiser and Jaillin move and live. All the harshness of their condition, their brutal living circumstances, so often described by the author, indeed is never truly analyzed, the resonance muffled by the author's claim of nostalgic re-creation.

> I suppose the story I really want to tell begins with Jaillin . . . . When I first met her I was a child, the last time I was with her childhood suddenly came to an end. Looking back she seems to appear in every picture I have of that short span of life. (19)

To be sure, there is in *Humming-Bird* the colorful depiction of youthful infatuation, to be sure the Edenic rural setting is often depicted in brilliant colors and brush strokes. Yet even as Alan can quickly shift from the harsh immediacy of the dismissal to a statement of nostalgic past, so, too, the Edenic is often transitory, the natural affected by the societal, the external beauty trespassed on by internal, reactive, emotional states. Perhaps Kaiser and Jaillin symbolize the natural. Alan, always wishing to be superior to Kaiser and Jaillin, challenges the natural. Thus, again, the friendship between Kaiser and Alan always operates on two levels, the instinctual or natural, and the contrived or societal. Alan consistently attempts to dominate, to control the space in which Jaillin and Kaiser move unhampered. Indeed, Alan, unable to control their natural freedom of movement, feels peeved, irritated, jealous, constantly becomes confused, a blush coloring his pale skin.

> I looked at them, amazed and envious. A red-sailed skiff bobbed further out on the wind-chopped sea and I focused my eyes on that, pretending to ignore those silly children.
> The next thing I knew they had come closer, and shrieking with laughter they splashed water over me fast . . . . I ran up the beach out of range, tears itching in my eyes, so angry at their fun. (99–100)

From the very beginning of the novel, Alan envies the ease with which Kaiser moves in his natural surroundings.

> He could run faster than I and was more active in every way. One day we ran a race from the old samaan tree up the pitch road to the plum tree near the railway line. He beat me by twenty yards and I was sobbing with lack of breath when I came up to him . . . . I watched him enviously. (7)

Alan attempts to compensate, so that throughout the novel there is an unstated rivalry between Kaiser and Alan and since Alan is the narrator, his inner feelings, his true motives, his constant need, if not to emulate, then to dominate, become fully externalized motifs of the novel. Alan wishes to triumph in all of their encounters. He says, "I found it easy to love them when I held the stage" (96).

Is Alan's need to triumph over Kaiser, to be superior to Kaiser and Jaillin, societal or is it an element of Alan's own character? Since the reality in which the novel unfolds is a divided one, the constant reinforcing by Alan's parents of superior-inferior values, of class distinctions, may account for his incessant and unmitigated need to be superior. Yet, so recurrent is this need that it must, in part, stem from his inner character. At every instance of confrontation deriving from the difference in cultural perception, Alan's reaction stems both from the societal and his own inner perceptions. When speaking of the Madonna, Alan says to Kaiser and Jaillin:

> "Yes, I expect anyone can ask her for things and she might answer because she's so good. But it's better to be a Catholic." I clung to my privilege. . . .
>
> "Why we are not Cat'olics?" Jaillin asked Kaiser.
>
> "What you asking me, chile? What we have to do wid Cat'olics? We have we own temple, we have we own prayer. What you want mo', eh?"
>
> . . .
>
> "But it was the first," I said. "God told us we were the first and only ones." (105)

This scene clearly emphasizes the cultural differences which beset the relationship of the three protagonists and further underscores the distance separating the privileged Alan from the servant class, Jaillin and Kaiser, who though poor, maintain a strong sense of their own East Indian culture.

Alan's father, though liberal, accepts and rigidly maintains class distinctions.

But my father, though so tolerant with the men who worked on his estates and though so well liked by them, took care to draw a strict line between benevolence and friendship. (46)

He is benevolent, benign, superior. Alan's mother, too, is superior, direct, assured of her own privilege, her own superiority. At every level she forbids Alan to indulge in social intercourse with Jaillin and Kaiser. She, like his father, is outraged when he takes Jaillin to church. "Alan, I hear you and Jaillin were in church together this morning . . . . Son, you must have more respect for yourself" (129).

Always, at the level of ritual or societal observances, class and racial distinctions are reiterated and underscored; on the one hand the pagan, on the other, the Catholic; on the one hand, the poor East Indians, on the other, the wealthy privileged white. Thus the relationship between Alan and Jaillin, their encounters and infatuation, are constantly shrouded by the play of privilege, the statement of that privilege and the visceral, instinctive reaction by Jaillin to that privilege. She is even wounded by the hypocrisy which she confronts in the Catholic church; the natural rhythms seem lost.

In the idealization of the external reality, the landscape is vibrant with color, ornate with shapes, is vital and lush. It is this landscape which momentarily negates the problematic, the discordant themes of class and privilege, and lets the young friends momentarily come together, dancing symbolically, in the rain. "It was a wild glory of boys. We were near to each other in the joy . . . . We vowed to be friends forever" (6). Momentarily, too, Alan and Jaillin touch.

"You skin feel smooth, boy."
"So does yours, very smooth. I like touching your skin."
"I barely see it is white at all, you could be a Indian."
"No. We both could be anything we wanted. Let's pretend we're purple or green or blue." (138)

But such moods snap very quickly, weighted down by the memory of the external societal reality. Alan here wishes to flee the truth of the reality, he wishes to alter the reality and transform it with new magic colors, but the transformation does not take place in this novel. Thus, the nostalgic re-creation of that reality is fraught with tensions, undergoes no deep subsurface transformation, no essential coming together, achieves little cohesion.

In *The Humming-Bird Tree*, McDonald paints the external reality with colorful brush strokes; paints the variegated colors, the lushness of the rural vegetation; captures the speckled varieties of birds and butterflies, the rich and myriad tropical fruits. The butterflies of the tropics are beautiful.

The fruits are luscious. Yet the presentation of nature is more figural than symbolic.

In Michael Anthony's *Green Days by the River,* the representation of natural phenomena is less lyrical and more actual, more immediate. Like *The Humming-Bird Tree, Green Days* traces a growth process, but the maturing of Shellie seems more closely allied to the immediacy of nature. Thus it is the Ortoire River that becomes a recurrent motif, an immediate space whose flow and contours Anthony charts. The mood of the Ortoire River is dreamy in its flow, "Dark, dreamy Ortoire eased along" (Anthony, *Green Days,* 118). The colors shift from yellow and brown when bathed in sunlight: "Now I could see the red boundary flowers, where the forest suddenly cleared and beyond that I could see the bank and the yellow-brown Ortoire, flowing by" (22); to a more profound earth, dark when the mood of the novel has shifted; then the river seems laden with assorted debris, "bits of dead leaves, and green leaves, and broken branches" (173), with discarded bits of nature.

By the Ortoire River, many daily functions are performed. It is there that Gidharee often washes and cleanses himself. It is from there, too, that he draws water to feed his dogs. Yet the river can become a threatening reality, sluggish, heavy, filled with alligators, feared by the protagonist, Shellie.

> After a moment I said, "The dogs does swim in this river?"
>
> "Swim? Here? I don't even want them to drink this blasted water, far less swim. Especially in this part . . . . This place have alligators like peas!"
>
> This made my blood creep. "And you does still wash your hand here."
>
> "Why not? Who 'fraid alligator!" (67)

Here, Gidharee's voice seems reminiscent of Kaiser's in its casual dismissal, for both novels attempt to capture the language, the body shift, the racial patchwork of rural areas. Further, both novels trace the maturation of young men of different races and the early seedings of sexual encounters, the problematic entanglements spun in the webbings of the external social reality.

Cedar Grove reflects the cycle and shift of relationships with intimations of lushness, of promise.

> Reaching [Cedar Grove,] we turned along it, and at once we were in a strange world of forests and shade and strongly-scented flowers and fruit, and in a world of birdsong, and of dry leaves almost covering the red macadam road. (22)

Later there are overtones of dryness, of problems: "The sun of the dry season had scorched the trees and many of them were brown and shorn of leaf" (172).

The novel *Green Days by the River*, as its title implies, contours the growth of the protagonist, his initiation into manhood, the forming of friendships with other young men, his growing awareness of his own physical maturing, his accepting the role of breadwinner for his family, his burgeoning sexuality.

Many of Shellie's relationships have their beginnings by the cashew tree, or during village rituals and observances. As a boy, he encounters Lennie and Joe by the cashew tree while they are engaged in stoning the tree and eating the cashews that fall. Later, his first meeting with the *dougla* girl, Rosalie, also takes place by the cashew tree as she stoops to fix "her dress . . . carefully to cover her knees" (31). In its time of flowering, the cashew tree becomes a symbolic indication of the growing relationship between Shellie and Rosalie.

> She bent back looking at the cashew tree and as I looked at her there were the two points pressing out the pockets of her sailor bodice, and it set me thinking how in one season we could be children, and in the next we could be grown. (130)

Even as the natural environment seems at times to be an indicator of budding relationships, holidays and rituals, Christmas and Discovery Day, also provide the occasion for personal interaction. Shellie first goes to the school in Mayaro on Discovery Day where, too, for the first time he not only meets Joan, the creole girl, and Freddie, but also gets drunk.

Michael Anthony repeats a novelistic motif which is central to his novel, *The Games Were Coming;* perhaps *Green Days by the River* does not refract the problematic fragmenting social reality of *The Humming-Bird Tree* because the rural society depicted in *Green Days* is native to the area, not injected with the presence of the white overseer class. To be sure, there are racial overtones, but the creolization of races is devoid of any hinting at the problematics of cohesion.

Rosalie is a young *dougla* girl who "is the sweetest thing in the *whole* of a Mayaro" (18), admired by many of the young men of Cedar Grove. Her father, Gidharee, is attracted to creole people, Negro people, and does not really stand in the way of Shellie's relationship with Rosalie. But Gidharee notes that creole people have a propensity to fool around.

> He said, "You know, it's funny, but I like *Creole* people . . . . Especially decent *Creole*—like you . . . . one thing about *Creole*, boy," he stuck his cutlass violently into the ground, "One thing with *Creole*, they like to play round but they don't like to get married. Never! Never!" (*Green Days,* 175)

Gidharee, ascribing a stereotype of the creole, makes Shellie aware of his responsibility to Rosalie by a covert threat. Later, again by indirect and covert warnings, the dogs that initially brought Shellie and Gidharee together are used as coercions to marriage.

> Mr. Gidharee said: "Perhaps they know something about Rosalie. Perhaps that's why. Dogs does know things, you know. Perhaps they mean to tear you up unless you mean to get married to her. Dogs funny, boy." (180)

Indeed, nature, the rain, animals, the people, Gidharee and Shellie, all intersect, crisscross, at the point of resolution of the relationship between the East Indian, Gidharee, the *dougla* daughter, and the creole, Shellie. Rain shrouds reality.

> There was the murmur of the rain in the trees and a few stray drops sprinkled me. As I looked up, the sky was shimmering with light rain-drops, and was very overcast. (181)

The attack of the dogs who initially were friendly is reflected in that half-light, half-shadow of the sluggish river. The river, as in many instances in the novel, is a symbolic indicator of shifts, of climaxes. Gidharee's statement that "Rain will fall" (177) acts as a harbinger to Shellie's attack by the dogs. After the attack, "there was a dull glow on the river, and the water looked as sluggish as oil" (181).

Gidharee threatens Shellie, and the dogs pounce on him; still, Shellie is acting shrewdly when he accepts the dowry of land and estate which his engagement to Rosalie offers him. His relationship to Joan, whom he met at the Discovery Day celebration, he expediently ends, even though he attempts to rationalize his action. He senses the great opportunity afforded him by the cocoa lands and plantation. Clearly, this possibility points to that social cohesion absent from *The Humming-Bird Tree*. That question of money, the financial straits of Shellie's family, will disappear with his engagement to Rosalie.

Perhaps Shellie's growth and maturing have derived from the close relationship between himself and his father, their "uncommon friendship," the latter's understanding, counseling and worldly wisdom. His father makes "life and love look so true and honest that it always made me wonder what people were so silly about" (102).

Shellie's contract with Gidharee to marry Rosalie seems, however, to derive more from expedience than from the honesty which he ascribes to his father's teaching. Indeed, the trajectory of Shellie's growth has arced from initially having to ask his mother's permission to work with Gidharee on his land to the point where he tells her,

"Look, Ma, you see Mr. Gidharee and me—we is good friends. Look, I have plenty to tell you but I don't know how to start. But let me sleep now—but don't worry about money because from now on we ain't hard up." (187)

Shellie's move is a steady progression toward physical and social integration into the rural society. He symbolically moves up the hill to Cedar Grove, a move which seems free of problematic entanglements, without the stumbling, the social searching of Tiger, without the harsh "greening" of Mumu.

S *ong for Mumu* by Lindsay Barrett is a rite of passage through symbolic space, through river water and the ocean, through strong green country and gray city, a passage from love to loss of love, a cyclical drama of lament and longing. An ironic paradox is that every man in Mumu's life, every celebrant of love, seems doomed to die, indeed to be a victim of a "quality of violence." *Song for Mumu* becomes a searching by Mumu through symbolic greenness for the true strength of love, a search not only for sensual love, but for an African love, for father, for brother, for lover. Barrett's novel embodies and expresses the character of whole circular images, effecting a testimonial of total truth. For Mumu is not only promise, full of youthful sap rising from the power of greenness, but, when linked with her, this power has the capacity to create the total image, and completing a circle, to arrive at a total truth. In the country, her father knew the greenness that she initially seeks.

> My father was well loved in this grey place and hated it, well loved in green regions and me, I am the ripening fruit of that green love, the fruit of the true tree. (Barrett, *Mumu*, 115)

Her mother, too, knows the greenness with Scully and later returns from the grayness of the city to the mountainside with Preacher Man to recapture and replunge into that greenness, "to understand the strength, the unseen blood that rains from the sky of dreams" (183). It is Mumu's inability to live the continual "greenness" that is the essential metaphor, an inability which she laments, forming the basis for her song. For just as she is ripening fruit, seeking green love, so too she is song, seeking to be sung. Indeed she is at one and the same time an object—symbol of promise—and an extended metaphor of possible fulfillment, for "a young girl's body is the shape of her sweet song" (127) and makes song.

> He was fascinated. At first with unbelievable grace the black blur swam towards the shore growing larger minute by minute until again the outline of her supple form and flesh was clear, a sweeping thing of

beauty, the shape of an immeasurably wonderful song. . . . Seen enough?, she asked this almost calmly, even without sarcasm. He answered. His tongue and lips could only say, A song, a song . . . . a veritable song. (128)

Yet the song which she seeks is never fully voiced, never really intoned. She never arrives at the true center of the song, the sensing of its larger signification. Even though Mumu often experiences singing and momentarily sings "the song of calm and soothing love, sweet relaxation now a spot of peace in a forest of confusion" (128), the totality of song eludes her. She never attains the song, symbolized in the flow of the river, through sensual interplay of sun and water, "sun as it struck clear silver through the river's water body to the sand bed that bloomed grey-blue in the light beneath the flow of all those years and songs" (5).

The basic melody of *Song for Mumu* has two parallel recurrent motifs. Mumu's song is really an echo of Meela's song, indeed is a sort of canonic imitation of the mother's song, to the point where the novel is undergirded not only by circular polyrhythms, but by a continuous nexus of cross rhythms. Perhaps we can say that Meela's song, the timbre of her voice, are already dark contralto, having carried the heaviness of pain and lament. Mumu's voice moves from that of lyric soprano in hills and mountains to a shrieking coloratura and finally, heavy with pain which she no longer screams, her voice becomes like her mother's, a dark contralto. The song is mother and daughter's song; the song is a song for Meela and for Mumu. So intertwined are the melodies, so unilinear the song, so symbolic their voices, that they descend into a watery grave together, thereby ending their song. But this final union of mother and daughter, of their physical forms, only closes the circle which initially came into being from one seed, from one body, Scully's. It is through him, husband to Meela and father to Mumu, that they have already attained a cross-pollination; the seed planted in Meela while she is still green bears a fruit, Mumu, whose greening provides the novel with its melodic structure. That Scully when implanting Meela was already crazy from a kick by a horse's hoof becomes the oft-repeated note, the haunting voice affecting both Meela's and Mumu's song. When Meela and Scully first meet and mate, all is music, all is lyric interplay, all is color.

> This is grass. Golden dry and soft. Acres of it. Eye cannot furnish the finish of it. Alone in this gold pasture black me. I lay here. Scully that you? It is me. Now she comes. All naked. She straddles my head. So beautiful. Oh goddess. Ebony. I am on my back in this golden ocean. It is warm here . . . . Standing spread-eagle observing me from a height. She beckons. I cannot rise. Meela. Meela. Come on down to me. Kneel! She is kneeling. An unbelievable black sun at my head. (11)

Later on in Scully's madness, a deep deviant rhythm enters, a note of discord heightens; the fertilization of Meela is violent.

> In that same month Meela did not have her bloodletting. She found there was a child in her womb. Rejoicing. Hugging him. He only pierced her again. Not seeming to comprehend what she tried to tell him or to care. (32)

The question that Barrett poses here for us and the question which remains unanswered is the origin of the deviant rhythm; does it originate in the impotence of the white landowner who, unable to impregnate his wife, drives her to seek sexual excitement from the motion of a horse's back; the horse which, maddened by the white woman's violent passion and desire, kicks Scully into madness?

Mumu, in a parallel statement, notes the impotence of the white man and implies the source of the white city woman's unfulfillment: "The only time . . . I've seen a white man naked, he didn' have no arms no legs and no prick!" (105). Later in a ritual cleansing, in a violence rooting the cause and purpose of Scully's madness, the white landowner is destroyed in a violent sacrificial act. The song is here a communal chorus, intoning the destruction of exploitation, celebrating the cleansing, the reacquisition of the earth.

> The Farmers on the far side gazed after the rolling bobbing progress downstream of their former master, silent and bewildered, until in a sudden fiery burst of rage and joy they leapt towards the clouds and screamed and shouted praises for the land that was theirs again. (51–52)

But there is no balm, no atonement, for Scully's madness. His voice is ever-present in the minds of the mother and daughter, a haunting melody which ultimately ordains the song, their search for maleness, for their own fulfillment. Together they are one ripened fruit and one ripening fruit; mother and daughter mate with father and son, Junji and Joker, and the two voices rise in lyric celebration of love. At this point of becoming and of fulfillment, the song becomes a lament, bemoaning the loss of father and son, their lovers. Even as Meela later leaps into the open watery grave to die beside her daughter, so, too, Junji leaps into the watery wastes—water which is both creator and destroyer. Mother and daughter lament, and, though the voices are different, Mumu's high-pitched coloratura and Meela's deep, heavy contralto, they sing together. Their song, merged, bemoans the loss of the male baritone of Junji and Joker, whose dying finds parallel atonement in the death of the old River Woman.

Is Barrett here lamenting the loss of their innocence and ritual power which the country breeds? The old River Woman embodies this lament in

Mumu's flight to the hills, as she intones a song of loss for the greenness, for the memories of innocence and of fulfilling love.

> Mother Meela can you hear me callin' . . . this place is nowhere in my achin' soul . . . I don't want to see the light of day in this green place another day. (69)

In a symbolic movement both mother and daughter are carried from the greenness of the hills to the grayness of the city by the cartman, Oboe. Their link to him, even as their link to Scully and their parallel song with Junji and Joker, becomes both release from pain, fulfillment after wanting, and a subsequent loss just at the high point of their city singing. The echo of Scully's haunting voice, the recurrent theme of his madness and loss, is momentarily stilled when both Meela and Mumu hear it. A contrapuntal interplay takes place; only after Meela knows of Scully's whereabouts in the city can

> her head [feel] free again and it was as if a spell had been raised out of her skull and great and open winds, currents of wild air flew through her dreams, she found she was open to new love. (85)

Mumu, in her search for her father, Scully, initially drowns her fear in meeting with Oboe. Then when she hears of Scully's whereabouts from Meela, Mumu, too, freely and voluntarily accepts Oboe as her lover: "Oboe, take away these fears from me . . . take me and leave me nothing . . . nothing . . . Oboe . . . Oboe" (97).

The theme of lament and loss recurs, the poignant melodic line is sung again, another male voice is lost. "A moan goes up into the heavens" (101) as the chorus in the city mourns Oboe's death; Mumu laments and questions her own tragic condition.

> Why Meg, why, why must I be doomed to this to live forever without a man and without a father even . . . or a brother and all the men who enter me die! (101)

Now the rhythms become deviant. Meela in a contrapuntal movement flees from the city with Preacher Man as she attempts to find again greenness of the mountains. Now Mumu's song is a song of the city, high-pitched and at times hysterical. She moves from admiring lover to lover, her losses wreathed both in tears and smiles. Her emotions tinged with a deceitful play of light and dark, of regret and an almost sinister satisfaction.

But the melodic theme of water and promise of greenness and freedom keeps recurring, keeps circling back: baptism of a lover in the water, a running free in the wind at the beach.

Rainbow myriads of the flying spray and distance of water, green green. Green was the colour [of] the ocean. . . .

. . . she spun him face downwards and began to plunge his head beneath the waves. I, she screamed laughingly even as Mumu was rolling with bright laughter in the sand, hereby baptise you and name you Poet, son of sun and sea and shit and piss and forger of songs and all things sweet . . . (his legs waved about) . . . and hope (again she plunges the spluttering head into the salt pond) to God you do the business right, and sing a pretty song in my Mumu songbox. (126, 129)

Indeed the song for Mumu and the song for Meela, constructed along one basic melodic line of love and death, the search for love and fulfillment and the counterpoint of loss, fuses many harmonic lines, opens out and swells with crisscrossing ritual rhythms, the vital interplay of country and city painted in contrasting greens and grays. The ritual incantation of race and heritage in the hills and the mountains that the old River Woman intones, choruses the memories and strengths of the race, and in the city, Preacher Man revives the spirit of Jaja.

The old lady in front in her bright blue gown that flows itself like the river around her in the calm stirrings of morning wind is carrying the song with her piercing voice. She is the single voice.

We go to the river
We got to go to the sea
We go to the river
The ancient blood to see.

The chorus seeming to sway in time to their answer.

We got to go to the river
We got to go to the sea
If we never come back
Turn the people free. (18)

Jaja is sunshine and the sun is light
Jaja believes that man is soul is nature.
Whoho jaja. (93)

However the gray city and green country are linked by Lindsay Barrett in the ritual of water, flow, death, life and ancestry. Indeed the ritual becomes a statement by the author of continuity.

CHAPTER 3

Entrapment and Flight

And after the spawning of villages, the spawning of an amorphous urban, or more precisely marginally urban reality, a formless inchoate social slum circumstance. . . .

In that ever-shifting, dynamic movement of peoples from one social ecology to another, certain transit points, certain conduit and transfer areas, become established as permanent. Though often amorphous concentrations of living, these conduit zones are arenas, at times become the battlefields, where the struggle to persist is waged.

So immediate, so personalized are the settings that often they are imbued with all the dominant intersecting and mobile interrelating of central protagonists with multifarious personages.

The action of these novels, then, unfolds at the intersecting of an ecological setting with the central protagonists and with those who inhabit the barrack yards, the tenements. It is in these locations, communal and rowdy, often viscerally vital in their shared raw living, that the novels of this chapter unfold. In the unfolding at their confluence, these works of fiction have their dynamic and relentless evolving, the plots their denouement: and the knotting together of their lives of characters living in their crowded contiguity results in a seemingly inevitable unspooling.

The sense of relentless inevitability that seems to dictate the lives of these characters, that seems to inhabit the topography itself, at times is a condition of entrapment, often resulting in an attempt to flee from those conditions. Thus, disintegration and flight become the basic modalities for these novels. From the very beginning of the novel, then, in a series of rhetorical questions, Roger Mais illuminates the condition of entrapment, the possibility of breakup, hints at the prognosis of disintegration and flight.

> who is there outside in the dark beyond the door, knocking, to tell his dreams? . . . there are so many empty rooms in the shuttered house that is yesterday . . . hamstrung at high noon, who is it at midnight wakes to madness and rattles his chains? . . . the sea is a weary old man babbling his dreams. (Mais, *The Hills Were Joyful Together*, 63)

In this cadenced refrain, in a poetic prose so characteristic of his writing, Roger Mais evokes the haunting mood, the unrelenting pathetic circumstances, the loss of dreams, and the fragmented lives inhabiting his novelistic universe. For so many uninhabited rooms remain after the loss of dreams, after so many characters, whose hopes are hamstrung at noon time, run their course to death or to midnight madness. Into what reality, into what rooms, does Roger Mais push his characters, who seem to be caught in the web of the spider, whose lassitude is the unending weariness of the weary old man of the sea? The sea, the moon, the wind, the moonlight, all animate and vital, chart the course of the rise and ruin of his characters. Clearly the landscape, which Mais daubs beautifully, shivers with the movements of those many elements pulsating in the Caribbean. Is this landscape doomed to sterility, to unending dying? Is its history one of rock hardship and endless dreams which never are fulfilled? As he philosophizes on the Caribbean reality, Mais poses this question, time and time again:

> Who are they that passed along weary beachheads and sang their songs before us? . . . they have hung their harps on the willows and gone their way . . . this curvature of rock was limned into being out of reluctant granite . . . these sterile grains of sand have told their tales before . . . the wind writes its tireless song along the stricken hollows . . . and the sea is a weary old man babbling his dreams. (63)

To be sure, in the world of Roger Mais, especially in *The Hills Were Joyful Together*, people and characters seem to be decimated, to be pushed into the shadows, in spite of their searching and in spite of their noonday or midnight dreams. In the novels of Roger Mais, there is so much loss of dreams, so many abandoned hopes, so many wasted lives that perhaps it is correct for him to conclude:

> The dark shadows beyond our ken crowd in on us and stand and wait unseen . . . they wait in silence and drink us up in darkness . . . they wipe their hands across their lips and pass the cup . . . they are the dark company that keep eternal vigil over life unto death . . . we are endlessly lost amongst a host of shadows that stand and wait. (150)

This play of light and dark, the shifting of mysterious shadows, all reflect the dim interlacings and reveal the unending life and death struggle of so many of Mais's characters. The elements, cohering with the shifting moods and grim circumstances of such characters, themselves become carriers of these circumstances, reflectors of fragmented realities.

For Mais, landscape and elements carry within them not history, as in Mittelholzer, but the inner landscape of individualized living, of communities groping for livelihood, for the barest of existence. Even as the elements are animated and vital, so, too, the communal groping for existence gives off its own intrinsic vitality.

Thus it is that in Roger Mais, the human, the societal and the elemental landscapes shade together, giving an uninterrupted dramatic movement to his grim, intensely alive reality. Images of light and shadow run through the rooms, the barrack yards, the lives; specter moods and dreams grow dim or glow in Mais's depiction of vibrantly harsh spatial circumstances.

At times Mais imbues the light and the shadows with larger philosophical signification, evoking the seeming anonymity of life and death, depicting the relentless movement of his characters to a death which can strike a thousand ways.

> Anonymous in his cloak of darkness each waits with the night . . . the thunderous acclamation of the stars, does not disturb the stillness. . . . what waits with such aplomb as the brother outside the door? . . . all the guests are gathered beneath the same anonymous shadow . . . each answers to his name, and all with one voice . . . death speaks with a thousand whispers, but a single voice. (132)

Perhaps to imbue the landscape with philosophical meaning attests to a novelistic vision which links together all realms of experience, all regions of reality. In this vision, moon and sea coextend, the one moving in and out the other, a shifting light play cutting across silences, or locating, through images of movement, the positions of people and characters. All realms cohere, night and shadow, sea and fish nets, tree and man, joined together by Mais's dexterous spatial wordplay.

> The moon rises red from out the still water of the bay . . . the hanging nets throw a dark shadow on the beach . . . the serried rows of nets have come to rest under the trees . . . and only the water is unquiet with the pull of the tide. (26)

Clearly, landscape, the painting of that landscape, the creation of mood through the reflecting mirror of elements, give to Mais's world a Caribbeanness. For in the Caribbean, moods, emotions, and living itself are all replicated in the landscape: so imminent all Caribbean landscapes, so quick the changes of elements, so furtive the movement of colors. Indeed, most Caribbean writers make landscape an integral part of the world they create.

In so many differing settings at so many different times, light and the play of moon shadow the novels of Roger Mais, giving them constant color contrast, making them mirrors of the changing fortune of the characters. The moon presides over the night, "riding high in the sky, lets down light, dividing the shadows, and walking in loveliness between them" (Mais, *Brother Man*, 59).

Yet at times, capturing the true vivid nighttime reality, the absent moon or the not-yet-risen moon allows the full luster of the stars to be experienced. Perhaps the absence of the moon may be but a mark of time suspending the impending movement toward a novelistic climax. The voices of the chorus, foreshadowing the impending conflicts between the principal characters in *Brother Man*, predicting also the possibility of a growing, albeit slowly rising affection between Bra'man and Minette, ring through a dark night, bereft of moon, lit by glittering stars.

At the critical juncture in Brother Man's ascendancy, when his powers of healing seem constrained and unable to flow freely, he opens the window onto the night, where the moon, though late in rising, will eventually appear and assert its presence.

> He felt suddenly that the room was close, with the smell of sickness about it, looked over his shoulder, saw the window was close-drawn. He got up and threw the window open from the bottom.
> He leaned through it, and gazed out into the night.
> The moon was late in coming up. The sky was a sown field of stars. (130)

Here the night and the absent expectant moon seem to fortify Bra'man's way: "a bright torch of moonshine went before him down the lane" (170). At times the moon "like a shield from behind a cloud" (171), becomes a protector, shielding him from inimical forces.

Clearly, Roger Mais, by imbuing the elements with symbolic meaning, ascribes to them a power, animates them with force, to such a degree that all his writings seem to be inlaid with these elements, which are at times not only a beacon guiding characters, but a structural signal, a commentator on the novelistic action. Thus it is that Brother Man, to find the way out through the gathering darkness, the oppressive uncertainty as to his curative powers, ascends "up in the hills" (175) where through ritualistic participation with the hills, he receives guidance, direction, and a new vision. And as though postulating the notion of linkage between forces and elements, of the continuous energizing flow of phenomena and their interactions, even as Brother Man receives his new vision, the elements themselves offer a response, give voice to his inner searchings.

> And the night darkened about him, and the moon was put out from the heavens, and thunder rolled among the hills, and it stormed that night, a great thunderstorm that came up from the east. (175)

It is not surprising that *The Hills Were Joyful Together* derives its very name from the landscape, that in the hills ritual worship is performed, and that the hills themselves become vital commentators and symbol reactors of climactic incidents in the novel.

On a hilltop mountain, the rising moon marks the climax of worship (*The Hills*, 109); the hills mark Rema's rising madness by seeming to threaten her with their ominous presence. To her the hills seem to "come prancing down from up yonder with a thunderroll" (207), taking on a menacing corporeal reality, threatening to "trample [her] to death."

Descending to the seashore and in jubilation, phenomena join together to celebrate the derangement of a human being and, as in a ritual dance, all phenomena participate in the downward spiraling, the decline of a living being.

> She could hear the far-away gurgle of water from up the spring, and it sounded like the muffled clapping of hands . . . and the hills put aside their veils and came out from behind the clouds, and they joined hands together and started to dance. They went dancing like that right down to the edge of the sea . . . and all the sea rose up in waves and they clapped their hands. (169)

The same ritual participation of phenomena in the depiction of human emotions, this drawing on old religious observance and on biblical references that attest to the ontological relationship between man and the elements, are all woven together to give Mais's *Black Lightning* its very structure, providing it with the very basis for the character depiction of its main protagonist, Jake.

Indeed, in *Black Lightning*, it is that omnipresence of lightning, accompanied by thunder, rain, and wind gusts, which injects fear into the very being of some of the principal characters, marking the transforming vision of their reality; and when the lightning appears black to Jake, his outer vision is sacrificed but his inner vision is heightened, investing him with growing spiritual awareness. Thus it is that lightning, like the moon and the sea, the hills and the wind, inhabits the novelistic landscape of Roger Mais. Their configurations lend movement and color to his idiom, at times indicating the shifting structure of plot, the changing moods of characters; then at times becoming ritual symbology, for the harsh social reality of *Brother Man*, for the grim social circumstances of *The Hills Were Joyful Together*, or for the novelistic meditation of *Black Lightning*.

Even though the omnipresence of the elements and landscape in Roger Mais is extended into distance, giving elaboration to his novels, all three of his novels—*Brother Man, The Hills Were Joyful Together* and *Black Lightning*—are set within narrow social confines, are located within specific microcosmic social realities, and have their intrinsic formulations within carefully demarcated areas where human drama, human conflict, become intensified by this very process of circumscription. It is not that the microsocietal circumstances are not endemic to the large external reality, it is that the fragmented society has not as yet achieved an inclusive cohesion wherein areas are not simply isolated pockets of societal experience but eventually must become cohering social entities. In *Brother Man* and in *The Hills Were Joyful Together*, the only instances in which two worlds are brought together are when the communal law comes into conflict with the societal law. *Black Lightning* unfolds within a novelistic landscape wherein human drama, not realistic depictions of external reality, is the dominant feature of the narrative. In *Brother Man* and *The Hills Were Joyful Together*, unlike in *Black Lightning*, the ever-present struggle for survival, the vital fusion and friction of lives and of people, lead to a materialistic presentation of reality. Living takes place within confined areas, street moves into yard, yard opens into living quarters, rubbing against one another; the rooms become windows to tumultuous lives within and without.

In *Brother Man*, these lives with all of their multitudinous emotional criss-crossings are conjured up for us in the ritual polyphony of the chorus. Skillfully, by localizing the various elements of the social circumstances, each grasped in the word play of that chorus, Mais overlaps the vital environmental chaos with human drama, paints the shifting economic fortunes of his characters, introduces us to the subsurface gestation of his reality.

From the very beginning of *Brother Man* the chorus, acting as the author's mouthpiece, voices the fatalistic vision of the reality in which Mais plunges his characters. Clearly chorus and environment, individuals and their fate, all coalesce into a baroque introduction to the microcosmic world where the novel spins out, with a guided inevitability: "all are involved in the same chapter of consequences, all are caught up between the covers of the same book of living" (*Brother Man*, 8).

Brother Man presents the inevitable movement of individuals rooted within a particular environment: a movement toward insoluble problems, toward unending woes, which the chorus, the reflector of the lives within this close environment, "clacks" everywhere, clacks all the time, demonstrating perhaps that all the people inhabiting this community are randomly and continuously caught up in a visceral, turbulent living.

> They clack on street corners, where the ice-shop hangs out a triangular red flag . . . under the ackee tree or . . . the Seville orange tree behind the lean-to pit-latrine in the yard, they clack-clack eternally telling their own hunger and haltness and lameness and nightness and negation . . . .
>
> Night comes down and the tongues have not ceased to shuttle and to clatter, they still carry their burden of the tale of man's woes. It is their own story over that they tell in secret, overlaying it with the likeness of slander, licking their own ancient scrofulous sores. (9)

Every element of this raw living is foreground. It is not accidental backdrop; it is an immediate and pressing reality defining and affecting the lives of the inhabitants. So that even as landscape and elements have been omnipresent in many Caribbean novels, so, too, the immediate corporeal environment injects itself into the body politic, into the emotional, the gut living of Mais's characters. Seemingly as a single line, Bra'man walks and the chorus clacks, linking together the unfolding lives, the adjoining living quarters, the multiple backyards and interacting human dramas of the novel, *Brother Man*.

It is this close communal setting that gives a skeletal plot its ribbing, gives presence to the confined space, the immediate reality. The closeness, the confinement, breathes communality of living; however, it is a communality that, though vital, is still bereft of the basic economic prerequisites for true harmony, and the plot, with its premonitions of doom voiced by the chorus, is pushed toward a climax through its many conflict situations stemming from economic and emotional frustrations.

The action revolves mainly around the Christ-like figure of Brother Man, as he is shown interrelating with the people in his "back-yard" environment. Each character is, in his or her own way, struggling for survival. The action is also carried along by various themes of searching: the search for spiritual revelation, for self-knowledge, for health, for economic comfort, and for sexual and emotional satisfaction. The search themes motivate the characters to action, as if they are blindly impelled by some superhuman force.

Each chapter opens with the click-clack tattletale gossiping of the chorus in the lane; which sets the tone and whets the reader's appetite with information about the events which will take place later in the chapter. They talk about sickness, prophetic forecast of the weather, crime and punishment and their effect on family life. They comment on inflation, prostitution and love affairs. In effect, the chorus keeps the oral history of this community and hints at its possible future.

In chapter one we see an accumulation of all kinds of faces, most of them mentioned by the chorus. They rise out of their own little corners but very soon their lives begin to touch one another.

Mais introduces Papacita and Girlie, engaged in a heated argument: Girlie is jealous about his unexplained absence, believing he is out with another woman, when in truth he has gone in search of an easy way to make money. His secret meeting with Fellows sets the stage for his ultimate downfall.

Also introduced are Jesmina and her sister Cordy, who is sick. She comes to believe that Bra'Man has healed her and wants Bra'Man to heal her sick son, Tad. It is her subsequent anger at Bra'Man for not healing her son that leads her to conspire with Papacita to have Bra'Man framed with Papacita's counterfeit coins.

We also meet Minette with Bra'Man and another conflict is established: her desire for his love and attention and his preoccupation with his work and Rastafarian religion. The three important pairs of characters are: Girlie-Papacita; Minette-Bra'Man; and Cordy-Jesmina.

The importance of the ties between the characters may not be immediately apparent; however, certain emotional attachments cause complex entanglements that plunge the characters into crisis situations from which only violence can result. Papacita lusts after Minette, who loves Bra'Man, who believes it his duty to help people first before satisfying his wants. Because each character's dreams or desires are not completely fulfilled, frustration, anger, and jealousy set in to cause conflicts and eventually disaster. Cordy hates Bra'Man for not healing her son; Bra'Man holds Minette off because he seeks greater spirituality; Minette flirts with and thwarts Papacita; Papacita, frustrated, seeks to get rid of Bra'Man and win over Minette; this only causes Girlie's anger to build to such an extent that she kills him in the end. Her man in prison and helpless to save her son, Cordy goes insane from loneliness and grief. Toward the end of the novel, after overcoming many social and psychological obstacles, Brother Man becomes more human and Minette more spiritual. These two characters seem to survive the violence and chaos because they acquire and integrate a humanistic vision which places the community above the individual and the spiritual above the material.

This powerful story is kept fascinatingly alive through Mais's dramatic style, the intensity of the characters' emotions, and the poetic beauty of his language.

In this skeletal plot, the characters, immersed as they are in a compelling immediate reality, seem unable, or perhaps powerless, to break out of that reality. In all three of the Mais novels, the preceding statement can be posited. In *Brother Man*, the immediate reality undergoes little change except perhaps after the near-sacrifice and crucifixion of Brother Man. His role as spiritual leader of the area is assured. Basically, the environmental reality, the material reality, though remaining static, is ultimately affected by Brother Man's spiritual consciousness. Thus a new awareness is injected into the consciousness of the lane and of the surrounding community.

Even as we witness the fluctuations in Bra'Man's spiritual power, we witness the parallel growth of affection and love on a human level between him and Minette. Perhaps it is this growth of affection, heralded by the breaking light of day, which presages the increase of human possibilities and human consciousness. Thus it can be asserted that in *Brother Man*, though not formally prescribing environmental change, Mais's vision does clarify the possibility of change within the human condition. There is compassion in Mais; there is also a solution to poverty and strife.

B ut in *The Hills Were Joyful Together*, strife and conflict between characters searching for emotional fulfillment and economic satisfaction determine the plot to such a degree that, though one or two characters may glimpse new social possibilities, may grasp at political consciousness, the majority stay trapped in unchanging social conditions. Implacable, Mais delineates the decay, the demonic reality, the rundown conditions, the grim communal presence of a pervasive environmental poverty. It seems that Mais is imbuing the reality with a foreboding determinism since from the very beginning of the novel he imprisons his characters within rundown yards. His novelistic lens first penetrates the external reality and then unerringly x-rays the inner reality of intense secreted passions, economic illnesses.

As if unearthing an archeological ruin, Mais explores the intricate pathology of ruin, reveals time's corrosion, geometrically mapping out former social conditions, previous existences. The present inhabitants are but the inheritors of an area once rich with promise. These inhabitants are now living in fragmented social circumstances.

> The building stood on the south side. A row of barrack-like shacks . . . with the crazily-leaning fence out front, enclosed what was once a . . . courtyard in the middle of which there was an ancient circular cement cistern and above it a standpipe with a cock leaning all to one side and leaking continually with a weary trickle of water. (*The Hills,* 9)

Here history does not crisscross with landscape, initiating that early dialogue of Caribbean man and his recent historical beginnings. Rather here history locates the decay and destruction of former societal affluence, an affluence in which the present community did not particpate. These are the squatters of history, these are the pariahs of changing urban history. All is baroque dilapidation. The present community still lives physically linked to the old dwellings from which ultimately it will have to break away.

As if mirroring the characters who struggle for survival within the tiny rooms, the external vegetation and the immediate environment struggle for survival, sickly, thirsty, each contending for a little bit of space, each fighting for a little sustenance.

> Near the cistern in the yard a gnarled ackee tree reached up scraggy, scarred, almost naked—branched to the anemic-looking sky . . . . A prickly lime tree struggled up from among the earthed-in, seamy, rotting bricks in the yard; it stood against the northern row of wooden shacks right outside the room where the three Sisters of Charity lived, and crooned and gossiped and cooked and sing-sang sad hymns of wailing the livelong day. (9)

The cistern, symbolizing the life-giving water, still cannot provide sufficient sustenance for the anemic residents in this starved setting. It is here that the drama of equally starved lives unfolds; lives housed in unattractive contiguous rooms where men, women and children love and hate, live and die.

The Hills Were Joyful Together is divided into three books with a number of chapters and subsections. We are first presented with a very evocative description of the physical environment in which the characters live. The perimeters as well as the decrepit contents of their world are poetically sketched, creating a vivid but bizarre mosaic-like setting that foreshadows the complexities of the social interactions that intensify the personal conflicts and give depth and power to the novel. The overtones of squalor and poverty accentuate the harsh reality of the people's lives.

The central location for most of the action is the barrack yard, which has the people boxed together, forcing them to relate directly and without pretension. In the first part of the novel, the characters pop out from everywhere, as if on a large stage. The majority of them are sitting, lying or waiting for something to happen. They are introduced and the conflicts are established.

All the characters are connected to different rooms that surround the barrack yard. Many of the main characters share rooms. Surjue lives with Rema, Euphemia with Shag, Pussjook with Goodie, and Charlotta with Bedosa. Certain other important characters like Bajun Man, who is Euphemia's lover, Flitters, who is a sneaky friend of Surjue, and Zephyr, a prostitute, do not live in any group whatsoever. Yet their actions affect greatly the situations in the other households. Just as rooms are linked, the lives lived within these rooms are linked together in a continuous dramatic unfolding.

The main elements of the plot are generated from the troubling circumstances in which two different groups of characters find themselves. Other conflicts involving other characters reinforce the tragic movement of the story to its unavoidable violent conclusion. The Rema-Surjue-Flitters triad and the Shag-Euphemia-Bajun Man triad provide the psychological framework for the novel. Shag loves Euphemia but Euphemia has a growing passion for Bajun Man, who uses the money she gets from Shag to subsist. Rema and Surjue love each other, but Flitters presents Surjue with the possibility of making large sums of money, which would not only make him self-supporting but allow him to leave the barrack yards with Rema. These characters, like the others, are tied to each other by passion and economics.

Euphemia continues the affair with Bajun Man, although Shag has hinted that he is capable of violence in case of betrayal. The frequent mentioning of knives and machetes foreshadows the violence to come. Shag eventually finds Euphemia with Bajun Man and soon after going insane with the anger and jealously, he chops her up.

Rema and Surjue seem to be the perfect couple even though Rema supports him. His tenderness and passion are always turned toward her. It is Flitters who diverts his attention by concocting a seemingly simple get-rich scheme: he proposes that they rob a safe and use the money to set themselves up in business. Surjue is reluctant at first but soon his desire for materialistic success brings him to agree on the venture. When they attempt the theft, something goes wrong. Flitters escapes but Surjue is captured. Despite repeated beatings he refuses to name his accomplice. Flitters is killed later on by Surjue's friends because of his cowardice and betrayal. Having lost her man, Rema goes insane from loneliness. Attempting to return to Rema, Surjue is killed trying to escape. The plot then grinds to a halt since the violence has played itself out, taking with it many victims of circumstance.

C learly the ruin and squalor so pervasive in *The Hills Were Joyful Together* do not trigger off countering political reactions even though they precipitate personal attempts to escape the oppressively constraining circumstances. *Black Lightning*, set in the woods, stresses the inner landscape of human reality in all of its changing weaknesses and strengths. The environment does not vibrate with human passion but merely provides a backdrop to the personal and psychological interrelationships. Indeed the landscape is unspecified, not particularized, is far different from the setting in *Brother Man* and *The Hills Were Joyful Together*. In *Black Lightning*, there is not the confinement and squalor of the barrack-yard interiors; rather there is all the airiness of open spaces, the lyric quiet of the countryside.

> The sound of pea-doves calling to each other under the sweet wood trees, the song of the axe, the wind soughing through the branches, were the only sounds in the wood. (Mais, *Black Lightning*, 32)

Even though the setting provides a harmonious locus for burgeoning conflicts, it is not functionally spun together or baroquely elaborated. It is externalized, natural, and indeed poetically evoked. Yet, the poetic landscape of "first brown smudgings of dusk shook out over the silent wood" (33) contrasts sharply with the dynamic configurations of the elements: lightning, thunder, rain, and wind. They become symbolic elements marking the internal emotional and psychological transformations of the characters. Yet this dramatic contrast between the almost pastoral quiet of the landscape and the charged power of the lightning and thunder is so characteristic of the Caribbean that it adds a quality of Caribbean realism. It is at times a realism which injects its transitory moods into the changing characteristics of the protagonists and their relationships. For it is this very changing pattern of inner character transformation which provokes an evolution of relationships, which becomes modal to the action of *Black Lightning*.

Like *Brother Man* this novel is arranged in chapters and sections. There is no chorus, but there is still the element of gossip and intrusion of people into one another's affairs. In general, the plot moves in a straightforward fashion. Chapter one introduces the major characters who will affect the movement of the plot. The characters meet in the woods that circumscribe their world and provide the novel with two of its motifs: nature and the elements. In the beginning of the novel, some of the characters are searching for others in the woods. The two young lovers finally meet because Miriam is led to Glenn by the sound of his axe. Bess, in search of her daughter Miriam, is led by the sound of his accordion to Amos—Amos, who wants to be left alone. The main protagonist, Jake, is also led to Amos by the sound of the accordion. At the same time, in another part of the woods, Jake's wife Estella is planning to elope with her lover, Steve. That they are searching for each other is essential because it becomes the most important psychological activity in the story.

The novel places emphasis not on the plot but on character development. The major conflicts are internal because the transformations start within. The external conflicts bring the subjective needs of the characters out into the open. Estella's flight precipitates the tragic movement that eventually leads to Jake's blindness. Jake is deeply hurt that his wife has run off with another man, and he reacts by pouring all of his energies into the creation of a wood carving of the biblical Samson, with whom he is intensely fascinated. His preoccupation with lightning and the Samson story increases until it becomes an obsession. He instinctively believes that his life will parallel that of Samson, who was also betrayed by a woman. He is blinded when struck by lightning during a storm. Somehow the villagers think that justice has been done because the excessively proud Jake has finally been humbled.

Because dialogue is such an important aspect of the story, the characters are usually grouped in pairs. Miriam and Glenn love each other, but they relate in a somewhat immature manner in the beginning of the story. Amos, a cripple and a loner, does not get along with Bess. They curse each other frequently and the only reason for the conflict appears to be the jealousy each has for the other's relationship with Jake. Amos and Jake have established a kind of hostile comradeship, with Amos almost always losing the arguments or accepting the insults. He does so because no one else will really talk with him. This explains his dislike for people in general.

As the novel progresses Miriam and Glenn try to relate to each other in more meaningful ways. At one point Miriam even seeks advice from Amos about love. Jake, because of his blindness, becomes more tolerant of Amos. Amos becomes more assertive now that he realizes he is needed, and this helps him become a caring human being. Jake's dependency on Bess causes a new kind of relationship to develop between them. Although he has lost his sight, Jake becomes more perceptive, intuitively understanding other people as well as the phenomena around him. However, he soon acquires a new vision and with it the courage to end his life, like Samson.

Lightning is not only a methaphor in the story, it is a powerfully present reality that shapes the narrative, foreshadows and causes blindness and insight. The isolated world that is described here seems to undergo a purge. The wind, rain, and lightning build to destructive intensity, and then abate to usher in a rebirth and a period of tranquillity and benevolence.

In Mais's novelistic world, especially in *Brother Man* and *The Hills Were Joyful Together*, body language of the many people leaning or sprawling on the backdrop stage articulates the visceral connection between the external physical and emotional world of the characters. So confined is the living, so close the very space, that bodies and dwellings and yards often become co-extensions, one of the other.

> The people come out of their doors; they lean against gate posts, sprawl on steps, hitch up against the brick walls that rise above the squalid sidewalks . . . . Some of the men smoke pipes, the younger ones reach for cigarettes, or wait until those who have, take a couple of drags of theirs, and pass them around. (*Brother Man*, 59)

The shifting positions, the changing relationships, the emotional movement, lead to unalterable variations in the fortunes of the characters. For implicit in the world that Mais boxes out for us is the truth that any displacement of properties leads to subsequent displacement of other properties. Thus if one character moves out of his circumstance and enters the mood space of another, this occasions a causal reaction, affecting the lives of all other characters. Given the closeness of living, this happens all the time. All the yard participates in or witnesses the fight between the brash young man, Manny, and Euphemia.

> The neighbors came out into the yard. First Bedosa and Charlotta. They stood on the doorstep, ineffective, not knowing how to proceed . . . . Rema standing behind Surjue and a little to one side screamed, but Surjue was right up to Manny already. He didn't make a grab for the knife but he just pushed his left palm outward into Manny's face and brought down his right fist sharply against Manny's wrist. (*The Hills*, 35, 36)

For clearly, such close and confining quarters necessarily demand an immediacy of reaction, of participation. This participation is not of necessity, in its inception, negative. People may not have to take sides. At times, whether festive or sad, it can bring together the people who populate the lanes and the yards.

That evening it was very hot and everybody came out into the yard and sat on chairs and stools and boxes and gossiped and cracked jokes and sang songs. And there was a big fish-fry . . . and the big fire lit up the darkness . . . and they . . . forgot their worries and their fears and their jealousies and their suspicions and the occasion took on all the aspects of a picnic, and they were like children again. (38, 39)

But such fish-feeds or wakes, communal mournings for the tragic death of a yard person, are rare occasions, are momentary manifestations of communal cohesion. So that in *Brother Man* and more so in *The Hills Were Joyful Together*, what defines the living of the characters is that visceral interrelationship of man and woman, of people struggling for emotional and economic fulfillment. Often this striving leads to conflict and strife, tragedy, and only occasionally to fulfillment, so confined is the space, so limited the economic possibilities, so intense the emotional relationships.

Despite the physical closeness of the reality which Mais delineates for us, the recurrent motif driving the characters' violent actions is loneliness. Some form of unresolved strife pushes a character into an interior searching, into a lonely place where feelings of helplessness and depths of frustration ofen culminate in destructive actions.

Indeed Mais the novelist, as he grapples with the meaning of individual man's life and death, postulates fear and terror and an ontological loneliness as the basis of the human condition. Is Mais suggesting that there is a basic irony of life in that the only validity to life is its affirmation by continuing to live? For even as he roots his novelistic reality within the confining space of a localized area, Mais gives a sense of otherness by probing after the meaning of existence within that very confinement.

This is the story of man's life upon earth that formed him . . . it shudders throughout from cover to cover with terror and pity . . . the demons of light and of darkness inform all his days and nights . . . it has been attested that he is of threefold dimensions . . . all his being is encompassed about from birth with dying . . . his separate death matters nothing . . . it matters all, that he has turned his back upon life. (184)

Yet in this probing after the fundamental significance of life, Mais affirms a vital concept: that despite oppressive sociological or psychological circumstances, life must be lived. In spite of this affirmation, Mais the novelist relentlessly pushes his characters into situations that lead to violence and destruction. Cordelia, a normal individual who is lonely because of her man's absence, reaches out for help, yet a seemingly inexorable doom propels her ultimately toward suicide. In a philosophical statement of doom highlighting her personal crisis, the imprisonment of her man and the subsequent death of her child drive her to suicide. She reaches out to Bra'Man, the healer, she attempts to seek help from Brother Ambro, she looks for comfort from her sister, Jesmina, but all these efforts to deal with life do not forestall her doom.

Like Cordelia, Rema of *The Hills Were Joyful Together* goes insane with loneliness; bereft of her man's presence, passion and tenderness, she too occasions her own destruction, a violent death by fire. Her man, Surjue, because of his consciousness of the destructive power of loneliness, is goaded into attempting escape from his prison cell. He, too, as if caught in a binary condition and driven by a parallel and connected circumstance, perishes violently. Through a skillful structural interplay, Mais correlates Rema's loneliness, her death by fire, with the loneliness and the abandonment of an old and dying prison inmate. Surjue's reflections on the meaningless and lonely dying of the old prison inmate, contrasting with the lyrical recall of Rema's presence, underlines the sense of personal helplessness, societal entrapment and philosophical doom that shrouds the narrative.

> Why the hell should this man's dying mean anything to him? . . . A hell of a thing to die in the night like this, for all practical purposes, alone. Her breath was like the good sweet smell of the deep forest mould . . . there were things worse than death. A thousand times worse. They were going to take her and put her in a strait-jacket. (247)

Even though there is a proximity of living and at times shared community actions, the recurrent motif of loneliness pervades the backyard reality of *Brother Man* and *The Hills Were Joyful Together*. Imprisonment with all of its resultant despair is but another manifestation not only of confinement but also of the oppressive interior aloneness besetting so many of Mais's characters. Rema, too, anguished and distraught by loneliness and terror, runs her course toward madness. Indeed Mais quite often reveals to us an inherent correlation between loneliness, violence and suicide. Parallel to Mais's presentation of the motif of loneliness is his depiction of the process of madness. We see this clearly in his portrayal of Rema's progressive emotional and mental decline.

> The loneliness and the night overlaid her, and she was defenseless, like one in a deep sleep menaced by the terror of a dream. "Nobody in all the world . . . just nobody at all . . ." but the words didn't mean anything, they were just part of the confusion inside her, part of the jumble of mixed-up images and sounds. The darkness and the cold and the stillness lay upon her like a great crushing weight. (170)

It could be said that Mais continuously analyzes the visceral relationship between abandonment bringing on loneliness and withdrawal leading to emotional and mental instability. In this regard, perhaps Brother Man is saved from possible emotional withdrawal by Minette's presence. Brother Man does not, by his spiritual presence, save Cordelia, nor does Surjue's concern for Rema allow him to forestall her doom.

In *Black Lightning*, Estella's abandonment of Jake leads to his withdrawal and his substituting an artistic endeavor for her presence.

> Jake was never the same since Estella run away from his home that night, and the difference wasn't something you could just put your finger on and say it is this or it is that; it was something other, and more. (*Black Lightning*, 46)

The element of causation thus becomes a principal method of character development in Mais's novel. Estella leaves Jake, Jake withdraws, uses sculpture as a spiritual therapy which eventually leads to his blindness. Blindness leads to Jake's further withdrawal, with consequences Amos fears. For he realizes quite clearly the correlation between aloneness and emotional decline and its ultimate possible consequence, death. Perhaps because Amos, a cripple, has led a life of seclusion and aloneness, he is able to perceive the tragic ramifications of loneliness and attempts to forestall its consequences.

> If only he could think of something to lift that cloud of despondency that had settled upon Jake. A man couldn't drag himself into a corner, and live alone, in the dark. And that was what Jake was trying to do. (191)

Through his efforts to ward off the menacing effects of loneliness, a fraternal bond is established between Amos and Jake which lessens Amos's loneliness and moderates Jake's solemn and solitary pride. Thus the characterization of Amos and Jake revolves around the growth of a fraternal communion which binds them together. Even though there is conflict of personalities it is a conflict which leads to self-analysis and growing self-awareness, occasioning a larger vision of their human condition.

Both the physical pressures and the psychological problems affecting the human condition become constant motifs in the novels of Roger Mais, receiving his penetrating scrutiny. For clearly Mais presents us with conditions endemic with strife and conflict, posing questions as to their causal effects. Brother Man, conscious of the possible effects of economic deprivation, laments the possible consequences of "trouble" as leading people "as though by a ring in the nose into all paths of violence" (*Brother Man*, 56). While in *The Hills Were Joyful Together* and *Brother Man* it is the societal, the communal influences that bring about the novels' denouements, in *Black Lightning* it is the external personal conflicts that shape and contour the resolution of the novel. On a larger and more philosophical note, Jake ponders the nature of deprivation, loss, and suffering made manifest in his carved statue of Samson.

> "Look, Amos, if you could gather up all the suffering there is in the world . . . of all the folks who had lost their way in some kind of darkness, and of all who have known any lack that human flesh and spirit can know . . . take all that suffering, and add it up . . . you should get something like that—that hopeless, uneven slump of the shoulders, that face. Eh?" (*Black Lightning*, 110)

Mais's characters confront the question of material or psychological deprivation and the burden of living in different ways. In *Brother Man*, Papacita, the hustler and womanizer, brutally states his doctrine of survival within a deprived social reality. He does not speak out for fraternal communion; rather he advocates that, in a strife-torn world, fulfilling individual needs and desires should be the supreme principle guiding one's actions, one's existence.

> Every man had to scuffle for himself—that was the law of existence as he knew it. It was a simple matter of individual survival, each man for himself. You only ball you'self up tryin' to think about things besides that. (*Brother Man*, 43)

In *The Hills Were Joyful Together*, Charlotta wearily and resignedly struggles with the meaning of her own deprivation, her own "trouble." Her existence is a continuing battle for livelihood, a battle which forces her to erect a hard protective barrier. Unlike Papacita who advocates belligerent survival techniques, Charlotta turns into a "bigoted and narrow minded" religious fanatic and

> the springs of her being that had flowed with love dried up, so that she was unjust and shrewish with everyone but Papa Bedosa whom she feared and Manny whom she spoiled outrageously, shutting out his faults from her mind and painstakingly glossing them over. (*The Hills*, 31)

The causal relationships that Mais establishes between loneliness and emotional instability, between abandonment and suicidal tendencies, between deprivation and survival reactions, all are further emphasized in the turbulent love entanglements affecting the behavior, the attitudes and perceptions of almost all of his characters. For it is in the incessant tug of love-hate relationships that jealousies and passions erupt, leading to conflicts, often violence. Indeed many of the plot situations derive from these conflicts of passion and jealousy.

So interwoven is the novelistic world of Roger Mais that physical passion and love are inextricably bound up with economic monetary needs and desires. Euphemia puzzles over her instinctive physical aversion to Shag, even as she reflects on his being "so gentle and kind and generous to me. He would give me anything I want" (88).

In these love-hate entanglements, relationships are visceral, reactions are often from the gut. Often characters are driven by brutal instincts, and the act of lovemaking reflects the struggle endemic to the lives of the characters. The love-hate relationship of Papacita and Girlie, which ultimately leads to Girlie's killing of Papacita, is perhaps foreshadowed by the violence of their lovemaking.

> Their mouths met in a savage kiss, and she took his bottom lip between her teeth and bit down on it until she tasted blood . . . she said: "Hurt me like that—hurt me—Love me and hurt me! Hurt me hard!" (*Brother Man*, 29)

In Mais's novels, passion, lust, and jealousy propel many characters toward violent confrontations. Papacita, lusting after Minette, resorts to treachery and is capable of killing to satisfy his lust. Perhaps the ultimate statement of uncontrolled passionate desire is uttered by Glenn in *Black Lightning*.

> And there was nothing he could do about it; it was something in his flesh. Like a ping-wing macca that had broken in there and couldn't work its way out again, and it was festering.
>
> He fought against it hard, God knew, but it had him licked from the drop of the cap. Women did that to him. He just couldn't help himself anyhow. (*Black Lightning*, 143)

Yet contrasting with such naked expressions of lust and brutal displays of passion is the sensitive presentation of the developing intimacy and love between Brother Man and Minette and the sensuous tenderness with which Surjue recalls the first time he and Rema made love. With body shifts, body language, with suggestive understatements and with Minette's clear yet often unexpressed yearnings, Mais skillfully sketches Minette and Brother Man's evolving intimacy.

> He took her by the wrists, pulled her hands down from her face. No words passed between them; but something did, something that went without words. Slowly his arms went around her, pulling her towards him. She opened her eyes, as in a dream, and felt his hot, panting breath upon her face. (*Brother Man*, 137)

This first real physical encounter between Minette and Brother Man is a shy though passionate embrace, the culmination of long seductive overtures. Surjue's recalling of the first embrace between himself and Rema not only brings him momentary comfort, it evokes a tender and sensuous experience. Shut away in prison, Surjue imbues this experience with eroticism.

> And in the midst of this he could think of Rema. Rema and himself, together, making love for the first time, under the silent trees. He remembered the taste of her mouth, her passionate response to his kisses, all the bright sweetness of her, the way she closed her eyes with her head back against the crook of his arm, . . . and how the corners of her mouth came up a little as she made her lips ready for his kiss. (*The Hills*, 245)

The tenderness and eroticism, contrasting with Surjue's present condition in jail, highlight the experience. Mais's novelistic technique—deriving from the interplay of present condition and past memory, presented through interrupted juxtapositions, through a skillful splicing of episodes separated in time or space—gives suspense and dramatic tension to his narrative.

Even as rumor and gossip often magnify conflict situations, exacerbating them, so, too, foreshadowings anticipate the climaxes of such conflicts, and intercuttings highlight them. Through the use of foreshadowing, Mais imparts a sense of the inevitable to the unraveling of many of the complicated relationships. Further, the narrative statements of the chorus awaken an expectation of conflict and violence. Similarly, through intercuttings and through skillful use of the interrupted narrative, Mais imparts a dynamic movement to evolving episodes. The element of foreshadowing takes on various forms which lend a ritualistic dimension to the narrative. Papacita's violent murder is intimated when he breaks a mirror and cuts his hand. The blood obviously signifies his eventual bleeding from the wounds inflicted by Girlie.

> He had carried that superstition with him from a child. He could not see his image in the mirror any more, and it was as though by his own violence he had effaced it. (*Brother Man*, 179)

Similarly when Cordelia, steeped in superstitious beliefs, pricks her finger, she accepts it as an omen of a possible tragedy. Subsequently she will take the necessary precaution to ward off a possible evil.

> She let the garment she was mending drop suddenly to her lap and sat for a moment looking down at her finger where a drop of blood was slowly forming. She was stricken with a nameless fear. (83)

Indeed the world of Roger Mais seems guided by a fatalistic vision; characters, even when sensing possible tragic occurrences, seem unable to avert them. Thus the chorus intones the possible outcomes of Papacita's lusting after Minette. Not simply the chorus but later on, through intuitive recallings, Brother Man senses the possibility of his being framed once again as he has been in the past. Brother Man's story to Minette anticipates the arrival of the police, his framing, arrest and imprisonment.

> But she kept her threat all right. She framed him, so that he went to jail. It was the boyfriend who showed her how she could get her revenge; she made a clean breast of it to him afterwards, when it was too late. They planted ganga in his room and went and informed against him to the police. (160)

Brother Man, though warned by Minette not to go out into the night, leaves to face a seemingly inevitable encounter with violence.

Not only is violence foreshadowed by rumors, not only is tragedy presaged through accidents that are charged with superstitious significance, but the use of a story as parable, indicator to future happenings, is frequent.

> It happened that Wallacy caught Susu in bed with her spiv, a little rat of a man with his belly and chest and hips all run into one like a snake and he went through the window in only his underpants, and Wallacy reached under the mattress where he kept his machete, sharp, and chopped Susu like cuts of meat. (*The Hills*, 53)

Shag's story of the violent ending of a love triangle in which the jealous lover kills his sweetheart with a machete anticipates his own action. The story, once told, seems to have an incantatory force that brings about its duplication. Shag consciously places his sharpened machete under the bed, a constant warning of a possible violent ending to their relationship. Often in Mais, once mirrors, machetes and knives are introduced into the fabric of the narrative, they become functional tools of "God-sent chance," "carriers" of eventual destructive actions. They are an ever-recurring motif in *Brother Man* and *The Hills Were Joyful Together*.

In *Black Lightning*, all the elements of foreshadowing give structural directions to Jake's eventual suicide. Jake's preoccupation with the force and power of lightning, indeed his challenging of that power, and Jake's constant touching of his rifle all trigger off a spiraling movement toward death. Perhaps that constant preoccupation with the Samson story will inevitably lead to a parallel occurrence. Here story or parable seems to ordain the character's existential freedom. For though Jake is highly conscious of his circumstance, his obsession with the Samson story pushes him to accept a similar fate, culminating in his death. However, Jake, unlike many other characters in Roger Mais's novels, is given the freedom to make a choice. He is conscious of alternatives. Because he is unable to accept the purposelessness of his life and after he has destroyed the essential product of his creative genius, Jake chooses to end his life with a meaningful act, perhaps to him, a courageous one.

> God forgive him for that—I wonder? Killing himself . . . . Jake said, somewhat irrelevantly: "It takes some courage in a man to kill himself." (*Black Lightning,* 72)

So intimate, so interlocked is the relationship between the stories told and the lived reality of the characters. Jake chooses to die, but many of the other characters in Mais's novel seem unable to know of and thereby choose the moment and manner of their dying.

So often in the reality depicted by Mais, conflicts are resolved by violent actions: Girlie kills Papacita; Flitters is murdered; Shag cuts up Euphemia with his machete; Jake kills himself. Is Mais stating that violence is the only way out of the seeming entrapment, the harsh social realities in which the characters are imprisoned, where they are groping toward economic and social stability? Clearly violence is not simply made to release the pent-up frustrations of the characters, but more importantly it disentangles, though tragically, the complicated relationships and situations. It can be claimed that violence is not merely an impasse, a dead end, but paradoxically becomes an escape valve to the entrapped characters in the novels. The penned-up living quarters in *Brother Man,* more thoroughly sketched in *The Hills Were Joyful Together,* lead to pent-up emotions which, needing some form of release, ultimately explode in passions and in violence.

Throughout Mais's narratives, brusque gestures reflecting anger or frustration relieve, if only for a moment, the characters' feelings of helplessness, or express intense emotions. As if attempting to break out of confinement, characters often strike out with a futile gesture to expel their frustrations. The young boy, Manny, having been teased and rebuffed by Euphemia, throws a tantrum:

> He took his upper lip between his teeth and bit it until he could taste the salty taste of blood in his mouth. He beat on the ground with the hammer . . . . Hot tears blinded Manny's eyes and he shut them tight and hit the ground with the hammer and bit his lip hard. (*The Hills,* 162–63)

Jake, after deep introspection, unable to unravel the enigma of his situation, strikes out furiously.

Suddenly he swung it up above his head with both hands and brought it down on the anvil a resounding blow. And the head of the hammer flew off . . . . (*Black Lightning*, 61)

Even though he cannot explain the reason for such a sudden and impetuous action—"Just felt to slap somep'n you know that way?" (65)—clearly these actions are but relief mechanisms, momentarily reducing the compressed emotions, emotions which are at times mirrors of the societal entrapment of the characters.

At times release does not come from such violent physical actions but rather from music and singing. As we see throughout Caribbean literature and life, singing, music and dancing provide not simply momentary panaceas from harsh social circumstances but indeed have become such an intuitive manner of reacting that many of Mais's characters automatically resort to these modes of expressions. Charlotta sings to ease the constant pain, the harshness of her life.

> That was Charlotta over the ironing board inside her room singing to keep from breaking down and weeping. It was she who gave Zephyr most concern when the terrible news had reached them. (*The Hills*, 141)

Girlie's humming becomes a clear indicator of a shift in her mood, an indicator that is easily understood by Papacita:

> She got up, cleared the used breakfast things off the table, started dusting and tidying the place. She hummed a little to herself. (*Brother Man*, 21)

With his accordion, and in the playing of his music, Amos gives expression to his inner pain and loneliness, releases his own lingering sadness.

> He played softly, to himself, a tune that came out of his head, making it up as he went along. In it he was saying all kinds of things, just as the thoughts went through his mind, without stopping to turn them over, just letting them go. (*Black Lightning*, 151)

Bess more so than any other character uses singing to express her feelings. Through singing Bess reaches a high point of happiness, transcending her immediate everyday reality.

> She sang *Sweet Little Jesus Boy*, because she was filled with a great sense of release and happiness. And she sang and sang, until presently she was swept up and carried away with the emotions she had generated, and tears came to her eyes. (210)

Almost unconsciously Bess arrives at a new level of experience which brings about fulfillment that transforms her immediate social circumstances.

In Mais many characters attempt to transform their own social circumstances, to break out of their own immediate reality, through a violent action or reaction, some through a spiritual searching. For even if the environment confines, closes in on, and seems to trap the characters, each in their own way fights to break out of the confinement. The fight may be at times an unconscious reaction, at times a calculated response to oppressive conditions. But always there is a search, even for those characters whose seeking ends in frustration or in death.

Yet it may be said that in spite of the harsh repressive social reality, in spite of the conditions of entrapment, in spite of the problematic emotional and philosophical dilemmas into which the characters are pushed, Mais's ultimate novelistic vision is an optimistic one. For within the larger philosophical debate as to man's ability to affect his social circumstances and his existential reality, there is a possibility of self-generated action. Estella, though unable to articulate this possibility, is intuitively aware of it.

> I believe we shape the circumstances that make us what we are—in the end. I can't explain it better, but I know what I mean. (*Black Lightning*, 217)

Yet to affect the immediate social circumstances or to chart the immediate condition may demand not spontaneous haphazard action and response but rather carefully planned action. Jake searches for a direction:

> Jake sat down again. He changed the subject abruptly. "A man should have his own life. And a plan. Nothing moves without a plan." (135)

But planned action or communal participation in reshaping or in aiding the spiritual development of one's immediate social reality may not initially affect the consciousness of the community or the immediate reality. Yet Brother Man, through a conscious spiritual effort, attempts to share his own spiritual strength in order to negate the immediate oppressive social forces. His efforts are initially rejected or misconstrued.

> Sometimes they forgot, some of these people, that he had helped and comforted them, and healed their wounds. Sometimes they secretly despised him that he cared so little for himself, and so much for others, that he would give what little he had to succour another whose need he thought greater than his. (*Brother Man*, 23)

Roger Mais, using Brother Man as his mouthpiece, advocates a vision of action, almost mystical in its self-negation. Regeneration of the self comes only after one has been able to divest oneself of the tangled vibrations deriving from chaotic social circumstances. Man must strip away the harsh resonances of the material world, go into an inner silence that taps inner strength and inner resources. But the question as to where the inner strength or inner resources derive their regenerative force leads to the larger question of man's faith in himself and his ability to give meaning to chaos. Through belief in an ultimate regenerative force, Man will knit together his fragmented personality and achieve a coherent self.

What a man needed above all was a clear vision. Sometimes what a man wanted to see stood in the way. A man must go down inside himself and search himself earnestly, and after that he should stand and wait. And when the call came he would hear it. What a man needed most was to be quit of himself, and be still, and wait the call. (56–57)

But does this waiting imply that in the final analysis, one's existential action is simply making the self ready to receive a spiritual charge, or is the ultimate existential action open to man only partially dependent on the creator? Jake poses the question as to man's role in shaping his particular destiny:

Oh, what's the difference? What you think about yourself, Amos? Did you at some time take over from God, in making yourself what you are today? Or does he have the last word in everything that is formed in all us—you, me? (*Black Lightning*, 123)

Yet the question that continues to haunt Jake is where does it all lead to?

But to what end, Amos? Where does the finger point? Down what blind road . . . through what blank wall . . . to what? Where will he take that burden to its last resting-place, and set it down? And be restored to himself again, whole? (110)

So that after the flight from entrapment; after the searching for emotional and economic stability; after the violent passions and reactions; perhaps the fragmentation will lead to a new cohering of the communal identity and open into an optimistic vision of reality.

Surely laughter must lighten, now, somewhere in the world to put the shadows asunder . . . waits, like a young girl, untaken, waits for her first kiss . . . waits like the unspoken beginnings of desire . . . waits like the sap waits to burst with bud from a tree . . . Somewhere in the world something to redeem them . . . resolve their doubts, blot out their deeds . . . resides something . . . like love trembles on a young girl's lips, unspoken . . . waits laughter to lighten, now, and right them . . . redeem them, resolve them . . . redress them . . . somewhere in the world. (*The Hills*, 200–201)

The social reality of Mais's novels, which palpitate with poverty linked to explosive passions and violence, differs from the reality central to *In the Castle of My Skin*. This novel by George Lamming tells of changes that happen to a village steeped in colonial values, still a replica of a slave plantation—a large land-owning house surrounded by the native population. The human condition of entrapment, so immediate in *Brother Man* and *The Hills Were Joyful Together*, does not play the same role in *In the Castle of My Skin*. Lamming with consummate skill makes his social history dynamic through a constant interplay between the elemental, the societal, and the personal realities. For Lamming imbues this interplay with a quality of duration wherein the continuous to-and-fro movement of interlocking phenomena, though promising coherence, dramatizes a shifting and amorphous social reality. The boundaries of the colonial order begin to give way; the uncharted movement from enslavement to freedom is as yet not clearly formulated. A society shifting from village to urban polity moves along uncertain and fluctuating courses.

Whereas in Mais, entrapment, breakup, and flight are the principal novelistic modalities, in *In the Castle of My Skin*, which charts the breakup of the social order of colonialism and of the extant plantation society, the main construct is disintegration.

The recurrence of this motif clearly highlights the central theme, the very movement of the novel. As he attempts to explore the notion of change, Lamming often presents social history through disintegration of physical phenomena. The village street makes evident the shifting reality.

> The village was a marvel of small, heaped houses raised jauntily on groundsels of limestone, and arranged in rows on either side of the multiplying marl roads. Sometimes the roads disintegrated, the limestone slid back and the houses advanced across their boundaries to meet those on the opposite side in an embrace of board and shingle and cactus fence. (Lamming, *In the Castle*, 2)

Not only in the physical realm is disintegration manifested but in the natural realm also. Sands shift, the motion of the sea changes abruptly, cloud formations cohere and disperse. It is not simply that disintegration occurs in physical phenomena but that the images refer to disintegration within the social order itself.

> The sun had scattered [the clouds] in several directions, giving them many shapes . . . a thick, white wave . . . seemed to be driven by some force outside it, but soon the wave burst from inside . . . . I looked at the other side of the sky where everything was more peaceful and the clouds were enacting a legend. (111)

Through the use of the word "burst," Lamming injects an active force into the disintegrative process. The cloud formation seems to replicate the social order in which colonialism brought the scattering of peoples and disintegration of previous social orders.

From the novel's beginning, author George Lamming calls witness to impending change and presages the possibility of disintegration. As is characteristic of the Caribbean novelist, he uses the landscape, the elements, to mirror the moods and echo the vibrations inherent in personal societal relationships. Through the elements, the dynamic interplay of Caribbean man and his circumstances are reflected in all their ceaseless to-and-fro changing patterns. "Rain, rain, rain," begins *In the Castle of My Skin*. Incessant, persistent is the rhythmic incantation of the music mystery of the elements. Here, then, Lamming is foremost a poet. In the very first paragraph, we hear the alliterative pounding of the rain: "Rain, rain, rain . . . but the evening settled on the slush of the roads that dissolved in parts into pools of clay" (1). George, a perspicacious and perceptive child, intuitively realizes the significance of that inexorable rain seeping through the crevices of his mother's roof. Folk belief that rain brings with it showers of blessings, a belief that the hero's mother voices in spite of the evidence of the immediate reality, is doubted and questioned by the boy.

> I wept for the waste of my ninth important day. Yet I was wrong, my mother protested: it was irreverent to disapprove the will of the Lord or reject the consolation that my ninth birthday had brought showers of blessing. (1)

Paradoxical, too, is the basic function of the elements; here, of water with which *In the Castle of My Skin* both begins and ends. For water, which can be both benevolent and destructive, becomes the dramatic recorder, prophesying the changes to come. Immediately there is sounded a note of inevitability, of unalterable sequences which will lead to change.

> As if in serious imitation of the waters that raced outside, our lives— meaning our fears and their corresponding ideals—seemed to escape down an imaginary drain that was our future. Our capacity for feeling had grown as large as the flood, but the players of a simple village seemed as precariously adequate as the houses hoisted on water. (2)

Clearly this seemingly preordained escaping "down an imaginary drain that was our future," contrasts with Estella's intuitive but inarticulated feeling, "I believe we shape the circumstances that make us what we are—in the end" (Mais, *Black Lightning*, 27) and with Jake's articulation, "A man should have his own life. And a plan. Nothing moves without a plan" (135).

Quite often Lamming makes the innocent the principal formulators of his social philosophy. Through them he is able to capture more vividly the shifting realities of the Caribbean social condition; naive innocence grapples with larger ideas that approach the legendary, the biblical. Thus Trumper articulates the static and seemingly unchanging communal relationship, which delineates a social condition.

> The way we is here . . . My mother over yonder in that corner, an' my father down there in that corner, an' me somewhere else. An' you get the feelin' you know, that everything's all right. 'Cause of the way everybody sittin' . . . an' for the moment you feel nothin' ever change. Everything's all right, 'tis the same yesterday an' today an' tomorrow an' forever as they says in the Bible. (Lamming, *In the Castle*, 120)

Thus the social realities are not only fixed in space, but extend far into time in a seemingly unchanging perpetuity. Later Trumper gropes after the possibility of change occurring within the village, then momentarily rejects that possibility by introducing the notion of the stranger. For him, continuity is a closed entity in which outside influences could be but minimal. "Everybody in the village sort of belong . . . we all live sort of together, except for those who don't really belong" (144). To belong is to be fixed in unchanging patterns of behavior, to be encased in tradition which, though maybe expanding quantitatively, qualitatively remains the same.

> There were more flags now, the school was bigger and the children more clever. They could take and give orders, and parade for the inspector. And they understood the meaning of big words, but nothing had really changed. (29)

Lamming describes a colonial relationship that has endured through history. This unadulterated relationship and stewardship is not only geographically illustrated in preparation for Empire Day, with the "flags . . . the same colour . . . Good Old England and old Little England," but it is also reinforced by the demeanor of the white inspector of schools and his benevolent speech.

> We're all subjects and partakers in the great design, the British Empire, and your loyalty to the Empire can be seen in the splendid performance which your school decorations and the discipline of these squads represent . . . . The British Empire, you must remember, has always worked for the peace of the world. This was the job assigned it by God. (33)

It is not surprising, therefore, that nothing seems to change. And as Lamming correlates the views of both the young at school and the aged in the village, he places his ideas in their idiom, giving an elasticity to his notion of time even when the reality is static.

Ma and Pa and Trumper are the two poles of a three-generational span of time, duplicated in the history of political governance of the village by the Creighton family, the physical manifestation of the colonized condition, the landlord. The Creightons, as inheritors of an uninterrupted tradition of plantation dominance, have always been lords of the village.

> [Mr. Creighton] had died, and the estate fell to his son through whom it passed to another son who in his turn died, surrendering it to yet another. Generations had lived and died in this remote corner of a small British colony, the oldest and least adulterated of British colonies. (17)

Their unending domination is underscored by the words "fell to . . . passed to . . . surrendered to . . . lived and died," and all these open with forceful irony to the word "adulterated." The rule has been pure, uninterrupted, total.

Through a spatial relationship Lamming articulates the totality of the sociopolitical reality. It is that reality between those who govern and the governed which, through a vertical-horizontal interplay, demonstrates who is on top, who has been ruling. Not only does the Creighton house dominate the village, but, though set in trees, it negates the natural vegetation by its mortar and its "high, stone wall that bore bits of bottle along the top . . . . From any point of the land one could see on a clear day the large brick house hoisted on the hill" (18).

The changing relationship between the house on the hill and the village becomes the central theme of the novel *In the Castle of My Skin*. In the first part of the novel, the author stresses the polarized and static social reality structuring the relationships between the lowly and the great and ordaining their lives. This has led to an unswerving pattern of behavior; thus the turning on and off of the lights in the landlord's house signals, indeed controls, the flow of activities in the village. "When the lights went out . . . the landlord had gone to bed. It was time [the villagers] did the same" (21). The white house on the hill is perceived as a castle in which the great are stationed in a superior plane of reality. From this house the landlord descends from time to time, dispensing with smiling condescension his benevolence, his "daughter seated in the back of the carriage . . . haughty and contemptuous" (22).

Figurally, the village, steeped in its own unchanging regularity, spreads out horizontally beneath the white hilltop house. During the day the shoemaker and others ply their trade with a seemingly unbroken monotony:

The men at cricket. The children at hide and seek. The women laying out their starched clothes to dry. The sun let its light flow down on them as life itself flows through them. (17)

Yet this village life has its own rich texturing for, with consummate craft, Lamming captures the polyphonic folkways of these village types in all of their rich variety, their incessant daily motion, their pathetic ebb, their humorous flow. With gentle whimsy, Lamming sketches the attempt by the boys to escape from a scolding through a transparent artifice, a disguise. With a wicked and explosive humor, he orchestrates an encounter between a little boy and a white gentleman. Perhaps Lamming is at his cleverest in this episode.

> "Well, he see a white gentleman standing at Bellville corner waiting for the bus, and he go up to the gentleman to ask if he would buy the fowlcock. Mind you, the white gentl'man dress for work, white suit, hat, shirt and shoe to match. Nat'rally, the gentl'man get vex, put his head in air and say to Gordon, 'Does you expect me to take a rooster to work?' Gordon ain't pay him no attention, he just hold up the fowlcock, saying look, what a pretty comb. Then he turn the fowlcock round and round in the air till the bird backside was staring the white man face." (12)

It is through the eyes, the prism, of Trumper and his friends that Lamming pastels in impressionistic inlays the varying moods of phenomena. The early morning venturings of the boys are marked by their footprints on the shimmering dew, "shivering over the edge of the blades" (116). At noon all phenomena—the birds, the sea, the wind, the very boys—seem to be inhabited by an all-pervasive silence.

> Everything was quiet and hot, but the wet and ooze of the sea . . . . On the side by the sea the shade was deep and soothing over the esplanade . . . . There were no parakeets in the trees. It was quiet like the esplanade beside the sea, and the morning star had resigned its place to the sun, burning bright in the sky. (157–158)

Unending is the boys' fascination with the precise details of nature, with the movement of the crabs across the sand, and their mating; and the surf awakens a thoughtfulness in the boys as they grasp the larger significance of phenomena, which supercedes the sociopolitical presence and reality. Revealed to them is the strength inherent in landscape, a strength which may not simply negate the immediate social circumstances but move them out of these circumstances.

> When something bigger appeared like the sun and the sand, it brought with it a big, big feeling, and the big feeling pushed up all the little feelings we had received in other places. (153)

Indeed throughout the narrative we follow the adolescent feelings, the uncanny perceptions, of the boys as they grow up, change, or go away.

> Like Bambi an' Bots and Bambina. They live alright for only God knows how long, an' as soon as one get marry to the other, it don't matter who marry who, as soon as they is that marryin' business, every thin' break up, break right up. (141–142)

Some of the villagers achieve a modicum of the mobility possible through political changes. But to Trumper's way of thinking those vital inner changes often do not take place; nor should they.

> People who teach an' work in the post office an' the bank . . . . they got to work an' go back home, an' they go out the next day an' go back home again, an' they keep they head straight . . . nothin' ever go pop, pop, in they heads, an' nothing' ever will . . . . Nothin'll ever change in the village. (145)

In Mittelholzer's *Of Trees and the Sea*, the sea, the sand, and the trees had affected the inner psyche of the protagonists, leading to various emotional entanglements and intercourse. In *In the Castle of My Skin*, the sea and the surf often reiterate the unchanging rhythm of people's lives; but with drastic political changes, those things going "pop, pop" in their heads must change. The historic strikes and riots that shook most of the English-speaking Caribbean in the 1930s and that ultimately led to the New Day, affect the very root beliefs, the ordained habits and perceptions of the villagers. Symbolically, the new men bring a new, foreign presence of challenge to the village.

The dethroning of the landlord results. Now he no longer views the village from the pinnacle of power or with benevolence. Now he is reduced to a horizontal space, a supplicant in his fear, a supplicant begging the old couple for assurance. Ma and Pa, the aged exemplars, are confused by the new talk of buying the land on which they have lived for decades. They cannot understand the concept of ownership, the motives driving all the violence and change. Ma is befuddled by the landowner's confusion, his fall from grace. Neither the old lady nor the landlord, both of whom have remained so long fixed in their own social space, can grasp the changes which are taking place in the sociopolitical order. The old woman is "ashamed" by the "disrespect, strife and threats silent but sensed on all sides"; the landlord is frightened: "He could bear anything except disrespect.

It knocked at the roots of his world. It made him feel that nothing would be too big, too wicked to be attempted against him" (184).

To be sure, remembrances of the old order are ritualistic and meditative. As Pa's mind recaptures, through ritual memory, the larger signification of his links to his race and his rootings, all is landscaped memory:

> Star in the night and stone in the shrine of the sun sideways speak nothing but a world outside our world and the two was one . . . wherefore was Africa and the wildness around it and the darkness above and beyond the big sea? (126)

But ultimately in their declining years, they are disinherited. Initially, the men are excited by the new notion of a strike. Later, however, the male pillars of the village respond with a perplexity, anger, and outrage at the threat, at the prospect of dispossession.

The boys, growing up, also drift apart, leading to the unalterable fragmentation of the group. They, too, discuss and are somewhat befuddled by the notion of ownership of land. All becomes confused, the old political order destroyed, the traditional relationships disintegrated. The consequences of the changes dampen Trumper's oft-repeated intention of going away, but later he makes good his threat; he does go away. On returning he finds himself the only remaining bond between George and the former band of friends. In reality, the group of friends, the band, has disintegrated. George is representative: he is going to the high school, and his entry into another place of social intercourse aids in the disintegration and begins that relentless process of going away.

The feelings about the inevitability of change, about impending separations, intimated through the incessant rain at the novel's opening, crystallize again in and through the landscape. George's sense of the impending changes culminates in an irrevocable separation from his mother, a seemingly final departing from the land, his going away: "I knew in a sense more deep than simple departure I had said farewell, farewell to the land" (303).

George's mother, like so many Caribbean women, seems to have dedicated herself to driving her son toward intellectual achievement, emphasizing that this is the single narrow door through which one can slip into a better life.

> My mother was unsparing . . . there was much talk about opportunities others had had and had wasted. My friends had drifted into another world . . . . None of them had gone to high school. (221)

Even as the rhythm of the village has changed, its tonalities altered, George's life pattern also changes. He enters into new space.

In *In the Castle of My Skin*, the oppressive nature of the colonial reality, though elaborated, though clearly specified, is yet so subtly presented that its harshness seems modulated, its violence somewhat attenuated. Perhaps this is because Lamming's novelistic voice exquisitely captures the oral and folk idiom, in all of its communal resonance. Before its disintegration, the village exhibits a communality of living and a contiguity of interrelatedness, a linkage that negates perhaps not simply privacy, but that brutal aloneness so evident in Austin Clarke's *Amongst Thistles and Thorns*. In the latter, there are no boys running on the wind and surf and sand, no camaraderie of spinning tales and sharing adventures, no togetherness.

Aloneness and fear, terror and rejection, dread and punishment, and an omnipotent darkness are the grim presences that inhabit Clarke's novel. They comprise the central metaphor of laceration so sharply connoted in the "thistles and thorns" of the novel's title. The very opening notes of the horizontally constructed narrative echo with the ripping apart, the tearing into the human flesh, with its attendant bloodletting, and resound with viciousness, with brutalizing and degrading violence.

> Each time the heavy knotted tamarind tree of a whip fell, it cut across the bruised landscape of my young tender back. (Clarke, *Amongst Thistles and Thorns*, 1)

> I thought I felt blood squirting all over the back of my shirt . . . Now the blood seemed to be rising like the waves in the sea, near the Hastings Rocks. (10)

Such scenes of violence with their attendant wishes for equally violent revenge are all pervasive, are recurrent motifs in the lament of the boy narrator, Milton.

Not only does the social reality resound with violence, but the landscape, too, incorporates the very mood and sense of violence. The landscape is pierced by the continuous cries of the boy protagonist. The village's morality is revealed as propped up by empty sententious sayings and maxims, so that contrapuntal interplay between appearance and reality registers the basic immorality, the unethical mores and behavior, and irrelevant educational ritual of the village.

The economic, emotional, and spiritual impoverishment of this Barbadian village is painted by Austin Clarke with thick daubs which give baroque weightiness to the novel. Indeed, both foreground and background of this grim canvas are painted in dark colors. Perhaps nowhere is the image of the blackness, the sense of gloom, and a mood of oppressive darkness more present than in Milton's inner mind processes, his undirected stream of consciousness, which is interspersed with random incidents and episodes to give *Amongst Thistles and Thorns* its loose narrative structure.

> I could feel the quiet; the quietness of the house; somewhere in that quietness, somewhere in that darkness, my mother was lurking for me. Somewhere, blended in with the darkness of the spirit of the house, were the anger and the wrath. And the wrath and anger would change into a horrible Thing; and the Thing would come at me. And the Thing would change into my mother as it got near to me; and like a crab—but larger then any crab I ever caught on the beach—the claws of darkness would reach out like prongs, like the prongs of a large ice-prong made of steel. And my mother would grip me. (152)

There is no real plot to the narrative. There is a series of social and interpersonal situations in which a number of village types find themselves forming a background to and fleshing out the central action: the trials and tribulations of a young boy, his anguish, fear, his terror, his outsideness; and the arduous life of his mother, Ruby, her shrewd juggling of meager resources to make ends meet, her devious juggling of Willy-Willy and Nathan to try to keep a father for Milton and a man for her bodily warmth. Perhaps the mother's juggling of the men comes closest to a plot formulation. Clearly the relationship between Milton and his mother differs totally from the ties that link George and his friends to their mothers, as depicted in *In the Castle of My Skin*. The tones and intentions of both novels are radically different, the mood-scape of *Amongst Thistles and Thorns* so dissonant, echoing with seemingly cacaphonic and converse rhythms. Even so, it is evident that Austin Clarke's basic novelistic preoccupation and intention is the depiction, in all its everyday random and problematic circumstances, in all its raw living, of an urban Barbadian village: the quality of its poverty, the shape of its oppression, the tone and mood of its realities.

The village itself comprises two societies, one open, one closed, two realities—a residual colonizing presence impinging on the depressed living conditions of the native village. This basically colonial condition remains static, and nowhere in the novel is the restructuring of this colonial relationship glimpsed, nowhere is the promise of its breakup envisioned. The colonial formulation undergoes no changes, as it did in *In the Castle of My Skin*. No character, no village type, endeavors to shatter this oppressive condition. In this instance, then, the author's vision does not open out to any promise of ultimate freedom; his intention is clearly to present a fixed, static, unshifting condition. Austin Clarke underscores the difference in the quality of life between Front Road, the white sector, and Bath Corner, the pivotal point for the Black villagers: Front Road with manicured lawns, clean streets, vicious dogs; Bath Corner with wooden ramshackle dwellings, the standpipe where countless quarrels and fights take place, and its public bath.

Through the mouths of the native population—men at the standpipe corners, women over fences, and boys repeating the overheated arguments of the grownups—Austin Clarke shrewdly parodies the white colonizing presence, its manners, its attitudes, its affectations. The parody receives its texture through counterpoint, through contrasts, through comparing reactions of the white colonizing presence with those of the native population. Thus it is that Ruby and Girlie, both of whom are employed by whites, and are exploited by them, marvel at the aberrations of certain white women, ridiculing them. In an over-the-fence scene, with piquant bawdiness, the two Black women belittle white consumer habits.

"Them white people, them blasted white people is some funny funny, smart bitches. Now, tell me . . . a black person . . . *iffing* she was in possession, if she was in a position, money-wise, to own and possess all these underwears . . . you think they would buy *all* in one colour? You think that any black person you know, or I know, in their right senses, would go down in Town . . . *catch a bus to go down in Town* . . . and come back with twenty-*fourrr* . . . twenty-sev'n pair' o' underwears, all in one blasted colour? And white ones at that?" (*Thistles*, 32)

Later on Ruby, who slaves for this woman, washing and ironing her clothing for a pittance, gives vent to her pent-up anger and in a moment of triumph, rips up the white panties, symbolically negating their dominance.

Thus, within the static condition of colonialism, in their minds and conversations and on occasion through their actions, the Black villagers reject the basic power imbalance. Indeed, it is the question of racial superiority that seems to color many of the arguments of the village men. In many scenes, Austin Clarke skillfully captures the debating style, the rhetoric, and argumentation intrinsic to "Barbadian old talk" where logic derives from irrefutable upmanship, not necessarily from first-hand knowledge. The discussions of the young boys seem but refractions, so that the debate between Milton and his buddy Lester as to who is greater, Winston Churchill or Haile Selassie, has all the texture, echoes all the tonalities, all the polyphony, of the village men. What is overheard is presented as fact and evidence by the little boys, the notions of superiority and inferiority infused with the consequences of visible social power and standing. The white vicar, with servants, maids, and butlers, is contrasted to the Black villager Willy-Willy, who has none of the social trappings of power. Yet his authority is incontrovertible; he is, in fact, "the onliest man in the village what went all the way up in Harlem New York City, America, and sit down and drink rum with the great Joe Louis" (165).

In this juxtaposition of Willy-Willy and the vicar, of Haile Selassie and Winston Churchill, of Joe Louis and Rocky Marciano, of the notion of black and white, Austin Clarke focuses on and highlights the interactions between the colonial presence and the native population. Perhaps nowhere is the juxtaposition more clearly etched, in all its sardonic interrelationships, than in the scenes between the Black headmaster, Mr. Blackman, and the white inspector of schools. The white inspector, arrogant and supercilious in his execution of the colonial will, and the Black headmaster, the middleman in the colonial village hierarchy, supine, cowardly and vicious, are vividly depicted by Clarke. The teaching offered and the education received by the children can breed no more than a group of robots, of functional illiterates who, battered by misinformation, drilled by rote processes, become as confused and alienated from their own reality as Milton.

> We began at the First Commandment; and we worked our way, slowly and in pain, right through to the Tenth.
> I did not know the Commandments very well. My mother never told me about them. I could not understand how or why they would apply to me; or to my father, or to my mother . . . .
> "How many Gods they is, though?"
> "Ask the headmaster!"
> "But suppose a man was to feel like having more than one God! Suppose he was a kind o' man like what they have in Africa!" (6–7)

Not only is the education irrelevant to the native reality, but it also reinforces through the image of the white inspector a colonial power and, more generally, a violent model of authority. The education is viciously administered by the Black headmaster, as the colonial middleman asserting the Britishness of colonial authority.

> "I going beat you till you have the decency to cry! I going beat you arse till it turn black-and-blue!" . . .
> "I going beat you till you cry, you worthliss black brute!" (37)

The socializing effect of this education on Milton, who is mercilessly flogged, is fraught with dire consequences. He attempts to answer the riddles of his existence, to formulate and resolve the dilemmas of the colonial reality, to find an explanation for and give coherence to his history. But no coherence comes, not even to the third reality, Milton's confused random merging of fantasy with his own immediate circumstances.

Milton's fantasy world provides him with an escape from his immediate circumstance which, brutal and oppressive, awakes in him thoughts of murderous vengeance. Repeatedly, Milton envisions the destruction of that circumstance. In his visions, there is distortion bordering on hallucination.

His first blow landed on an old wound. I thought I felt blood squirting all over the back of my shirt; and between my tears, I imagined the blood squirting all over the schoolroom, drenching the boys and the assistant masters . . . . The second one: *whapp!* In the same place as the first. Now the blood seemed to be rising like the waves in the sea, near the Hastings Rocks. And they rolled and came and smashed against the concrete walls of the schoolroom; . . . And all the boys and all the assistant masters were scampering to the sides of the room, trying to escape from the drowning turbulence of the waves and the sprays of blood. (10)

His vengeful mental landscape is not only flooded with water and waves but is often illuminated with fire that would consume immoral authority figures. The Pastor Best Church loudly enshrines an overtly holy morality but one that is invested with an actual sordidness. Even as the church burns down, so too Milton, in his dream consciousness, burns the overtly moral, basically corrupt, despicable headmaster and sets on fire unethical, lonely Miss Brewster.

Two conditions ordain Milton's figure: a constant hallucinating state brings together a disparate unconnected series of images that take on the qualities of a dream state, that assume the proportions of a randomly expressed stream of consciousness. Through this stream of consciousness, Milton liquidates the reality that presses in on him, threatening him.

Constant running away provides Milton with an actual escape hatch from that threatening reality, creating the second condition, a central metaphor of Milton's reality; flight, escape, concealment. This metaphor of flight recurs through many of the novels in this chapter, as the protagonist attempts to apprehend a shifting, fragmented, disintegrated reality. For even when the immediate condition remains unchanging, the restlessness, the mobility of the novelistic reality can no longer achieve social coherence, is not yet infused by a communal vision so necessary to locate the potential of the vengeful protagonist. Milton flees through the darkness and the night, searching for a resting place. But though resting places elude him, the very act of fleeing and hiding at times liberates him, giving him a sense of temporality, a momentary sense of freedom.

And her voice, like the voice of a church bell in the distance, disappeared from me as I ran across the street, our street, away from her, to be free . . . . (63)

From his many hiding places, Milton is able to overhear conversations that involve him. He has the power of the unobserved observer. Concealed in the darkness under his house, he overhears the truth of his paternity. Indeed his hiding places give him an insight into the many moods of his mother, of Willy-Willy, his true father, and of Nathan, his assumed father. The life of Milton's mother, Ruby, with her arduous toil and her scheming to keep a man as a bedmate, designs the fourth reality.

For many years, Milton's mother has refused to have intercourse with any man. Her constant toil is alleviated only by emotional participation in the shake church of Pastor Best. Milton has observed his mother's abstinence, her chastity, and later on, when she finally enters into a sexual relationship with Nathan, Milton, the novel's narrator, observes the dramatic changes that come over his mother's body.

> The way she walks about the house is different already. Her footsteps are lighter now. . . . Love has now placed a dancing-ness, a feeling of expectation in her footsteps. My mother is a woman once more. She is moving about the house like a woman expecting her man, my father. (115)

Yet the total novelistic reality of *Amongst Thistles and Thorns*, the relationship between inner and outer realities, undergoes no real change, nor does the basic social condition of the main protagonists, Milton and his mother, Ruby. The relationship between the outer and inner realities is best captured in the creatural image of two dogs, one black and one white, locked in intercourse. Here Austin Clarke dramatizes the indecency of the intercourse between the colonial presence and the colonized.

> Two dogs, a white dog and a black dog, came from opposite ends of the road, smelled one another, jumped on one another, and then were stuck together in a frantic whimpering game. But suddenly, one dog, the white one, wanted to leave. But he could not, because he was still stuck to the black dog. The white dog was pointing in the direction from which the black dog came; and the black dog was looking in the direction from which the white dog came. And except for the thing which joined them, they were free of each other. In the whimpering tug-of-war which followed, neither one was winning. (36)

Indeed, no reversal of the social order takes place; Clarke suggests a symbiotic immobility dooming the native villages to a cycle of servitude from which neither their education or their action will extricate them.

In *Miguel Street*, V. S. Naipaul presents a social condition, depicting and satirizing its foibles, its follies, satirizing its reality. But unlike Austin Clarke, who does present causation though minimally, Naipaul notes no political origin, points to no historical power relationship, that dooms the characters in his novel, *Miguel Street*, to a condition of unchanging, paralyzing social stagnation. Only the boy narrator moves out of his immediate social condition. Only for him is there intimated a hope of realizing a better life. The basic condition of the characters in *Miguel Street* opens out to no future, offers little hope for realizing their dreams. Rather it is these very aspirations which hamstring many of the characters whose lives are cut through by Miguel Street. When magnified these aspirations become character flaws leading to ultimate frustration, loss, decline, flight. These excessive hopes, idiosyncratic and often the cause of the essential failures of the characters, are satirized by Naipaul in all their comic absurdities. Yet the basic tone and mood of *Miguel Street*—the events, pathos, sadness—all underscore a tragic social and human condition.

In *Amongst Thistles and Thorns* Milton's social condition undergoes no change, there is no upward-thrusting communal action which would change the contours of the basic social reality. So, too, in *Miguel Street*, though there is camaraderie, a sharing of both laughter and pain, there is no communal, no concerted social action by the characters to affect a new vital reformulation of their social reality. Indeed, the immediate social reality does undergo change, not through cohesion but again through breakup, through disintegration.

Despite *Miguel Street*'s robust and strident *fatigue*, its roguish and bawdy *picong*, its *posing*, its mobile pain and pathos, its essential configurations and features undergo change: things fall apart, the community of Miguel Street breaks up. As in *Amongst Thistles and Thorns*, the essential metaphor is flight from the immediate reality, departure from the immediate surroundings of *Miguel Street*. The novel's trajectory describes an arc from an initial camaraderie and community of main characters to a point of breakup, loss, and the drifting apart of that initial community. Even as the trajectory of *Miguel Street* describes a downward arc, so too do the lives of the characters, so, too, the structure of the stories: Characters move upward, a characteristic or idiosyncrasy highlighted, almost assuming identity, possibility, a hope; an erratic dream is almost realized; then like the fireworks of the pyrotechnicist, they arc downward, fizzle into nothingness.

The lives of the characters are fraught with lost dreams, and even the realization of dream is presented with ironic fatality. Morgan wants to make the greatest fireworks ever.

> Morgan would say "Make what? Make nothing. By this time so next year, I go have the King of England, the King of America paying me millions to make fireworks for them. The most beautiful fireworks anybody ever see." (Naipaul, *Miguel Street*, 82)

However, after most of his fireworks have gone up in smoke and have constantly fizzled into nothingness, ironically, Morgan achieves his dream. All is pathetic irony, all a grim representation, counterpoint of absurdity.

> It was the most beautiful fire in the Port-of-Spain since 1933 . . . . What
> really made the fire beautiful was Morgan's fireworks going off. (91)

Just as ironic is Laura of "the Maternal instinct," who has casually
produced "eight children by seven different fathers." With resignation, she
says that "you get used to it after the first three, four times. Is a damn
nuisance, though" (107). Still she cannot accept her eldest daughter Lorna's
first pregnancy. With a brutal pathos, and, again, with a contrapuntal finality,
Laura shrieks and cries when Lorna tells her she is "going to make a baby."

> Laura's crying that night was the most terrible thing I had heard. It made
> me feel that the world was a stupid, sad place, and I almost began crying
> with Laura. (115–116)

Bogart, who apes the screen star, tough lover-boy Humphrey Bogart,
ironically is jailed for bigamy. Popo, whose great pride, an absurd comic
dream, is to make the "thing without a name" (8), becomes a cheerless
person when he begins productive work.

Thus in *Miguel Street,* irony shades into pathos, comedy etched with
absurdity shades into sardonic grim humor. Living seems futile, as dreams
or idiosyncratic ambitions explode, dissolve. Almost all the characters either
flee from Miguel Street, or are removed from it through jailing or commitment to an asylum; some lose their own unique inner quality; others die. It
is against this backdrop of ultimate departure and loss of dreams that
Naipaul satirizes Trinidadian societal attitudes and many individual idiosyncracies. He makes ludicrous the grand boast or ambition, and, with telling
understatement, highlights folly or stupidity.

The overriding effect derived from Naipaul's depiction of Trinidadian
society during the war years is comic. For even though his vision of the
social reality is rooted in cynicism, even though there are real moments of
pity exibited, *Miguel Street* is not nurtured by a compassionate vision which
would make the cynical achieve the tragic, which would give the comic a
deep effective poignancy. Skillfully, Naipaul unmasks the pose, the boast,
the mimicry which he ascribes to so many Trinidadian attitudes—attitudes
that all seem based on the need to achieve some modicum of status within
the society. Humorous moments intertwine and overlap.

Naipaul constantly parodies the attitude of Miguel Street residents toward
education. Clearly education would provide, in lieu of money, a certain
respectability, and those who do not have it, feign it. They take on airs,
pretend to be knowledgeable. B. Wordsworth, perhaps one of Naipaul's best-
drawn characters, claims that he will write "the greatest poem in the world."
Deftly, Naipaul ridicules both his aspiration

I have been working on it for more than five years now. I will finish it in about twenty-two years from now, that is, if I keep writing at the present rate, . . . I just write one line a month. But I make sure it is a good line. (62)

and his speech:

His English was so good, it didn't sound natural . . . he spoke very slowly and very correctly as though every word was costing him money. (62)

The attitude toward education and learning of the residents of Miguel Street causes them to label many of their fellow residents as brainy or as possessing genius. Thus when the "brain" or the "genius" who has accepted that label fails to live up to the ascription, a comic, farcical situation ensues. Uncle Bhakou, the mechanical genius who pulls cars apart and then is unable to put them back together, always blames the design. Elias, the "brain" who initially failed his Cambridge Examination, states to his friends:

"Yes, boy. I think I going to take that examination again, and this year I going to be so good that Mr. Cambridge go bawl when he read what I write for him" . . . .
In Elias's mouth litritcher was the most beautiful word I heard. It sounded like something to eat, something rich like chocolate. (41)

Status-seeking through association provides Naipaul with many moments of whimsical humor. Eddoes, the best street scavenger, boasts about his association with "high class people."

He said he knew everybody important in Port-of-Spain, from the Governor down.
He would say, "Collected two, three tins of rubbish from the Director of Medical Services yesterday. I know him good, you know. Been collecting his rubbish for years, ever since he was a little doctor in Woodbrook, catching hell. So I see him yesterday and he say 'Eddoes (that is how he does always call me, you know) Eddoes,' he say, 'Come and have a drink.' Well, when I working I don't like drinking because it does keep you back. But he nearly drag me off the cart, man. In the end I had to drink with him. He tell me all his troubles." (120)

Not only does Naipaul seize on the comedy inherent in status-seeking through association, but he constantly exposes and holds up to ridicule characters who rely on exaggerated machismo to achieve status in the eyes of their comrades. Constant motifs in *Miguel Street* are wife-beating, bigamy, adultery, attitudes toward parentage. So endemic is wife-beating to Miguel Street that Naipaul chucklingly relates that Mrs. Bhakcu, though she is big and strong, keeps "a cricket bat, with which she was usually beaten by Mr. Bhakcu, well oiled and greased and she refused to lend it out!!" (154). And with the caustic wit characteristic of Naipaul, inherent in his writing, we view the following assertion:

> "Why? Why? Why you have to get married?"
> "She making baby."
> "Is a damn funny thing to say. If everybody married because woman making baby for them it go be a hell of a thing. What happen that you want to be different now from everybody else in Trinidad? You come so American?" (190)

Even though many of the attitudes toward wife-beating and toward parenting are presented in their comic possibilities, such characteristics lead to the dilemma of many episodes and to disillusionment of some characters and the ensuing breakup of the Miguel Street circle. Bogart, jailed for bigamy in the first episode, is the first to leave the street. Hat, too, the chief commentator, the cog around whom the episodes and the characters revolve, is jailed for beating his lately acquired common-law wife, who left him for another man.

Like George in *In the Castle of My Skin*, the boy narrator of *Miguel Street* also goes away. Having captured and presented the breakup of a community of characters—even as it breaks up, even as it undergoes radical changes— his life, too, changes; his horizons widen. He does not remain trapped in static immobility as does Milton in *Amongst Thistles in Thorns*, nor does he go running through the Trinidadian landscape in quest of a modicum of essential living as does Walter Castle in Earl Lovelace's *While Gods Are Falling*.

During the three years of Hat's jail sentence, the boy narrator's perception of Miguel Street undergoes radical changes, the essential nature of Miguel Street is irrevocably altered.

> Hat's homecoming fell a little flat . . . . Hat too had changed. . . .
> . . . I no longer wanted to be Eddoes. He was so weak and thin, and I hadn't realized that he was so small. Titus Hoyt was stupid and boring, and not funny at all. Everything had changed. (214)

The robust though ultimately barren lives of the characters, their expectations and their failures, their departures and their abandonment of the street, the ultimate futility of their lives, are captured by Naipaul in the total disappearance of B. Wordsworth from the scene, as if he never lived in the street, as if he were merely a fantasy, a fiction.

I walked along Alberto Street a year later, but I could find no sign of the poet's house. It hadn't vanished, just like that. It had been pulled down, and a big, two-storied building had taken its place. The mango tree and the plum tree and the coconut tree had all been cut down, and there was brick and concrete everywhere.

It was just as though B. Wordsworth had never existed. (65)

Clearly the episodic novelistic landscape created by Naipaul is corroded by a cynical vision of reality, so that the social reality of the war years, the time frame of *Miguel Street*, is not presented in all of its upward surging movement. The social ramifications of that period, the inner texture of Trinidadian society, the shifting class configurations are not made evident; they are but shadowy, gray outlines in Naipaul's rendition.

Miguel Street does not palpitate, does not have the incessant throbbing pulsebeat of a period that saw the emergence of a steel band, that underwent social changes because of the presence of the American military in Trinidad, that would bear witness to a social elasticity concomitant on the new possibilities inherent in adult suffrage and consequent political independence. *Miguel Street* is devoid of social philosophy, is but a social commentary where characters merely disappear as if never having lived, or more importantly, do not translate their idiosyncracies into any meaningful social action. Though characters are presented, in truth they are but caricatures, puppets of the author's cynical vision.

While *Gods Are Falling* also develops against the backdrop of a street, Webber Street, situated not in Woodbrook as was *Miguel Street*, but in Belmont, another marginal area of Port-of-Spain. From the very beginning of the novel, it is evident that Earl Lovelace's social notions and consciousness affect the rendition of his material. He attempts to implant social causation in the analysis and depiction of the social reality. Here too—as in *Amongst Thistles and Thorns*, as in *The Hills Were Joyful Together*, as in *Miguel Street*—characters are trapped in environments that seem to close in around them, circumscribe their aspirations, thwart their dreams. As in the other novels, the motif of flight from the immediate threatening reality qualifies the actions of the central characters of *While Gods Are Falling*.

Walter Castle, the novel's protagonist, while still an adolescent, flees from his family in a rural sector of Trinidad, goes to Port-of-Spain in search of a livelihood and meaningful work, then returns to another rural sector of Trinidad for employment and for the peace of the countryside, then runs back to Port-of-Spain. At the beginning of the novel, we find him debating whether he should leave Port-of-Spain again and return with his wife, baby, and younger sister in an attempt to find again the peace and quiet he ascribes to the countryside.

The immediate plot spins around his attempt to resolve the dilemma of living in a small tenement apartment in Webber Street, a crowded, poor section of Port-of-Spain. Indeed, the fabric of the novel, its emotional contour, is Walter Castle's groping toward self-identity, toward self-realization through political actions, through communal participation. In this respect, Walter Castle—and by extension, author Earl Lovelace—views the individual's role in the rehabilitation of an unequal society as different from the apolitical, uncommitted, and disinterested consciousness of the characters in *Miguel Street.*

Walter Castle, after a great deal of self-wrangling and unending bickering with his wife, Stephanie, stumbles with his bandy leg toward a liberating political communal awareness. Through a series of interior monologues presented in flashbacks, we are introduced to the principal episodes in the bleak, unexciting life of the anti-heroic protagonist. We are introduced to his rural childhood with his family, his interrupted schooling, his running away to the city, and his itinerant wanderings in a lonely frustrating search for jobs, to his nonparticipant life in the boisterous rural lumber village, Nugglee, and finally to his marriage to Stephanie and the problems confronting him in his job.

The birth of his child, the oppressive living conditions, his hard unrewarding job without the promise of promotion, the crowded violence of Webber Street, its rundown conditions—all these are fully externalized, primarily through an interminable series of conversations with his wife, with a one-legged neighbor, Mr. Cross, and with a Baptist preacher and Bible salesman. The central question vexing Walter Castle and further accentuating his inner tension, his pent-up anger, is whether he should chuck everything and do what he has been doing all his life, run away. Should he resign himself to a dead-end job, where men trained by him are promoted over him? Should he leave Webber Street, where there are no gods, where the gods have fallen, and flee with his wife and his child and younger sister to an imaginary bliss and the hard-working peace of the countryside?

The abandonment, the wasted lives, of those whose existence is circumscribed by a reality running to ruin are captured in the image of the hodgepodge collection of debris littering the dry river, which often forms the demarcation line between hope and hopelessness.

> It is Sunday morning . . . . Four corbeaux hunched like judges on the drooping branches of the solitary coconut tree in the yard look at the dry river swollen with water and boiling with tin cans, old boots, strips of wood and other unassorted debris. (Lovelace, *While Gods Are Falling,* 9)

The vivid contrast between the rotting social conditions symbolically presented here and the luxuriant greenness of St. Clair, the visibly wealthier area of Port-of-Spain, is sharply underscored, palpably demonstrated by Earl Lovelace. St. Clair and Webber Street seem to have the same contrasting configurations as Front Road and Bath Corner in *Amongst Thistles and Thorns*, but here even the landscape, the elements are figurative representations of this contrast.

> . . . St. Clair with green-roofed, white Victorian houses in yards with green shade-trees, mown lawns, well-trimmed hedges and pedigree dogs . . . . Look at the Laventille hillside where damp small houses balance . . . . Above the tangle of black electric wires, tops of taller buildings rise under the . . . skies cluttered with thick black clouds. (7)

Clearly the environmental contrast, so reflective of a colonized reality, is refracted, repeated, in the sociopolitical conditions affecting both areas. The relationship between poverty and crime, between law and the maintenance of the status quo, becomes a constant point of reference in Earl Lovelace's depiction of the social configurations of urban Port-of-Spain. Lovelace ascribes to these configurations of poverty, of crime, of fear, an endemic quality affecting the moral perceptions, the existential fabric, of the lives of people in the Webber Streets of Port-of-Spain.

> There is no decrease in disorder and crime, and no end to fear, even though more policemen with more revolvers are patrolling the areas . . . though priests are saying more masses . . . And alongside this . . . around St. Clair . . . people are buying more motor-cars, TV sets, washing-machines. (8)

It is against this sociopolitical backdrop that Walter Castle sketches, through reminiscences, the emotional contours of his childhood, the disintegration and breakup of his family. At times, though rarely, a touch of blue colors the basically gray depiction of the lives of his father, mother, brothers, and sisters. Walter Castle does remember a time when he shared his father's laughter and received from him tidbits of wisdom garnered from many experiences, although those experiences have not all been rich ones. "I'm just a bee with a broken wing," Pap says, and elaborating on the nature of life, he reflects:

> "All a man get from it is experience . . . . You know, boy, there's a lot to learn. You learn that you're just a man. A man is the greatest thing in God's earth, and a man is the weakest in God's earth." (36)

Pap's life arcs from a time when he was a strong man, a "womanizing man," a drinking man, who had land to work, but ultimately there is a downward arcing decline: he loses his land, becomes crippled through an accident, turns inward, sad and silent. His physiological and emotional crippling, then his refusal to assert his parental authority, lead inexorably to the breakup of the family. His daughters, Carmen and Ruth, become pregnant, get engaged or married without his consent.

Even though Pap as a man in his prime seems fiery, the picture we are given of his wife is that of a long-suffering, dour, mirthless woman. The mother is a picture of resignation. She displays little maternal tenderness, exhibits little sympathy for her daughter's behavior, or for her husband's attitudes; her judgment is unyielding: "Ma looked on, furious and grim, her gaze accusing them both: the daughter for her sin, and the father for comforting the child" (32). Despite her harshness, she carries with her an air of bewilderment and surrender. Only momentary signs of affection for her son Andrew are displayed by this figure of a woman burdened down by loss of dreams and continual sadness.

With the death of Walter's father, the last coming together of the family takes place before its ultimate disintegration occurs. Boysie leaves for England; Andrew becomes a policeman in Port-of-Spain; Walter, later on, flees to Port-of-Spain in search of work.

Even as the theme of breakup and disintegration characterizes the pattern, the quality of life, of Walter's family, alienation and flight structure his individual development and character. For Walter Castle, like so many of the protagonists in this chapter, finds the immediate environment at times threatening or hostile, and the method of coping with and sometimes combating this environment becomes the raison d'être as well as the articulation of broken dreams and aspirations. Initially, as a boy in school, Walter Castle challenges the status quo, finds himself alienated from the school and his peers. His challenges are futile in most instances, though he does "sometimes [get] a good punch and [bust] a fellow's mouth . . . but those times were rare" (38).

But something truly changing occurs: we see the beginnings of his incessant questioning, his attempts at finding solutions to his own puzzle-ment—qualities that eventually lead him even farther into isolation, loneliness, alienation.

> At school, he was puzzled and sometimes outspoken and self-opinionated to the point of actual conceit. He lost friends much faster than he made them, and wondered why everybody was against him, why they all had to argue with him . . . . He was very lonely. (38)

His constant need to exhibit maleness and independence makes him repel condescension or any attitudes which would undermine his pride.

He rejects Andrew. His relationship with his stiff, unbending, authoritative brother becomes a constant series of challenges, of duels. He rejects Andrew's condescension and in a scene so reminiscent of Milton's running in *Amongst Thistles and Thorns*, Walter, too, runs into the night.

Leaving school, going to Port-of-Spain, does not end Walter's constant running and his constant searching for something that would stabilize him, for employment that would not be exploitative. Any seemingly unjust treatment, any unjust accusation, stirs up an angry reaction, an impetuous action which leads to yet another flight, another running away. When unfairly accused of stealing by his employer, Walter angrily throws a bottle and then runs: "he had been running for three weeks; running even when he was walking, even when he was sitting or sleeping" (52).

Thus, at the beginning of the novel, we find Walter Castle debating whether he should once again pack up and run away. Not simply because the immediate living conditions are harsh and violent, but more so because he is reacting against an unfair threat on his job. Much of *While Gods Are Falling* is shaped through Walter Castle's complaint against personal injustice or affront, and through Lovelace's constant complaint and protest against the social conditions in Trinidad and Tobago, which affect the lives of people such as Walter Castle.

Through Walter Castle's conversations, discussions, and arguments with his wife, Earl Lovelace is able to present—while giving stage directions to their dialogue—his ideas and thoughts about pride, maleness, politics, and the societal configurations of the islands. Walter Castle debates whether his pride, his maleness, his sense of fair play, could withstand his not being promoted.

> "Patience. I've had that for years. I'm sick with patience. Work. Keep on. Keep it up. Don't give up . . . Christ! A man must have some pride . . . . That's all a man has. Like his two balls. When he loses them he's not a man any more." (15)

Lovelace makes *While Gods Are Falling* a novel of protest whose ultimate statement is that one has to stand up and fight in order to change the ascribed police brutality, the criminal justice system, the rampant bribery and corruption, the prevailing poverty and violence. In a series of protestations, Lovelace bitterly comments on the essential texture, on the emotional contours, of the urban environment in Trinidad. In a rhetorical question, Lovelace asks

> What is wrong with this city? . . . There is something wrong in this city
> . . . something dark, poisonous and stinking, something like a sore in this
> city. (9)

This darkness, this poverty, seem to affect the body politic in Trinidad.
Symbolically, Lovelace arrives at the central metaphor of his novel, injecting
a feeling of hopelessness, ascribing a sense of larger doom, of fatality to the
urban reality of Port-of-Spain.

Shifting from the horizontal image of flight characterizing Walter Castle's
constant running away, Lovelace ascribes a vertical image to his bleak vision
of social reality confronting the circumscribed lives of the youth—their
unemployment or their jailings and the entrapped living of people eking out
a meager existence surrounded by poverty. In a rebellious note of protest,
Lovelace lashes out at the social reality of the hills surrounding Port-of-
Spain.

> Look, and feel anger building within you, bulging your neck veins,
> bristling your neck hairs, feel the blood of anger thumping in your ears
> . . . On those hills there, it is not only poverty. It is disorder; it is crime.
> (8)

And through the voice of Walter Castle, Lovelace ascribes an existential
responsibility to the inhabitants of those hills to stand up and fight for one's
rights through communal participation.

Walter Castle realizes that flight is not the answer. It will not allay
personal frustration, will not resolve or ease social problems.

> A man has to fight right where he finds himself or lie down and let them
> walk over him . . . . What do you have to match against reason? Disgust?
> Fear? Anger? Man, you're crazy to think about dragging that poor
> pregnant woman and that small child somewhere behind God's back away
> in the country. Man, you're real crazy. (128)

Finally Walter Castle, through what seems "crazy" to others, attempts to
resolve the dilemma of his living. The central debate is whether to pick up
his family and sink into a romanticized peace of the country, or whether to
stay in Webber Street where the gods have fallen. He dreams of being able
to live a life of self-sufficiency in the countryside among wet earth and grass,
green and glistening with dew and sunlight, the corn tall with long ears and
blond tassles. He chafes at having to live in a community pitted with
corruption, gripped with an ever-lurking and gratuitous violence. The
resolution of this debate, however, comes not through Walter Castle's
wrestling with it, but rather from an external incident that becomes a catalyst
for his participation in the community. He stays to help organize a commit-

tee of community residents to help raise money for the lawyer's fee for the defense of a young man unjustly arrested for murder. Thus it is that from being principally a commentator and one who kept fleeing from his circumstances, Walter Castle becomes participant, involved and committed to a larger communal struggle. He accepts the dictum that "if you want to live and life is to mean something, you must be involved with people" (214).

Now indeed as he walks through the city to the first organizational meeting, Walter Castle at least begins to sense and note its robust vitality, its visceral rhythms, its human throb. Now there's a purpose to his living in Webber Street. Thus from the personal and social chaos, Walter Castle arrives at a personal resolution through purposeful action.

No such possibility lies within the grasp of the characters in *The Children of Sisyphus*. Their doom, their entrapment within the physical confines of the Dungle, is assured not only through actual physical barriers, but is even more decisively ordained by symbolic, psychological circumscription. For Orlando Patterson in *The Children of Sisyphus* gives a corporal reality to his naturalistic depiction of the Dungle, makes it animate. The relationship between Dungle-dweller child of Sisyphus and the Dungle with its inevitable, inescapable confinement is total, becomes the symbiotic binary in Patterson's symbolic title. Though by social decree the gods may have fallen in Lovelace's novel, by personal endeavor and commitment there is a possible revocation. In *The Children of Sisyphus,* the title's mythic and symbolic propositions ordain inflexibility, decree immobility. All the novels of this chapter depict the characters' attempts to flee from entrapment in various social and political topographies, yet each author's private vision shapes the texture of the flight, the strength and pull of the topography. For Patterson, one can never leave the Dungle. According to Rachel, the old Dungle dweller and voice of prophecy:

> Once you born in it the world was the Dungle. The Dungle was the world. You were condemned to roam and wander freely there. But you couldn't leave. That for certain. (Patterson, *The Children of Sisyphus*, 181)

Dinah, one of the younger Dungle dwellers, believes, "The Dungle was an obeah man and it would cast a spell on those who fall prey to it" (94). Dinah's attempt to flee from the Dungle becomes one of the principal narrative ingredients of *The Children of Sisyphus*. Indeed it could be said that the theme of flight pushes the characters along into their cycle of unending entrapment. Even the smell of the Dungle is inescapable. It enters into the body, becomes a blotch, a stain that no distance can wash away. Patterson makes the smell of the Dungle animate, effective.

"You come from a Dungle . . . ah can smell it 'pon you . . . .
"De only sin me ever commit is when me find meself in a Dungle,
an' me no responsible fo' dat." (59–60)

To be from the Dungle is to be forever stigmatized. Here Patterson, true
to his symbolic interpretation of the Sisyphus myth, ascribes a finality to
origin, injects a naturalistic inevitability to the lives of his characters. Thus
the odor of the Dungle, while becoming a repulsive social stigma to the
Dungle dweller, conversely provides a sense of refuge to those repulsed by
the outside world: "She never knew the stale stench of filth could smell so
sweet." It is as if the Dungle is a world unto itself with its own protective
shell, a reality separated from the larger social reality of Jamaica. The two are
juxtaposed, but the Dungle has its particular landscape of poverty.

in the Dungle poverty was a way of life . . . . Where she came from there
was complete poverty, and so there was no poverty . . . . They were all
little pieces of garbage thrown aside by their worlds. (98)

Patterson naturalistically depicts the Dungle's outer reality, its origin, its
filth, and its growth with the piling up of garbage. It is the dumping ground
for refuse; it is where wrecked lives have their habitat. Rachel, the Dungle
recorder, narrates her part in its beginnings.

I 'member when dis place was a swamp . . . . An' I 'member de firs' time
de donkey-cart start to carry de shit an' dump it right here . . . de last cart
dat dump . . . shit here . . . from dat time is only garbage dem dump here
. . . me was de firs' person fe' hit on de idea [to live here]. (39)

The motif of garbage, the process of its dumping, and the recurrent sense
of abnormality are baroque opening configurations giving to the novel its
dense creatural overtones.

Patterson, as if luxuriating in the depiction of these overtones, takes us
slowly on a journey to the Dungle. We see the Dungle through the suffering
eyes of the garbage men, we see the human aberrations who inhabit this
festering world of the Dungle. Elaborately Patterson creates the horror of
their poverty: the introit is measured and ghastly, the Dungle dwellers seem
almost predators, ritualistically awaiting their daily offerings.

Any moment now he would begin to see them. Yes, yes. Already there
was one of them. Ragged thing. Black skin, scaly with exposure. Hair
peeling off. Eyes yellow-brown and dark, deep and sallow, piercing. Bang-
belly, bang-belly. One, two, three of them creeping from out of their little
darkness. (24)

Even the garbage man, as he views the landscape of poverty and the children of Sisyphus, concludes that the creatures of the Dungle

> weren't human. If anyone told him that they were human like himself he would tell them that they lied. Those eyes peering at him. Deep and dark red and hungry for what he carried. And for his own blood, too, he was sure. (20)

The various attempts to flee from this world of abject poverty externalized with its high-piled garbage give structure to the depiction of Dinah, provide us with images of induced dream, drugged fantasy flights, through presentation of the Rastafarian brethren. Through the inducement of ganja smoke, Brother Solomon not only escapes the reality of the Dungle, but actually makes the poverty lyrical, the Dungle a garden. Not simply through the ritual of smoking the chillum pipe are the Rastafarians able to endure this ghastly world but also through the promises of their beliefs. For the Rastafarians, Ethiopia is the final resting place calling them and taking them away from their exile in Babylon. Here the theme of exile and return only to Africa, in this instance to Ethiopia, takes on figural significance, releasing power and energy, confirming dream and belief.

Thus the theme of moving away, of flight, as seen in *The Children of Sisyphus*, when containing the Rastafarian dream of returning to Ethiopia, is endowed with a ritual significance beyond the immediate threatening reality. For indeed the immediate reality, the Dungle, circumscribed by Babylon, signifies a period of bondage whose end is ordained.

The possibility of going back to the land of their forefathers seems to efface the effects of Dungle living, to release the Dungle-dwelling Rastafarians from physical entrapment. A feeling of ecstasy liberates them from their immediate reality; the elements, mountain, moon and sea, provide transcendental landscapes of freedom from bondage.

> [They] soared up to the top of the high mounds of filth and grappled for the sky, and, when they could not reach it, screamed: "Africa! Ethiopia, I come." And still others, in sheer deliriousness, dashed for the black, murmuring sea and, fully clothed, plunged themselves in. (118)

But to Brother Solomon, the ecstasy of his brethren—the transfigured landscapes on which their dream, their frenzied joy, play out—seems to awaken different responses, assumes different intonations. So that to him, at the high point of the Rastafarians' ecstasy, the sea does not give off songs of assurance but rather seems indecisive in its to-and-fro movement: "black sea, wide sea, endless, remote and haunting sea; he could hear it going backward . . . forward, backward; forward, backward" (120). Here the to-and-fro movement of the sea seems to be a pulsebeat registering not simply

Brother Solomon's feelings, but anticipating the shifting nature of the hopes and dreams of the brethren. The question that arises is whether in truth they would leave Babylon or whether their hopes of leaving would wash ashore and dissolve. Often Patterson uses the elements, relies on landscape, to measure the beat, to indicate the rhythms of emotions, to bear witness to deep feelings and actions. Thus, as the sea witnesses Dinah's passionate acceptance when possessed by Cyrus, her initial ambivalence and fear, which come to characterize her actions, almost reflect the sea's to-and-fro movements which wash the sand where she and Cyrus mate.

Like the Rastafarian brethren, Dinah also attempts to leave the Dungle, rebelling against its hold, in search of her own identity, her own essence. Initially she thinks:

> It was cruel the way she going to leave her pickney. But she had to be cruel. If she was going to leave the Dungle she had to be merciless. (35–36)

Driven by the need to find her own self, or maybe by ambition, Dinah initially is able to leave the Dungle. An ambivalence between intention and "true feeling" characterizes Patterson's attempt to ascribe an existential paradoxical quality to Dinah's behavior, to her reactions. Dinah's flight from the Dungle takes her through many experiences, through many emotional encounters, but each is characterized by a paradoxical inability to totally grasp any single emotion. Through his presentation of Dinah, Patterson attempts to locate the existential relationship between pain and pleasure, suffering and joy, and the essential nature of deep experience. Clearly in this novelistic attempt to present aspects of the philosophy of being and nonbeing, there is a disassociative quality. Not that the analysis lacks philosophical depth, but at times it seems novelistic imposition, addenda. Dinah's reactions are always fraught with ambivalence, so that perhaps Patterson is ascribing totality to ambivalence. Dinah's flagellation by the Shepherd Man, whose flock she joins, awakens contradictory emotions in her which border on the masochistic. Later on, when Dinah is told of the possibility of leaving Jamaica for England in the company of the Shepherd Man, Patterson injects a philosophical debate on the nature of desire and consciousness.

> She was ever more conscious of the happiness she should feel. But her very consciousness was the wind that blew away the soil on which the moment had planted . . . . She knew she could not experience it. She knew the very act of trying destroyed itself. (187–188)

Thus, this child of Sisyphus, Dinah, is never able to fully enjoy her deep experiences, to apprehend their true meaning. At the philosophical level, even at the level of enjoying material requisites, Patterson ascribes almost unreal ignorance, indeed total cultural deprivation to Dinah. He goes to just such an extreme:

> Her eyes suddenly caught sight of the eggs. They were such curious objects . . . . Fry them, yes. But not with this thick shell, the oil would never get into it. (189)

Clearly this note of deprivation attests to the incorporation of the harsh reality of the Dungle, its ordinance over the behavior of the Dungle dwellers.

The Dungle is metaphor, designating a social reality from which characters are unable to extricate themselves. The plot of *The Children of Sisyphus* revolves around the attempt of the various characters to extricate themselves from that threatening landscape: the Rastafarian brethren to leave the Dungle, to leave Babylon for Zion; Dinah to leave the Dungle in search of material and emotional well-being; Rosetta, the little brown daughter of Mary, in search of upward mobility brought about through education and through color. Rosetta is the only Dungle dweller who seems ready to leave; but is she ready because of her color or because class mobility can only come about through education?

> "What I mean is that Rosetta has to leave the Dungle. It's a miracle that she has achieved anything under the conditions she was brought up and with you leading the life which you have. She has to make a clean break. She needs a good home and a good Christian upbringing from now on if she is to achieve anything. The board has arranged for her adoption." (176)

Rosetta, like the narrator in *Miguel Street*, like George in *In the Castle of My Skin*, leaves her circumscribed surroundings, escapes the entrapment of the Dungle, achieves going away.

In the social ecology of all these works of fiction, the essential development of a social order seems unstructured, even unchartered. Yet the fortuitous mixing, the visceral touchings of the people living in crowded conditions seem to have produced their own unique communality. Even though the authors depict that emerging order as pathetic, they still locate and imbue a certain quality of vitality to that order.

To be sure, the condition of entrapment leads to many lost dreams, to many violent endings, as many characters run into "midnight madness." To be sure, too, the initial topography of many of these works of fiction undergoes a relentless breakup and disintegration, a disintegration often mirrored and reflected in the patchwork changes in the elements.

Yet ultimately through that inner dynamic quality resident in all social order, a transformative process, as in *Miguel Street* and *In the Castle of My Skin*, ushers the narrator/protagonists away from the confines of their social reality into the essential modality and condition of chapter 5—movement away and exile. A transformative process also intimates the breakup of an old colonial order, as in *In the Castle of My Skin,* and the beginning of new political institutions, a "new day."

Many of Mais's characters are violently released from their conditions of entrapment—some go mad, some die. Other characters, like Milton in *Amongst Thistles and Thorns,* seem to remain rooted in that condition of entrapment—his only recourse constant flight. Others like Rosetta in *Children of Sisyphus,* move away from the harsh reality into one that promises to offer less entrapment, more opportunity, more material ease. But the promise is open to question: the new social condition and circumstance may usher in a situation wherein race, class, color and sex may bring aloneness and alienation—an exchange of communal living for isolation. Will the characters who leave have to ponder, as did the boys in *In the Castle of My Skin?*

> "Tis good to dream," said Boy Blue, "but it ain't good to dream all the time . . . . There is something real in this kind o' dreaming."
>
> "It ain't good," said Trumper, "cause sometimes you get a kind o' nightmare like way we did feel now an' again when talk 'bout the loneliness." (Lamming, *In the Castle*, 53)

CHAPTER 4

The Fragmented Reality: The Separated People

Sprightly little black boy
Playing by the shore,
Mild of eyes, and laughing
By the white surf's roar.

Hello, little black boy,
Heaping sand on sands;
What may you be doing
With so small dark hands?

Laughing little black boy.
Answer me will you?
"Building castles surely
As other boys do."

Ah, sweet little black boy
Playing by the shore,
As the ships are passing
Through the dark sea's door.

Harold M. Telemaque, "Little Black Boy,"
Anthology of West Indian Poetry

. . .

I take again my nigger life, my scorn
and fling it in the face of those who hate me.
It is me the nigger boy turning to manhood
linking my fingers, welding my flesh to freedom.

I come from the nigger yard of yesterday
leaping from the oppressor's hate
and the scorn of myself.
I come to the world with scars upon my soul
wounds on my body, fury in my hands.

. . .

Martin Carter, "I Come From the Nigger Yard,"
Poems of Succession

"**X**avier! I spoke to you!"

"To hell wid you!"

It went through the office like a prong of lightning. Mr. Jagabir dropped his pen with a soft clatter on the blotter.

By the safe, Mr. Murrain, putting on his coat, paused and turned.

Miss Yen Tip glanced at Mr. Benson to make sure that the scowl on his face was directed at Horace and not at her.

"To hell wid all o' you!"

Horace was on his feet. He kept looking about him in jerks.

Mr. Reynolds perspired.

"Because I black? You-all not better dan me!"

The door to the Ladies' Room opened a trifle.

Horace strode through the barrier-gate with a crash. He was at Mrs. Hinckson's desk in three strides.

Mr. Jagabir half-rose from his chair.

Horace snatched the paper from the File tray.

"Boy! You gone off you' head!" shouted Mr. Jagabir . . . .

He was trembling all over.

"You hear me? It's mine! Nobody can stop me from taking it!"

He went toward the barrier-gate at a half-run.

(Mittelholzer, *A Morning at the Office*, 244–245)

This scene from the social documentary novel, *A Morning at the Office*, climaxes the principal plot of the novel—bringing together many of its motifs. It is a scene charged with all the elements of the persistent themes and the intricate inner workings of racial conflict. Here, Horace Xavier, the Black office boy, ascribing racial overtones to the office's reaction to a love poem which he has sent to Mrs. Hinckson, indicts the office personnel. It is an office which, though not segregated, is completely compartmentalized along the varied lines of class and race, fragmented along inflexible stereotyped classifications.

Horace's dramatic, if somewhat hysterical exit through the gate, though not in itself a transformative gesture, has in it suggestions of a liberating action. For this gate is also the barrier that has separated him, a Black office boy-messenger, from the rest of the office. Indeed, the gate is not simply a physical divider, but has also been a visual and social indicator separating him from the rising hierarchy of the office. He takes his exit from this stage, wherein all the actors are held as in a frieze, rigid in stereotypic social and class positions. They manifest diverse ethnic and class roles enshrined in the society of Trinidad and Tobago during the 1940s, roles that in many cases still ordain behavior.

Clearly, Mittelholzer uses linear space to show the racial, class, and color patternings of the society of that period. Thus, the young, ambitious Black boy is closest to the commotion of the street: he is, as it were, on the outside. Behind him, in a linear progression according to the color of skin, the texture of the hair, all the way back to the "frosty glass door" behind which the white manager Mr. Waley sits, appear all the many players acting out their own societal stereotypical roles, displaying their personal idiosyncrasies and ambitions. Like actors who have been given a fixed, unvarying role, their lives crisscross but never blend together. For in *A Morning At the Office*, the personal, the idiosyncratic, the particular of each character seem to be subsumed in societal expectations, rigidly controlling the perceptions of all the actors. Yet, though the personal is subsumed in the societal, the societal has not cohered into the communal by bringing all the modulations of class, all the tonalities of race, together in one amalgam. Mittelholzer captures not only the singular undertones, but indeed the deeper resonances echoing and rumbling throughout the society, using what resembles stage techniques, as so many Caribbean authors do.

The same barrier that serves as stage exit for Horace serves as a very different entrance for white Mr. Murrain's wife, and the contrast effectively dramatizes both the attitudinal underpinnings based on race, and the unmasking of white stereotypic behavior.

> Without a glance at Horace, without a word of greeting to anyone, Mrs. Murrain walked into the office and headed for her husband's desk. . . .
>
> "Where's Mr. Murrain?"
>
> Miss Henery went on typing as though deaf. Deaf and blind.
>
> Mrs. Murrain, tallish, thin, pretty in an English, narrow-faced way, not very well dressed, repeated the question—this time sharply.
>
> Miss Henery typed on. Her mouth tightened, her eyes grew steely.
>
> "You!" Mrs. Murrain pointed at Miss Henery . . . . [who] stopped typing and looked up. "When you learn manners," she said, "I'll listen to what you're saying. Not before." She went on typing.
>
> Mrs. Murrain's eyes and complexion reacted perhaps less expressibly than the stiffening of her body.
>
> "Do you know who you're speaking to?"
>
> "I'm perfectly aware whom I'm speaking to." (Cheap, thought Miss Henery, but I couldn't resist putting her right on her King's English.)
>
> "You're impertinent!"
>
> "You're disturbing me at my work!"
>
> Mr. Jagabir's hands were clasped together tight. His eyes were the eyes of a man hypnotized.

Miss Yen Tip was silently convulsed—a convulsion of delight and approval.

Mr. Benson muttered, "Good. Good," with anguished approval. His eyes glittered. "The unmannerly white pig!" (143–144)

The whole office witnesses these actions, and the reactions and comments of each member of the office staff become deft barometers of the prevailing climate affecting all their lives, indeed, represent larger societal reactions.

Mittelholzer, by showing the reactions of the various members of the audience to the encounter between Miss Henery and Mrs. Murrain, sheds light not only on the seething dislike of whites by some local coloreds, but also on the expression of an indigenous sense of independence. In a similar fashion, the reactions of the various office members to an act of political protest reveal the relationship between the local and the foreign perceptions of political and economic enfranchisement, emphasizing further the preferences of particular class, color, and racial groups. Mr. Benson's reaction, though prompted by an attempt to efface his cringing subservience to the white manager's wife, underscores the growing indigenous awareness of the exploitative colonial presence, the quest for ultimate political independence.

A Morning at the Office is more than a presentation of class conflict. In it Mittelholzer introduces that visceral, upsurging quest by the workers for social justice, equality, and indeed independence from that colonial rulership to which they ascribe their poor working conditions, their basic oppression. For the novel takes place at a time of increasing strikes and demonstrations by newly formed unions seeking their own enfranchisement and, by extension, the political enfranchisement of the whole colony.

Such political demonstrations focused not only on winning political and economic freedom from colonial domination but also addressed the question of the formation of a federated Caribbean unit. The banners carried by the workers, as Mittelholzer describes them, also indict the small ruling elite, and the few dominated, though elected, local representatives as well, portrayed as stooges in connivance with the colonial authorities. The demonstrators are almost entirely Negroes and East Indians, with Negroes in the majority.

Clearly, however, the urgency in the streets seems to barely affect the atmosphere within the structured hierarchy of the office, as evidenced in Mr. Waley's discussion with Mrs. Hinckson. She, though basically in favor of the demonstration, still seems removed from the concerns that prompted it, and does not viscerally relate but objectively debates its relevance. The subsequent discussion of the pros and cons of the nationalization of the oil industry, of the nature and use of the profit from that industry, and of the foreign presence underscores race relations in *A Morning* and their central point of derivation: the white colonial presence.

There is little novelistic tension or drama in the long palaver between Mrs. Hinckson and Mr. Waley. So "civilized" is the discussion that the urgent need for political and economic transformation which would usher in local control and independence is reduced to casual debate.

> "Do you agree with the sentiments the banners express?"
>
> "Not with all of them—but one or two said things I'm definitely in favour of . . . . nationalizing our oil industry."
>
> ". . . You're really in favour of nationalizing the oil industry?"
>
> "Most certainly! Don't you think it a scandal that millions of our dollars should go . . . [to] England and America every year while . . . we get next to nothing?"
>
> "Next to nothing! Do you know how much royalty the Government collects?"
>
> "How much! Not half as much as they should." (185)

Clearly here, as in so many scenes, the novel takes on a discursive tone in which novelistic plotting gives way to social discourse and commentary. So it is that the set design of *A Morning* is not only constructed with racial, class, and color frames, but held together by political and religious constructs—indeed, all the myriad societal underpinnings of that period come into play. And though subplots tell of personal histories, the novel *A Morning* is really the elaborate presentation of the social history of Trinidad and Tobago—and to some extent, of the entire Caribbean before independence: Here, races and all the blendings of race; here, miscegenation and all the results of miscegenation; here, too, illegitimacy and all of its pervasiveness—all blend together, a warped, intricate societal mosaic. Mittelholzer stresses in his character development the controlling pull of blood, the tug of memory, seeming to ascribe an immutability to the social condition. Mr. Benson thinks Horace is "efficient and alert; no fool." But while, "That nigger would get on," Mr. Benson believes, "socially he will never get far, that black skin will always hold him back." Horace's own personality seems to be totally controlled by a fear of olive skin, which lurks just behind the walls of his black skin, because of a gang attack on him several years earlier. Horace's ambition, the conduit for any social mobility, makes him attempt to educate himself by reading Shakespeare, but his perception of color and class remains unchanged. He continues to admire girls with "loose hanging dark hair . . . genuine white-people hair; not kinky hair straightened with a hot comb like Miss Henery's" (50). And others' perceptions of him are determined by his Blackness and his "social position." He remains Horace, the office-boy. He will never be able to mix with those of wavy hair and light complexion, those who are said to come from privileged, educated, genteel backgrounds.

Believing his color and class to be ill-fated gifts from an unkind destiny, he challenges that destiny to attempt to mediate those gifts.

> He breathed deeply, and told himself that nothing would thwart him. He would smash his way through and beat Destiny. Beat God Himself and Jesus and the Virgin Mary if they tried to hinder him from getting what he wanted out of life. (50)

Mr. Benson, too, "three parts negro," is destined to be self-deprecatory, a petulant misanthrope with a continuous racial hatred.

"He hated negroes, but white people he hated twice as much" (146), and "He hated coolies as much as he hated niggers" (161). Further, he seems unable to resist what Mittelholzer portrays as a genetic inheritance.

> The day when he had stolen a sixpence from the dinner-wagon to buy half-share in a sweepstake ticket, she had screamed at him between blows: "You can't help stealing! It's de bad blood what your mother put in you! It must come out one day!" (167)

Historical circumstances or past personal preferences keep influencing present behavior; thus most characters are charged with a sense of historical causation. Mr. Jagabir is unable to free himself from the constant fear of being sent back to work on an estate, a condition that once controlled the lives of many East Indian indentured laborers. Consequently, he reacts with ingratiating subservience and manipulative deference. Indeed, he slyly takes in everything that occurs in the office, to assure his controlled participation and to secure his position.

Mrs. Hinckson's stated sexual history of attracting writers, intellectuals, artists, now undergoes a change; she yearns for an animal type. She attracts many of the male workers in the office. Horace has written her a love note, thus providing one of the main plots of the novel. Mr. Lopez dreams of having intercourse with her: "Lucky fellow if he's sleeping with her . . . . He conjured up a breath-taking picture of himself in bed with Mrs. Hinckson" (235). Mr. Lorry intends to, and is certain of seducing her. Mr. Lorry's confidence, indeed his very attractiveness derive from societally stereotypic perceptions of what is attractive. Though "he [is] not particularly handsome . . . no girl ever refused him a date." Like Mrs. Hinckson, his sex life is the dominant and controlling feature of his characterization.

In this tableau where race and class and color and sex are operative and effective conditions, ordaining attitudes and behavior, controlling and guiding the actions of characters, there is little cohering of different groupings of people. Still evident is all the discontinuity particular to the separation of

races, classes, and peoples. Thus it is that in *A Morning at the Office*, Mittelholzer's characterization is on two separate yet integrated levels, the one
societal, the other more personal. These two levels crisscross and converge
at one and the same time, setting the characters into a type mold even while
particularizing them. In all of this, one of the more sensitive characters is
Mrs. Bisnauth, who attempts not to stereotype, to characterize her colleagues
without understanding their situations. She tries to move beyond stereotypic
conditions, to move beyond the barriers of race and class. Her Hindu parents
had adopted all the trappings of Western society but they still reflected all
the ambiguities of race and class. Though Hindu, the parents do not speak
Hindi, have become Christianized, and have assumed behavior as exemplified and practiced in the India Club.

> Hinduism had ceased with their grandparents, the sugar estate coolies—
> but they were still clannish; it was as though this trait had continued . . .
> from the seed of their forebears so that whenever there came a decision
> that involved a mixing of racial strains it rose to the surface. (78)

This notion of separation structures the plots of many of the novels of this
chapter, qualifying the actions, the attitudes of the characters as they move
through different societal realities; societies that as yet have not cohered.
Many experience, as with Cynthia in *Crick Crack, Monkey*, a feeling of
alienation.

In *Crick Crack, Monkey*, Merle Hodge deftly exposes the absurdities
inherent in the acceptance of English morals and attitudes and the
adoption of English culture. She pinpoints the basic inanity of their use by
supercilious, pretentious, native Trinidadians and by members of an evolving
Trinidadian society. Such behavioral absurdities receive full elaboration
through a series of personal confrontations, shifting episodes and occurrences,
replete with rollicking comic overtones, animated by tragic/comic undercurrents relative to cultural deprecation, cultural mimicry. By overtly contrasting
the rural folk, the oral flair of their indigenous reactions and morals, with
stilted, unnatural adopted attitudes of the urban middle class, Hodge
highlights the cultural differences, underscoring the absurd behavior of the
latter group and its attempts to transplant English habits onto the local
landscape. Her contrast of the foreign mores with the internal indigenous
ones illustrates two contrasting modes of societal perception, and Hodge
makes quite clear her non-elastic preference, expresses her rejection of those
attitudes that reflect a continuing neo-colonial cultural condition. The society
of *Crick Crack, Monkey*, like the one of *A Morning at the Office*, has not yet
achieved a sense of itself, has not yet cohered.

The main protagonist of *Crick Crack, Monkey*, Cynthia, bridges two inherently differing social realities—a poor unsophisticated urban community where she intially lives with Tantie, and an affectedly sophisticated urban middle-class community where she subsequently goes to live with Auntie Beatrice. Through the development of Cynthia's character, Merle Hodge uses every opportunity to pinpoint the contrast between the two communities, a contrast heightened by the snobbery, the classism saturating them and negating social harmony, social and communal cohesion.

Through the eyes of Cynthia, a participant observer, we see the unfolding of one of these communities, a rowdy and vital neighborhood. Through this neighborhood Tantie's voice trumpets, vibrant with all the visceral colorings, seasoned and richly spiced with all the flavorings inherent to that vernacular and idiom particular to *buseing* in Trinidad. We join Cynthia's tentative meanderings through a maze of irrelevant educational and religious experiences in A.B.C. Kindergarten, primary school classes, and Sunday school.

> I was given a place among the chanting which went on and on and became more and more disorderly as more voices either dropped out, chanted at half a second's interval after the confident voices or simply became a drone, keeping in time with the rhythm. Mrs. Hinds embroidered. After some time, at around the seven-times table it must have been there were only about four tenuous voices articulating anything, the rest were rhythmic drone . . . . When the noise came to a complete halt Mrs. Hinds said, "All right, recess," and I nearly fell off my end of the bench as all my colleagues rose abruptly. (Hodge, *Crick Crack, Monkey*, 37)

In such scenes, we are presented with the figures of teachers, of ministers, and their pedagogical idiosyncracies. They stand in sharp contrast to the rural figure of Ma, with all her indigenous folk savvy, her oral presence. Running with Cynthia and her country cousins during their school holidays, we are introduced to and enter into the folk orality of rural Trinidad. How Cynthia pleasurably receives the teachings of her rural grandmother contrasts sharply with the mood and her attitude at school. In a delightfully etched scene, Merle Hodge presents the mood-space wherein folk wisdom is transmitted through the folk tale. Clearly it is from this scene that the author derives the title of her novel.

> At full moon there was a bonus and then we would light a black-sage fire for the mosquitoes and sand-flies and the smoke smelt like contented drowsiness. And, when at the end of the story she said, "Crick-Crack?" our voices clambered over one another in the gleeful haste to chorus back in what ended in an untidy shrieking crescendo:
> "Monkey break 'e back

On a rotten pommerac!" (25)

Here the comfortable drowsiness bursts into a gleeful chorus, contrasting sharply with the abrupt ending to the school scene that "nearly makes [her] fall off the seat."

Ma, who we see in all of her native wisdom, her firmness, her warmth and affection, is a figure of strength, of assurance, of abiding continuity. Both Ma, stern yet gentle, and Tantie, rowdy but equally gentle, represent an indigenous rootedness which initially cushions Cynthia's growth. The novel's trajectory describes Cynthia's movement away from this rootedness, her going to live with another family member, Auntie Beatrice, an affected, lonely woman in an alienating and sterile space.

After winning her scholarship to a secondary school, Cynthia moves away from that natural warmth and assurance to an uncertainty, a sense of not belonging, steadily disassociating her from the earlier world of storytelling, of belief, of wonder. Life in the unnatural household of Auntie Beatrice, her exposure to class prejudice and snobbery at her new school, at church, at home, at social functions, all bring on confusion and loneliness. No longer does she feel the vital throb of the street where she grew up and where Tantie held sway. Cynthia's moving between these two contrasting social realities, between two contrasting lived circumstances, gives an elasticity and a spatial tension to the novel.

The beginning of the novel introduces to us the voices of the street where Tantie lives, voices that are raucous but tinged with the underlying humor of the Trinidadian idiom. The scene is typical of the grassroots urban condition—a condition Merle Hodge sensitively represents through its inner rhythms and incessant undertones, capturing all the plasticity of meaning, the mobility of speech and behavior.

> Then I heard singing and knew it was only Miss Terry taking—dragging—Mr. Christopher home again, Mr. Christopher being stone drunk and singing at the top of his voice, "Gimme piece o' yu dumpling Mae dou-dou!" We crouched down instinctively . . . . many a youngster had had his tongue washed with household soap for launching into the refrain of "Gimme piece o' yu dumpling Mae dou-dou!" (8)

Tantie's language and behavior resonate with all the plasticity, the piquant bawdiness, the drama inherent in that urban condition. When her nephew Mikey tells her that he is going to New York she explodes.

> "But what the arse it is you have to do up there, what the shit up there have to do wid you? . . .
>   . . . any damn place yu is yu does have to haul yu arse out the bed when the mornin' come; yu vest does ha' to wash yu ears does get wax

an' if yu ain' shit yu belly does hurt yu. Me ain' know if yu think yu does come different like if yu cross-over the blasted Jordan or what." (94)

Her constant wrangling and quarrelling with Mikey are not seeded in bitterness, though, but seem to derive from her own character, her sharp, quick responses to any and every situation. Perhaps one of the most touching scenes in the novel is played out by Tantie after Mikey has defended her honor from his street companions. Mikey has engaged in a fight with Audie Murphy, and this news is breathlessly related to Tantie.

> We ran up the path as fast as our legs could carry us. Tantie had come home and excitedly we delivered our account of the baffling affair.
>
> It was when Tantie's features began to knot themselves hard together that I remembered with a plunge of dismay that we should never tell her that we had been down at the bridge. But it was too late . . . .
>
> . . . She moved about the house in silence, setting the table, going to the window every few minutes and peering up the dark road. . . .
>
> . . . Mikey was surely coming home to his execution this time.
>
> When we heard his step in the gallery my heart and my stomach exchanged places. Mikey slouched in . . . .
>
> "Water in the bedroom, Mikey," was all she said. And then she hurried into the kitchen to heat up the cocoa. And when the sound of water could no longer be heard in Mikey's room, she called to him in what seemed to me a reverent voice: "The tea on the table, Mikey." (18)

Tantie's reaction is surprising to the young girl, Cynthia, but in truth hardly surprising at all if one accepts the inherent good nature that lurks behind the sharp and biting tongue. This good nature is again cleverly revealed in her dealings with the Chinaman shopkeeper, Ling, so typical a figure in most Trinidadian neighborhoods. *Crick Crack, Monkey* introduces so many of the characters that mirror and create that incessant mobility of local color within the burgeoning indigenous society of Trinidad and Tobago. The interplay between Ling and Tantie is in itself a drama so typical, so prevalent in all levels of Trinidadian interpersonal relations.

After Tantie breaks her tooth on a pebble buried in a slice of cake she returns to the Chinaman's shop:

> Tantie grimly untwisted the paper bag and turned it upside down on the counter. . . .
>
> "What yu t'ink o' all that, Ling?" she inquired. . . .
>
> "How yu mean, Miss Lrosa?" asked Ling, his eyes darting nervously from the display on the counter to Tantie's face . . . .
>
> "Awright, awright, wha' 'bout mih teet' way fall out?" . . .

> . . . When we went back to Ling it was the Friday night after Uncle
> Herman had sent Tantie to get her gold tooth put in. Tantie was in the
> best of humour, flashing smiles all around.
>   "Ah! Miss Lrosa! So yu come back from the country!" beamed Ling,
> with his eyes creased with joy.
>   "Yes, man," said Tantie; then leaning across the counter she confided
> to him in a thunderous whisper: "You' pig-tail sweeter!" (61–63)

Merle Hodge captures, too, the effervescence and vitality of the street boys
through images of figures borrowed from and mimicking Hollywood movies,
which gives an immediacy to the social reality she delineates. So much of
this interplay becomes theater, street theater at its best.

> There was one memorable time when Mikey took us along to the
> bridge. When we arrived a discussion was in full swing. Lamp-post was
> enthusing.
>   "Western in yu arse, boy, Western in yu arse!" and Joe was recreating
> the climax with a lively pantomime; "'ey boy, forty-million o' them
> against the star-boy and the rest o' them ridin comin then he bullets run
> out . . . ."
>   "An' then the other guys reach, an then, ol'-man, then yu jus' see
> Red-Indian fallin dong all over the place—ba-da-da-da-da—pretty, boy,
> pretty!" mused Krishna. (16)

Yet clearly Hodge fails to indict their mimicking, their showy borrowings
from Hollywood.

Her sensitive rendering of the interplay between the street boys and the
teacher, Miss Hinds, shows her social preferences; for the figure of the
teacher, like others who parrot the British colonial manners, receives no
sympathetic treatment, is caricatured, becoming cartoon.

> Like any proper lady (it seemed to me) she had a high, stiff, bottom and
> spectacles and stockings. . . .
>   "Mind the buses and them, too, Mis' Hinds, yu might overbalance
> with all that weight in front there," in a sing-song lady-voice.
>   "How she go overbalance," contested another with irritation, "that is
> what the bottom there for! Yu never hear 'bout ballast or what?"
>   And Mrs. Hinds would turn and lecture them with the most careful
> enunciation on the moral evils of vagabondage, a lecture which the boys
> punctuated copiously with dramatic sighs of "Oh yes, Lord!" and "True-
> spoke, sister, Amen!" and "Glory, glory be!" (16)

The religious and the academic education to which Cynthia is exposed—
and which typifies so much of the schooling still received by the vast

majority of Caribbean people—is farcically depicted by Merle Hodge. Cleverly and wittily she reveals the parroting of foreign cultural symbols which marks so much of the education imparted to formerly colonized peoples.

She reveals all the perniciousness of borrowed cultural symbols with their inherent racism, all of their irrelevance to the native culture, as she shows the school girls' song:

> Til I cross the wide water, Lord
> My black skin washed from me
> Til I come to Glory Glory, Lord
> And cleansed stand beside thee,
> White and shining stand beside thee Lord,
> Among thy blessed children. (46)

But it is the very mimicking of foreign culture that determines the movements, aspirations, and attitudes of Auntie Beatrice, and that are virtually palpable in her household and in the social circles through which she flits.

Unsympathetically and indeed with a certain ruthlessness, Merle Hodge draws the character of Auntie Beatrice with flat, dull, passionless colors. Her responses, her language, are rooted in affectation, replete with a predictable snobbishness, to such a degree that her character becomes one dimensional. Essentially Auntie Beatrice is a lonely woman, not particularly liked by her two brattish daughters, who demonstrate little affection for her. Neither does she receive affection nor any measure of sympathetic intercourse with her passionless husband. There is no vibrant energy flow or stimulation from her husband. These emotional relationships receive little in-depth elaboration, are illustrated without giving resonance to Auntie Beatrice's characterization. Even in the scenes where her emotional isolation is clearest, Merle Hodge fails to give resonance or any novelistic sympathy to this essential pathos. In all her dealings, Auntie Beatrice stands as a figure of ridicule, rejected through her vulgar classism and inane snobbery. Perhaps nowhere is this more clearly represented than in the following scene, where the absurd flights of fancy are deftly represented in the uncoordinated body movements in a pretentiously elitist dance class.

> "Afternoon Miss de Vertueil, how are you."
> But Miss de Vertueil was talking again, her back half turned to us. Auntie Beatrice cleared her throat.   "I have my little niece with me," she said somewhat apologetically. Miss de Vertueil had now taken hold of a nearby child and was twisting its arm and neck here and there like dough. . . .
> "I was wondering if you could try her out for the troupe" . . . .

"All right, we'll give her a rhythm test," said Miss de Vertueil absent-
ly. . . .

"Go, on, dear," Auntie Beatrice was urging worriedly, "dance!"

. . . What both Miss de Vertueil and Auntie Beatrice meant was that
I should promenade about with my feet twisted at unlikely angles, waving
my arms about and occasionally reaching towards the ceiling, and this I
was permitted to do at any tempo I pleased, for obviously the music was
not of any relevance to the proceedings. (107–108)

In scenes like this, the novel *Crick Crack, Monkey* becomes a serious
indictment of snobbery, the affectation, the elitism, riddling the social fabric
of the Caribbean, which make for a dysfunctional, disassociated social reality.
The rejection that Beatrice suffers in the preceding scene Cynthia, too,
experiences upon entering school, where the same girls are selected for the
"choir," the "Dramatic Society," and the "tennis courts," selections that
seem to have little to do with talent.

Even as she details them, Cynthia rejects all the normative qualifica-
tions—participation in ballet, the singing group—which are made to attest
to class, to aristocratic upper-class behavior. So pervasive, so widespread and
deleterious are the mimickings of the colonizing habits, attitudes, and
prejudices, that even in the church and religious observances they are
embodied, sanctified.

> At school I was taking in the catechism pages at a time, and Auntie
> Beatrice said I was to be christened into the Catholic Church. But for the
> moment crossing myself and genuflecting and bowing and kneeling and
> rising and sitting at the appointed cues while keeping track of the stream
> of murmuring which I was assured was printed in the little book I held
> in front of me, presented a challenge of the most terrifying order. (113)

Thus it is that Cynthia's going away from the bawdy security and warmth
of Tantie's household and of the community takes her to a new space,
unnatural, lacking in spontaneous warmth and generosity. She moves into
educational and social institutions steeped in snobbery and pretentiousness,
stuffy with affectation. In her aloneness, Auntie Beatrice attempts to draw
on Cynthia's company for a measure of companionship and warmth, at times,
in effect, as a shield from her children's brattishness, from her husband's
disregard. She puts her arm around Cynthia as much to "protect herself from
the madness all around" (105) as to console her. But, essentially Cynthia's
life with Auntie Beatrice, though materially easier, is lonely.

> On that first night it was comforting that Auntie Beatrice firmly
> patrolled the two rooms where we got ready for bed. And when we were

in bed and she kissed me on my forehead I could not wait until she was
out of the room before I rolled over and buried my face in the pillow.
    It was the first time in my life, too, that I was to sleep in a bed all by
myself. (106)

In her aloneness, Cynthia gradually moves from a nostalgic desire for the
warm and raw living of the neighborhood that she left, into a groping for
acceptance by those who continuously snub her. Her process of going away
from the first warm certainty of her childhood is manifested through her
incipient rejection of the behavior and the enjoyable memories of her youth.
She's disgusted by the presence and display of food that she formerly
enjoyed, indeed by the presence of her family and friends.

Her memories of Carnival become distasteful to her as she slowly,
irrevocably moves toward the coldness, the sophistication of the figures and
institutions of the so-called upper class.

> Carnival came, and I discovered that I did not even want to go home
> for Carnival. We went to the stands on both days, where we sat primly
> and watched the bands in the company of the tourists . . . .
>   And sitting wedged against an American tourist, he in a hot shirt of
> many colours, Bermuda shorts of many other colours and a broad panama
> hat with a polka dot band, we in our sober and tasteful jeans and jerseys,
> I remembered in a flash of embarrassment Ramlaal's inelegant truck into
> which we used to pile with a herd of neighbors and neighbors' children
> for the trip to Coriaca to see Carnival there. . . .
>   All this I was seeing again through a kind of haze of shame; and I
> reflected that even now Tantie and Toddan must be packed into that
> ridiculous truck with all those common raucous niggery people and all
> those coolies. (123–125)

Her values and her perception of her social reality undergo a change that
perhaps will continue by her going away to England. The very idea of
abroadness seems to give validity to Cynthia's existence, in Beatrice's
household at St. Anns, in the social arenas in which Beatrice moves, and to
which she aspires.

> Auntie Beatrice threw a party for me and invited all the nice people's
> children she could think of, so that the news got safely around to all the
> nice people. She took me shopping for clothes and managed to communi-
> cate to every shop-clerk that this was her little niece who was going to
> England so we were just getting a few things together, you know. (141)

The theme of going away seems to inhabit the dreams and clarify the
aspirations even of the so-called upper class. The motif of going away, the

prestige of abroadness deriving from the patterning of attitudes and behavior on foreign models, becomes recurrent, and evolves into the theme for the novels of exile. The very title of the novel, *Crick Crack, Monkey*, is the author's response to this recurrent notion of abroadness: this folk idiom— which Hodge employs in ways that often clash with her own novelistic explanation and analysis—symbolizes her attempt to contrast indigenous with foreign formulations of existence.

L ike *Crick Crack, Monkey*, *The Year in San Fernando* has as its narrator- protagonist a young person, Francis, who presents his impressions and evaluations of two distinct disassociated realities: the first, his life in his poor home in a rural seaside village, Mayaro; the second, his new and often complicated life in an overtly comfortable middle-class house in the town of San Fernando. The raison d'etre of the novel becomes the essential contra- diction between material form and inner spirit: Francis leaves the warmth, the family togetherness of a materially poor home to live for a year in a materially comfortable house split apart by a never-ending feud between a mother, Mrs. Chandlis, and her son, Mr. Chandlis. The ensuing quarrels between mother and son, as narrated by Francis, become central to the novel's action, providing it with a modicum of suspense as Francis attempts to unearth the reason for that conflict.

However, *The Year in San Fernando* is a simple, uncomplicated narrative neither deeply analytic nor charged with suspense. It revolves around the daily activities of the young boy—at dawn, at midday, at nightfall; its themes center on his learning about the town, San Fernando, his entry into and his growing awareness of a new social reality. In linear progression, Francis moves toward new vistas, fresh experiences, which occasion expressions of aloneness and self-pity, punctuated by incomprehension and a yearning for home. Nostalgia and homesickness highlight, indeed emphasize, the contrast between the two homes, the two realities.

On an invitation from Mr. Chandlis to serve as help and companion to his aging mother in San Fernando, Francis reluctantly agrees to going away from his mother, sister, and two brothers. Francis's mother considers the offer a fine opportunity, for she in her impoverished condition is struggling to raise four children. Immediately we are introduced to notions of class, its outward trappings, its pretensions, its more subsurface goings-on. Moving from the warm security of home to the impersonality of the Chandlis house, Francis comes up against the reality behind appearance.

Mr. Chandlis's outward appearance, his vested suit in the warm weather, is taken as indicating his having class; his condescending attitude as reflect- ing an aristocratic leaning. His initial request that Francis become the companion and servant to his mother in far off San Fernando, though opening up a possibility of Francis's receiving both training and remuneration from that household, is not really examined by Francis's mother, but rather is welcomed by her with immediate excitement. Francis is going to live with people of class, with superior people.

So excited is Francis's mother at the prospect of her son interacting with these people of class that she indecorously slips under the wire fence separating Mr. Chandlis's building from her family's poor dwelling, a fence that spatially demarcates the class distinction:

> She hurried down the steps and made for the forestry office.
>
> Again, she did not go out into the road and enter the building from the front, but instead she ran towards the tiger-wire fence and held the spiky wires apart and eased through, then disappeared towards the back of the building. (Anthony, *The Year in San Fernando*, 12)

Of importance here is not the acceptance of the offer, but rather, the way in which the offer is received. The mother's expectations are fraught with all the absurd notions of what constitutes class, the unquestioning acceptance of what passes for aristrocratic behavior. So circumscribed are the possibilities of social and material mobility open to Francis and his family that they pay an excessively admiring regard to Mr. Chandlis's show of class, to his seeming prosperity. Thus, Francis moves from his small seaside village, Mayaro, to San Fernando, as did Cynthia in *Crick Crack, Monkey*, not in search of heroic adventure, but rather with expectations of living with class. Although Michael Anthony's novelistic intention may not be to articulate an analysis of class snobbishness, perhaps implicitly Anthony underscores that pernicious classism so damaging to social cohesion, so negating of the self.

The journey from Mayaro to San Fernando, a journey reminiscent of many journeys of "going away" from rural conditions to urban realities, affords Anthony the opportunity to contrast the living conditions and styles of Mayaro and the town. In the bus, Francis begins to reject his buddy, the conductor, Balgobin. Francis is silent and confused by the speed of transition, blinded by the lights and activity into which he is rushing, amazed at the hubbub of the town.

> Here was an even giddier world than Rio Claro. Outside, lights twinkled like candle-flies. Cars, bicycles, people, rushed about. Here, life was not settling down for the night. Life was teeming . . . . The noises rose and fell and the feeling was very similiar to what it was when you were on Mayaro beach in the night. (17)

That he compares the rise and fall of the noise in the town to the sound accompanying the rise and fall of the waves shows that his images still derive from his rural village life. Continuously throughout, when confronted by rejection or assailed by feelings of loneliness and consequent nostalgia, images from his rural life are imprinted on the immediate reality of his year in San Fernando. This recall not only offers solace, a way of cushioning any oppressive present conditions, but indeed, nostalgic recollection becomes a recurrent motif, an often-employed novelistic construct for many Caribbean novels which treat the theme of going away, or running away, the theme of exile.

The material comforts of the Chandlis house are negated by the emotional tension which inhabits it. The quarrels between mother and son, bitter and unrelenting, make for tense living conditions, especially when Francis becomes a scapegoat for the anger and hostility of mother or son. Initially, Francis doesn't even enjoy the material comfort of the house, for ungenerously Mrs. Chandlis offers him a bundle of paper and old clothing for a bed. From this bed and later from the refuge he finds under the house, he views the many to-and-fro movements of Mr. Chandlis, whose departures he always greets with relief.

Yet, Francis slowly begins to identify with the household, feeling ashamed when a particulary explosive quarrel takes place between mother and son on Good Friday.

> I lay there listening. I had never heard them quarrel so fiercely before. I wondered if the neighbors were listening. Mrs. Chandlis sounded like the screeching of some wild bird, and Mr. Chandlis, in his anger was loud and booming, and you could almost feel the house shake when he talked .... It was Good Friday morning and most people were rising to go to church. I felt we were a disgrace to Romaine Street. (68–69)

The "we" of his observation reveals his identification with the house's occupants. Clearly also, he begins to identify with Mrs. Chandlis, anticipating her behavior, her bouts of stinginess, her infrequent displays of generosity. With Mrs. Chandlis, he begins to share his adventures in the school which he has begun to attend. In order to please her and to ward off abuse, he quickly learns how to buy the goods she likes, often taking pleasure in her own pleasurable responses. Learning the market, learning the town, making friends, all contribute to his growth to awareness, to his settling into his life in San Fernando. After six months, Mrs. Chandlis declares, "You is nearly a San Fernando boy now!" (98). Not only has Francis learned to manipulate the situation, but he becomes more and more aware of the natural landscape of San Fernando in all of its varying moods. Whereas formerly his image references of landscape derived from Mayaro, now he seems to apprehend and capture images of the San Fernando setting. Thus it is that the visualization of San Fernando, the representation of its landscape, of its urban condition, all become foreground. Francis notes the passage of his days in

San Fernando through the changing foliage, the dryness of the soil, the watering of the flowers, whose habits he has learned. But now this is marked by a new element, the discovery and exploration of another landscape, that of the emotions.

> I would watch particularly, the anthuriums, for their thick leaves drooped right down as if they had lost hope, and so did the begonia leaves . . . .
> But with the evening's waterings they took strength again and a little freshness, and all of them prevailed against the sun. (106–107)

Now, beyond merely perceiving seasonal changes and growth, he also interprets them, injects them with his own sensibility. Now begins that active incorporation of the surrounding environment that precedes reacting to external stumuli. And thus it is that Francis starts to become aware of and to be attracted to Julia, Mr. Chandlis's girlfriend. This is but another stage and another manifestation of his growth process.

Mr. Chandlis's affair with Julia is but one of the reasons for the enmity between mother and son. The conflict between them, though bitter, does not preclude Mrs. Chandlis's performance of what she considers her maternal duties. Whereas before, Francis merely reported on Mrs. Chandlis's actions, now, as an indicator of growth, he begins to assess them.

> Mrs. Chandlis hurried about the kitchen and I knew she was trying to get Mr. Chandlis lunch quickly . . . I could not take my eyes off Mrs. Chandlis hobbling about. The truth was, she sickened me. It was hard to picture anyone more foot-kissing. (47)

With her other son, Edwin, however (and he may be another cause of the enmity between Mrs. Chandlis and her son), she is effusive and demonstrative, receiving from him a kind of assurance, a shield. Michael Anthony, through his narrator, Francis, sketches Edwin sympathetically, imbuing him with an easy, unaffected egalitarian attitude. Thus it is that Francis is not only assessing attitudes, but in a voice much more mature than his earlier one, he also begins to make distinctions between persons of the Chandlis household.

> I was looking outside but there was growing within me a strange, close feeling for him. It was coming home to me that at this late hour we were becoming friends . . . I could feel it strong and real . . . I wondered how come he felt he could talk to me like this and be friends with me. I knew he was no tyrant now and I was feeling easy with him. (176)

Francis's year in San Fernando provides him with certain psychological insights into behavior and character. He learns that appearance or class is not an indicator of a person's inner quality, that it does not necessarily dictate the morality or ethics of relationships. Yet returning home, Francis becomes aware of the impoverished life that his mother leads, of her hopes for her children's "making it," their material betterment. He sees more clearly, too, how that impoverished life brings on his mother's aging, graying her hair, creasing and wrinkling her smile.

The following three novels: *The Life and Death of Sylvia, The Games Were Coming,* and *Pan Beat,* enunciate the experiences of three young women and their emotional and social relationships principally to the male protagonists and other characters. In the novel, *The Life and Death of Sylvia,* Mittelholzer intimates that Sylvia's death results not from a personality flaw or a defect in character, but from aberrations of race, class and status. Indeed, she is a victim of a fragmented society, of a dislocating social process. The fragmentation, the dislocating inferences so evident in the social fabric affect Sylvia's very origins; they also influence the development of the relationship between her mother, Charlotte, and her father, Russell.

Charlotte, is not only portrayed as a lower-class Black woman, but as one who is poor in spirit, deficient in confidence, devoid of language. She has accepted the status into which she has been thrust by birth, accepting all of its negative qualities detrimental to growth, to self-assurance, to any measure of self-fulfillment. Not only is she segregated from Sylvia's father's circle, but she accepts the separation without questioning, without even attempting to intrude into it. Further, she ensures that her own friends do not come in contact with Russell: "in her cringing inferiority, [she] saw to it that Russell did not come home and find them in the house" (Mittelholzer, *The Life and Death of Sylvia,* 26). Within their very house, shut into a back room, she leads the life of an inferior being. Sprung from such a caste situation, it is not surprising that Sylvia shows more appreciation for her white father and instinctively turns toward her father's circle. Since Sylvia accepts her father's perception of a social order built on race and class, she does not—and clearly cannot—accept her mother's cringing personality, in essence, her mother's color. She "always sides with" (66) her father. On no level can she accept her Black mother and her "low class" behavior. Social stigmas deriving from color, class, and racial differences make Sylvia aware of these differences. The rejection of the Black mother is indeed the beginning of the movement toward Sylvia's self-denial, which ultimately marks self-destruction.

Initially, her father and his circle act as a shield and bolster for Sylvia against the evident aberrations of race and class crippling the Guyanese society of that period. Later when her father dies, Sylvia loses that shield and is exposed to the viciousness endemic to that society. Though her father initially reacted with a modicum of surprise at the social hierarchy, he never really attempted to change it in any way. In a long, explanatory statement,

Russell depicts the social aberrations, the ethnic fragmentations, indeed the economic compartmentalizations skewering the Guyanese society.

> Russell laughed. "I've never seen a more complicated social set-up. Such a tangled mass of cliques and clans and sub-cliques and sub-clans!
> . . .
> "Positively astounding how life goes on at all. There are the whites in an exclusive little corner of their own. Then the high-coloured coloured in various little compartments. . . . Take two steps aside and you're up against the East Indians in another cluster, with a hierarchy of their own ranging from rice miller to barrister-at-law and doctor and then down to busdriver, chauffeur, provision-shop-keeper and sugar-estate coolie . . . . My God! If it isn't bewildering!" (35)

By his advice and fatherly counsel, he not only points out the underlying inequalities withing the society, but seems to accept and instill into Sylvia such notions of inequality. Even as he tries to prepare her for the corrosive effects of social stigma deriving from race, class, and color, he participates in those constructs. He himself tells Sylvia her Black and Arawak mother caused the family not to be "rated as much," but reassures her that

> "If you can succeed in marrying a man of good family you'll be all right, because I'm white, an Englishman, and I'm no pauper. That will count heavily in your favour. Mother will be forgotten and overlooked in the general reckoning." (61)

Russell validates the foreign colonizing presence, and by taking his advice, Sylvia would be rejecting not only her Black mother, but also the indigenous part of herself. To be sure, a fragmentation would take place, but totally opposite to that which is necessary for the ultimate cohesion of the Caribbean society, its realization of its indigenous multiracial self. In order to achieve that indigenous self, what must be fragmented is the external colonizing and formerly colonized presence: what must come about is the casting away of any and all effective physical or moral remnants of that colonial presence, especially those parts which have brought about the degeneration, the dismemberment, of the indigenous.

Clearly, within the Caribbean, the notion of the fragmented personality in its essence makes for wholeness. At its most radical, it posits the negation of the foreign, in this instance, of the English, and any of their normative values implanted in Caribbean society that may be inimical to that society. Jack Sampson, one of the characters in *The Life and Death of Sylvia*, states forthrightly:

"We got to wake up. We still dazed. We still stupid. Look at you and your upper middle-class! All you-all strive to do is to be cultured and polished—cultured and polished like de English. I don't say culture and refinement isn't a good thing. But de English people clever. They encourage you-all coloured people to be cultured and refined like dem! Because . . . de more loyal you will be to the British throne! Yes! . . . Dat's why it will be hard for us in dis West Indies zone to be independent." (175)

Sylvia's father Russell is caught in this web of ambiguity and often reacts ambivalently to the social order. Sylvia, on her part, also becomes aware of the absurdities, the pretentiousness within the fragmented social order. And even with her father as shield and protector, she suffers the rejection consequent on her class, her color. She is unable to enter the convent school, to which the lighter-skinned young girls from well-established families have unquestioned access. "No, you couldn't go there. Your complexion is just a trifle on the wrong side," her father tells her. (39) Indeed, this representation of the social order in the novel—with its hierarchy, its affectation and snobbishness, its segregated and dislocated reality—is but a reformulation of the rigid structure of class and privilege which Mittelholzer portrayed in *A Morning at the Office*. The social order forms the nexus of commentary in the novel, providing the underpinnings for character and action to a point that the novel becomes a social canvas through which Sylvia moves to her death. All the interactions of characters, all the episodes and events, radiate from the play of color, class, and race. All of Sylvia's movements, her actions and reactions, her responses and emotions, refract from a cracked social reality, a mirror that gives back false images.

Thus, though aware of the essential boredom and absurd mimicry that is the genteel, affected imitation of a foreign class, Sylvia still aspires to this, believing that her entry into society offers her another shield, another protective barrier. In a long interior monologue, Sylvia's ambivalence to the social order and the ambiguity of her position reveal not only an inner confusion about the social order, but one derived from Oedipal emotional feeling for her white father. Thus Sylvia at this point is totally affected by, indeed trapped in, a web of class and race.

To-night, felt Sylvia, she had arrived. To-night she had become a lady of the good coloured middle-class. She had nothing to fear now for the future. She would live down the shoddiness and nonentity of Mother's pedigree. The thought of Benson, however, troubled her. Of course she was not in love with him, but — well, just suppose he did, some time in the future, ask her to marry him. Could she? He was only a Portuguese. . . .

. . . Hadn't she decided that her father would always be the one man on whom her heart could be set?

The cantata bored her. This kind of music did not appeal to her. She liked dance music and sentimental airs. Nevertheless she applauded enthusiastically because everybody else did. She was a lady of society and must do what was considered the correct thing. (106)

Her interest in Benson springs not from affection, but from her wish to have a liaison with a man of Portuguese descent. Now, thinking that she has arrived at the inner circles of a higher class, Sylvia sees such an affair as a liability. The social order, though static, in fact monolithic, does not provide Sylvia with a sense of stability or offer any liberating freedom; rather, she seems to be entrapped by it, lacking the sense required to extricate herself. It is only in her interaction with the natural order, in her sensitivity to external phenomena, that Sylvia achieves any freedom, that she can move to the rhythm of phenomena unhindered by barriers. She can note variations without being dislocated by the variety. Indeed, only through phenomena does she find a proper mirror of herself, of her personality, an unbiased reflection. At times she is at one with nature, in harmony with its rhythm: "The concord between them was complete" (101). Unlike the social order, entry into the environment is unencumbered. Thus at times, Sylvia totally identifies with natural phenomena.

> "I feel really good to-night, just sitting here and remembering our talks, and it's a lovely night, too, plenty of stars and the air smells of leaves and dew and jumbies hiding under buckets. I can hear the sea plainly, it's loud at the minute and dark-blue and brown all mixed together like what I'm thinking and feeling at the moment." (254)

Here there is no need for falsehood, for deceit; she can freely merge with reality, can freely enter its flow. Here there is no dislocation, no sense of fragmentation. In this interplay with natural phenomena, the elements—whose ever-changing forms she always seems to sense, to capture—soothe her, providing her with moments of rest, periods of tranquility.

> Going home leisurely on her bicycle, she could appreciate the soft fleecy array of clouds in the sky. She watched them change from bright yellow to purple, then to grey-brown, the fan-like rays of sunshine behind them dimming all the while . . . . A soothing sadness passed through her spirit as though it were mist that emanated from the residences of Main Street, and in the deep twilight she could feel the solid presence of the samaan trees, rough trunked and aged, guarding her with a secret umber intelligence. (176)

Indeed, all the variations in the landscape of Georgetown awaken varying responses in Sylvia, arousing inner sensations. External sensory phenomena and internal personal emotions merge. Here Georgetown is accessible to her; it is not fraught with all the social rejection, proposals of sexual exploitation for the procurement of employment. Here Sylvia does not feel threatened by the Georgetown of that era with its chicanery, its manipulative dishonesty. But after the death of her father, Sylvia is left unprotected, exposed to many situations that are overtly exploitative, blatantly manipulative. Inherent in all these situations is exploitation deriving from class, race and sex. It is this combination of such social forces resident in a fragmented and dislocated social reality that ultimately leads to Sylvia's total self-denial, to her death.

> There could be no doubt at all, she told herself, that the easy, carefree days were over. It was a certainty now that life for her would be one day-to-day, week-to-week struggle. She had to forget her dreams of being a lady of the upper middle-class. She had to suppress her illusions. The High Street times lay irrevocably in the past. (182)

And eventually unable to aspire toward a respectable life among the wealthy coloreds, aware of the status which accompanies her seeking employment, the drying up of a small inheritance through the corrupt practices of her father's friend, Sylvia stumbles upon the destructive effects latent in this dislocated social reality.

Her future is uncertain as she confronts the dawning awareness of her true position within a society where all is measured by one's racial mixture, where all is gauged by one's class, by one's origin, all encompassed in the structures of color. Having lost her shield, indeed having lost the only man whom she truly loved, her father, Sylvia searches in vain for an answer from external sensory phenomena—an answer, which the hierarchical social order does not offer.

Although the principal modalities structuring the novel *The Life and Death of Sylvia* and governing Sylvia's character are race, class and color, yet sex with all of its discriminatory implications also becomes an effective catalyst propelling her to her tragic end, her own destruction.

Another Sylvia, in Michael Anthony's *The Games Were Coming*, is not only manipulated by discriminatory sex attitudes, but she, too, manipulates those attitudes. In spite of this, however, she essentially remains acted upon and responding, not initiating and controlling. She too, like Mittelholzer's Sylvia, is in essence a pathetic figure.

In *The Games Were Coming*, sex becomes a more dominant factor in the shaping and characterization of Sylvia, the principal protagonist, whose sexual urgings not only guide her behavior but also determine the principal novelistic situations.

San Fernando, the setting for *The Games Were Coming*, is imbued with a certain maleness by Sylvia, as protagonist of the novel. She responds instinctively to "the sun . . . blistering down, the sun . . . red on the water" (Anthony, *The Games Were Coming*, 97). Its allusion to virility with all of its overtones of sexuality makes her pause before the seemingly indelicate nature of such a reference, fraught with suggestion, charged with immediacy. Sylvia is missing the physical interaction with her lover, Leon, and is unconsciously yearning for some physical excitement. Leon, too, the champion cyclist whom everyone expects to win the main event at the coming games, yearns from time to time for that same physical interplay with Sylvia, but refrains from sacrificing his assiduous conditioning. Instead he releases his pent-up energy by pounding the pedals of his cycle, which Sylvia resents, as her thoughts pendulate between prudish surprise and mounting brazenness; " 'Bicycle is his woman!' she said aloud. She smiled brazenly and she felt very cheap for carrying on this way" (119). In *The Games Were Coming*, both Leon and Sylvia achieve in their respective ways physical release of their differing energies: He self-centeredly drives toward his goal of winning his cycling race; she moves, with a degree of hesitation, toward an intimate affair with her boss, the store owner, Mohansingh. In spite of Sylvia's vacillation between feelings of guilt and mounting desires, between her sense of what would be socially labeled "shameful thoughts" and her own stifled sensuality, she moves irrevocably toward an eventual seduction by her boss, Mohansingh: "Not that anything had happened yet. But it certainly was coming" (117).

The novel's plot is the steady progress of parallel actions toward this resolution, indeed, the propelling of characters toward concurrent release of pent-up energy. In *The Games Were Coming*, events, episodes, occurrences, move along parallel lines that lend to the novel a structured immediacy and coincidence when such lines converge and intersect, when they shade together. Thus many actions take on duality, contemporaneity, predicating one another's impending movements toward climax. The coming of the games, their attendant colorfulness, the tension and anticipation building to a fever pitch; all of these things are reflected through Leon. He becomes a clear manifestation of that mood.

> He watched the days fade away one by one and his restlessness was almost too much to bear. . . .
> Now, in the night, he was lying on the bed. He was trying to think of all sorts of things to keep the tension out of his head . . . . he wanted to keep out the sky-full of released pigeons. His head was full of music and

pigeons and club colours and bicycles. He was feeling giddy and harassed. (194, 196)

The games become the central metaphor of the novel.

Time and time again, chapters begin with the refrain, "the games were coming," a refrain that is repeated, elaborated, fully externalized, and orchestrated. Descriptively, the games spurt along to their climax, peaking to a crescendo. Leon's triumph is novelistically assured and totally necessary for the plot resolution. His family, too, accentuates the build-up by their own expectation, goading him on toward triumph.

> "If you healthy you must sweat—that ain't have nothing to do with weakness." And he grinned. "I wish I had your weakness," he said. And then he said, "Listen, boy, you in form. Don't worry with all those stupid people!"
>
> Leon felt reassured. It was as easy as that for his father to convince him. (38)

Just as Leon's winning of the race is assured, so too is Sylvia's seduction. Although her thoughts are marked by vacillation, Sylvia's movement toward the climax of her "game" is unerring; though punctuated by inner dialogue and debate about the propriety of actions, their societal decorum, their seemliness, her movement toward that seduction is uninterrupted, does go forward, in fact, seems novelistically inevitable.

Initially Sylvia is characterized by Leon and May, acquaintances, as "really cool and easy going" (77). She accepts this label and attempts to maintain if not reinforce it, an action which belies the strength of her pent-up energies. Thus it is that appearance and inner reality, social responsibility and the manifestations of her inner feelings, tug against one another, taking on the quality of an inner dialogue by which she is principally characterized. Thus her walk along the streets of San Fernando the morning after her first physical encounter with Mohansingh is measured by the to-and-fro movement of her inner debate, as well as by the changing play of colors in the carnival costumes displayed in the shop windows. The sun's movement down the Naparima mountain, divesting it of shadows, seems symbolically to evince a clarification of her inner dialogue which centers on a feeling of guilt—guilt not derived from any deep moral conviction but rather from notions of respectability and good behavior.

Sylvia's consideration of May as lacking in propriety, devoid of respectability, is phrased with false sophistication:

> May was of little consequence to her. In fact, what could one expect from such a girl? She had two or three children and she wasn't married, and she wasn't even ashamed. They were two different sorts of people. (75)

And when Sylvia surprises herself by privately indulging in thoughts which seem less than respectable, she uses May as comparison. She is righteously annoyed

> the first time Mr. Mohansingh had put his hand on her shoulder. . . . She did not like this at all. . . . Thinking about it she got quite worked up about his having put his hand on her. (71–72)

But this action breaks into a period of boredom for Sylvia. Thus in her restless state, Mr. Mohansingh initially provides a measure of excitement. She feels relieved when he appears and later accepts without any struggle Mohansingh's kisses, an embrace whose imprint she cannot erase and does not attempt to block out.

> She could not get rid of the sensation of last evening of his hand on her chest and his lips against hers. She had pushed away his hands but he rested them there again. (119)

The following morning, knowing full well that she would have to give up something in exchange for arriving late to work, and though realizing that she was playing with fire, she still goes leisurely to work.

> Only yesterday when Mohansingh had called her into the office to discuss show-window displays for the Carnival he had said she was always rushing in to work, she could take her time and come in any time she liked. . . . Now, the very next morning, she was arriving in late. She knew this was playing with fire. She wasn't so naive that she couldn't understand. She knew Mohansingh expected returns for his favours. (121)

She compares Mohansingh to a "bloody maniac!" (119), the same words she uses to describe Leon in his preoccupation with his cycle. Unconsciously, a physical association has been made between her lover and Mr. Mohansingh, which is but a prelude to a physical action. Sylvia is totally aware that she is moving toward a "precipice." But she is unable or unwilling to escape: "in a way she felt powerless to turn from it. And yet . . . the reason why she did not turn away was because she did not want to" (118). As she moves toward her seduction she invests San Fernando with a visceral quality of robust maleness.

> You could not dispute there was a certain grace about the town but there was also a certain toughness about it. She could not understand the people referring to San Fernando as "She." San Fernando was male. San Fernando was like a man. Virile and tough. (78)

Sylvia experiences all the throbbing excitement of the coming Carnival, a secular ritual which is both a reflector of and a mask for her true feelings.

> Her face looked very clean and black and then there was the slight redness of her lips. . . .
> . . . "Let's face it—you're a dam' nice-looking black girl!" She was greatly thrilled with herself.
> . . . she felt the Carnival spirit surging into her again. It was strange how certain things put certain feelings into her mind. (122–123)

The element of hiddenness so characteristic of Carnival, the ability to let loose while being masked, affords her the opportunity to give in to Mohansingh's embrace quickly and without resistance. Once the masking has allowed her a seemingly sacrosanct respectability, once the debate has been clarified by action, she enters without reserve into her affair with Mohansingh. That Anthony attempts to use linguistic symbology is evident; the Sunday that marks the build-up of excitement for the "heats" anticipates Sylvia's, Leon's, and Mohansingh's interrelationships. It all seems to be a game whose final episode is Sylvia's manipulating Leon into a promise of marriage. The early manifestations, the quick signs of Sylvia's pregnancy, which are used by Anthony to bring a resolution to the game and to the novel, can only be credible and acceptable within the context of the "game."

Sylvia's respectability is assured, Leon has won his race, and now his manipulative game can end. He can no longer use his having to train as an excuse for not entering into a deep relationship with her.

> He said, "After the games, look girl, if I only win this Blue Riband, I'll marry you *right* after the games."
> "When?" she said.
> "In a month. If I win."
> He did not tell her that if he lost he would have to ditch her again for another year, as much as he loved and wanted her. He did not tell her that as weak as he was to her, if he lost he could become strong and cruel again.
> She was thrilled. She saw victory was in her hands. If he married her a month after the games she wouldn't be the first girl to have a premature baby and everything would be nice and respectable, and she liked it. (204–205)

That Sylvia is placed in situations initially not of her own making shows how circumscribed were the avenues offered to young women at that time, those being only sex and marriage, as Anthony implies. Even though it is her inherent sexuality that leads her, she doesn't plan the situations in which she finds herself. Nowhere does Anthony present Sylvia with a way out.

Sylvia's affair with Mohansingh, her sexual involvement with him, is not so powerful, so overwhelming as to liberate her from her stifled desires. So steeped is San Fernando society in the pressure to maintain its trappings, to have women conform to its mandates, that ultimately shame, hypocrisy and deviousness are the corollaries of whatever is labeled "bad" by that society. To be sure, the "games" have come and gone; a marriage will take place. But given the societal attitudes toward sex, it seems unlikely that a genuine resolution of the relationship between Leon and Sylvia will be achieved.

Thus it is that both Sylvias, in *The Life and Death of Sylvia* and *The Games Were Coming*, are victims of their societies. They are trapped in the race, class, and sexual discriminations inherent in those societies. Few avenues seem to be open to them for achieving selfdom, for realizing potential. For indeed both have been presented as refractors of the external societal realities. Their characters have been drawn with little inner tonality, devoid of personality and potentiality. It is not surprising, therefore, that both characters are essentially, though not intentionally, pathetic. For these societies have not as yet cohered, and the Sylvias as yet have not been allowed to exhibit their own true feelings.

Many of the female characters in the novels of this chapter are portrayed through their sexual involvement, their marital prospects or experiences. For instance, Beatrice in *Crick Crack, Monkey* was relegated to social climbing, was involved in a marriage devoid of any warmth, any affection. A barrenness in these emotional experiences, which lack honesty and affection, seems to characterize so many female/male relationships.

Yet, with all, in *The Games Were Coming*, it is Sylvia who is the central character of the narrative; her inner psychological debate indicates a measure of preoccupation by the author with the role of the woman in interpersonal relationships between men and women. Though thrust into a situation, Sylvia does manipulate it. Clearly the questioning of ethics or of social morality finds little treatment in this novel, *The Games Were Coming*, nor in many of the novels of this chapter.

Here, then, society has not as yet moved to a situation that exhibits the social cohesion necessary to knit together the sexes, the classes, the races. Involvements seem devoid of any liberating passion, lacking in deep inner convictions which should ordain an ethical society. Yet, that an indigenous secular ritual, Carnival, has been rendered novelistically, indicates a movement toward the acceptance of the indigenous, a fundamental element of the possibility of that cohesion.

In *Pan Beat*, Marion Patrick Jones uses an indigenous musical form, the pans, the steel band, as her novelistic point of reference, at times her novelistic metaphor. Here, too, the central character, the person through whose eyes we see the passionless living of many of the characters, is a woman, Earline. Her life has been touched by one true affection, her relationship with David Chung. Yet, the lives of most of the characters portrayed by Jones through recall, flashbacks, and sociophilosophical dialogue seem unfulfilled, somewhat barren, contributing little to society's evolution toward a measure of social and cultural coherence. Yet, that the socially rejected "pan," the steel drum, is the principal motif of the novel, attests to the development of indigenous ritual and cultural forms through which classes and races may cohere.

Thus it is that Marion Patrick Jones, in the final statement of *Pan Beat*, envisions a society in Trinidad that achieves sociocultural coherence, strong in its dreams, fulfilled in its promise, and rising to the call of its own indigenous rhythms, to the beckoning of its own music, its pan. Clearly, then, the indigenous pan here can bring about a measure of cohesion between landscape and society wherein the hills give a soul sense of the social reality. Further, death as symbolized by the Lapeyrouse Cemetery, and life after death, provide a context wherein the seemingly senseless deaths of Angela, Dave, and Louis can take on meaning and relevance. Thus, meaning and purpose can be ascribed to living in the island world, to the human condition; a measure of clarification can be given to the spatial and spiritual equation between the here and the hereafter. Further, the final statement, while not redeeming the essentially empty and unfulfilled lives of a lost generation, gives a historical and social continuity, an intergenerational relevance, to those caught in that shifting, uncharted, transitional period prior to political and cultural independence from colonial rule. The presentations of the lives of that generation, their interactions, their existential stumblings in search of life's meaning, are the subject matter novelistically spun and pulled together in *Pan Beat*.

For in *Pan Beat*, Marion Patrick Jones attempts an imaginative analysis of an important period in the social history and the cultural evolution of Trinidad. She traces the lives of a group of students and friends, fuses together their emotional and intellectual interrelations, their entry into some form of professional life, their societal existences, their going away, their coming home. The cultural movement is marked by bloody and continuous gang warfare between rural steel bands from different but topographically similiar areas. John-John, Picadilly, Laventille, areas labelled "Behind the Bridge," the domain of the poor, of those labelled low class, are the birthplaces of the steel band, prototype of fragmented social reality.

Separated from other areas by perceptions of class, disassociated from them by a seeming lack of educational opportunities, adjudged to be socially discontinuous areas by imported normative value systems, yet these areas spawn this most important vital cultural creation. Clearly Marion Patrick

Jones's final statement in her novel is a negation of the normative value system by which these areas have been judged. She proffers a vision of a cohering social and cultural reality in which validation does not come from away, from abroad. Indeed, her final statement points to these areas of possible indigenous sources of a social cohesion, vital and necessary. The pan, the indigenous musical form, is accepted into church.

> It was the first time pans had beat at a funeral, and they beat softly, tune after tune: "Ave Maria" . . . Handel's "Messiah." (Jones, *Pan Beat*, 143)

In this culturally integrative process, the indigenous is still subservient, the church still the dominant cultural artifact. It is this same church from whose subjugating, foreign, un-Trinidadian influence Leslie Oliver, turned priest, feels alienated, separated.

> For Leslie it was not a better life, it was a day by day putting up with being ostracized in one's own country, with a loyalty to an order dominated by a people for whom he had the same mistrust as his West Indian pupils. Irishmen would always be strangers to him. He would have to eat potatoes when he would prefer to eat rice, rice pudding when he wanted ice cream; it would be impossible to make friends of the priests with whom he lived, without remembering that they belonged to different countries and were of a different colour. (73)

This church, as presented by Marion Patrick Jones, has not only helped to shape the aesthetic image of beauty—Maria being the perfect representation—but also seems to give deleterious personality to some of the young, convent-girl students. Denise, for instance, in her earlier years, is injected with false piety by the abrasive religiosity of the nuns. Denise "was one of those who was made a prefect in the third form. . . . After three years in the convent, Denise was walking like a nun" (63). Thus it is that Denise's early perceptions are shaped and guided by church ritual and dogma to such a degree that the notion of miracle is never far from her consciousness. This type of moral training and education can hardly prepare girls such as Denise to understand the quality of life of those behind the bridge. In fact, it only succeeds in dividing those who go to the better schools and those who live behind the bridge. Many of the better-school types, though seeming to associate with folk behind the bridge, cannot really understand the robust communal living of such an area. Thus Denise thinks that only a miracle can make even the grass grow there. Later, her husband, Louis the egalitarian—socialist, exponent-dreamer deemed communist—also believes that only a miracle can bring about change to these people in Laventille.

"The sort of miracle I am looking for," he said, "is the loaves and fishes
type. A whole heap of loaves and fishes, and roti and saltfish, to serve a
heaping lot of Black people . . . . Give them something new to work for,
a society in which they can be real people, instead of this sham in which
one has the choice of being a hypocrite or a criminal." (144)

Even as Louis makes this pronouncement he still seems to stand outside of
that particular social reality; indeed he seems somewhat supercilious. Alan,
the son of a whore, now a relatively well-off petroleum engineer whose
mobility derives from his education, also seems to stand outside the very
social reality from which he sprang.

Thus in *Pan Beat*, neither Leslie the priest, Denise the artist, Alan the
engineer, or even Louis, the committed participant in the everyday living of
the Behind the Bridge steel-band men-workers—none of them can bring
about the miracle and by transformative action change the fragmented
reality. The novel's central protagonist and principal narrator, the brown-
skinned Earline, has just returned to Trinidad to find her roots, to rekindle
the memories, to enter again the still magic of the rhythms of the pan, to
track the unspooling lives of the Flamingoes.

I . . . suddenly feel the need to come back to Trinidad, to find myself
and discover my roots. It has something to do with the trees and the
sharpness of the hills. I heard a real steel band last night for the first time
in ages. It has left me dizzy and weeping with emotion . . . . It makes me
feel nostalgic for the days when I was very young and the Flamingoes
were a band. (16)

Through discussion with members of the Flamingoes group, Earline tries to
recall those youthful days and to relive those youthful memories. She
becomes the narrator/participant who acts as a conduit for the narrative, and,
by linking together different eras, gives an elasticity to the narrative time.
The refrains of the novel and the cadenced rhythms introduce the members
of a small, privileged group, intensely involved in a socially nonconformist
action.

Flamingoes was the first of the sixth form steel bands . . . a sixth form
middleclass steel band. Most people put the blame on Louis Jenkins.
Louis was a tall thin boy with freckles and yellow kinky hair, . . . Some
people . . . placed the blame on Alan Hastings. Alan, tall, handsome with
his shirt open at the neck and his pants resting on his hips, had this to his
discredit: his mother was a prostitute . . . . A very few people blamed
Dave Chow . . . because that Chinese man couldn't be trusted. (23)

Here, Marion Patrick Jones not only gives a brief sense of the social history of the growth of steel band in Trinidad and Tobago, but by depicting the physical make-up of the members of the band, she is able to present many of the racial variations existing in Trinidad. The privileges of this group of sixth formers derive not from class nor wealth, but from education, with all the societal expectations imposed on young men and women who have achieved the distinct possibility of going abroad, of going away to become professionals. That the members of this group later do not achieve distinction or open the way toward social, cultural, and political change is a measure of the imposed societal expectations. Almost all their lives are subsequently devoid of that earlier intensity with which the pan beat energized them—their lives will seem empty, all in vain, societally nonparticipant, dysfunctional.

Through the eyes and words of Earline, Marion Patrick Jones locates each member of the Flamingoes within a particular niche even while exposing the existential emptiness of their lives. Further, the author notes the corrosive effects of the passage of time on various members of the Flamingoes.

> [Denise] was acutely aware of the passing of time and of how little she had done in her lifetime. Thirty-two, and the only thing to her credit a pile of a second-rate paintings . . . and a husband who spent most of his time making a scrap book of Trinidad Guardian cuttings. (124)

> Leslie was thinking that Louis was a boy with a hell of a lot of talent, it had just fizzled out along the way. He nearly got a scholarship; he nearly got through his American degree . . . he was just one of those people that never quite made it. (130–131)

The author not only underscores the existential barrenness pervading the lives of the members of the Flamingoes, the corrosive effects of their aging, but further suggests that they have indeed failed their society.

> We were the first ones with a real chance, and most of us have got all the material things of living, yet we thresh ourselves about, wearing ourselves out, trying to build up our little selves by the foolish process of changing our cars each year or getting a new fridge. Some future generation. (139)

That emptiness, that unfulfillment and inability to participate in the sociopolitical reality, become weaknesses that cause them to be branded as a "lost generation." Indeed, their very failure may have been seeded in, and now be a mere outgrowth of, that very education that gave them a position of privilege.

Pan Beat does not emphasize the theme of education, which is surprising, given the fact that so many other themes are debated and discussed. In fact, the education that sixth formers received at that time, though relevant in itself and intrinsically analytic, did not really prepare those sixth formers for a participant role within the larger society of Trinidad and Tobago. That is not to say that the education was dysfunctional, but rather that it was irrelevant to the evolving sociopolitical demands of a country moving toward political freedom and independence. To be sure, the education could make for individual growth and fulfillment, for macro-abstractions such as evidenced in Louis's political formulations and in Leslie's inner debate as to the relationship between life and death, spiritual purification with its corollary passion. Yet, it was an education that did not essentially locate the indigenous potential latent in the evolving society, in the evolving pan culture; it was an education that, in its essence, did not make the magic necessary for the miracle.

Thus, in the protagonists' evolution, the movement is from the externalization of highly individualized characters, to characters who become representational states attributable to particular professions: the artist, Denise; the clergyman, Leslie; "big shot" businessman, Alan; the civil servant, Joseph; the radical, Louis; the housewife, Marjorie.

This evolution is marked by pendulations between the past and the present—the time of the articulation of the novel and of the final prognosis of hope in the shiver of new relationships. By the shading together of time past and time present, and by the interplay of recalled past events, the lives of the characters are revealed to us in dialogue, in discussion, through questions whose answers awaken memory or outline current episodes. The play of memory and the use of flashback re-create the episodes and occurrences, emotional and personal interrelationships shared by the characters in their younger years. Earline listens to the rhythms of the steel drum. The pull of the rhythm, the intense reaction to those rhythms, the worshipful reverence before the pan beat, all are sharply etched:

> She would sit for hours absorbed in the music, intensely interested, . . .
> Most of the time when they met to beat, he and Anthony Joseph and
> David Chow and Leslie Oliver, and Louis Jenkins, she would be there.
> She would warm up by swaying a bit . . . her face turned towards the
> pans as if she were praying to them. (31)

Louis, too, when "the rhythm had moved from the pan and his hands to the whole of his body," Louis is equally intense. In their youth, all participation seems intense as the characters gulp deeply of life, answering the call of their feelings, their urges. Marjorie gives free vent to her sexual urges, "always wanting to go to bed with him . . . everywhere, on the grass on the savannah" (109). Yet almost as counterpoint to Marjorie's sexuality, Dave has already begun his final movement toward ascribing irrelevance to life, an absurdity, a meaninglessness.

> His pan needed tuning, he never joined the cadets and he had won a scholarship . . . He had gone to London then nothing . . . . What was there after living? (31)

Thus, during this earlier period, despite the intense participation, the free sensing of rhythms and life, the characteristics that develop to haunt certain members of the group have already taken seed. Leslie, who eventually commits himself to "the complete apartness of a monastery," was always "inclined to be lonely" (109). Even from his youth, he has already moved into his ultimate loneliness. Alan, disturbed by the social stigma attached to his mother's profession, was already dreaming of making it to erase that stigma, of making himself "a somebody" (26). Denise, later on the unsuccessful artist, when she was young painted

> little girls with yellow hair and pink stockings; now she was turning out what she called "Modern West Indian Art." Earline had watched the pictures being hung, and to her they were still little girls in stockings, only now the little girls wore brown stockings with their yellow hair. (65)

The novelistic time affects the structure as well as the development of the characters: death, love and the meaning of love, the premature loss of dreams consequent on loss of love, all become motifs whose formulation and argumentation not only mirror attitudes but indeed depict whole characters, portray entire representative states of being. Often then, *Pan Beat* takes its shape from a series of these formulations through which the past and somewhat melodramatic activities and the present human condition of its characters are eternalized and elaborated.

Louis's violent death ushers in the plot's denouement. Leslie ascribes deep signification to that death which shatters the barrier that has earlier prevented him from praying. With Louis's death, Denise's list of perfect people falls apart, unravels itself, because the central figure, according to her, has been uselessly destroyed. No longer does she indulge in the search for perfection in Jesus, His sacrifice, His work on earth, Louis's dream of a perfect society, and the apparent vocational purity and self-sacrifice attendant on Leslie's priesthood. Now, indeed, it seems as though the beat of the pan is muffled with Louis's death, the Flamingoes have disbanded, and the rhythms and the pan beat have ended.

Although Dave Chow's suicide in England and Louis's seemingly useless death in Trinidad do not necessarily point to a tragic vision of reality by Marion Patrick Jones, their deaths do highlight an essential loss of the dream which resounded in the rhythms of their pans. In *An Island Is a World*, a pivotal character also commits suicide.

Toward the end of Samuel Selvon's *An Island Is a World*, Foster, its central protagonist, arrives despondently at an ultimate realization of the purposelessness of his search. His window onto the world makes the world recede, seem unattainable, remote. Here, Selvon intimates that Foster's search for purpose, for meaning, for ultimate coherence, has abruptly ended; an end impelled by the unexpected suicide of Father Hope, who seemed to be so assured in his faith, so strong in his beliefs.

Father Hope's suicide is dramatized in symbolic color and ensuing darkness. Foster's search ends in that dramatic termination of Father Hope's faith and beliefs. All is shadow now; all the divergence of color, all the ramifications of a search, come together in an ultimate obscurity.

> He lit a cigarette and looked for a moment at the sinking sun. The sky was ablaze with a riot of color . . . . "Father Hope?" he shouted stupidly . . . . When he looked down all he could see was the deep green of the vegetation . . . . Darkness was swiftly falling . . . . In the gathering darkness every object looked like Father Hope to his frightened imagination. (Selvon, *An Island Is a World*, 280)

Significantly, the sun has set on one part of the world, on Father Hope's life, perhaps, too, on Foster's giddying search for the meaning of life. Yet the sun has not set on another part of the world where Rufus's brother stands. Simultaneously, as Rufus moves into his own space from Trinidad to confront and build a new life in America, his father-in-law, Johnny, sets sail for another world, India, the world from which he came. Here all the configurations of search through space and time for meaningful, purposeful living, come together—with some arriving at new harbors, some setting forth for new vistas.

> They came towards the city the night before the ship was due to sail, because they were afraid that it might go away and leave them behind . . . . And all of them had a light in their eyes, as if salvation had come at last . . . people were leaving the country in which they had worked their lives away, to go to distant India purely for sentimental reasons, to stand on the banks of the Ganges, to walk on holy land. (255)

Thus it is that both Johnny and Father Hope leave their own island space, moving out in the darkness and the night into new spaces. Time gives a structural chronology to the novel wherein the fortunes of characters begin at dawn and move into an end space, nighttime.

The novel opens with dawn breaking on the central protagonist, Foster. He is unable to marshal his thoughts, a quality that proves to be a recurrent and distinguishing mark of his character: "Whenever Foster tried to pursue one thought to the end (at the same time thinking, what end?) the end never came" (8). Thus, it is that Selvon frames the beginning of day in images of perception, indicating perhaps that varying methods of perceiving the immediate reality outline the shapes and movements of the characters.

Foster locates himself within the island, a speculative point that is magnified by its extension into the other convergent realities through which the characters pass—England, America, Europe, Asia. The delineation of the lives of his West Indian characters affords Selvon the opportunity to present ideas about living in these distant places.

Rufus will perhaps find meaning in the United States, living with the American woman, Sylvia. For him, Trinidad and the Caribbean are too small, too confining. Earlier, in his initial experience in England, he has come face to face with the notion of the smallness of his island world—of its anonymity.

> I will tell you, that important as we West Indians think we are . . . there are people in this country who have never heard of our existence . . . . Over here you don't say you come from Trinidad . . . . You have to say the West Indies, and then they take it that you are from Jamaica. (131)

Foster, in his searching, has physically discovered England and momentarily arrives at an emotional resting place there with Julia. When he returns to Trinidad he locates through his perceptions of varying cultures the notion of going home. For he has discovered that all peoples have their own cultural history which, by assuring their inhabitants a point of historical reference, becomes a testimonial for their communal selves.

Father Hope has gone out into the world striving to attain a profession, an education. He returns to the sanctity and safety of an island world in a beautiful valley of Trinidad. Far from the maddening crowd he builds his church, his world of sanctuary, a refuge from an earlier gratuitous crime. Andrews, rooted by his participation in politics, and his subsequent love and marriage to Marlene, also makes Trinidad his world.

The lives of the characters, then, intersect different separated geographies; dreams spool apart to encompass these new worlds, then bring them together, providing conduits for many emotional entanglements.

The catalysts of the novel are the many tenuous, problematic love-and-sex involvements that bring the characters together in various combinations. At the center of the emotional involvements of the three male protagonists— the brothers Foster and Rufus, and Foster's friend, Andrew—is the figure of Marleen: Rufus while married to Rena has an affair with Marleen before leaving for America; Foster impregnates Marleen before leaving for England; Marleen eventually becomes Andrew's wife. These entanglements, cogs and wheels for the various novelistic actions and their resolutions, all unerringly revolve around unexpected, and indeed unwanted, pregnancies. Thus the philosophical speculation, the search for meaning with which the novel is weighted, is counterpointed by the pervasive and recurrent theme of sex, and the willy-nilly siring of children.

All of Rufus's movements from one space to another, the development of his character in one part of the world or another, revolve around his affairs with different women; his impregnation and subsequent marriage to Rena in Trinidad and Tobago, his impregnation of Sylvia in America, and his marriage to her. His whole development, his movement to the north, seem based on gratuitous, irresponsible actions. He marries Rena not out of love, but because she is pregnant. His relationship with Marleen stems from boredom with Rena and his inability to satisfy her need for a good time. Later, his involvement with Sylvia, the problems besetting her abortions, his subsequent marriage to her while not divorced from Rena, become goads for his return to America. Thus, we can conclude that the cardinal points of his world seem ultimately to derive from carnal involvements.

For, indeed, *An Island Is a World* is constructed along intersecting episodes linking characters' spaces. The perimeters telescope outward from the island, representative of a Caribbean historical reality, to other geographical realities (Europe, Asia) from which the population of Trinidad orginally derived, to which many people of the Caribbean immigrate. Then through interlocking events extending into interlocking structural formulations, Selvon brings together characters and their geographies, their actions and cultures crisscrossing; but ultimately these do not fuse into a coherent social community.

By dividing the novel into three parts—the first set in Trinidad, the second in Trinidad, the United States, and England, and the third centered in Trinidad but extending outwards to India, the United States, and England—Selvon posits a triangularity of relationships between characters, a triangular movement of characters from one geography to another, a structure that underscores the notion of going away and of going home. Further, he assesses and analyzes the societies and the cultural relevance of the three areas. Thus, even as we glimpse and derive a sense of the Trinidadian's reaction to the American cultural landscape—its vastness, its seeming possibilities—through Rufus's entanglements and his attempts to become a dentist, similarly, we derive a sense of the cultural differences between England, the behavior of the English people, and Trinidad through Foster's eyes, through his constant analyses and reflections. For Foster's character, through an unending series of questions about his immediate social reality, is governed by self-searching, self-doubt. Even though Foster's search for meaning about the nature of life, the reason for living, is often tinged with self-doubt, his constant analysis of the social reality borders on the self-indulgent, becoming habitual. The constant analysis, which in itself coats Foster's character, at times takes on the quality of plot, so making the narrative action somewhat turgid and lacking in passion. Often analysis becomes a random existential assortment of circular streams of consciousness, grasping at a seeming absurdity about living. Yet perhaps these circular and elaborate meanderings take Foster out of his condition of inhabiting the "dot" of Trinidad.

> Every morning when Foster awoke, it was the same thing. The world spun in his brain . . . [he] imagined Trinidad as it was, a mere dot on the globe . . . he saw himself in the dot. (8)

Later on, when faced by the tragic reality of Father Hope's death, Foster becomes more rooted in the spatial reality of the island world, less of a random searcher for some meaning of existence. For "the Universal kiss" negates neither racial prejudice—which stands in the way of his being able to marry white English Julia—national idiosyncrasies, nor the ironic absurdity of Father Hope's suicide. But this wider perspective may bring Foster the ability to grasp specific situations: initially and slowly he notes the similarity and, indeed, the inane regularity of homogeneous actions, the seemingly purposeless hurrying of crowds in England. Slowly he comes to the realization that perhaps each hurrying person may have a simple purpose for living, for their individual rooting activities. Foster keenly captures the harsh social circumstances in which many emigrant West Indians live in England. Further, his suggestions to Andrew about political campaigning in Trinidad seem precise, accurate, and derived from a clear understanding of the political reality of the island.

Foster's analyses, argumentations, and mental formulations provide the link and make for the nexus of his friendship with Andrew and his relationship with Father Hope: Andrew, who is attempting to instill ethics and morality within the political arena of Trinidad; Father Hope, whose writings search for a universal religion. Through these discussions with Andrew and with Father Hope, through his exchange of correspondence with Andrew from London and Trinidad, the novel becomes a representation of the sociopolitical reality of the 1940s and early 1950s.

Unlike Rufus, who seems impelled into relationships, Foster drifts into them seeking solace, stability and refuge. His relationship with Julia in England initially affords him a point of rest from his anxious searching in the possibility of an unquestioning, soothing relationship. Julia's cool and seemingly casual aborting of her pregnancy does not, as would be expected, trigger a series of meditative explorations about the nature of life and death, childhood. Rather the casualness and the reasons for her casualness are explored by Foster; the effective act and not the essence of the event becomes important. In his search for significance, indeed for existential truth, Foster never seems to examine and explore the inner meanings of affection and instinctual love, nor the nature of protective affection.

Jennifer can easily and unselfishly offer love to Foster, and comes to offer affection, after many years of silence, to her father as well. Their worlds converge and link in Trinidad, even as Father Hope's world crumbles, even as he joins the universal spirit by suicide. Clearly the movement from going away to coming home is assured by these two linkages, this coming together of contiguous personal and spatial realities.

As Father Hope goes to rest in the valley of Caura, in his island, he offers Foster his dream, his congregation of simple peasants, his ideas, writings about the universal religion.

> "You see how easy it is. Simple minds, simple people who believe only in right or wrong, and do not allow the world and its ways to intrude on their lives, like you and me. You will like these people, Foster." (278)

There is also a measure of fulfillment and continuity of dream as Jennifer's father, Johnny, on leaving Trinidad in search of a home in India, offers her his only treasure, his idea about gravity.

> I have nothing more to give you but this idea. . . . Now Gravity does only pull things down, but suppose a man could invent something so that Gravity pull things sideways . . . . That would be a great invention. (261–262)

Johnny's character is sketched in all of his shifting moods, in all the immediacy of his actions and reactions. His essential loneliness is suffused by bouts of drunkenness, and even as he offers Jennifer, his daughter, the inheritance of his dream, he finally inherits what he has dreamed of having— a young boy child, his grandson, Tim, who is immediately taken by his parents to America. Others are going away, too: Rufus to America, Rena to Venezuela, and Father Hope to his own rest. Andrew and Marleen, Foster and Jennifer, remain in the island world, attempting to make it home.

The island world that Selvon presents collages many shifting and ever-changing relationships between characters, and portrays various processes of going away and returning to the island reality. Garth St. Omer's novels, with settings principally in St. Lucia and Jamaica, also present characters moving between an arena of "awayness" in England, and a locus of going home, of return to the islands. St. Omer's canvas is kaleidoscopic, the many relationships between characters refracted in the prism of the island world and its geographical nexus, England.

In *A Room on the Hill*, through a series of confrontations between John and his father, John and his mother, John and Miriam, John and Rose, Garth St. Omer attempts to trace the patternings, the flux and shift, of John's character. His drifting between illusion and reality is accentuated by the notion of the transitoriness of things, to such a degree that he accepts, even projects, the ultimate dreamlike quality of his experiences, which in turn dance between illusion and reality, between sleep and waking.

> During those five years, John thought he had been like a somnambulist waiting to awake. Nothing he did then had any significance, except the pain of his waiting. For the pain, like his somnambulist state, was transitory. It could only last so long as he had not awakened. . . . the memory of not even a single [action] gave him pleasure or satisfaction now. (St. Omer, *A Room on the Hill*, 97)

Even when an action is in progress, he sees it change before his very eyes. It is the tracking of change, the actualizing of a sense of the transitory, that gives complexity to the style of debate that informs St. Omer's prose. There is always action followed by discussion followed by reaction to discussion. Thus, after making love to Rose for the first time, John perceptibly not only tracks his diminution of the happiness of that moment, but even anticipates the loss of the essential moment.

> The subdued exhilaration for him after the act of love, Rose's presence on the sand next to him, perhaps, too, the unfamiliarity of the beach— everything seemed to suggest an unreality he was imagining only. (41)

The loss of that essential moment is accompanied by an increase in his sense of hysteria; a countermotion is taking place, the voices are crisscrossing, a contrapuntal disharmony begins. At times John orchestrates this disharmony. After his mother's death, the scene with his father, who wishes to sell his mother's possessions and their house, is dramatized by a series of orchestrated steps while John moves from smiling to being angry to saying nothing.

Again, using the pull of opposites, St. Omer attempts to make distinctions between thought and feeling, that is, extending the notion of reality and illusion, of awaking and dream. He etches in dramatic dialogue John's need for inner privacy, his attempt to reject feeling, even while reacting to emotionalism, to demonstrations of feeling.

> Her love and concern sprang out at him and he recoiled. It was not the protection of love he wanted but the reason of understanding. . . .
> He would have liked to expose everything, not to her love, but to her understanding, not to her sympathy but to her admiration. (35)

John's reactions are not simply tense, not simply emotional, but indeed seem to be impelled by uncontrollable impulses. In one of his confrontations with Miriam, a sadistic impulse controls his actions.

> He wished to see her as she had been when she came to his house the day Stephen had drowned, distraught and showing her pain . . . . his desire to see her unhappy and his shame at the thought were simultaneous. (64)

And since John seems to be often pulled by contrary emotions, the sadistic need to hurt Miriam manifests itself in a personal need for flagellation: "He was like a monk being flagellated and yearning for the silent admiration of those who beat him" (35). This clearly manifests John's complex but subtle need for recognition by others, a recognition that takes note of his demonstrated feelings. To be sure, he has requested appreciation manifested more by head than by heart; but at the same time ambivalently he wishes that his gift to his mother be appreciated by her, not with the head, but with the heart.

> That achievement, which he was about to set out for, was to have been the bouquet he would place at her feet, to let her hold with her calloused hands and to look upon with her tired eyes, to caress if she still remembered how. (32)

This sharply contrasts with his loss of dream, his drift, his lost ambition, consequent on the death by drowning of his friend, Stephen. John has been frozen, unable to act, either consciously or unconsciously, to come to the aid of his friend; reminiscing or so often remonstrating with himself, John ponders about cause and effect, about the far-reaching consequences of that moment of inaction.

> Stephen's death, now, had another, more special, relevance. After it, the aspirations . . . became a dream. His remorse, his anguish, had become the only reality. (98)

Often St. Omer notates thought processes through the rhythms and beat of the elements, through environment. Thus the sun or the movement of shadows, the play of light or the movement of the sea, accompanies important happenings and decisions and thoughts of consequence. John's mother's burial is reflected in "palpable dusk," between the times when "[a]ll shadow had gone with the sun and the true dark had not yet fallen" (18–19). And as John ponders on his reactions to Stephen's death, the sun, the shadows, the sea, slip in and out, as shifting background to those thoughts.

The sea was now only the sound of itself breaking and running up the sand. Gradually his eyes became accustomed again and he could see the white luminous crests of the waves as they broke beyond the area of light, and, in the distance behind them, the flat darkness of the sea. (98–99)

John's sense of freedom, albeit a momentary condition, is reflected in the free flow and movement of water, its drift, its apparent freedom of choice. All is liquid image, unhindered by thought processes that often dam the flow of action, often negate it. "He felt as fluid as they. An absence of tension, a suppleness of spirit, . . . the very symbol of peace" (90).

Stephen, his friend, more assured as to his goals, more aware of the direction in which he wants to go, in fact, more controlled by material elements, is consequently deeply afraid of insubstantiality and of death. Through his suicide, then, through that underlying tragic irony which St. Omer posits, so much of action is rendered inconsequential, dreams transitory, hopes illusive. It is not surprising, therefore, that he begins and ends the novel with scenes of death.

The delineation of John's character is imaged in elements of disintegration. The very title, *A Room on the Hill*, is evidence of John's choosing to be alone and separate, so transitory he considers relationships. Woven throughout the prose are the intertwinings of threads of contradiction so that reality loses its immediacy, the possibility of arrival always slipping away, denied. "'We are happy now,' he said, 'very happy. But afterwards. I don't know'" (41).

Indeed, John's need to constantly analyze action, to always ascribe motive to action, not only devitalizes the action, but can even negate it. In this way, St. Omer attempts to ascribe a "non-ness" to the moment. Often, the present takes on an immediacy of action, unraveling in an air of the insubstantial, of dream. John's perceptions are veiled by dreams: actions become unreal, deceptive, "each one . . . a trick" (184).

It is not surprising, therefore, that many of John's relationships are transient, relationships demanding little responsibility, requiring no deep commitment.

Thus he neither commits himself to a deep and consequently responsible relationship with Rose, shunning an active involvement with her, refusing its inherent possibility, nor does he consider the possibility of its disintegration. Like so many of the characters in St. Omer's novels, John has no deep social commitment, nor does he attempt to alter the fabric of the society around him. Though by no means unconventional in attitude or behavior, his actions are highly personalistic, rooted in self, lacking in concern for the societal. His alienation can color his perception of society without demanding of him the responsibility of action, thus he can glibly say the world is full of

> "Imitation, . . . always and everywhere imitation, now and forever, amen. A race of imitators. . . .
> "Cows. Big, fat, ugly cows. . . . Chewing the cud of other cultures, other habits, other religions. Other everything." (107)

And he can boast, "Stephen's death never touched me . . . . And Stephen was my best friend" (79).

Even as he did not act to save his friend, he seems incapable of controlling his own clearly perceived drift. Indeed, having accepted drift as a quality of his own character, he is able to indulge in it. He feels himself "a very small piece of wood drifting on a wide sea" (101). Perhaps the self-perceived drifter thinks himself free of any social responsibility.

John's highly personalistic analyses of action and thought, of feelings and emotions, can easily lead to and rationalize rejection of togetherness; can, as he participates in action or relationships, let him off the hook. There exists a solid "wall" between John and Rose, "of human selfishness and misunderstanding, of imperfectly explained and imperfectly understood motives" (45). A wall also separates him from his father, who never married his mother. He is shut off from both of his parents; "he knew that forever his parents would be a closed book to him" (83). Though often apologizing, he fights with Rose, with his father, and continuously with his mother. And as John pushes his self-imposed alienation and aloneness to its limit, he resents not being able to live in the room on the hill and finds himself touched by the deaths of his mother and his friend, Stephen: "feeling acutely the effect of the deaths of Stephen and of his mother . . . it had been intolerable that he should have to" (118).

Even while wishing to remain untouched by their deaths, John can't let go of having been part of their living and, indeed, part of their dying; he is blamed for his mother's death; Stephen's death, too, weighs heavily on him.

In the novel, *The Lights on the Hill*—symbolically, just after Stephenson's and Thea's decision to end their two-year love relationship—the lights on the hill go on and then are turned off again, just before the coming of another day, another time.

> Something about the hills he was looking at again caught his attention. Then he saw what it was. The lights had been switched on again. He was about to mention it to Thea when, abruptly, they went out. (St. Omer, *The Lights on the Hill*, 108–109)

And indeed, another day begins as if curving backward to another time, arching downward to a familiar space. This arching time plunges Stephenson, the novel's central protagonist, into aloneness. So many incidents of his life are presented through flashbacks and reconstructions of the island reality that at times the novel seems situational. The novel presents that ever-shifting movement of people journeying between the Caribbean islands. We see Stephenson's youth and his working in the coal pits in St. Lucia, his Christmastime with Meme, his schooling, his dreams of going away, his employment with the civil service, his bribe-taking conviction, his going away to St. Lucia, his attending the university in Jamaica, his two-year love affair with Thea. These random incidents in his life seem unplanned, occurring by accident. Now

> Thea . . . seems unique, different from . . . his temporary alliances . . . working in the customs, the whores and the women on the fringes . . . . She was different from any woman he had come close to before. Always restless, always dissatisfied, hovering on the fringe of things, avoiding the center or the depths. Confused, too, and wondering, and forever envious of people who have achieved something. (21)

With Thea during their love affair he no longer feels like a rat drowning and suffocating, like a "snail in its shell refusing to come out"; he feels free to put "his antennae . . . out again" (86). But later, as their love affair is coming to an end, again under a luminous moon, he breaks the silence about his life, brutally illuminating pain. Unthinkingly, like an animal, as if by reversion to his younger days Stephenson brings hurt to Thea's gray eyes while brutalizing her with his past. Earlier described by him as having canine teeth, she bares them, snaps back at him both in self-defense and in self-assertion.

Perhaps this self-assertion is that unique quality that has attracted Stephenson, for many of the women with whom he has his random and indulgent experiences seem to be cowed, boxed in by limiting social circumstances, trapped by sexual exploitation. Thea is unlike Moira, a former lover whose eyes are like those of a hurt animal. Nor is Thea like Rosa, whose sexual involvements with various visitors from other islands are cloaked in secrecy, deviousness, and though not wanton, have elements of promiscuity. Nor is Thea like Laura, Roland's wife on the small island where many women seem to live trapped lives, entering into random sexual relationships while waiting for the few returning professionals. Laura does not fight when Roland, in pursuit of his profession, casually rejects and abandons her.

At the end of the affair, Thea fights back with the strength that she has exhibited all through the relationship. Though sometimes feeling unwanted, she has still been able to exert such control over Stephenson as to free his trapped spirit, making him miss her while he walks in the hills during his vacation, making him feel, and "[write] all that he did and saw that was strange to Thea" (62).

Stephenson and Thea's relationship is played out against the background of university life in Jamaica during the late 1950s. Indeed, the university life takes on the quality of foreground, actualized in the movement of students at the student center; the dancing, beer drinking, flirting; the bull sessions in the rooms, the heated discussions about politics in the West Indies at that time, talks about the projected Federation—the sheer excitement and newness of campus life in which young and not-so-young were brought together from many distant West Indian territories. All of this vital activity is embodied in the accompanying moonscape, so vital a feature, so present an element, in the university life at that time, accompaniment to Stephenson and Thea's loveplay. It is not by chance, then, that Stephenson illuminates his earlier life in the light of the moon, in the valley of the university. So present is the moon, so strong the pull it exerted on university life. But the moon, with its shimmerings and mystery, sheds its light on other episodes in Stephenson's life as well, becoming an ever-present motif in the novel. In Castries, walking down the hill, "Moonlight glinted on the wet grass on either side of the road," reminding him of when

> on a similar night, and after a dance, too, he had kicked his heels over the wet lawn on the way to his room, swinging his arms and smiling at himself under the moon. (88)

Even as the moon sheds light on many events in Stephenson's life, so, too, his walk reveals much of the social reality of differing areas.

> He began, then, to walk.
>   Sometimes he spoke to a policeman he had once played football against or once had bribed. They smoked cigarettes, the policeman taking care to hide his . . . he headed for the part of the town where he lived near the market. He walked along the littered streets past the rancid smell of small shops, past the smell of fried foods, past rumshops and the smells of urine and of vomit. (104)

After his conviction for accepting bribes, Stephenson walks to the hills for relief, there to sojourn briefly before his nightly walk throughout the city of Castries. This nightly walking affords St. Omer the opportunity to externalize many social features of Castries at that time. We learn of the segregated area, Columbus Square, where the old and dying colonial representatives live.

> He looked at the clean, two-storeyed houses with electric lights, . . . Cars were parked in the quiet empty streets. He heard voices on the verandah

. . . Their accent was different. Some of it was foreign. They were lawyers and doctors, held executive positions in the larger business houses. A few were white, none was, as yet, black. (102–103).

This exclusive neighborhood stands apart from those neighborhoods where poverty sleeps at night under verandas of small houses, where the air is redolent with odors and decay. But the city is more than contrasting neighborhoods. This city is where so many women live, their lives ruled and regulated by color and class, their expectations few, their hopes and dreams confined by lack of opportunity. Color and caste dictate their choices of mates.

St. Omer presents but does not analyze the recurrent incidence of children born from transient sexual relationships. Stephenson himself, the *ti beche* born from one such relationship, claims to suffer from it: "The girls and boys he played with, the girls especially, called him 'ti beche,' little white man" (97). From this social reality, many men flee, go away to work in refineries on other islands or seek their fortunes elsewhere.

And most of the men who leave do not return. Their exile, with all its ramifications for the loneliness of the women left behind, becomes permanent.

Carlton could not go home again now, even if he admitted that he wanted to, except on holiday or after he had retired. He had joined that ever-growing list of young men who left the island and went elsewhere to work and could not return because the island could not cater to them. They were exiles forever. (49)

Thus it is that after Stephenson's walkings through the city he, too, accidentally, goes away to an equally small neighboring island. There, Moira, Rosa, Edith, and the other women remain trapped in a stultifying loneliness that so often makes for devious sexual relationships.

Stephenson, transient and with no social responsibility for his behavior, involves himself in the lives of these trapped women. His life on this island is a "holiday," lacking in responsibility, lacking in effective social participation.

Remembering his episode with Rosa, Stephenson thought how characteristic it was of his existence . . . on her island . . . . He had come here to work . . . It was not difficult work, required no thought, no preparation. It offered no prospects either. Nor gave any satisfaction. (33)

Only the sea and the sun charge him with excitement, bring him moments of true fulfillment. His intercourse with the elements there on that small island liberates him momentarily. Mornings on the beach give him the sensation of space without end, of a sea and a sky without any limits to them. It seemed also there were no limits to the pleasures he derived from his body. (33)

But Stephenson's freedom and exhilaration in the sea are soon to be replaced by his walking huddled in the rain: "he suddenly felt small, futile . . . insignificant. He hunched his body even more under his raincoat" (46). All is problematic, devoid of meaning, everything seems to be gray rain. Stephenson is, "committed to his pursuit of futility" (115). There is no liberating swimming or running in the night wind, no Thea, no Eddie to envy. The replay of his personal life merely points to future possibilities. The island's social realities, especially on St. Lucia with its dead-end opportunities, its prognosis of boredom, of useless living, is fully externalized, taking on all the qualities of a dirge, the sound of requiem. The configurations of his personal reality, like those of the social reality, seem limiting not limitless, seem throttling not liberating; bordering on insanity, echoing the cry from the lunatic asylum.

Stephenson recalls the figure of Mr. Jones and his cul-de-sac life which seems to close in around him before he has fulfilled himself. Jones, forty-nine, married with five children, says he should have gone back, there's nothing to stay in the dreary foreignness for. His figure makes Stephenson recoil, makes him fear becoming a replica of Mr. Jones.

Similarly, in *Another Place, Another Time*, Derek refuses to follow the dead-end career of secondary school teaching, which the figure of Old Archie so clearly manifests.

> If Archie had a future once, he had none now . . . He had been teaching for many years, would get neither gratuity nor pension, nor any consideration for his years of service except perhaps a book token. (St. Omer, *Another Place, Another Time*, 215–216)

Here, this man, aging it seems before his time, living a promise which is a lie, has secretly turned to drink for temporary fulfillment.

Derek will not accept such a life, will not become entrapped by the promise of a job whose boundaries are circumscribed even before he enters it. In this circumscription, all the elements of dysfunctional colonialism are subtly demarcated. Obviously, the Irish priest wears all the guises of the missionary to the colonial outpost. In this assumed role of martyr, he, like the other teachers on the island, lives a privileged life, despite "his grave tones, his lean face, the crow's feet, all [making] him seem tired" (222).

Yet, this very privilege the priest would deny to the ambitious islander, Derek, directing him into the cul-de-sac of teaching, rather than into an open-ended medical career. That Derek totally refuses to become "martyr, saint, patriot," that, further, he sees behind the Irish priest's duplicity, makes him refuse to participate in any societally functional enterprises. He will work for his own betterment and that of his immediate family—not for the larger society and its improvement: "He had no cause nor any country now other than himself" (222–223). Derek negates his generation's responsibility, saying "his children will do it" (223). This answer seems to echo the statement in *Pan Beat*, which signals the losing of a generation of social activists who might fashion a new community, a new and vibrant island.

John Lestrade in *A Room on the Hill*, Stephenson in *The Lights on the Hill*, and Derek in *Another Place, Another Time*—all three main protagonists in these novels—though commenting on the colonial situation on their islands, refuse to become committed to or even involved in changing the shape of that colonial structure, of uprooting it by their actions. Clearly, then, this recurrent attitude of not attempting to change the basic status is evident in the characters' leaving, in their going away to acquire a profession or an education, which can make them part of the privileged class. Stephenson is not involved in the politics of the Federation. His friend, Carlton, however strident and however false, does participate in it. Derek, through a dysfunctional education, is not aware of the political process evolving in his own country.

> They had taught nothing of [the elections] in any of the schools he had attended. And perhaps they were right, for it did not concern him. Neither he nor his mother could vote. He was still too young and she was too poor. (*Another Place*, 134)

In these instances, then, both at the level of ambition and that of functional participation, all three characters demonstrate either the pursuit of selfish inclinations or the lack of responsibility that affords them the opportunity to drift and to introspect about their drift. As in *Pan Beat*, where the education of the sixth-formers has not prepared them for vital involvement in the sociopolitical evolution of their island, so too in these St. Omer novels, the colonial education has made of the protagonists uninvolved observers, participating only at the peripheral and personal levels in the communal aspects of their island country.

Derek's absent father and his friend have glimpsed the need for Derek's education. Miss Elaine, the woman who earns a living from selling sweets, souse, and black pudding, also sees the value of education. She laments only having gotten an education up to Standard Three, and realizes that Mr. Du Cote, whom she knew as a young woman, has arrived at his position in the society because of education. Berthe, her daughter, is studying for her pupil-teacher exam. The need for education is clear; the nature of education, however, is in question. Indeed, Mr. Du Cote, through education, has moved into a position of privilege, inheriting the privilege that the colonial masters enjoyed and that made for segregated living, segregated peoples.

St. Omer, though not analyzing the nature of colonial education at length, demonstrates its pernicious and harmful effects on his central characters. Education, then, becomes one of the central thematic schemes of this novel. Derek lives caught in its ambiguity, shifting between his privilege of secondary school education and the underprivileged conditions of his living.

> And over the years he had behaved as if he really had belonged to that race apart he had moved with, with the blue blazers and brass buttons . . . . Yet, always, he had returned to his home on the street where not one of them lived; to the smells and sounds of the shops, the noises from the rum-shops, the women who loitered in front of them or walked arm in arm with white sailors off ships refuelling in the harbour. (197)

Obviously, he cannot enjoy his privilege as a student of the leading secondary school. He not only is rejected by his neighborhood friends, but he learns the snobbery of privilege, rejecting because of her blackness a young woman whom he has formerly idolized, when "at college he discovered she was ugly, too black . . . he was ashamed of, and thankful no one knew what she had been to him" (161).

This evident acquired snobbery makes him walk between two separated realities, divided by space and by conditions of privilege. Here, even as in *The Lights on the Hill*, Derek's walk through the city telescopes the spatial separateness between the privileged and the poor, which St. Omer neither romanticizes nor scorns, but simply presents in each one's robust interactions.

Yet, that spatial separatedness has clearly affected Derek, who is caught between performance and his mother's expectations—expectations heightened by her sacrifice, her hard work.

> He could not be a tailor nor a master mason now. He must supply, if her efforts were not to have been a waste, the other half to the equation of which his mother's mistake, sending him to college, had been the first. It was too late for either of them to stop. He was a soldier in a war he had not caused nor wished to fight. (198)

Lying on the wall, apparently his favorite vantage point, Derek's jealousy of the boy rowing and fishing is but a manifestation of his lack of choice, his being pushed into a circumscribed place devoid of the naturalness of the young boy's actions.

Derek felt a spasm of inferiority . . . . The boat drifted, the boy was eating. He looked comfortable, uncaring, seemed to face no contradictions. (197–198)

The second central and palpable theme of these novels, providing both foreground and background, is random sex and its corollaries, illegitimacy, abortion, and fatherless homes. In *Another Place, Another Time*, Berthe's mother, Elaine, is not married to her father. Her reason:

"It's only the opportunity we didn' have. I left school in standard three. At [Berthe's] age I was selling sweets already with my mother." (132)

Derek's father, mostly absent, married his mother when Derek was eight years old. Derek's uncle, Beaurire, fathered the tubercular Cecil, whose mother, Edith, had many other random relationships. Sybil, now irascible and promiscuous, maintained her respectability and her job by marrying after she became pregnant. The father has returned to Trinidad and is absent. Her sister, Babsy, with whom she shares an apartment, eventually dies after having a series of abortions. In all of these instances, the men seem to accept no responsibility for their haphazard and random sexual relationships with the women. In the novel, there is a sense of licentiousness, where women are trapped, entering into relationships that have little future and no promise except for abandonment and exploitation.

St. Omer underscores the theme of aberrant sex by paralleling Derek's sadistic abuse of Berthe with the occurrence of Babsy's fatal abortion.

It was no different than he had expected. He was soon up and putting on his clothes again . . . .
"Yes, get angry. Then you can just walk out. Just like that."
Her toneless voice was not even angry . . . .
"You were going to take care. That's how. Everything in me."
She was right. He had taken absolutely no care. Well, it was going to be the last time . . . .
She was gone. He was alone in the room . . . went across the corridor into the dining room. He could hear Sybil talking to Berthe in the drawing-room. Babsy was dead. (209–210)

Berthe's rape by two of Derek's college colleagues does not awaken his sympathy or pity; rather it arouses feelings of rage, a desire for vengeance deriving from a selfishness and insecurity. His relationship to Berthe, which provides one of the central actions of the novel, is marked by his brutality and sadistic streak. Initially, he regrets not having deflowered her as they walked on the beach. He worries that he has been a fool, a sentimental idiot . . . . Once he had begun to struggle there was one thing he should have done—continue struggling, harder the more Berthe resisted. (151)

He berates himself for what he calls his "silly sentimentality." Later, when he chauvinistically believes that he is the first to make love to Berthe, her unexpected and inopportune confession to having been raped awakens all of Derek's sadistic brutality. All he can think of is the shattering of his own fragile ego. Why Berthe confesses to the rape at that particular time after offering herself to him is not analyzed by St. Omer. Her reason is not even speculated on, only the result is revealed: Derek's continuing craving for her and his continuing desire to hurt her in order to repair his shattered male self-image.

> He was brutal, taking her again. And desire for revenge was only a little satisfied when he saw her crying afterwards on the bed next to him. (188)

His continuous and unabated brutality makes meaningless the long introspective inner dialogues with which St. Omer girds his character: the introspection seems out of context, dubious and novelistically out of character. Both the substance of the novel and Derek's portrayal derive from his involvement in education and his involvement with sex. Derek's introspective crisscrossed interior debate about mother and lover does not have that vital tension, does not resonate with dramatic intensity, but seems indulgent, pathetic. In *Another Place, Another Time*, the overwhelming mood is one of anguish, the social reality fragmented, disassociated, barren of promise.

Through a series of interlocking relationships, the character of Peter, the central protagonist of St. Omer's novel, *Nor Any Country*, is delineated. Through introspection and the constant analysis of situations of cause and effect, of motive and origin, Peter's personality is leisurely but relentlessly shaded in. For this novel, like all of St. Omer's other novels, is constructed on the charting of character rather than on the narrative action; more on analysis, the outlining of personality, in all of its minute sociopsychological contourings, than on the rapidly shifting configurations of plot and subplot. Thus, in the novels, little is left in doubt: all is exposed, externalized through analysis of action, of the comparative correlation of situations, of the interplay and fusion of time. Through flashback and by the use of recall, temporal correspondence is given to episodes, shading, drawing them together, making them elastic and immediate. Relationships between Peter in England and his accepting, understanding white lover, Daphne; between

Peter and the volatile artist, the intriguing Black woman, Anna, are recalled and compared with Peter's social and sexual intercourse with his mulatto wife, Phyllis, whom he left behind on the island of St. Lucia, while he pursued his studies.

> And the prolonged touch of their aroused bodies becoming normal again together under the blankets was something he had never known in his brief, insensitive couplings with Phyllis or in his intense, lustful and brief contacts with Anna. (St. Omer, *Nor Any Country*, 13)

St. Omer makes their sexual intercourse, or rather the methods of their participation, extensions of their differing personalities. Daphne is all uncritical acceptance, displaying total allegiance, unswervable identification with Peter. She unquestioningly accepts every experimental sexual position. Peter remembers "the world of sexual improvisation he had discovered with Daphne" (81). As she follows his sexual initiatives, she also patterns her social responses to fit what she perceives as his concerns.

> The cause of all spades had seemed to be hers. She would come into their bedsitter, sucking her teeth, and tell her latest story of intolerance and prejudice. (83)

Anna, on the contrary, is volatile, passionate, and impetuous. She is more self-assured, more conscious of her heritage, more traditional. In lovemaking, she is less experimental, more in control of all situations, with "a certain carefulness, an instinct for avoiding unpleasant or uncomfortable situations [that] had always qualified her" (81). Assured of herself, she reacts with confident arrogance to racism, is guided by potential artistic excellence, not snobbery. Anna will not brook duplicity and, on discovering a concealed photograph of Phyllis, inscribed "To my dear husband," she walks away from the bedside.

> She had been calm listening to his explanation, her things on the bed, her empty bag beside them. Before he had finished she was putting the things back into it. (39)

In bed, Phyllis is subservient, self-effacing, willing to take crumbs, to be used and abused. Only once, it seems, does Phyllis challenge Peter's abuse and tyrannical behavior. Bravely, if but momentarily, she refuses a marriage of convenience.

> "I won't have an abortion. You don't have to marry me if you don't want to."
> He remembered single-mindedness, the tears forgotten now that had accompanied it, angered him. (42)

Except for that one instance, she moves to the winds of Peter's actions, insubstantial, weak, nonassertive. So that she becomes, when Peter returns, not simply an obstacle as she seemed while he was in England, but an object to be taken and mounted at will. No tenderness here, no respect for another day; only, it seems, a willful and vengeful brutality, as Peter "finally turned to that body which did not attract him, his lust aroused, and mounted it" (56). Similarly, out of bed, she is subservient and a bit of a hound dog.

> "What's the matter?" she asked . . . . "Have I done something?"
> He resented her humility, her apparent readiness to assume blame.
> (40)

All three female figures move through intersecting phases of reality, affecting Peter's action, his reactions, indicating and becoming signposts of his character. Daphne's constant, uncritical giving with its attendant clinging control, irritates Peter, his deceit at not telling her of his impending return to St. Lucia heightened by his not being able to fault her generosity.

> In the dark, he found again his mood of self-indictment, and his assumed exploitation of Daphne loomed more clearly, more accusingly, than his deception of Anna. (15)

Anna's assurance challenges Peter; Phyllis's obsequiousness, her patient, dumb waiting, strikes anger, awakens brutal instincts. That he finds her "at once insolent and accusing" only heightens her weakness. She is long-suffering, pathetic. She, like Peter's mother, has never been shown tenderness nor honest affection. Like so many women in St. Omer's social reality, she seems totally dependent on any form of even transitory gratification, on the whimsy, the wanton pleasure of brutal irresponsible males. Woven into these novels are women, often debased and exploited victims, who turn to religion or, more often, to sex for fulfillment. Often what results is not fulfillment, but impregnation, forced marriage, illegitimate births, at times suicide.

The social reality represented by St. Omer is one of unrelieved gloom, as women live truncated lives, totally lacking in gratification. The social position of these women is so grim, so desperate, the social reality so stark, so rigid, that few of the many female characters—even those who have received on the island an education similar to the male characters—analyze or even protest their predicament. Such analyzing would give at least a modicum of movement to a rigid pattern.

Occasionally, the men suffer for their sexual irresponsibility. Peter's brother Paul refuses to marry Patricia, whom he has impregnated. His refusal stems not from any radical societal notions, but rather from a desire to maintain a rigid independence. For his refusal, he is dismissed from his teaching position at the college and is ostracized, which leads him downward to loneliness, then to drink and prostitution, later to a semblance of piety, which the community accepts as redemptive, and finally to acting as if he were mad, which offers him a retreat and shield from the society's accusations. Paul, through assiduous discipline and training, has triumphed on the playing fields. He seems driven by one desire—that of excelling, of winning. The shape of Paul's character, which dictates his position in the small society, has been determined largely by his success in sports and the prestige that emanates from achievement, as in other novels. That his sexual involvement with Patricia and his subsequent refusal to marry her now negate his achievement, his successes in sports demonstrates how important, how effective, is the role of sex in the social reality delineated by St. Omer. Thus it is that sex and its consequences determine and control the lifestyles of the two brothers, Peter and Paul, whose characters are central to the novel's narrative structure.

As with Derek in *The Lights on the Hill,* Peter, while brutalizing Phyllis, demonstrates some concern, some filial affection for his mother. Her welcome to him on his return is sketched with warm colors and his acceptance of the welcome is affectionate and gentle. She waits on him and fusses over him, seems always to stand near the table while he eats.

> As she held him silently, he heard the familiar roar from the market place, the familiar beat of the station engines, the noises from the street, and smiled upon the grey in the hair which was all that he could see now as, her face buried in his abdomen, she recited the *Magnificat Anima Mea Dominum.* (19)

Also, on his return, Peter's relationship with his father takes on a cordiality, indeed, a geniality. For the first time they eat at the same table, a gesture that is so lacking in St. Omer's novels. But clearly, since his conviviality is not founded on a deep and binding affection, memory alone will not suffice to give it a solid foundation: "And when they had exhausted their memories, they found they had little else to say to each other" (30).

The relationship between Paul, who stayed on the island, and his mother, who has always been constrained, now becomes tense with the open feuding between Paul and his father. Paul is willful, stubborn, and refuses to be placated by his mother's affectionate gestures. And he challenges his father at every turn, ultimately wishing to destroy by his display and pretense of madness his father's new-found prosperous status as superintendent and his father's dreams of acquiring a new house. Confessing to Peter, whose self-righteousness he bridles over, Paul states:

"I can never be a disgrace now, to her or to anyone else. Except your father. It is only for him that, dead to myself and to others, I am very much alive. When I put on a suit and go and sit in that dirty warehouse and people stare and snigger, it's he that's tainted . . . I hate him." (105–106)

Peter's return affords St. Omer the opportunity to present an outline of the past relationships between mother and sons, between father and sons, between Peter and Paul. The motif of return also affords St. Omer the opportunity to present, if not analyze, themes of race, class, and color that pervade the society and direct the movement of the members of that society. The social reality seems static, unchanging, perhaps unchangeable for the plantocracy as represented by Desmangues. The essential classism remains unchallenged even by the avowedly brilliant Austin. Keith Austin, a successful and wealthy Black lawyer, despite his sophistication, his taste, is shackled by feelings of inferiority vis-à-vis older mulatto-like families. Indeed, Austin, who is to enter the privileged segregated circle of the social club, wishes further to achieve the lightening of his color by marriage to a mulatto woman.

On the other hand, Desmangues, a member of the old plantocracy, has with total freedom and license trespassed on the space of the Black woman, mother of Phyllis, with whom he cohabits. But Desmangues cannot bequeath his power and the means of his wealth to her family. Her daughter as well as her other children consequently live in reduced circumstances in the big house, now rented out for wild parties by prostitutes. But the notions of class and color privilege are depicted figurally by St. Omer, rather than analyzed in depth, or explored in detail.

Again it is through the play of memory that the static nature of yet another sociocultural element, religion, is presented in the figure of Father Thomas. He, like Louis in *Pan Beat*, lives in the ambivalence deriving from his color, his origin. Here, Father Thomas realizes the ambiguity of his situation, caught as he is between a rigid, dysfunctional religion which nourishes the soul but does not provide for the body, and his own inner feeling of responsibility to the people of the community where he was born, to which he belongs. He questions his role as priest, realizing its perogatives of privilege. With Peter, whose visit to the island is a short one, he freely discusses his ambivalent situation, stating,

"Being a priest seems somehow abortive. I should have been a bridge, like you, a link between our parents and the children you alone will have . . . . Now you alone, of the two of us, are that bridge. I am like one side only of a bridge. I project from one bank and I end over the chasm." (101)

The theme of going away and going home appears throughout the novel. Peter is not initially recognized by the boatman, Antoine, because Peter's faltering native patois and his nonisland English accent already make him stand out; he already seems differentiated by language: "He was a stranger" (87).

Recognition, however, when it does eventually come, immediately erases any alienation. Now Peter can enter the native laughter. Yet, in his relationships with former classmates and friends, many of whom are now civil servants, Peter cannot really enter their professional idiom. Is Peter, the Ph.D., able to come home again? If he's a doctor but does not cure people, "Why they calling you doctor?" (62) questions Father Thomas's mother.

Peter is peeved at Phyllis's and his new nephew's patois, as well as his nephew's uncritical attitudes toward religion—attitudes that vitiate rather than vitalize the social reality. But Peter remains unable to effect change. The question here is: is Peter, given his own moral, sexual, and ethical proclivities, equipped to bring about any change in that seemingly static sociocultural reality? Does his nonbelonging derive from his own inner character traits, or from the inability of the static society to accept him? The societal condition, the island's social values remain unaffected, since the men who go away never seem to return and, like Peter, must travel outward again.

Thus, the fragmented sociocultural reality, fragmented and dysfunctional through the unsolved strictures of race, color, class, and sex, seem unaffected either by those who stay at home or by those who go away. Clearly the social reality of this set of novels has not as yet achieved a cohering communality— its separateness persisting at many levels of intercourse, its potential lessened by that separateness. The process of going away is still operative, so an indigenizing cohesion has not as yet become an effective possibility, making the society whole.

CHAPTER 5

I Going Away:
The Exiled Ones

Oh shuttered exiles,
When will you be home again
To fan and light again
The cold, wet coal-pot fires.
. . .
Oh shuttered exile son
When will you come back
To read that yellow parchment
For a mother,
Shuttered exile
All alone at home.

Wilfred Cartey, *Waters of My Soul*

These are The Emigrants.
On sea-port quays
at air-ports
anywhere where there is ship
or train, swift
motor car, or jet
to travel faster than the breeze
you see them gathered:
passports stamped
their travel papers wrapped
in old disused news-
papers: lining their patient queues.

Where to?
They do not know.
Canada, the Panama
Canal, the Miss-
issippi painfields, Florida?
Or on to dock
at hissing smoke locked
Glasgow?

Why do they go?
They do not know.
Seeking a job
they settle for the very best
the agent has to offer:
jabbing a neighbour
out of work for four bob
less a week.

What do they hope for
what find there
these New World mariners.

Edward Brathwaite, "The Emigrants," *Rights of Passage*

Be not afeard; the isle is full of noises,
Sounds and sweet airs, that give delight, and hurt not
Sometimes a thousand twangling instruments
Will hum about mine ears; and sometimes voices,
That, if I then had wak'd after long sleep,
Will make me sleep again: and then, in dreaming,
The clouds me thought would open, and show riches
Ready to drop upon me; that, when I wak'd
I cried to dream again.

William Shakespeare, *The Tempest,* Act 3, Scene 2

The details of this ceremony are very elaborate; but the outline, the conscious style of intention, is quite simple. (Lamming, *The Pleasures of Exile*, 9)

And indeed, the structure and intention of George Lamming's *The Pleasures of Exile* do take on these very configurations, extended details, and fully externalized situations,

> to make use of *The Tempest* as a way of presenting a certain state of feeling which is the heritage of the exiled and colonial writer from the British Caribbean. (9)

Later, in *Water with Berries*, Lamming novelistically, but with all the central elaborate structurings of the architect, of a master craftsman, joins historical stone to stone, constructing an elaborate relationship between the heir of Prospero and the descendant of Caliban, between the Old Dowager and the children of Caliban, whose blasphemy tears apart her way of feeling. In that novel, the destruction of the Old Dowager attains to that ultimate fragmentation of reality—the assumption of Caribbean presence is possible, indeed realizable.

Here in *The Pleasures of Exile*, even though we wander with the narrator through many turnings, leisurely move through, at the pleasure of the exile, many literary episodes, a recurrent and insistent motif is the divestment of historical domination, the uncementing of an unequal cultural symbiosis which would ultimately negate the exiled search for meaning, for belonging. *The Pleasures of Exile* is a solemn communion, attempting to unearth the secrets of the colonial past, to sift and clarify them, making them relevant to the lives of the living, the Caribbean peoples, offering possible prognoses for the future.

> My subject is the migration of the West Indian writer, as colonial and exile, from his native kingdom, once inhabited by Caliban, to the tempestuous island of Prospero's and his language.
> This book is a report on one man's way of seeing. (13)

Is the writer, then, here a priest deciphering the enigma of the colonial past, sanctifying by imaginative and ritual ceremony the purgatory of that past, mediating the present, actualizing it, then prognosticating through the presentation of details of evidence a future of hope, of possibility? In the Ceremony of the Souls, in that ritual, the "sign, like a cross," transforms, reminding the Haitian peasants of their needs, then signifying again:

Through the medium of the Priest, the Dead speak of matters which it must have been difficult to raise before; and through the same medium, the living learn and understand what the Dead tongues have uttered. Revenge, guilt, redemption, and some future expectation make for an involvement which binds the Dead and the living together. (10)

Lamming outlines through his allegorical reference to the ceremony of the Souls his idea of the role of the West Indian writer. "Prayer," he states, "will assume whatever needs these peasants whisper" (10). And, "It is the duty of the Dead to return and offer, on this momentous night, a full and honest report on their past relations with the living" (9).

In setting up the "narrowest and widest terms of reference" (11) within which to judge colonial history and to adjudge the encounter between Prospero and Caliban, Lamming introduces the continuing paradox of the symbiotic relationship between master and slave.

For deep down, Prospero may want to change. Prospero's reluctance is but a part of his fear, and that fear is only the measure of his own self-colonisation.

For colonisation is a reciprocal process. (156)

The colonial condition as presented in *The Pleasures of Exile* is functional and unresolved, and much of the argumentation itself seems to remain rooted in the colonial condition.

Lamming draws on *The Tempest* as "prophetic of a political future which is our present," as if, conversely, the theme of "the migration of the West Indian writer, as colonial and exile, from his native kingdom" (13) intersects with that first exile of Prospero and Caliban. From this intersection, *The Pleasures of Exile* derives its own analytic tension. This is the historic encounter between Prospero, caught in but still possessing his magic (be it in the BBC), his knowledge; and Caliban, still innocent, still slave, however subtly defined. The ensuing symbiotic fusion, the relationship, seems to remain static, fixed. But *The Pleasures of Exile* still stands out as a bold effort to explain the nature or cause of departure of West Indian writers to England—the historical and cultural reasons for that exile, much of it rooted in the ambiguity of the relationship between Caliban and Prospero.

Ambiguity is swept away, is absorbed in the deep resonances, the polyphony, the polyrhythms of narrative sequences, evidence of some of Lamming's finest, strongest writing, indeed of some of the best lyric prose of any Caribbean writer. The bass drums boom out, and their echoes secure the rhythms of the hills, the mountains, of the islands, and their resonances roll over the dancing seas and waters of the surroundings, the islands reiterating their history.

"'Twas like in that time when the world know only nature and noise
. . . ."

". . . An' the fish dancin' wild an' makin' faces at the bottom o' the
ocean, an' only the sun get permission to say the time, an' the moon only
makin' plans to decide the size o' the sea, or makin' fun at some mountains which couldn't climb no more, an' sometimes collapse if a new tide
turn upside down, and shake up the sand." (19)

And the tenor pans sing out the melody, telling the story of beginnings,
of origins, in sweet ringing notes whose harmonies urge belief.

"Like in Genesis," Lee said.

"As in the beginnin'," said Bob, "before sense start to make separation betwixt some things an' some things."

"An' food was free," said Singh, "'cause there was no han' to hide
what it take." (19)

And all the time the modulated cello whispers and hums the mystery of an
evolving drama.

"Well just so it was," said Singh. "Exactly the state o' the island when
the Tribe Boys arrive. Right here on San Cristobal. Nobody know where
they sail from or how they favour here from home. But just so. They set
foot on San Cristobal, see it was empty, and say there an' then that it
belong to them." (19)

Then it is in the voices of the little boys that the legend of will and the
resistance to conquest and domination is chorused, a pan folk song weaving
together fact and fiction, a contrapuntal choiring hymning the virtues of
peace—

The peace which touch the Tribe Boys at night take them in a trance to
the top o' the world an' to the beginnin' an' end o' the ocean. (20)

—celebrating the courage of belief, ordaining:

"Where a man work," said Lee, "you can't always tell what turn his
reward will take. So with the Tribe Boys. They put a seed in the ground
expectin' nature to raise it up an' train it with time to make a certain
taste, and sudden so, like when the Kings come, something say that taste
is one thing, but what now sweeten the tongue must turn to a kind o'
terror. An' the Tribe Boys use simple food to fight with." (20)

". . . The pepper trees just burn and the Kings crawl like cripples who
can't find their crutch, 'cause when that smoke wrap round them, it put
the fire o' hell in every eye." (21)

This legend, fashioned in and celebrated by the voices of Bob, Lee, and Singh, three young Caribbean boys of African, Chinese and Indian descent, is a narrative, testimony to Lamming's assertion that the phenomenon of the emergence of West Indian novelists' writing is of great significance and stunning import. To be sure, these writers have located and given shape to the condition of the peasantry of the Caribbean, their abiding strength and their uncertainty. They have also located and given voice to the nature of that condition, the awareness, the sensibility of the peasantry. Yet the West Indian writer has found no place in his native land for publication of his works—the stranglehold the English held over the curriculum prompts Lamming to lament:

> How in the name of Heavens could a colonial native taught by an English native within a strict curriculum diligently guarded by yet another English native who functioned as a reliable watch-dog, the favourite clerk of a foreign administration: how could he ever get out from under this ancient mausoleum of historic achievement? (27)

But though most of the West Indian writers have come out of that peasant condition, their flight to the Headquarters may often represent an attempt to abnegate that origin. Indeed, the writers are faced by the unconcern of the middle class, most of which read mainly for the purpose of passing examinations,

> [examinations] which would determine that Trinidadian's future in the Civil Service, imposed Shakespeare, and Wordsworth, and Jane Austen and George Eliot and the whole tabernacle of dead names. (27)

Yet Lamming's statement, "to be in exile is to be alive" (24), is a manifestation of a need for entry into a presumed vitalizing space which clearly England is not. The notion of getting away, of having to get away, is depicted here:

> . . . *to get out*. That is the phrase which we must remember in considering this question of why the writers are living in England. They simply wanted *to get out* of the place where they were born. (41)

The act of going to the Headquarters at its most extreme can be seen in the novels of V. S. Naipaul, even though the West Indian writer, as Lamming suggests, is subject to that

> instinct and root impulse which return the better West Indian writers back to the soil. For soil is a large part of what the West Indian novel has

brought back to reading; lumps of earth: unrefined, perhaps, but good, warm, fertile earth. (46)

Yet that fertilizing force can hardly be gained in the thoroughly British Institute of Conjunctory Arts, can hardly be grasped in the leisurely presentation of debates about pubs; or drawing room poets can hardly be sustained by the bird discussion between English scientist and American professor. Lamming ascribes a more serious task to the emerging West Indian leaders, that task of decolonizing the mentality and culture of Caribbean peoples, a decolonization which can then provide the necessary space and oxygen for the returning West Indian writer.

> They can encourage the schools at the earliest possible stage to turn the habit of reading for examinations into the more intelligent habit of reading for exploration and discovery. (49)

> This may be the dilemma of the West Indian writer abroad: that he hungers for nourishment from a soil which he . . . could not at present endure. (50)

Throughout *The Pleasures of Exile*, Lamming offers prescriptions for change, for altering a colonial way of seeing or for changing a racial condition—a condition which stifles growth. (40)

Yet in many of the anecdotal episodes that bring together the descendants of Prospero and Caliban as projections of possibilities, there is no true interdependency relative to that change. For Caliban in these episodes remains dependent on Prospero. He becomes a reaction, he is acted upon, does not indeed act. It can be said that Caliban's change is the change of contemporary reality. In exile in Prospero's land, he loses his initial will to protest, to rebel. His rebellious spirit has been muted: David Pitts's inability to show anger may have derived from this muting of a rebellious spirit. He has learned, too well, perhaps, the art of that very diplomacy with which Peter meets the threat of Notting Hill. For Peter, who has lived long in London, does not openly rebel against a possible racially motivated attack against him. His response, still within the boundaries of respect for English law, is flight. Thus Lamming's, as well as Peter's, acceptance of Prospero's legal generosity leads into a false acceptance of Prospero's benevolence.

> Why didn't the Home Secretary intervene, positively intervene? . . . Either he did not think the situation sufficiently urgent and calculated that the matter would solve itself, or he realised its urgency, but had reasons for postponing his decision about intervention. (82)

Perhaps it is this danger that Lamming warns against when he argues that the West Indian student . . . should not be sent to study in England. Not because England is a bad place for studying, but because the student's whole development as a person is thwarted by memory, the accumulated stuff of a childhood and adolescence which has been maintained and fertilised by England's historic ties with the West Indies. (25)

Lamming is certainly aware of the impact of colonization on the behavior of the colonized. For he bluntly states that the assumptions, the myths become

a part of the actual texture of behavior itself. Sometimes it will take the form of a calculated aggressiveness; at other times it may take the form of sulking. At its worst, it is the soil from which the perfect lackey is born. (26)

And in the case of Peter and Lamming himself, both exiles in London during the Notting Hill violence, they seem to have been devitalized rather then vitalized by their exile. Neither is able to admit to himself the possibility of violence at the hands of the children of Prospero.

I recall a feeling of utter stupefaction; for I had argued in America—a year before—that it was difficult to draw parallels in spite of prejudice, for Georgia or Alabama just could not happen anywhere in England. (80–81)

Even the humorously told episode of the factory girl's curiosity about the nature of the Jamaican workers' sexual organs demonstrates a devitalizing of that Jamaican worker. In this factory, there are many descendants of Prospero, many factory Mirandas, whose naked curiosity about "the beast" exposes them to that beast.

Sam related one incident which had to do with English factory girls creeping up behind the Jamaican, trying to lift his jacket in the hope of discovering his tail. The Jamaican peasant was deeply shaken by this reduction of his person to the status of an ape. (77–78)

But the Jamaican factory worker does not react with Caliban's raw vitality. Indeed, he reacts with the same stupefaction that Lamming and Peter demonstrate in their reaction to racial disturbances in Notting Hill. Here Lamming, with his gift of language, does not speculate on a contrary contingency based on all the rules of English fair play. What would have happened had the Jamaican, equally curious about the color and consistency of the factory Mirandas, lifted their dresses to investigate? Could he then be described as a child of the backward glance or would the legal authorities have met this with a stiff upper lip?

Yet in spite of the muting of the spirit of rebellion, Lamming constantly emphasizes the continuity of that spirit, of the struggle for survival, of the continual challenge against Prospero's dominance. In a delightfully incisive discussion of the possible cohabitation of Caliban and Miranda, Lamming speculates on the political significance of Caliban's reaction to the false charge of attempting to rape Miranda: "Did Caliban really try to lay her? . . . Could Prospero really have endured the presence and meaning of a brown skin grandchild?" (102).

The spirit of rebellion—the same spirit that provoked Caliban to reply that, had he not been stopped, he would have actually raped Miranda—is explored on a much graver level when Lamming juxtaposes C.L.R. James's *The Black Jacobins* with William Shakespeare's *The Tempest* in order to explore the significance of the overthrow of Prospero. Adducing from James, Lamming enumerates the methods of survival, the dynamics of rebellion. But a precondition of Caliban's successful revolt is the transformation of language.

> We shall never explode Prospero's old myth until we christen Language afresh; . . . James shows us Caliban as Prospero had never known him: a slave who was a great soldier in battle . . . full of paradox but never without compassion. (118–119)

Although Lamming credits James with having exploded the myth, of paramount importance in this discussion is the question of generosity and indebtedness. Caliban's generosity lands him in a rock prison. Later on, Toussaint L'Ouverture's basic humanism, his generosity of spirit and aristocracy with which C.L.R. James seems to imbue him, land him equally in a rock-cave in Fort-de-Joux, where his exile does not lead to life but to a lonely death. L'Ouverture perhaps has not appreciated the brutal contract between Prospero—that is, Napoleon Bonaparte, his commissioners—and himself, still viewed as slave by them. For it could be argued that Toussaint's humanism, which James lauds so much, may have been more of a defect than a virtue in his relationship with Prospero's descendants, whose inherent brutality he knew, but did not honestly believe.

Unlike Dessalines, Toussaint has not experienced all the brutality inflicted on him by Prospero's descendants. For a month, Toussaint does not join the slave rebellion. In his generosity of spirit, he stays behind to protect his master's family. Throughout his narrative, *The Black Jacobins*, James, though stressing the inherent nobility of Toussaint's character, alludes to that nobility as if it were an inheritance of the Europeans, a language more proper to them than to the slave. Of interest here is that the brilliance with which Lamming analyzes *The Tempest*, with which he orchestrates Caliban's benighted condition, is missing from his analysis of *The Black Jacobins*. For instance, did Toussaint L'Ouverture really owe to the Abbe Raynal's writings his participation in the revolution, his leadership of that revolution?

> Where is he, that great man whom Nature owes to her vexed, oppressed and tormented children? . . . Everywhere people will bless the name of the hero who shall have reestablished the rights of the human race (126)

Or could Toussaint's intention to liberate the slaves have come about by having witnessed, if not suffered from, Prospero's brutality?

All the modulations of rhetoric and argumentation fuse together as Lamming articulates the symbiosis of past relationships, of an ongoing but changing intercourse between the descendants of Prospero and Caliban. The author locks them into an interdependency in which any change in the spatial movements, any shift in the psychological conduct of the one, leads to a correlative, if not corresponding change in the other. The victory of Caliban signals a new order, a new relationship with new rules. Lamming declares that:

> The old blackmail of Language simply won't work any longer. For the language of modern politics is no longer Prospero's exclusive vocabulary. It is Caliban's as well. (158)

Although Toussaint may have misjudged the generosity of Prospero and lost his own life, the transformation of Caliban has been achieved. "The ploughs had spoken" (125). And it is with that revolutionary act that Lamming balances the reciprocal relationship that perhaps is at play in his brilliant explication of *The Tempest*. In that energetic and vital analysis, Lamming grasps the nature of Prospero's deceit; his use of camouflage to obscure history, his use of propaganda to implant falsehoods. Yet Lamming, the descendant of Caliban, sometimes seems to accept, in his vital analysis of the relationship between Prospero and Caliban, the way of seeing which ordained Shakespeare's writing of *The Tempest*. He often appears not to challenge this way of seeing; indeed by his gift of language, with a blinding clarity, he accentuates it to such a degree that he illuminates Prospero. Rather than presenting his brutality, he stresses the brutishness of Caliban.

Prospero acquires the proportions of king, philosopher, and priest, and even though the illumination is underscored with irony, it is done. On the other hand, Caliban's total brutishness, his dependence on Prospero for the gift of language, engage all the dramatic intensity of language at Lamming's command.

> For Language itself, by Caliban's whole relation to it, will not allow his expansion beyond a certain point . . . .

Such is Caliban, superfluous as the weight of the earth until Prospero arrives with the aid of the Word which might help him to clarify the chaos which shows its true colours all over his skin. But he can never be regarded as an heir of that Language, since his use of Language is no more than his way of serving Prospero. (110)

Yet for Lamming to use the language he does—and not to serve Prospero—suggests that the emergence of West Indian writers represents a transformation that hails no less than the creation of a new language, the presentation of a revolutionary way of seeing—and speaking of—things. Further, he removes these writers from the crippling necessity of seeking approval or validation from Headquarters.

What the West Indian writer has done has nothing to do with that English critic's assessments. The West Indian writer is the first to add a new dimension to writing about the West Indian community.

. . . the West Indian peasant became other than a cheap source of labour. He became, through the novelist's eye, a living existence, living in silence and joy and fear, involved in riot and carnival. It is the West Indian novel that has restored the West Indian peasant to his true and original status of personality. (37, 39)

Thus, this liberation of the personality is almost simultaneous with the liberation from the prison of myths imposed during the reign of Prospero.

Having established Caliban's freedom, Lamming allows the landscapes for his discourses to range from the Caribbean to London, through Africa and the Americas. His voyaging to Africa, like that of the main protagonists of *The Scholar-Man* and *The Leopard*, is fraught with a lack of knowledge and weighted down with expectation based on a visceral connection, as yet undefined, between him and the landscape to which he is traveling. The West Indian traveling to Africa is perceived by Lamming to be in a less secure position than a white American traveling in Europe.

His relation to that continent is more personal and more problematic. It is more personal because the conditions of his life today, his status as a man, are a clear indication of the reasons which led to the departure of his ancestors from that continent. (160)

Lamming's discovery—that the fundamental link with the land and language has never been broken—means that "[The Africans] owed Prospero no debt of vocabulary . . . their passions were poured through another rhythm of speed" (162). As his journeys continue, Lamming seems to achieve a kind of personal liberation through insight into the particular forms of exile of the two-thirds of the world held captive by a perception of debt to Prospero.

> The world from which our reciprocal ways of seeing have sprung was once Prospero's world. It is no longer his. Moreover, it will never be his again. It is ours, the legacy of many centuries, demanding of us a new kind of effort, a new kind of sight for viewing the possible horizons of our own century. (203)

Throughout *The Pleasures of Exile*, Lamming often appears to be pleading for Prospero's reform, even while urging that the capacity to be shocked by his continued brutality and deceit must not be lost; yet Lamming, in his realization that the fragmentation of self—the shedding of the colonial self—has not occurred, intimates that the reformation of Prospero may be a lost cause, and his writing takes on a quality of grimness, a tone of gray despair. And though Lamming sees a prognosis for cohesion in the Caribbean, based on the multiracial composition of its nationals, his distrust of Prospero's capacity to function democratically leads him to warn against

> a similar method of blackmail . . . attempted through the language of Science and Technology. Science is no one's secret; and the modern Caliban is a greedy learner. He can learn methods of investigation as thoroughly as any Prospero with similar facilities. Moreover, he comes to these disciplines with a freshness of eye, a sharpness of curiosity; for their results still have the fascination of magic for his own landscape. (159)

Lamming, through his exploration and analysis of the conditions of exile, arrives at an intellectual and cognitive method of formulating that condition. He, in fact, though participant in *The Pleasures of Exile*, becomes the objective edge cutting through the various threads in which the colonial personality is still enmeshed. However, *The Emigrants* who come, journeying from their landscapes of magic to Prospero's kingdom, to occupy his space, to learn his form of magic, on arrival there do not come upon an island full of music, of songs and sweet smells that give delight, rather they come stumbling and fumbling through the fog, plunged into a benighted condition that numbs their sensibilities. Gone is the leisurely discourse of *The Pleasures of Exile*. Now actualized in *The Emigrants* is a setting that

> was dingy and damp, a hole which had lost its way in the earth; and they put their hands out along the wall and over the floor like crabs clawing for security. (Lamming, *The Emigrants*, 127)

The alienation the emigrants suffer is shrouded in an inscrutable darkness. That confounding fog is continuous and does not lift. Their arrival, the journey on the train in which already they begin to locate the differences between the landscape they left and that unto which they wander, ends in a stammer that presages a groping and incoherent entry into an unknown and uncharted reality. Lamming, by truncating the language, by affording it a disjunctional quality, dramatizes the break with their own certainty, their own native idiom: "So cold . . . so frightened . . . so frightened . . . home . . . go . . . to go back . . . home" (122).

They are refugees who have left home to be met by that crowd, that gray crowd, and the only voices that speak with certainty are those strange to them.

> Only these voices speak clearly. The strange ones. The men working on the platform. The others talk as though they were choked. (122)

Already the beginning disassociation from the reality of their home, from the certainty of their belonging, has taken place. The stammer, the stutter of language has already been preceded by a stifled tear that silently rips apart Higgins's dreams and hopes.

> Higgins was crying and no one knew, but in his resistance, it seemed that he had become the dormitory itself. He was crying over himself and the others. For in the dormitory it was as though they were in a cage with the doors flung open, but they couldn't release themselves. (105)

The cage is opening out to a nothingness, a barrenness, for they have come—moved by the instinct of possibility, herdlike—to England in search of what they know not. Ironically, it is Higgins who has been so certain of his reasons for coming, and who has during the voyage attempted to instill a measure of certainty into his fellow passengers. It is he who undergoes the first searing loss of hope. He was going to become a master chef—of that he had been certain. On his arrival his dreams explode and he is lost in the facelessness of his exile. Tornado, who in his condition of exile has lost that visceral quality of certainty, wonders about the nature of chance, asking whether the nothingness to which man is reduced is an ordained quality, whether chance or one's particular fortune is irreversible. This discussion between the Jamaican, Higgins, and Tornado intimates that this new space into which the emigrants have entered seems devoid of the hope with which they had invested it, seems barren of possibility.

> "They come expectin' to find some kind o' chance, an' then they find out that the same kind o' misfortune is in the place."
>
> "An' something more than misfortune . . . a kind of disaster which we wouldn't 'ave known at home . . . . They learn that the picture of the

place they choose to make men o' themselves, that picture wus all wrong." (189)

In London the condition of exile operates slowly but relentlessly on the emigrants, reducing them, closing in around them. The cage into which Higgins transforms the dormitory, shrunken into a room, shuts them in on themselves. Here there is no societal remedy to their personal dilemma; they cannot reach out to the certainty of experience to cushion their aloneness or to provide them a reprieve from the boredom of their lives. Even though in the regions they have left, their banter had no particular direction, resolved no particular problem, at least they could rely on it for momentary pleasure. But here there is no pleasure in the exile. Forced in on themselves, they are made to confront the meaning of self, of relationship. The play of memory tugs them between their immediate condition of exile and the nostalgic re-creation of the landscape they've left. Their sensibilities swing and pendulate between the conditions to which they've come and those they've left. Here, in this condition of grayness, of being caged in, there is not the red and yellow explosion of the *poui* and immortelle trees that "stand at the very top of the hills, so that above and beyond them there was nothing but the empty, expanding air" (12). The emigrants have fled that accessible landscape, have gone away from a known experience, and through a reversal of the middle passage, as it were, they are arriving at another condition of exile.

Their journey to that exile is both filled by the certainty of the experiences back home and shrouded by the uncertainty of their going away to an unfamiliar destination. The middle ground of the journey, which is taking them away from home toward that uncertain future, describes their coming together in groups and a breaking away from one another—each emigrant pursuing his own particular thought. As the ship leaves Martinique and the other islands, already a barrier begins to separate this group of emigrants from their homes, from the variations of color of their seas, from the rituals of religion and belonging.

> Now there was nothing between the ship and its port of call but a partition of night. The city lights went on like candles at the Feast of Paschal and the ship drifted with the sad certainty of the music that told those soldiers there was no parting. (20)

And even though now they are curtained off from their home by the distance of water, their coming together is rooted in memories, stories and discussions about conditions at home. Slowly and leisurely, Lamming describes the various members of the emigrant group. Initially, a confrontation derives from unfamiliarity, when Collis confronts the silence of Dickson.

"Say man, what's it you reading?" He was sure Dickson heard. Dickson raised himself higher, looking across at Collis as though a sin had been committed . . . . He glanced over his shoulder and was reminded of the space between them. . . . he felt that Dickson's body was speaking, warning that it shouldn't be touched. (33–34)

Slowly, however, the men and women group together. Tornado, who is returning to England for a particular purpose but who does not like England, offers information about England. The Governor, the other person who has been there, attempts to show in his own dominant fashion the interrelationship of their journey, the lack of difference between the realities they have left.

"Lemme tell all you something," he said, "education or no education, the whole blasted lot o' you is small islanders."
". . . I know Kingston like I know Port-o-Spain, ol' man, like the palm o' my hand, an' I say the whole lot o' you is blasted small islanders . . . . 'doan lemme hear any more o' this bullshit 'bout small islan' an' big islan'." (41)

One and all, however, speak with certainty about the condition of home, and since most seem to use education or the acquisition of education as a barometer of accomplishment, education becomes a subject all the emigrants seem to debate.

"Education an' qualification an' distinction is the order o' de day . . . . 'Tis why we all here on this boat. In search o' some way to make the future better." (62)

"Dat same education is a rope they givin' you to hang yuhself wid. An' when all said and done you end up where you begin, nowhere." (64)

The journey affords Lamming the opportunity to explore the relationship of the emigrant to the condition he is leaving, the ramifications of that condition, its promise, its inability to fulfill dreams.

For the Jamaican, Higgins, history of the islands takes on a characteristic particular to the experience of those who have but badly understood history. He gropes after the meaning of the colonial condition linking the Caribbean to Africa to Asia.

England, France, Spain, all o' them, them vomit up what them din't want, an' . . . . the vomit them make Africa vomit, an' the vomit them make India vomit, an' China an' nearly every race under de sun . . . . the books ain't tell me yet 'cause my readin' not finish, them stir an' stir till the vomit start to take on a new life. (67)

It is this same lack of understanding of the history of the place to which they are migrating that makes the quality of their arrival tense; a tension deriving from their own deep uncertainty and their impending confrontation with the unknown. On the journey all the emigrants except Tornado, the Governor, and Higgins seem to reiterate that uncertainty, that doubt. They all know why they are leaving the Caribbean, but they do not know to what they are going.

> No one knew the place they were going to, but everyone talked about the place he was leaving . . . . Whatever the island each may have come from, everything is crystal clear. Everybody is in flight and no one knows what he's fleeing to. (52–53)

Thus, the closer they get to their point of arrival, the more the tension mounts, the grayer the colors of their space become; a grayness which on their arrival shrouds each of them, yet also makes them huddle together.

Their journey from the Caribbean to London and the development of the dilemma of arrival follows, in spite of the pendulation between the Caribbean and London, a fairly linear progression. This linear progression changes drastically toward the end of *The Emigrants*, where Lamming attempts to pull together all the disparate adventures of the many emigrants, pulling the strands together in an attempt to achieve a tidy ending. Thus, the linear changes to the circular, a radial structural movement that makes for a merry-go-round of episodes. Perhaps here Lamming is positing the inevitability of the pull of one's past activity. Thus it is that the light-skinned Miss Bis, who has fled Trinidad after being jilted by her fiancé (an episode which is wryly presented in a calypso), unwittingly finds that fiancé, Frederick, in London. She has changed her name to Una Solomon; he has changed his appearance. His impotence becomes the convenient subject of a minor plot in which an African character, Azi, attempts to cure him. Azi becomes a point of reference for many of the episodes toward the end of *The Emigrants*. It is he who gives a vial of medicine to Higgins, which the police view as drug paraphernalia, landing the latter in jail. After this, Higgins's decline is steady, his movement toward paranoia ordained.

> "'Tis the reason they follow me all the time," Higgins said. "Since the day I set foot on this soil, they follow me without end."
>
> "Nobody followin' you," the Governor said, "an' nothin' can't happen to you in here." (234)

As subplots intertwine, it is intimated that Phillip, the student, is Higgins's son, born out of wedlock. Again, it is Azi who performs an abortion on a married woman, Julie, with whom Phillip has had an affair. After the abortion, we see Phillip moving tensely with Dickson, "silent and solitary under the sky. The stars looked down, grinning at their discomfort" (271). For Dickson has become crazed when thinking that of all the emigrants, he was chosen by the sunburnt white woman who travelled back with the emigrants. He realizes that she and her friends were but curious about his sexual organs: "She said they only wanted to see what he looked like. . . . The women . . . devoured his body with their eyes" (256).

As if no longer in need of clothing, he offers his wardrobe to Tornado and Lilian for safekeeping. Ironically, Tornado and Lilian, who have gotten married, begin to pawn articles of the wardrobe circuitously, and by chance Lilian meets in the pawnshop the "I," the narrator of the earlier part who is never really defined, whose role as narrator is never clarified. The Governor and the African, Azi, are co-owners of a club that has taken the place of the ship's dormitory, becoming the meeting point for the emigrants. When the Strange Man and woman enter the club, the story that the Governor has so humorously told on the ship circles back now with "A terrible foreboding . . . drowning the music, putting out the lights" (270).

Thus, it is that the final part of *The Emigrants,* which describes the settling in of the characters, becomes an interweaving of many subplots through which the emigrants bob up and down. Indeed, perhaps this very bobbing up and down symbolizes the instability of their settlement in London, their awayness, the fragility of their exile. Clearly the very humanistic hope expressed by Andrews to Phillip has not really taken place. For the lives of the emigrants all seem to arc downward, spooling out into seemingly tragic conditions.

> . . . When I see these strange people from so many different lands, the English girl and her Zulu boy-friend, the German and the Sudanese, when I see them walking arm in arm, trying to make a kind of conversation . . . between them there is a long dark passage of all kinds of differences . . . . The real bond between them is the mutual passion of those bodies. (207–208)

And even though the part-time narrator of the story states that perhaps unwittingly all the emigrants are moving toward a part of their heritage, they all seem to flounder in the space that that heritage has allotted them.

> There was a feeling, more conscious in some than others, that England was not only a place, but a heritage. Some of us might have expressed a certain hostility to that heritage, but it remained, nevertheless, a hostility to something that was already a part of us. (228–229)

Clearly, the fragmentation of the personality has not yet taken place; perhaps the hostility to one part of the self, to the heritage which produced that hostility, has not been visceral enough to bring about the fragmentation of the personality. Indeed, the entrapment in the exiled condition has become irremediable; Higgins's attempt to go back home, to stow away, is thwarted, and perhaps this same fate will meet any similar attempt by the other emigrants. Only when that part of the self which produces the hostility is shed can there be a wholing of the self; only when the pernicious elements of that acquired personality are cut away can the movement toward presence take place. Only then can the feeling of awayness, of exile from self, be checked, be interrupted, ushering in a possibility of return to the self, the going home.

I n *The Emigrants*, the principal journey is that of the migration of Caribbean types from the Caribbean to London; the central thematic construct is the delineation of the passage from one space to another country, wherein the exiled condition occurs. Often the emigrants, through recall, present the social and natural ecology from which they are migrating. Many of the novels of exile, however, present the chief characters and personages constructing their lives within the country to which they have migrated. Clearly then, two separate spaces, the countries of origin—the Caribbean—and the countries to which they have migrated—England, Canada, the United States—become the figural polarities linking together the condition of awayness, the going away.

In *The Last Enchantment*, Neville Dawes takes the principal character, Ramsay, through two spaces, Jamaica and England, but he seems to pay more attention to the topography of Jamaica, its social, cultural, political and ethical configurations. Consequently, what is highlighted is the arena from which Ramsay migrates. His stay and exile in London are not as fully externalized or represented as his growth and life in Jamaica.

However, in *Escape to An Autumn Pavement*, in *Water with Berries*, in *The Lonely Londoners*, and *The Housing Lark*, the migrant characters are already settling into their condition of awayness. They are structuring or coping with the new realities to which they have migrated, in which they are living, to their condition of awayness. Thus, these novels take on the configurations of settlement, the topography and reality of that settlement being the country to which they have migrated—England.

In a series of situations and episodes, *The Last Enchantment* delineates the political dimensions, textures, the social mood and environment of Jamaica in 1946, just after the introduction of universal adult suffrage. Dawes's delineation of that sociopolitical reality, tinged as it is with an underlying sarcasm and irony, offers little prognosis for the situations, nor do episodes resonate any excitement that would open out into an organic political development. Little vitality seems evident in the society; indeed, the emotions of the characters lack urgency, are devoid of any thrusting morality. Political involvements are not vitalized by any ethical commitments; indeed, they have a grim, toneless quality because action and emotions are passionless.

In the first part of *The Last Enchantment*, the external reality, the sociopolitical landscape, is inhabited by characters whose main preoccupation seems to be only tangential participation in relationships. Intercourse, whether sexual, social, or political, is presented by Dawes as lacking intensity, for so much is surface, so many desires mere posing and posturing, so many relationships based on race and color and respectability.

The novel begins with the death of Alphonso Tull, the father of Ramsay, the main protagonist, an incident that in itself has no pathetic overtones, but perhaps symbolizes the passing of one era, the beginning of another. The father has lived by certain basic codes:

> His philosophy, incoherent and distorted, was that of a hard-working negro prospering by white man's grace in a white man's world. His heroes were Booker T. Washington and Dr. Aggrey, and he tried to make Ramsay, barely nine, read *Up From Slavery*. (Dawes, *The Last Enchantment*, 10)

Ramsay, who, with his friend, Cyril Hanson, represents a new hope, a new era, is barely affected by this code, barely affected by even his father's death. That new era, the contemporary social reality, is fully externalized by Dawes, as he presents the attitudes and behavior of civil servants, the social landscape of parties and receptions, the random sexual involvements of personages, the cultural and political expectations consonant with a new political era.

In this presentation, characters become essentially representative types: the radical socialist politician, Capleton; the well-manicured, middle-of-the-road politician, Dr. Phillips; their youthful followers; the light-skinned social climber, Mrs. Hanson; the Indian creole, highly sexed secretary, Mona Freeman; the bright young scholarship winner, dark-skinned Ramsay; the clever, light-skinned social climber, man-about-town, Cyril Hanson. In this gallery of characters so reminiscent of *A Morning at the Office*, actions seem dictated mainly by surface appearance, by position within the society, by the wish for social mobility within that society.

Productivity in the civil service, as symbolized by that office, seems to be of little concern to the civil servant.

> When the Courts were in session and the Clerk and Deputy Clerk were out of the office, the temporary clerks stopped working. Mona Freeman went into the inner office to chat with Miss Bodden, the typist. Donald

Stevenson, who was preparing for bar examinations, began to read a book on Roman Law. (19)

At the higher level, there are instances of corruption within that civil service. Mona Freeman has gotten her job by sexual favors. Cyril Hanson, having access to the Rhodes Scholarship Committee, tries to manipulate his way into a scholarship: "We can't have any colour discrimination these days—isn't that true? The Minister of Education is on the Committee, isn't he?" (23). Indeed, Ramsay's drunken brother Bobsie underscores the essential corruption of the civil service.

> Bobsie was fascinated by Ramsay's cleverness at winning a scholarship without pulling strings; he didn't know it could happen in Jamaica and this must be a record. (114)

But, more than that, Dawes ascribes a positive insanity to the upper echelons of the civil service. The Scholarship Committee that interviews Ramsay is presented with deliberate sarcasm.

> "Yuh seh here, Missa Tull, dat yuh waant to work for Jimayca. Why yuh sey dat?" . . .
> "Yuh mean yuh want to work for the peeple of Jimayca, don't it?" the Minister said to assist him.
> "Yes, that's what I meant, sir."
> "Tell me again, now," the Minister said, enjoying himself hugely. "Yuh seh you come from country. You ever eat shad?"
> "Yes," Ramsay said, quite confused. The Board laughed. (75)

This is the same undertone of sarcasm that echoes throughout Dawes's portrayal of the leaders of political parties; all their speeches seem devoid of ethics, lacking in a deep political awareness, merely hollow-sounding words, little concerned with any political development of the people. Dr. Phillips of the Moderate Party makes a speech laced with platitudes about democracy. Capleton, the Socialist leader of the PPL, though portrayed as being charismatic in his honesty and naturalness, appears to Ramsay as "fantastically naive." What he says is "unsound half-heard theory" (27). Even the prayer of the bishop, as well as the speech of the ruling Merchant Party, is presented by Dawes as meaningless, insincere rhetoric.

It is not surprising, therefore, that the political scene is shot through with violent encounters between overzealous and hustling party followers.

Nor is it surprising that radical actions are manifested in dysfunctional, destructive societal proportions. Irresponsibly, the youthful followers of Capleton set fire to buildings in Kingston.

Personal relationships are just as superficial, and they, too, move toward violence. With no deep emotion or even any show of passion, Mona Freeman and Ramsay have sexual intercourse. Later Ramsay violently possesses Sweetness.

> *He's a nice boy*, she thought, *but he's trying to do that!*
> "Leave me alone!" she shouted, angry and selfish. She jumped up and he grabbed her ankle and they struggled, like trying to wake from a nightmare, like drowning, and he tore her underwear and it was painful. (124)

Perhaps even more violent, more irresponsible is the relationship between the Black man, Dr. Kendall, and Mrs. Hanson, whose inane racism, whose dislike for Black people, disappears before her sexual yearnings and appetite. Dr. Kendall, like so many characters in the novel, is not simply egotistical, but a charlatan and brutishly honest. Their contract is a bond of sexual urges and momentary satisfaction on which a snobbish Mrs. Hanson becomes dependent. For Mrs. Hanson is portrayed by Dawes with little sympathy. Through her snobbery, her classism, we are introduced to the various color and class gradations "in all shades from ebony to apple-blossom" (48), and to her version of Jamaican culture. Her expectation of that culture echoes with the same unexciting, uninvolved platitudes that mark the political speeches. Dawes presents rather than analyzes the various attitudes of his characters, their feelings, their conversations, for so much of the early part of the novel is a representation of the social and political reality rather than its analysis. To be sure, the author's novelistic intention is clear: a linear description, underscored by ironic and sarcastic undertones, of the sociopolitical environment at that time. The main protagonists, the two young men to whom perhaps implicitly will be given the responsibility for political development and fruition, lack depth of commitment, intensity of involvement. Ramsay often appears self-righteous, acting it seems not out of conviction or sincerity, but basically out of a self-serving need to do the right thing at the right time. His actions spring from opportunity, from convenience, even though this opportunism, this duplicity is often veiled by an avowed intention to change the society.

His friend, Cyril Hanson, equally unconcerned about social and political ethics, is overt in his actions, clearly shows that he will pander and benefit from any situation. He displays "an opportunism that was remarkable for its shrewd moderation" and even makes his friend "Ramsay's scholarship a personal triumph for Cyril Hanson" (105). Hanson is careful to "[go] to the beach and the Myrtle Bank pool with apple-blossom girls who had names like Myers, Hopwood, Brandon, Fonseca" (116).

As does each character Ramsay encounters, Hanson helps to elucidate perceptions of race and class, helps to situate Ramsay within a particular response, usually one that denotes an absence from self, an absence of certainty, an absence of awareness of his being Black and West Indian. This absence from self he attempts to evade by advancing philosophical treatises, a reaction that in its essence demonstrates a feeling of inferiority about his race, his color.

Two episodes in England with two English women reveal Ramsay's seeming inability to come to grips with his color, to feel at ease with his inner self. In one episode, he reacts with impotence to the overtures of a young woman; in the second, with vicarious violence to what he perceives as an insult to his manhood. With Marjorie, the young English girl, he skirts a possible sexual involvement by abstractly discussing literature. When she tries to touch his hair, he freezes and becomes so uncomfortable that "she thought, 'He is excessively shy and alone in this country and so much in need of friendliness'" (168). The virile sexuality he has exhibited in Jamaica becomes inoperative; indeed he is seized by a kind of paralysis of action. He cannot jump this girl as he jumped Sweetness.

Similarly, in his first encounter with Deidre, who has much sexual experience, Ramsay takes refuge in abstract discussions about romance and love. Ultimately he rationalizes an insult, rather than acting forcefully:

> I didn't feel indignant that she called me "nigger" like that. I had passed beyond niggerness now, because of her, to a kind of mastery of the white world. But she was trying to destroy me by subtly inverting the myth. (199)

Ramsay's impotence and lack of action have their roots, it seems, in the deep psychological dread of confronting the white face. He writes the story about the encounter, substituting thought for direct action, perhaps attempting to negate the presence as destructive to him.

> Earlier this evening, after she told me everything was over between us, a white man came in and they went into the bedroom together. Later he came out and went away .... I looked up and saw her face and I strangled her, and her body is there on the sofa and she is dead. I had to destroy that face. It was the face of the salesman, the priest, the sailor, Guy Horne. It was the face of my blackness and my inferiority and my ambition. It was my own face. (199–200)

Thus it is that in Dawes's depiction of Ramsay's life at Oxford, the series of encounters with different types and prototypes who are quickly sketched becomes representative of a particular political and social condition. One of Ramsay's first friends is Guy Horne. He is

a classless Englishman, a product of the war and statistics and evacuated
schools and levelling up, a working-class Londoner who had always
spoken with an upper-middle-class accent. (161)

Guy nestles Ramsay away, protecting him from the racism that confronts
them as they travel out together. Here clearly Guy is representative of that
working-class Englishman, who, understanding the nature of the working-
class space, enters into comfortable dialogue with the colonial West Indian
searching for himself.

These encounters in London elucidate Ramsay's inner relationship to
Prospero, highlighting interdependency, symbiosis. His relationship with the
African prince is qualitatively different, seems to be not one of dependency
but rather one of envy. Clearly Ramsay is accepting a position of nonbelonging to a larger African presence. In a stereotypic assessment, he
grudges the African prince his "simplicity of purpose," his assurance, his easy
identification with his origins.

> To the Prince questions of racial discrimination and imperialism, though
> extremely important, were subordinated to his personal responsibility to
> return and work for his people . . . . Ramsay was ashamed that he had
> ever enjoyed the monstrous caricature in Waugh's *Black Mischief*. (169)

Again, reacting stereotypically, Ramsay feels a cultural deficiency in his
relationship to European culture; his reaction is stereotypic only insofar as
it has become a recurrent novelistic motif in so many West Indian and Afro-
American writers. Ramsay ponders:

> The "world" was made up of bits chipped from European philosophy,
> music, art, poetry, an esoteric vocabulary, the nice conduct of a clouded
> cane, of a sherry glass. For Guy these things were not serious: for Ramsay
> they were serious but had no personal permanence because the back-
> ground from which he judged them was borrowed. (182)

The seeming lack of cultural perspective based on origin and history is
repeated again by the Trinidad psychologist:

> "The negro wants a new art form," the Trinidad psychologist said. "Any
> of the existing art forms are already a projection of white sensibility."
> (206)

Clearly this seeming cultural deficiency suggests a terrible sense of exile
from self, since it is based on an absence of information and knowledge
or perhaps a nonacceptance of African institutions and history. Here the self
has not undergone that essential fragmentation so necessary for accession to

wholeness. For even as Ramsay seems to be aware of the throttling effects of his schooling at Surrey and later at Oxford and the limitation of that education, yet he is unable to place in proper perspective his own cultural roots, unable to define himself, his personhood. Ramsay's exile, then, is an exile from self, from race, and less from country. He differs from Johnnie Sobert in *Escape to an Autumn Pavement*. Sobert's search moves along an emotional, personal axis, his escape from self radiating into a seeming acceptance of a homosexual relationship. Ramsay does not escape to an autumn pavement; Sobert, however, through search, achieves a measure of self-awareness, a prognosis of possibility.

> Then she began to lead me gently . . . .
> I was hers again . . . . because I had hurt her; rejected her; despised her . . . . I had come to her, not knowing why . . . . accustomed to her world of make-believe; I had come to her because I was dead inside. (Salkey, *Escape to an Autumn Pavement*, 194–195)

This is a game fraught with the direst of consequences for Johnnie, for his sexuality is in question; if Fiona were to arouse him physically, while proving her feminine control, her power, she would also, and more importantly perhaps, allay Johnnie's fear, if but momentarily, of being homosexual. But *Escape to an Autumn Pavement* describes the turbulent downward spiral of an ambivalent middle-class Jamaican into a possible homosexual encounter. What was once an elaborate game, a play, a kind of soap opera—in which Johnnie seemed not only participant-actor-scriptwriter, but indeed stage director and critic—has altered drastically, has undergone fundamental and visceral changes. He has been a smug participant-observer, clinically, incessantly analyzing motives, anticipating gestures and actions. Overbearing as subject, grossly indulgent as object, he now acts as both recipient and donor, using and being used:

> "Johnnie, you've made me so happy. So wanted. So much a woman, full and desired. Don't say anything. Don't spoil it." . . .
> But she doesn't know that something's dead, does she? (108)

As it is fully externalized, the whole love play between them—Fiona's voracious melodramatic sexuality, Johnnie's glib, self-satisfied acceptance and dissection of her need for passion—becomes boorish, repetitive, tiresome. The pacing of the relationship between Fiona and Johnnie is narrated by Johnnie as a third voice, which often becomes the author's voice, and this blurring of voices robs the narrative of that dramatic tension in which expectation and anticipation reside. Thus where the playacting meets with the intense, urgent depiction of Johnnie's predicament, the action slips into a stage rehearsal with explanatory notes.

In short, Johnnie was being a damn' "hard case," and enjoying every moment of it, he believed. He was refusing, not terribly unlike Miss Otis, to dine with either of his admirers.

In short, again, and perhaps less flippantly so, things could be summed up as follows: Fiona loved Johnnie. Johnnie was free with Dick. Dick was prepared to take over Johnnie completely if only he'd acknowledge his homosexuality ....

They had made a farce of freedom .... They made me know ... that truly "whole people" ... were tagged, always have been, pigeon-holed. (190–191)

Yet even this statement is essentially melodramatic, false. For the farce of freedom is partially, if not wholly, scripted by Johnnie himself. In his sex play with Fiona, even as he realizes its gamesmanship, he enters into the game and enjoys it almost to the end.

This Christmas Eve mating, the love play between Fiona and Johnnie, initiates another playact between Johnnie and Dick, the intense seriousness of which dissolves into a play of wits, a brittle confrontation. Indeed this is the first extended meeting between Dick and Johnnie. Fiona's personality has been portrayed in action, its voracious consuming sensuality fully detailed. Dick's personality (his true motives are not presented in actions until this scene) for every meeting, every possible delineation of their relationship, has been interrupted by another presence, a third party—twice by Shakuntula, once by Fiona and then by her partner, Trado, the butt of Johnnie's sarcasm. Dick's personality, then, the nature of his relationship to Johnnie, has been mainly circumstantial, all the evidence supplied by Johnnie himself who, while decrying Fiona's overpowering possessiveness, has always praised Dick's seemingly honest and nonconfining, indeed liberating friendship: "it's the freshness and sincerity of approach to each other which Fiona refuses to understand .... there's a kind of loyalty, a bond, which doesn't make slaves of us" (137).

Perhaps Johnnie's adulation of Dick, his uncritical regard for him, has but postponed the inevitable merging of the principal characters on the same set on Christmas Day. But the postponement of the confrontation between Johnnie and Dick could only be temporary, for all the central characters, as in a play, have their moment on stage, a meeting, a confrontation of sorts in a regularly structured dramatic format.

At the very beginning, the personae of the novel are introduced in a quick series of meetings, encounters; all of this dialogue and repartee is brisk, illuminating the various members lodging in the Blount house. A program-list enumerating them:

one faint-hearted student lover-spree; an unmarried married couple; a ... chauffeur ... who drives a fleshy, over-dressed, upper-middle-class tramp

. . . and the owner of the house, a jagged, sophisticated dragon who reigns on her damp throne. (11)

Johnnie's interaction with all of them is swift and deliberate; with Mrs. Blount, "the dragon on her damp throne" (11), it is full of flippancy. His dialogue with Shakuntala is incisive, blunt, aggressive:

> The third time I pass the Indian on the stairs . . . she speaks. The thing actually speaks!
>
> "Where you come from, Sobert?"
>
> "A place damn' far away from India, Miss Goolam." (13–14)

No such aggressiveness characterizes Johnnie's encounter with Trado. His performance there in the presence of the white man's insults is unaccountably spineless, subservient, cowardly.

The setting, the principal backdrop against which Johnnie's drama of escape, of exile, evolves, comprises four interiors; Miss Blount's house; the Jamaican barber shop owned by Lennie; the club where Johnnie hustles tips and over which Sandra prevails; the flat to which Johnnie and Dick go to share their undefined friendship. All these hangouts, among which the main plot shifts, have their own texture, their own words investing them with particularity.

Lennie's barber shop, the meeting place for the West Indian migrant exiles, resounds with talk, with laughter, with stories of back home. Lennie's role is as confidant, as a survivor, the elder who seems to grow in understanding. He is the migrant who has experienced much and is still hustling with grandiose dreams, but who is now astute and wise in the ways of the autumn pavement.

> "You know how much I just count on this cold Christmas morning already? I just count [29 Spades] . . . .
>
> "White or Spade, neither belongs in this blasted cold, if you ask me, Larry."
>
> "I like to hear you talk like that, Johnnie boy. That is real first-class dishonest talk, eh! That is the clever side to all of we who live here long enough, you know. You talk in one big compromise fashion; just like how *they* talk to you in the first indication of racial pressure. Why should you bring the white side into it? Can't you see that you doing something that is not your duty to do? . . . You look like you sell out to the other side." (176)

The club attracts another kind of exile, too, the Black American GI, who continuously slakes his awayness in drink, in white women, in smoke.

The naked exploitation, the hustle, the swindle in the club rises to hysteria:

> Tips. Tips. Tips. I could see nothing else. And that was as it should
> be: Christmas or no Christmas, tips should flow . . . . Tips for the rental
> of the flat; tips for spending money; tips for the hell of it. (160)

In this novel, the tone of the exile suffered by Johnnie takes on an increasingly strident timbre, turning downward into choked neurosis; perceptions of the external reality alter. Even though the love-bed seems a battleground, the somber grayness of Trado's apartment deepens, its mood taking on a quality of death:

> Finchley Road looked moth-eaten and raw. Very raw. (150)

> Everything about the sitting room looked raw and diseased. (193)

With all, Johnnie's predicament continues. Possible causation of Johnnie's homosexual predicament and probable evidence of sexual maladjustment are blurted out in a series of cacaphonic statements, exclamations, questions. All is anticipated in the novelistic directions.

> Fiona had helped me to make my decision. She had, without intend-
> ing it, put the idea of leaving the Blount establishment into my numb
> head. I, in turn, had deliberately infected Dick with it, and off we went,
> leaving Trado the Tramp, Shakuntala, the old lady, and a bleeding Fiona,
> into a world of freedom and blissful, wishful thinking. (145–146)

But to search for a house in London is to come up against overt racial prejudice and discrimination; to be greeted by scorn and insults from white landlords. Johnnie's reactions to these insults and the demeaning suggestions of all the white male personages are insipid and pointedly weak. Salkey offers no reason, no explanation for this cowardice, for Johnnie's completely emasculated attitude.

As if he were a lackey, Johnnie suffers racially insulting venom from Trado, who heaps scorn on him. He spinelessly tolerates the lewd insinuations, the insulting suggestions made against Black women by a drunk who accosts him on the London street.

> "You've got some very beautiful women, haven't you? Wonderful skin.
> Nice, high backsides. Strong devils, I bet?"
> "Yes. Yes, of course."
> . . . How can I get out of this? Just walk away, of course . . . .
> . . . "Couldn't you and I get a party going at my place? . . . All you'd
> have to do is get a couple of your girls to come along."

"Sorry." (36–37)

Indeed, many of the random and generally out-of-place dialogues—with Biddy, the barmaid at the club, with Fiona, who awaits his arrival in the dark of his room, with a random white stranger whom he meets on the street—all these duets discuss race, allude to interracial sex, ask of Johnnie the reason, the why of his exile.

Biddy's implication is harsh without the chuckle of earlier camaraderie: "You're also bloody well finished as a man. No woman in her right senses would want to know anything like you!" (169). Intimations that his sexual maladjustments may derive from a muted, overpossessive mother's love run through Biddy's letters to him, which echo with discordant notes.

In jagged utterances, there are suggestions that Johnnie's need to escape and its consequences result from his boring, pretentious, middle-class upbringing. He claims he must shed "a certain first coating, an insulation of household tricks, deceit, false pride, intolerance" (172), to survive London's "hustling and hardknocks." As the novel progresses various explanations are adduced for Johnnie's escape to the autumn pavement, for his movement toward homosexual liaisons.

Such psychosocial undertones seem contributory but only partially explicate Johnnie's personality, do not really substantiate the gut, the visceral reasons for Johnnie's possible homosexuality. Nor do Larry's lucid psycho-cultural notions:

"I see myself in a clear-clear light, Johnnie, and it is the same light which I taking now to see you.

". . . You feel lacking in all that because you're a colonial boy with only slavery behind you. So you bound to be confused. You bound to want to escape. You bound to get involved in all sorts of social things." (199)

But Johnnie's homosexuality still remains in the realm of speculation. Dick, though explicitly referring to evidence of Johnnie's homosexuality, adduces no such evidence.

"At Hampstead you showed certain signs, certain signs, shall I say, of latency. I watched you carefully, but still I wasn't sure." (181)

Fiona, too, remains uncertain about his sexuality. "Frankly, Johnnie, I do think you're homosexual, but I can't say to what extent or anything" (188).

Thus Johnnie remains suspended between two pulls, with his movements along the street, the pavement as pivot, with Piccadilly Circus as radial point. To emphasize Johnnie's disorientation, his ambivalent relationship to the arena of his exile, he flees his pad on Christmas Eve, goes aimlessly walking,

like many exiled spades. Again, early on New Year's Day, Johnnie runs
frantically through the streets. Maybe his walk on the winter pavement
crystallizes his emotions.

> I felt compelled to get out and go for a long walk. Anywhere. . . .
> I was heading nowhere in particular. I didn't even feel as tired as I
> should have . . . .
> [I had a choice of lives before me. A choice of loves. And, perhaps, a
> choice of enemies.] . . .
> . . . I had to wait. For the truth about Dick, about Fiona, about
> myself. About my next move. That and only that was worth waiting for:
> the truth about myself, and the courage and ability to recognize it when
> it came. (208)

Clearly it seems as if Johnnie has resolved on this New Year's Day to
carry through his choice of action with courage and determination—
whether this be to enter a homosexual relationship with Dick or to live with
Fiona. Yet his escape to an autumn pavement seems to have webbed him
into a paradoxical situation from which he cannot easily extricate himself.
Derek, however, one of the characters in George Lamming's *Water with
Berries*, through a demonstrably violent action, destroys the binary situation
in which he has been caught.

As in the case of Johnnie, explanations for Derek's initial ambivalence
have been deduced.

> "Always fucking right," Roger said, coming quickly to full voice, ". . .
> always you feel you have to look honourable. In your friends' eyes. In the
> enemy's eyes. You have to be honourable. In the eyes of every fucking
> living creature you pass by." (Lamming, *Water with Berries*, 138)

Derek's behavior is rooted in a religious upbringing with the admonitions to
be virtuous, "to be and to come and to keep always clean" (240). Toward the
end of the novel, Derek, the little actor for several years in London, the
actor corpse, springs into life, ripping away the trappings of the past,
breaking out of the prison of his conscience, raping, violating white presences via Desdemona, in front of an audience made impotent by their lack
of warning before so uniquely brutal an assault. (241–242).

Derek's escape to an autumn pavement, the seven years of his sojourn
in London, has turned to acid in his mouth, has acquired the "taste of aloes"
(219). The city of London, its historical monuments, have become mausole-
ums, burial grounds of his exile, his journey's final epitaph. The images
toward the end of *Water with Berries* are all of death, of destruction, as the
early scenes of the London journey, the principal settings of the sojourn—

the Mona Pub, the dwelling house, the Circle Theatre, the Old Dowager's cottage on the moor—all go up in flames, cremating past dreams, the history of exile. The mood of the novel becomes funereal, a succession of corpses, a procession of bodies. The relentless unraveling of the histories of the principal characters, as if by novelistic ordinance, leads to the coincidence of past and present, to the obliteration, the purging by fire of that past.

Also toward the end of the novel, Teeton, like a crab, scuttles over the rocky desolation of a barren, windswept island north of London, an island that has been refuge for himself and the Old Dowager, refuge, too, and solitary home for his crazed brother-in-law, Fernando. He moves with clawing motions, like the crabs watched by the boys in *In the Castle of My Skin*. This motif of crabs is but one of the many recurrent image forms in Lamming's panoramic, textured depiction of the sociocultural history of the Caribbean. Teeton is on his way back home to meet the revolutionary band, the Secret Gathering, waiting in a London basement, a rendezvous whose projected hope and purpose is to bring about the liberation of San Cristobal. The leader—ironically named Prospero—tired of his exile in London, does not doubt that Teeton will keep his rendezvous; Teeton himself knows that to miss the rendezvous would make for a never-ending exile, which would ruin his chances of going back home.

> For this was his last chance to return to his own roots. He knew that this need would never bless him with its passion again. And if he failed it now, there could be no remnant of hope in any future which remained to him. He must be off this island soon. Now. (Lamming, *Berries*, 184)

To accomplish this, Teeton has freed himself by killing the Old Dowager and burning her house on the moor, has exorcised her presence, her control over his consciousness. He has, indeed, rid himself of the threat of blackmail, and cleansed his own conscience. The possibility of blackmail initially came between Roger and Derek, whose need to be solicitous, to do the virtuous act, eventually leads to the turbulent, fiery end of their relationship.

Flames, too, earlier in the novel, bear witness to the Old Dowager's loss of her way of feeling, her privilege, her innocent ascension to power. Her dominion over the natives of the Caribbean in their exiled home is brutally severed and ripped apart by the savagery that the natives have experienced and incorporated during their years of servitude.

> [The island's] history had been a swindle of treaties and concessions. Its sovereignty was no more than an exchange of ownership. There had been no end to the long and bitter humiliations of foreign rule. The battles for ascendancy were too numerous to be remembered. (18)

It is at this intersection of history that the descendants of Caliban break, rip away the privilege, the purity, destroy Prospero's daughter's virginal claim and relationship to the Caribbean island.

> "I could only see the flames," she said, "like a million tongues licking and sucking up the night. That's how it was. They'd made a bonfire to celebrate the rape of me. Right there, in the open field, with the flames sizzling and spraying everything with heat. God! It was so hot. . . . And soon I couldn't tell any longer which was worse. That fire screaming and crackling about my ears, or the terrible pounding that started up inside me. There was only that tearing apart, like instruments opening up my insides." (150)

Here, one of Lamming's principal themes, the cultural and historical confrontation of the descendants of Prospero and those of Caliban, is actualized through the rendering of generational history in the explosive imaginative power of his narrative prose.

Before her baptism by flame and water, the Old Dowager has learned all the geography of the island, its fauna, its flora; has explored every nook and crevice marked on the map; has traversed the entire landscape of the domain over which her father lorded.

> "He taught me everything . . . . Not a single bird or beast could escape Father's curiosity. The rarest creature, the moment he saw it, would soon be subject to his learning. Never showed any interest in personal fortune . . . . He must have been a saint. The estate would have gone to ruin if it had not been for the care his servant lavished on him. He was the only school I had ever known. Until the day he died." (145)

She seems to belong there and Teeton visualizes her there, a symbiosis of person and landscape: "Her face had become part of the rivers and the mountains which his maps had kept alive" (148). These maps provide Teeton and the Old Dowager the means of an elaborate game. They usher in a set of rules, of words, of meaning, of intention and motive reaction. Teeton, the artist, having experienced prejudice in his search for housing in London, finds a place of refuge in the Old Dowager's house. There these maps bring a momentary consciousness; they structure the relationship and chart the elaborate game at which they play. They establish symbolically for seven years a game whose development and analytic delineation provide the novel with its central structural contrast.

The method of Teeton's coming to the house, the slow but steady nurturing of their relationship, the boundaries and the confines of the game that protects that relationship, all offer Lamming the opportunity to decipher the true meaning of dialogue, to leisurely track the changing temperatures of rhetoric, to trace the changing configurations of argumentation. Skillfully and clinically Lamming pinpoints the steps leading to an interdependence between Teeton and the Old Dowager—perhaps more accurately her growing control over him—to such a degree that the narration of the story of her rape liberates her, frees her from the shackles of her silence, from her own personal history, but correspondingly shackles Teeton to her. He seemingly accepts the guilt of her history. She assumes the privilege of her new freedom.

Indeed, their game comes close to being transformed from a relationship of dialogue and wordplay into that of tactile sexual interplay. So much does Teeton recall the Old Dowager's husband that perhaps a historical transference takes place: Caliban takes on, except for color, the proportions of Prospero. Now, more than ever, he is bound to her, a bond that tightens and constricts him. After the Old Dowager promptly shields him from the possibility of being accused of and charged with Nicole's death, she, affected by memory and led by the past, totally identifies herself with Nicole's body, with Nicole's form. During the ten hours that she guards Nicole's body, she recalls her grim, deadly experience, but also her husband, whose mannerisms Teeton seems to exhibit.

Another dimension of this intersecting of form and history, the play of past and present, surfaces through the ritual of relationship between the living and the dead embodied in the Ceremony of the Souls. Recall is so close to history, legend lying just below the surface of the immediate moment, that Teeton is paralyzed after he learns of his wife Randa's death. The announcement of her death creates a dream state, a condition that, though demanding responsibility for action, postpones immediacy, seeming to open out into an interior debate over the what and the why of his exile: "[Randa's] suicide had made San Cristobal more than a place of birth . . . . The what and the why. Would he ever be rescued from the tyranny of these distinctions?" (110).

The presence, the pull of the English island also overshadows the game. For Teeton postpones his departure for fear of destroying the game, for fear of once more betraying a cause, a trust, as he has accused himself of doing on the island of San Cristobal.

It was desertion. There was no other name for his escape from the island. After seven years the word had lost none of its terror. (18)

Was your safety more important than your allegiance to the men you left behind? . . . Were you more important than what they were trying to do? . . . There is no service that can compensate for your desertion. (109–110)

Haunted by his memory of desertion, accused of it by Jeremy, a desertion that may have led to Randa's death, Teeton postpones his departure, thus affecting the set routine and pattern of the game. And when he finally discloses his intention of leaving, he shatters the game and with it destroys once more the Old Dowager's will. He leaves her "all crushed up inside" (224).

The interplay between the Old Dowager and Teeton takes on all the configurations of ceremony, postpones the inevitability of separation, of departure. Teeton can only be free when the ceremony, their game, has played itself out; his guilt at postponing a statement of the truth of his relationship to both islands will only be expiated by his responsibility to the Gathering, to the freedom of the present.

Nicole, too, the white midwestern young woman, raised in a Christian fashion, sees the reflection of her father in the figure of Roger, and like the Old Dowager who has been succoring Teeton, controlling his freedom of movement, Nicole comes to Roger's aid when he is on the brink of emotional and personal danger.

> She had met . . . [Roger] in some desolate region of himself which he had never visited before; had never dared to explore . . . . Vulnerable, afraid, he might have gone dead in his pride if Nicole had not arrived. (80)

Roger becomes totally dependent on her, yet must free himself of a possible future guilt. For Nicole's unborn fetus, the fruit of miscegenation, may retain the stamp, the color of the descendant of Prospero; Roger denies responsibility, denies paternity. Once again, that paradox of relationship, here between indentured Indian slave descendant and white Christian figure, plays itself out in a turbulence of guilt and dependency. It is this relationship that destroys the close bond of friendship between Roger, the musician, and Derek, the actor.

With all the argumentation and debate about motive and intention that Lamming uses to develop the relationship between the Old Dowager and Teeton, he delineates Roger and Derek's friendship, analyzing emotional and physical reactions to statement in a leisurely externalization of the hidden ramifications of relationships. Like all the other relationships, it undergoes violent convulsions, breaks up under the weight of interdependency, under the need for expiation. Roger, who has severed ties to his judge father, Capildeo, and has gone seeking his own freedom and independence from a colonizing situation, ironically journeys into an exile wherein he is dominated by the affections of Nicole. He attempts to free himself from his past turbulent exile in London, burning all the evidence of his stay there. His manuscripts of music born in the Circle Theatre, his moments in the Mona Pub, are consumed by fire, and the body of Nicole is buried in the yard of the Old Dowager's house, cremated. The intertwined lives of the descendants of Caliban and those of Prospero all seem to spool into a kind of nothingness.

Now Roger's exile, like that of Derek, has come to a dead-end future; the wind on the moor sweeps away the last vestiges of the Old Dowager's history, scattering it, symbolically erasing her presence:

> The Old Dowager's body was behind [Teeton]; her face had finished in a cloud, a white shadow that moved in circles. The wind had washed her smell away; the odours of scorching tissue; the acrid remains of her hair. The wind had made a total killing; . . . had snatched her smell; drowned her putrefaction; baled her odours up from the grave and dirt of the valley; her smell was adrift, a tide of air drowned in the wash of the sea. (247)

And Teeton, freed from this presence indeed symbolically, may move across the waters to his home, freed from the presence of a descendant of Prospero.

> But he was calm; no pulse to his blood; no whisper of a beat from the cage of steel that covered his heart. Calm, Teeton was so calm. (248)

Man, the elements, and history come together at this point of intersection. At this climaxing of the turbulent breakup of the relationship between the Dowager and Teeton, the wind image is that of war; there is no suspense in this clash, in this historical confrontation; there is only a grave foreboding of imminent disintegration. This process of disintegration is evident in the breakup of the friendship between Roger and Derek, reflecting the changing configurations of shape and form in fog and the clouds, a disintegration and breakup Lamming characteristically captures and traces, step by step.

> The fog was breaking up. A moment ago he had marvelled at the huge edifice of blue air which occupied the street, obliterating houses and the telegraph poles. His gaze had grown weary with looking for the first row of houses which would announce the heath. It was such an unlikely start to the day: this black. dawn erupting from the heart of September. (11)

So too the author links the relations of history to the present, to the future, to the incessant changing inherent in all relationships, as *Water with Berries* in its essential structure delineates relationships, tracing the breakup, the possibility of cohering.

E ven the old veteran, Moses, the chief raconteur of *The Lonely Londoners*, the main counsellor, the elder of the boys, even he is assailed by nostalgia on revisiting Waterloo Station—the gateway during the 1940s and

'50s that admitted countless West Indian immigrants to their condition of exile in Britain, the doorway perhaps to opportunity, seldom to future.

> And right away in that big station he had a feeling of homesickness that he never felt in the nine-ten years he in this country. For the old Waterloo is a place of arrival and departure, is a place where you see people crying goodbye and kissing welcome. (Selvon, *The Lonely Londoners*, 11)

Here the station is linked to home, to memory, and is a vicarious point of communication and news for those starved for news through which the touch, the feel of home is retained. And Samuel Selvon, in his own inimitable style, always charging an episode, an incident, a setting, with a visceral immediacy of reaction, of emotions, intimates a possible end to Moses' exile in London, perhaps his exile on earth: his going home. Yet Moses is the veteran who now comfortably straddles two worlds; he is social historian initiated into the ways of London, noting the racial discrimination, but without assuming or knowing its origin.

> It had a time when I was first here, when it only had a few West Indians in London, and things used to go good enough. These days, spades all over the place, and every shipload is big news and the English people don't like the boys coming to England to work and live . . . as far as I could figure, they frighten that we get job in front of them, though that does never happen. The other thing is that they just don't like black people, and don't ask me why, because that is a question that bigger brains than mine trying to find out from way back. (30)

But Moses, too, was a newcomer before his initiation—for the life of each of the characters in *The Lonely Londoners* is really an initiation into exile, a season of trial and error, learning to cope, to survive in a new terrain, in the vaguely perceived landscape of London. Uncritical, expectant, clothed in a mask of self-assurance, easily identified, dressed as they are with all the cultural trappings of the West Indian homeland, they come. Their arrival is unexpected, sometimes unannounced, sometimes almost completely unprepared for. Such a group is Tolroy's family:

> "All of we come, Tolroy," Ma say. "This is how it happen: When you write home to say you getting five pounds a week Lewis say 'Oh God, I going England tomorrow.' Well Agnes say she not staying home alone with the children, so all of we come." (16)

The settlement of the many types who flit through *The Lonely Londoners*, their survival techniques, their coping, at times their making it, are the principal motifs and themes that Samuel Selvon presents with consummate artistry. He possesses a keen ability not simply to delineate the tragic consequences of the exile condition, but to use the colorful and metaphoric home talk and folk idiom of Trinidad and Tobago, to locate the comic overtones within every tragic condition. Thus the harsh condition of exile in *The Lonely Londoners* seems muted by the use of an idiom that often captures the piquant laughter lurking just behind the tear. Through fatigue, through *picong mauvaise langue*, Selvon weaves together a series of ballads whose essential formulations unearth the laughter, the comedy resident in any situation. Thus many of the characters in *The Lonely Londoners*, their attitudes and reactions, are presented in fully externalized episodes tinged with lyrical pathos that underscores the comic tragic condition of their exile. Through Waterloo Station come Moses, Galahad, Big City, Cap, Five, Tanty, and so many others, characters whose idiosyncracies do not simply structure the ballad but also enliven the narrative.

The initiation of characters, the transference of certain cultural habits particular to the Caribbean onto the landscape of London, offer Selvon many opportunities to structure episodes and relationships that border on the farcical. Tanty, perhaps one of Selvon's most vividly drawn characters, not only settles in—"Tanty used to shop in this grocery every Saturday morning. It does be like a jam-session there when all the spade housewives go to buy. And Tanty in the lead" (83)—but soon begins to implant West Indian cultural mores and practices on the London scene. The name Tanty retains all of its meaning, its West Indian attributes.

> It was Tanty who cause the shopkeeper to give people credit.
> ". . . Where I come from you take what you want and you pay every Friday."
> . . . Then one day Tanty buy a set of message and put it in she bag and tell him: "You see that exercise books you have in the glasscase? Take one out and put my name in it and keep it under the counter with how much I owe you." . . .
> And Tanty walk out the white people shop as brazen as ever. (83–84)

Seemingly untouched by her exile, she can cope with what basically is an unsocial reality whose configurations of poverty have outlines similar to those she knew in Jamaica.

But the reactions of the characters to a condition of awayness differ. While Tanty colonizes her environment, Galahad seems to merge with it, at times bemoaning his condition but always seeming to flow with it. Initially, however, on his first morning alone, Galahad is assailed by a deep feeling of loneliness:

He forget all the brave words he was talking to Moses, and he realise that here he is, in London, and he ain't have money or work or place to sleep or any friend or anything, and he standing up here by the tube station watching people, and everybody look so busy he frighten to ask questions from any of them. (33)

To him the elements of London assume configurations totally different from those he has left behind, and his feeling of loneliness is increased by the quality of these elements. Selvon often uses the weather, changes of the seasons, the fog, the cold, the summer, as motifs structuring the attitudes, behavior, motives and conditions of the immigrants in London. That first morning:

The sun shining, but Galahad never see the sun look like how it looking now. No heat from it, it just there in the sky like a force-ripe orange. When he look up, the colour of the sky so desolate it make him more frighten. (34)

Galahad sets out totally unequipped and ill-clad for his adventure into exile.

A fellar would land up from the sunny tropics on a powerful winter evening wearing a tropical suit and saying that he ain't have no luggage. (22)

Later Galahad comes to imbue Piccadilly Circus and Marble Arch with magic realism. Simple meetings and assignations take on the quality of romance. But on first entering the space of his exile, a hostile field, unable to cope with overt challenges, he responds only with brusque reactions, conciliatory gestures. "'Mummy, look at that black man!' . . . he bend down and pat the child cheek" (96). Despite the hostility of some of his encounters, so ill-prepared and uninitiated is he that his reactions to prejudice are masked even more with off-handed, tolerant, bemused questions.

Galahad talking to colour Black, as if is a person, telling it that is not *he* who causing botheration in the place, but Black, who is a worthless thing for making trouble all about. "Black, you see what you cause to happen yesterday? I went to look at that room that Ram tell me about in the Gate, and as soon as the landlady see you she say the room let already. She ain't even give me a chance to say good morning. Why the hell you can't change colour?" (97)

Even when he learns the terrain and manages to equip himself, to clothe himself in his finery, proof against the disdain of London, he moves like a courtier, a knight, through all encounters gracefully, still supercilious.

At times, so heavy is his ordeal and so unending the trial that Galahad lapses into despair; then, disconsolate, he bemoans his condition of exile, his peculiar circumstance. The exile for the boys is, though grim, recounted by Selvon in ballad style, remaining at the level of calypso song. Yet so humorous and poignant is Selvon's depiction of the exiled condition, that the grimness lurking just below the surface does not evoke a continuous lament, a sob. Perhaps by using the everyday speech of many Caribbean peoples as the medium of his narrative, Selvon negates the alienation, the awayness of the exile, rendering the episodes more immediate and giving them all the texture, all the tonalities of home. Paradoxically, however, that everyday speech seems to accentuate their loneliness.

> This is a lonely, miserable city, if it was that we didn't get together now and then to talk about things back home, we would suffer like hell . . . . In the beginning you would think that is a good thing, that nobody minding your business, but after a while you want to get in company, you want to go to somebody house and eat a meal, you want to go on excursion to the sea, you want to go and play football and cricket. Nobody in London does really accept you. They tolerate you, yes, but you can't go in their house and eat or sit down and talk. It ain't have no sort of family life for us here. (154–155)

Here Moses bemoans the loneliness of the exiles and recalls pleasures that offer a firm point of nostalgic reminiscence. Herein lies the dialogue of the islands, the dialogue of exile. Nostalgia sifts from the past the Caribbean conditions that initially prompted the migration into exile, even though now they make the present condition of exile seem less tolerable.

The migrant has undergone a change in perceptions, a reversal of preconceptions. The condition of the West Indian is rooted in a colonial ambivalence, which has driven the colonial to the capital, to the very mecca from which his erstwhile colonial master had come. This mecca is a lonely one for thousands of immigrants from the Caribbean seeking either the glamour of a "Waterloo Bridge," or the ballads that come in the warmth of summer. Perhaps it's the glamour that calls them to the city, where they are rejected, lonely, and forced into exercising the qualities of survival—qualities embedded in their own West Indian soul and spirit. But though their ambivalence is tinged with loneliness and rejection, they stay, writer as well as worker, to enjoy the paradoxical pleasures of exile. They know full well that the cruelty of the islands prohibits the return of the exile who has not made it—who has not been accepted by the world of the colonial master. The writer claims that the world from which he came denigrated and lessened his power of articulation by its middle-class inanities, inactions, and unconcern, causing men to flee to this city hardened by time, in which faces are expressionless—all wearing the same mask. The road they all tread to psychological exile is far removed from the sameness that they see in the Caribbean, from the sterility they claim existed there. But they can't appreciate their home until they're too far down that road away. In the Caribbean, there was community. There was the familiarity of language and gesture, the certainty of belonging. To transfer this community to London is to build a refuge against its overt prejudice, and the dialogue of the exiles is a two-fold one. The harshness of the city offset by memory is transferred backward in time; present time recalls the nonchalance, the pleasurable activity of life back home.

Even though the community in London, as that back home, makes for the "minding of your business," Moses realizes that there is community. There is family life in its own amorphous way. There is "the talk" and the "ballads" and the attitude of laughter and the language of *picong* and *fatigue* and a giving tone at someone else's distress even while deeply sympathizing with that person who provides all of these sustenances and prevents the exile from plunging into despair. Nostalgia, too, holds him and keeps him afloat—there is always the thought that there is a possibility of return, so the exile moves between two worlds. An island is a world spanning two worlds— the Caribbean and England. For this is the span which embraces the writings of many Caribbean novelists. Most are in physical exile. The novels move between the colonial master's home and the Caribbean from which the exiles came. Selvon's dialogue is a dialogue voyaging between London and Trinidad.

> "Ten years, papa, ten years the old man in Brit'n and what to show for it? What happen during all that time? From winter to winter, summer to summer, work after work. Sleep, eat, hustle pussy, work . . . . Boy, if I was you, I would save up my money and when you have a little thing put by, hustle back to Trinidad." (153)

Exile offers material advantages but seldom affords any deep spiritual solace. The condition of exile is rooted in a symbiosis between Caribbean persons, their history, their culture, and those of the former overlord; fragmentation—the breaking away from the insidious control of that over- lord—has not as yet taken place, ridding the Caribbean person of that part of self that negates the shaping of a new presence, a new person.

Moses' rhetorical questioning pinpoints the possible future extension of not only the worker but also the Caribbean writer. A too prolonged exile means a lessening of awareness of the Caribbean area, which is so rapidly changing, means a loss of the sense of the rhythms of the languages with the myriad flowing images and new slang. Too prolonged an exile means drawing over and over on what by now is a past historical moment, the time spanned by the youth of the writers. Indeed, most of Selvon's novels are set in historical moments—the mid '40s, early '50s—and like so many other writers he doesn't capture the contemporary society of Trinidad, even though all the same Caribbean attitudes still persist. Indeed, this land and landscape of the Caribbean—its fruits, the sea and sky and stars; the flora and fauna; the land caught in its different moods, at mornings or in the noonday sun, in drought or in hurricanes—all coalesce in the writings of the Caribbean novelists and form a point of looking back. Thus it is that Moses yearns for the peace and repose provided by one of the Trinidad valleys so dear to Selvon.

> "Boy, you know what I want to do? I want to go back to Trinidad and lay down in the sun and dig my toes, and eat a fish broth and go Maracas Bay and talk to them fishermen, and all day long I sleeping under a tree, with just the old sun for company . . . . That is life for me, boy. I don't want no ballet and opera and symphony." (154)

It is in such a valley that Father Hope, in *An Island Is a World*, sought refuge, consolation and peace from that world of restless searching of the exiled; clearly Selvon is in love with the landscape of his country; in love with the *poui* trees blossoming, the immortelle trees. This is the background against which he often places the folk—simple peasant people—of many of his novels. But such peace seems open only to those who do not doubt; and so many of Selvon's characters at various moments are plagued by the essential motif of doubting, of questioning.

The characters who stream across his London works are less prone to this kind of questioning than those who bestride their two worlds and become immersed in the dialogue of the self, in the search for the meaning of the individual caught in the crowd, the meaning of the very small islands planted amid vast continents. Those in London momentarily still their anguish by laughter, by nonchalance, by the swagger of the *saga boy*, characteristics brought from the islands.

> Behind the ballad and the episode, the what-happening, the summer-is-hearts, he could see a great aimlessness, a great restlessness, swaying movement that leaving you standing in the same spot . . . on the surface, things don't look so bad, but when you go down a little, you bounce up a kind of misery and pathos and a frightening—what? . . . As if the boys laughing, but . . . they only laughing because to think so much about everything would be a big calamity. (*Londoners*, 170)

Here are revealed not only the essential nature, theme, motifs, and style of Selvon's London works but also his deeper hidden meaning. We laugh at many of the ballads and episodes, yet behind it all is the pathos and the tragedy of the exiled West Indian—or more so, the worker—in his many poses as he seeks to eke out a living in England. To be sure, it is only through his deft mastery and style, using all elements of Trinidadian talk, that Selvon captures the nuances of feelings, the depth of emotions, the indomitable "kiff-kaff laughter" of his London characters.

These "lonely Londoners" differ from the characters in *An Island Is a World,* who attempted to reflect on the Caribbean person's spatial and philosophical position within the geography of the world. Only once does Moses achieve this state of reflection. Unable to articulate and to give depth to their innermost feelings, many of the characters in *The Lonely Londoners* seem to act out these vague feelings, revealing them in gesture, in movement, capturing them in language, in the ballad, but never able to explore them with deliberation.

Many characters drift across the stage of *The Lonely Londoners.* There is Big City, who as his name implies, has a feeling for cities, and, like so many of Selvon's immigrants, is unable to live in a village again. There is Five Past Midnight—loud, brash, always on the point of borrowing, but always at the same time looking for a good *fête.*

Laughter acts as the *fête;* the laughter, the *fatigue,* the communality, all emerging out of and shot through their communal exile and their communal searching for a livelihood that sustains the individual exile in the broken-down suburbs. It is this laughter that enables them to survive grim, cold winters, their living in the face of discriminatory attitudes and stereotyped opinions of the English about the migrants, which allows them to endure the general dilapidation, the conditions of poverty:

> This is the real world, where men know what it is to hustle a pound to pay the rent when Friday come. The houses around here old and grey and weather-beaten, the walls cracking like the last days of Pompeii, it didn't have no hot water, and in the whole street that Tolroy and them living in, none of the houses have bath. (76)

But Selvon sees the brighter side of the sun, sees the sunlight which summer brings to the harsh midnight of the immigrants and poor whites. Selvon has an eye for brightness of colors and seems to love the sensuous warmth of summer.

> Oh what a time it is when summer come to the city and all them girls throw away heavy winter coats and wearing light summer frocks and you could see the legs and shapes that was hiding . . . what a time summer is because you bound to meet the boys coasting lime in the park . . . everywhere you turn the English people smiling isn't it a lovely day as if

the sun burn away all the tightness and strain that was in their faces for the winter. (115)

Selvon shows the magic effect that summer has for those struggling for a living—joy, sensuousness, and laughter beam, radiating far and wide. There is always a ray of sunshine.

The summer recalls the ways of sunlight, the warmth of countries from which the migrants have come. In Austin Clarke's *The Meeting Point,* the harshness of winter marks and highlights dilemmas faced by Bernice, the main character. There, too, when the summer comes, such dilemmas seem more bearable. The sun brings with it a kind of freedom of movement, awakening memories of warmer times. In these novels of exile, the rhythms of land and man still coincide, still throb. The being of the Caribbean person itself provides the Caribbean novelist with a landscape and relationship to landscape unique to the Caribbean.

For exile assumes the putting on of different clothes, the assumption of another landscape, which, in its essence, has different rhythms, cultural resonances distinct from those of the Caribbean. To divest oneself of this acquired clothing is, perhaps, to begin the process of going home, to begin the process of investiture in one's own still-evolving heritage.

As its name implies, *The Housing Lark,* set against the headiness of summer, is a lark. Indeed, it has all the contours of an elaborate and protracted skylark, that Trinidadian sociocultural phenomenon of imbuing a situation, an episode, with an element of levity, of banter, thereby reducing and lightening the seriousness of that situation, that episode. But it is not the ballad, the "ole talk" with all the immediacy, the fresh clever undertones spicing the narrative, that structures *The Housing Lark*. It is dialogue, it is more so the skylark game giving the novel a playful shifting texture, where characters dart in and out, run on and off stage, the city of London, and come together on the main set—the basement room of Battersby, 1317. For in its essentials, *The Housing Lark* is a play presenting and staging situations and episodes which some ten characters, principally Trinidadian by origin, live through, experience, romp. Indeed, the novel toward the end even takes on the more structured quality of a morality play as Teena center-stages, upbraids the men, the boys for their levity, their skylarking, with all of its seeming lack of respectability.

Everything is a skylark and a fete and a bacchanal. None of you ever get serious; if I didn't take Fitz in hand, he would gamble every night and go sporting and looking for white girls. You all can't even get serious about a thing like housing. You know the distresses we have to go through, you know the arse black people see to get a roof over their

heads in this country, and yet, the way you all behave as if you haven't
a worry in the world. (Selvon, *The Housing Lark*, 145)

Yet, the novel remains a lark, a skylark. "A little later [Bat] produce a pack
of cards and all the resolutions disappear as they start up a session of rummy
at a tanner a corner" (147). So Selvon explains that cultural inheritance, that
Trinidadian, indeed West Indian attitude, that quality of perception which
negates the inherent tragic condition of exile, robbing it of its harshness.

So customary it is for the exiled Caribbean to skirt the tragic by extract-
ing the humorous, to avoid the serious by the skylark, to run to the sun,
accept the pull of summer rather than moving to the dark, the cold, that

> another thing was the summer. If to say they had let the summer pass
> and then begin to save, it might have stood a chance, as in the cold
> months have less temptations. But Bat came up with this scheme a few
> weeks before the sun start to shine and flowers and things come out to
> greet the summer. No wonder them boys want their money back!
> Because now is the time when fellars have to stretch their legs and look
> around for birds, and smoke and drink and lay down in the sun and enjoy
> the pleasures of life. (88)

The novel, then, becomes both a midsummer night's dream and a tale
of two cities. For one of the constant motifs is a dream, one of the principal
structural elements, the tug between the memory of the Caribbean reality
and the actuality of the London experience. For many characters, saved by
their own cultural clothing, by the ballad, by the skylark, the exile in *The
Housing Lark* even seems pleasurable.

In a semi-dream state, Battersby at the beginning of the novel, awakening
down-and-out in his dingy basement room, wills the "genie" on the falling
wallpaper to provide him with food, riches, women, rum—his prerequisites
for happiness. Later, while stroking Matilda, his sister Jean's upstairs
roommate, whom he has been eyeing for some time, he cries out in ecstasy:
"Geni, you are great!" (67). At the end of the novel, with a promise of
fulfillment of his dreams, enough money to purchase their house, Battersby
tears off the wallpaper, his talisman, the genie.

> He went across by the fireplace where piece of the Aladdin wallpaper did
> sever relationship with the wall and was dangling. He tear it off gently
> and put it in his pocket . . . . You could see as if he wishing he could
> strip the lot and carry it go in the new house. (154–155)

This is one of the many dreams that urge and direct the hopes of many
characters, their fantasies.

In the morning fantasy, the genie grants Battersby's wishes, obeys his summons. But clearly the genie comes from a different cultural bag than his West Indian master. He is of another city, his tastes fundamentally different. The contrast in taste between Caribbean Battersby and his European slave genie offers Selvon an opportunity to exploit the full range of his fanciful, comic style by which he shatters the immediate reality. Battersby, broke and unable to pay his rent, teetering on the brink of eviction, bolsters his postponement of rent payment by citing the Englishman's own similar devices in a long excursive about

> [these Nordics] say red sky is shepherd's delight, and if the dog fall asleep that mean rain coming, and if the cat start to play frisk that mean sunshine. (10)

Similarly, another excursive, a ballad, humorously narrates Battersby's method of fund raising.

> And Bat had a way, he used to be so cool and casual that before you know it he tap you for a quid. "I don't think of money at all," Bat used to tell the boys. "I mean, what is money? It only get you in a lot of trouble—" and right here he splice in with "see if you have any change in your pocket and lend me ten bob,"—an carrying on with the topic as if there wasn't any interruption. (14)

These frequent breaks into ballad style, so characteristic of Selvon's writing—with their leisurely interruption of the narrative, the depiction, the bringing to the foreground of some attendant tangential object, the unhurried return to the central narration—all lessen the immediate harshness of being broke in London.

Swiftly Selvon introduces the motif of shelter, of obtaining housing, the specter of eviction from that housing, in the figure of a fellow of exile, the rent collector, Charlie Victor, who will survive at all costs, at anyone's expense.

> Well, all I believe in, is what bringing me money, because money is the thing that I got to have to live in this world. If you vex with me, what happen? The sun stop shining? Snow stop falling? No. But if I ain't have a job, and if I ain't have money, I might as well be dead, because I can't live without it. What the arse I really care what you think of me? (17–18)

The idea of the boys getting together to buy a house originates quite casually from Harry Banjo who begins to share the basement room and its expenses with Battersby. Thus the motif of housing, so critical an element in the exiled reality of Black migrants continually exposed to, continually rejected due to, racial segregation, is spawned and immediately becomes a lark. The search for lodging by two of the prospective house buyers is narrated with all the comic overtones, the humorous quality, exploding into farce.

> One time Syl was catching real hell to get a room. He walking all over town reading the notice boards in the sweet shops and tobacconists, but all he could see is "No Kolors" or "Sorry, Uropean only." Syl was thinking how is a hell of a thing these people don't want him, when they can't even spell. (29)

He hears of an "English landlord who taking Indians. He don't want any West Indians, mark you but he taking real Indians" (29–30), and the farce deepens as Syl tries to convince the landlord of his nationality.

> "I am straight from the banks of the Ganges," Syl say. "I am a student from the Orient seeking a roof over my head."
> "You are not wearing your national garments," the landlord say.
> "When you are in Rome," Syl shrug.
> "What part of India do you come from?"
> "West India." (30)

Often Selvon in his depiction of characters, in his delineation of fanciful situations deriving from certain idiosyncracies, pinpoints the sham, the assumed stance. Then unmasking the sham, the boast, he explodes it with a burst of laughter. Indeed this unmasking of the braggart derives from the Anancy folk tales, an immediate element of the Caribbean folk tradition on which much of Selvon's narrative is based. Thus it is that Syl, who has set himself up as being knowledgeable about the form and figure of women, though actually having little firsthand intimate knowledge or experience, is burnt by the experienced Battersby, who in a comic episode walks off with Syl's date.

In another episode, Fitz Villans, the braggart who boasts he is "a professor of womanology," makes everyone believe "that Fitz would rather dead than get married" (41–42). However, quite soon he marries Teena, who promptly places him under wraps:

> Every time we go by Fitz for a game, he either scrubbing or washing or sweeping. And all this time, Teena only looking at we, ain't saying a word, just rocking in a rocking chair and keeping an eye on Fitz to make sure he don't sweep no dust under the carpet. (44–45)

The other characters who take part in the housing scheme are rapidly introduced at the beginning of the novel in all their idiosyncratic attitudes. Their identifiable behavioral patterns, their quirks, the peculiarities of action or reaction, form the basis of their comic presentation, a presentation at times bordering on the pathetic. In most instances, though, they all seem to be hustling in their own particular way to achieve a measure of livelihood, to make ends meet. Gallows won his nickname in Trinidad:

> Many years ago in Trinidad a calypso make up about Gallows. What happen was a feller name Johnny thief Gallows girl, and the calypso quote Gallows as saying, when he catch up with Johnny, "the grave for Johnny and the gallows for me." (45)

Now he walks with his head down continually looking for a five-pound note that he lost some time ago. This constant search, though providing some humorous episodes, is indicative of the penurious lives led by most of the migrants to London.

Poor-me-one, who initially joins the group but eventually leaves it again, represents the consummate hustler, the pusher; he slips in and out of London, always eluding the grasp of the law. Poor Hustle is a cool one—he remains seemingly unruffled by his forced furtiveness, but he keeps "his hands in his pocket, as if inside them he holding on to something what give him inspiration to continue living" (52).

Battersby, who, as we have said, dreams, seems to symbolize the character who wishes for material possessions but who never really works gainfully to acquire them. He hustles the savings set aside for the buying of the house. He lives partially supported by his sister Jean, a prostitute, and her roommate, Matilda. Both Matilda and Jean are sketched in colors that mark their real intentions, their hopes, their aspirations. Jean, who prostitutes herself for money, really wants to be settled and married. Matilda, brought up strictly along Christian lines, deep down yearns to lead what she thinks is the glamorous life of the prostitute, wishing to acquire all the clothing and external trappings of glamour, but without prostituting herself to get them.

These are the characters whose lives in London Selvon comically and humorously sketches, whose aspirations and hopes he alludes to, who are impelled by dream, often tugged by nostalgia and memories of the Caribbean. They all live on the border of poverty, which is assuaged by their camaraderie—card-playing, drinking, stroking. The camaraderie and coming together soften their loneliness and their exile, and eventually it is the sharing of dreams and hopes that in *The Housing Lark* opens out into the acquiring of a house. Clearly Selvon's novelistic intention is not to satirize or to cauterize their dreams and aspirations or the robust boisterousness and quality of bacchanal that provide momentary relief from their day-to-day existence.

In Austin Clarke's *The Meeting Point*, the quality of the exile in Canada is not softened by the momentary laughter, not relieved by the fatigue, the ballad, the lark evinced in *The Housing Lark* and *The Lonely Londoners*. Here the exile is harsh, bitter, and shrouded in ambivalence—at once tentative and ambiguous. It is tracked through Barbadian characters: a domestic in the Burrmann household, Bernice; her sister, Estelle; her friend and a domestic in the Hunter household, Dot; the latter's husband, unemployed Boysie; and his unemployed friend, Henry.

Even as the relationship of Bernice Leach, the central character in the novel, and of Dot with Mrs. Hunter, her boss, is rooted in ambivalence and uncertainty, so, too, are their opinions of and reactions to the quality of their lives, to their exile and that of other West Indians during the 1960s in Canada.

Yet no such uncertainty discolors the harsh experiences suffered by these Black migrant West Indians. The ethos of the exiled condition finds figural representation in two interracial liaisons: the passionate affair between the newcomer Estelle and the impotent—initially, that is—Mr. Burrmann; and the quick coupling between the long resident of many years, Henry, and Brigitte the German maid. At the end of the novel the two Black migrants lie critically ill. Estelle, in the emergency operating room, from complications arising out of a self-induced abortion following Mr. Burrmann's caustic disclaimer of responsibility for her pregnancy; Henry, seriously wounded from a savage, methodically brutal beating inflicted on him by two white policemen—one of whom is Brigitte's lover.

To be sure Austin Clarke gallantly attempts, in his portrayal of the main white characters—Mr. and Mrs. Burrmann, Brigitte and Agatha, Henry's regular lover—to present them in multidimensional, humanistic contours, noting predicaments, explaining—sometimes too assiduously, it seems—their foibles, their psychological problems, their engrained prejudices, the monolithic stereotyping of white attitudes toward Blacks. Yet in spite of all this, for migrant West Indians, the arena of exile in Toronto has all the makings and retains all the conditions of an elaborate plantation society.

Through Bernice's eyes, through her recalling, her recounting of situations and of episodes in which her wide-grinning overtly servile responses mask her true feelings toward Mrs. Burrmann, all the various multiple maskings of the great house are exposed. The house, typical of wealthy homes in the rich Toronto suburb, Forest Hills, conceals behind its obvious opulence, its privilege, the lonely, alcohol-dependent, sexually unfulfilled wife, Mrs. Burrmann: the problematic marital relationship, her clandestine love affairs, her many parties and dinners, his absence, his long hours of work, his clandestine affairs.

In the house, Bernice, who has been exploited and hurt by constant abusive reminders of her Blackness, learns the art of masking her true feelings, her Barbadian freedom. This element of masking, which characterized the behavior of the slave, ordains Bernice's character and commands her relationship with her employer, so that Bernice constantly operates at two levels. Scenes with Mrs. Burrmann assume a bifocal reality: her protestations over long hours, poor salary, exploitation, remain but empty, stifled, cowardly questions; her curses of Mrs. Burrmann only in her mind:

> Behind the smiling face, Bernice was telling her: . . . *Be-Christ, look woman . . . . You in here from daybreak to dusk sitting down on your fat behind drinking drinks, whilst I out there, in that hot kitchen working off my fat, for peanut-money. From the time I come into this country, I been working. Working, working, working hard as hell, too . . . .*
> "Leach!" Mrs. Burrmann was screaming. "Have you gone deaf?" It was a long time before Bernice heard her voice . . . .
> "No, ma'am."
> "Well?"
> And that was all it took to defeat Bernice, once more. (Clarke, *The Meeting Point*, 13)

Bernice doesn't even react violently when the Burrmann's child fingers her person:

> "Then, as I telling you now, I feel this thing running down my leg, right from up under the middle o' my behind . . . in the soft part o' my behind. Christ! a fright take a hold o' me . . . . And Jesus God, Dots! When I turn round that little white bastard was *up under* my uniform . . . .
> "I turned round and I say, but Miss Ruthie . . ." (61–62)

Not only does masking make her mute, lead to a sullen impotence, but it reduces her to a thing—an uncomprehending thing. As thing, indeed as one devoid of sensibility, she clearly cannot comprehend music. Hearing the Beethoven symphony that Mrs. Burrmann plays incessantly, reflecting and refracting her moods, her loneliness, Bernice says she is reminded of

> "women back home reaping corn, and putting that corn on their heads, and singing all the time they putting . . ."
> "I am sure, Leach, that you don't really understand this symphony, dear."
> ". . . and, a moment ago . . . I could swear that the music was telling me 'bout winds blowing, and a storm gathering up in the clouds and the skies . . . ." By this time Bernice was talking to herself, because Mrs. Burrmann had left the room. (24–25)

Clearly Mrs. Burrmann's departure negates Bernice's presence, makes irrelevant her thoughts and emotions, denying her personality, her being. Invisibility is but a shade away.

From her vantage point, present but not seen, Bernice can observe all the boredom, the basic unhappiness and attendant excesses and indiscretions giving meaningless particularity to the lives of Forest Hill types. As a Black woman she resents their singing of Negro spirituals at the height of their revelry. As a church-going woman, Bernice is scandalized by their goings-on. As a domestic identifying with the fortune of the house and its occupants, she resents her mistress's indiscretions. For Bernice, after thirty-two months of service in the Burrmann's household, not only identifies with it—its occupants—ascribing blame to Rachael or Sam Burrmann for the obvious breakdown of their marriage, but she begins to have, indeed to adopt, a proprietary attitude.

> With her own two black hands, she would tuck the lily-white linen under the chins of Serene and Ruthie. She began to move like a conqueror round the table, and about the house. (4)

But to identify is not to belong. Her clean, personally furnished apartment, with more material comforts than she had ever considered possible in Barbados, cannot assuage her loneliness, cannot be transformed into male companionship, cannot be a balm to her larger alienation. Her space in the great house is bounded, rather confined, by her kitchen, her radio, her princess telephone. Her kitchen, the domain where she rules, is her tiny principality. And as her sense of identification with the household grows, Bernice begins to wonder why, given Mrs. Burrmann's skills and adeptness at housekeeping, she is needed as a domestic. She ponders whether Mrs. Burrmann's need is an expression of that aberration, that neurotic need of many whites to dominate, to feel superior, to make others feel inferior. For, indeed even in her loneliness—her constant need of whiskey as bulwark against an empty, though wealthy life—the white queen bitch, who could easily have done the household duties performed by Bernice, needs to have someone of an ascribed inferior status working for her. This constant need to dominate, to lord over an inferior, attests to a neurosis leading to a superiority complex. Bernice escapes from this domination, from this assertion of superiority, by turning to religion or by reducing Mrs. Burrmann's show of superiority, and by stressing the latter's unethical and immoral relationships.

Through the telephone she can reach out to her friend, Dot, with whom she discusses the morality and ethics of the Burrmann household, to whom she can confide an anger suppressed, a frustration so deep that she trembles on the border of violence. "I think I hate that woman so much that . . . that I could have *kill* her this afternoon" (29).

This expression of violence frees Bernice from her suppressed anger, giving it an escape valve. Bernice escapes from her exile in the Burrmann house through the reading and rereading of letters that she receives from Mammy and Lonnie. These recall her life in Barbados, her relationship with Lonnie, her memory of her mother, but to recall is to accentuate her aloneness, her lack of bodily contact. Memory of Lonnie's body awakens in her desires that momentarily stimulate masturbation, along with a guilt, a feeling of "worthlessness" that shames her.

> And she imagined Lonnie on her, making love to her; and she began to pant and breathe heavily, in rhythm to which she remembered so well; and she was feeling good, as if it was real and she was coming to the end of the race, with the tape in front of her eyes, and then she jumped up from the bed. (159–160)

Living in the Burrmann house offers Bernice material comfort; working there affords her the opportunity to have her very own checking balance of $3,000. Her amply stocked wardrobe is evidence of a measure of prosperity hardly attainable in Barbados. Yet she does not belong; her alienation is mirrored in the winter cold and snow, which she dislikes totally. Her reading of *Awake*, her visit to a predominantly white Unitarian church, do little to lessen her alienation, to feed her spirits. For there in Toronto, the overriding sensation, the ever-present element, is that of nonbelonging, of being visible in her Blackness. The West Indian immigrant is conspicuous, the object of stares, of ridicule on subways.

> Bernice never liked to be by herself when travelling on the subway . . . . She would imagine that they wanted to push her under the wheels; that she was unclean; that she was some kind of interloper; that she was without rights to sit on *their* subway. (200)

This feeling of paranoia that overwhelms Bernice while travelling on the subway is neither casual nor random, but rather derives from an indignity she once suffered while riding the subway, an indignity that haunts her memory. That incident awakened a murderous anger in her that she has only expressed through frustration, through tears.

> A small child raised its eyes from its mother's and saw Bernice opposite and said, slightly too loud for it to be a secret, "Mummy! *Look!*" . . . she hogged her way up the cement steps to the exit . . . . She asked . . . for the ladies' washroom, . . . entered it; bolted the door behind her; shut out all the white noises, all the white people in the world; sat on the clean, detergent-smelling toilet bowl (which was white) with the cover still down, and covered and woolly; and she cried for fifteen minutes. (202–203)

The clearly demonstrable racism that greets Estelle on her arrival in Canada makes her adventure in this new country a hostile, brutalizing, and degrading occasion, justifying Bernice's paranoia. In a humiliating search at the airport, the attitude of the customs officer seems to trespass and demean Estelle's person. On the other hand, she is rejected, too, and negated by her fellow Blacks, who turn away in embarrassment, clearly attempting to hide, to efface themselves, to negate their *own* Blackness. "The black family held down its head in shame and embarrassment; the black woman . . . averted her eyes" (46).

The outer society, the migrant's way of seeing, his perceptions of the new reality, seem completely controlled and dominated by race and sex.

The male characters, Boysie and Henry, because of their race are unable to find employment, but paradoxically also because of their race are able to indulge in sexual liaisons with white women. Discussion, dialogue, gatherings of the immigrants, all pivot around, all seem mired in race, in sex, to such a degree that almost all of the episodes, many of the subplots governing the narrative and directing the action of the *The Meeting Point*, are based principally on the circumstance of race, the element of sex. These, then, are the two basic ingredients shaping the lives of the West Indian migrants, the development of their characters, contouring their reality, their exile.

Mr. Burrmann's rape of the naive newcomer Estelle is reminiscent of and has all the wanton brutal configurations of the sexual exploitation and abuse of Black slave women by white masters. A successful white corporate lawyer, Burrmann uses his first sexual encounter with Estelle as an attempt to regain his lost maleness, to shed his fear, his impotence.

Clarke attempts, by orchestrating Estelle's restlessness, her boredom, to anticipate the rape. Indeed, the author even implies complicity, intimates acquiescence. But the intimations of nonresistance by Estelle can in no way explain Burrmann's unsolicited and brutal trespass. Her reaction of thinking "she had made him suffer long enough; she would have to save him now" in no way nullifies his "standing over her like a landlord . . . the passion and the lust in his body, which turned his smile into a criminal's grin" (13).

Clarke's spate of lyricism, in which he attempts to give esthetic dimension, even spirited aura, to the violent act, functions only to obscure the author's perceptions, his own interpretations of the rape, and its true signification.

> She was the land through which he had to travel like a man exploring, cutting through a jungle of veins that obstructed his path and vision. He was a traveller through this land, searching for the end at the other side, for enlightenment. And she, like the land, possessing *the* power did not insist on blocking his path; but allowed him the arrogance and the

comfort of trampling his feet on the black soil of her body. She was the land. And he, the explorer. (139)

Indeed the image of the land, the landscape, has undergone an essential debasement, for here the anthropomorphic relationship between Black woman and earth, an incessant image in so much of Black literature, has been utilized by Clarke to bring about a defilement of a Black woman. Clarke's lyricism about the rape becomes perhaps as obscene as the rape itself.

While Henry, the Black man, is beaten up by jealous white cops for having an affair with the German maid, Brigitte, the white man, Burrmann, not only escapes punishment but, in fact, is liberated; regains his manhood by frequent sexual intercourse with the Black woman-mistress for a while. With his newfound potency, Burrmann can now satisfy the sexual urges and temper the frustrations of his white wife. "He loving her up, and she loving him up, just as if they going on a second honeymoon" (239), Bernice notices.

The affair between Estelle and Burrmann is brutally ended when Burrmann realizes that Estelle is pregnant. He disowns his paternity—the evidence of his newfound potency. In a scene that brings together all the class, race, Barbados-Canadian implications, in a discussion that recalls a history of rape and miscegenation, the duplicity in the relationship between Estelle and Burrmann is exposed.

> When Estelle heard what the man said, she asked him to repeat it. He repeated it; and still she refused to believe she was hearing properly.
>
> "Is that what I mean to you?" She had already sensed it.
>
> "Is that *all* I mean to you, Sam?" . . .
>
> Sam disowned the child. . . . She had found out that she was just a woman, another cheap woman. Yet, had she been back home and this had happened, she would have chosen to keep this child as the forceful weapon to remind him of his past. . . . But she could have told him a long time ago, all that she meant to him. Her own grandfather had told her grandmother what *she* meant to him. (217)

The novel describes an arc whose trajectory seems to lead to the regaining of marital bliss for the two white protagonists, Mr. and Mrs. Burrmann; in a counter movement it traces an essential movement in the character of Bernice, who reins in her anger and simmers.

> Violence had always been close to Bernice. Frequently in her dealings with Mrs. Burrmann, and with the children, this violence seethed beneath the surface of her smiles. . . . Even at times, when violence seemed to her the only honest, dignified solution to a problem, . . . she had still kept it off. (242)

And for Estelle and Henry the trajectory arcs downward, leading not to regeneration but to an ultimate state of degeneration, to a state of ultimate loss.

Unlike the principal characters in *The Meeting Point, The Lonely Londoners,* and *The Housing Lark,* who suffer through a condition of exile in England or Canada, arriving there as mature individuals, the principal characters in *The Friends* and *Brown Girl, Brownstones* are young people whose growth of awareness, whose maturing, are notations of, and refract from, an exiled condition. For even as these characters arc into a new space, new arenas, they stumble through their conditions of growth into an uncharted space.

Any growth of awareness, that unordained movement from childhood through adolescence to young womanhood, is fraught with uncertainty, with the problematic, for the past must be abandoned for a future that's uncharted, unknown. The predicament of growth increases even more when the arena of that growth is also unknown, limiting. This is the predicament facing the central protagonist of Rosa Guy's *The Friends,* Phyllisia, who has recently arrived in New York with her sister Ruby to join their parents, Calvin and Ramona.

Phyllisia passes gropingly through many emotional states and crises as she explores and attempts to adapt to the new alien landscape of Harlem. Having stumbled over personal and societal barriers, Phyllisia finally attains a true and genuine friendship with Edith and now confronts the anguish of loss. They realize that the reality of the future awaits them: "there was no time left for the little games that children play or dream of—not any more" (Guy, *The Friends,* 196).

They both have undergone a harsh, often brutal initiation that has left scars now transformed by ritual trials into strengthening satisfaction. The lives of these two young girls have intertwined, linking them together in friendship. At the end of the novel, now that a true and honest relationship, a spiritual communion, is established, they can each face the future. Edith enters a foster home where she joins and helps her surviving younger sisters; Phyllisia challenges her father's decision to send her and her sister Ruby back to Trinidad. She must attempt to get to know her father and, for the first time, to communicate with him.

> All the way home I had been trying to think of words that would force him to listen to me, words that would make him change his mind about sending us away . . . . What was it I could possibly say to a man I had never really spoken to? (198)

Through the ritual trials, Phyllisia's physical growth has taken place, and she begins to sense the ramifications of her correspondingly expanding responsibility: to her friends, to herself, to her family.

> I *was* almost sixteen and I had never accepted any responsibility. I had even blamed Calvin for *my* treatment of Edith. But I was the one who had made her suffer. (190)

The quality of exile that Phyllisia encounters is textured differently, possesses a different cultural weave, from the exile of those who seek their fortunes in London, in Toronto. Phyllisia's initial alienation is cultural and personal, rather than principally societal. The outer reality, Harlem, though disconsolate, does not select her out because of race, does not regard her with surprise and amazement because of color; rather in Black Harlem she is most often indistinct, faceless, customary.

Phyllisia's aloneness derives from and is accentuated by the sightlessness of the adult world and the adults' mode of participation. Their method of relation differs from that experienced and expected by the children. She "[stares] hard into the faces of grownups, searching for a look of pity" (14–15), but finds none. Ironically, her feeling of alienation derives from her inclusion in that formless, enforced condition of mass. She is, in essence, but a digit, an unconnected cipher blending colorlessly into a social reality splattered with blood from fights, from dog-eat-dog hustle. Phyllisia in her exile moves through a space scarred by riots, poverty, by a reality that Rosa Guy portrays without romanticism as deformed, compartmentalized, lacking community, unsanctioned.

This mass condition ordains, it seems, a herdlike community that does not distinguish its members, negating the possibility of escape from it.

> Like a roaring wave, bodies slammed against me, pushing me backwards, forcing me off my feet, yet holding me upright by sheer numbers . . . . Policemen . . . broke up the wall of human flesh into smaller, more manageable knots. My support gone, I fell to the sidewalk. . . . Twice I tried to scramble to my feet, was knocked down and crouched, holding both hands over my head. (56)

From this perilous situation where her safety is threatened by that external, formless mass, Phyllisia is rescued by Edith, who, strong in resolve and strengthened by a generous friendship, places her body between Phyllisia and the rioting mass. Edith and Phyllisia pass from this external and violent anonymity of the streets into an interior, gloomy and dark, just as threatening as those streets. Edith's home is a scene of loneliness and desolation, a compartmentalized, individualized family tragedy, unknown to the men on the steps and indeed of little concern to them.

Rosa Guy skillfully and poignantly reduces Edith to human proportions, for she is indeed a child who too early has assumed the adult burden of taking care, singlehandedly, doggedly, of a poor and abandoned family. She is "not young anymore—not old, just not young" (59). In spite of her efforts, relentlessly the family breaks up, unseen, unheralded by the mass. Some of them fall by the wayside as wounded members of the herd community: her formless, silent father disappears—presumably dead; the angry, disoriented teen-age brother, Randy, is gunned down by the police—brutal and undifferentiated, an inhuman arm of society.

> A policeman shot him. Said that he was running across a parking lot and told him to halt. Shot one in the air, he said, but the boy never stopped running. Shot him in the back. They say the boy died instantly. (152)

In a well-paced, artfully orchestrated scene, Rosa Guy highlights Phyllisia's alienation, her fear, her ambivalence, her constant inability to carry out a resolution, a decision. Phyllisia's West Indian accent, her educational training, her own need to stand out—to achieve, to demonstrate superiority—set her apart from the group, the herd whose reactions against her are instinctual, swift, venomous. When she answers in class "despite a sixth sense warning [her] to remain silent" (7):

> I felt a dozen needles sticking my stomach. I leaned back in my seat. The fingernails of the girl behind me dug into my back . . . . I found myself staring into the eyes of the thick-muscled girl with the breasts . . . . As our stares locked, she balled up her fist, put it first over one eye and then the other. The needles in my stomach multiplied by the thousands. (8–9)

In the classroom, Phyllisia is not nameless and faceless. She is good at her studies and answers questions correctly, but she must pay the cost for this loss of anonymity. Her accent, her very language is viciously labelled, branded. The other children "called me names—'monkey' was one of the nicer ones" (5). Even the teacher taunts her, calling her a "Miss Cathy" when she calls on her, implying she is superior and snobbish. To increase Phyllisia's misery, the red-faced Jewish teacher, ridiculed by the class and fearful of the students, redirects their restless anger, channeling it away from herself. The young girl realizes her teacher is

> setting me up as a target. Any fool would feel the agitation in the room. But that was exactly what [Miss Lass] wanted.
> I knew it suddenly . . . . *Miss Lass was afraid!!* She was afraid and she was using me to keep the hatred of the children away from *her*. (8)

It is Edith, the little girl with the dark, quiet eyes, a character whom Rosa Guy portrays with a tenderness, a touching sympathy, who, in a highly dramatic scene, challenges big-breasted Beulah, the leader of the herd that cornered and beat Phyllisia after school the day before.

"I hear tell that some of you been messing with a good friend of mine. Well, let me tell you one thing. If anybody in this room feel like messing with a monkey chaser, I got your monkey and I got your chaser. So come on and try me." She chewed hard on her gum, hands still on her hips, one foot patting the floor. (40)

Yet Phyllisia snubs Edith, the only person offering her friendship. Phyllisia's attitude is not singular, not peculiar to her alone; rather it is a manifestation, a cultural inheritance passed on from her father, Calvin. It is rooted in that inherent need to swagger, to pose, to conceal one's weakness, to survive the brutal outward reality by pretending to be the grandee. Thus a person is judged by his pose, his swagger, more by appearance, by show, by surface attributes, than by inner quality. This mode of perception, of evaluation, derives from societies such as those in the West Indies where color and assumed class were the barometers of privilege, the requirements for acceptance. It is this mode of perceiving that dictates all of her father's behavior, colors his attitudes, shapes his judgments. Calvin is a "Miss Cathy"; the people around him, on whom his business depends, are dismissed as ragamuffins. Phyllisia, too, is a "Miss Cathy," and Edith—on whom her life depended during the riot, and on whom her rescue depended at school—is a ragamuffin to be despised because of her poor clothing. As Phyllisia notices her friend's clothes, her "feeling of gratefulness changed to one of annoyance" (41).

Phyllisia, never suspecting, indeed not being able to believe, that her father works in a sweatshop of a restaurant, glamorizes him because every morning he dresses up to go to work. Calvin's external appearance not only belies the conditions in which he works, but in fact is intended to mask them. Phyllisia also "longs for" the friendship of Marian, who "wore the prettiest dresses to school and those thick, ribbed socks that were all the rage" (27). And Phyllisia yearns for the "glamour" of her sister Ruby and her friends, while neglecting Edith. Phyllisia's attempt to selfishly impose her own ideas on another, indeed a seeming egocentric self-assertion, is apparent in her behavior and evinced in her initial relationship with Edith. Her petulant anger, her withdrawals, her incessant feeling of being the outsider in the home, are all qualities that also shape and contour her father's behavior, impel outbursts of anger, lead him to inflict punishing beatings on his children, and ultimately spark a confrontation between father and daughter. But initially, when Calvin orders Edith out of the house because of her appearance, Phyllisia, jealous of the attention Ruby and Ramona, her mother, have shown Edith, does not come to her friend's aid and totally rejects her.

The movement that urges the novel to its climax is Ramona's illness, which leads the central protagonist to a critical self-evaluation, a self-analysis, to a confrontation with the essentials rather than with the surfaces. The suffering of Ramona demands that her family come to grips with reality, confront the truth rather than continue to accept only surface appearances—a confrontation that exposes Calvin's posturing.

> A savage cry came out of his throat, "You know me, Ramona. I play the fool sometimes. I make things big—bigger than they are sometimes. But I never lie unless I can make a lie come true! Ramona, I can never lie to you!" (96)

Ramona, too, has lied and concealed the truth from her daughters. By violently ripping away her external clothing and exposing the wound that has replaced her missing breast, she then rips away the artifice, the falsehoods which have tempered Phyllisia's friendship with the unfortunate Edith. Ramona confronts Phyllisia with the knowledge of her own impending death and expresses her regret that she has allowed Phyllisia to absorb and act out her father's prejudices in her treatment of Edith. She makes Phyllisia aware not only of her own pretentiousness, but of her father's, too.

Ramona's death then triggers a deep rebelliousness in Phyllisia against her father, perhaps intensified by her own sense of guilt and remorse for her treatment of Edith. She is "haunted" by "that voice which plagued me whenever I fell ill and was alone in the room" (186). But Phyllisia ignores her mother's voice coaxing her to assume responsibility for her actions. In her grief, she continues to blame her father, who has become tyrannical in his determination to keep the family away from any outside associations. The situation deteriorates between father and daughters until Ruby, desperate, summons Ramona's friends. The elders, Cousin Frank and Mr. Charles, are members of the extended family, whose role, whose presence and intercession, Rosa Guy depicts in all their Africanity. Here, in these friendships, is the visceral relationship that makes for family, for clan, eventually for community. Frank and Charles are characterized with a sympathetic and affectionate attention that gives veracity to the possibilities of the extended family. They are summoned to act as mediators between the irascible father and the girls, who are attaining their womanhood. Aware of the pressures of that growth into womanhood, Frank and Charles can modulate the harshness with which Calvin deals with his daughters and can at the same time attempt to direct the course of their growth.

"We know that it's not easy, Calvin," Mr. Charles agreed. "And we know we have not helped. I think that I can talk for Frank as well as myself when I say that we will take more interest. We will be here much more often. But even with that, Calvin, you have to be able to trust your children." (169–170)

Rosa Guy offsets the willfulness, determination, and impatience of Cousin Frank with the quiet understanding and diplomacy of Mr. Charles, imbuing them both with facial expressions and attitudes that act as indicators of their modes of intercession, of any possible tensions. These two men have shared a friendship with Ramona that eased her hidden pain, have manifested a tenderness and affection absent from and in contrast to Calvin's overt swagger and bombast. The relationship among Frank, Charles, and Ramona is drawn with pastel strokes that have all the singular delicacy of a caress.

His gentle approach [did] more than complement [Ramona's] beauty. It forced consideration of the fragility that lay just beneath her surface appearance. It reminded me that I had been shouting at her a moment before. I was ashamed. (24)

Their attentions to Ramona signal their role as trusted family members in their demonstrated tenderness with the ailing woman. "They hovered over her like two hens, rubbing her hands, her feet" (104). The strength of their caring gestures makes it seem natural that when faced with Calvin's intractability, the tenderhearted Ruby would call on these dear friends of their deceased mother, whose softening influence is no longer there to act as a buffer. Clearly the novelist's intention is to show the cushioning that can derive from the concern and affection inherent in the true friendship possible in a genuine extended-family relationship. Rosa Guy has drawn the household, though rocked by tension and incessant confrontations, as a buffer zone against the mass condition of the outside world.

But in the absence of her mother, Phyllisia begins to seek solace in the streets. Here she is away from the pain of both home and school, seeking a new environment in which she might be able to exert some control. Although her wayward behavior is adopted initially to goad Calvin into sending her and Ruby back home to the islands, Phyllisia changes her mind when she realizes that her friend Edith needs her. She also realizes that she has become "hardened—a part of the concrete buildings and sidewalks of the city" (165). This newfound hardness helps her in her resolve to confront her father and thus to confront her own alienation. Thus, it is at the intersection of home and street, at that axis of interior—which retains the possibility of community—and exterior—which seems to have negated it and sunk to the level of a mass—that Phyllisia begins to lay hold of both realities. Now she does not "cringe, melt or wilt" (199) under her father's gaze. And she finds the courage to put her thoughts into words.

Though Phyllisia has not transformed the arena to which her family migrated, she has begun to apprehend it, to locate herself within its perimeters. Indeed, though the essential conditions of the external reality have not undergone any transformation, Phyllisia's perception of those conditions has altered. Thus the feelings of estrangement and alienation that contoured her initial arrival in Harlem from Trinidad undergo a fundamental change, and thus diminish.

To be chained, yet always fighting to be free; to be circumscribed, yet never contained; to be hemmed in, yet finally to break loose; to be caged, yet eventually fly out of that cage in search of light and air—in each instance, to go beyond the point of tiredness, seeking for the free flow—such is the vital shunting and essential motion of the unfolding lives of the men and women in *Brown Girl, Brownstones*. The emphasis is not simply on development, but rather on that unique quality that makes for persistence in spite of the stressed pervasive images of imprisonment in Paule Marshall's novel. Here the self-doubting, thin-shanked, flat-breasted young Black girl stumbles and fights her way to a point of liberating awareness from which she may be able to soar freely and easily away from her cage.

The bars of the cage are in some instances self-made and family-constructed, but the cage itself is the brutalizing outer environment of the larger society, which presses in on and attempts to contort the life of the protagonist, Selina. Paule Marshall's narrative is continuous and intricately laced together, taking place in a Black middle-class community in Brooklyn in the 1940s.

Basically, the outer reality remains threatening and uncompromising, with control just outside of Selina's grasp. Not only Selina but her family and many other characters who move through the novel are trapped mummies within their own brownstone tombs. Here in a series of images of imprisonment Marshall quickly etches their confinements.

> Perhaps everyone had his tomb: the mother hunched over the table all night might be locked in hers, her father, stretched out on the cot, might have been sealed in his, just as she was shut within the lonely region of herself. She might never find a way out, but like Miss Mary, move from one death to another. (Marshall, *Brown Girl, Brownstones*, 168)

The trajectory of *Brown Girl, Brownstones*, however, describes the way in which Selina, unlike Miss Mary, does not move from one death toward another, but finally toward escape.

The novel depicts the interplay between the outer environment pressing against the protagonist and her attempt to shake loose from it as she grows in awareness. In *Brown Girl, Brownstones*, the outer material circumstances mirror the internal psychological conditions of the characters whose changing fortunes are, in turn, reflected in the changes that take place on Chauncey Street in Brooklyn. Perhaps the collapse of the family unit is marked by the deterioration of the brownstones. The other material circumstances change: from a cool, green park full of trees to a desolate and wasted park; from shuttered brownstones—enclosures in which the few remaining, seemingly embalmed whites and aspiring Blacks struggle—to ravaged, crumbling brownstones devastated by encroaching projects. The once-genteel brownstones will be abandoned by middle-class Blacks to newer Black and Spanish arrivals, and will increasingly take on the characteristics of Fulton Street, which before was separated from Chauncey Street by the fresh green of the intervening park. Fulton Street—crowded with people, cars, and trains that seem to move uncontrollably and violently, loud with shrieks and noises, garish yet alive—used to differ so much from the hushed monotony and dead silence of the genteel Chauncey Street.

The acquisition of brownstone houses on such streets as Chauncey becomes the consuming passion of the majority of Barbadian immigrant families who are the central characters of this novel. In wartime images—for the time setting is around the Second World War—Paule Marshall skillfully chisels out the brownstone house in which Selina, Ina, Silla, and Deighton Boyce live. The row of houses, like "a fortress wall guarding the city," stands with all its defenses ready, "reared against the sky" (1). The external rigidity and embattled appearance of the houses reflect the internal struggles compressed within the family ranks, contained within the shadowy interiors of the brownstones. The monotonous, undifferentiated exteriors proclaim the dull, oppressive boredom, the ceaseless grinding weight borne by the striving occupants of the brownstones.

Within one lives the Boyce family and their tenants: an old invalid of a white woman, Miss Mary, a relic of the previous white occupants of the house; Maritze, her frustrated daughter, bitter with hate, frozen by religious zeal; and Suggie Skeete, an earthy immigrant Barbadian woman whose only enjoyment and relief from the weekly servitude of working for rich white folk is in the licentious abandon of sensual intercourse with random lovers.

The part of the house occupied by the Boyce family lies dimly hushed under the weight of ponderous and seldom-used furniture, all of it, except a huge bed, inherited from the former white occupants. The whole interior of the house, its rooms, its corridors and its occupants, is revealed through the eyes of Selina, the principal narrator of the story, who, waiflike, haunts the corridors and sifts through the histories of rooms and people. The outer reality impinges on and seems to control the inner histories of things and people. Here the vital pervasive presence, the all-controlling force, is the brownstone.

> Her house was alive to Selina. She sat this summer afternoon on the upper landing on the top floor, listening to its shallow breathing. (8)

But, although alive, the house is spectral, is shadowy in the summer heat, and seems to have entombed and trapped the ghosts of its former white owners. And outside the brownstone, those who form the world around that brownstone, they, too, live set, confined, in narrow niches or stifled in limited aspirations with which their lives are circumscribed.

Miss Thompson, tall, aging, alone, bearing on her foot a festering sore—her symbolic inheritance of the white world of the South—toils incessantly, boxed within the narrowness of hairdressing booths; or then again, exhausted, she lies caught within her bedsheets, a masklike statue, vitalized and warmed by the small bodies of abandoned children whom she has taken for her own. It is to Miss Thompson that Selina often turns in her loneliness for comfort and solace; she seems to represent for the growing Selina a spirituality, a point of spiritual refuge, whereas Suggie evokes the sensuous, representing the physical.

Beryl, Selina's childhood friend, is encircled by a family obsessed with pursuit of gentility and driven by the desire to acquire material security. Like the other characters, Beryl, too, seems trapped within the confines of a world structured by the savage, driving determination to acquire a brownstone, a world dominated by the importance of appearances with all their figural attitudes. She and not Ina, Selina's sister, provides Selina with youthful companionship, with camaraderie. Yet at times Beryl seems a foil, a youthful representative of an older generation whose goals are basically incomprehensible to Selina. In her house, there is no loosely strung together gathering of individual tenants, but rather a family, rigidly controlled and harshly ruled over by a patriarchal father. Indeed, to Selina, Beryl seems to live within this orderly house "like a small, well-lighted room with the furniture neatly arranged around it" (17).

The immediate outer reality of Selina's house seems controlled and dominated by the haunting presence of dead and dying white people.

> She rose, her arms lifted in welcome, and quickly the white family who had lived here before, whom the old woman upstairs always spoke of, glided with pale footfalls up the stairs. Their white hands trailed the banister; their mild voices implored her to give them a little life. (9)

The irony here is patent, for it is the desire to acquire such a house which leads to the tragic and pathetic breakup of the Boyce family.

The peculiar condition of the Boyce family's exile is reflected in the inability of Deighton and Silla, most often referred to by the author as "the mother," to reconcile their individual expectations and aspirations within the context of the myriad prisons imposed by a hostile and foreign environment. While the mother takes refuge in the relative safety of the Barbadian community, which approves and supports her efforts to achieve her material goals, Deighton most often takes refuge in his dreams, in the arms of his "concubine," in his preening.

Indeed, the tragedy that overtakes the present occupants of the house may have been foreshadowed by the lives of the former occupants, whose remnants and spectral presences seem mummified there, mocking the aspirations of the new arrivals, denying them possession.

> She did not belong here. She was something vulgar in a holy place . . . it belonged to the ghost shapes hovering in the shadows. But not to her. (9–10)

This sense of nonbelonging to this house with remnant whiteness, the feeling of alienation haunting Selina, is not particular to Selina alone, but in its larger signification indicates an essential difference between the lifestyles of Selina's immigrant family and those who lived muted by "friezes of cherubs and angels."

For indeed the configurations of the house contour the activities and demarcate the characters of its inhabitants, the internal material atmosphere forming a nexus and merging with the inner human mood. The last old white occupant of the house, living still on memories of her past, lies in that gray, fogged zone between life and death, her decay and rot reflected in and blending with the phantasmagorical yellow:

> The light remained a tarnished dust-yellow. It was always like this . . . .
> In the midst of this dust and clutter, Miss Mary's bed reared like a grim rock. She lay there, surrounded by her legacies, and holding firm to the thin rotted thread of her life. Her face was as yellowed with age as the air, her eyes smeared with the same stale light. (21)

There is here a total sense of dereliction and waste, of an all-pervasive, all-encompassing emptiness that claims Miss Mary's daughter "as empty of life as the room with its dust-yellow fog" (35), as yet another victim.

As an offset, it seems, not far from the empty death chamber of Miss Mary is the room of full-blooded, sensuous Suggie. Her room, though as crowded with objects as Miss Mary's, is vital and alive, not dying but wanting to live. In one room, the enclosed stifling atmosphere is exhumed by "boxes of old clothes"; in the other the wished-for, free-flowing movement is imaged in all the liquid perfumes: "all shapes and sizes of bottles waited there, cool glass without, warm amber perfumes within" (20). For Suggie, though trapped in her small blue room, is still liquid movement, vital light,

> her wide red skirt falling like red-glazed water from her hips. . . . and the earring under her thick hair flashed with amber tints as her body swayed. (26)

Lying "sprawled amid her rumpled sheets, sluggish from the rough pleasures of her night" (46), she exudes all the vital signs of life. Yet like Miss Mary, she, too, is essentially unfulfilled: an immigrant Barbadian woman, living with memories of the past, who seems unable to cope with the abrasive, relentless competitiveness of the alien and foreign lifestyle of urban New York. That Suggie is pictured lying sprawled and sluggish is no mere accident, for Paule Marshall pinpoints each posture, giving an essentialness to it, translating it into a definition of each character, so that character, posture, and setting all blend together, cohere. It is this constant interpenetration of character and setting, of life and situation, of mood and atmosphere, that gives such density and fullness to Paule Marshall's character depiction.

In the sun parlor where "sunlight [that] came spilling through the glass wall, swayed like a dancer in the air and lay in a yellow rug on the floor," Selina's dapper, sensitive, seemingly carefree father lies, "stretched dark and limp on a narrow cot like someone drunk with sun" (12). While Deighton languidly gives himself up to the warm sensuousness of the sun parlor, hanging free and easy in the sunlight, his wife Silla seems always to be poised, attentive, either "cool, alert, caged in sunlight from the barred window" (46) or standing "in the relaxed, unself-conscious pose of someone alone" (23). Both are alone, but their differing postures within their individual and different habitats already announce a fundamental incompatibility in their approach to life, foreshadowing conflict.

Silla and Deighton's estrangement is highlighted by their chosen settings within the house. Silla's stark white kitchen intimidates Deighton, challenging him "to impose himself somehow on the whiteness" (23). Silla, like the kitchen, is unwelcoming. Her resentment of Deighton's lack of ambition and lack of fidelity prevents her from yielding to her natural desire to communicate with her husband. She and Deighton are often depicted in attitudes of mutual but unverbalized longing. Of the prisons and spaces that enclose them, none seems so restricting as their own inability to move beyond the void which separates them and touch.

> He thought how cool her skin would be despite the heat and his fingers suddenly ached for that touch. He might find the words tonight to bring

trust again to her eyes; his hands might arouse that full and awesome passion they once had. (23)

As the kitchen is Silla's domain, the sun parlor is Deighton's, eventually keeping them locked away from each other in reality, as their separate goals and needs divided them initially. "He slept in the parlor each night now with the tall sliding doors locked between them" (126).

The unhappy couple's alienation deepens when Silla devises an elaborate deception, which she uses to fraudulently sell Deighton's "piece of ground" back home in Barbados. She is determined to use the money as a down payment on the deteriorating brownstone they now lease. The house is ever an intruder, ever a source of conflict between the two, and comes to symbolize their conflicting philosophies.

> "You put aside anything this week toward the down payment on the house?"
>
> "Not one penny!" he cried and wanted to wind his arms tight around his head to shut out her voice, wanted suddenly to strike her into silence.
>
> Silla's wrath broke and she whirled from the sink, her voice flailing across the kitchen. "You mean it all gone on fancy silk shirt and shoes caterwauling with your concubine." (25)

But Deighton has been building his own dream house. He has confided to Selina of a house built out of good Bajan coral stone that he plans to paint completely white. Silla's betrayal—her single-minded determination to get ahead in the chosen place of her exile—means the death of Deighton's dream.

> He moaned, breaking inside as the dream broke. Yet . . . it was as though Silla, by selling the land, had unwittingly spared him the terrible onus of wrestling a place in life. The pretense was over. He was broken, stripped, but delivered. (97)

But though Deighton may secretly be relieved, he is compelled to seek revenge. With the consummate skill of an actor, he breaks down the barriers between him and Silla long enough to deceive her into trusting him with the bank draft.

Deighton, only on this particular day, is able to master Silla and the starkness of her kitchen. After a one-day shopping spree with the money that he has agreed to use for the brownstone, he returns to Silla's kitchen for the last act of his performance and he showers his "lady folks" with gifts bought with the ill-gotten money. Silla remains immobilized while Deighton dominates her space, throwing the "bold red coat with a collar of dark fur" (109–110) at her feet in a magnificent act of revenge. Then he retreats to the parlor and Ina to the safety of her bedroom, leaving Selina with her mother, moved by her grief.

> Obscurely she knew that this was her place, that for some reason she would always remain behind with the mother . . . . she gazed around the kitchen . . . It might be invaded by a band of revelers, she thought. They had dyed the air with their laughter and dropped bits of gaudy costumes as they danced, then rushed out, leaving the trumpet twisted on the floor and the mother's red coat like a raw pool of blood there . . . .
>   . . . there was a part of her that always wanted the mother to win, that loved her dark strength and the tenacious lift of her body. She asked, "You want me to fix some tea?" (112)

Paule Marshall displays a continuously evocative sense of color and space in this scene. The mother's defeat is seen in the "raw pool of blood" and the destruction of the rigid order she has always maintained in her space. The littered kitchen expresses her inner desolation and leaves her still surrounded by the remnants of the useless fragments of paper and wrappings where order and well-laid plans should have reigned.

Thus it is that both *The Friends* and *Brown Girl, Brownstones* are built around their young protagonists, Phyllisia and Selina, who go questing for self-awareness in an unknown and uncharted space, which ultimately they begin gropingly to understand. Their initial alienation from their immediate reality lessens as they grow in self-awareness; the space through which their characters are chartered grows then, too; though impinged upon and seemingly controlled from without, they begin to be defined within their own growth.

The principal modality of *The Scholar-Man* by O. R. Dathorne and *Other Leopards* by Denis Williams is not growth but rather a search for presence, a grasping after new interpretations of a distant landscape, an African ethos. These two novels show the quest for self in identification with Africa; for both of the protagonists of these novels, Adam Questus and Lionel Froad, pursue the long road of return from Guyana to Africa. They are in search of a freedom in which all times fuse—past, present, and future—leading them to an instant of truth.

Adam Questus, on flying to West Africa to become a lecturer at a university, realizes that

> for most of the passengers, it was just a journey across two continents, but for him it went across past, present and future. (Dathorne, *The Scholar-Man*, 10)

Lionel Froad is caught in the enigmatic web of time where he feels the past was ashes; a mystical future sending wave-impulses back to a hopeless past. The future hardening, tick-tocked like an alarm clock to its hour. Everyone saturated, the alarm would work off to the ultimate consummation: the orgasmic flood, the freedom realized, the old thing butchered, the new thing born. (Williams, *Other Leopards,* 74)

But before this new thing could be born, Adam Questus and Lionel Froad must go through triple baptisms—sprinkled with the creek waters of their Guyana; lashed by the doubts and questionings about African independence and their place of belonging in this freedom; and finally washed clean by consummation with the rhythms of Africa.

For Adam Questus, the past is the remembrance of Egor, whom he comes seeking and who gave him the first baptism in Guyana: ". . . he dreamt of Egor, cutting through brown river waters, and swimming naked in the sun" (Dathorne, *The Scholar-Man,* 23). For the witch doctor and for the villages to which Egor has come, Egor is an aberration, an oddity to be shunned.

Well—the witch-doctor shifted—he was different. He stopped, and started again suddenly, Why should a normal person want boys and lame women and—"What?" He left the village. We drove him away. He was no good for us. (169)

Yet it is this very "difference" that Adam admires in Egor, whom he states "was a man who had to get every ounce out of life, even if he had to squeeze it dry" (166). This difference, this aberration, is but one motif of the novel, one recurring theme often captured in a language whose dramatic or lyrical overtones run totally contrary to the major theme of the novel. The depiction and presentation of university activity in West Africa takes shape through mock satire, broad farce. Thus it is that the novel operates on two levels whose narrative formulations construct the central argument; the search of Adam Questus for his relationship to Africa.

The first baptism in the waters of Guyana is consecrated in images of strength and warmth, of entry into greenness. Here, there is light, a rhythmical fusion with the rhythms of the Guyanese landscape.

The river hurried from the jungle and here on the coast the brown water dissolved into the sea. The river bank was purple and palms knelt close to the edge of the water. . . . He was smooth and beautiful and they used to race for the water, tumbling together and capsizing the grey sea foam and mingling with water and wet in this first baptism of life . . . glorious and fulfilled. (1–2)

Then Adam, who comes to Africa in search of Egor, his mulatto lover, a teacher from his grammar school days in Guyana, now consecrates his search by his copulation with Egor's "second wife," Adam perhaps being his "first wife." It is with her, in a spiritual copulation with the possessive madness of the African mud and earth, that he receives his third baptism

> driven by a kind of mad desire and love, power and hate. . . . The lightning spotlighted his coarse animal movements over her and the thunder came from her spine, the lightning from her spasms. Then the rain fell and he lay lost in this, his third baptism of mud and water. (179)

But the past is not only Egor; it is three hundred years of separation that have brought with them forgetfulness of the ways of Africa. Although he is the only African type in the plane load of returning expatriates—and he is constantly taken for an African—he is labelled an expatriate by Farrar at the university because of his inability to truly enter the rhythms of Africa.

> Adam asked, "Do we drive across?" He was surprised that Farrar went to his car, as the distance was only a few yards. "Oh yes," Farrar said, "expatriates don't walk." (42)

Neither can he be correctly situated nor can he situate himself or find a locus of belonging. Adam Questus initially cannot apprehend the significance of the African rituals, so, too, he seems unable to understand or cope with the natural effects of an African ecology.

> Was it not strange? Of all people, he had to get malaria—the white man's curse in the tropics, the illness that made this the white man's grave. And he had come so full of hopes, looking for light and the sun. (108)

His entry into the village, the space that counters the European-style African university, finds him unable to hold up under the pull of Comfa drums or to bear the sting of the whip. Now Adam Questus fears the dark African night, no longer understands the spiritual sacrifice by which an African servant saves his life. In the dance of the Comfa, the Guyanese Adam symbolically feels the lash of the whip, whereas those who were never separated from the earth rhythms only feel its caress. To be sure he has, half-dressed, given himself up to the rhythms of the darkness and the drums; but here, too, he faints. He has forgotten their essence. Again he seems unable to apprehend the symbology of an African ritual.

> [The drumming] took him back, snatched him and ripped off his prim sophistication, and sweating, swelling with its roughness, it tossed him half-naked into the circle. And he was dancing in the centre of the crowd moving his hips, his buttocks, his hair, his feet, forgetting his reason and

reasons, consigning his concerns to the terror of the message and the beat and the sound. . . . And then suddenly . . . there was the screech of a hundred women's voices and the terror of the men, and the leader . . . flashed his teeth and his whip . . . But Adam felt it. (177)

The theme of sacrifice, that is, of something dying for the regeneration of another, finally hinted at in the burning of the university, takes another form here. Henry, the servant of the Farrars, becomes a sacrifice for Adam Questus's acquisition of an ultimate knowledge, "and in the madness of that rainy moment, in the slush and the lighted dark, the wet and the testimony of thunder, he knew" (181).

It is at this level of sublimation that Adam Questus, in his search for Egor, on his first night at the university dreams of Egor. And always when in intercourse with Helen, the paradigm of the young white expatriate woman, he recalls Egor. This confluence of parallel themes—his affair with Helen and his search for Egor—though presented with an element of seriousness, splits in melodramatic overtones, wherein Helen, whose morality is but questionable, is made to mouth ethical statements about the African historical movement.

"Well, what is the new Africa? Shall I tell you? . . . The new Africa is the wonderful wild life locked up in the zoo for a shilling, the savannahs being used as a golf-links, and goggle-eyed Negro Americans living *à la primitif* in the villages, and signs going up: 'Virgin Jungle. Tread carefully. Do not litter. No loiterers.'" (163)

On the level of the depiction of university life, however, there is no melodrama, there is melodic farce. The relationship between Farrar and his wife; the interaction between Farrar and his servant, Hannibal; the classroom scenes between Adam Questus and his students; the mock seriousness of the debate over the students' strike; all these are told with relish, sketched in broad comic strokes. But even though these strokes are comic, they pinpoint many elements of absurdity that characterize the presence of expatriates in West Africa, characterize, too, the mimicking of European attitudes by some West Africans. Farrar, is portrayed within an obsessive fear of "horrible local diseases." The farce of the scenes with Farrar and Hannibal is structured on the type of relationship between a European expatriate and African servant that once was customary, that once prevailed.

Farrar, the knowledgeable expatriate, that figure who knows all about Africa and Africans, who has learned so thoroughly their psychology, explains in his book, *Non-European Mind*, in a chapter entitled "Africa at Work and Play,"

> Africans sometimes work and sometimes play but unlike Europeans their
> work is part of their play and their play part of their work . . . . (124)

He has suggested that Adam Questus begin his introduction to literature
with the nursery rhyme, "Mary Had a Little Lamb." But this scene with
Adam and his students reveals another level of the European-African
relationship. The classroom scene is cleverly paced, picking up on the way
all the nicknames that label the students, picking up what the labels
represent and the statements of the students, and opening out these
statements into an infectious comical interplay.

> Adam said, "I want to start off by discussing a poem with you."
> Someone jeered, "Heh! Scholarman!" . . .
> Another student, a tall well-built fellow, said to him, "My nomen-
> clature is Talkfada—that signifies the Father of Talk, the progenitor of
> all conversation." . . .
> . . . A student sitting near Talkfada, apparently a disciple of the latter,
> said, "I detect in these an imperialist insinuation. . . .
> "In these country no one is called Mary, we do not like little lambs."
> (43–45)

Here there is broad and expansive, irreverent laughter. Later on, with
Byron's poem, the scene takes on the quality of rollicking, earthy laughter
as the students make interpretations of the poem that border on the bawdy.

> "The poet is now old and he makes excuse to his wife. The sword is the
> male organ which he shows her and which is now important, but unfortu-
> nately impotent . . . ." (124)

This romping banter, which characterizes Dathorne's presentation of the
students, develops into a mischievous, but caustic and ironic guffaw as
Dathorne ridicules the vice-chancellor's person and his entire administration
at the university. There eventually emerges a serious indictment of the
behavior of many of those who are responsible for the functioning of
independence. The meaning of independence is denigrated to a "big day for
Government people, like Christmas" (166) when a trader can double his
prices for eggs. The meaning of independence to the politicians as well is
ridiculed.

> The wireless was full of independence and in between the advertise-
> ments the politicians spoke and the imperialists did a bit of congratu-
> lating, and the firms talked of expansion and prosperity, and then another
> advertisement was heard. (166)

But *The Scholar-Man* is saved from preaching and high-sounding ethical pronouncements about the nature of African independence by the many elements of farce and by the rowdy laughter that accompanies most episodes. This quality of offsetting one condition against the other, of presenting two parallel but distinctly different moods and themes—that of life in the university and Adam Questus's search for a subliminal relationship with Egor, for belonging, for identification with Africa—at times robs the novel of clarity of purpose, veiling its novelistic intention. By highlighting the farcical proportions inherent in the figure of the expatriate in a West African university setting, by depicting the pretentiousness of the African vice-chancellor, by highlighting what is essentially the bull sessions of the students in class, Dathorne seems to reduce university life to its ultimate absurdity. Thus he seems to be denying the evolutionary possibility in the development of West African university life. When the advocate of "Mary Had a Little Lamb," Farrar, takes over the university, the students, even the future of the country, are made into negatives.

As the university buildings burn, a voice in the pidgin idiom ritualizes the destructive force of a bush-fire and echoes the promise of fulfillment as a resurrection from the ashes.

> Bush-fire na thing what dey come for night in hot season. It no dey ask question, it no dey give warning. It dey come late for night when the sky empty and the moon gone for house, and bush-fire does wake up and walk. It be the light eberyman want to light his darkness . . . . It no know what be European man, what be native man—it no care. In the morning ebery man have to wake up and plant again. (177)

The bush-fire is indiscriminate, but its promise of fulfillment ordained. It is this promise of newness with which Dathorne concludes the action of his novel, *The Scholar-Man*. Clearly the promise is but wished for, for nowhere in the movement of the novel, in its spoofing of action and episodes, in its mockery of university life, is that promise held out or even barely envisaged. Thus it is that the fire takes on the proportions of a bonfire, ironically representing the circus of independence. For Dathorne makes of independence, of university life in West Africa, of students' participation in that life, of the role and presence of the expatriate, a circus, a mockery that teeters always on the brink of laughter, descends to the level of farce, whose effect is a total reduction of that university life, of the seriousness of independence.

The questions that remain are: Can these negatives help to rebuild the university from its ashes? Can Adam Questus's exile, his repeated feeling of aloneness, his sense of nothingness, can all these be sublimated by his final encounter with the raw elemental form?

Like Adam Questus, the protagonist of *Other Leopards* comes in search to Africa. Lionel Froad is an archaeological draftsman, a man of Guyana living in Jokhara, in the Sudanic region of Africa, and pursuing the unravelling of the ruins of Old Karo, an offshoot culture of Meroe. His past is linked to the three thousand years from which some of these ruins date. The past and the present merge for him in the figure of Eve, the daughter of an African Christian minister. She seems a replica of some figures of old Meroe that he has seen in drawings, and to him becomes a concrete representation of Queen Amanishakete. But this merging of figures reveals the paradox of his relationship to the past—the not-knowing, the enigma of its pull.

> I looked at the gold figurine of Queen Amanishakete and sensed something of the same confusion and depth agitation that had first surprised me in the pages of the Lepsius. I knew that this image of Eve, this persistent female, would never leave me as long as I lived. And I resented this. (Williams, *Other Leopards*, 134–135)

Thus he is impotent to fertilize Eve, to locate her in time. Yet since she is also the evocation of Guyana waters and foliage, he grasps for her essence:

> I liked to compare her to physical things: . . . to the immense black rivers of my South American home; the virginal strength of our equatorial forests. But Eve should more accurately be compared to certain sombre psychological states: to the nausea of inspiration, say, or to the nameless yearning for origins that beset most of us. (90–91)

Lionel is not even able to decipher the enigma of his own second self, Lobo, a baptismal Guyana name given him by his sister. He feels himself "Lionel, the who I was, dealing with Lobo, the who I continually felt I ought to become" (19). Thus, like Adam Questus, Lionel-Lobo is searching in Africa for that other self. But both have been caught by their relationship with and opposition to their second baptism. Adam Questus, even though leaving the "darkness of London for the light of Africa" (9), returns in his memory to his seven-year stay in England and constantly juxtaposes the material problems faced in Africa with a certain sense of "at homeness" in England. In addition, it is Helen, the daughter of an expatriate English lecturer, who, symbolizing England, brings about his second baptism, and to whom he almost becomes wedded.

Lionel Froad, too, almost accepts the comforting embrace of Catherine, the Welsh expatriate and, like Eve, the daughter of a minister. For a long time, Lionel is also dominated by his disciplined, rational-thinking, pragmatic English boss, the archaeologist Hughie, who symbolizes Western success and who has definite directions and beliefs. Hughie attempts to make Lionel validate the past cultural existence of Sudanic Africa even though Lionel is totally resistant to giving himself to the task of justifying his race and by extension himself. Hughie has injected a feeling of inferiority into Lionel, who in turn has ambivalent feelings toward Hughie, alternating between deep resentment and admiration, an affection approaching love. But at the point where he has almost deified Hughie, Lionel frees himself from his boss's control by an act of violence.

In *Other Leopards* the style unfolds in ironic asides, in an impressionistic and satirical way in which thought and word sequences collide and clash. Williams, too, views with skepticism the shrewd manipulations of political leaders, the tension between the Muslim part of the country and the Christian, the certainties of the black-skinned Christian minister, Chief, and the assuredness of the army colonel, Hassan. On the other hand, Lionel's quest for self is a continuous interior monologue, taut with doubts and uncertainties and multilayered with symbolic imagery.

However, in his double absence, his double exile, from both self and origins, Lionel Froad stumbles through his own ambiguity, even the ambiguity of region, of circumstance, to arrive perhaps after the fragmentation of his historical reality to a transformed liberated self. But to liberate himself, to enter into a state of wholeness, he must physically destroy that part of himself, that alter part whose cold, constant, ruthless presence—the West European presence—has disfigured the Black Western-educated man, separating him from his African cultural heritage, his cultural mores. Lionel wilts under the trauma of his own interior tension, under the insidious self-contempt, feels it to be an incessant statement of inferiority, a continuous goad and challenge to his person, being, manhood.

Indeed Lionel with all of his Western training, or because of it, seems to accept the role of lackey without a culture, a lackey constantly whipped, needled, goaded into accepting the burden of his race, into accepting what seems to be the dead weight of his culture. Thus, Hughie bludgeons Lionel, who cringingly accepts the former's taunts, parries them from time to time, but mostly resigns himself to that whipping.

> Take your ease, man, take your ease; not afraid of him, are you?
> Who the hell's Hughie to be afraid of? If I'm late I'm late; tell him straight. If he says, "Morning, Froad," with the faintest rebuke in his eye
> . . .
> Stopped again to calm himself. Useless. (36)

So long has his exile been, so total his indoctrination, his absence from self, this exile, his awayness. But Hughie in his conceited assurance believes that scientific materialism can replace and dominate the human will, the spirit. With a conscious effort Lionel attempts to break away from the Englishman's throttling presence, his smug intellectualism, his scientific

determinism. The act is at once brutal and necessary. It is an act fraught
with the deepest signification for the enshrining of the Caribbean presence.

> I have achieved a valuable state: a condition outside his method.
>   . . . No one can now expect me to make the faintest gesture towards
> a civilized language. I am a savage, shadowless. In my own time I can
> make my way back to the Fellata village. Only remains now to remove
> my consciousness. This I can do whenever I wish. I am free of the earth.
> I do not need to go down there for anything. (222)

The actualization is not a spurious act but a vital liberating one, without
which emancipation from the colonizing imperialistic presence is not assured,
by means of which the personality is fragmented, that part of the self which
has occasioned ambiguity dropped off, shed. But an integrating resolution is
no easy accomplishment, and even as he realizes the implications of the
ambiguity of baptism, of the naming, realizes and accepts the ambiguity of
his origins, of his essential geography, of the consequences and issue of
Kaywana's first bedding by the Dutch adventurer, he is beset by a paralysis
and inertia.

> All along, ever since I'd grown up, I'd been Lionel looking for Lobo. I'd
> felt I ought to become this chap, this *alter ego* of ancestral times that I was
> sure quietly slumbered behind the cultivated mask. Now on that after-
> noon I came consciously to . . . the attitude of involuntary paralysis . . .
> as the Uncommitted African. (20)

A supercilious pose and a lack of true commitment have resulted from the
inherent ambiguity. In an evening on the hillside of the Sudan, in the midst
of a fragmenting imagistic reality, and when all is the play of light, of
shadow, Lionel realizes his lack of commitment, of involvement, and
rationalizes his historical space moment. Lionel, unconnected, articulates the
notion of self unrelated to race, to community.

But Eve perceives the essential dilemma making for that articulation. Eve
is at this instant a shadow presence, rooted in an evocative landscape:

> She folded herself moodily into the kind of night-bag-overall thing she
> was wearing, and wrapped the shadows round her, moving in her own
> stillness like a Bacongo carving. (94)

Unlike Hughie, Lionel cannot deny the pull of race. Even after three
hundred years of absence, a part of him can still enter the natural African
rhythms. All is shadow, silhouette, concealment; his entry into "sweet
rhythms" natural, but still not free, free from the white man's supercilious,
cold scrutiny. He enjoys his dance not for itself, but as a weapon of exclusion to Hughie.

And his adventure into the past, into his race, comes continuously under Hughie's cold, measuring scrutiny. Indeed *Other Leopards* argues in all of its contradictory impulses that Lionel's confrontation with his history, his past, is as a supplicant; he must validate that past to himself, to the clinically negating eye of the white man, who is intent on questioning the origins of Meroetic civilization, refusing his provenience in African civilization.

Uncertain, tentative, with a cavalier attitude covering his confusion, Lionel moves toward his confrontation with his history. Clearly to the supplicant such a confusion is perilous, so fearful that it causes the seeker's steps to waver, even to seek flight. But, symbolically, the presence of Europe, in this most intimate reunion of mother and son, is witness to it, forces it on.

> A minute from her pyramid, guts unaccountably failed. I came to a stop, stood gaping, a supplicant after all, before an inscrutable oracle, making excuses, telling myself what the hell, it didn't matter a damn, that I could turn on my heels and never see her and not care. . . . The South Cemetery pyramids stonily returned my gaze. I turned, made a resolute little run up the hill to number six, and came bang up against her chapel pylon, towering above me. This was it: the crucial, the reluctant confrontation. (150)

All is vital "green sky," all is royal purple rock-towering presence. His confrontation with his past, with this statue, is marked not by the entry into presence, not by mythic wonder, nor by the investing of myth or sacredness in it; rather the statue is figuratively represented, its ethos delineated, its mere personality articulated. Having ascribed no mystery to it, he cannot communicate sensation, emotion; feeling confounded, dumb, he cannot baptize it with water, with pure language, for he wants to render its spirit, his corporate oneness with it, in the logic of words. Unable to do so, perhaps because of a Western reductionist approach to his reality, Lionel not Lobo reduces the meeting to an absurd nothingness:

> She had died and gone, yet she was still there, filling and emptying vessels. But how could that be! How could real water exist at the heart of a mirage! How was I to believe *that!* I wished for the words to assault those stone ears with some claim of my very own, mine, me! But time passed, wind blew, sand settled, gloom deepened, and I could think of nothing; nothing at all. (155)

Perhaps Lionel's long exile, his saturation in a ruthless clinical perception of reality, a perception akin to Hughie's scalpel-like analysis, has made him bent on stripping the person naked. He has approached Hassan, Eve's husband, using cruel objectivity. An equal ruthlessness marks his treatment and his dialogue with Catherine. With Catherine, he has sardonically planned his offense against her rejection of him that he predicted. His plans are cold, calculating, and devoid of any emotional intensity; all seem to be surface reacting. Even with Eve, even as deep passion erupts, he is brutal, ruthless, and clinically recording her reactions to his violence.

> I shouted, "Mind y'talk!" and belted her another; good hard one this time. "Mind how y'talking!" She must've been seeing stars by now, because she bent over and made no move to dodge the third blow. "Don't talk me back that way!"
> She screamed and leaped up and started clawing, so I palmed her face and shoved it back downwards. . . . Trembling something silly. "Shut up, I tell you," holding a back-hand poised over her eye. (92)

Thus, during the time of his second baptism, as he searches for self and roots, Lionel Froad not only evinces deep doubts about those roots, seemingly unable to confront even their archaeological representation, but also, in his search for self, he demonstrates feelings of ambivalence, and at times, uncontrolled bouts of sadistic behavior. Thus, at this stage, he has neither achieved a wholing of self nor has he entered into that symbolic space and time of return to roots.

After periods of doubt, after the parody and irony, after the homosexual yearnings of Adam and impotent spasms of Lionel, in both novels the protagonists undergo their third baptisms, a freeing of selves in a return to the earth rhythms. With Lionel,

> I thought of . . . Original Sin: the New Baptism: the Cleansing from Menace. There was this Cleansing from Menace before us all. I . . . felt the anger rising again. But I didn't want this anger: it didn't comfort: it was no longer mine. I'd done with it. I was free of even that. (Williams, *Other Leopards*, 219)

and with Adam:

> Then the rain fell and he lay lost in this, his third baptism of mud and water: and he lay flat clutching her, feeling the shape of her huge breasts and the rain tickled his eyes and smoothed his face and the blessing of water poured down his mouth and his nostrils and the lightning itched and the thunder eased and the wind blanketed them; and in the madness of that rainy moment, in the slush and the liquid dark, the wet and the testimony of water, he knew. (Dathorne, *The Scholar-Man*, 181)

PART TWO

I Going Home:
An Evolution of the Caribbean Presence

CHAPTER 6

The Search for Polity:
The Fashioning of Dream

No!
I will not still my voice!
I have
too much to claim—
if you see me
looking at books
or coming to your house
or walking in the sun
know that I look for fire!

I have learnt
from books dear friend
of men dreaming and living
and hungering in a room without a light
who could not die since death was far too poor
who did not sleep to dream but dreamed to change the world!

And so
if you see me
looking at your hands
listening when you speak
marching in your ranks
you must know
I do not sleep to dream, but dream to change the world.

Martin Carter, "Looking at your Hands," *Poems of Succession*

Music is swelling in my ears as I go over to the east window. Our people are marching from the Bay, and now I can glimpse the torches carried by those taller ones. I listen good, and can hear the words . . .

Onward, Christian Soldiers . . . .

Funny how my mind turns back and I can remember it well.

'Sixty-five, it was. October morning; sun-up is fire and blood, and fear walks with my family. Remember, I remember, that this was the tune Pa John told us to sing that time when we came down out of the mountains.

Hear my father: *Sing, family O! British redcoats do no' make war on Christians . . . .*

Hear my bro' Davie to Father: *Do no' go down, Father. Stay up here in the mountains. Mr. Gordon and Deacon Bogle are hanging by their necks from the court-house steps.*

But how my father was stubborn! His head was tossing leader-bull fashion as he walked out in front of us.

Come behind me, Tamah, he said. *Sing after your mother, you pickneys.*

So, we went out of the mountains down into Baptism Valley, a-sing. . . .

Now they round the foot of the hill and come up to our house. Candlewood torches make our road as bright as day. (Reid, *New Day*, 3–4)

Here, through dramatic temporal juxtaposition, singing makes history lyrical. The present shivers with the echoes of the past. The night trembles with the ritual promise of a new day. Thus from the very beginning of the novel the historical movement of Caribbean peoples toward a "new day" is symbolized in the candlewood torches that burn bright to light the way.

You know how you make candlewood shine? Go into the woodland and find a limb as big as your wrist and a half. Strip the bark partways down, and leave it hanging over your hand to keep off the sparks. Sharpen the point, then light it with a lucifer-match. And then how it will burn bright! (4)

Here in the beginning of Vic Reid's *New Day*, symbol and form coalesce, merging together a holistic possibility emblematic of a new social order. But yet *New Day*, though still a repository of the historical turbulence, enshrines the mighty deeds through which that new society was conceived. The chronicle of these mighty deeds is vitalized through the alchemy of distilled memory and is imbued with corporal immediacy through the vision and the presence of the old narrator-griot.

At the confluence of time past and time present, history and landscape conjoin, echoing in memory's chamber. At the confluence of song, through

314

an actual celebration of future dreams, the disjunction between past losses, past rights, and the present is bridged.

> I hear the singing now. Our Party people are coming to our house at Salt Savannah, marching with torch-light and mighty hymns. Make them come.
> Bring your torchlights and your voices and put fire and music in the soul of an old man tonight! (3)

In the soft Jamaican night, in Morant Bay, in the parish of St. Thomas, rich, deep voices of men, women, and children resound in the Blue Mountain wind. These voices herald the coming of a "new day"; the granting of the new constitution to Jamaica awakens all the vast layered memories of the narrator-griot, old John Campbell.

The night is redolent with all the smells of the Blue Mountains—

> Through the half-opened window near where I sit, night winds come down the Blue Mountains to me. Many scents come down on the wind, and I know them all. I know all the scents o' the shrubs up on the mountains. There are *cerosee*, mint, mountain jasmine, *ma raqui*, there are *peahba* and sweet cedars. I know that the bitter *cerosee* will drive away fever, that *ma raqui* will heal any wounds—even wounds from musket balls. (1)

—a night filled with the echoes of history and resonant with the possibility of future days and new awakenings. In history there is both sorrow and jubilation, but the voices that sing in the night are rich with the promise of a dawn.

> The song has changed and softer it is now. From their throat the song sobs, but with no sorrow in it. A plaintiveness like a January nightingale winging through the Cuna Cuna Pass, and yet with deepness and richness, like cloud robes wrapping an evening sun. (4)

Through lyrical memory, in the very lyrics of the singing Vic Reid imbues the introit to *New Day* with pathos that is at once sob and celebration. The mood is in the plaintive because so many generations of people have fought and died to make that new day possible. If only some of them could be present, the old man wishes.

> Then now! Pa John and Ma Tamah, father and mother o' sorrow—are you hearing? And my brethren, Emmanuel, David, Samuel, Ezekiel, Ruth, Naomi, are you hearing?
> Are you a-hear, George William Gordon? And Paul Bogle, Abram M'Laren, and the good Doctor Creary?

And you too, bloody Governor Eyre and your crow Provost-Marshal Ramsey, are you hearing wherever you are? Tell me, Bro' Zaccy O'Gilvie, are you a-listen of me tonight?

Then, now! All o' you Dead Hundreds who looked at the sun without blink in your eyes, you Dead Hundreds who fell to British redcoats' bullets and the swords o' the wild Maroons, the wild men o' the mountains; tell me, you Dead Hundreds o' Morant Bay, are you hearing that tomorrow is the day? And that sorrow and restlessness are here with my joy, for I am standing here alone?

Aie-me, John Campbell, youngest o' Pa John Campbell. (2)

Here the old narrator skillfully introduces all the chief protagonists of the novel, *New Day,* awakening them, urging them into novelistic immediacy through the vital repetition of "Are you a-hear? Are you a-hear?"

This refrain brings about a sensory correlation which dramatizes the singing in the soft night wind. Clearly John Campbell's direct appeal to the voices he hears in the soft Jamaican night is both ritual evocation and celebrative lament.

Edge up yourself sharp, Coney Mount tenor-man! Roll it out, big-bone bass-man from Cedar Valley! Roll it out, for the girls from Morant fishing beach must ha' something solid to pour molasses from their throats on. Sing, my people, for good this is. (4–5)

The lyrical use of geography—Stoney Cove, Cedar Valley, Cuna Cuna Pass, Coney Mount—links the present night in 1944 to the October days of 1865, the time of the Morant Bay uprising, precursor and initiator of the new day, for the men who went to sing and march with Deacon Bogle came from the same geographies as those now singing.

Every Sabbath-day there is a big *met* at the Gut when Deacon Bogle preaches to his people. From day-cloud broke this morning they should be trudging into the Gut, from Morant Bay and Yallahs and Bath Town. There will be big mountain men a-come through the Cuna Cuna Pass from the Rio Grande Valley. (41)

Through the use of ritual geography, such men who comprised the Dead Hundreds seem to live on in the voices of those now singing, attesting to the notion of sacrifice, loss, and regeneration. All is underscored and quietly intoned by Davie Campbell as he finishes his deposition to the British.

"Representative government will come back to our island one day, one day. And mark me, Your Honours, there will be no *buckras* making the laws then, but the said poor like whom they have killed, and a Governor of the people will be sitting in St. Jago. For we will ha' learnt that sympathy for the poor must come from the poor. Then who can say that time that St. Thomas people died in vain?" (195)

The notion of loss and sacrifice, the historical cycles and generation that all are motif, theme, and construct of the narrative, lend the note of plaintiveness and pathos, not only to the beginning, but indeed to the whole novel, *New Day*—"A plaintiveness like a January nightingale winging through the Cuna Cuna Pass" (4).

Clearly, then, the notions of sacrifice and regeneration—which in *New Day* ritualistically lead to the enactment of new constitutional arrangements, to the registering of new societal formulations, to the commencement of possible indigenous polity—differentiate *New Day* from *Children of Kaywana* or the Kaywana trilogy. The latter—though presenting cyclical changes within a family and within the history of Guyana—does not enshrine that family nor that history in sacrificial possibility, does not spiral upward into dreams of a "new day." But the landscape of *Children of Kaywana*, the layered forest leaves, is witness to the conceptual beginnings of a historical process that symbolically terminates in the promise of a new sociopolitical reality: the "new day."

In *New Day*, a narrative totally vitalized by a holistic vision of indigenous reality, all phenomena interpret both the human emotional and physical landscapes; the elements decipher forms, reactions, forces present in and native to that landscape. This all coheres in the figure, the being, of the narrator, whose maturing vision is consonant with the maturation of the political reality and reflects his own circumstance and growth. His language changes from a boyish wonder, lyrical, evocative impressions, a piquant excitement and freshness, into an increasingly more reflective metaphoric and proverbial discourse. Indeed as the narrative unfolds, Reid, as if paralleling the transformative process that prophesies a wise government, spirals the narrative upward from richly woven landscape simile to the metaphoric, the contextual, the symbolic.

The narrator, John Campbell, becomes the repository of wisdom, of his family's and of his island's historical process. Unlike the *Children of Kaywana*—indeed developing beyond them—he is not an individualized though linked product of historical and imposed cultural determination; rather he is the mask whose wrinklings are ritual lines tracing the cycles of age to innocence; he becomes custodian and emblem of generational continuity, the assumption of commonality. Reid's novel is conceived in a series of large frames wedged together by prognosis of dreams and dramatic memory. The history is engrained in simile, and metaphoric symbols engrave it.

In the sound of the shells echo the incantatory dreams of the Morant Bay
revolutionary followers of Deacon Bogle. Clear and pure upon the wind the
dreams ascend to the skies.

> Hear the shells how they blow! First a-moan with sadness and
> loneliness, of earth heavy with sorrow; then there is the swift ascension
> and no longer near the earth but is leaping from tree-top to tree-top, a-
> leap to the wild stones high on one another, and your head is twisting all
> about, sending your eyes up after the sound of it. So till reached, your
> eyes have reached the highest crag and there against the sky is the shell-
> blower.
> Watch how he leans against the wind, his cow-horn shell curved away
> from his lips, taking your eyes with it, till you forget the crag is there and
> believe the shell goes to shake hands with God and is a-carry the blower
> with it.
> *Are where those shell-blowers now? Shepherd Jesus—how they could blow!*
> (93–94)

Here, too, as throughout the novel, a sense of loss pervades the narrative—"Are where those shell-blowers now?" This sense of loss gives
poignancy to Reid's novel and lends a pathos; its plaintive noises create at
once epic and tragic moods. At the center and pivot of the extended space
stands the shell-blower carved in time, suspended in wind, the whole scene
presented with novelistic mastery: All things conjoin—earth and man and
sky; all symbolic geography and mystical history, that same mystical geography with which the Blue Mountains were imbued.

> Young men must be strong like boar and quick like goat and with breath
> like racehorse of St. Dorothy's parish if they would use the mountainside
> to go to Kingston. I do not know the trail, but Davie has been there, and
> great tales I have heard of the bush where man can touch man and still
> not be seen, of mighty stones with which Jehovah played marbles and left
> helter skelter for by-and-by; of cracks in the earth where you throw rocks
> down and no sounds come back until you draw fresh breaths; . . . Tales
> I have heard of the Blue Mountains, where Davie says God is no' far
> from man. (59)

The link between man and mountains, between man, space, earth and
sky, demands a consummate energy. By this means, man can enter into
vertical space, vertical image, thereby attaining a concordance with his spatial
reality. But since the mood of this spatial reality can be affected by societal
implications, that visceral link between man and that reality undergoes
constant change. The basic artifact that brings about this linkage is also in
a continuous state of change, responding to the particular societal and

historical moment. Thus the intrinsic sound of the shell undergoes constant changes as it refracts from the particular societal happenings.

As the revolutionary action between Bogle's men and the militia is joined, these shell sounds, no longer lyrical in their intensity, take on the wildness, the frenetic quality of the encounter.

> Funny it is to me how the shells sound different when I hear them in Morant Bay town. There was a wildness when I heard them in the hills, but there was beauty in the wildness, a clear length of sound that did no' snarl at me as it leaped from earth and curved through blue spaces. But now when I hear them in Morant Bay no cleanness is there. (101)

Clearly the shells and the sound of the shells of that historical moment notating the Morant Bay uprising, snarling out broken rhythms, are reflective of a fragmented social reality. The transformative coherence is missing. Later on—generations later, as a societal coherence is taking shape with the inception of labor unions—the shells sing out a confident reveille, mustering together the workers in the early dawn.

> Next morning before day-cloud Garth and me were at the gate of Garfield's property. We ha' got some old shell-blowers with us. We are no' allowed inside the gates this time, but that does no' bother us at all.
> For, up goes Garth's hand, and shells are a-talk loud to the dawn.
> Blow, they blow; around and up the sounds wind. *Coo-ee . . . coo-eee . . . ooee . . . coo . . . coo . . . coo-eeee* . . . a-talk again in St. Thomas parish, but no wildness in their throats this time. . . .
> The shells are sounding loud, and men and women and children on Garfield's estates are running to the gates where the sounds come from . . . . Shell-blowers take their pipes from their lips, and quietness comes on the land. Dawnlight is soft on us. Easy-easy, I hear a *john-to-whit* bubbling in his throat. (318–319)

The foregoing scene is obviously one of peace, reflecting an assurance attendant on the coming of the new day, prognosis of a possible holistic transformation of a social order. As the sound of shells and the coo-eeing of birds harmonize, there is harmony here between idea, the work which led to that idea, and the dawning day. Later, the death of the old trooper, Timothy, who, like the narrator, has lived through the ever-changing sociopolitical reality, echoes in the music of the shells, a symbolic farewell to the spirit of a rebel fighter:

> "Uncle John, he came to march with me. He said the shells were blowing but I couldn't seem to hear them."

Timothy O!
Timothy went with evening star. I was with him all the time until he crossed the river. . . .
. . . Knowledge of me did no' come to him at once, but after our eyes had made four for a while, a little smile touched his mouth . . . .
We took back Timothy with us to Salt Savannah, for he must lie near to where one day I will lie. A long way we ha' come together, Timothy and me. (327)

Indeed, *New Day* registers and delineates the configurations of the long way that Timothy and John Campbell have walked together, from the beginnings of the Morant Bay uprising in 1865 to the promulgation of the new constitution in 1944. The novel describes the movement from fragmented social reality to the possibility of coherence of that reality. As is symbolically shown in the motif of the shells, a series of transformative actions has taken place.

The central construct of the novel, then, all the undergirding motifs and themes, the fortunes of the principal characters and personages, pendulate, undergo constant change. Through a series of dynamic formulations, all individual characters and events point ultimately to a cohering reality, to a new day. Like the sound of the shells in Bogle's headquarters before the central conflict is joined, the motif of singing with which *New Day* begins can reflect either fragmentation or cohesion in the immediate social reality. The singing reflects harmony, attains a soothing silence:

Only the singing I can hear and see and feel . . . .
. . . I walk across the square, and is a cassava-strainer, me, and the rich ripeness of the song is pulping and pressing through me, and I am a-throb to it.
But they come to the long-metre *Amen*, and the wind is a-run through the trees again, and nightingale is a-talk to the dusk again, and men are clearing their throats again, and I am Johnny again. (65)

The configuration of the voices raised in song, the fragmented reality discerned in "I going away," undergo harmonious transformation, defragmentation, which opens out into a holistic vision in *New Day*. The elements, the balm of a Blue Mountain night harmonizing with song, ritualizes the senses of the old man-participant-narrator, John Campbell—"I am Johnny again"—making them elastic so that the immediate present vibrates with all the tremulous history of the past, shivers with the expectations of the future new day.

Now the closing night of history—symbolized in the figure of Johnny—moves into, merges with, the light of a new day. The ritual of passage between granduncle and grandnephew is enacted, assuring historical continuity. Here all things cohere—the elements, man, and history merge. Through the cogency of pure memory, the history of Jamaica is rekindled, emblazoned, and enshrined in the landscape by the evocation of elemental images of indigenous symbols. Thus, the historical content, sensitized by an indigenous language and orality, resonates with promise, with deep-layered hope. History is actualized in the figure of Garth Campbell, symbol and promise of the new day. The passage and the dying of many of his ancestors, the rise and fall of each generation, are heralded in significant disasters that befall Jamaica. Drought, hurricanes, fires, epidemics take on epic proportions in which the history of Jamaica is celebrated.

Clearly Reid's novelistic vision is vitalized by a transformative intention that negates fragmentation, placing even these disasters into regenerative cyclical epochs. Natural disasters, so prevalent in the elemental geography of the Caribbean, are located within the regenerative process, a rhythmic cycle of that geography. It is this cyclical regeneration which imbues *New Day* with possibility, with potentiality, and as ordained with all regenerative cycles, there is the element of the pathetic ever present: loss and pain, suffering and death, destitution, immediate, palpable.

Thus often throughout the narrative the narrator cries out: "do no' make him cry, Mas'r God, for if my father brings eye-water, Johnny will be dead" (148). Here in a pathetic appeal the young boy witnesses his father's pain, his agony, tries desperately to hold on to that image of strength, of unswerving faith, with which his father is endowed. Earlier, the narrator, as if intoning a precise poem, bears witness to that strength.

My father is a great boar-hunter! . . . My father has the strength of ten! If there is sorrow a-tear through his throat now, do no' believe is a sign of your victory, that. (145)

The tears and the praise song tinkle and resonate, reecho and reverberate in the movement of the Caribbean toward a new day: "The song has changed and softer it is now from their throat the song sobs, but with no sorrow in it" (4).

Unstated but clearly implied throughout *New Day* is that ultimate notion of sacrifice assuring a rebirth, ordaining a new Caribbean day. The notion of sacrifice and its hoped-for corollary, beneficent change, vibrates at the end of the main protagonist's deposition to the Commission of Inquiry:

Common talk it is now that at the next session, Governor Eyre will ask for Crown government. But yet still I am thinking that even if the little is taken from us, time will show that St. Thomas people did no' die in vain. (195)

Later the narrator bears witness to the efficacy of that sacrifice in the prognosis of a new day.

> Tomorrow I will go with Garth to the city to hear King George's man proclaim from the square that now Jamaica-men will begin to govern themselves. (1)

Thus it is that the novel circumscribes an arc that moves from lament, loss, conflict, from drought, resistance, repression, and colonial domination, to the beginnings of trade unionism, the emergence of party politics, the struggle for adult suffrage and national political freedom. The novel's central construct—whose elaboration follows the fortunes of four generations of one single family, the Campbell family—narrates the deep-rooted changes the Campbell family undergoes even while particularizing the specific changes each of the main protagonists experiences. Both the novel and the family move toward a cohering Caribbean reality.

Though genealogically there are four generations of Campbells, in terms of the basic novelistic agenda only three generations are central to the process of regeneration and growth. All are held together by the presence of the narrator, who is at once participant-observer, actor, and narrator-griot of the story. Through his eyes we witness the to-and-fro pendulation of his father, of his brother Davie, of his grandnephew Garth, each of whose development is central to one of the three parts into which the novel is divided. Further, each part is differentiated from the other, not only by the character of each personage, but rather by the intensification of the narrator's vision, his deepening perception of the social reality about him. This perception moves from the initial sense of lyric wonder and drama of Part 1—in which he describes his father's ultimate anguish and the dispersal of the family—to Part 2—in which he is actor, sharing in his brother Davie's and his adopted mother Lucille's deep relationship, the decline of that relationship, the development and loss of a dream colony—to Part 3—where a ripening man becomes counselor and guide to his grandnephew's development: to his grandnephew's evolving perceptions, his training for political leadership, and the now realizable dreams for a new day, a new social order. Clearly, then, central to this novelistic construct are the elements of continuity and change, of generational recurrence. Here of utmost importance is the movement of the people toward their own initial self-governance, toward an indigenizing of their possibility.

The novelistic action begins in 1865, when drought grips the land and hunger stalks the poor. Here there is no celebration, no joy. Only a dirge-like refrain reiterates the sorrow, echoes a lament:

For three years now, no rain has come. Grass-piece and yam-vines are brown with dryness, cane-leaves have not got much green to them. Thirst and hunger walk throughout our land . . . .

For three years now, no rain has come and only the rich laugh deep. (6–7)

Here the elements not only vividly emphasize the great disparity existing between the rich *buckra* planters and the poor peasantry of St. Thomas but act as additional goad to the basic resentment of the poor against continuing oppression. Their grievances are many; the ostentation of the wealthy *buckra* planters and the seeming legalization of overt exploitation further deepen their resentment:

"What happens when hard time comes on us? Some poor people borrow money on their crops from *buckra* estate owner . . . . estate owner takes them to court. But since poor people ha' not got any money, since dry weather is here and no canes will grow, *buckra* magistrate tells *buckra* estate owner that he must take the land, for poor people will no' pay . . . .

"And if you ever talk o' injustice, is to prison they send you . . . . to the crank and the treadmill, or you get the gallows for treason." (21–22)

The drought that has scarred the land and the dreams of the poor peasants serve as catalysts to their resentment against this injustice. Deacon Bogle's call for secession from English-style justice, when heeded by many, becomes the pivot and hub for the conflict which not only further dislocates the social reality, but even destroys close-knit family entities:

Father in a temper, Davie in a temper, Mother worrying, Manuel worrying. . . .

"Wickedness? . . . Wickedness to want even rice and flour and *osnaburg* while *buckra* Englishman eats bacon and wears Shantung silk? Why do they no' make us govern ourselves and see if we would no' eat bacon too? Why they will no' give the vote to all o' us and make us choose our own Council?" (14–15)

The first part of the novel presents not only the dislocation of the Campbell family, its dispersion, but also the very conflict between the followers of Bogle and the militia and troops of the British government. Conflicts in the household are registered by images of wind and water and rain and their changing configurations, representing visceral emotional changes, vivifying parallel physical alterations, consequent to those emotional changes.

Even as "outside in daylight, and sea-breeze is putting anger-marks on the face of the Bay" (11), inside the Campbell household thunder and lightning and wind are images depicting the deep, wrenching conflict between father and son, who are so much alike: "Now there you see Father, a-face his ownself across the table, 'cept that one face is smooth, while t'other has seen many mango seasons" (14). The exchange progresses at a lightning pace, each response evoking another like a "fall in the Plaintain Garden River, where water tumbles down in deep-voice quickness" (14). The scene in the Campbell household, charged with all the explosiveness of the social conflict, mirrors the volatile elemental changes present in the Jamaican landscape. Knowledge that Davie has answered Bogle's call and is participant in the Stoney Gut meetings unleashes the father's fury, which explodes like thunderflash. Equally explosive is the son Davie—"thunderhead for day-cloud and the sun peeping through blackness on grey water in the Bay, so is Davie's eyes" (14).

This dramatic beginning to the novel dramatizes the deep fragmentation that has scarred the social reality of Jamaica, leading to the Morant Bay uprising. In this dramatic confrontation, all the characters are caught up, and even on the sabbath day there is no peace in the household, but rather a distressing powerlessness, as of small birds caught in strong winds:

> Mother rushed out . . . screaming like *kling-kling* bird homing on evening wind. Fright was there on her face, but she held on to Father's arm and was up and down like kirk bell before he stop using the trace-leather.
>
> "Pa John!" comes from my mother, "Pa John! Done—you hear? Enough that—ha' done!" (16–17)

Here there is no warmth, there is little of the laughter that marks the relationship between the young narrator, Johnny and his sister, Naomi; little of the respectful warmth that characterizes the relationship between the father and the mother.

> Mother is talking to Father, and I see her take the trace-leather from his hand.
>
> Now Father has got her to one side. Quiet, he talks to Davie now but north wind blows cold in his voice. (17)

An ideological difference is central to the confrontation between father and son. Vic Reid portrays the father as a proud, strong man unswerving in his convictions: a believer in the sanctity of the Bible and in the fairness of British law and justice.

> My father said: "I will go down. Mr. Gordon can no' die in vain. I will ask to see Governor Eyre. I am no' a Stoney Gut man. The English will no' make war on Christians." (153)

His stubborn belief in British justice is exemplified in his conversation with Dr. Creary, whom Reid makes out to be a balanced, sensible and just vestryman.

> "Justice! Justice! God Almighty! . . . Eyre has shown the manner in which he intends to settle this business, and right now Ramsey is building two gallows at Morant Bay. There will be no justice, Campbell. . . .
>
> "God forbid!—but your name has been given to the proscribing registrar by Zaccy O'Gilvie himself." (140)

This unswerving belief ultimately leads him to his death. On the other hand, his son Davie rejects any notion that there is morality or ethics in British justice, pointing out in his many lessons to his younger brother, Johnny, a basic dishonesty inherent in that justice.

Skillfully Reid presents the disintegration of the Campbell household and the inexorable movement of the father toward his death. His worry, his aging, his being proscribed, his leaving his home in Salt Savannah, his climb into the mountains and his descent from those mountains to his death in Baptism Valley, all are etched in the changing visage of the landscape, which reflects the father's very transformation. The father's movement toward his death and the dispersion of his family echo with the sound of contained tears and are marked by a vertical movement, a tragic ascent to a sacrificial grandeur, epic in proportions, pathetic in essence. The young narrator is witness to his father's pathetic grandeur and strength:

> Father took off his hat and turned to face the sun and we. A wind is a-search the strands of his hair. Down in the Bay the sea kneels on the shore.
>
> *Our Father which art heaven, Hallowed be thy name* . . . .
>
> If I keep quiet and bite on my lips, I will no' sob like Naomi. Heavy with tears is my father's voice. . . .
>
> Father O! You can no' fool me, tears are there in your throat. I must no' listen to you, I must think on Davie . . . . Davie is a-march the Blue Mountain Valley with a hundred Stoney Gut men . . . . Davie is there on the Windward Road, leading his men to Bowden. (143)

Just as the bay reflects the father's moment of prayer, so, too, the mountains bear witness to his strength, his ascent, his movement toward his point of glory. The narrator hymns a praise song to his father's power, physical strength and leadership. The song is epic, lyrical in tone, evoking a symbiosis between man, the elements, and heightened emotion:

> Mountains, you must fight like mad! My father is a great boar-hunter!
> Mountain-mists, you must wrap us tight-tight in your shrouds! (145)

All is celebrative, all is praise, but as is typical of Reid's character delineation, moods and tones and emotions pendulate rapidly, the celebrative mood
becomes quietly shot through with tragic implications. On learning of his
daughter Ruth's pregnancy, given his own exalted sense of morality and
ethics, the father, in a rage, strikes his wife and descends from his mountain
hiding place:

> Then my father is raging. Never I have heard him so before. And I see
> him strike my mother.
>   Mother lay crying softly. . . .
>   So Father gets up and says: "Come again, Tamah . . . .
>   . . . "We will sing *Christian Soldiers*. Sing, everybody, so I will keep my
> faith." (147–148)

Ultimately the father, with his flock, rejects the warnings of his own son,
Davie, rejects, too, the voice of reason, and marches bullheadedly to his
death in the valley.

> "But, Father, you do no' understand," said Davie . . . . "Your head is
> in the lion's mouth, so take time and get it out. Wait till they ha' lifted
> this martial law." . . .
> "I do no' die if my boys live," Father said . . .
> . . . "Sing all!" . . .
> . . . Power is my father's voice.
> *"With the Cross of Jesus going on before* . . .
> "Father O! Father O! Come back! Come back!" . . .
> Then I see flame born on the valley floor . . . .
> And Father is no' standing any more. (153–156)

Clearly Reid not only uses phenomena as image and symbol, but he
imbues certain locations with characteristics that respond to human moods,
which reflect all the array of emotional changes of his personages. Thus in
the midst of the deepening conflict and confrontation gripping St. Thomas
parish, Maroon Hole becomes a refuge of cool and calm for Davie and his
brother Johnny. In the quiet of Maroon Hole, the little brother is told about
many searing historical events, but here these harsh happenings shade into
softness. So it is that landscape, given a dynamic function, responding to
alternating moods and patterns of history, captures all the rapid changes and
shifts in each particular current in the novel, *New Day*.

Perhaps by demonstrating the interplay between history and the landscape of Maroon Hole, Reid is already anticipating the presence of the

Maroons in the conflict of the Morant Bay uprising, anticipating already their swiftness and stealth. Here, too, Davie moves easily from seriousness and sternness to laughter, from heavy discussions about slavery to shared companionship with his brother. After the initial quarrelling with his father, at the beginning of the breakup of the Campbell family, Davie steals away to Maroon Hole, where his brother Johnny finds him:

> I lay down like [Davie] with my feet in the water say: "Poor Davie."
> Davie quiet, then he turned on his face and looked down on me for a long time; looking like I am no' there. But presently his eyes made four with mine and he laughed and said: "Cho, man, nothing!" (19)

Maroon Hole is presented as a kind of oasis in the midst of all the conflict that grips the land. It is a cooling interlude before the conflict is joined.

> Cool and sweet is the water, and you take off your pantaloons and swim from bank to bank and the water hugs you close. Like say when you dream at night that duppy-ghost is a-chase you and you cry out and Mother hugs you and you wake up and her breasts are a-kiss your face and there is a peace on you. Is so Maroon Hole. (18–19)

Like Maroon Hole, Lucille is first presented to us in soft twinkling colors that light up her face, her very being. She, too, initially is a point of rest and promise; she is all dance and fireflies, giving lyricism to the young narrator's perceptions. Her lightly changing moods and sensations are captured in quick pastel strokes in which colors flash and lights dance: "Moon is a-shine on white sea-sand as Miss Lucille reached for her throat. Her mouth is a two-day *kling-kling* a-beg for air" (60). Thus it is that the changes that take place in her in the second part of the novel by contrast seem more intense, seem starker, more pathetic. Similarly this contrasting shift in her mood parallels the change that comes over Davie of the Maroon Hole. In the lockup, Davie seems to his young brother like a monkey:

> Wildness is in his eyes, flax stand straight up on his head. See my bro' Davie there looking through the bars like monkey at August Fair! They ha' caged Davie, my poor bro' Davie! (53)

Gone is that feeling of freedom Maroon Hole has given Davie, but here, still, "There is a grin from him, and softly: 'Cho Man'" (53).

But as the narrative intensifies in the second part, Davie loses that flexibility to grin in the midst of trials and becomes like his father—stern, inflexible in his purpose, self-righteous—to the point where he destroys Lucille's soft nightingale laughter and ultimately destroys himself. For indeed he becomes obsessed by an idea, that of disproving the words of Pastor Hamphrey who said:

"Over a quarter century ago our good Queen Victoria in her great wisdom gave freedom to her darker children of Africa. Men there were who questioned the wisdom of that gift and asked whether people who were clearly unfit for responsibility should be made citizens . . . .

. . . Because Almighty God has seen fit to visit His wrath on these people for their laziness and hardness of heart . . . they have rebelled against His ordinance and seek to supplant those whom He has set in authority over them." (42)

In what could be considered his secession—that is, his flight to the cays and his building of the colony of Zion on these cays—Davie, by hard work and steady discipline, converts the formerly barren cays into a fertile productive land. But even as he does this, by his insistence on sternness he destroys qualities eminently necessary for a holistic vision of social reality—joy, enjoyment, and laughter. For although the land thrives, human emotions shrivel, and an emotional drought as severe as that which made barren the land in 1865 ensues. Clearly then the reality of Zion is as fragmented as was that of Morant Bay earlier in the narrative.

An attempt is made to disprove the notion that descendants of slaves are lazy, are undisciplined. Indeed, initially the land and colony are productive:

Davie has planned our planting well. Over in the next three-acre we can hear our people singing as their forks bite deep into the soft bottom . . . . Seven days it will look up at the sun, gathering strength before the mating with the seeds . . . . By the time the autumn rains ha' watered the land young shoots will be waving in the wind. No idleness in Zion for man or his land. (213)

Yet by his insistence on stern puritanical behavior—"every Sunday-day Davie goes to the pulpit and tells us o' Zion above" (203)—he ultimately becomes a captive of that very behavior, destroying the freedom of Maroon Hole, putting a shade over the firefly light of Lucille, who confides her misgivings to Johnny:

"Johnny, Davie has gone crazy with an obsession and would like us all to go the same way! . . .

"Johnny, your brother is building a Tower of Babel. By the time he is finished we might not speak the same tongue!" (212–213)

Johnny is aware of his brother's change, his brother's transformation, for he has heard his brother "praying by himself . . . . Like Father's was his voice" (202). Johnny—caught between his love for his brother and his love for Lucille—can but sadly reflect:

How can [my bro'] no' see that sadness has come to the beauty of her?
   I could ha' told my bro' that nightingale will no' sing as sweet if bamboo *springe* has caught her feet. (215)

Clearly Reid builds his characters by orchestrating shifts and changes, by imposing transformations which give to them a density, a deep resonance and heightened tonality. A generational continuity is established in which Davie's father's dominant qualities reappear, are reflected in Davie, and through generational symbiosis possess him:

> My bro' scrubbed too, then he took out Father's Prince Albert. When he is finished with the buttons it is my father with years off his face who is standing before me. (197)

The very wearing of the Prince Albert coat shrouds Davie in the mantle and character of his father. To be sure, as the oldest living son of his father, he should ritualistically bear responsibility for the family, should be its continuum and "put his hand to the plough" (212). Yet to totally adopt the Book, to have the plough and frock dominate and envelop him, is self-negating and fragmenting.

This self-negation and fragmentation ultimately destroy him, his wife, and later his colony. The death of Davie, the main protagonist in Part 2, is occasioned by a catastrophic elemental happening: he is crushed to death during a violent hurricane. Lucille later dies in a fire that sweeps through Kingston; and James Creary and his wife die in a cholera epidemic. Reid uses disaster to dramatize the change in the family's fortunes, to chorus the deaths of its members. Phenomena in their grandeur add epic quality to the narrative, give a sense of epoch to the history of the family.

Here, dying comes through natural disaster, whereas in Part 1, the deaths of the main protagonists come at the hands of other men. Bogle and his followers, in their quest for freedom, die at the hands of the British redcoats and the Jamaican Maroons, some through battle, some through brutal hanging: "Whole families ha' been taken from their homes, flogged, and hung from trees while soldiers set fire to their homes" (50). In Part 2, Davie's followers and he himself die not through conflict in search of an initial freedom, but through natural disaster and intrinsically through Davie's own puritanical intransigence.

Clearly each of the larger structured formulations of the novel comes to a close with the death of one of the central characters. The manner of dying, however, differs, marking perhaps a change in the social mode and context of the particular epoch. Pa John and the Stony Gut men signify the violence of the confrontation between British rulers and the Jamaican freedom seekers. Davie Campbell is crushed by a falling tree, thereby marking the

epoch when the landscape, the elements, and the earth were being cultivated and worked in order to produce the wherewithal for a new community.
In the time of the "new day," when the violence in the social order seems
to have given way to the possibility of a new cohesive polity, Timothy, the
old trooper, dies peacefully.

> His eyes are closed, asleep I can see, but my heart comes to my
> mouth, for nobody has to tell me that Timothy is near the river. His
> breath comes out with noise. I turn to Garth and speak with tears thick
> in my throat. (326)

Timothy, whose life has spanned the three epochs and whose participation
has in some measure helped to bring about the new day, does not celebrate
its dawning.

> Sad I was that Timothy was no' here to see how men can march with the
> banner o' the law waving over them 'stead o' shells talking of blood and
> fire. (337)

The narrator-griot John Campbell not only celebrates the dawning of a new
day, but indeed he has become the elder statesman and voice qualifying the
transformative process and vision leading to that new day. All is generational
remembrance and recalling. Everywhere the narrator locates the figures of
the generations who have gone by, locating the blood heritage with which
his grandnephew, Garth Campbell, is invested. In a lyrical celebration of
generational participation, the narrator notates not only the history but also
the deeds of Garth's forebears.

> He has come down from a man who . . . was a mighty boar-hunter. His
> grand is a man who . . . went in and out 'o Morant Bay when redcoats and
> Maroons, thick like fleas on dogs, were seeking for his blood. He is a man
> who took his bro' and the woman he loved and sailed blue water to his
> own island, where he built his land with his own two hands and made the
> sand island to flourish with green. (338)

Not only, then, is there a heritage of blood and valor in Garth Campbell but
also an inheritance of form and temperament. But now even as the mood
reflected in the manner of dying has changed, so, too, have the temperament
and political attitudes of the chief protagonists of this third epoch.

> Davie's voice is a-talk to me, but there is no helpless bitterness in this
> throat; he is running his race with confidence. And if there is quickness
> in his voice, it is only 'cause racehorse can no' sprint his race if excite-
> ment does no' build his nervousness in his flanks. (257)

His training for this race has been assiduous and undertaken with a purpose and vision; his education has prepared him for his work in transforming the political and social arena of his country. It is not surprising, therefore, given his family heritage, his assiduous training, that Garth Campbell is endowed with all the qualities necessary to attempt a transformative action. Thus he begins the running of his race on his family's estate, learning how to mobilize workers and practicing his egalitarian approach to labor. He takes over his family business, bringing into practice his knowledge of international economics, which makes the estate thrive.

But he shares the earnings more equitably with his workers than do the many other planters around. To be sure, he is a member of the plantocracy, but Reid imbues Garth with egalitarian principles that ultimately bring about a transformation of the worker class, and thus the planter class. Garth teaches his workers the power of collective bargaining by encouraging them to form a union.

"This union will be the first apostle of the Campbell creed . . . . They in turn will preach the gospel according to the Campbell Estates all over the parish. From here it will travel all over the island. . . .

. . . Our work-people will soon feel the power in their union and ask for certain benefits." (296)

Here, then, Reid places the growth of collective bargaining within a narrative framework whose essential configuration and theme is the formation of unions, their power, and the catalytic possibility inherent in their organization. What is stressed here, as a condition necessary to transformative action, is careful planning, foresight, and an unswerving but steady motion toward one's objective. Reid sees the need to use the wisdom and understanding derived from the past, but he knows that understanding and wisdom must be energized by the present, by "the young ones, the almost children" (288). Through his cohesive energizing, Garth assures not only a stabilizing force, but also a creative energetic presence. "It's the only way out of this mess, the only way out of these centuries of darkness. They must grow tall and strong, fearing no man" (257).

Using maxims and proverbial statements through which he incapsulates his eldership, the old narrator shows how Garth puts into practice his own sense of the grafting of knowledge with energy.

"All young barristers should go in with an older man. That way you can learn the ropes faster." (251)

When [young colt] goes the first time, an old mule must be there to steady him. Otherwise your harness will be torn and torn. (251)

> Garth is a wise one who has learnt that knowledge o' things to come is
> no spoilt by learning the past. (253)

Thus, for the transformative process to succeed, the past must be made to
fertilize the present. But the present must also be approached with, if not
caution, a clear sense of how to pace an action.

> Secession was what Bogle asked for—and what he got? Constitution taken
> away and the Crown a-rule from Whitehall. (253)

Using the image of a steam train, the narrator-griot counsels the young
transformative agent about the nature of that pacing, its function, its efficacy.

> "Take steam engine, Son. When they are drawing our canes to the
> factory and the engine is going downgrade with too much steam a-boil
> inside, the driverman reaches hand for a lever. They call it the safety
> valve. You ha' studied the laws o' our country, Son. You ha' got educa-
> tion, so the safety valve you are. Mount the footplates if you can and
> drive off from where your grandfer left. But remember this safety valve
> and you will no' hear this—pouf!" (254)

Thus the past wisdom, when handed over to the younger man, Garth,
often reduces his confusion, steadying him.

> When dark-night comes on Garth, he travels to the old one at Salt
> Savannah. (333)

> As I talked daylight came to his voice. (334)

Given all this advice and wise counsel, it is not surprising that Garth's
advocating of collective bargaining to the workers on the Campbell estate
and his egalitarian approach to labor bear fruit both for the estate—enlarging
the sugar crop—and for the workers: "our cottages ha' been fitted with
showers and . . . electric light are making their nights brighter" (299).

His unionization of the estate brings about a transformation of the quality
of life of the workers on those estates. The larger unionization of the
corporation sector initially brings with it a conflict situation that somewhat
dampens Garth's ardor, exposing him to the possibility of arrest. However,
Reid, as he presents the conflicts inherent in the trade union movement in
Jamaica—the riots that took place consequent on the movement—seems to
minimize rather than highlight those riots. The initial triumph of the unions
comes after a number of workers whose case Garth has successfully pleaded
are freed. The winning of the case, however, comes about only after Garth

with his immense legal astuteness goes into the past to abstract legal constructs, which lead to his success.

> He is gone a-walk through musty old books, seeking for the marks that generations o' freedom ha' made for us to walk by; marks that tells us why we are free who live under the Jack . . . . Garth gets his writ, and his men are looking at the sun again. (277–278)

Although at this point the union movement seems to have run out of steam, Garth's grand design and the quality of the "running of his race" lead step by step to the transforming of the political consciousness, both of worker and employer. The riots consequent on the growth of this transformative movement have their own dynamic force, leading ultimately to political cohesion, the promulgation of a new constitution, the dawning of a new day. With skill and determination and foresight, qualities with which Reid endows Garth—and which by extension Reid posits as essential for the undertaking of a transformative action—Garth argues for the fragmenting of the political order of some two hundred years. These are new times, he states:

> "The old days of benevolent master and dependent servants are passed. These are days of capital and labour, not master and servant. The days are gone when at Christmas a few steers are slaughtered and served with hogsheads . . . .
> . . . The workers themselves aren't sorry that those days are passed. They are grown up and their sense of values have changed. They prefer to stand on their own feet, to handle their own cash—to buy their own Christmas gifts." (306–307)

With the fragmentation of the old political order, with the rejecting of old hierarchical controls, the transformative agent demands a new order, new political alignments. The vision is a transformative one, articulating the indigenizing of the political reality, advocating a new political cohesion, a new wholing of the social order.

> "We must have a new constitution. This archaic system of Crown government must go. We want full representative government within the British Empire . . . . and every man and woman in this island must be allowed to share in the shaping of this destiny." (331)

Thus it is that Reid, faithful to his narrative technique of showing the dynamic interpretations of generational linkages, establishes the notion of generative possibilities.

"I would tell you that for 200 years before October gone, men were a-march on Morant Bay court-house. Say it was not from Stoney Gut they marched, . . . nor Port Morant, nor Cuna Cuna Mountain. Say that they marched from all over the island, and ha' been marching for 200 years." (190)

In Part 3 of *New Day*, Reid almost outlines all the training and preparations necessary for the assumption of leadership. Clearly Garth's initiation and vigorous training, linked to the wise counsel of his granduncle and grand-aunt, are posited as stages assuring not simply the ushering in of a new day but indeed the building of solid foundations on which that political, economic, and social phenomenon can be based.

In *Of Age and Innocence* by George Lamming, the new day stands as a wish and a promise whose attainment vitalizes the will of the people of San Cristobal, and whose execution demands an all-embracing and cogent vision of nationality and freedom. And differing from *New Day*, this all-embracing and cogent vision, transformative in its possibility, is presented, not in a series of didactic examples, but, rather, in dramatic all-possessing speech:

"Nationalism is not only frenzy and struggle. . . . The national spirit is deeper . . . . It is original and necessary as the root to the body of the tree. It is the source of discovery and creation. It is the private feeling . . . of possessing and being possessed by the whole landscape of the place . . . the freedom which helps you to recognize the rhythm of the winds, the silence and aroma of the night, rocks, water, pebble and branch . . . . It is the bond between each man and that corner of the earth which his birth and his work have baptised with the name, home." (Lamming, *Of Age and Innocence*, 174–175)

Here Lamming is demanding a total identification of man with the essential landscape of his island, an intense vital symbiosis cohering landscape and societal performance. This urgent need for identification with the landscape is not casual but rather becomes a recurrent cohering motif throughout the novel, *Of Age and Innocence*. The drifting movement of water, of wind, of clouds, the constant extension of mood as action into landscape of trees, of leaves, of tendrils and vines, verify the author's injunction of the necessary visceral interpenetration of man and land.

The landscape of San Cristobal carries within it its very history, its very geography. It is lasting evidence of the elemental transformations that have occurred in San Cristobal. The carriers of innocence—Bob, Lee, Singh—representing the basic ethnic groupings in San Cristobal—African, Chinese, and East Indian—bear witness to this evidence:

The boys paused, staring over the ridge of the hill at the wild, green cone of vegetation . . . . The sides were thick with trees. The wind had carved it hollow . . . the huge hole which made a circle extending from the top, wide and deep within, to a black, dead crater of bush at the bottom. It reminded them of the legend which told of their island's formation: the ascent of the land from water which now surrounded the peaks and valleys and inactive craters of San Cristobal. (113–114)

In the preceding, time is the cipher of landscape and of the changes it has undergone. In the following, the swift changes that Lamming captures in this particular space-time are dismal:

The sun was beginning to label the leaves with its quick and customary mixture of crimson and gold . . . this interval of light would not last very long. It never did in San Cristobal . . . [this] interval between two major items of time: daylight and darkness. (115)

Small wonder, then, that given all the changes in landscape, daily, seasonal, or millenial, Shephard, the principal protagonist of the novel, upon returning home from England, clarifies the temporal presence of San Cristobal. In a moment of hallucination, he summons it:

"San Cristobal, San Cristobal . . . . You let rumour argue against reason in a voyage to San Cristobal which every race has reached and where the sea is silver and the mountains climb to the moon. You do not know San Cristobal, coming up by accident one morning from water, the tiny skull of a mountain top which was once asleep under the sea." (58)

Here race and history commingle with geography and open out into a political promise in which the returning Shephard locates his dream, his adventure into leadership, which becomes the theme and action of the novel, *Of Age and Innocence.*

Through landscape, through his characters, Lamming ritualizes the ontological link between age and innocence, between the old and the young, establishing, as did Reid, a generational continuity, spatial as well as spiritual. Thus time becomes a symbolic carrier of legend: the old woman, Ma Shephard, mother of the main protagonist, Shephard, embodies age, and the three young boys who have formed a secret "Society" partly patterned on the new political party incorporate youth and innocence. The middle generation of Singh, Lee (fathers of the boys), Shephard, and Mark use the oral legendary presentations of the young boys and Ma Shephard as foundation stones for their present political activity in San Cristobal. Time for Ma Shephard is elastic, stretching from the lived past to a politically tense present and to the possibility of a cohering political future. Like the griot

John Campbell in *New Day,* she is the bearer of an oral wisdom: "her memory stretched the distance between her and the boys" (68). Her wise counsel attempts to guide their footsteps into a communality of all the major ethnic groups in their adopted country, San Cristobal:

> "An' I talk to you like a duty tell me the four must be part o' any prayer my lips make concernin' San Cristobal.
>
> ". . . An' if your heart keep a right respect for age; the little wisdom my time collect can help your understandin' too. Never you look to the ways that teach those round how to hate, an' different as you be in name an' nature, 'tis the same love my prayers will ask to favour any wish you make." (71)

In this way, Ma Shephard attempts to contain the political excitement affecting the boys and sweeping the entire island of San Cristobal before its elections with full adult suffrage.

As Ma Shephard has seen so many years and lived through so many experiences, to be precise about dates is of little consequence to her: "A number will name the years, my son, but no mind can contain the time. The measure is too great" (64). In this regard, she differs from the narrator John Campbell in *New Day,* who, since he was dealing more with historical events, located history in the landscape, recalled dates and years of actions and catastrophes leading up to the new day. We heard of the great hurricane of 1874 and of the fire in Kingston in 1862. The catastrophes that have afflicted San Cristobal have for Ma Shephard more of a moral texture, more of a legendary quality. The tidal wave that buried San Cristobal for many years is located within nonspecific, airy space and time. As she narrates the deluge to the boys, past time is made immediate and present; a sense of immediacy imbues the oral narrative. The backward glance, a motif and technique which gives structure to Lamming's novelistic vision, ordains the past in a ritual linkage to the present:

> "'Twas a day with a face like today, they say, with the sky unkindly lookin', an' the water movin' silent in a malice no man can watch. These same sands you tread now . . . slip like ice . . . . They say the rain itself loose an' burst upon us like a harvest of thorns, an' the poor lan' cry till the tears that cover it like a lake of water stretch in every direction to shake hands with the sea." (64)

Thus, this very immediacy enshrines a continuity between not only Ma Shephard and the boys, but between Ma Shephard and the landscape, the boys and their land. Ma Shephard tells Bob, Lee, Singh, and Rowley of the flood as, before their time, she told an earlier generation about it. Then not only as a midwife did she bring Rockey, the fisherman, into the world, but as oral historian, she introduced him to the legend of his island.

> "'Twas you who tell me all I know 'bout the islan'," said Rockey, "how it rise from water, an' what tribulation it meet in the days before I was born. An' 'twas you too who bring me in the world." (402)

In this way, Lamming makes time elastic; a link between generations is established through oral history, which in its way becomes a structural device knitting together the narrative. Ma Shephard's story of the fire that swept San Cristobal when she was a girl presages the fire that destroys the mental home, killing Marcia, Penelope, and Rowley, the new initiate to the boys' secret Society. This fire at the mental institution is the point and climax of the Society's endeavors: the pivot and climax of the success of the People's Communal Movement, led by Shephard, Singh, and Lee. Further, structurally the fire marks the decline of the fortunes of the main protagonists and the movement of many toward death. Vividly Ma Shephard recalls the first fire, "the fires crack with every blade o' cane an' spread wild with wind all over the town" (68). Later on she is the central witness to, the bearer of evidence about, the mental home fire. Then the testimony and evidence bring about a dislocation of an ontological relationship between her and the boys of the secret Society—Bob, Lee, and Singh.

> "Nine nights I wrestle with the Lord," she said, "but my will would not last, an' I offer up what I find that terrible evening." . . .
> And Singh screamed at the top of his voice: "You lie, you lie," and the others carried the chorus like a sudden lunacy had possessed them, "You lie, you lie, lie!" (408)

Similarly the legend of the Tribe Boys (Carib Indians) and the Bandit Kings (Spaniards), the telling of which makes the Society celebrated, becomes functional in the political campaign, rooting it to history.

Mark, in his speech, locates the connection between the action of the Tribe Boys, their will to be free, with his definition of freedom. The story of the Tribe Boys and the Bandit Kings, an oral polyphony, initially sang out a testament to the natural, to the will to be free. In the legend of the Tribe Boys, as told by Bob, Lee and Singh, a total societal coherence is made manifest. Lyrically the story is chorused by the three boys:

> "'Twas like in that time when the world know only nature an' noise."
> "Bird noise and wind," said Singh.
> "An' plain animal talk," Bob continued. "An' the fish dancin' wild an' makin' faces at the bottom o' the ocean, an' only the sun get permission to say the time, an' the moon only makin' plans to decide the size o' the

sea . . . . Like such a time it was for San Cristobal, long, long before human interference." . . .

". . . The day was for doin' . . . an' the night was for knowin' what happen in the day. That is peace, real peace." (95–96)

Clearly this initial idyllic condition corresponds to a time of innocence, of beginnings; later with the coming of social experiences and age, that peace, that idyllic condition is shattered. War ensues between the Tribe Boys and the Bandit Kings. A struggle is climaxed with an act of freedom. A homage to man's will:

"They swear in whisper one to the next never to take defeat from the Kings, never to be victim complete. An' they walk without stoppin' . . . right to the top o' Mount Misery. An' there they kiss on the cliff for ever, an' then lean their heads down in a last minute dive to their own funeral." (99)

It is a restatement of this action, a will to freedom, that Mark uses during a political meeting as his definition of ultimate freedom:

"Freedom and Death, like opposites and contradictions working in harmony, are the two facts which we cannot bargain, the two great facts . . . . But here we can choose. And our choice is not complete until it becomes an act." (173–174)

To Lamming freedom is a human and universal quality, the prerogative of all who seek it. Freedom defined in such a way could be a transformative and cohering element and even as it is "a nerve," "an instinct" (173), when fired by passion, even martyrdom is not too high a price to pay for it. Thus it is that, driven by his need to change a dislocated and fragmented reality in which his forebears and he himself barely existed, Singh becomes impassioned, totally imbued with that quest for freedom:

"I am prepared to blunder and die, and let another like us blunder and die . . . until we blunder into hell . . . or into a different kind of life in San Cristobal." (246)

Legend, the tale of the Tribe Boys recited early in the novel, enshrines a ritual, offering a possibility of regenerative hope. The orality of legend, even while linking past and present, even while replicating historical action, offers a ritual temporality to the novel *Of Age and Innocence.*

The earth grew light where they stood. Their gifts still made a quivering fire over Rowley's grave, and they felt that it was he who kept their candles alive, that they would burn forever in a legend which told San

Cristobal and the world why they had followed their wish to climb that steep and pitiless cliff which carried the Tribe Boys to their death. (412)

As San Cristobal celebrates the feast of All Souls and the nine nights for Shephard's death, as the island lies under a military curfew, as Singh, Lee, and Bob mourn the death of Rowley and the imprisonment of their fathers Singh and Lee, the legend of the Tribe Boys is actualized. The four groupings—Mark and Marcia, Penelope and Bill; Shephard, Lee and Singh, leaders of the People's Communal Movement; Bob, Lee, Singh and Rowley of the secret Society; and governmental representatives like Crabbe and Paravecino—provide a structural regularity to the novel. Their coming together leads to ultimate friction, wherein the plot of the novel surges. Of these four groups the only one that seems to survive with a possibility of promise is the boys, who have developed from boyhood to manhood:

> "The Society start as a game," Lee said, "but it ain't a game no more."
>
> "Once a man always a man," said Bob, "and hard as hard can be, a man got to stop his eyes from makin' water." (406)

Earlier, however, during the early days of the Society, in that period of their initiation, they pondered the relationship between boyhood and manhood.

> Once a man twice a child, Bob was thinking . . . . Twice a man once a boy like now when man and boy happen at the same said time without dividing line . . . . Age is nothing if there aint no doing . . . . Age is the Society start young and behaving old without any show of numbers. (116)

This conclusion becomes prognosis of the future of the Society, indeed is realized at the end of the novel.

The actual time of the novel, then, circumscribes a movement from innocence and youth to age and manhood. The "new work" that the Society undertakes early in the novel actually is beginning for these three boys at the end of the novel. They will attempt not simply to free their parents, who were involved in the killing of the most hated symbol of white colonial domination, Crabbe, the English Chief of Police, but indeed to bring about a social and racial cohesion in which the son of this very Crabbe will symbolically be present in death: "While we last, he can count himself with the livin'" (405). That prognosis of social coherence is already manifested in a sense of newness which has qualified the mood of the island of San Cristobal during Shephard's ascendancy and the rise of the People's Communal Movement to power.

Many voices of the people chorus this possibility of newness. Some, like Thief, accentuating a racial coherence:

"Friend or foe, Baboo, we goin' lie down in the same future," said Thief. . . . "an' we goin' join the same dream that wake with the Chinese too, an' any white who willing . . . . So you votin' with me Baboo, an' the Powers who want to humble pride with learnin' goin' salute Thief an' Baboo in the same mornin' . . . . You smiling, Baboo? . . . Smile!" (81)

Others comment only on the new mood that has manifested itself in San Cristobal:

"Was like a new day o' deliverance," someone said. (76)

"Tis a next day o' deliverance he goin' bring." (77)

". . . a new set o' power." (82)

In the minds of the populace, this possibility of newness is engendered principally by the words and actions of Shephard. To the police inspector, "Shephard is not only a man . . . but a kind of magic which caught everyone asleep" (113). To Thief he "is a engine without any brakes . . . . Nobody ain't stoppin' him now" (164).

Clearly, then, Shephard not only captures the imagination of the people, but is also, as stated by his own presence, molding and shaping a new mood, a new feeling in San Cristobal. He has prophesied during his moment of delirium on the plane the creation of "an old old land inhabiting new forms of men who can never resurrect their roots and do not know their nature" (58). And indeed in spite of the many statements made about Shephard, Shephard's own remarks, his own words, seem always to be charged with a tension, a pendulation from calm to passion, at times transformed by hallucination. Thus his character depiction is more an allusion to some man who creates an illusion of power not illustrated in his own actions, not demonstrated by his own speeches. Singh is friend, admirer, and disciple. Impassioned by Shephard's killing, he extols Shephard's influence on him and Shephard's contribution to the new mood, almost a revolutionary mood, sweeping San Cristobal:

"There never was a man who make me feel more deep than Shephard . . . an' never will be . . . . Such a man never happened in San Cristobal before, never. He take the struggle which I start and turn it to a movement that was now more than losin' or winnin' . . . . I learn for the first time what it could mean to feel loyal, not only to the cause but loyal to the person too." (379)

In contrast to this description of Shephard's strengths, Lamming more often than not presents Shephard teetering between sanity and delirium, swinging between realms of reality and unreality, gripped by recurrent nightmarish dreams brought on by feelings of paranoia. At times he demonstrates a kind of schizophrenia; at times he seems possessed of unhuman characteristics: a head rising out of a seat, a head that scares Rowley, the little English boy, son of Police Inspector Crabbe; a head that also scares Marcia, the English woman on her way to San Cristobal with her native born lover, Mark. Here Shephard seems not simply to be bogey man, but is depicted in creatural, indeed in animalistic terms.

> The enormous black skull which had been wagging from side to side like a clock's dull tongue rose gradually, showing its heavy thick neck, and the ample shoulders that sloped abruptly into arms. (48–49)

The scene explodes in Shephard's brutal and savage attack on Penelope, an act with obvious sexual overtones:

> "I should like to see you in another form . . . .
> . . . "I should leave your legs in all their natural lechery, but I'd have fat snails, out of their shells, slide plentifully into your womb, leaving you heavy and full with a lasting slime." (57)

Later, on Bird Island, in the quiet of an early afternoon, Shephard, after saving Penelope from drowning, calmly, yet at times excitedly, explains to her his behavior on the plane. Not only was he attempting to purge himself of the memory of an unfortunate love affair with an English woman, but to him that act was necessary in order to destroy his perception of himself as colonial man, and to bring about a new self-awareness, a new confidence.

> "When I saw you, it was another woman who was standing before me, and when I attacked you as I did, it was neither you nor the woman I was attacking. It was myself." (200)

> "Until that experience, I had always lived in the shadow of a meaning which others had placed on my presence in the world, and I had played no part at all in making that meaning." (203)

By presenting his notion of a colonized status and condition, and indeed by perceiving it, Shephard should have been able to, if not free himself from that condition, at least to manifestly control the effects of such a condition. Indeed he asserts that by accepting the condition of the colonized, he, like a chair, was but a passive recipient. But as participant in that condition, he can but alter it and drastically reverse it:

> "When [meaning] suits my purpose I shall use it, when it doesn't, I shall be hostile. . . . I am at war. . . .

"... I am the one who now sees them, not they me ....

"... my rebellion begins with an acceptance of the very thing I reject, because my conduct cannot have the meaning I want to give it, if it does not accept and live through that conception by which the others now regard it." (204–205)

Yet Shephard seems totally unable to free himself from the glance or the perception of "the others," a perception that resurrects itself at every point of emotional stress. Consequently he is plagued by recurrent nightmarish dreams that immobilize him, or he is imbued with hypersensitive emotions that accentuate his delusions of grandeur. On the eve of the elections, trapped, it seems, like so many of the other characters, within a room, Shephard confesses to his mother, Ma Shephard, the recurrent nightmare of the trains. In this state of being seen but not seeing, Shephard is absent from himself, indeed, symbolically is absent from the world:

"Every eye in that carriage just turn on me. Like lights or spears fightin' to pierce through me, everyone lookin', lookin', lookin', till I feel I was shrinking, all of me shrinking to nothing." (293)

This wanting to be seen by others, this inability to withstand the glance of others, of those who seem to have colonized his mind, lead him inexorably to demand attention, to demand that others see him not only as himself but as having achieved control over others. Even as a boy he demands that Mark witness his control over the chairs transformed by his dream into children:

"... Children in darkness, do not ask to change, and do not be angry that you cannot of your own accord make a change in your condition. Be happy to serve and if you serve well, there will be reward for your service .... I shall give love and punishment as I see fit." (109)

Later on, goaded by the same need just prior to his own death, he confronts Mark. In a lucid semi-rhapsody, in the ritualistic rhythms that characterize so many of his speeches, he almost attains his wishes for grandeur, almost achieves a state of apotheosis:

"I shall hold this land in the palm of my hand, and bend it like a wheel to meet my intention. I shall call on the earth to clap and the water to sing and every living thing shall tell its pleasure in a humble service to my sovreignty on an island that once slept under water. But tonight, Kennedy, I shall walk the water and for a moment consult with my Maker." (316–317)

Yet if Shephard is the metaphor promising a defragmentation of a colonial reality, guiding a people to a possibility of newness and social coherence, given his own inner emotional turbulence, his own fragmented personality, it is hardly likely that he could truly shape a new presence or indeed significantly transform the sociopolitical reality. That is not to say that in the transformation of colonial reality into a coherent political entity a leader is required who in himself is totally self-contained, self-assured, self-reliant. Yet, neither can the volatile and erratic grandeur of a Shephard successfully bring about that transformation. Throughout the novel *Of Age and Innocence*, many of the characters are transformed by the very gestative and fragmentary sociopolitical environment in which they are plunged, while some, given their own particular personalities, deepen those characteristics that qualify their personality. Thus, for instance, Mark's quality of disintegration intensifies as he plunges into the turbulent political arena of San Cristobal. At a high point of political intensity, after his speech about freedom, he hallucinates uncontrollably:

> He felt imprisoned by this hallucination which now possessed his senses
> . . . . It was as though a terrible heat had dissected everything . . . . He
> was part of a constant and perceptible disintegration of things . . . .
> . . . He thought his hands had turned pink and soft with the heat, and
> it seemed that his feet would soon melt and make red puddles from
> which his bones would emerge like poles in water. (175–176)

This "disintegration of things" qualifies many of the relationships between characters in the novel, indeed leads to the breakup of various groupings, bringing about a dissociation, a falling apart of things and people. At the center of the novel is the relationship of the four groups, their intersecting emotions, and at the point of interlocking loyalties, disintegration of various kinds ensues. Dramatic confrontations deriving from personal and social intrigues become the raison d'être of the novel, the cog and center around which the action and plot revolve. The four principal groups are like secret societies with their own codes of ethics, their own rituals, their own allegiances and loyalties.

The disintegration of the first group of migrants to the island—even though Mark was born on the island he left at the age of ten, now returning at the age of thirty—is principally occasioned by Mark's silences, his temperament and his eventual separation from his lover, Marcia, from that group. His mood leaves a void in his relationship with Marcia, which Penelope, impelled by a feeling of group loyalty, attempts to fill:

> She widened her embrace. Marcia drew closer, sobbing heavily. But
> Penelope did not speak. She thought for a moment only of Mark and the
> role which his absence had now assigned her. She had to play Mark's
> part. Her voice soothing Marcia with a chosen comfort had to be Mark's

voice, and her arm feeding Marcia's body with warmth was Mark's arm. (106–107)

The inexplicable nature of this homosexual feeling plunges Penelope into a self-analysis, into a debate which she is unable to share with Bill, Mark, or Marcia. Thus from an attempted act of loyalty, Penelope moves to become secretive and silent, to a secrecy and silence that change the basic relationship of the group. She perceives herself as different, becoming Penelope, in spite of herself.

In parallel formation, Mark's inability to open up heightens Penelope's anxiety, increases her doubt about the situation vis-à-vis the group. Mark, on the other hand, is unable to extricate himself from his own secrecy, his own disinclination: "They were both silent, retreating with grave and similar reminiscence into their solitary and different worlds of understanding" (183).

Even as secrecy and silence diminish the relationships of the first group, secrecy and silence are the catchwords of the Society of Bob, Lee, Singh, and Rowley. Their secrecy, their oaths of allegiance, imbue the boys with sensations that make them feel in some way superior to their parents:

He was no longer a prince in a crowd which could not guess his secret. He was bigger and better than a prince, an equal in the house which his father ruled. (133)

Rowley's oath of allegiance to the boys' Society underscores the recurrent motif of loyalty that defines the behavior and reactions of almost all the characters. Even Crabbe, the police inspector, is made to declaim about his own particular brand of loyalty: a loyalty, paradoxically, to playing the game fairly and to appearing as a loyal colonial administrator. It persists even when facing Singh's impassioned wrath:

He wanted to redeem the cause which he served .... to avoid the slander .... he would be loyal to his mission .... His mission in San Cristobal was larger than his life, more urgent than his death. (380–381)

The motif of loyalty operates at all levels whether pertaining to ethical or unethical behavior, to moral or immoral conduct. Baboo, who double-crosses almost everybody, who kills Shephard and shoots Crabbe before the latter can betray him, pleads loyalty to his obsession, his own cause:

Baboo .... A saint whose martyrdom served no purpose. His loyalty had betrayed him. He wanted to go closer, but the body lay between them, and he saw Singh's face like two uneven profiles divided by the light, beyond recognition. . . .

"Was only for you, Singh, was only for you I do it, . . . from infancy
I dream to see someone like myself, some Indian with your achievement
rule San Cristobal." (384)

Bill's incipient wish to help San Cristobal, his initial reaction to save
Shephard, all are obscured by his maniacal wish to be loyal to the corpse of
Penelope, who has been burnt up in the fire at the mental institution. For
this he attempts to punish Shephard, indeed to murder him. He accepts this
as a duty to Penelope's memory:

It defined his duty. (307)

But the memory of Penelope had obscured the politics of San Cristobal.
He wanted to deal with Shephard directly. (309)

Lamming conceives the novel *Of Age and Innocence* in a series of interpersonal spatial relationships consonant with the movement of the action, with
the tightening of plot, with the heightened intensity of mood. Environment
and phenomena correlate and correspond to the movement of the story.
Initially most of the action, most of the meetings, take place in the open air
where the mood is warmer, where the light still shimmers: the group of
Penelope, Marcia, Mark, and Bill crystallizes during their sojourn on an
island during a period of tranquillity; Rowley is initiated into the Society in
Paradise Woods on a warm sunny day; Penelope and Marcia hear the story
of the Tribe Boys while sitting outside on the pier; Shephard's and Penelope's meeting on Bird Island takes place under a tree in the afternoon. All of
these meetings occur in the open air. The mood is not intense; rather its
texture is lyrical, its pacing leisurely and given over to analyses, speculations
and musings. Later in the novel, the fire at the mental hospital seems to
climax and bring to a close that earlier mood. The fire is presaged by a
squawking bird, and darkness seems to shroud the land:

The night would probably be black and heavy with rain. A huge macaw
strayed over the wall . . . . The sun made a blazing circle of flame with
the scarlet ring of feathers . . . round its neck . . . . . the air was suddenly
rent by a violent spark . . . the bird had flown out of sight, leaving an
echo of panic. (261–262)

The latter part of the novel is shrouded in mist and rain and drizzle. The
recurrent mood is one of gloom, the time is night, closing in on rooms with
characters in a semi-somnolent state pushed on by dream, or by passion, or
by hallucination. Shephard, feeling a sense of doom and tragedy around him,
attempts to keep his old mother awake to watch with him:

He wanted her to stay awake. He needed someone to save him from the danger which was luring him slowly beyond control . . . . He did not want to tire her, but he felt it was unsafe to be left alone. (292–293)

Singh, locked in a room with Baboo, who is bent on murdering Shephard, tries to intercept that intent, but like Ma Shephard succumbs to tiredness and sleep. Thief dialogues with the dying monkey in his half-lit room. The two policemen talk drunkenly about betrayal, Christ and death. Here, then, as the novel moves from a baroque kind of music through litanies and dirges to a kind of mass, or requiem, all of the landscape accompanies these changing moods, choruses the voices of the characters raised in rituals of emotion, of passion, of hallucination. Indeed the notion of evening closing and of night ordaining the future, transforming reality, is underscored in Mark's diary. Man and atmosphere cohere and become locked in a blend of anguish and terror:

> The day does not slink away as though it wanted to stay. It cannot. The evening arrives . . . . with a show of militant displeasure and it declares its wish for solitude and the absence of light. . . .
> Deprive the day of its incredible need to return, and teach a new terror, bloodless and unfamiliar. (311)

Toward the end of *Of Age and Innocence*, "The season had returned, and the town had honoured their promise to celebrate the souls of the departed" (404). The celebration of the soul of Rowley opens into a ritualistic promise and cohering dream. The boys—Bob, Lee, and Singh—honor their fallen comrade, locating him within the reassuring and mythic strength of the Legend of the Tribe Boys. To be sure, the Society "was no game no more" (408), but since the origins of the Society, its embryo, was fertilized by the Legend of the Tribe Boys and hatched in the dream of possibility of a new political order taking shape in their island home, the corporate memory of that Society seems to offer the prognosis for the realization of a new order in which the boys may play a part. In the rain and the flickering candlelight, the boys reiterate the mythical sense of the Tribe Boys, echoing the possibility of regeneration in the repetition of the word tomorrow.

> The earth grew light . . . . Their gifts still made a quivering fire over Rowley's grave, and they felt it was he who kept their candles alive, that they would burn forever in a legend . . . .
> "Tomorrow is the trial," said Bob.
> "Tomorrow and maybe till a next tomorrow it last," Singh said . . .
> "tomorrow an' a next tomorrow." (412)

Here, though the boys feel a sense of anguish and noncomprehension of the tragedy that has befallen Shephard, their political leader, and Rowley, their friend, the future of San Cristobal seems ordained: its history vitalized by myth, its earth by regenerative legend.

The Mimic Men by V. S. Naipaul offers no such expression of regenerative possibility; indeed Naipaul posits instead an absence of historical and mythic presence. In this novel, the fictionalized political leader, the character Ranjit Singh, offers no legacy to his island space. Rather he stumbles through his own idiosyncratic devitalized ambiguities:

> It is with my political career as with that gesture. I used to say, with sincerity, that nothing in my life had prepared me for it. To the end I behaved as though it was to be judged as just another aspect of my dandyism. Criminal error! I exaggerated my frivolity, even to myself. For I find I have indeed been describing the youth and early manhood of a leader of some sort, a politician, or at least a disturber. I have established his isolation, his complex hurt and particular frenzy. And I believe I have also established, perhaps in this proclaimed frivolity, this lack of judgement and balance, the deep feeling of irrelevance and intrusion, his unsuitability for the role into which he was drawn, and his inevitable failure. From playacting to disorder: it is the pattern. (Naipaul, *The Mimic Men*, 220)

Here the narrative voice attempts to underline and emphasize the author's narrative intention and to define the perimeters of his endeavor, thus qualifying simply the presentation of the protagonist, the latter's reactions and attitudes. Using, as it were, his statement, the author attempts to validate his creative intention, presuming that his novelistic intention in all of its manifold formulations is so accurately executed that intention, expression, and outcome shade finely one to the other, correspond and dovetail. And indeed in *The Mimic Men*, the author attempts through persuasion, through sympathetic cajoling, to impress his narrative intention and purpose on his reader. The reader is asked to follow the youthful meanderings of the narrator through his schoolday relationships with Browne, Hok, Eden—fellow students at Isabella Imperial—and to enter his relationship with his father and extended family.

Through a series of encounters in the first part of *The Mimic Men*, the youthful artist-writer trespasses on the threshold of various affairs with women in London and later as a married man on the island of Isabella. The encounters are with groups of upper-class, cosmopolitan returning professionals. To be sure, the author has been delineating the youth and early manhood of a "leader of some sort" (220) and has attempted through a series of sociopolitical extrapolations to locate the inner personality and inner character of his protagonist. But the establishment of frenzy claimed by the narrative voice seems to derive more from the inner fabric and texture of the narration. Thus it is that often there is disjunction between extrapolated statements, philosophical structurings, and the interweaving of relationships. Yet the political events and happenings of *The Mimic Men* climax in a search for self. *The Mimic Men* is basically the sketching and the constant filling out, through numerous encounters, episodes and relationships, of the personality and character of Ranjit Singh. He attempts to locate the modus of his reactions, the locus of his emotions, the reason for his attitudes, and to understand the seemingly intrinsic irony underpinning his character delineation. At the center of Singh's adventuring toward selfhood is a basic irony derived from ambivalence and ambiguity wherein conflicting claims of reality converge in a contrapuntal disharmony and dissonance. Cause is followed by ironic effect; play-acting extrapolates into disorder; political action seeded by drama ends in disaster, rather than in disharmony; the very thing that made for success is endemic with seeds of ultimate failure.

Throughout *The Mimic Men*, almost every event, episode, encounter culminates in a feeling of unease, disorder, dislocation, loneliness, indeed in a kind of nausea. But again that feeling of nausea is more of a statement issuing from the narrative voice, more of a philosophical motif and tenet assumed and imposed. The externalization of the feeling of nausea, a feeling often not intrinsically woven into the episode, the encounter or particular event, robs the nausea of its essential quality: a deep disgust and despair. Thus the character or personality of Ranjit Singh never really achieves or assumes a deep pathetic quality; indeed so much of both is statement.

Here the narrator, Ranjit Singh, states his reaction to a fight which has been staged by a sibling uncle to whom pleasure "appeared to lie in an increase in self-violation . . . like a man testing his toleration of the unpleasant" (198). To the staging of the fight, a reaction of nausea:

> I again had that sense of being forced to eat raw flesh and drink tainted oil . . . .
> . . . I asked for a drink. They gave me rum. It was raw and sickening. (193)

It is the same stated reaction of nausea that he experiences at the ritual killing of a race horse, the ritual killing attributed to his father.

> What I . . . heard chilled and sickened me and gave me more strongly than ever the sensation of rawness and violation: rubbery raw flesh, tainted holy oil. It was more than a death . . . . An ancient sacrifice . . . now rendered obscene. (167)

Ultimately in *The Mimic Men* Ranjit Singh's personality is established principally by statement. His essential self and presence are not deeply ingrained into the mold; the frieze remains without deep inlays and etchings. The many patternings and contourings of Ranjit Singh's personality equal the many and varied situations and circumstances from which these patternings, these contourings, emanate. Further, the reason the narrator turns to writing as a way out of his particular predicament, though ironic and ineluctable, seems based on self-deficiencies and personal dilemmas, urgently and compulsively reiterated.

The author or the narrative voice of Ranjit Singh—one is never sure who is speaking—adduces reasons for undertaking the narrative statement that writing would serve as a clarifier, would perhaps impose an order to a seemingly endemic disorder and frenzy:

> my presence in this city which I have known as a student, politician and now as refugee-immigrant, to impose order on my own history, to abolish that disturbance which is what a narrative in sequence might have led me to do. (292)

This imposition of order is also stated as a need to arrive at the truth and to give authenticity to half-truths, which have been the stamp and seal of his character and his actions:

> It was the first of many such pieces: balanced, fair, with the final truth evaded, until at last this truth was lost. The writing of this book has been more than a release from those articles; it has been an attempt to rediscover that truth. (226)

Yet in that rediscovering of the truth, in the stated attempts to clear the balance, the narrator realizes the possibility of distortions endemic to the writing, distortions that ultimately would modify the truth: "writing, for all its distortion, clarifies, and even becomes a process of life" (301).

It is not surprising, then, that the author relies on statements and pronouncements about reactions to deeds and actions even when those reactions are in themselves contradictory, even when pronouncements about the same event or phenomenon vary in their connotative applications. Thus it is that elements of play-acting, bluff, sham, all of which can be collected in the word "drama," release ambivalent and contradictory responses, shift and vary and change in their inner truth and meaning. Perhaps these inconsistencies derive from an expressionistic treatment of narrative detail. Even though the total orchestration of Ranjit Singh's character resounds with the melodramatic, with acting, with contrived responses, there is a stated fear of drama and its use: "I feared drama. My dream of the cocoa estate was not the dream of eviction; and it was more than a dream of order" (43).

The same drama the narrator fears takes on another quality, assures for him a differing dynamic, so that the narrator's attitude regarding drama is left in doubt, becomes open to question, as are many of the stated reactions. As politicians, Ranjit Singh and Browne are said to rely on drama for their successes. Here Ranjit Singh does not fear drama, rather in one of the pronouncements he glorifies it. Similarly the narrator, while claiming "frenzy" as an operative dynamic in his reactive mood, states that he was never really in that very condition of frenzy: "I never was a politician. I never had the frenzy, the sense of mission, the necessary hurt" (43). The pronouncements about frenzy seem insubstantial echoes, creating a mood, a setting, for the relationship between action and reaction, or episode and pronouncement. In this shifting novelistic reality, analysis seems to derive from prior intentionality rather than from the very fabric of the deed it records:

> I no longer seek to explain; I merely record. For eight days, during which whatever reputation I had left was being destroyed, I stayed on in London, held by what I had detected in Stella's manner at our first meeting. Frenzy was what I had first thought it to be; and frenzy it was, of a sort. (275)

So that often *The Mimic Men* becomes a series of recorded attitudes and responses to episodes and events through which Ranjit Singh—actor, narrator—lives. In this summation, attitudes and episodes during his student days are tied together. Here the operative words are "player" and "dandy." Ranjit Singh, the player, the lover, the dandy, created by Lieni, a London charwoman:

> We become what we see of ourselves in the eyes of others . . . . It was Lieni who told me that my eyes might disturb and that my dark, luxuriant and very soft hair might be a source of further disturbance . . . . Her background was . . . concentrated in her memory of an affair with an Indian officer in Italy . . . . It was disquieting, yet . . . oddly flattering, to be cherished as a substitute; I became her apt pupil. (25)

Quixotically Ranjit Singh rides out to make his conquests:

> It was Lieni who told me that I ought to spend the extra half-crown two or three times a week to arrive at the School in a taxi, having travelled by public transport the better part of the way. It was Lieni who dressed me. (25)

He evinces disgust at imperfect breasts; later, as a "great lover," another assumed pose, even while his marriage to Sandra is breaking up, he publicly play-acts to love:

> In public [Sandra and I] would commune. It was the word we used. I would say, "Shall we commune?" "Let's," she might reply . . . . On a high settee she might then sit . . . her feet hanging loose over my shoulders as I sat on the floor below the settee; and I would be content, kissing and stroking those feet and legs which twitched and squeezed in answer. (83)

As politician, too, his initial contribution to the party stems from his vaunted dandyism: "I never abandoned the character of the dandy. In this was neither honesty nor dishonesty; it was the easiest way out" (247). Evidently, then, so many of Ranjit Singh's attitudes are built on play-acting, on pose, pose that often takes on the quality of bluff. His participation in politics "began in bluff" (249). But these qualities are not recently acquired; rather they have been in evidence even during his youth. Imitation and pretense qualify his youthful preparation for sports and track. Likewise his participation in cricket, his bowling, is qualified by a seeming need to call attention to the self. Clearly here is displayed a tongue-in-cheek attitude, a measure of self-mockery:

> I took up sport. I put my name down for cricket. I thought I would be a bowler and needless to say I wished to bowl very fast. I took a long run and not infrequently at the end lost control of both the run and the ball. I did not last on any side. But the effort was not wasted. I lost some of my selfconsciousness. It takes some doing, after all, to put on the absurd garb of the cricketer and to walk with a straight face to the middle! (135–136)

This need to be seen, indeed to participate and belong, to be accepted, give definition and label to the pose, the affectation. However, this definition in itself seems necessary, intrinsic and vital to a personality which in its essence attempts to place a mantle and covering over a basically shy and insecure nature.

> The public speaker was only another version of the absurd schoolboy cricketer, selfconsciousness supressed, the audience ignored, at the nets of Isabella Imperial. (136)

This insecurity of the outsider, of the other, gives his self-definition texture and shape to the point where he ascribes power to the eye, to the regard of the other, the outsider. (25) It is by this means that he actively becomes a politician.

A man was only what he saw of himself in others, and an intimation came
to me of chieftainship in that island. This was my political awakening.
(121)

It is, then, the acceptance of the others' perception of the self, the stated
need for the external regard and validation, which in their elaboration make
for pronouncements and claims such as "in a society like ours . . . no power
was real which did not come from the outside" (246). The notion of the
outside, the sense of the other, perhaps coalesces in statements of yearning
for other landscapes, of a feeling of shipwreck on the island, Isabella, so that
the motif of landscape linked to the theme of escape becomes central to the
narrative, charting and directing the narrator's journeying into self-discovery.
For the axis of *The Mimic Men* is the voyage toward the self, not the movement toward coherence and communality.

Initially as a young man, Singh finds escape in his reading, which opens
up vistas of heroic Asiatic history to him. In this historic dream world of
wonder and knight errantry, through a transformative process, the dreamer-
narrator-author leaps over spaces to assume a chieftain's role in his island.
Clearly, then, this preoccupation with chieftaincy, which culminates in the
momentary assumption of that role in the politics of that island, is an embryo
that develops fertilized by the imagination and later finally hatches.

> In my secret life I was the son of my father, and a Singh . . . . of Rajputs
> and Aryans . . . . I lived a secret life in a world of endless plains, tall bare
> mountains, white with snow at their peaks among nomads on horseback
> . . . . And I would dream that all over the Central Asian plains the
> horsemen looked for their leader. (117–118)

The narrator, then, lives through many landscapes, the landscape from
which he originates, and those through which he travels in imagination or
actuality. Thus, the visualization of landscape in *The Mimic Men* pendulates
between these various regions, these shifting environs, to the point where
this pendulation makes for an ambivalence of his response to successive
landscapes:

> Even as I was formulating my resolve to escape, there began that series
> of events which, while sharpening my desire to get away, yet rooted me
> more firmly to the locality where accident had placed me. (142)

But the accident of birth cannot simply be accident; it is actual and
compelling, demanding its own inevitable allegiance. The narrator's reaction
is at one and the same time, then, paradoxical, ambivalent, and in some
instances confused, for he is caught willy-nilly in the rootings of the accident:

I abolished all landscapes to which I could not attach myself and longed only for those I had known. I thought of escape, and it was escape to what I had so recently sought to escape from. (36)

Unable or perhaps unwilling to accept the pull of his roots—perhaps because he has ascribed to those roots unromantic beginnings, shrouded as they are in slavery and indentured labor—the narrator correlates a vision of order with that of belonging. He colors his origins "picturesque Asiatic" and pronounces a vision of disorder:

A man, I suppose, fights only when he hopes, when he has a vision of order, when he feels strongly there is some connection between the earth on which he walks and himself. But there was my vision of a disorder which it was beyond any one man to put right. There was my sense of wrongness, beginning with the stillness of that morning of return when I looked out on the slave island and tried to pretend it was mine. There was my sense of intrusion which deepened as I felt my power to be more and more a matter of words. So defiantly, in my mind, I asserted my character as intruder, the picturesque Asiatic born for other landscapes. (248)

The dandy or the notion of the dandy is an uneasy bedfellow with the indentured Asiatic. The narrator is unable to rid himself of a feeling of inferiority, even when he assumes a romanticized notion of his immediate point of origin, Isabella; even when he transforms the attendant conditions of serfdom of his furthest origins. Thus even as the narrator lyricizes the landscape of Isabella and in flowing strokes apprehends the beauty of that landscape, he dissociates himself from the historical reality of the cocoa plantation built up and maintained by slave labor by projecting himself into a position of chieftaincy—an estate manager living in a baronial house.

The cocoa plantation is presented in all of its residual beauty, a landscape that is vital even though deriving from a static historical mode. With lyrical strokes the author captures all the luxuriant, variegated colorings and flowing beauty of the cocoa plantation.

And cocoa: it is my favourite crop. It grows in the valleys of our mountain ranges, where it is cool and where on certain mornings your breath turns to vapour. There are freshwater springs that make miniature waterfalls over mossy rocks and then run clear and cold and shallow in their own channels of white sand ... giant *immortelle* trees ... set every hillside ablaze with bird-shaped flowers of yellow and orange which then, for days, float down on the woods ... the tormented black trunks of the cocoa trees rise, their shining cocoa pods, in all the colours from lime green through scarlet to imperial purple. (39–40)

In such a landscape, then, the narrator sees himself as estate owner possessing all the trappings which accompany that position of privilege and of exploitative power, enjoying its luxury.

> Cocoa and papaw and fried plantains, freshly baked bread and avocadoes; all served on a tablecloth of spotless white, still showing the folds from its ironing; the clean napkin on the polished plate; . . . The rest of the morning would have seen me at my desk, slowly patterning the white paper with the blackest of inks. (40)

It is not from this landscape that the author wishes to escape. Later a devitalized London stands counterposed to the lushness and flowery greenery of the cocoa estate. From that vantage point he recalls with a seemingly deep sense of nostalgia the cocoa plantation.

> Beyond . . . the wallpaper in my room, which has a pattern of antique motorcars—there is a ceaseless roar of traffic; the tainted air vibrates. No cocoa trees! No orange-and-yellow *immortelle* flowers! No woodland springs running over white sand. (41)

The eye of the narrator seems restless, shifting from landscape to landscape, always indeed seeming to locate and settle on the greenness on the other side of the fence.

Yet the narrator is caught and trapped by a romantic vision of self activated by the play vision of dandy. He is unable to accept his rooting to the tree and the earth, unable to come to grips with his heritage and past; the eye of the other, of the outsider, is always required to validate his person, his very being. For him the white snows of the Laurentians, contrasting with the perceived fragmented reality of Isabella, provide the only true landscape, a landscape mimicked and imitated by the natives of Isabella. Dramatically the narrator in wanton fashion makes his grand proclamation and claim to the title of his book, *The Mimic Men:*

> There, in Liege in a traffic jam, on the snow slopes of the Laurentians, was the true, pure world. We, here on our island, handling books printed in this world, and using its goods, had been abandoned and forgotten. We pretended to be real, to be learning, to be preparing ourselves for life, we mimic men of the New World, one unknown corner of it, with all its reminders of the corruption that came so quickly to the new. (175)

This questioning of his education, his tutelage, his roots, indeed the very rejection of them in the avid grasping for validating spaces, shrouds the narrator in another mantle, in another pose of ambivalent nonbelonging. The narrator's rendezvous with his history has not brought about a fragmentation of his personality, rather it has made him seek even more to ape the foreign cultural ethos, the very cause of his ambivalence, the origin of his alienation from himself.

This quality of ambivalence also characterizes his relationships to his sisters, his family. While the father is unheroic, the author's relationship to him seems ambivalent, rejecting. His perception of his father and his attitude and relationship to him shift and pendulate. At one and the same time embarrassed by his father's not having paid back a debt of $30, he yet defends his father's good intentions and fights to protect them.

> Tears came to my eyes. So suddenly I had taken on my father's pain. It was a debt that had to be repaid . . . it had once been needed . . . once been asked for. (194)

Later on he redeems that debt in a somewhat propitious gesture of atonement.

> [The debt] couldn't really be repaid, but the gesture was necessary . . . .
> I gave her three ten-dollar bills. "My father borrowed this from your son Dalip." (211)

Yet that feeling of sympathy, the gesture of atonement, are actualized more so by memory than by a constant and assured attitude. The memory of the father's gentle touch evinces a feeling of sympathy, actualized by a nostalgia for something lost.

> I remembered the embrace of his arms before, the day he towed me on the crossbar of his bicycle . . . . The sympathy that remained was for the idea of him. (211)

Clearly, then, in *The Mimic Men,* in his representation of the cultural and sociopolitical reality, V. S. Naipaul adduces little possibility of a coherent order wherein the dialogue between man and landscape, between man and society, will lead to a holistic vision of that reality. His vision opens into no cohering possibility but rather becomes an advocacy of a continued dependency on foreign cultural and ecological patternings. The dialogue between man and his landscape, indeed the very argumentation, seems to posit an indigenous polity devoid of vitalizing energies. John Hearne, however, on his novelistic canvas makes the notion of excellence a qualification in which his characters and his landscape move and are enshrined. His notion of the heroic derives from a vision of reality in which characters, though at times not rooted in the immediate social reality, always grasp after an ideal. Thus, often the representation of the reality becomes an idealization of the indigenous in which resides the representation and prognosis of possibility.

Yet in some of Hearne's novels, this idealization of the external reality does not come to grips with the actual inner societal workings; by positing idealization the author already raises the societal condition to a higher level, wherein deep social trauma is really absent.

Hearne's preoccupation is the interrelationships among people, but his novelistic vision is rooted in the macrocosm. The author always seems to seize upon the grand action, imbuing even base gestures or things with their most vital resonance; he postulates excellences of action and reaction, depicting them on a grand scale. His lenses penetrate deep within or elevate upward, far upward, focused on an ideal as he moves away from the trivial and the mundane. His interpretations of human actions, often coming as parenthetical coda to an episode or action captured in flashback, are all as exaltations as they grasp after essences. To postulate excellence in behavior or even to attempt to capture the highest nature of misdemeanor, attests to a transformative vision which posits attitudes relevant and vital to societal transformation. In these novels, these attitudes become oft-repeated motifs, indeed thematic constructs structuring the narrative action, shaping the character depiction. These attitudes can only be operative within the context of societal reformation, in sociopolitical conditions that have already begun to undergo a transformative process.

Hearne is not indifferent to the larger society, but he often leaves us in doubt about what kind of total society he advocates. For Hearne reserves his moral judgments for man acting as individual within society, not for society reacting and controlling man. It is not surprising, therefore, that the fortuitous, the element of inexplicable accident (the sort of accident issuing not from society but rather from a novelistic unknown), often guides or gives direction to the denouement of his novels.

In these novels of Hearne, *Voices under the Window* (1955), *Stranger at the Gate* (1956), *The Faces of Love* (1957), *The Autumn Equinox* (1959), we may devise four structural formations, four principal settings: man moving within society, the island Cayuna on which the characters move, the particular social structure of that island, the physical landscape. The author's vision holds all these together with his particular stylistic and structural underpinnings.

Man, committed and evolving through commitment, arrives at a stage of fear or doubt, becomes involved in politics or social action, plunges into love and emotional crisis, at times achieves fulfillment. But his action, to be most effective, must be undertaken alone; the individual man, acting alone, by his commitment, participates in that phenomenon, the public. Even as he acts, he is beset by doubt and fear and the compelling ties of friendship, which demand their own generosity. And all of these culminate in an irony of shared relationships, for in Hearne's novels, the ties of friendship compel generous action toward a friend that often leads this friend into destruction. At the point of its winning, the love that has been sought often cannot be enjoyed. At the very moment when, for the first time, Mark Lattimer in *Voices under the Window* has, freely and without fear of too much giving, offered himself in love to Brysie, he meets with a tragic and fatal accident. Thus the basic irony is that even though commitment is essential to bring about transformation, often commitment ends in unfulfillment or destruction.

In all of man's relationships, particularly in love, Hearne demands total commitment. At the center of relationships lies woman. In general, all of Hearne's women possess an abounding maternal instinct, which manifests itself in their relationships with men. In *Land of the Living*, the relationships of the expatriate university lecturer Stefan with both female characters, Bernice and Joan, seem to stem from their maternal instincts toward him. Joan eventually marries him when her protective instincts are aroused. She wants to "take care" of him. Bernice's relationship with and love for Stefan are also rooted in her maternal instincts, which are not only exhibited toward Stefan, but also revealed in her relationship to her old father, Marcus Heneky. In *The Autumn Equinox*, too, Eleanor Stacey in her love for Jim Diver manifests all the elements of the maternal:

> All morning I thought about Jim and the way he had looked. I guess life really sets a trap for women: we find it so difficult to know where we start being mothers and stop being lovers. That's why men are able to take advantage of us so easily. Half the girls I know who have had to marry before they meant to, or who were unlucky and couldn't persuade the men to marry them in time, got caught because they suddenly felt an overwhelming pity and tenderness in one night—not passion. (Hearne, *The Autumn Equinox*, 182)

Thus pity and tenderness, not passion, seem to be controlling factors in the love that Hearne's female characters display for their men. Though Rachel Ascom in the *The Faces of Love* is motivated by a desire to control and almost consume her various lovers, she eventually offers herself most completely to a man for whom she feels some tender pity.

While this "maternal instinct" seems ultimately to direct the behavior of many of the female characters, commitment becomes functional, an operative quality, in the depiction of many male characters. It is an ever-present motif in the novels: commitment through love or friendship, commitment to a larger society, to a cause, to one's belief. Marcus Heneky in *Land of the Living* is completely committed to the cause of his race; he zealously gives himself to the liberation of the Black man. In *Stranger at the Gate*, Roy McKenzie requests Carl Brandt's help for a cause to which Roy is committed even to the point of death. Carl helps to harbor the political exile, with whose ideas he disagrees; his action springs not from belief or agreement with Roy's self-imposed mission but rather from the cult and the call of friendship. Similarly Nicholas Stacey, bound by ties of friendship and loyalty to Luis Corioso even after years of separation, generously gives his help to aid the cause to which Corioso has committed himself, even though Stacey cynically notes that the cause will end, like all other causes, in larger disillusionment. Commitment, then, must be demonstrated through action, but often the very act brings about destruction. The end result of Nicholas Stacey's action is that his friend Corioso, pursuing his commitment to the cause, has his hands cut off. Carl Brandt's act of generosity leads eventually to Roy's death. And Marcus Heneky, in acting out his commitment, loses his life. These ironic results exemplify Hearne's statement: every action carries in it the germ of its own decay, its own lack of meaning.

Perhaps because of this paradox, commitment and action must not be hindered by rational thought. Hearne claims that actions coming from the heart and not from the head contain a deeper degree of truth and are, in essence, more efficacious. Emotion, the heart, feelings, stand juxtaposed to thought, the head, and logic. And even though Hearne seems to luxuriate in words, he indicates that words minimize the essence of action. Thus action that responds to the call of friendship, the pull of deep emotion, or the throb of the heart, not the reason of the head, is the type of action that most contributes to societal transformation. And action that stems from the head rather than from the heart can bring with it a sense of anguish and inadequacy.

> "He's given his allegiance from the heart. I gave it from the head. And that's why I was afraid this morning; I didn't have any heart to fall back on." (Hearne, *Voices under the Window*, 114)

In Hearne's view, fear, which can paralyze a man's center of action, comes from the head, whether it be a fear of losing oneself through too deep a commitment to another, or fear of violence and its corollary, death. Mark Lattimer, when faced with the specter of death, cannot help crying out and revealing his anguish to his friends. On many occasions, Lattimer has been afraid of giving himself too completely. Thus, as he lies dying, he berates himself for the many instances in which his actions were marginal, for the inadequacy of his actions.

> You've bitched up and spoilt the people you wanted to love most, because always you were afraid of something. Afraid of what? This time it was dying. And the other times? I don't know. Having to really care

about them, maybe. Having to love them so the consequences didn't matter. I was afraid of that, of having to give too much. (*Voices,* 122)

Hearne claims that unless a man gives without rational reservation, a man must be afraid and alone, for in feeling and in the heart resides community; the heart reasons the community of men.

Community can issue also from camaraderie and shared participation in action. Like commitment, camaraderie becomes an oft-repeated motif in these novels, binding together many characters, irrespective of their racial or national origins or positions in the society. In *Voices under the Window*, there is the friendship between Mark Lattimer, brown—almost white—and the East Indian, Ted Burrow. There are bonds of friendship between Carl Brandt and Roy McKenzie in *Stranger at the Gate*, between Jojo Rygin and Oliver Hyde in *The Faces of Love*. Joint participation in any endeavor seems to negate the stratification of society, positing a possibility of cohesion.

Hearne does recognize the various strata making up the society of his novelistic island, Cayuna, which closely resembles Jamaica. To be sure, he does not give a deep sense of analytic historicity to the social elements which he presents. He describes these strata, often making them operative and essential for the release of action. But despite the representation of inequities in the social fabric of Cayuna, Hearne does not seem deeply preoccupied with them. To be sure, the various attitudinal motifs—commitment, camaraderie—have within them an intrinsic potential, offer with them a prognosis of change, of transformation. Yet Hearne doesn't posit through these attitudes any resolution of the existing social inequities.

In general, the class and caste of the principal characters of Hearne's novels are professional or island aristocracy. There are two kinds of aristocracy: those who have for generations lived and prospered on his island (for example, the Brandts), and those who are aristocratic in a spiritual sense because they exhibit those principled attitudes of friendship, commitment, and action (as, for example, Marcus Heneky). Those in the latter class are distinguished by strength of character, strength of purpose, which drives them on to almost superhuman feats of endurance and action.

Hearne presents the traditional aristocrats living in a certain splendor, where manners are genteel, meals are sumptuous. The owners of this type of household, with its "old polished wood" and "old, winking silver" (Hearne, *Stranger at the Gate*, 28), though living an active life, do not, of necessity, participate in the activities of the smaller settlers and farmers living around them. They extend a gracious yet still feudal generosity to the settlers. If we accept the statements of Roy in *Stranger at the Gate* and of Jojo Rygin in *The Faces of Love*, this manner of living does not harbor the seeds of regeneration but rather breeds its own decay. The regenerative force stemming from new approaches and more vital interaction is missing. The servants in this type of household are depersonalized by the very rhythms and seemingly generous attitudes of their masters. The principle of reconstruction is not operative. Some members of the old traditional families who, for one reason or another, have been bereft of their prosperity, become involved in an arduous attempt to amass money in order to regain the ease and assurance of landed gentry. In these novels, the new people of power are those like Jojo, men of action, strength, foresight, and ruthless awareness of the potential of certain areas of Cayuna: Jojo becomes a master builder and drives himself to establish control over vast tracts of land and sums of money; Rachel Ascom ruthlessly and dynamically uses her vast knowledge of the island's potential to amass her own fortune.

Those of another stratum of society represented by the professional man—lawyer or politician—achieve stature by their own resources and by championing the cause of the socially deprived. This type of man seems to be most conscious of the problem of the poor and is committed to social reforms through political action. However, Mark Lattimer and Roy McKenzie, characters who are examples of this type, are still not rooted in the people. They have come from, if not wealthy, at least comfortable and well-established households. Thus they, like many of Hearne's major characters, do not typify the people, but rather a few select and aristocratically inclined individuals.

The political dimension does enter at a certain level in these novels, but mostly as a background, the arena in which individuals act. In general, Hearne seems to be disillusioned with politics, with its efficacy, its practitioners, and its goals. In *Voices under the Window*, Lattimer, probably speaking for the author, still retains a certain belief in the possibilities of economic betterment for the poor through political action. There is obvious sympathy for the riots and the mob's actions, and, to the author and to Lattimer, their anger at the poverty of the mob's situation seems completely justifiable. In *Voices under the Window*, the conditions in which the mob lives are not simply described; they are integral to, and functional in, the opening action of the novel. In *The Faces of Love*, however, the lower level of this stratified society is simply presented, without functional, analytical penetration. In *Stranger at the Gate*, Hearne emphasizes the violence and the predatory nature of the people in this slum jungle. Implicitly, he is critical of the sordid meanness and grasping greed of the people who live in this area, and in the figure of Tiger Johnson we see the epitome of predatory meanness.

At times Hearne develops a sharp and incisive skepticism about the usefulness of political action. Not only is that cynicism applied to the smaller local dimension of Cayuna politics and society—on the personal level we are introduced, through the figure of Littleford, to political bribery and corruption—but that cynical view also extends into the larger dimension of political change through revolution. In *Stranger at the Gate*, Etienne, the political exile from a neighboring island, still preserves a high degree of idealism, justifying his past ruthlessness by emphasizing the idealistic nature of his goals. In *The Autumn Equinox*, Nicholas Stacey, perhaps again speaking for the author, cynically comments:

> I am only sorry that, at his age, Luis Corioso should still be wasting his energy and experience on this sort of revolution. Surely he must have learnt by now how ephemeral is the life of what passes for justice which such revolutions achieve. A change of governors is all that happens; no change of government. A brief intoxicating week-end in which those who have fought for truth and liberal catchwords use up their honesty and then the take-over bid by the realists. (100–101)

The political dimension is often related to problems of color and race in Cayuna, and Hearne is not idealistic about such problems, either. He states the equation between color and class and the snobbery that stems from the prevailing attitudes toward this equation:

> "Edna Hyde. She's never quite believed that she has a black daughter-in-law."
> "The old fool."
> "She won't be the only one . . . . People like Oliver and Andrew and me were always 'us' and people like Sybil were 'them'." (Hearne, *Land of the Living*, 26)

This equation means that the Black man remains at the bottom of the social and economic ladder unless he can rise through his own very powerful and concerted efforts.

> As in most crowds of this sort on the British islands, only a few of them were probably white, and nobody was black. They belonged to the subtle poker school, in which as far as a certain shade you were dealt much the same cards and played on equal chances. It was only the black man who had to try and draw a wild card of exceptional talent or wealth. If he could do that, then he could sit in on the game, too. (*Equinox*, 78)

The problem of color is a small part of the large complexity of race. In the minds of Marcus Heneky and his followers, the equation and its solution are obvious: The Black man is oppressed as a race; only the vision of Africa (more precisely Ethiopia) holds out any promise to him; rejection of the white man's rule becomes essential. Within the conflicts of the island, the many sects (obviously those that have been called the Rastafari) live apart from the ruling class, which is, in their equation, the white and brown peoples, and seek salvation in an almost bibical return to Israel and Ethiopia. In *Land of the Living,* Hearne presents these movements not as simply insular, nor as any intruding political tenor from neighboring islands; rather Marcus Heneky incarnates the deep spiritual and messianic bond which has been created in the minds of these many sects. It is obvious that Hearne sympathizes with them, presenting even the violent Son of Sheba as possessing a powerful, elemental total belief.

Hearne subordinates the role of society and political alignments to man's power to act as an individual, but the physical locale in which man acts enlarges the arena, extends the focus of action for his characters. For in his novels many of man's actions are performed outdoors. The landscape of Cayuna is painted in all its diversity and moods, captured at different moments, in bright or dark colors, at rest or when disturbed. However, Hearne notates man's intrusions on landscape, the inroads he makes: the land reddened by bauxite, the land explored for oil, the land under plantation. Here, even while painting for us the colors that mixed together, reveal the brightness of the landscape, Hearne deftly gives us a sense of the cultivation of the land. It is a functional description of the landscape of the island, the cultivation of crops being smoothly and unobtrusively worked in.

> From New Stamford down to the Weeping Women River it is all cattle grass, bush, or small fields of cash crops. Then, as you go across the iron bridge over the river, you see the bright, green, soft glow of banana trees filling the broad, high valley floor, receding ten miles down to the coast, and the grey road winding among the glossy, smooth stems and disappearing round a bend in the valley. (Hearne, *The Faces of Love,* 85)

Cayuna is a land of rivers and waters, of ravines and valleys, of mountains over which clouds, pink and orange or purple and dark, float and swirl. The sky over the island is vast, star-studded. Hearne also captures the sea in its various moods. He imbues his novels with a sense of water—in the woodlands or playing around the shores of the island. And the mountains are hewn out of the land as the author spirals his landscape upward. Hearne's painting of the Cayuna landscape is impressionistic; he catches it at all times of the day and night, noting its shade and color tones, its various moods. The noonday heat, which so many West Indian novelists depict, brings with it lassitude or the harsh glitter from the direct overhead sun:

> It was really hot now, with the sun climbing to the top of a pale, hard sky. There was the midday feeling of stillness, the slowing down and rest. (*Stranger,* 34)

In the islands, afternoons and early evenings bring their own respite from the harsh midday sun and offer the promise of cooler moments before the swift fall of night:

> In the late afternoons, sometimes, you sit on the terrace of the little cafe overlooking the gorge with bright sun bringing out the gold in the lawns of the Gardens and long streamers of mist filling the high forested valleys between the peaks and the mountains going purple as the mist thickens. (*The Faces*, 50)

Night in the islands may be jet black with myriad silver stars, or may be "washed with silver under it" (*Equinox*, 60) by the huge moon. Hearne's sensitivity toward the landscape of his island and his love of it get deeper and deeper. The appeal to sensory stimulation from nature is lush and more detailed in the later than in the earlier novels; so are his descriptions of interiors, his stress on the sensory details of an action, and his elaboration of the appearances of his characters. This elaboration of material phenomena often provides us with an almost baroque canvas: Adjectives and images are splashed all over and saturate the canvas to the point where at times one loses sight of the central image, the high point of relief in the picture, so that Hearne seems more adept at capturing the physical and the sensory than at conveying psychological nuances. For instance, in an early scene in *Voices under the Window*, where Mark Lattimer lies mortally wounded, Hearne's indulgence in elaboration of detail vitiates the novelistic mood. For when a man lies near death, what purpose does it serve to dwell on such minor details as "the cheap, soft iron key in the lock"? (*Voices*, 211). Of course, it may be claimed that the author is attempting to give us a total sense of the poverty of the room in which Lattimer lies dying, yet doubtlessly, we lose sight of the essential happening: a man dying on a bed. On the other hand, at times Hearne's elaboration of detail, seizing every single action, paints a total picture. For instance, his description of a man getting out of bed in *Stranger at the Gate* (9–10) captures the essentials of the scene.

Hearne often notes the smells of bodies, of clothing, of various kinds of interiors, of the earth, of food, indeed of almost anything that has a smell. In describing the interior of Nicholas Stacey's shop, he extracts all the various odors that commingle:

> Standing at the back of the store, you felt little eddies and surges of scent on your face: the tough smell of the saddles, the coarse, clean odour from the sails and rope, the stifling sweetness of ginger and the heavy, new smell of tweeds and silks and shoes. (*Equinox*, 63)

We get the "heavy exciting smell of tropical earth freshly watered just before sunset" (*Equinox*, 42), the smells of flowers and coffee. Foods and the delights they offer the senses are motifs which occur very frequently in Hearne's novels. We see, too, the deep sense of luxuriance as Hearne's characters sink back into sensuous enjoyment, for Hearne always, perhaps too often, tries to capture the deepest and the most sensuous experiences enjoyed by his characters.

Thus it is that a sense of the superlative—superlative of sensory reactions—lends a grand dimension to Hearne's work. Of course, one may always ask whether this vision of the largeness of things ever takes into consideration a sense of the average. The continuous emphasis on superlatives seems excessive as we enter the land of the never-nevers:

Never in my life would I see anybody as clearly. (*Equinox*, 67)

I had never seen such a ravaged battlefield of shame and arrogance on any other face before. (*Equinox*, 161)

Yet the stylistic excesses, magnification of the sensory, the detail, are vital to Hearne's vision as a novelist. As an idealist, he wants his characters to feel deeply and experience intensely. All his larger-than-life average characters want to reach to the center of perceptions and feelings. Thus, Eleanor wants to be deeply seen:

Sitting beside him, I want to do something to make him see me. Really see me . . . as I see him. He is so bright and definite it almost hurts to be near him. (*Equinox*, 80)

The intensity of feeling often stems from reflected excellence in the other:

And to me, "kicks" meant being able to see Eleanor again; being able to enter that new, tremendous world where the face and touch of only one other was all you could experience, all you needed. Thinking of her, I suddenly felt limp with happiness so intense that I couldn't grasp it all at once. (*Equinox*, 190)

Hearne seems principally interested in the actions of strong people, devoting little attention to the mediocre.

This total sense of the overpowering or the large or the intense finds its finest expression in Hearne's depiction of characters. It is essential for us to realize that Hearne always seizes upon the exceptional physical feature of each of his subjects. Clearly in these physical traits may be isolated a transformative element, which may serve as a catalyst for a measure of change. For indeed he does not limit his selection of exceptional physical traits only to his major characters or only to people of the upper class. Democratically, he endows even many of his workmen, fishermen, and settlers with powerful physical qualities. Jackson, a boatman, was a huge man, big enough so that even Carl always felt little beside him, and he moved with the shambling, fluid sureness of a great ape. His size too, was all bone; the flesh was so thin over the rough cut, gigantic frame that it was stretched like the skin of a drum; and even the muscles which bunched if he so much as lifted his hand were lean and flexible like hose-pipe. (*Stranger*, 225)

That Jackson shambles and looks somewhat like an ape in no way detracts from the impression of power and strength which he conveys. In *The Autumn Equinox*, despite Pierre-Auguste's gauche appearance and build, he is also presented at his most graceful:

Rowing is the only thing he does without fuss. It is . . . with one long, lovely movement like the end of a whip, with the blades biting out two absolutely equal whirl-pools and the boat surging into the thick of the water. There is never any jerk or unevenness when Pierre-Auguste rows: it is just one long wonderful flow of power, with the oar blades going like dancers' feet. (22)

That Jojo Rygin "came across the road with his fast, light stride his toes turned in slightly, as he had always walked, like a bear" (*The Faces*, 84), is not a purely accidental observation, for Hearne always emphasizes the bestial, the animal quality that his characters exhibit in action or in manner or in appearance. The examples are many:

Her body, as I held it against me . . . had the unbelievable delicacy and warmth of life you can feel throbbing beneath the plumage of a little bird. (*Land*, 27–28)

The old man's soft face was troubled. He looked like a large broad-faced fish that has sensed a change in the climate of its tank. (*Stranger*, 50)

Often the animal image becomes a representation of an essential quality inherent both in the animal and in the human. By this correlation of spheres the author achieves a further elaboration of detail suggestive of a cohering of realms and regions.

In his use of the heraldic image, Hearne brings about another correlation between spheres of reality suggestive of a linkage, a continuity between these spheres. Here the landscape extends outward, achieving through this extension a religious symbology.

The coconut palms were scoured by the little rain of the night, rank after rank of bronze pillars curving round the bay like a temple. (*Equinox*, 263)

Here man's form and face acquire a mystical representation.

For a moment, the face of Marcus Heneky formed itself before me, raw, declamatory, as starkly obsessed as a face in a cathedral window. (*Land*, 17–18)

The straightforward statement of the "what" of the characters in *Voices under the Window* and *Stranger at the Gate* undergoes modifications until the "what" and the "why" begin to merge in his later novels, *The Faces of Love* and *The Autumn Equinox*. In a character like Marcus Heneky, the what and the why, skillfully blended, form a portrait in which Heneky's motivation can be perceived springing from instinct that guides action, instinct rooted in a framework larger than the purely material or sensual. Instinct, motivation, and action create desire and merge in the evolution of a character. The sympathetic contract between author and character has indeed taken place.

To be sure, this is not the case with all of Hearne's characters nor even with many of them; the actions of characters such as Andrew Fabrieus, Rachel Ascom, Jojo Rygin, Eleanor Stacey, Roy McKenzie, and Mark Lattimer are seen from the outside, but in a few characters, such as Heneky and Nicholas Stacey, we find an inner interplay and analysis in Hearne's characterization, a penetration of the smoke screen that often obscures the real man. He moves away from statement and presentation of action to interpretation and penetration of motive.

Yet, in spite of Hearne's idealization of gesture and figure, the polity of Cayuna in its principal social manifestations of race, class, and color does not yet achieve that coherence consequent on the fragmentation of the personality or on the dislocation of an oppressive and continuing racial-class domination. Thus two advocates of possibility and coherence, indeed two visionaries of that possibility, Mark Lattimer and Marcus Heneky, are both struck down by men who have accepted and hold to a vision of reality which though seemingly fanatical may contain pure notions, pure though static notions of race and color.

In Marcus Heneky's attempt to divest himself of a purist and intense vision of independence for African peoples, he's struck down by one of his disciples, Ralston, son of the Queen of Sheba, who intones:

"The sword of Zion find two traitors to strike down. 'I have pursued mine enemies, and overtaken them . . . . I have wounded them that they were not able to rise.'" (*Land*, 278)

Here Ralston is driven by a certainty, motivated by an unswerving passion, by the urge toward total rejection of compromise with things of Babylon. Indeed he has accepted and internalized Marcus Heneky's earlier statement about racial distinctiveness:

"No man can ride two horses. . . .

. . . "History dig a gulf between us . . . an' it don't fill in yet. Not yet." (*Land,* 248)

But Heneky's statement, his purist position on race, seems to be tinged with a personal sense of regret, regret at a seemingly unchanging historical social condition:

Like the glint of a bright accoutrement seen for the merest registration of the retina in a wall of forest, a flicker of what might have been kindness, regret, liking or perhaps pity passed across his face. (*Land,* 248)

This manifestation of regret, underscoring a basic humanistic vision of reality, does not permit Marcus Heneky to carry to its ultimate conclusion his cohering vision of a social reality. At the point of severing himself away from this vision of an ultimate social reality that would empower his race, Marcus Heneky is cut down before he can betray that vision. For though Marcus Heneky's actions have seemed to be unswerving and though he has gathered around him a large band of trusting followers, Sons of Sheba, who all came to him to replenish a concept of themselves, Marcus Heneky himself has not totally accepted that unswerving position at his death. An inner debate still seems to be ongoing. That total liberating passion is not quite assured:

He looked as if he had died in the middle of some absorbing conversation and was holding himself still as though to surprise an echo meant only for the living. (277)

That consuming passion is clearly manifested in Ralston's actions, as it is in the statements of the Rasta:

"Dis land an' de whole eart' belong to de white man, an' de black is his slave . . . . Our God will come . . . . Black an' shinin' an' terrible. . . . Africa's children will turn and rule . . . . It is written . . . each colour will have its day of glory an' dat de black shall be de last an' for evermore. . . . All nation shall bow down to Africa and to de Emperor of Ethiopia an' to his people . . . ." (49–50)

Here this Rastafarian vision of future political order is lessened by no inner personal debate. It is clear, unequivocal, and harsh. It is this clarity of purpose and harsh execution of that purpose that Mark Lattimer, in *Voices under the Window,* ascribes to his assailant. To Mark Lattimer, so persistent and so endemic to Cayuna is the question of racism and its corollary, racial enmity, that he views the assailant's action, not as a result of his ganja smoking, but as a consequence of this historical racial dynamic:

"I'm just the sort of fair, almost white, that chap has wanted to kill all his life. He's hated me and been afraid of me more than anything. Just as I've hated him and been afraid of him and his colour more than anything else." (*Voices*, 27)

Clearly Lattimer's statement points to the coincidence of race and class, exploitation and suffering, that brutal coincidence, that brutal coming together of races at the point of superior, inferior. The man who cuts down Mark Lattimer is anonymous, depersonalized, random—"a man came out of the crowd suddenly" (18).

This very indefiniteness, this depersonalization, however, accentuates the subsequent action, underscores a latent racial enmity and class hostility pervading Hearne's Cayuna polity. This polity, though basically idealized by Hearne, is still devoid of a social and racial coherence so necessary for the creation of a new presence. Many of the characters come laden with historical and social personalities, perhaps ordaining a separateness. The whole social canvas seems shot through with indelible stretch marks separating groups along color and class lines, lines that seem to indicate there is, as Hearne stresses, a correlation between color (Black) and one's position within the Cayuna social hierarchy.

In these novels, there are many statements which, though not functional to the action of novels, become backdrops to some of the relationships of the personages. Indeed a motif of separateness recurs, though mainly as statements, rarely through deep analysis of the searing problematic consequences, implications, of such attitudes. This endemic class distinction is replicated by Hearne at several levels, even though in *Land of the Living*, Oliver and Andrew have seemingly cut across class and color lines. Yet in the main, this cutting across is not acceptable, hardly customary, still accidental not universal. In *Land of the Living*, Stefan is portrayed as being regenerated by Bernice; it is from her that he claims to learn the purity of love and the generosity of total giving. Yet despite his close call with the Jewish Holocaust he is unable to cut across these barriers of color, class, and education:

> She prepared me as carefully for the demands of love as we prepare a child for the adult world . . . . I felt a throb of guilt for the inevitable break . . . . the difference in our ages, the fatal inferiority of her education, the very attitudes of our society—would gnaw the foundations of . . . something permanent and public. (Land, 90–91)

Here the reaction of Stefan, the sensualist, the seeker after authenticity, offers no regenerative perception, no cohering vision of new possibilities, and like Nicholas Stacey and Carl Brandt, indeed like the social polity of Cayuna, he remains fixed, his attitude seemingly ordained. The "dem"—the privileged—remain in unregenerative fixed and unchanging sociopolitical reality. Carl Brandt's life is a "familiar pattern of . . . bright flowers, airy dark-polished rooms and intimate relationship" (*Stranger*, 108). Nicholas Stacey and his circle, too, have all the stamp of careless privilege and unchanging, seemingly gratuitous ease and comfort:

> When I walked on to the veranda at the Staceys' it was like entering a cage of old eagles perched in a tight circle of grey arrogance . . . . I remember Nicholas Stacey and his four friends . . . . old, creased faces . . . the bleakness in the face that comes when you have been assured too long of what you are. (*Equinox*, 140)

These are the "dem" distinct from the poor, the Dungle dwellers differentiated from the class that they serve. To be sure, Hearne's representation of the physical reality of the Dungle has all the vividness so characteristic of his descriptive talents:

> It was densely populated . . . . These shelters were made of old kerosene tins, motorcar chassis . . . and rusty sheets of zinc . . . . There wasn't any water except for two stand pipes on the edge of the area . . . . it smelt bad . . . the sweetish stink of bodies which don't get enough food . . . .
> . . . people quarreling and laughing . . . . a lot of light, but fitful . . . glare and heat to shadow unexpectedly . . . . men, sitting in front of shacks . . . drifting . . . ragged. (*Stranger*, 74–75)

It is this poverty, such social surroundings, that gives rise to the riots in the novel *Voices under the Window*. Yet perhaps because of Hearne's idealization of his social reality, the corrosive effects are not presented in all their inner dynamic overtones, in all of their essentiality. Indeed Hearne in his novels does not come to grips with the oft-repeated motifs of poverty, race, and class. His idealized vision of reality, his notions of commitments and involvement, prohibit such a presentation. He accepts and, again with bold lines, presents also the racial admixtures that give graphic particularity to the physiognomies of the people of Cayuna, "disturbing mixtures—not black, not brown, not any conventional formula of stirred colours" (*Land*, 41). Yet this biological admixture, such an ethnic cohering, this racial intermingling visible in the outward form and mien of the people of Cayuna, seems not as yet to have realized itself in the social and political reality. Hearne underscores the harshness of poverty by ascribing a historical and continuing generosity of spirit to some less privileged people of Cayuna. Like the biological admixture, like the seemingly monolithic nature of privilege, here, too, Hearne idealizes "brutal and gluttonous" history, the condition of poverty as having "nourished a peculiar gentleness and habit of charity among the humble and obscure" (*Equinox*, 239).

Here, then, environment becomes a phenomenon. A social condition is idealized and made into continuous history, yet to Sonny, the heavy, chocolate-brown face in the Stacey household, generosity deriving from privilege awakens no gratitude, has no intrinsic claim to respect, but instead should spur the recipient to change, ultimately negate the donor's position of privilege, to reject his charity and to seek for one's own selfhood:

> "Dere is two people in dis country. One stay like me an' one stay like dem . . . . If you want somet'ing den you mus' tek it for yourself. Like dem have always done . . . . What him give me couldn't buy shoes to put 'pon Eleanor's foot . . . . der oder servants, tell me say, I must be grateful . . . . Grateful don' bring respect . . . . don' put clothes on your back . . . .. It's de grateful ones who work an' buy dat for oders." (*Equinox*, 210–211)

Clearly Sonny has come to the ultimate realization that only with a transformative action will any social polity undergo fundamental change and achieve a holistic reality.

In John Stewart's novel, *Last Cool Days*, Marcus, the chief protagonist, also comes to this realization and, through a liberating though violent act, achieves the fragmentation of his personality that brings with it a holistic presence.

Marcus Shephard, through a brutal, yet vital and necessary act, transforms his historical reality, shatters the binary relationship between himself and Anthony, symbol and presence of white dominance. It is a liberating act that brings with it freedom; the self fragmented from a symbiotic intercourse achieves a wholeness, attains to purity. He hears the warden's pronouncement

> as only a pure man receives his challenges—with neither fear nor visions of glory; with neither a wish to die, nor a wish to conquer, but simply a recognition that he was himself committed to an unchangeable shape, an immutable action that might be deflected but never denied. (Stewart, *Last Cool Days*, 35)

The feeling of purity is clarified in the brilliance of electric charges that momentarily brings Marcus closer to his fellow prisoners at the height of a storm.

> [They] continued making wagers as to which streak of lightning, which thunder blast, would spell the end to Carrera . . . . They were all in prison dress now . . . [Marcus] was in prison dress too . . . . he had come

nearer; though not so near as he had come to feeling his own purity, the purity of an elemental streak of lightning . . . . Marcus thought that really, the other prisoners had come a little nearer to being pure like him. (33)

Later the sense of impending danger, the immediacy of participating in an action fraught with peril, ushers in a feeling of freedom, of being disconnected from his immediate reality. Yet this very sense of being disconnected unifies him, is a spiritual center devoid of materiality, yet fixed and seemingly assured. He, along with prisoners on the rock-island jail of Carrera, is swept up in the excitement of a storm and its liberating force. They move, chanting to their confrontation with the night of storm:

> "Ride, ride," they cheered. . . . Marcus was . . . intoxicated with the
> danger of the moment, his own sense of facing it with no qualm, no hope,
> no reserve. (35)

Yet unlike his fellow prisoners, who hang on to some "will," wanting "to survive and be free" (34), at this point in his life, Marcus Shephard, having been sentenced to ninety-nine years for his killing of Anthony, feels no compunction about dying but rather anticipates it: "He was happy to be in the storm, and took excitement still in the danger around him" (39).

That Marcus Shephard has attained to a condition of inner peace which allows him to accept the embrace of the storm and move toward his apotheosis with the sea. His final intercourse with waters of the Dragon's Mouth takes him down to a quick death that sweeps away the baggage of imposed history and dominance of the "overseer type" and introduces the mating with his own particular rooting: "Marcus never came up. He went down with the first impact, and was sucked under forever" (40). Marcus disappears into the sea that for him is

> a connection between the several stages and states of myself that were
> scattered about the world . . . in more or less of a triangle from West
> Africa to Europe to America. I longed to gather up these various deposits
> myself—for I was but a shadow without them—and the sea was the only
> avenue. (68)

Thus through the dematerialization of his social and historical reality, through an initial fragmentation of a historical self, he achieves wholeness, continuity, and moves toward an ingathering of his dispirited soul selves. It is this movement toward an ingathering of the self, the methods by which he breaks out of his symbiotic and throttling relationship with Anthony, that constitute the theme and action of *Last Cool Days*.

When he finally kills Anthony, it is as a result of an accumulation of incidents where the principal preoccupation is race and that colonial relationship between white and black. The killing is but the unshackling of the chains that have bound Marcus at every turn and movement of his body. Only with the killing does he attain an inwardness, a silence, a state of quiet peace. For him peace is both death and life. It is an assurance, an instinct visceral to the condition of freedom, indispensable to the wholing of the fragmented personality.

Peace holds with it a promise of presence:

> "Peace is death," had been one of his grandfather's constant aphorisms, but even as a child Marcus knew the reverse was nearer the truth. Peace was life . . . . Peace was living in the full knowledge of your fate . . . . Grandfather was afraid of death, but Marcus wasn't afraid of peace. (23–24).

He has yearned for such peace, he's wished for its silence. Even while being sentenced by the judge in the packed courtroom he moves into a self-introspection, protective and assured, and, when the judge says ninety-nine years, he "felt a great relief . . . . For ninety-nine years he would have silence, and perhaps peace" (18–19). Paradoxically, then, jail for Marcus is not circumscription of his spatial reality, but rather an extending of the self into a space wherein there is no need to self-destruct through feelings of envy or jealousy, nor a need for vengeance against the part of himself that has to be fragmented, which has to be destroyed. And the rendezvous with time and his destiny has been ordained, prescribed:

> Long before Anthony, Hille or I had been realized in seed it had been determined precisely how our lives should flourish or bend in the moment of that meeting. (172)

But the conjunction, the coming together, of Marcus, Anthony, and Hille produces a period of nonpeace, of unbearable jealousies and ambiguous intercourse, which seems to deny "that vulnerable, corruptible but inescapably unique oneness glimmering through the vision of reprieve. No peace" (172).

There is no peace within his relationship with the white woman, Hille. To be sure, there are moments of happiness, periods of shared erotic delights, pleasurable memories of physical togetherness "little leapings of joy on the inside" (178) at the the sight of the other. But most of the encounters between Marcus and Hille, most of the momentary happiness, seem always marred by a social nonpeace, the result of racial bigotry, intolerance, and at times naked hostility. In a quiet moment of intimacy in which their hands touch affectionately, the mood is shattered.

We knew what together meant . . . . Until four brawny sailors trooped their way up onto the verandah from the bar . . . . Yankees from the nearby naval base . . . . "Back in Carolina, do you know what we would do . . . in Illinois—take her out and feed her to the boars!" . . . our fingers fell apart. (107)

Similarly, epithets and slurs follow them as they walk through the streets of Port-of-Spain, slurs hurled by the nationals. Neither is the relationship accepted by the director of the orphanage:

"This nonsense you're carrying on with Miss Hille has got to stop. Do you realize what will happen if her father hears of this? He is a rich man. His daughter is teaching here. You know our Home is supported by Charity. Put your mind to work, man. What will he think if he hears about her going here and there with you?" (100–101)

So much of the relationship, then, must be surreptitious. Not only does the relationship suffer from the external social forces impinging on the two, but the very inner racial texture they both bring to the relationship seems unnatural, unwholesome—in many instances, unhealthy. Hille gushes over Black native beauty, evincing all the stereotypic reactions which, even while appearing laudatory, in their essence are contemptuous. Everything in this landscape is new to her—and beautiful, from the canefields to

the women—not so dried as the men, some even audaciously fat, bloated. Draw-string skirts hugged tight beneath their breasts falling away over fertile and tragic wombs like voluminous mysteries . . . . "How beautiful they are!" she said. (165–166)

Clearly it is this "beauty and the beast" complex which drives her to enter into social and physical intercourse with Marcus, defending herself against the bigoted, overt hostility of the white sailors. Though it is to anger her attackers that she asks, "How come black men are so free? . . . How come black men have such beautiful, free bodies?" (108), these sentiments are rooted in the racial ethos from which she has come. She makes a distinction between the "regular niggers" in the town where she grew up and the "real black men and women who were so different from the niggers at home" (105).

To her, then, Marcus is somewhat of a curiosity, perhaps somewhat of a stud. Ultimately and ironically, Hille's penchant for Blackness, the sense of animality underlying her curiosity, is brutally portrayed and harshly realized in the village from which Marcus came. Her high point about Blacks parallels Marcus's growing awareness.

Hille came along, and somehow it seemed wrong when she saw so much to love and be proud of in my village . . . . Once they start loving they love everything, from man to cockroach without distinction. (136)

Marcus is caught at the intersection of history and self, trapped at a crossroads of paths whose turnings all abut onto ends of racial injustice, disharmony, dominance, and inequality. But Marcus forces a way out of the cul-de-sac into which his grandfather walked with unchallenging dignity, wearing a mask of acquiescence to an aberrant, fragmented social order.

Behind his eyes Grandfather had it still, . . . behind his gleaming eyes . . . his self-assurance, his confidence, his manhood . . . . It was reassuring . . . to know that dignity and self-confidence were integral parts of my own make-up. (52)

The prevailing social order is relentless, continuously ruled over by generations of Red Ones coming to a cancerous head in the figure and presence of the overseer. Marcus's grandfather knows implicitly that the social order in the village is based on continuous slavery, on unending subservience, "forced . . . labouring in the fields" (84).

But for his grandfather, Marcus would have been orphaned by the flight of his parents—his mother and his artist guitar-playing father—from an intolerable condition of servitude, a dead-end, demeaning life. And even his grandfather, though he has maintained some dignity, has led a hard life.

I, [Grandfather] was determined, would have the opportunity to write a book of truth, the likes of which he would himself have written had he not been forced to spend so many of his years labouring in the fields, and were he wiser than to have spent so many others chasing his hands beneath the skirts of various women. (84)

To the growing Marcus, the replicated symbol of superiority, of unchallenged, of, indeed, unbridled authority, is white, principally the overseer who cares little for the lives of even the children. Marcus realizes that even the undertaker, paralyzed as he is, is

a white man without any legs who sits in his parlour all day looking like a giant from the waist up . . . . It is good I cannot hide from myself the way he attempts to hide from his. (43–44)

All the replicas of this symbol are portrayed as from some unwholesome culture, if from any culture at all, in images at once unlovely and creatural. Even Hille is unattractive and creatural: "She walked like a bird—mincing, pigeon-toed steps, her shanks angled forward, slight points at the knee and rear" (178).

From his boyhood Marcus has realized that the only way out of the social order and cul-de-sac in which his forebears—grandparents and parents—and he, too, have been mired and imprisoned, is to "smash" in the face of the living representation of this class of people: the overseer, his constant bugaboo: "the fear through which his father ruled mine was already alive in me but that I was determined to fight it off!" (61). The first encounter between Marcus, the son of the laborer-descendant of slaves, and Anthony, son of the overseer, descendant of white privilege, is demeaning and traumatic for Marcus, and serves as a catalyst and unending goad to his need for revenge. To that first encounter Marcus brings an initial naivete and generosity, while Anthony and his brother prove to be shrewd exploitative natures, already warped and socialized by a degrading stereotypic value system and perception: "Father says you people spend all your money in rumshops" (47). This encounter leaves a wound so deep, so continually reopened by subsequent encounters, so easily infected, that only with bloodletting or an infusion of blood can it be healed.

> White blood. Rage. White blood. To feel my knuckles into a real redface. Feel his flesh tear. Hear him groan in pain. I had to do that. Nothing else would do. Dream inherited from my race, nothing else would do. (48)

Any and every social encounter and relationship in which Marcus thinks that he has been bested by Anthony makes the wound fester even more, increasing Marcus's need for an atoning vengeance. His need for revenge becomes an obsession presented at times with melodramatic fervor, always feeding on every incident deriving from a violent love-hate relationship between himself and Anthony. He envies Anthony: the shape of his head, the color of his hair; he is jealous, too, of Anthony's ability to serve in the war, to join the military. That Anthony rides in his father's car, heedless of Marcus's presence, after they've cycled from school together makes Marcus seethe with resentment, a resentment that is echoed when Marcus is rejected by the servant Cleo in favor of Anthony, who can provide her with valuable gifts and money. Cleo even brags to Marcus of how she benefits from Anthony's higher status:

> "And what will you bring me? . . . I can get all I want . . . from your friend . . . . Want to see what your friend brought last week?" (95)

Here, then, at the level of social intercourse, Marcus, while envying Anthony his largess, suffers from his inability to provide an equal largess.

Later Anthony's relationship with Betty, who carries his child, further intensifies Marcus's jealous and vengeful attitude. In a scene that anticipates the final encounter between Anthony and Marcus, Marcus's attempts to pull Anthony out of his car fail and terminate in "The white man hit him! The white man hit him!" (150). In a scene streaked with the color red—red of blood, red of Betty's dress—Marcus is unable to control his anger, which borders on madness: "Tonight you acting like a madman. What got into you? ... You should know better than to fight Anthony—he can kill" (153).

But the conflict situations between Marcus and Anthony, the evident rivalry that seems to be at the level of the personal, derive from a larger historical context and are deeply rooted in the pathological socioeconomic phenomenon of slavery and its corollary, colonialism. Marcus and Anthony are but players in a larger, more endemically violent contest. Even as Anthony has inherited certain attitudes from his father and his forebears, so, too, Marcus's self-perceptions derive orally from his grandfather and experientially from historical documentation, his exposure to the social reality and, ironically, from the library of a white reverend father.

> I am grateful to him for the other people I found in his library, those
> whom he never invited me to know .... I remember well the first day
> I laid hands on Raynal. (62–63)

Marcus's voyagings through the library of the reverend father deepen his awareness of race as a factor in the universal flow and movement of events.

From his grandfather, who ingrained in him a deep sense of dignity and self-worth, he not only realizes the need for education but he also gains access to landscape through the voyages of his grandfather's searchings:

> "Someday you're going to get the chance I missed, the chance to write
> a book that tells the truth. I'll be dead and gone, but remember what I
> say. You can't write the truth if you don't see it. A man's got to see first.
> Learn what these schoolbooks say, but don't let that blind you ...."
> I did discover that many of the things I knew or seemed to know began
> and ended right there inside me ... if I could ever make that inside
> knowing known on the outside, that would be a truth. (87)

Clearly to bring about this association, this cohering of the inner self and the outer society, would mitigate the disjuncture between external personality and inner presence. Located in such a binary association, in such a cohering, is the transformative vision that in its essence, even while it minimizes the influence of the external proscriptive societal mode, would also change it.

Like all the principal characters in this chapter and in Chapter 7, Marcus attempts to locate the center of possibility would bear witness to a cohering truth and sanction a transformative vision. Though his act is a liberating one, bringing about the fragmentation of his own personality, leading also to the rejection of the imposed personality, that act is mostly personal and does not have the larger societal ramifications of actions by some other characters. But through the cogency of its liberating force, the act unerringly leads to Marcus's movement into presence, into selfhood.

CHAPTER 7

The Rootings of Self:
The Adventure of Communality,
The Shape of Myth

Holy be the white head of a Negro,
Sacred be the black flax of a black child.
Holy be
The golden down
That will stream in the waves of the winds
And will thin like dispersing cloud,
Holy be
Heads of Chinese hair
Sea calm sea impersonal
Deep flowering of the mellow and traditional.
Heads of people fair
Bright shimmering from the riches of their species;
Heads of Indians
With feeling of distance and space and dusk:
Heads of wheaten gold,
Heads of peoples dark
So strong so original:
All of the earth and the sun!

George Campbell, "Holy," *Caribbean Voices*

I turn to the histories of men and the lives of the peoples.
I examine the shower of sparks the wealth of the dreams.
I am pleased with the glories and sad with the sorrows
Rich with the riches, poor with the loss.
From the nigger yard of yesterday I come with my burden.
To the world of to-morrow I turn with my strength.

Martin Carter, "I Come from the Nigger Yard," *Poems of Succession*

And so, the principal characters in this movement, this "I going home," journey through dynamic space and ritual of time, seeking an essentiality of being. All undergo in their journeyings toward selfhood an ultimate transformation inducing a new relationship of hero to his vital space. Space, then, achieves a ritual presence, symbol.

The whole modality posits a motion indigenizing and cohering realities, symbol engendering myth. Personality vitalized by indigenous rhythms shades into presence. The fragmented self, the new presence modifying its ethos, coheres, accedes to wholeness, signifying, indeed sanctifying a Caribbean mythos.

All is ushered in as the characters begin their runnings into a season of adventure, begin, through a dramatic, rhythmical coursing into ritual space, up the secret ladder, into the palace of the peacock.

In *Season of Adventure*, George Lamming offers us a prognosis of the potential inherent in the concordance, in the rhythms of the steel band. The music is indigenous, is vital, and becomes a medium of resurrection, the conjurer of dead presences.

> But the music was there, loud as gospel to a believer's ears. It was the music of Steel Drums, hard, strident and clear: a muscled current of sound swept high over the *tonelle*. The women's voices followed, chanting a chorus of faiths that would soon astonish the night. They sang in order to resurrect the dead. (Lamming, *Season of Adventure*, 11)

It is a music calling forth the most instinctive emotions. Lamming ascribes to this music origins that spool back into first beginnings, into a mythic space resident in the waters of the Caribbean sea.

> It seemed this music had always been there, immortal as the origin of water swinging new soundings up from the sea's dark tomb of noise. (19)

They are drums that summon the most spontaneous reactions. This music summons the most fundamental reactions, calling, urging, transforming the immediate, liberating a deep, essential rhythm and movement.

> [The women] had lost control over their passions. The bodies seemed to stretch beyond this moment of the dance. Perhaps the gods were there, waiting for the dance to prove their presence in the *tonelle*. (29)

It is subliminal music mediating the spirit consciousness of the young.

> The child was wide awake. It seemed she had seen everyone and everything inside the *tonelle*. The dance was an instinct which her feet had learnt. (29)

Impelled by this music, Fola moves into her season of adventure, into her search for her own essential unprivileged presence.

This search for an essential presence ordains the movement and trajectory of the main protagonists of the novels in this chapter, as they move through their adventures, as they seek their indigenous rootings, as they venture through generational history into the landscape of the palace of the peacock. But the season of adventure is so recent:

> As a child treads soft in new school shoes, and a man is nervous who knows his first night watch may be among thieves; so the rhythms are not sure, but their hands must be attentive: and so recent is the season of adventure, so fresh from the miracle of their triumph, the drums are guarding the day: the drums must guard the day. (367)

Thus the search for an essential presence, the venturing into an evolving indigenous landscape, is fraught with dramatic uncertainty climaxed by a tragic regenerative fragmentation. The bands have come home, their music, their rhythms, changed but triumphal, still pure in their ultimate regenerative cohesion.

At a high point in her transformation at one of the stages along the road to otherness, to that vitalistic future of essential being, Fola and "other than," her other self, perceive a symbolic change in the relationship between the new moon and the old.

> Under the wide vault of sky, the old moon had lost half of its face where the new moon emerged into a dubious splendour of yellow light, hard and clear. There was no subtlety of difference as the moons exchanged their vigilance. The new moon was thrusting up through little clots of blood which mottled half of the old moon's face. It was the only sign of movement in the sky. (243)

Here a dramatic cohering of realities between the human and the elemental is established. The transformation in Fola's essential character is reflected in her perception of the moon's face.

At the confluence of the old personality and the new presence at that dramatic intersection of choice, blood markings, scarifications of new possibilities register, and an absorption akin to death results: "The new moon looked like bone, exact and without any of the shadows which were closing over the old moon's retreat" (243). Fola's choice has indeed propelled her, after an intense momentary hesitation, from a past order of privilege into a new chosen self, into a new self-directed space of freedom. Putting an end to the authority/father figure Piggott has as its corollary Fola's yearning for her matrix root, a seeking for an instinctual natural bond between mother and daughter. Uncontrollably, Fola summons her mother's presence.

She cared for no one but her mother. Some old and dormant bond of blood had come alive . . . . She wanted to coil herself to an infant's size and nestle calm and forgetful in her mother's arms . . . . She was whispering through a salt, white froth of spit and tears: "Aggie . . . Aggie . . . Aggie . . ." (282)

At this juncture there is none of that paradoxical antipathy, that festering enmity, that has characterized Fola's relationship with her mother, Agnes, divesting it of any filial affection. There is only a hypersensitive instinctive need. This hyperemotional reaction seems to dramatize the culmination of each particular stage in Fola's quest for a new awareness, for a distinctive presence, for otherness. This emotional condition is so recurrent, so typifies her character delineation, that often, even as that character delineation is so carefully orchestrated, it takes on a quality of insubstantiality, teeters on the brink of feverish unreality.

Yet acceding to the insubstantial, denuding of the self, are prerequisites to any mystical experience, so Fola's search for her biological father takes on—with all of its attendant dynamic fervor, its dramatic emotionalism—many of the elements of a mystic voyaging. Further, since Fola's voyaging necessitates a dramatic rupture with her position of privilege—since, too, her adventures demand a loosening of habit, a destruction of a past perception, a fragmentation of self—each stage of this voyaging, each step of her adventure, must be accompanied by feverish, high-pitched, and dramatic tensions, must result from states of hyperemotionalism derived from a heightened sensibility.

From the very beginning of her season of adventure, Fola's search is fraught with tension, heavy with paradoxical relationships. As witness to the Ceremony of the souls, she begins to evince uncontrollable states of emotion.

Fola had lived in the shadow of two terrors: hypnosis and the sight of rats. She thought of both and the dancing made her shudder. (25)

She has ironically been led to a ritual observation of her own mythic folk roots not by a mere stranger, but by a stranger of mixed European ancestry, himself in search of rooting, of his heritage. Charlot, the foreigner, quests analytically as historian for self, for group identification. Considered white in San Cristobal, he uses Fola as a guinea pig, seeing in her a "perfect example of his own displacement."

"I come because there are things that remind me of myself," he said. . . .

"But what's it about the island to remind you of yourself?" she asked. . . .

"My father was a Spanish Jew," he said, "my mother some part Chinese and half French. I was born by chance in West Africa, but learnt all that I know in England." (26–27)

Thus Fola unwittingly arrives at the first stage of what is in essence a spiritual communal quest as a guinea pig, to be clinically observed by this stranger, her teacher, with whom she has an undefined, ambiguous relationship. The foreigner insists on locating the roots of Fola's being within the spirit and movement of the people in the *tonelle*. Instinctively, Fola reacts to this suggestion of root relationship.

"I'm all these," said Charlot, "just as you're a part of those women there." . . .
"You want to suggest that I believe in all 'that,'" she said. Her voice was low, distant, closing on a note of quiet disdain. (27)

At this beginning point of her adventure, the reality of her roots is not just totally foreign to Fola, the idea itself is abhorrent. Charlot, however, stresses the associated link, the inner rhythmical pulse flow, between Fola's dancing on the beach, the Ceremony of the Souls, and the music and art of the steel drums.

"But I've seen you dance, Fola. . . ."
"It's the same rhythm," he said. "And the music of the Steel Drums. You yourself have said no music makes you feel the same way . . . ."
"There wouldn't be any music without the ceremonies," said Charlot. "You couldn't do your dancing without those women." (27)

The ceremony of the souls, in which is located all the elements of resurrection, begins its unrelenting pull on Fola.

Her questions were other than an interest to examine. She became aware of their contagion in her mind. The prayers were a conspiracy against her doubt. The voices grew loud and louder in their prayers, each prayer like a furious bargain for her faith. (33–34)

Here at the *tonelle* the foreign tutelage begins to lose its hold over her, the fragmenting process begins, the unlearning of a foreign, despiritualized, analytic perception of Fola's root reality. Fola realizes that Charlot is indeed a foreigner who can discuss her root relationship to the Ceremony of the Souls but who cannot be affected by that ceremony because he does not belong. She resents his ability to remain outside the pull of her roots, outside the compulsion of the ceremony of the souls. Fola wilts under the burning eyes and vision of the true guru, the aged exemplar and medium of San Cristobal, the new republic's essential historian, Aunt Jane.

Yet their prayers couldn't touch Charlot. They couldn't arouse the slightest fear in him. He wasn't near to anything they felt. . . . She resented his safety. She wanted Charlot to take her away; but she dared not move while the old woman's eyes blazed upon her, old and sure and purposeful in their scrutiny. (34)

The simple fact is that those of the race of Charlot, though having had a hand in the shaping of the external historical reality of San Cristobal, cannot reach into its ethos, do not affect the true inner spiritual center of that historical reality, its mythos: "Only who belong to the dead got any right inside" (30). Only those who, like the little girl Liza, have a votive link to the dead can chant with the passionate intensity of the women, can be conjured into instinctive, innocent, and primal possession; only they can enter into the very crucible of their ritual history, as the aged spirit-medium Aunt Jane does in her tormented, anguished writhings.

The old woman had risen to her full height, thrusting her weak, black hands above her head . . . . Tumbled in the dust, she rose again, her hands spread wide, snatching at the air. (39)

Only the hands of great Gort can intone the miracle of watery resurrection, the mystery of invoking the passion, and the inner mystery of the ritual night.

Each chant was an errand chased by the drums' stern clap of steel. . . . The voices were tired but the drums came to their aid, swelling each pulse with a loud refrain, feeding new energy to the night. . . .
. . . the drums rode their message through the night, moving deeper and deeper in dialogue with the dead. It seemed this music had always been there: a sermon of rhythms in revolt over the *tonelle*. (19–21)

When free, uninhibited, Fola knows and feels instinctively the music of the drums and can enter the sensual ordinance of those drums: "She hadn't lost their rhythm . . . [the] sense of physical delight" (24). However, here in the *tonelle*, all the inhibitions deriving from societal privilege interrupt her free participation in those rhythms, making her initially an observer refusing to participate in the essential raw ecstasy of the ceremony. For belonging seems to be the unreserved, uninhibited giving of oneself to the kinetic energy and force of the music, to the ritual power of the ceremony of the souls.

At this point in her season of adventure, Fola resists being mounted by the spirit force of the ritual and the drums, by their spiritual power. Those who unreservedly belong, when exposed to the rhythmical incantation of those drums, to their ritualized sexuality, without realizing it, are mounted by watery spirits.

> "Ride me spirit! An' comin' I comin'! With it! . . . Sea cool O spirit clim' me an' I come, done come! Cool, cool, sea-wet cool all in an' out, cool . . . ." (35)

Yet in the beginning of her season of adventure, seduced and trapped by the Ceremony of the Souls, Fola loses her essential psychic control and as climax to her tension, wets herself.

> But it was too late to move, too late to talk, too late to stop the slow, hot, slow tautness of muscle under her thigh. Her muscles were giving way to a slow, hot trickle of water sliding down her legs. She was wetting her pants. (34)

This watery flow becomes manifestation and symbolic actualization of that central primal metaphor, water, with all of its attendant images of linkage, of continuity. At this ritual celebration, which dramatically begins the novelistic staging of *Season of Adventure*, the principal contrasting yet complementary motifs come together and coalesce. Here in this particular observation of the Ceremony of the Souls, the two souls seeking freedom from their residence of water talk about the origin of the wealth that enshrines that oppressive privilege of the main ruling elite of San Cristobal.

> "So it was the diamonds . . . . What Titon do that for? Why Titon put his knowledge to such evil purpose?"
> "Money, money . . . is money make him do it . . . ." (35)

The shadowy, doubtful origin of the money that enshrines the sense of privilege leads to a false authority, to the classism of those who live in Federation Park or in Maraval.

Fola, in her quest, attempts to deny the self—the personality of classism—and to reach out to make a new self. Fola eventually rejects that privilege which, before her visit to the *tonelle*, she had assumed as a right. Conversely, the dead spirit's search for his natural mother, the boy's excruciating anguish at not finding that mother, propels Fola into a search for her natural father. At this juncture, the *Houngan* for the first time is unable to enact the ritual summoning and evocation of a soul yearning for its mother.

> The dead boy had precipitated rebellion against the gods. The soul had tried to free itself before the *Houngan* could authorise its release. It had driven the old woman to her possession. (40)

For the first time, too, Fola in her season of adventure, in her search for her origin, demands to know the truth of her paternity.

"You never ever hear me call you daddy. Never." . . .
"All right, you say he's dead," she shouted, and Piggott felt the treachery of other ears behind him. "But even the dead used to be. Who was he, Piggy, tell me, Piggy, who was my father?" (127)

The question of paternity becomes one of the novel's principal motifs, the search one of the main drives to its action. Fola's season of adventure is a ritual movement into her space, into otherness. Folk ritual—the Ceremony of the Souls, to which is ascribed the origins of the folk music of San Cristobal and the indigenous art of its painter, Chiki—ordains the beginnings of that journey into otherness. Almost in a trance, Fola is led away from the foreigner by the *Houngan* and begins her initiation into the mystery of folk self, into her spiritual redefinition. In the *Houngan's* secret chambers, Fola libates the earth with gin "instinctively as she had seen the women do" (44). There, she is thrust into darkness, a darkness symbolic of the first break with her immediate external reality. She becomes dematerialized, seeming to turn to stone, and not only is surrounded by the cathartic images of her childhood memories but also attempts to locate her mother, the matrix root.

Now everything turned dark. She could feel the pain where he was pommelling her with his fist on the gin-wet socket of her arm.
It burnt and stung and pushed like an acid into her body. There was a stiffness in her tongue; a noise like water running out of her ears. Fear had turned her to stone. She was too weak to cry. She could hear nothing but the remembered echo of the mad voice wailing above the tent. The rats of candle flame wriggled round her eyes, as she tried to call her mother's name, but no sound came. (44–45)

Thus, wrapped in the primal voice of the circling wind, plunged into the vital center of the shadowy sanctuary, Fola begins her shedding of foreign teachings, her rejection of analytic history, of Charlot, and ultimately of the social reality of privilege. Thus begins her ritual transformation.

Bewildered but beyond the reach of the stranger man, her former teacher, Fola walks back from the Ceremony of the Souls, returning to her home in the embrace of the night, and symbolically shuts out the foreign presence. All of the phenomena—flowers, earth, ceremony, music—seem to participate and indeed to rejoice in this climactic break from the foreign cultural control and presence: The fragmentation has begun.

"Good night," she said, and turned away.

The conventions of respect had been lifted forever from this pupil's restraint. She didn't even wait to hear what Charlot would say. A breath of jasmine blew up from the garden, and lingered where he turned in retreat from the silent colours of white marble.

The earth breathed with insect noises. The familiar rhythm of steel had pursued them through the wide, black spaces of the night. The rhythms of steel were riding in triumph over the *tonelle* as Charlot walked under cover of darkness, and watched the sky open upon a skeleton of stars dancing to the ceremony of the drums. (50)

The next stage in Fola's journey is marked and blurred by a fever, which brings with it not simply physical weakness but hallucinatory interplays of memories and pictures. The elements, too, seem to participate in and bring about this purging and cleansing fever.

Lightning burnt a crack over the pane of glass, and a wind whipped the trees into a storm of leaves falling heavily outside her window. The rain hadn't stopped. The fever boiled upwards through her veins and spread across her forehead. Her throat coughed a weak dry sound like shells. (65)

In the grip of this fever, the image and picture of the foreign teacher break and are displaced by the vital immediate presence of the little girl Liza. At this point, differing worlds confront each other, the world of privilege as framed in the picture on the wall, and the world that Liza seems to inform and embody. Symbolically, Charlot's framed picture breaks, falling from Fola's fever-weakened hand as did the gift that signified the condition of privilege of the ruling class of San Cristobal.

The fever had shaken the picture from her hands. She tried to stoop, and felt the sudden thrust of pain twisting like a chisel through her skull . . . . Yesterday a similar thing had happened. She had dropped a large plate glass tray which was her mother's birthday gift from the Vice President of San Cristobal. (66)

Thus begins not only the dissolution of the foreign tutelage but also the questioning of that essential privilege, with its attendant denial of those less privileged.

In the feverish state, water and sweat and blood seem to take on the same properties: "When the sweat broke, dripping like rain into her mouth, she started to imagine the taste of blood" (66). Now her world of privilege, as exemplified by the foreign tutor and the ruling elite, collides with a new world, as exemplified by the presence of Liza. Slowly but insistently, the presence of Liza routs the image of Charlot, guiding Fola backward into an infancy where the foreign presence was nonexistent: "She could see Liza in a frenzy of rhythm that tossed her around the bamboo pole" (75). In her feverish state, Fola wishes to trespass on that infancy with her mother, negating thereby or attempting to decipher the beginnings of her denial of her mother: "She would have liked them to trespass upon the past together" (79–80).

As the fever breaks, Liza's image hardens into reality. Fola perceives the root presence and influence of the Ceremony of the Souls and the relationship to an essential freedom: "The ceremony was a soil from which the child would grow, natural and sure as plants" (75). As the fever finally breaks, Fola's perception of her true cultural prominence clarifies and hardens. She becomes totally assured of the role and function of the ritual celebration in the *tonelle*, and is awakened to the cultural formation of an indigenous sentiment and belonging: "And her reason now emerged harsh and clear as the violent pounding of the drums in the *tonelle*" (93).

At this point of clarification, Fola's relationship both to the *tonelle* and indeed to the music itself does not have the earlier stridency, nor the frenzy accompanying her departure from the *tonelle*. Rather, as she takes the first step of her journeying to a new presence, the drums wrap her in their soothing embrace.

> She had heard [the drums] on her return from the *tonelle* that night; but the sound was different now .... The rhythms came soft, more soothing as she slipped deep and deeper into the moisture of the sheets. (94–95)

In the next step of her journey, in a well-orchestrated, passionately violent and poignant scene, Fola—in a cold rage, not a burning fever—rejects the formerly effective cajolings, the warm affectionate generosities, of her powerful commissioner stepfather Piggott, and by so doing begins the dissolution of his power, the negating of the significance of yet another authority figure. In her search for her natural father, for origins, Fola brutally shatters the unfulfilled yearnings, the longing of Piggott for a natural daughter. Sterile Piggott is at one and the same time warm, attentive, and affectionate to Fola and his wife, Agnes, but, as commissioner, cruel and brutal to the poor, to the steel bandsmen; Piggott, even as he yearns to be progenitor, father, rejects his origins in the Forest Reserve, his patrimony. Fola disinherits herself from Piggott, shattering his world of assumed fatherhood, leading him to expose his duplicity, his two-facedness. Fola's affection for her stepfather Piggott was up to this point unquestioned and assured. Whereas Fola would with equanimity reject her mother's offers of a party, she would hesitate to say so for fear of hurting her stepfather, because of her affection for him: "She was too attached to Piggot to see him hurt; and she knew how hurt he would have been if she had spoken out" (119).

In spite of this affection, Fola's search for otherness, her new clarity of vision, bring with them a certain innerness, a new kind of silence that not only perplexes Piggott, but indeed shuts him out. He is unable to grasp the meaning of the silence and the restlessness that begins to mark Fola's behavior.

> He had thought, with a father's assumptions of knowledge, that it had to do with growing up. Now he had his misgivings. Fola had become at once more restless and more aloof. Her questions had acquired a certain tone of calculation; and her silences, which were becoming more and more frequent, contained some agonising and unspoken urgency for those who were around. (117)

Piggott has hoped that Fola will be unique and distinct and has wished that this distinctiveness will give her her own selfhood, one not linked to him or to her mother Agnes.

> He tried to imagine a time when people would say: "there goes Fola . . . distinct, separate and pure, like the sky." (116)

For Fola, however, the distinctiveness, the unique otherness for which she begins to quest, leads her back to the root image and recurrent presence of Liza and her own beginning otherness, brought on by her experience at the Ceremony of the Souls. Both Liza and the ceremony of the souls become the focal point magnetizing her new perception, pulling the images of father, mother, teacher, into their center.

> She thought of the child, Liza, dancing round the bamboo pole, and tried to see him at a ceremony of Dead Souls, waving the *Houngan's* axe, or entering the tent alone to hold mysterious concourse with the dead. Would he have been embarrassed about her interest in his past? She had lived with Piggott as she had done with her own past. Until these last few days she had never known the tendency to make *that backward glance.* (120)

This "backward glance," Fola's journey into otherness, propels her into a rejection of the accumulated weight not simply of her education and privilege, but clearly of the history and personality of that past. Fola's need to unearth the true sense of her past, to uncover the hidden sources of her personhood, to unmake the veneer of privilege, all catapult her into a deep visceral emotional explosion.

She experienced an utter loss of control, a furious release of feelings: doubts, angers, a sense of expectation forever denying her grasp. Fola felt this blinding urge to drag herself from under the huge accumulation of things that pressed her down, covering her with a silence like a grave. (125)

Uncontrollably, and frantically, she forgets her affection for Piggott, her wish not to hurt him, and directs to him the most imploding question: "Who was he, Piggy, tell me, Piggy, who was my father?" (127). The magnitude of this question and the dramatic intensity of their encounter, shatter Piggott's immediate reality and force him backward to search for the roots of his barrenness. Clearly, the barrenness is loaded with symbolic intent, suggestive of material acquisition in the midst of an inner loss and deprivation.

> "And it is Fola," he cries, "it is Fola who drives me back. Good God, how is it that a girl still child to my own years can drive me back, drive me back into such black infancy?" (131)

Again, in a starkly brutal confrontation, Fola strips away the notion of motherhood from Agnes, reducing the instinctive relationship of mother-daughter to its raw materialistic dimension of thing, of bitch, of "this woman." Drizzling rain witnesses this dissolution, this step in a journey toward the fragmentation of assumed personality into otherness, into presence.

The scene between mother and daughter, its stark and brutal passion, is preceded by the explosiveness of the elements: "Soon the clouds will burst and clap with rain over each acre of the republic's soil" (149). The elements, especially the rain, become participant and witness to the dread encounter between mother and daughter, enclosing them, shutting them off from any intervention.

> That final crash of rain had ruled the neighbours out. No one could hear beyond the wide, repetitive hoof of water striding each roof. (150)

Their encounter is as powerful as the uproar of the rain. Fola symbolically repossesses her own garments, forbidding her mother to ever use them.

> Each time Fola said: "don't ever touch my things," some nerve had collapsed within Agnes. Not from the words which, at some other time, might have been a harmless threat. It was Fola's tone: the dry, ripe, bone-clean certainty of her will towards a chosen enemy. (151)

The passionate intensity of their encounter leads to the stripping away, not simply of garments, but indeed of any material bond. Fola rips apart that bond to the point where, denuded of any filial affinity, she arrives at a stark and shattering perception: mother becomes thing, "this woman," bitch.

"You've been more trouble than profit since the day you born."

And Fola stood rigid, feeling the change from mother to *this woman* give way to a more appropriate description of her rage. "The bitch," she thought. (150)

The power of the confrontation between mother and daughter—their anger, their rage, and even more so, Fola's need to unearth the past and her origins—catapults her into a new condition, which fragments her from her immediate reality, pulsing her into a new state of being. Here, the elements, the landscape, all cohere, locating Fola in a beyondness. Clearly the emotional encounter and confrontation serve as a catharsis, imploding and leading to a new liberating condition.

Her rage had given her an impossible strength; freed her from any loyalty. . . . Fola wanted to outstrip the wind in an obstinate pursuit of something she had to know . . . . She was *beyond* error; she was *beyond* fear; she was *beyond* shame; *beyond, beyond, beyond.* (154)

The fragmentation from her past reality of education and privilege ensues, and the transformation, begun in the *Houngan's* sanctuary and in the Ceremony of the Souls, reaches the initial point of climax, which synchronizes with her acceding to womanhood.

Like the dead souls in the *tonelle*, Fola was *beyond* her past. She was free; dead to the accidents of her past, dead and free. Fola was a freedom which now reached *beyond* the grave, *beyond* the sky. Dead and free on her eighteenth birthday. (154)

To complete the stages of her search, to attempt to apprehend her furthest beginnings, Fola tries to relive that condition, those circumstances evinced by her mother Agnes during pregnancy. To sense those beginnings, that embryo-ripening time, simulating the circumstances of her mother's pregnancy, Fola visits the outpatient's maternity clinic.

Fola tries to see herself there in the shape and skin of their recent disfigurement. She wants to feel in the natural pulse of her own bowels the life which had increased their size. Her hands travel slowly up and down, searching the corners of her skirt, reaching to span the curves of her stomach. (172)

There she is horrified at the casual, the cowardly responses of pregnant women to the demeaning, brutal debasement that they undergo at the hands of orderlies, unmannerly nurses, and callous doctors. At this juncture, this moment of revulsion, Fola sees with clarity the starkness of the condition, and the word *bastard*, like the word *bitch*, hardens into form, takes on meaning.

> "Let it rot in her guts," the doctor's voice shouted. "It'll teach them to have some kind of *standards*." . . .
>
> Fola recognised Camillon's voice, cold and aggressive in its authority. . . .
>
> . . . For the first time in her search for a father, the word bastard was born in Fola's mind. It existed in its own right . . . . Fola was thinking: "I am Fola and other than Fola, meaning bastard: *and other than, and other than, outside and other than.*" (174)

From this moment, Fola the character begins to author and fictionalize her own reality, create her own being, her past, and—rejecting her circumstances of privilege—enters into a new fictionalized social circumstance, and into, as well, the shaping of her otherness, the molding of her new future.

Swept along by her need to create a new self, a new image, Fola invents a dramatic story of sexual possession by Powell, the leader of the Forest Reserve Steel Band and a relentless foe of all the privileged. In her new "otherness," Fola not only simulates her first possession but indeed depicts it with such visceral intensity as to make it seem a real happening, a violent sexual act in which she was participant.

> She made Veronica feel the sting of the wind as she rode with her drumming lover from the *tonelle* through miles of deserted night, feeling lust, expectation and the terror of delight as she recognized a madness in his limbs. . . .
>
> "And there he lay me down," said Fola, "to batter me with all he had. I cry, and cry with pain all inside me, 'cause it wasn't love make him do it. I beg him to let go, let go, but my begging only add to the murder he was making inside me." (183–184)

Fola's invention, the story of her violent mating with the head of the steel band of the Forest Reserve, when narrated and acted out to Veronica, the daughter of the vicepresident of the Republic, climaxes the fragmentation of her social reality of privilege, and completes her transformation, her movement into otherness.

> But this was not Fola whom Veronica now saw, and she didn't know there was another Fola; Fola *and other than*. This Fola had started on a history of needs whose details she alone would be able to distinguish: a season of adventure which no man in the republic could predict. (184–185)

Clearly the metaphor for *Season of Adventure* is finely interwoven with and correlated to the Ceremony of the Souls, the ritual unearthing of truth, the ritual search for one's beginnings. The spaces of the adventure, the radial points of action, comprise two opposing planes of social reality, the residential districts of the privileged and the Forest Reserve, the back-yard residences of the steel bandsmen. Fola journeys between these two principal spaces in her quest for an indigenous cultural identity.

Fola's story about her visceral intercourse with Powell intimates a copulation between the most extreme poles of the society, between the privileged and the Forest Reserve. Indeed, such a great gulf separates these two social entities that the privileged seem unable to perceive any interaction between their world and the world of the Forest Reserve. Thus, Fola's story not only profoundly shocks her friend Veronica's sensibilities, but its very invention climaxes the fragmentation of her own personality.

Later, when Veronica, distraught by the murder of her father, President Raymond, relates Fola's fictionalized tale to Piggott, he goes berserk, his rage inflamed by the thought that Fola has not only debased herself but that she has pulled him back into a space, a gutter, from which he had extricated himself.

> To have been made pregnant by a ruffian from the Forest Reserve! All his achievements had crumbled. Fola had dragged him back to the forgotten squalor of his past. . . . Piggott had gone berserk. . . .
> Therese and Agnes watched, their eyes made impotent by the thunder of his fists on Fola's body. (306)

Piggott's rejection of his roots is equalled by Powell's dislike of the privileged. And the steel-band leader's hatred of the ruling class is not only equally brutish and violently visceral, but seems almost preordained in his attack on Fola. Powell's hatred of the privileged is stronger than Piggott's, and is capable of awakening more vicious, more destructive, more vengeful instincts.

> She had seen in the force of Powell's presence the fury of hatred which was old as Powell himself . . . . Her memory was still fresh with the rage which had driven Piggott to go berserk on her body; but this had been reduced to childish petulance by the weight and meaning of what Powell had intended to inflict on her. (320)

Whereas Powell seems to be the raw-boned conscience, the vengeful spirit, of the Forest Reserve, Chiki seems to be its voice, its political and cultural conscience. After Piggott has allowed Gort's drum to be smashed in, an act which echoes with desecration, Chiki raises his voice in protest, reminding Piggott of his roots.

Earlier, as a young student, that same voice was raised in protest against the colonial authority, an act for which Chiki was expelled from the prestigious public school. To attend such a school would have opened to Chiki endless privileges, possibilities of acceding to the highest social and political positions. Aware of the privileges consequent on Chiki's winning the scholarship, the vengeful articulator of the Forest Reserve Steel Band imposes a communal mandate and responsibility on the young Chiki.

> "Now listen, Chick, don't think I can't talk to you no more, 'cause you still live here, is still Forest Reserve you got to call your home . . . . it ain't you alone what goin' up, is all the Boys what have no scholarship, Chick. We can't all go up there, but we with you, Chick, like those big books what on your back. Remember all the Boys waitin' to hear." (228–229)

Fola, too, later rejects that condition of privilege assured by such schooling. Belinda, the prostitute who sells her body to assure her twelve-year-old son's education, remarks on Chiki's and Fola's abandonment of that education.

> Those two, woman and man, only different in age, but alike in the way they treat that future which they have swallowed like a pill; swallowed, and, it seems, forgotten like the result of every pill. (229)

Chiki seems not simply the social voice of the Forest Reserve, but the exemplar whose every departure and absence either shimmers with the communal spirit, or shivers with a deep sense of tragic loss.

Clearly George Lamming's principal preoccupation is Fola's movement into otherness, her assumption of a new presence. Integrated to this presence, to its assumption, is her acceptance of a root relationship with Chiki, the painter. Her adventure, her searching, embodies a quest for indigenous societal roots, free from a residual colonial condition of class and privilege and power derived not from any intrinsic personal distinction, but rather from crass materialism.

Chiki's existential condition—as a young rebel against the colonial and privileged class, as a gifted artist, as ultimately a friend and confidant of Fola—structures the second principal novelistic formulation of *Season of Adventure*. Chiki, too, is searching for coherence of origins. Whereas Fola's search is more societal, Chiki accepts the nurturing of true folk influences by attempting to delve into the indigenous sources of art and culture. His artistic representations derive not only from subliminal childhood memory but also from biblical sources. Even though his instinct guides his art, his artistic representations evince and are shrouded in paradox.

He looks away, but every glance is cornered by a memory . . . .

. . . Nothing can be more willing and ready to be told than the knowledge his childhood knows . . . Lazarus is not so easy, but his legend is familiar. . . .

. . . Chiki has no faith in the Christian promise, no need for humility, propitiation or dialogue with the other gods. But the weight of his paradox is greatest when he looks at his parable of the talents. (188–189)

His backward glance brings with it a Christian past, which even as it informs and invests his awareness, evinces a paradoxical relationship to his art. His artistic potential blends with the indigenous ritual Ceremony of the Souls to produce his artistic mastery, yet the very past to which he is intrinsically bound prohibits his leap beyond.

Chiki will not paint because he thinks he is a man imprisoned in his paradox for all time: the paradox of what he is and what he cannot do. (366)

Gort stands in counterpoint to Fola and Chiki. Lamming ascribes to him a pure condition of illiteracy, untainted by a foreign tutelage as in the case of Fola, uncluttered by external cultural and complicating influences as evidenced in Chiki's paradoxical relationship with his art. Unlike Fola, Gort does not see his personhood through otherness, through a backward glance, for his selfhood is secure, his ties to the past assured and intoned in his music. Quite unlike Chiki, who is hamstrung by the cerebral quotient in his brilliant luminous art and standing perplexed before his canvases, Gort's relationship to his steel drum, to his music, is akin to worship.

The music is asleep, but he can awake it at the slightest whisper of a finger nail . . . . The universe is asleep under his hands, dreaming some harmony which will perfect tomorrow's drumming. (51)

As spiritual as his ties to his drum are Gort's friendships with Liza and the children of the Forest Reserve, with the band, with Chiki. Just as deep were his ties, his affection, and adoration of his master, Jack o'Lantern, symbol of the revolutionary cultural spirit of his steel-band music. It is in music that Gort demonstrates the depth of this affection and adoration. Through his own spirit music, Gort celebrates the death of his master. In this music—on his tenor pan—there is no paradox such as that which besets Chiki, the artist. To Gort the pan is imbued with a sacredness, is medium and celebrative conjurer of his dead master's spirit. Indeed here Gort is *Houngan*, unearthing and giving corporate presence to that spirit. It is Gort whom they choose to play the exhumed pan of Jack o' Lantern.

The bands played together all the calypsoes and digging songs which had made Jack o' Lantern famous. Then Gort alone played the hymn which every childhood in San Cristobal had learnt from infancy:
Work! for the night is coming
When man's work is done. (318)

Gort's relationship to his music and to his poem is deeply personal, emotional, and pure. Thus when his tenor pan is wantonly smashed by the police who raid Forest Reserve, his reaction, his anguish, is instinctual, deeply pathetic. As the lyrical adieu to his master evokes a deep, almost sacred emotion from Gort, the destruction of his tenor pan elicits deep pathetic grief. The loss of his drum takes on all the qualities of a tragedy akin to death.

> Gort was alone; alone with a mystery that collected only evil in his head . . . . It made him hear the chime of bells telling a funeral in the Sargasso cemetery. . . .
> . . . Gort wept for his loss; he wept because he could not understand.
> (289)

Just as deep as his spiritual music is the language of his heart, his soul's alphabet and idiom; it tells with deep pathos of his friend Chiki's absence.

Lamming ascribes to this music a quality of linkage, an indigenous cultural texturing of diverse musical inheritance. This music does not embody the syncretic element that stymied Chiki's creative gift, but rather enshrines a new dynamic, a changing and revolutionary cultural expression gifted with prophecy. Through the medium of Gort's music, Lamming traces the existence of cultural linkages and flow, ordains the notion of continuity. The central symbolic metaphor, resurrection—which gives novelistic coherence to *Season of Adventure* and which provides the principal thematic formulation of that search for roots, for belonging, provenience, and for indigenous selfhood—achieves its ritual completion. It becomes charged with regenerative potential, restorative energy, when Gort disinters his master's tenor pan, intoning on it a musical revolutionary challenge to the polity of privilege and power, celebrating a message so crucial, so vital for the Caribbean work. For the night is coming when man's work is done.

Like Fola, whose season of adventure involves a journey in search of her indigenous roots, the title character in Harris's *The Far Journey of Oudin* also engages in a search for self that is intertwined with the history of his people. Oudin's journey starts at the creative center of the world's beginning, in the humus and mud of the earth. From an energizing interconnection of body and mud, Oudin sets off on his pursuit of the child-daughter

Beti, rising and standing to begin his journey. Emerging from this mud beginning and indistinct almost featureless form, he enters through the doorway of Beti's half-dreaming consciousness to ultimately crystallize into a presence of freedom and conscious existence. Almost from a fetal position, Oudin rises to begin his journeying.

> Oudin's extremities—hands and feet—had turned to mud. He had crawled and crept far. He had risen to his feet to follow her, but he carried with him rings around his ankles, and islands off the foreshore, and it was with difficulty he still uprooted and extricated himself. (Harris, *The Far Journey of Oudin*, 34)

Beti's first vision of Oudin is of a disembodied being whose brittle presence has been violently repelled by her father just before his death.

> He had looked like a bundle of death then—as wild and terrible as he looked now—and her father had thrown him out, swearing he wanted none of him. (35)

But in the still pure, childlike consciousness of Beti, Oudin's presence, though seeming to incorporate a history of feud and ancient controversy, embodies promise and freedom. From the very beginning of the novel, Oudin's origin and presence bemuse the others. Seen in the half-light of morning, his figure moves and shifts between reality and fantasy, perplexing Mohammed. What is the essential link between Oudin and himself, Mohammed wonders.

> Certainly this was *not* Oudin. Who was *Oudin?* Where had the name sprung from? . . . His feeling hardened, hating the thought of the true relationship, wanting the unknown to be real—since he might be able to banish that—and the actuality to be a fable. (38)

From these two initial visions of Oudin, Beti's and Mohammed's, Oudin becomes reinvested within the procreative cycle of regenerative harvesting, entering and taking on the very presence of cyclical time. Here, man and earth co-penetrate in a seemingly continuous cross-fertilization leading to a harmonizing of energy and presence. Clearly, Oudin has emerged from the ringed mud by which he was initially burdened. Now a part of the cycle of reaping, he takes on the pulse and rhythms of seasons, becoming their very essence.

> Oudin knew it was still a dream, the dream of the heavenly cycle of the planting and reaping year he now stood within—as within a circle— for the first time. He felt his heart stop where it had danced. It was the end of his labour of death. (11)

Thus, Oudin in his journey shifts from an insubstantial presence and featureless form into a being, aware of its own inner linkages not only to the elemental, but indeed to the very consciousness itself, to a grasping of primal principles. The journey, then, can be seen as the unfolding of Oudin's awareness of his historical circumstance and folk condition. Indeed, his journey becomes the intuitive apprehension of his place within the larger historical phenomenon of the group.

Oudin's journey not only takes him across the vast landscape of Guyana and becomes his search for self, but finally is symbolic, in fact representative, of the historical journeying of peoples of East Indian origins in Guyana.

> He felt in a stumbling intuition of self, that the pattern of a lifetime
> of migrating from province to province, was now being set, and the
> coming journey was a crucial rehearsal, a rehearsal that would be repeated
> once again over thirteen dreaming years of his marriage to Beti. (100)

In this journey, then, in the threefold movement into self, across space, and through historical time, the fabric of dreams and their configurations create correspondences of oppositions; and, destroying the material barriers between phenomena, bring about the cohering of spheres and realities. Death and life shade together; fantasy and reality commingle; man and land merge.

The configurations of a simple journey—undergoing the same enlargening transformative vision with which the woodsman imbues his limited reality—take on larger signification. Indeed, the woodsman seems to be stating author Wilson Harris's creative processes and formulations—

> It was his habit to make the simplest story into something of far-reaching,
> dramatic significance . . . as if the grotesque lives huddled in a room and
> a cabin were deserving of universal attention and value that outweighed
> by far the mere character of open lust and simple treachery. (122)

—to such a degree that the perceptions of each of the characters, their interpretations of simple phenomena, become an orchestration of the historical, the ecological, and the personal.

> It was a recurring and unwelcome vision he seemed unable to
> interpret and stop, of subversion and opulence, misery and well-being
> resting upon no one and nothing . . . . looking outwards and inwards in
> the dreaming conspiracy of time and history and migration, with a threat
> to convert him, and everyone else, into the relative image of a child. (38)

And as characters attempt to interpret their own particular historical and physical realities, each individual interpretation, reflecting and refracting with all others, undergoes a transformation. It is the shifting orchestration that gives a particular substantiality to the changing reflections themselves, so that physical forms, emotional reactions, and elemental qualities, transforming one another even as they refract, create permanent representations. As Beti sees her reflection in the river she seems to achieve a quality of permanence.

> Her eyes were round and black in the river, almost falling from her head, and the smoothness of her skin was an intent and naked particle of freedom like one who had been stripped in truth at last. The unexpected face she saw was guarded and protected in the glass of the river and it stood beyond a touch where no material impact could break it, vulnerable as it looked. (23)

Here the interplay of human form and the elements, of woman and earth—their interpenetration—is not simple anthropomorphic representation, but is indeed a conduit to the assumption of essential being, to the substantiation of form, to the embodiment of external reality. Oudin's journey toward self-realization is accompanied by Beti's journey toward her assumption of essential self: "She clung desperately to her plank of living emotion seeing a crumbling vision and image in the mirror within her" (23). Initially Beti, in her uncomprehending relationship to the external reality in which she journeys, takes on the uncomprehending dimension of that reality and becomes an enigma.

> She had begun to live in such closeness to the jagged uncertain cloudy picture of her world that she had become part of everything she hardly knew, and this was the stage where every form and parting footstep were charged with the hysterical imagination of grief belonging to an illiterate woman who had lost every conventional art of self-expression to become an enigma to herself. (124)

Subsequently, however, as Beti journeys toward her own self-awareness, the external reality is no longer incomprehensible to her, its jagged edges no longer adding to her uncertainty; now she merges with that external reality in an enfolding embrace, leading to coherence, to awareness, to the sensing of her essential being. The transformative process has effected an essential change in Beti.

> Beti felt a curious sensation . . . in her limbs, and a sense of relief in standing above the bottomless swamp. It was an essential uplift and bond in the midst of all figurative flight and chaos. (115)

At the beginning of Beti's journey she lives in a world of insubstantial forms and spirits toward which she gropes. Beti's stretching toward unknown presences attempts to resurrect them by denying their absence.

> Her outstretched hands writhed and struggled to seize a spirit that had
> always eluded her and the heart of Ram stared, hanging on her breath.
> (17)

Her journeying, then, is that movement from an initial grasping of insubstantial form to her arrival at being the possible generative force, the progenitor of a new breed. The end of Beti's journey is not only a denial of Ram's lust, his attempted control over her, his attempt to possess her, but clearly also an entry into self-awareness and creative regenerative possibility: "Beti was another name for 'daughter,' the daughter of a race that was being fashioned anew" (136).

Oudin's journey takes him from the material vision of poverty to the hut that gives the first corporate sense to his beginning perceptions. Clearly the distance he travels stretches from that initial vision of material poverty to his apprehension of his role and responsibility in the possible shaping of a folk presence. In the morning light, he half-sees the hut, and its material dimensions momentarily take on a spiritual dimension.

> Oudin saw it in the corner of his eye as if for the first time: so clearly
> he might never have seen it before. The stark light in which he beheld
> it was a mystery to him, the first real mystery and power of apprehension
> he possessed. (12)

The distance he traverses from that initial point of awareness is not simply quantitative material space but a qualitative searching for his essential place within the larger schema. Yet only through the cycle of death and rebirth, through an acceptance of the notion of sacrifice, is his journey ultimately illuminated.

> It was the first shell and hurdle and offering of repentance and sacrifice
> he must accept in himself and must overcome, to be the forerunner of a
> new brilliancy and freedom. (105)

Only through the deaths of Hassan, Rajah, and Kaiser, deaths that destroy the curse which has hung over them, can succeeding generations arrive at a new point of regenerative awareness. Here, Wilson Harris does not postulate sacrifice as the essential philosophical basis of regeneration but rather by accepting the cyclical motions between life and death, their regenerative link, he foresees and prophesizes a rebirth. For Rajah, Kaiser, and Hassan, the immediate moment of journeying (like Oudin's journey that leads him to a new brilliancy and freedom) opens out into promises of new beginnings and new assurances, illuminating a new freedom.

> His grandchildren, perhaps, Rajah grumbled, might live in a different
> self, or his grandchildren's children. They would have little reckoning of

the womb and the curse from which they had sprung to life, and of the vast relative dreaming canvas in which they found themselves, pinpointed and cocksure like stars, as though destiny had made the past and the future theirs all right. (81)

The landscape in which all these journeyings take place is of endless savannahs, of swamps and corridors, of rivers now in flood, now in drought, of forests in their never-ending shadowy configurations. This landscape not only is depicted in its material and oppressive substantiality, but often assumes a presence deriving from the particular action in which protagonists are involved. Thus, the space of the journeyings in all of its changing moods and manifestations becomes co-extensive with changing human sensibility, with evolving time. Indeed the presentation of the landscape and the representations of the elements take on the qualities of the novelistic formulations inherent in *The Far Journey of Oudin*.

They were held on the circuit of rain that wreathed itself into a transparent blowing mist on which the face of time evolved as though it had been forgotten, and was miraculously painted afresh. (123)

At times the landscape is presented in its very immediate materialistic dimensions. The savannah in all of its vastness exudes a debilitating heat, enervating both man and his primal emotions.

The savannahs were a white and blazing fire, circulating like a breathless sultry blast of unchanging wind across the dry earth and the brown cropped fields. (80)

In the rise and fall of the river, marking the seasons of rain and drought, the mating and marriage of characters finds historical reflection, evokes memories of loss, awakens hopes of fulfillment.

Rain recalled the procession . . . of Oudin and Beti. It was the year of the great flood, surpassing the previous one of his childhood recollection, and he recalled it as if what he had seen then was the dream and reflection of misery, and what he saw now was the launching and freedom of a release in time. (27)

The wedding of Oudin and Beti is a sequel to their first meeting in the *couridas* and swamps. Here landscape is presented as space where an initiation takes place and that later opens out to and crests on the river waters. The aged and twisted trunks of the *courida* vegetation are witness to a youthful meeting between Beti and Oudin.

Beti met Oudin for the first time in the middle of the *courida* on the foreshore that always awoke her apprehension, the trees were so gnarled and twisted in their extremity. His face was new and strange to her and yet he seemed like someone she had seen before. (33)

From this beginning in the *courida* swamps to their marriage on the river, the journey of Oudin and Beti, their flight, takes them into another landscape, into the forest with its unending shadowy and changing contours. Oudin takes Beti across the barrier of the forest, through its heartlands, emerging from their shadowy entanglements into a new space. Their entry into the forest is no simple penetration into material space, but rather takes on all the spiritual, indeed mystical, qualities of covenant, where their true union takes place—an essential mating of man and woman with a landscape in "the tropical dawn of the longest twilight in the world" (106).

Here the ageless gestation and the perennial creation that marked the beginnings of the forest, the ceaseless struggling and gestation of elements, are mirrored in Oudin's struggling movements toward the true beginnings, toward a symbiotic relationship with Beti. In a series of vertical images, Oudin's feet enter into the very center of the forest earth so that the in-and-out shuttling movements of his limbs embody the procreative rhythms which engendered the forest bed and now lead to climax and embrace between Oudin's and Beti's bodies. Indeed, Beti, now weighted down with the very mud and humus of creation, is the vessel that Oudin must carry in order to bring about the covenant.

> He carried himself as if he were bearing a corpse, stranger and relation at one and the same time. In reality he bore the transparent memorable body of Beti, whom he had lifted from the ground to cover a very bad patch. In this region she became heavy as lead. (107)

In this journeying through the forest bed, Oudin and Beti almost seem to take on the quality inherent in the formation of that bed. The representation here is of a cycle, a death and rebirth, in an unceasing regenerative energy flow. The elements, the landscape, are not simple indicators of their passage, their journeying, but indeed are essence of that journeying.

Often Harris reveals, or rather elucidates for us, the essential structure of his writing. Through the fundamental use of his lexicon, through the alchemy of words, the author brings about the mergings of different realms, the cohering and correspondence of different phenomena, locating their dynamic intersecting and the consequent transformation of their essential qualities. This interplay and cohering of realities, and the subsequent dynamic transformations, give credence to the transformative vision that leads to new formations, new possibilities, to a new presence. Through Kaiser, the author presents the transformative power of words, their cohering function; the words themselves take on their own essential structures, becoming paraphrase or soliloquy. Their intersectings become the creative parable of the author's craft, so that language, phenomena, and perceptions all undergo an inner dynamic transformation and change.

Kaiser moistened his burning lips, searching for the ruling love and parable in the nature of words. A tree was a word, a river was a word, a man was a word: yet they were—all three—as imperishable and wordless as all substance, which is compounded of fire and reflection, smoke and husk. (74)

Even as elixir transforms Kaiser's vital blood flow, so, too, through the alchemy of words Harris postulates the artist's vision of a new reality and fuses together into a new becoming the creative sperm of life with the unfolding scientific knowledge of mankind.

There was an esoteric yearning for the mother's shell and womb, and there was a technical longing for the mined and subjected earth. It was this secret and this technical understanding, whose marriage could make life new and desirable again. (74)

The egg, the embryo, and the womb become essential motifs in this transformative process, affecting the vision and the perception of many of the characters, promising, underscoring, and accepting a subliminal and unending procreative process. This creative unfolding is perceived in nature and the elements as the basic ordinance of a new societal possibility. All is a cohering of different realities, so that the vertical perception of the forest from the sky not only transforms the essential mood of forest but locates the very conception and formation of the forest itself.

When one's eyes strayed down from the blue sky-light at last . . . . The impression of darkness and concreteness in looming phallus and tree and sky faded again, and turned into music and the rustling blind whisper of streaming leaves. (115)

Here sky, forest, stone, leaf obey that transformative power of words. This vertical image of penetration, of phallus intersecting with tree and turning into music, this metaphor suggestive of the procreative act, recurs at many varying levels through *The Far Journey of Oudin*. The song of soliloquy seems to become a conduit leading into the very matrix center of procreative time, into the womb. The promise is held out of new creation, by the symbiotic merging of image and metaphor, of Beti and Oudin.

The words struck an intimate note in Oudin's heart, and he forgot where he was; the figure before him had become an image of trans-parency through whom he looked across the river and into the distance, as into a timeless womb and unconscious landscape. Or it might have been soliloquy he had been conducting with the hunted reflection he had drawn in the river of himself and Beti. (104)

Essentially Oudin's journey ultimately takes on the quality of a mystic illumination leading to soft conceptions of new realities. At the beginning, the forest gloom (the darkness that is symptomatic of that condition) is streaked through and pierced by a procreative shaft of light; the darkness is illuminated even as the egg is fertilized.

> He searched the remarkable gloom everywhere, following threads and lines of sepulchral vision, pale and fluid, rising and falling. The leaves rustled like feathers and tender illumination shifted and pooled and changed all the time. The forest was settling as a hen settles, or standing as a hen fluffs and stands to dry its raining feathers and circulate the light like a hatching cushion of eggs. (130)

Forked lightning witnesses and illuminates the mating and intercourse of sky and earth. The creative act ensues.

> Then the far track of lightnings came closer, without warning . . . the sacred embryonic beasts of the sky crouched. The table of creation began to dislodge itself and to fall with the greatest crash. (88)

Harris, in his presentation of the principal racial group—the East Indian, who is central to *The Far Journey of Oudin*—indicates change that leads to a transformation of the essential nature of a given structure of that group, leading eventually to the promise of new order. So that underscoring Oudin's journey is the initial breakup, the changes and transformation of an old and established order and culture. Both Beti and Oudin, in their journeying toward self-awareness and new presences, shed some of the old cultural trappings by which their childhoods and their formative years were molded. The ceremonies and rituals that guided their spiritual relationship to their group become less immediate, less important, but even as this change is occurring a dynamic process of transformation seems to ordain a new ritualistic order. The journey of Oudin and Beti, then, is a journey toward freedom from the old established past and culture. But since all phenomena are linked in a continuous unfolding, the new presence embodies some of the old ritual. Beti, even as she is on the point of assuming a new self, a new presence, attempts to enter as deeply as possible an old ritual presence.

> He looked at Beti, until she felt the beating heart of ancient alarm and lust beneath his rags and flesh. She saw horns reflected on the tiger's head in the devil's searching eye. It was another piece of the unconventional jigsaw she had always adored; and she was indulging

herself in her last flings now the parting of the ways had come for the bride of spiritual fantasy and the mother of actuality. (125)

In her journeying, Beti arrives at a heightened sense of perception and awareness in which she achieves a dynamic cohering of realities; fragmentation leads to coherence, a process ordaining continuity, establishing a vitalistic perception of reality.

> What dominated the phantasmogoria and cosmopolis of experimental life was a shattering and constructive mystery, rather than an ultimate and dreadful representation and end. (122)

Even as Beti attempts to reenter a ritual past from which she is moving away, instinctively she attempts to retain it. Yet her journey takes her into her own liberating space, which she enshrines on the sand as an emblem of new freedom, indicating to Oudin her arrival at a new presence.

> What she had to do was to make her kind of secret mark on him—the obvious mark an illiterate person must make in lieu of a signature and a name. With her toes she drew in the sand an incomprehensible, fertile figure within a hollow cage at Oudin's feet. . . .
> . . . It was a crystallization and acceptance . . . of the dark logic of ultimate separation and division. (113)

Through this act, Beti achieves the crystallization of her presence. Beti, who at the age of fifteen would have been pawned out to Ram, her virginity traded away, now as signatory establishes and confirms her own selfhood. Her journey heralds a new order, a new relationship between East Indian woman and man. The transformative act has taken place, an act that also proffers and ordains a new presence.

Oudin, too, promises a vision of a new order. But this new order is often beset by searching and doubt. Oudin, still partially tied to an ancestry that has preordained so much of his past, wonders:

> How could he hope to plant and invent a human brain and cosmopolis— of sublimation as well as of nerves—and to ingrain it into the fibre of a race whose darkest crime and brightest destiny had long since ceased to count . . . . Yet if he was unable to do this, how then was he to rise from the grave of the world? (112)

But Harris has already, in a long expository statement, articulated the inner falling-apart of the traditional culture of the East Indian, the process of its inner dynamic changing—its shifting, faltering hold on its descendants. The whole inner structure of kinship, and authority based on kinship, the ceremonial of family ties and loyalties, Harris states, is in a process of endemic change. Its etiology Harris does not expound on or analyze; rather he states that some "secret participation and magic of ancient authority and kinship, father, brother, daughter" (51) had been broken beyond repair. Now Kaiser wishes for a freedom from the intrinsic authority of his culture and of his belief in and adherence to the ceremonies and rituals of his culture. He wants only "the freedom to die when and where he pleased, and to love whom and what he wished" (72).

It is not surprising, therefore, that Oudin's journey as charted by Harris is the search for freedom from authoritarian culture, freedom from the initial beggary that has marked the wanderings and journeyings across the savannah of his forebears, an indentured band of laborers.

> No one knew where they were going, or where they had come from, and what their ambiguous mission was, whether it was death or whether it was a new symbolic birth and life. (84)

Perhaps the attempt to move out of this wandering beggary by assuming and entering into a new materialistic endeavor, which eventually leads to an embracing of hyperacquisitiveness and a neglect of the land, may have initiated the decline and ensuing rot of a cultural past. Mohammed laments his journeying away from the land into a new materialistic order whose only motivating principle is the acquiring of power.

> Mohammed knew the page had been written and finished . . . . Every word of meaning within them was rotting . . . . Their partial neglect of the land was contained in the seed. Their disfiguring and vulgar quest for new ways of making money . . . were all a beginning and a rot in the womb of subversion. (52)

Ram, too, in his quest for power arrives at the state of confusion in which the fragmentation, the disintegration, of his material reality, when followed by a reintegrative process, further heightens that confusion, making him unable to apprehend or give meaning to his journey. His perception becomes a blurring of phenomena whose edges run together, leading to bewilderment and to regret about his journey. The blurring edges do not produce a cohering reality, but rather lead to uncertainty and reduction.

> "I so bewilder I can't place nothing no more. What I used to value and what I used not to value overlapping. . . . And yet all is one, understand me?" (91)

Oudin's far journey, however, opens out into a cohering possibility. In order for Oudin to achieve his existential reality and arrive at his own essential being, he has to undertake his journey of indenture, of union with Beti, of fatherhood—a journey that clarifies the past and illuminates the future. This future ordains a new beginning, a new presence, and by extension new cultural possibilities in which the self is sacrosanct but still joined to the communal.

> It was this foresight and incipient universal compassion, lighting up the near future—as though each dark year ahead was alive with brilliant possibilities—that had fired Oudin into becoming the slave of Ram, and the labourer of Mohammed; and later the husband of Beti, and a father of one child and another still unborn. . . . It made Oudin conscious of the dreadful nature in every compassionate alliance one has to break gradually in order to emerge into one's ruling constructive self. (101)

Wilson Harris, through his own magical artistry, through his singing, achieves a coherence not only of the ecstatic, but of the spiritual and the philosophical. We arrive at *Palace of the Peacock*, where symbolic communion takes place, a sacrament leading to essential self-possession, to a cohering and to an assumption of presence.

> I felt the faces before me begin to fade and part company from me and from themselves as if our need of one another was now fulfilled, and our distance from each other was the distance of a sacrament, the sacrament and embrace we knew in one muse and one undying soul. Each of us now held at last in his arms what he had been forever seeking and what he had eternally possessed. (Harris, *Palace of the Peacock*, 152)

Harris, using the vast landscape of Guyana with its multiple races fused in space, sets out to locate the radial center of that landscape, to shade together its seeming oppositions, and by so doing, to present a harmonious possibility of new beginning to the land and to its people. Thus, Harris establishes a cyclical regenerative process that ultimately ordains the arrival of a mythic crew to the cohering reality of *Palace of the Peacock*.

Clearly Harris, in his attempt to grasp the essential meaning hidden in the ecological landscape of Guyana, fuses together all times, all realities, all seeming oppositions, investing them with an ultimate creative possibility and unity. His vision, therefore, is essentially transformative, negating disassociations and attesting to a holistic interpretation of that ecological landscape. Through his own creative muse, Harris gives substantiality to the abstract, locates the elastic linkage in corresponding realities; finally, in his search for universal meaning, he proffers ultimate optimism, an assurance of a never-ending and everlasting creative process, obedient to the longing, to a yearning, to endow the vast historical canvas of Guyana with universal meaning.

A longing swept him like the wind of the muse to understand and transform his beginnings: to see the indestructible nucleus and redemption of creation, the remote and the abstract image and correspondence, in which all things and events gained their substance and universal meaning. (130)

Harris, by using a technique of reduction and accumulation, gives signification to the most minuscule—the atom—and extends that signification into enlarging macro-perception to the total landscape of his novel and to the method and substance ordaining his novelistic technique: "He longed to see, he longed to see the atom, the very nail of moment in the universe" (130). Thus Harris reflects and reenacts the very creative process that fired into beginning the landscape of which he is writing. Harris, too, accepting an ultimate trust and interrelationship between the initial spark and the finished product, accepting, too, a continuous and unbroken umbilical link with that spirit force and presence, can but reincarnate that spirit force. It is as if Harris imposes on himself the extreme responsibility of re-creating through words and language the very creation of Guyana itself. Creative form, therefore, responds to the essential process.

I had never before looked on the blinding world in this trusting manner—through an eye I shared only with the soul, the soul and mother of the universe. (146)

Here Harris seems to be postulating that the artist derives his essential creative inheritance from his landscape and then can imbue a further cohering quality in that landscape as he seeks its essence. This intradynamic process assures continuity, gives credence to a regenerative process and presence. For essentially *Palace of the Peacock* provides narrative evidence of cyclical regeneration, where fantasy and reality are textured together, where life and death mediate, where the structures sprung from the seeds of historical reality dematerialize and a possibility of new beginnings for the folk is reestablished in all of its dynamic variations. In a richly colored texture of landscapes and seasons, a promise of new beginnings is embodied in the blood flow and in that pulsating life-current of the universe, impregnating the bodies of the folk with the same vital ceaseless flow as the spirit nature of streams and rivers.

The trees on the bank were clothed in an eternity of autumnal colour—equally removed from the green of youth as from the iron-clad winter of age—a new and enduring spiritual summer of russet and tropical gold whose tints had been tenderly planted in the bed of the stream. The sun veined these mythical shades and leaves in our eye. (76)

Here all the splendor, the brilliance, and luxuriance of a tropical essentiality hum with the promise of summer greening; all is resonance, and echo, and vibrating sound, charging landscape and character with harmonious and rhythmical becoming.

> He felt the fine stringed bars of a universal ecstasy tuning within him beyond life and death, past and present, until they neither ceased nor stopped. (78)

Evidently the essential action of *Palace of the Peacock,* though located in a voyaging quest toward arrival at Mariella's settlement, is really the search across space, time, across spirit space, to arrival at selfhood—at presence. The novel's action delineates that total process of becoming, of arriving at one's existence; after the questing, after the pursuit that characterizes the novel's action and spans eons and ages, life force and death cohere, so that each character arrives at his own ultimate essence. The gulf separating the material beginnings from the first frail physical and corporeal reality, from that spiritual insubstantiality, is bridged time and time again through the connecting link of that pursuit. Carroll enters into a universal ecstasy; Vigilance, into the fullness of space, indeed into the mythic center of that space.

> Vigilance winced a little and rubbed his eyes where he climbed and clung to the cliff wondering at the childish repetitive boat and prison of life. What an enormous spiritual distance and inner bleeding substance lay between himself and that crust and shell he had once thought he inhabited. . . . He tried to convey across the span and gulf of dead and dying ages and myth the endless pursuit on which Donne was engaged. (104)

Donne arrives through figural disintegration of self into the void and center of nothingness by a process of regenerative apprehension of that void.

> He focused his blind eye with all penitent might on this pinpoint star and reflection as one looking into the void of oneself upon the far greater love and self-protection that have made the universe. (140)

However, arrival at this ultimate cohering necessitates a metaphysical creative journey in which the vastness of Guyana is apprehended through accumulating brush strokes leading to the essential linking of forms, of matter, of spirit. The journey, therefore, is an attempt to imbue the material reality of the land with metaphysical meaning, with philosophical existence. Here, as often in Wilson Harris's creative writing, he articulates this metaphysical plotting of his landscape.

A metaphysical outline dwelt everywhere filling in blocks where spaces stood and without this one would never have perceived the curious statement of completion and perfection. (144)

The author's initial premise and statement, therefore, takes shape as a journey toward that point of perfection, and ultimately, the chase, after traveling the brittleness of experience, approaches a point of universal love.

I stifled my words and leaned over the ground to confirm the musing footfall and image I had seen and heard in my mind in the immortal chase of love on the brittle earth. (31)

Thus, it is that the pursuit, the voyaging, the chase, takes place across an earth-space that has all the contourings and patternings of radial but cohering shadows and forms. Indeed, the pursuit becomes the essential evocation of that earth-space of land, of Guyana. All becomes, then, the finite creative process in which the basic skeletal forms of things, the stone and bone structures, merge together in a holistic corporate design.

Across the crowded creation of the invisible savannahs of newborn wind of spirit blew the sun making light of everything, curious hands and feet, neck, shoulder, forehead, material twin shutter and eye. (146)

Even as the earth-wind spirit has promised new beginnings, initial consciousness and pre-memory become the creative modalities for leading to the structuring of metaphysical designs. How does memory, or indeed pre-memory, affect the conscious creative process? Harris questions, "Could a memory spring from nowhere into one's belly and experience?" (53). At what point do memory and consciousness, experience and perception, coalesce into precept, into vision? Clearly, then, through such rhetorical questions Harris premises a linkage of methods and phenomena, postulates the weaving of space and time in a continuous flowing. Clarification derives from this premise, this postulate, to such a degree that the creative impulse takes on a quality of revelation that will complete the metaphysical design, that will paint in the drifting half-shadows. Through the disintegration of material vision the creative artist arrives at the point of unique inner perception of reality.

He saw nothing, he saw unselfness of night, the invisible otherness around, the darkness all the time, he saw the stars he knew to be invisible however much they appeared to shine above him. (140–141)

Clearly, then, reductionism, creative disintegration, leads not to fragmentation of reality but to a cohering of reality. In this instance, seeming opposites cohere; the creative process becomes a vitalizing energy flow, cyclical promise ordaining a second coming; thus, the death of form, the disintegration of substance, opens out to new beginnings, to a new living. The whole structure of the novel—the reappearance of a second crew bearing the names of the men of another crew, all of whom died in a similar pursuit of the folk—testifies to this information.

> The odd fact existed of course that their living names matched the names of a famous dead crew that had sunk in the rapids and been drowned to a man, leaving their names inscribed on Sorrow Hill which stood at the foot of the falls. (23)

This constant re-creation of matter and form not only gives structure to the novel, but also conditions the perception of many of the characters. To a man, they locate their journey within the context of reincarnation or their reappearance in another time, which is essentially the same time. They all experience a constant resurfacing in a vertical motion, which undoubtedly links them to the undying experiences of the previous crew.

> So it was, unwitting and ignorant, he had been drawn to his death with the others, and had acquired the extraordinary defensive blindness, ribald as hell and witchcraft, of dying again and again to the world and still bobbing up once more lusting for an ultimate satisfaction and a cynical truth. (42)

Thus it is that the second chase, the journey upriver, leading ultimately to the "palace of the peacock," seems to have been ordained, as it celebrates an essential community of differing ethnic types of Guyana. The narrative voice, therefore, is unable to attach itself to this second voyaging. The second voyaging promises arrival, offers a possibility of fulfillment, a fulfillment that perhaps has been enshrined in a further beginning; Harris seems to underscore the circularity, a recurrence not simply of action, but of phenomena. The second crew foresees its drowning, but even as the men drown they live again.

> "Ah telling you Ah dream the boat sink with all of we," . . . "Ah drowned dead and Ah float. All of we exposed and float . . ."
> . . . "Ah dream Ah get another chance to live me life over from the very start. Live me life over from the very start, you hear?" (110)

Predictability seems to assure promise of recurrence and of self-generation. Thus, even as the second crew voyages upriver and its members meet their various deaths, the deaths themselves seem to reinforce, indeed, seem to be absorbed by, those who are still living.

They shuddered and spat their own—and his—blood and death-wish. It had been forcibly and rudely ejected. And this taste and forfeiture of self-annihilation bore them into the future on the wheel of life. (102)

Embedded, then, in the death-life formulation is a promise of futures opening out to ultimate possibilities. Thus, in the pursuit and chase of the folk, though they become victims, they remain imperishable, indeed, indestructible. Clearly Harris is stating that a folk essence girds and fortifies continuously the larger Guyanese life and presence: "His victims had never perished, constantly moving before him, living and never dying in the eternal folk" (68). In fact, even those who pursue the folk arrive at their essential being through the motif of recurrence, of self-regeneration.

> In this remarkable filtered light it was not men of vain flesh and blood I saw toiling laboriously and meaninglessly, but active ghosts whose labour was indeed a flitting shadow over their shoulders as living men would don raiment and cast it off in turn to fulfill the simplest necessity of being. (34)

Not only are the folk imbued with an imperishable nature, but those who have toiled to build Guyana, dying in the process, are revived, their ghostly figures reclothed in living forms, their deaths a dream leading to ultimate being.

Harris's metaphysical conceptualization of reality derives not simply from his notations of an existential space but also from the very vital shape and mood of the Guyana landscape itself. From this vast landscape, from the very heartbeat of tropical reality, emanate so many varying perceptions, so many illusive shapings, to such a degree that the essence of any form is only apprehended through the impressionistic ceasing of that form in all of its multiple moods and variations. The eye, though perceiving the external material reality, doubts its own perception, questions its vision as to the nature and substance of reality. Optical illusion and optical veracity combine in a uniquely changing vision shared equally by the "dead seeing eye" and the "blind seeing eye":

> The sun blinded and ruled my living sight but the dead man's eye remained open and obstinate and clear. (13)

"My right eye—which is actually sound—goes blind in my dream." (18)

The question is through what narrative eye is this creative landscape presented or even apprehended? Small wonder, then, that the novelistic landscape becomes a kaleidoscopic series of shifting and mutating representations, in a reality already imbued with its own kaleidoscopically shifting power and mutations.

> The solid wall of trees was filled with ancient blocks of shadow and with gleaming hinges of light. Wind rustled and leafy curtains through which masks of living beard dangled as low as the water and the sun. My living eye was stunned by inversions of the brilliancy and the gloom of the forest in a deception and hollow and socket. (26)

Yet Harris gives the reality of Guyana a certain historical solidity and permanence by an interspersing of direct historical and naturalistic statements into his metaphorical searching. This direct representation of historical and social formation is the scaffolding necessary for Harris's metaphysical architectonic structurings.

> The names Brazil and Guiana were colonial conventions . . . . I clung to them now as to a curious necessary stone and footing, even in my dream, the ground I knew I must not relinquish. (20)

That the narrator sees the vital need to hold on to that scaffolding is clear evidence of Harris's awareness that without the random references to precise historical and societal formulations, his vast metaphysical creation would take on a metaphysical insubstantiality and incomprehensibility. Thus, the map of Guyana, though imbued by the author with all of his dream and contourings, is fleshed out, is given substance, through corporate dimensions.

> They were an actual stage, a presence, however mythical they seemed to the universal and the spiritual eye. They were as close to me as my ribs, the rivers and the flatland, the mountains and heartland I intimately saw. (20)

So old, so eminently ageless, is the land of Guyana that in itself it embodies the marvelous, the magical, and entry into it can be entry into mythic history and the ageless ritual of changing phenomena. Indeed, the whole voyage upriver to the palace of the peacock, in an unquestioning search for a mission hanging over the vast waterfall systems, is but a search for a soul and spirit of the land and rivers of Guyana. Small wonder, then, that shadows move among them. The tremulous animation of this landscape vibrates their very consciousness.

> I stopped for an instant overwhelmed by a renewed force of consciousness of the hot spirit and moving spell in the tropical undergrowth. . . . The whispering trees spun their leaves to a sudden fall wherein the ground seemed to grow lighter in my mind and to move to meet them in the air. (27)

This landscape engenders mutations in a constant unfolding; and this dynamic engendering leads to vital transubstantiation of form and of being. All provide Harris with constant anthropomorphic imagery in which all phenomena are interlaced, form and feelings, bodies and emotions, commingle in an unceasing movement of the river, the central metaphor and essential landscape for the crew's and the author's metaphysical searchings. The unceasing gestations of a river are but reflectors of the creative mutations of body and mind. Images then become prismatic and multidimensional, wherein all phenomena are transferable, wherein an essential linkage is ordained. So easy it is to merge fantasy and reality when the reality itself is spun fiction.

> The river hastened everywhere around it. Formidable lips breathed in the open running atmosphere to flatter it, many a wreathed countenance to conceal it and half-breasted body, mysterious and pregnant with creation, armed with every cunning abortion and dream of infancy to claim it. Clear fictions of imperious rock they were in the long rippling water of the river. (32)

In turbulence and in the flow of the river is all the refracted history and power of the folk, in the texturings of that flow all the embroiderings of their vestments, and in the mutations of form, all the spirit and bodily mutations emblematic of the folk. In a brilliantly extended image unfolding and radiating ever outward, Harris weaves together the essential metaphors of *Palace of the Peacock*, the spatial and spiritual intercourse of river with land, of the miscegenated peoples of Guyana with folk. The whole crew is caught in the dramatic embrace of river and of the folk woman Mariella, an embrace that ultimately leads the crew to death and to essential being in the palace of the peacock.

> Her crumpled bosom and river grew agitated with desire, bottling and shaking every fear and inhibition and outcry. The ruffles in the water were her dress rolling and rising to embrace the crew. This sudden insolence of soul rose and caught them from the powder of her eyes and the age of her smile and the dust in her hair all flowing back upon them with silent streaming majesty and abnormal youth and in a wave of freedom and strength. (73)

Clearly the transformative notion and element so important to the recreation of form and personality, and so ultimate for the searchings of essential presence, all come together here in a majestic architectural structuring in the flow of the river; images are of necessity liquid and mobile. In the hard substructurings of stone, in order for the image to retain a mobility, a disintegrative quality must sometimes be injected. Here Jennings and Cameron seem carved in rock and stone; their gestures and action, history and character, with underlying premonition of crumbling.

> They were turned to stone stung to the bitterest attention by what they knew not. Jennings remained powerful, thrusting, the air of a primitive republican boxer upon him, and Cameron stood, heavy and bundled like rock, animal-wise, conscious of a rootless superstition and shifting mastery he had once worshipped in himself and now felt crumbling and lost. (98)

Later, the carved rock disintegrates, loses its solidity, its immediate history, and, changing into a crumbling abstraction of its former self, becomes a hollow shell and ancient relic.

> He had held the husk in his hand and it had given a dry brittle harp's cry of relief, mummified and mystical and Egyptian, melting at the same time into an inner dust that crumbled to an ancient door of life. (119)

In the novelistic landscape, then, all phenomena seem to be in a constant state of transformation, of dynamic change wherein myriad correspondences occur in constantly shifting configurations and patterns, to such a degree that external matter is presented as less than essential. Harris then attempts to imbue that matter, that form, with a correspondence that locates its essence. The frailty of bones and flesh as they crumble takes on the appearance of paper and ink.

> His bones were splinters and points Vigilance saw and his flesh was newspapers, drab, wet until the lines and markings had run fantastically together. His hair stood flat on his brow like ink. (122–123)

The elements, the animal kingdom, the human species, all of nature in its multiple manifestations, refract and reflect the incessant alterations of form, the transitoriness of image, the fleeting quality of shapes. Imagery, therefore, in Harris derives from a rapid succession of mobiles ever dancing in the cosmos; thus we have the impression that all things are in a constant state of motion toward a creative center, which in itself is in a constant state of change. At times this motion is turbulent.

> The sky turned into a running deer and ram, half-ram, half-deer running for life . . . . Leaves sprang up from nowhere, a stampede of ghostly men and women all shaped by the leaves, raining and running against the sky. (136)

At times the motion is a cohering of forms leading to a point of metaphysical repose, of spiritual quiescence; then, and only then, Harris seems to postulate the arrival at that point of centrality, of essence, clothed in the beautifying plumage, the brilliance of the peacock.

> The enormous starry dress it now wore spread itself all around into a full majestic gown from which emerged the intimate column of a musing neck, face and hands, and twinkling feet. The stars became peacocks' eyes, and the great tree of flesh and blood swirled into another stream that sparkled with divine feathers where the neck and the hands and the feet had been nailed. (146)

Before arriving at the palace of the peacock, however, the crew, in its mad pursuit of the folk, also undergoes substantial metamorphosis, even as each of its members becomes critically aware of his own particular ambiguous ancestral heritage, his own particular link to his fellows. A growing awareness of their ancestral linkages exposes all the rawboned emotional and spiritual discord wherein these linkages originate. Not only are the crew members linked to one another, it seems, but they are linked to the land whose history is turbulent, whose folk ancestry seems to contain a collective emotional and spiritual discord. The plot of the novel, then, becomes the unravelling of that ancestry, the grasping of that history, the metaphysical harmonizing of that emotional and physical discord; symptomatic of this discord is a recurrent drought in a land of waters.

> "They accustom to move at this season, sir," . . .
> "Some kind of belief to do with the drought—once in seven year it bound to curse the land." (60)

Here, old Schomburgh explains the movement of the folk to the leader of the expedition, Donne, from whom the folk, remembering the legend of a former crew, are shrinking and fleeing. Donne, the exemplar of a colonizing spirit (that is, before his symbolic entry into the palace of the peacock), realizes how harsh and brutal the actual novelistic landscape is.

> "Life here is tough. One has to be a devil to survive. I'm the last landlord. I tell you I fight everything in nature, flood, drought, chicken hawk, rat, beast and woman. I'm everything. Mid-wife, yes, doctor, yes, gaoler, judge, hangman, every blasted thing to the labouring people. Look man, look outside again. Primitive. Every boundary line is a myth. No-man's land, understand?" (17)

It is from Donne and his assembled crew that the folk flee, in a seeming reenactment of former history now turned into living legend. Thus it is that history and legend take on a pattern of belief leading to an intuitive, instinctual reaction to the presence of Donne and his crew. The previous drowning of the crew agitates the folk.

Everyone remembered that not so long ago this self-same crew had been drowned to a man in the rapids below the Mission. Everyone recalled the visits the crew had paid the Mission from time to time leading to the fatal accident. (37–38)

This memory of the drowned crew and its seeming reincarnation and representation cast gloom and awaken an uncontrollable dread in the hearts and minds not only of the present crew but also of the folk.

It was an ominous and disturbing symptom of retiring gloom and darkened understanding under the narrow chink and ribbon of sky. They shrank from us as from a superstition of dead men. (38)

This reaction to the presence of Donne and the crew, leading to the flight of the folk and their subsequent pursuit, becomes a central motif, guiding and catalyzing the emotional structure of the narrative, indeed leading to its action.

Donne had had a bad name in the savannahs, and Mariella, to their dreaming knowledge, had been abused and ill-treated by him, and had ultimately killed him. Their faces turned into a wall around her. She was a living fugitive from the devil's rule. This was the birth and beginning of a new fantasy and material difficulty and opposition. (38–39)

The interplay between the crew and the folk, alternatively pursuer and pursued, becomes the structural element not of a linear action but of interweaving plots and motif. In these interlocking motifs, all the various strands and threads of miscegenation and unknown family ties spin together. The crew is thus

one spiritual family living and dying together in a common grave out of which they had sprung again from the same soul and womb as it were. They were all knotted and bound together in the enormous bruised head of Cameron's ancestry and nature as in the white unshaven head of Schomburgh's age and presence. (40)

Here, the oppositions of races and the divergencies of ambiguous ancestry symbolically come together within one frail vessel. Their collective survival is dependent on the expeditious use of all their individual skills; yet, quartered together, emotions in all their instinctual immediacy surface, clash, and collide. Yet these collisions and clashes seem subsumed in their collective venturing; cross-energizing binds them together in their common venturing.

After a while this horrifying exchange of soul and this identification of themselves with each other brought them a partial return and renewal

of confidence, a neighbourly wishful fulfilment and a basking in each
other's degradation and misery that they had always loved and respected.
(100)

The communal questing, the common awareness of each other, even
while underscoring their individual ancestries, liquidates the need for
individual names and uncertain personal histories. In this, Harris postulates
a rehabilitative possibility making ambiguous heritage meaningless.

> It was a partial rehabilitation of themselves, the partial rehabilitation of
> a tradition of empty names and dead letters, dead as the buttons on their
> shirt. It was all well and good they reasoned as inspired madmen would
> to strain themselves to gain that elastic frontier where a spirit might rise
> from the dead and rule the material past world. (100)

Yet in each individual conscience and memory, in the consciousness, there
still vibrate all the interplay, the shifting tremors, and the elastic shivering
of their births and of their birthings.

> There had always been a thorn in acknowledging his relationships—an
> unexplored cloud of promiscuous wild oats he secretly dreaded. His
> family tree subsisted in a soil of entanglement he knew to his grief in the
> stream of his secretive life, and Carroll's arrival brought the whole past to
> a head before him. (77)

The question of paternity, so insistent and repeated a question and motif
within the context of Caribbean societies and Caribbean social and family
structures, cannot be stifled by the collective rehabilitative questing but
keeps echoing, keeps on resonating. It is a question that pulls at the
memories of each of the members of the crew, unearthing intricate relationships, sublimating the incestuous.

Through a transformative novelistic vision Harris negates the initial
stereotyping of the native Guyanese-Amerindian woman, then stamps on her
the quality of wisdom derived from a millenium of experiences. By this
transformative process, the author, after initially disintegrating the physical
reality of phenomena, in this instance of the woman's face and soul,
reclothes them in folk wisdom, majesty, and power. Initially, Mariella's
features are etched in all the familiar forms attributed to the Indian folk.

> The stiff brooding materiality and expression of youth had vanished and
> now—in old age—there remained no sign of former feeling . . . . the air
> of wisdom that a millenium was past, a long timeless journey was finished
> without appearing to have begun, and no show of malice, enmity and
> overt desire to overcome oppression and evil mattered any longer. (71)

Thus, it is the folk who are pushed through cycles that inexorably turn and turn in a movement toward essence. They have all the power of endurance, of eternal constancy, of immortality.

> In reality, the legend and consciousness of race had come to mean for her—patience, the unfathomable patience of a god in whom all is changed into wisdom, all experience and all life a handkerchief of wisdom when the grandiloquence of history and civilization was past. (71–72)

Kaywana's children have shed the stereotypic, have cut across the history, and, stripping their personality, have finally achieved presence.

A s in *The Far Journey of Oudin* and *Palace of the Peacock*, Harris employs the element of the chase, of pursuit, to delineate a structure and trace the action of *The Whole Armour*. Here, however, Harris implants his sociophilosophical ideas more into the action and the dialogue than into elaborate, existential formulations. The landscape in *The Whole Armour* is also more immediate, closer to material reality, and thus more actualized. The principal characters act out the shuttling motions between fantasy and reality, between ever-evolving forms and fixed experiences, to such a degree that the line between the theatrical and the actual shade together, fiction and reality commingling. From the very beginning of *The Whole Armour* this interplay of fantasy and reality affects Abram's perception and notates the transubstantiation of form. The motif of the tiger, the principal element directing the plot and structuring the action of *The Whole Armour*, is immediately introduced and actualized, dramatically represented.

> Abram dreamed he was crawling in a wood—on the high branch of a tree—and had reached the extremity of a curious twisted limb. The leaves of the tree turned into black swooping birds, obscene and terrifying. He surveyed what appeared to be a beach beneath him, on which lay an old rotted tree-trunk, or ancient tacouba, hard as iron. He knew he must jump but felt he would cripple himself in landing upon it. He sprang from his perch, meeting softer ground. (Harris, *The Whole Armour*, 11)

Thus, not only is the human transformed through this method of transubstantiation, but phenomena also undergo changes. It is this constant shifting of phenomena that often structures the characterization. Mattias, for instance, through his mode of perceiving reality, sees phenomena as an ever-shifting insubstantial yet dynamic interplay of forms. Clearly this mode of seeing, this method of patterning reality, characterizes Harris's design of his novelistic canvas.

Compulsive eternity stood while every disjointed upturned picture and impression revolved in his mind—a series of revelations, engagements and disengagements, each pattern appearing the very unstable antithesis of another and undermining even itself as it dawned. (67–68)

This shifting insubstantial canvas, then, is not only backdrop but affects the essential behavior of all the characters. Magda, the main protagonist, can shift with facility between the real and theatrical, to such a degree that one cannot truly say whether her actions are dramatic representations or a presentation of fact: "Cristo stared at her, feeling bound and gagged before her theatrical and blinding performance—more real than life itself" (22). Throughout *The Whole Armour*, Magda's actions swing between the theatrical and the actual. Like a director, Magda makes the players and actors change costumes and take on other realities, impersonate other characters, directions that become the catalyst for the novel's action.

She appealed to her policeman of the jungle, drawing him into a conspiracy of senseless and sensible deception and woe. Her mourning was a double-edged sword of keenest theatrical pretension and of hopeless buried reality. (38)

In her role as actor-director, she creates fantasy out of reality in the minds of characters, actualizing then the haunting presence of the tiger.

"Before that happen I was so bewitched a tiger been running with me like a corpse in his jaws. I dreamt I was Abram-self." (63)

The recurrent motifs of life and death that provide Harris with an essential philosophical statement in *The Whole Armour* are introduced through music, elaborated through ritual culture and beliefs, actualized through conversion of forms and costumes, and finalized in the dynamic projection of continuity, of life and death. In the strings of guitars, the whole configuration of the dying and birthing of generations is introduced.

A nervous throbbing came across the distance from a guitar, followed by the shrill complaint of a reveller—the coincidence of a skeleton of musical sound flying with the fading protesting senses and Abram could not help recalling the dying and newborn generations of the Pomeroon in his mind's eternal eye. (14–15)

But this formulation is elaborated through a conceptual acceptance of the duality of life and death, of eternal processing through a ritualistic participation. All phenomena seem involved in this magical transformation: the elements, the actual day-to-day living, the very relationship between man and his societal circumstance.

A fine distance appears between oneself and everyone until the prosaic living one had always taken for granted—turns into one's own model of uncertainty, and the prosaic dead one has always ignored begin to hang their features of necromancy in the rising clouds. (97)

Yet it is not magical transformation or necromancy that acts as the essential link between life and death. Perhaps it is the cultural belief enshrined in the ritual celebration of a wake. Here death is not mourned but celebrated in a ritual that seems to reject the very notion of death. Thus, the presence of death is really denied and transformed through the ritual participation of a whole community.

The wake was a way of cementing a fissure in the ranks, repairing a seam that had opened, driving home a nail where one was missing. It was a collective roll-call, an amiable meeting, often the frantic smoothing of a grieving brow. (43)

Since the presence of the dead is vitalized through the celebration of a wake, Cristo's presence could be summoned, his reincarnation actualized by the very wake itself. For, indeed, though Cristo has been shrouded in death, or in the clothing of death, in Sharon's mind he is still alive and present.

Might as well believe Cristo had come back to life at his own dead wake to take Sharon in his arms, and that one's true clock of fate ticked in the breast of the tiger as it beat in one's own heart. (80)

The formulation of the duality of life and death, the linkage between the two, seems to underscore the process of gestation and fertilization, assuring the notion of the unending unfolding of a procreative process. There seems to be little hiatus from this process.

The eternal bridge that stretched across limbo—from the "dead" to the "living"—had always been there, conjoint with time and eternity. (68)

So that even as Peet (who has also oscillated throughout the novel between a sense of life and death) finally dies, he, his image, and his form seem to assure Cristo's essential assumption of life after his impending death.

Peet's dead eyes were staring at her. . . . The hand descended slowly and gravely, signalling the naked impetus of flight from self-reproach and insensibility. Cristo would be free in the end, it seemed to state, in an armour superior to the elements of self-division and coercion. (128)

This assumption of life is not only spiritual, but is actually embodied in the promise of a new life, of a new birthing. Through Sharon, Cristo lives again as he waits, "listening at the door of the womb for Sharon's musing child to begin and crow" (123). As with life and death, so, too, the notions of fertility and drought, renewal and chaos, flow together in a continuous negating and writhing rhythm. Landscape becomes here an essential presence wherein this dynamic rhythmical process is assured. Even as Cristo has sensed and listened to the creative continuity in Sharon, an unending possibility is affectively enshrined through love.

> The inhabitants of the region had not properly wakened to the slaying of the dragon of drought by the spidery feet of the rain which left their trail in every thread and green shoot on the land. The stern winter of hardship had yielded to the spring of fertility but the roots and branches of transformation descended and arose only in the starred eye of love. (93)

The cyclical movement of phenomena—societal, human and elemental—is established through this pendulum swing: Life-death, fertility-drought, societal-coherence-societal chaos. Thus the transformative process assures a vitalistic presence. The vital process is reflected not only in the linkage of substance but also through the linkage of human presence. It is as if the commingling of forms establishes cohering of realities,

> the smell of a mingling of roots and leaves and branches all turning into a web of cognition that entered their blood. They walked with their newfound arms twined together, making a light almost aerial touch and step. (92)

Through this energizing linkage of form, the landscape and elements are no longer reflections of reality but rather here take on an essentiality of their own, creating an anatomical presence in which man and woman, man and landscape, copenetrate and fuse into a holistic and integral presence. Here again new love leads to a dynamic transformative motion.

> It was along this very mysterious backbone and watershed—between ancient terror and new-born love—that the frightful jaguar of death had roamed, leaping across emotional tumbling rivers from crag to crag. (82)

The whole landscape of Guyana in all of its extensive and vital presence seems to pulse and vibrate with the jaguar's elastic power and energy, surging with all of its primal motion. The jaguar, the animate and animal essential presence of the vast landscape, jumps over space and time, linking the past of his rulership to the present rulership of lore. All phenomena are made vital, all, the total landscape of Guyana and the South American coastline, is animated.

> Her fingers travelled across the map of Cristo's skin, stroking the veins in every ancestor's body. It sought to establish the encounter with the lost

soul of all generations, the tiger roaming through the trackless paths, rapping at every jungle door, calling to the sweet meat belonging to the dead sleeping flesh of the night, pausing by every pool of meditation. (82)

Here is established the primal presence of the tiger or jaguar—keeper and guardian of the societal, the elemental, the meditative inner soul of the region. The tiger is the very backbone and spine, the embodiment, of the whole elemental landscape. In this presence, in this animated phenomenon, the essential history and settlement of Guyana, too, are given a corporeal reality, a metaphorical presence. Here history and land and the human condition assume an existential coherence. Yet the postulate of coherence demands a certain struggle, a certain resistance, to an uninterrupted encroachment of landscape on the human condition, whose beginnings in Guyana embody all the qualities of wanton growth and luxuriance of the jungle.

A weak link in their armour . . . was tantamount to a surrender to the jungle they were called upon to face boisterously and to overcome. . . . It meant the rallying of all their forces into an incestuous persona and image and alliance—the very antithesis of their dark truth and history, written in the violent mixture of races that had bred them as though their true mother was a wanton on the face of the earth and their true father a vagrant and a rogue from every continent. (43)

In *The Whole Armour*, through the medium of the fabulous, Harris imbues the immediate landscape with a quality of the marvelous, transforming history into fable, fable into myth and legend. Thus, the whole novelistic canvas takes on emblematic qualities and, trembling through this transformative process, merges together the real, the marvelous, the mythic, and the legendary. The folk element of the people (which enters at every level in this transformative process), their history, their beginnings, their miscegenation and projected cohesion, all are subsumed in this transformative process. History shades into myth, personality assumes presence, the rite of passage becomes a ritual ceremonial. The gestation of races coheres into a collective folk self. Indeed, Harris seems intent on imbuing the whole novelistic canvas with an ultimate presence.

The Pomeroon region in which the novel is centered is made out to be the primal heart and center, the womb of the Guyanese heartland, so many nations and tributaries come together here. In this heartland reside all the vegetal possibilities of Guyana. Cristo elaborates on this, ascribing to this region and to its earth an essential possibility and nurturing presence.

"Pomeroon is the best place to be born to know this whole country, the whole of Guiana, British, Dutch, French, everything. . . . First, to know

we're all mixed up, East, West, North, South, every race under the sun.
Second, to know that what we possess comes from the ground up—
coconut, copra, plantain, banana . . ." (108)

Yet, even as the Pomeroon is vital with promise, its foreshore may be
disintegrating; its heartland and primeval jungle, constantly threatening with
their incessant and encroaching growth, demand a collective will to interrupt
that growth. Onto the primeval landscape, Harris imposes that spirit and
presence of a primal beast—the tiger—whose presence assumes the quality
of legend, whose historical predatory journeyings assume a fantastic quality.
The tiger in *The Whole Armour*, is not simply a presence but actually
becomes, like the jungle, a powerful symbol, a legendary presence.

> The visitation of the tiger was a feature that accompanied everyone's
> growing years . . . . always on the frontier between changing fantasy and
> the growth of a new settlement. (31)

In part, the movement of *The Whole Armour* is the voyaging through
fantasy into a New World promise; Cristo changes from Abram's dead clothes
into the tiger's emblematic attire, thereby entering into the heartland and
primal center, into its primal essence. All the characters of *The Whole Armour*
are caught up in this movement, this transformation. Sharon moves between
the world of fantasy and that of reality, her dreams and perceptions arching
always upward into the fabulous. Indeed, she eventually seems to acquire a
quality of the fabulous in whose realm from early childhood she seems to
have lived.

> It was Cristo's turn to laugh. "You love all the fables, don't you, my
> little one? You were born like that." (113)

In her relationship with Cristo, Sharon evinces that very quality of fantasy
to which Cristo has alluded. Here the Pomeroon is not primeval but takes
on a quality of fantasy. Sharon, as it were, transforms through her own
perception the immediate violent reality, rejecting it and re-creating her own
fantastic landscape. Her perception is not only transformative but in the
process she, too, seems transformed, takes on the quality of wizardry, which
in itself is the transformer of history. For Harris, in attempting to present the
essential history of Guyana, fusing that history with fantasy, regenerates it
with myth, asserting the dynamic energizing interplay between them.

> "Don't forget history is a fable, baboon man. You read it in school like a
> monkey, little girl. The mountains turned valleys and the valleys turned
> mountains and everybody was running from cataclysmic disaster. Glad to
> hide in the trees and look down on the lost Incas and the dead kings of
> Spain." (119)

Harris seems preoccupied with the movement of the folk who become essential presences in his nonrealistic canvases, notating the past, reiterating the motif of pursuit and the pursuer already evidenced in *The Far Journey of Oudin* and *Palace of the Peacock*.

In *The Whole Armour*, Harris is not simply exploring the history of Guyana, but more particularly the dynamic ritual history of the folk. History is not simply fable but more accurately it becomes the essential re-creative element. The ritual—the wake—becomes the radical center of a historical regeneration in which the folk participate. Thus it is that the killing of Sharon's lover, a seeming breach in the collective armor of the folk, must be cemented by the ritual workings of the wake. Indeed, Harris seems to make the wake the axis of his notions of history and fable.

> There was the problematic fable of history in a nutshell. It was a murder and breach the whole community alone could repair by sponsoring a rough protagonist out of the heart of the innocent party. (49)

The folk participation in this healing ceremony, in this knitting together of a folk communal presence, is not simply reiterated but reflected in the cohering linkage that knits together the clan and family structure.

> Each group possessed this stamp, dogmatic kinship and approval . . . . superior landlord redeemed by inferior slave, proud indigenous folk married to the economic emancipation of tyrants. In spite of everything that continued to happen it was an archaic sanction that constantly sought to reassert itself and bless every flood of enormity in a present and past life. (45)

The nexus of the indigenous and the foreign, the link of past and present, even as they represent the historical miscegenation of the folk, establish the folk presence. Here, however, the interplay between the folk presence and the ritual can reduce that folk presence into diverse personalities which, freed of a spiritual bond, loosen that cohering bond. Once the ritual sense of folk diminishes, the violence that has brought about that miscegenation and has led to the initial folk personality, seems to re-establish itself.

> It was the birth of a universal discontent and the shadow of the death of the past. . . . The figure of speech dawned on him like the infectious misery and involuntary dreadful conceit of the wake. (63)

This new perception or presentiment of the wake reveals to Mattias the turbulence that characterizes the history of the folk, that seems to ordain their lives: the "contemptible murder, petty jealousy, pretensive orgies of corruption and secretive theft" (67). The wake, with its ritual promises, its convention of kinship and presence, its spiritual force, can but mask an endemic historical personality forged by centuries of turbulent growth, of strife, with its groping toward a presence.

> Hundreds and thousands of years they had been laboring against the sun and the river, betraying each other and stabbing each other, hounding their free spirit deeper into all of themselves and searching for the man and the maid who lived in the desert of the moon. (81–82)

The ritualization of history thus takes on an affective quality, transforming the historical personality and historical phenomena through a mythic presence and a legendary emblematic action. Harris suggests that the myth-making process actualizes history making; those who participate in the evolving history become creators of that history. Thus, since "They needed to have a witch in the neighborhood" (103), they perceive Sharon as a witch, and thereby establish that mythic element necessary for the creating of history.

> She was a bewitched one, they swore, a witch, yes, the evil kind of woman who drew all her menfolk into the shadow of the gallows—even those who loved her and wanted to protect her. (94)

This transformative process, the perceiving of Sharon as witch, secrets in itself a re-creative element altering Sharon's essential history and reality. She takes on the quality of insubstantiality and otherness.

> She was being uprooted from all the fixed assumptions she had shared with everyone and everything into an order so tenuous and fleeting it aroused a terrible insubstantial uneasiness. (96)

Even as Cristo in the very beginning of *The Whole Armour* assumes an otherness by putting on the clothing of the dead man—Abram—thereby initially being transformed into another character, a character who is actualized by Magda's theatrical representations, so too Sharon's otherness is ordered through rumor and misrepresentation.

> "[She] could take on any shape she wished." (96)

> "This swelling tide of helpless rumor grew in the tiniest whisper of dew in the grass." (96)

Cristo, too, assumes different forms embodied in different garbs, is clothed in different raiments throughout *The Whole Armour*. Even as Magda dresses him in Abram's clothing, so too he dresses in the vital skin and raiment of the tiger. He accepts the myth-making action that attributes to him the killing of the ancient and legendary tiger. Clearly here Cristo's journey into legendary presence has all the contourings of a mythic fleeing from an act that stems from the love of a bewitching woman. Cristo's initial personality undergoes a transformation when he acquires Abram's clothes— he descends symbolically into the tomb, later to kill the elemental creature-predator of his people, and finally to assume and bring back to his lover the prized skin and raiment of the creature. The cycle is complete. Cristo's initial personality has taken on, through a transformative journey, a presence.

> "The truth was—I was dead tired. Fitted me together again. Chest and stump. Broken neck and skull. Gave me *this*." He held up his tiger's coat helplessly, almost shamefacedly. "Said the last thing I had done was to shoot the beast. I didn't believe them, of course. I told them it wasn't me but they who had killed the ancient jaguar of death. Older than any conquistador." (121–122)

That the elemental creature, predator of the folk, predates the newer and more immediate predator, the conquistador, imbues Cristo's action with a larger signification, adding a heraldic time to history. His action assumes not only heraldic proportions, but enters into the legendary future. Sharon, the witch woman, sings and creates the legend of Magda's man-child. Legend will assure history through a myth-making process.

> From Sharon's tower of perception the landscape had come alive with Cristo's fabulous adventure and the treasure of the victory he had won. One day it would become the legend of the new schools of the heartland—how Cristo had killed Abram's tiger and the lovely striped feminine skin of the devil was the coat he now wore wherever he went. (83)

In *The Whole Armour*, Cristo's journey assumes the nature of legend as he brings back to Sharon the skin of the legendary tiger of the jungle. In "The Secret Ladder," Bryant, through the promise of new progeny, runs with Catalena into a new space radiant with promise. Clearly, then, Harris in these novels ascribes to the metaphor of journey a myth-making possibility. Not only is the journey undertaken, not only is the search entered into, but often after a beginning fraught with problematic circumstances, the characters run their race toward new possibility, toward new presence.

In "The Secret Ladder," Fenwick's meeting with the ageless form and spirit-man, Poseidon, initiates a change, begins a transformation, which affects the perception of his reality and alters his essential consciousness. That Bryant can apprehend the seeming dichotomy in Poseidon's utterances and that Fenwick initially cannot, suggests that Fenwick's perception of a form such as Poseidon either has been historically altered or is in need of alteration. The meeting with Poseidon is no mere and simple incident, rather it is fraught with a powerful transformative energy that, in the space of seven days marking off the creative cycle, leads to a new awakening. As he begins to perceive Poseidon's inner potential and identity, Fenwick becomes aware of the element of linkage and of the spiritual presence embodied in that ageless form:

> He listened, no longer with a sense of contempt, to the agitated crooked voice of the creature he had caught, trying at the same time to follow the silent accents of an ageless dumb spirit . . . . Poseidon had been hooked and nailed to a secret ladder of conscience however crumbling and extreme the image was. (Harris, *The Guyana Quartet*, "The Secret Ladder," 371)

This confrontation suggests the coming together of two seemingly contradictory representatives of historical time; contradictions, however, that ultimately merge, fragment, and reform in that ceaseless to-and-fro movement of phenomena. For Wilson Harris in "The Secret Ladder" postulates the shifting movement of consciousness and of historical phenomena and their dynamic and incessant alteration of form. Clearly this dynamic alteration of form affects not only Wilson Harris's perception of reality, but indeed illuminates the style and language of "The Secret Ladder."

All phenomena participate in this incessant alteration and dynamic re-formation. Things are linked together in tenuous and insubstantial relationships, but in relationships that affect not only the substance of external reality, but also vibrate through Fenwick's inner consciousness. Thus Fenwick's attempt to apprehend his own essential identity is reflected in the seeming insubstantiality of changing form and refracts in that dynamic formulation of fragmentation, coherence, crumbling, re-formation.

> An air of enormous artifice rested everywhere . . . naked leaves pinned fortuitously to the sky, these worn materials of earth stretched almost to the limits of enduring apprehension . . . . All was an artifice of mystery to which one addressed oneself often with idle and pretentious words. The shape of mystery was always invisibly there, each representation the endless source of both humility and parody. Nothing lasted that did not show how soon it would crumble again. . . . (406–407)

How to apprehend this "artifice," how to seize his own consciousness, to achieve his particularity and identity in the face of this "mystery," this "artifice," are all questions that shape and articulate Fenwick's actions and his character. Clearly Harris realizes the increasing immediacy of change that not only alters the creative instant, but can immediately affect the essential purity of that creative instant, even diminish the initial spark that fires the creative instant, the pure beginnings of a relationship of love. Thus, even as Harris charges the moment with an ideal possibility, so evanescent is that moment, so open to diminution, that all thought, all movement toward essential consciousness can be tarnished by the transitory, by the momentary. What, then, is the relationship between the initial intuitive and internal creative moment—whether of thought or of love—and that impingement of the external reality on that moment? And again as Fenwick gropes toward his identity, his essence, there is an ironic apprehension of the quickness with which that essence—canvas of life—can crumble, gather dust:

> The pure paint of love scarcely dries on a human canvas without a modicum of foreign dust entering and altering every subtle colour and emotional tone, which affects the painter as well as the painted property of life . . . . (453)

But that questing for identity or essence cannot only be impaired by the transitory and by the quick gathering of dust, but it is also exposed to the increasing groping after consciousness, after freedom, and the need to perform the responsible act. Thus at every moment Fenwick seems to question his mode of acting, his basic apprehension of external forces and stimuli, his formulation of action and thought. His character, then, is structured in an ongoing process of inner reflection, doubt, questions, intentionality.

In the landscape of the heartlands where the action of the novel unravels, where everything dissolves "into the mirage of a desert and a jungle rolled into one" (360), where "you never know who make who or what make what in this tangle-up creation of a world" (442), Fenwick's search for identity and essential self is continuously affected by the external vibrations of other forms, of other people. He wonders about the nature of his authority and whether that authority over the crew is slipping, along with his basic relationship to that crew:

> He began to suspect a depth of conflict and exacerbation he could not sound. It was a humiliating bottomless extremity to find oneself in. Indeed it was as if their design was a technical and theatrical parody of the hellish nature of their work and existence. Fenwick wondered whether he had begun to credit a crew of ignorant men with the most sinister enduring talent. (361)

Fenwick's continuous introspection and his misreading of immediate phenomena touch not only on a basic question of his authority and his relationships with the crew, but lead him to explore more fundamental relationships, deeper relationships of his position, his attitude, and link to the spirit of the heartlands—Poseidon. In this, Fenwick is grappling with the unanswered, perhaps even unanswerable, question of the relationship of Guyanese people to the spirit of the Maroons, their essential freedom symbolized in the figure of Poseidon.

Fenwick wonders whether the possibility of ancestor worship can energize his present circumstance, and, by implication, affect the present and future condition of Guyana. Here Fenwick does not accept a static vision of ancestor worship. Even as he explores the nature of his own relationship to it as a "trapped condition," he infuses a new dynamic possibility into a possible relationship, visualizing a merging and consequent energizing of new forces:

> "Yes, I confess I owe allegiance to him because of his condition, allegiance of an important kind, that of conscience, of the rebirth of humanity. And this is the highest form of allegiance of all. It is the kind a man gives to a god. But surely this does not mean I must reduce myself to his trapped condition, become even less human than he, a mere symbol and nothing more, in order to worship him! I would be mad." (396)

Just as Fenwick in "his trapped condition" is unable to accept Poseidon, so too he is unable to decipher his relationship to Christian dogma or its artifacts. In his continuous questioning of how he and his present sociohistorical circumstances relate to the past social history of Guyana, Fenwick always seems to escape acknowledging his inability to come to a definite decision or to arrive at a logical perception of those social circumstances. Thus Fenwick's own personal reactions to other characters often merge with his questing for answers about social history, a merging that seems to accentuate irresolution or indecision. The role of Christianity in the history of Guyana, though not dwelt on or elaborated, remains unclear to Fenwick:

> He felt a ripple of shame, insecurity almost, and loss of face. It was involuntary the way one instantly shrank before derision, acknowledging uncomfortably in oneself how weak was the threshold of consciousness leading into a new age which might prove both solid and Christian, after all. (405)

It is not simply that Fenwick is unable to derive answers from his inquiry into the social history of Guyana, but that given his sensitive nature, his sensibility undergoes constant and continuous transformation by all external stimuli, which he in turn transforms through his particular way of probing. Thus the jungle, dreams, books, all seem to affect his mode of seeing, to heighten his sensibility, and to affect his relationships to other characters, to environment, to ideas. Fenwick ascribes a powerful affective quality to the jungle, whose presence seems able to contravene the amenities that social progress may offer in it: "Everything and everyone could become threatening, even strangely privileged and demanding" (373). Even as the jungle's presence is affective, so too is the general atmosphere of the brooding ancient river, which not only has a presence of its own, but a presence that can impinge on human thought: "It was nearly impossible to think within such a landscape of burning farce" (386).

In this landscape, then, all the elements are charged with this affective quality, or with a transforming possibility. Clearly, this affective transformative reality and landscape, where the river's movement takes on the slitherings of a snake, where the sky can be seen to change into "a flying fist of rock" (440), is charged with historical signification and qualified by the central and essential metaphor designating the New World quest for El Dorado. In this landscape, then, time and space take on a symbolic elasticity, linking together the past history of the New World adventure and the present mapping and investigation of that space by Fenwick. His new entry into this landscape, circumscribing a space of seven days, takes on, then, even a larger symbolic and figural representation—perhaps that of a creation of a New World sensibility. On the first day after Fenwick has confronted the spirit of that landscape—Poseidon—he, a New World explorer seemingly sensitive to the ramifications of history, awakens from a dream that affects his consciousness. Fenwick's dream of a vanishing horseman and a headless horse on the edge of the savannah—

> a tall nameless person mounted on horseback, armed with a sword or a spear. . . . the obscure horseman vanished and there remained a white decapitated mare, prancing on the ground vibrantly amidst her companions. (379)

—seems to have been triggered by the spirit presence of Poseidon: a spirit presence that not only affects Fenwick, but also affects his crew. Like the jungle, like the river, Poseidon's presence seems imbued with affecting and continuously transformative qualities, though both Fenwick and the crew, and by extension Guyana, are unable to come to terms with or comprehend those transformative elements:

> The binding ancestral apparition of Poseidon contained a new divine promise, born of an underworld of half-forgotten sympathies. And yet who could tell whether it was not the old monster of deception everyone secretly feared in themselves?
>
> Here was the ambivalent *lapis* of all their hopes of ultimate freedom and archetypal authority as well as the viable symbol of inexhaustible self-oppression. (379)

Poseidon's presence, then, takes on the quality of a spirit medium whose archetypal energies affect and transform Fenwick's initial certainty and his exhilarating entry into this historical jungle landscape. Initially Fenwick penetrates the center and womb of that landscape with a clarity of intention, with the excitement that all questing releases. In the bosom of the Canje River, he cuts through the jungle space naming "his dinghy *Palace of the Peacock* after the city of God" (367), symbolically climbing the rungs of a ladder "to climb into both the past and the future of the continent of mystery" (367), the metaphorical history and metaphysical geography of Guyana.

Thus symbolically Fenwick is questing for a present sense of El Dorado, is attempting to interpret the present condition and contemporary circumstance of that historical, metaphoric space—El Dorado. His journey essentially becomes a questing for self and a groping for identity in the Guyana heartlands. What, for instance, is his relationship to Poseidon and, further, how has the quest for El Dorado affected his own existential condition?

But clearly the search, the quest, is fraught with uncertainties and doubts as his consciousness is transformed, and as he transforms the external reality and the conditions through which he ventures. The initial dream of the horseman and the headless horse, he claims, may have been due to excessive reading, to his late-night analysis of "the network of surveyor's data" (378). These dreams become recurrent motifs affecting Fenwick's perception of immediate reality as well as infecting a sensibility questing for historical clarity. So that even as Jordan's head appears, Medusa-like, so effective, so immediate is the dream condition that Fenwick's perceptions are coated by his dream:

> Jordan had now dismissed the last member of the crew. His hands resembled a dusty parody of the writhing horseflesh in his dream, Fenwick thought in a flash of revulsion, with a crude coating of flour. (380)

So recurrent and insistent is this dream state that Fenwick's vision of form in the landscape is actualized and transformed by the dream motif of the horseman:

> He recalled instantly something he had almost forgotten—the moving naked design and the nameless horseman in his dream.
>
> The view altered as he approached across the savannahs. The neighing spirit of a horse addressed him (this time from right ahead under the rider's arms in the tree). He thought he saw her bare flanks vanishing into the roots of a deeper winding trail in the bush. (407)

Later, as Poseidon lies dead and the woman Catalena hallucinates with fear, the motif of Fenwick's dream is again actualized; dream, the past, the disappearance of that past, and immediate novelistic time merge and charge "The Secret Ladder" with a highly symbolic but insubstantial meaning:

> She screamed again to repulse every foundation in a monster of self-knowledge to which she was allied from the very beginning, equally real as unreal, artifice or folly as well as misery and cunning. There was only the drooping shadow of the mare whose tail fondled her breasts with the masquerading brush of pleasure. (459)

In this novelistic landscape where forms merge and the constant transformation of phenomena lends an insubstantiality to those very phenomena, Fenwick's search for identity seems to reflect this very process, his being transformed even as his perceptions transform the external phenomena. Thus, as external presences constantly affect his mood, reshape his attitudes, and transform that immediate moment of perception, Fenwick becomes unable to apprehend with certainty or to believe totally in his grasp of the external reality. So often does he doubt that reality, as it shifts between fantasy and immediacy. The search for self and identity, then, becomes a shifting sequence of ever alternating and transforming forms. Fenwick's perception, his ability to judge and make decisions, all undergo this process of alteration, to such a degree that ultimate responsibility, which action demands and which derives from certainty, that, too, undergoes change. The demands of history and the tenets of responsibility blur, become indistinct.

> "I understood Poseidon perfectly today." He knew that he lied, but his vanity and self-possession had been strangely shaken. "I shall investigate all the complaints he made against the members of the crew. And until I have cleared the matter up, it will remain my burden and responsibility. The facts, however, are far from being clear. Time and history seem to have made us all equally ignorant about who really exploits whom." (375)

In Harris's novelistic world, where all phenomena are knitted and woven together, a vast complex of reflected images emerges—Fenwick's character assumes its essential modality from mirroring those changing external phenomena, be they human or vegetal or, as in his own dream, heraldic animal. His own intentions—and often his responses, his leadership—refract from his relationships with people or the external reality. His crew senses his fluctuating, refracting responsiveness. This characteristic of being sensitized and changed by an external reflection and image, gives a certain volatile quality and adds an insubstantiality to Fenwick's already introspective, sensitive nature. External presences become the barometer of Fenwick's fluctuating moods, tempering and modulating his sensory reactions: "The frame of the tent and the placid river mirrored his own uneasy shadowy reflection" (389). But no such uncertainty marks his surveyor's appraisal of the underlying economic and social conditions at issue in the novel.

Poseidon and his African community of faithful, spiritual adherents are not simply heirs to the swamplands through historical settlement, but Poseidon himself is rooted to that land, seems to have merged with that earth: "His ancient feet—webbed with grass and muck—were bare . . . and his hands were wreathed in a fisherman's writhing net of cord" (394). This earth presence, the spiritual heir to the land, senses the possible dislocating attributes resident in the scientific tools and personality,

> seeing in them the heartless instruments of science which were aimed like sentient forces at him (and whose monstrous profession would turn the tables on him, and rob him of the last freedom he possessed). (395)

Indeed, these scientific tools not only dislocate Poseidon's reality and rob him of his spiritual freedom, but ultimately dislocate his land-settlement and rob him of his material possessions.

Fenwick, with his surveyor's knowledge, is aware of the counter-productive—in economic terms—nature of that settlement.

> "The land isn't all rich up here—in fact it's a mess—and they wouldn't want to keep it in face of a scheme that would do untold benefit to the sugar estates and ricelands of the Courantyne and Berbice coasts." (381)

But Jordan the cook, with his own clear perception of social reality, counters:

> "You asking too much," Jordan said stolidly and unimaginatively. "They can't see it. They may be living hand-to-mouth but this wasteland . . . everybody long since abandon except them, is all they've got. . . . And to make it worse they believe because they black you want to punish them, and the crafty East Indian man on the Courantyne savannah going get what they lose . . . ." (382)

Fenwick further suggests that economic benefits would accrue to all, but clearly the main beneficiaries would be the East Indian farming community and the white planter class.

> East Indians on the Courantyne and Berbice coastland . . . had never penetrated up the Canje. Nevertheless the aging Canje River was invaluable to the absent East Indian rice farmer and the European sugar planter. It provided their rice and sugar-cane plantations with a storehouse of irrigation water in time of drought. (388)

This larger social, economic, and racial signification underlying the novelistic plot remains, however, undifferentiated and unelaborated background. Fenwick's search for self becomes the principal thematic formulation.

The suggestion or hint of continued exploitation of Poseidon's African community for a general economic good leaves totally unanswered the essential question of the role and function of Poseidon's spirit and presence within Fenwick's inner consciousness and being and, by extension, in the core, the body of Guyana. Of extreme significance here is that Fenwick has no doubt—nor does his creator, Harris—about the rightful role and function of Christian presences and relics. Even though the mission house

> had an air both foreign and native, ideal and primitive, at one and the same time; yet it seemed so precariously and absolutely right . . . that the thought of an imposition, of pretentiousness or absurdity in the life of the crumbling building, seemed equally ridiculous and impossible. (411)

Even though Fenwick sees no "imposition" to evidence an exploitative element in Christianity, though he accepts the inherent syncretism, he still seems incapable of applying that notion of syncretic nonvoluntary integration to the role, function, and nature of the African presence as embodied in the figure of Poseidon and his community. Harris shunts the question about the African presence into the pages of a letter from Fenwick to his mother; a letter in which a statement about the African element is articulated but evinces no response, remains totally in the realm of the epistolary, the circumstantial, the purely rhetorical.

> To *misconceive* the African, I believe, if I may use such an expression as *misconceive*, at this stage, is to misunderstand and exploit him mercilessly and oneself as well. For *there*, in this creature Poseidon, the black man with the European name, drawn out of the depths of time, is the emotional dynamic of liberation that happened a century and a quarter ago. (385)

Van Brock deals much more cryptically and dramatically with the question, the dilemma, of ancestry. Van Brock, though still speculating on his relationship with ancestry in a highly symbolic descent into the pit, reestablishes a linkage with his ancestor.

> Van Brock descended into the grave pit even before she did, searched for the ring and restored it to her finger as a dutiful high priest at the wedding of memory. Was it an ancestor of life or of death he had created at that moment? He was obsessed with the self-indulgence and ordure of love as with the ghost of glory. (452)

This symbolic renewal of ancestral linkage through the retrieval and investiture of a ring for the ancestor's finger posits an unbroken continuous circularity to that linkage. The death of the ancestor figure, Poseidon, at the hands of his disciple—newly received and recently ordained into Poseidon's lineage and race—seems rooted, however, within an inexplicable historical irony. To be sure, the whole episode of Poseidon's death is rooted in symbology, but it is a symbology that, given its figural representation—given the *nommo* Poseidon, Perseus the Gorgon, the horseman and the presence of the unbridled horse—is more so classical Greek or European.

Clearly Harris is unable to place the African ancestor figure within a tradition of an African ontological continuum, where it is not that the grandfather's death and sacrifice are prerequisites for the grandson's birth and presence, but rather that the grandson's existence is ordained through the vital ancestral presence. Thus, in the end, Poseidon, assuming a shifting, ambiguous state of apotheosis, does not arrive or ascend through vertical vital space into a condition of ancestor-god, but remains devitalized, lying in horizontal inert space, powerless and devoid of that vital energy with which to change and infuse the spirit and being of his flock, with which to continuously reenergize his own spirit presence.

> The great judge of themselves was dead, and they alone could judge the relics of security or insecurity he had left. . . . The fire of desire that had been lit emphasized the black void of the night and the black face of the judge, godless now as well as godlike, lying mute and uncreated amongst them. . . . the fire that flickered within and without his countenance. . . signified the lie in their hopes as well as the creation of a jewel of light without self-evident generation or action. (458)

Here, Harris, through a series of oppositional formulations—"godless now as well as godlike"; "they alone could judge the relics of security or insecurity he had left"—seems to cancel out, to negate, not only Poseidon's presence but indeed that ultimate influence and power that vitalized and energized his followers.

Bryant, threatened by death, attempts in a fiery confessional to restore an ontological and unbroken link between ancestor and grandson through the promise and progress of his progeny begotten through his love with Catalena. With Catalena—who has been symbolically anointed three ways, through the unbridled kisses of the folk, the swishing caressing tail of the horse in Fenwick's dream, and the blood splattering her dress from the dying falling head of Poseidon—with this Catalena, Bryant will enter, will run into a new universal love space radiant with promise, with "Time for Bryant and Catalena to appear to run and make swift love on every trail across the earth" (463).

Fenwick, somewhat freed from the trauma, the six days of heightened drama subsequent to his first confrontation with the African-spirit root sense of himself, and having partially labored for six days to come to terms with that self as necessary affective presence, enters into a creative space of rest on the seventh day. His journey through the heartlands of Guyana, his movement into selfhood, has been accomplished in a symbolic numerological context, a creative cycle of seven days, and this numerological time has contained in it a cyclical notation:

> The instant the prison of the void was self-created, a breath of spirit knew how to open a single unconditional link in a chain of circumstance. . . .
>
> . . . the echoes of annunciation grew on every hand and became resonant with life . . . . In our end . . . our end . . . our end is our beginning . . . beginning . . . beginning. Fenwick awoke. It was the dawn of the seventh day. (464)

This same cyclical notation ordains Nebu the Hunter's journey across the vast heartland of Kenya in Vic Reid's *The Leopard,* for in Nebu's journey to his end, dying in a cave, is his beginning, his reentry into traditional wisdom and confidence. After the fragmentation and the rotting away of part of his body, the wholing of the self: "It was morning in his arms and shoulders" (159). With this line Reid not only climaxes the end of Nebu's journey into selfdom, but clearly offers the prognosis of entry into new presence after the fragmentation of a former personality.

Now at this high point of the novel, Nebu, even as he enters into the shadows at the point of physical death, achieves a kind of apotheosis, promising regeneration, offering a new beginning. Symbolically, the cycle of regeneration and rebirth is postulated by Reid, who makes his protagonist journey from dawn to dawn. The journey, however, is no simple one, but is fraught with loss in which the question and the paradox of change and development are explored, an exploration that delves deep into natural imagery for its formulations. However, since at the center of natural elemental imagery there is coherence and continuity, natural imagery gives a coherence and wholeness even to paradox.

Thus it is that even as Nebu sits rotting in a cave—metaphor of the beginning, the womb—as the lower part of his body decays, the upper limbs and shoulders breathe power, swell with all their potential. At this juncture of man, cave, vision, the protagonist once more reaches into the wholeness of his tradition, into the majesty of his land, sings of its recurrent power which ultimately negates his physical death, symbolic, too, of the death of some traditions.

> Nebu had grown out of the cave. He was three days' journey out of
> his sickness. The wanderobo twanged and the seven-foot spear sang, and
> game ran wailing through the bush that Nebu the Hunter was back. (147)

Images of verticality and of horizontal space cohere in the protagonist's dying
vision, lifting him out of the cave in which he rots, in which his crippled son
lies broken, in which the leopard lies dead, and in which the arrogant
symbolic representation of the leopard—the white lieutenant—stands ready
to be made beautiful by Nebu's spear.

> He stood out hard against the light from the door, a lean-waisted, wide-
> shouldered, tawny bull leopard. And Nebu chartered the curvature of his
> chest through the khaki bush jacket and marked where the breast-bone
> swelled above the heart, and the certainty that he had the target well laid
> flowed sweetly through him.
> "*Great One*," the African sang in his head, "give us long knives." (159)

At this historic confrontation, as Nebu reverts to his indigenous weapon, he
sings of the glory of his land and the richness of his traditions.

> Mine was the ridge of Nyeri, in the village of Kitusi, where the cook-fires
> were never out . . . . We herded the goats in the day and learnt to set
> traps for the coney and lesser *kudu*, for the smaller antelope and the bush
> pig, and in the evening we sat at the feet of the elders and learnt the
> steps for the ngoma and the words of the old songs . . . . And we obeyed
> and grew and were taught the spear and the bow and the panga and not
> to lie. This was the law. (141–142)

Yet endowed as he is with lyrical certainty of the law of his people; given,
too, the hunter's assurance which comes with his knowledge of the panga,
the spear, and the bow, Nebu's journey into the cave has already begun, in
his quest for a weapon, the foreigner's power. The novel depicts, then,
Nebu's inability to come to terms with the foreign tool that, ultimately, he
rejects for his own spear.

> "You will kill the leopard too," the boy said quickly. "I know you
> will."
> "Easily," Nebu said.
> "Especially if you use the rifle. Take the bolt. I will show you how
> it is to be fitted."
> "No, toto," Nebu said gently. "I know the spear. A great warrior is
> sensible. He does not ride a strange horse over a narrow footbridge."
> (148)

Here at the climaxing of the novel, Nebu's half-caste son, issue of his mating with the foreign white woman, attempts to give back to his father the bolt that has made the rifle dysfunctional. During Nebu's journey, his half-caste son has goaded Nebu about his inability to use the rifle, an inability that supposedly testifies to his native lack of intelligence. Here in the cave as the leopard is about to strike, Nebu rejects the rifle bolt, rejects, too, his half-caste son's duplicity. To revert to the spear, to sing his traditions, is to achieve a fragmenting of his reality, is to reject symbolically both the gun, the foreign tool he has craved, and the questing for which he began his journeying toward his physical death. But it is not simply a question of physical death. By rejecting the foreign tool, Nebu thereby transforms a vision of reality, moving into his own known space.

The question, however, is the method by which he achieves his entry into indigenous space. It could be argued here that Nebu's attempt to atone for having wronged Bwana Gibson—first by having intercourse with his wife, and second by killing him to get his gun—follows a negative perception of tradition and does not take into consideration the immediate historical reality created by the foreign man, the white settler with his gun and his thirst for power and greed for land. Thus it is that the journey, though powerfully delineated, even as it apprehends the power and glory of the earth and land of Kenya, is initially rooted in an unchanging, even static, perception of tradition—in a perception or vision that ultimately, however, apprehends the changing historical reality. As Nebu lies dying in decay he muses:

> Perhaps I lay here, hurt and alone, because I had not the strength to lose the old customs but must go to Nairobi to pay the recompense. (156)

It is at this point that his vision is transformed, a transformation that notates change itself—cyclically inevitable but also assuring and ordaining continuity.

> *The strength to lose an age and gain a generation.*
> To lose customs, women, land, life to the ring of change . . . . Each year, in the spring, change marched across his country, from Mombasa to the big mountains, and new flowers opened and new foals kicked wounds into the tender land. Change was invincible. (156)

Reid imbues Nebu's journey not only with a diurnal but a chronological temporality—having Nebu journey from dawn across evening into dawn, from his youthful beginnings to his dying in the cave. Nebu's journey begins in sunlight.

> Sunlight in shafts ploughed into the earth, pressing up into his nostrils the smells of the bitter purity of the womb where coal was smelted into

> diamonds. Nebu tightened the thong holding the panga about his waist.
> The great wanderobo bow was secure and comfortable at his back. (14)

Later, as he lies dying in the womb of the cave, there is evening song in his loins.

> He only knew that the evening, the long brown shadow of the Aberdares,
> had entered into him and was disposing itself in much of him. (156)

But even as evening is closing about Nebu, a dawning returns. A continuity, a cyclical return to panga, spear, now takes place and "It was morning in his arms and shoulders" (159).

But Reid further imbues Nebu's journey with a spatiality, taking him across the land wherein his feet move from youthful vigor, strength, and certainty to an inescapable rot, an irrevocable decay wherein they are no longer in tune with the rhythms of the earth, in touch with the inner throb of his land. In this journey, images of verticality root Nebu to his land, link him to its innermost rhythms, so that even in his decaying, his feet, his body, still sense the innermost motion of his land.

By the use of excursus and flashbacks, by the correlation of past and immediate time and action that intertwines past and present, Reid unfolds for us the total life of his protagonist in all of its rituals, its traditions, its indigenous customs and laws, its conflicting with the white foreign presence, in its searchings for the meaning and resolution of that conflict. Essentially the journey is a search for innerness, and the predominant images are those of entry, of penetration, of moving inward.

The essential metaphor is the procreative, in which all forces commingle and cohere, negating the historical conflict, postulating linkage, flow and intercourse.

> The long rains come, impregnating the earth with frightening fecundity,
> and the ancient wounds spread their lips again and new shoots spring
> from them.
>   . . . It is a land of immense folds and rolling parks; of water and forest
> and game; of huge valleys so vast. (15–16)

In beautifully cadenced prose, Reid captures the power and force of the elements, the majesty and grandeur of the land. In lyrical polyphony, he recaptures the essence of ritual and traditions of love-making; in sparse and dramatic language, the rhythms of the conflict between races, the epic struggle between man and beast, so that although the prose is spare, it resonates and achieves a musicality that echoes the fullness of the elemental.

It is a rich land: rich in humus and equally rich in hate, for all men crave it. Know, therefore, it is a land of feud: for the white challenger wants to conquer it, and the black man to keep it. (16)

This land which was rich in "feud" was made fecund by the long rains whose rhythms beat out the cadences, the changing meters, of Nebu's journey into the cave. He has danced the dance of his people when the long rains thunder over his land. The metaphor of the rain seems to design the motions of the hunter, of the traveler, Nebu. In his youthful vigor, the rains are long and powerful—a power equal to his own initial grace and power. This rain marks his mating not only with the woman of his tribe but also with the foreign woman.

The wind blowing on his nudity was the sweet-skinned girl whom the elders of the tribe had chosen for him at that half-forgotten Dance of Puberty when he had proved his maleness. (21)

Two parallel and yet converse rhythms resound in the play of rain on the land and the motion of winds accompanying that play. Even as the long rains have marked Nebu's power in his youthful time, now too in his journeyings across the land of Kenya to the cave, that constant rhythm of water notates the beginning of his decline, the sharpening ache of his wound. Reid imbues the rain with symbolic content, underscoring its ever-changing intercourse and interactions with man. As Nebu's pain sharpens his moralizing increases. Idea and symbol fuse. Nebu's travail finds its correspondence in the increasing dullness of the day.

The wound had burst into light, shedding pain in him. He held it and sweated. Nebu listened to the agony talking in him and waited for it to be silent. . . .
    The day dragged itself down through the trees, pale, sickly, the sun had no blood for it . . . . Nebu knew it would strike down again, for it was so long rains fell. (85)

In alternating patterns, Reid accepts the shifting nature and the correspondingly shifting moods the rain symbolizes. Even as the falling rain heightens the gloom, as his agony increases, Nebu, through recall and memory, creates a contrapuntal movement, negating that gloom, conjuring up the memory of the beauty of his land. In the pounding of the rain, Nebu recalls all the rhythmical power of his dance.

For the thunder of the rains was the drums, the whistle of the wind was the pipes . . . .
    He danced full of power and able to perform impossible feats of agility in time to the rhythm of the rain drums. (21)

And through the naming of the animals of his land he celebrates that land.

> And he wondered, as he had always wondered when he was a child, where did the lions and the buffaloes and the rhinos cower in the storm? . . . And did the eagles and the heavenly flamingoes kill their pride and weep among the rocks when the long rains loosened? (97–98)

The evocative language celebrates not only the animal but all the sensory richness of the vegetal, of both fauna and flora.

> The rain had let up, but the small trees showered when the wind shook them. The wind slipped, when it could, furtively out of the underbrush, bringing to Nebu the scents of his land, the slow sweet scents of the night-blooming jasmine and the mutoma and the musk odour of the soaked hollows. (102)

The rain not only paces Nebu's agonizing pain but also beats out the relationship between him and his gray-faced son, so that action and character and the essential ecology of the land have their mergings. Later as the gray-faced son lies dead and Nebu sits rotting in the cave, the flora and fauna recede and the land is now a watery waste. Under the rape of the rains the land has become increasingly sullen: "The land no longer rejoiced in the rain. It took its beating sullenly, gloomily, turning uneasily when the wind blew" (125).

Throughout *The Leopard* Reid attempts to invest all things with their essential force and potential, so that the style is elevated, the reality heightened, to such a degree that at times the argumentation seems weighted down—especially toward the end of the novel—with rhetoric and moralizing. Yet, in its totality, the novel is well-orchestrated, its language texturing fauna and flora, its tonality seizing the inner rhythms of all the insect and animal life of the earth, its images sculpting the vast sweep of land and space, the shapes of the limbs and the trees. However, the elements are not simply descriptive and figural notation of the land of Kenya; time is not simply a cyclical metaphor for Nebu's journey into the cave. But often the elements and time notate and give a specificity to important actions in the novel.

> He knew that stand of *mwena* over there. They flourished dark and tall and stout in their trunks and wore bright yellow spikes stuck fetchingly in their foliage. He knew the great grey baobab too. Under such a baobab had the tribe held market-place and council-place. (121)

Dawn witnesses the heightened conflict between the Mau Mau and the foreign settlers, bringing with it swift death and punishment for past deeds.

Thirty were in the band which hit the Loman farm before daybreak. They slew all in the household and looted it of food, guns and ammunition and vanished into the bush again, and nobody shouted "There they go!" because it was a sweet time for them to strike, when the morning ebb had drained the vigilance from the beleaguered settlers. (9)

The long rains witness the beginnings of another conflict born in an act of mating. The rains mark and herald the rhythmical interplay that takes place between the Black man and the white woman, uprooted from her land. In this interplay, the penetration of the long rains into the land has intonations of the sexual interplay that takes place, ultimately leading to the birth of the gray child who goads Nebu on in his journey to the cave. Thus it is that natural elements not only accompany the acts of man but, indeed, as though correlating different spheres and realms, mirror them, echo them.

Outside the windows the earth was in a joyous uproar beneath the rape of the long rains. The rain found all its hollows and embraced the hillocks. It soaked the trees to the roots. (21)

Nebu's mating with the foreign white woman is dramatized, with "the rape of the long rains" accompanying the interplay between the sculptured Black male form and the foreign woman etched in her horsewoman's body and her hollows. The mating has been anteceded by two physical actions that particularize both Nebu and the white woman, the former the dance of the *ngoma*, the latter her hard riding in the rain. Even though the *ngoma* precedes the act, its true celebrative moments appear at the time when Nebu's clan is intact, and when the ritual dance celebrates the relationship of a man to his group, with all of its ritualistic implications.

In presenting Nebu's mating with his chosen bride, the scene is less dramatic than Nebu's encounter with the white woman, yet in his dialogue with his new wife is intoned all the ritual certainty of promise and fulfillment, is notated the adventure of a first mating of new passion, the intrinsic harmony, the pure concordance.

"I will hunt and fish and work in our garden," he had said. "And by the winter I will have earned the cattle and sheep for the dowry."

"I will wait while my man does all these things," the new-made woman said, "and bear his children when he returns."

"They will be great men, these children," said the new-made husband.

"And faithful women," she said. . . .

. . . He wondered at it. He wondered at the strength there and was awed that he had heard her whimper. And he wondered at the composed mouth and unruffled forehead and tender eyes and he felt safe with her. (98–99)

To be sure, all this ritual promise of mating, of living within the ordinance of the group, of nurturing, providing and sharing, all sing with soft harmonies enshrining a life of contentment and fulfillment.

In his youth, a time of certainty and assurance, he is monolith and stone and sculptured form. He has the beauty of ebony, "his head arrogantly cocked back on the column of ebony throat" (21). He has the emblematic quality of stone, its agelessness and silence. He is a figure of vital energy and strength, but he also receives energy and strength from his vital link with and knowledge of the land. The link is physical, intuitive, acquired, ontological: "The land was a book you learned to read. Men, beasts, fowls, moonrise, the shape of trees were all explained in the book" (25). The knowledge of this book directs all of Nebu's actions leading to an instinctive, intimate relationship to his land. For this knowledge is law. This law was enshrined knowledge directing motion, "carefully written inside his head" (16). It is a law that also has sharpened all the senses attuning him to the innermost rhythms, the minutest sounds of "the earth . . . the squeals of grass, the crush of pebbles, the angry whine of discommoded insects" (37). He is all controlled silence and stillness linked to the inner rhythms of his land: "Trained to be still at the unexplained flutter of a leaf, the negro was fixed" (55).

Even as the rain marks the cadence of Nebu's journey so too do his changing form and representations.

> He danced full of power and able to perform impossible feats of agility in time to the rhythm of the rain-drums. . . .
>
> Nebu danced nude, narrow-hipped, the strong calves and plough-widened shoulders like dark old wine catching what light there was about. . . . he seemed to claim the room: running his hand over the bedsheets, touching with his finger-tips the things of her on the dresser. (21)

This certainty marks the beginning of Nebu's journey toward manhood, eventually interrupted by the death of his clan and the loss of his new bride, events that start him off on his journeying, leading him both to the dawn raid and to his work in Bwana Gibson's house and his subsequent mating with Gibson's wife. But here is intimated the beginning of paradox of identity and choice. Even though he sings often of the dreamlike state of his ritual mating, he rhapsodizes on the acquisition of the foreign woman. Nebu's description and recalling of his mating with the white woman soars beyond the idyllic, beyond the soft harmonies that intoned his mating with his chosen bride.

> She was a woman who lived beyond my ridge, a thought of last year's thunder, a whisper of a drum in the night, a bird that flew up from a far bush, a long forgotten garden in which you planted your young trees . . . .
> . . . She was the forbidden road on which Nebu walked. It led to the hut of the king. But should a warrior be afraid of his king? (140)

This same paradox of identity marks his later acquisition of the gun.

> The rifle was everything it had promised in his dreams to be . . . . for an instant you held an eagle in the steel-framed windows; . . . A godlike feeling. The thing balanced in your hand faultlessly, built for you from the commencement of time. It was such that you wanted to sing.
> . . . He could go to bed with such a gun. . . . He was gifted with destruction. (50–51)

These two happenings are fraught with larger signification, not only for the structuring of action of the novel, but for its ultimate climaxing in the cave. Nebu's mating with Bwana Gibson's wife resulted in a gray-colored crippled son, symbolic of an ill-fated merging of opposing cultural representations, the Black native servant and the dominant foreign presence.

After the dawn raid, Nebu, bemoaning his seeming ill fate at not getting a rifle, picks up the trail of a white settler whose boot prints tell Nebu the Hunter that the white settler carries with him a cherished rifle. The white settler turns out to be Bwana Gibson, who indeed is armed with a rifle but who also carries with him the crippled gray-faced child. Nebu, after killing Gibson with his native weapon, inherits a wound in the flesh, a rifle which has been made dysfunctional, and a crippled son, all of which become disabilities and burdens for his subsequent journeyings. The festering wound and the crippled representation of cultural miscegenation attract the attention of the leopard, which shuns the strong and stalks the weak. Yet Nebu is still certain of his physical prowess, assured of his relationship to the law of his clan. His tracking reiterates the certainty that marked his entry into his first great adventure with his new wife.

> But his speed must be tuned to his strength too; for when the time came for close stalking he must be fit and capable of closing with the quarry. He had all this carefully written inside his head, for it was the law. (16)

Here his strength is as one with the rhythms of his journey. His stride is still unbroken, his self-knowledge and his knowledge of the land are still ordained. Indeed, he seems to exult in his own power and strength.

Nebu dropped back into the hill man's style, the legs swivelled outward and cut forward in a half-circle that added up to a huge stride without great muscular effort, storing his strength. (22)

As the pain from Nebu's wound increases, that strength and stride no longer assured, he attempts, through a ritualistic entry into the healing pool, to restore that strength. But already he is at the midpoint of his journey—his running no longer swift; his walking slow and uncertain.

The Negro carefully peeled away the clothes from his swollen limbs and stepped into the pool. . . . It clothed and fed him and sheltered him. There was a wound throbbing, but it was pain happening in another house. . . .

The body that the black burdensomely raised from the pool was heavy as an elephant's. He was an old woman, stepping from the pool. (110–112)

Nebu's movement toward presence derives, however, not from any transformative action on his part. Indeed, some of his actions, his deeds, seem to be abortive, ill-timed. A slavish monolithic interpretation of his own traditional lore ordains a journey that initially leads him to a detached, somewhat cynical, interpretation of that lore. His personal attempt to remedy his seeming ill fate leads him on a search where his error of judgment causes his wound. Toward the end of his journey when he sits dying in the cave, only his spirit, his upper body lives, while his lower limbs have already rotted and died.

At this point, however, all is symbolic reference, all cultural and symbolic inference. His spear and his upper body still fuse together breathing an essential power, returning him to what he was taught in his childhood. Once more he exults in the youthful vigor in his arms and celebrates his strength and power. In the evening of his walking he seems once more totally assured of the resilience of his first running.

"Oho, Brother Leopard, evening is in my belly but bright morning is in my arm," he said softly. And the formidable spear rose easily to his shoulder and power flowed along his arm. (157)

In a journey that brings together lyrical symbolic space, novelistic ritual time, and dynamic history, Nebu arrives, returns to a centrifugal soul—a cave residence of ultimate being. It is a vital link between man and his land, being and earth.

Nebu is ". . . all the tribes in all the land from the borders of Ethiopia and Uganda to beyond mighty Kilimanjaro" (21). The "I" is transformed by vital motion into the "We"; all things cohere and a communality, a togetherness of a people, is established in Nebu's dance.

In the morning of his life, Nebu's running is swift, certain, all the tone configuration of dawn choreographing the litheness, the splendor of his movements. Later in his walking toward the evening of his life, the vital tonality of dawn is lost—a slow funereal march into the shadows of a cave. In his trajectory toward decay and rot, physical decomposition brings with it a growth of the spirit, a clarification of vision. His perception of reality undergoes a transformation, a dematerialization of his historical condition ensues, a shedding of inessentialities, the negating of acquisitiveness "of a tool," the gun, the achieving of presence.

From the very beginning of Michael Thelwell's *The Harder They Come*, we are introduced to the essential character traits—traits shaping the figure and orchestrating the movement—of the main protagonist, Ivan Martin: his willfulness, his daring, his own unique rebellious spirit subsumed in the still unassumed name, Rhygin. These are qualities silently applauded by Miss 'Mando, the strong, dominant grandmother figure of a Black woman; these also are the qualities she fears.

> Miss 'Mando did not know whether to be amused or concerned. There was something about Ivan that fit the name Rhygin. He was so full of life and energy, so full of questions. There was nothing that didn't interest him, and nothing that he didn't think he could master. Though he was quite small for his age, he seemed to give direction to his playmates. Maybe too much so for his own good. (Thelwell, *The Harder They Come*, 17)

Indeed, like Nebu, in *The Leopard*, Ivan moves from that early certainty, the demonstration and celebration of young energy and tonal physicality, and curves through a vital indigenizing cultural space to his rotting and dying in a symbolic womb space, a cave. Before his movement into the cave, Ivan, however, imbues the name Rhygin with presence, making it symbolic of rebellion or, rather, of an enduring spirit of resistance to a social and political order rife with corruption.

> The phrase *Rhygin was here/But 'im jus' disappear* was picked up and began appearing on walls over the city. It became the opening lines for nonsense doggerel that children chanted to keep time playing bull-in-the-ring and jump rope. (356)

At the end of his journeying he has indeed actualized and made celebrative the name he proudly adopted in his boyhood in Blue Bay.

The exuberance, the sense of motion with which Ivan runs down the hill at Blue Bay, characterizes the actions, indeed imbues the motions of most of the personages, perhaps of almost all of the protagonists, of Part 1 of *The Harder They Come.*

> In the soft soil he gave himself up to the momentum of the slope, running rapidly down, his legs churning, leaning back at an impossible angle to keep his balance and avoid falling forward on his face, leaping sideways to avoid trees, and shouting and whooping in exuberant glee. (62)

It is with a lyric mastery that Thelwell captures man at his intersecting with his space, with his landscape; his word paintings evoke the essentiality of the actions, of the particular phenomena, in a total cohering—of phenomena with man, of the flowing river of spirit with the sheer power of the body. Rafael, the boatman, merges with the river mood, a sculptured embodiment of harmony.

> Me know dat when the sun bright and the breeze cool an' the mountain dem purple, an' the sky blue, an' river water heavy an' cold an' green . . . . Me one an' Gawd on the river? Have Mercy! Just the wind ina me face an' the sun 'pon me chest, an' on both side is mountain and cliff-face just a rise up sudden so? . . . Me say, dem time deh, when Ah coming down, me one an' the river? Man can hear Gawd voice, you know? Yes, an'see him face too. (66)

This notion of space and distance, the interpenetration of man with spirit world, are clearly evident when Izaac, the votary voice of the hills, their spirit medium, proclaims the news of Miss 'Mando's death, voicing it far into the night. From a steeple tree on the hilltop, Izaac laments the passing of Miss 'Mando, in whom was invested the very soul, the continuum of the African hill presence.

> He rocked back and forth, making the top of the tree sway as if in the grip of a soundless storm, and turned a rapturous gaze to the sky. And with the veins in his neck swelling and bulging, he began a howl that filled the night, silencing the crickets and setting the dogs to barking and howling too, a drawn-out unearthly sound: "BRIMSTONE AND FIRE!" (78)

Here in this voicing of the death of the ancestral figure, Miss 'Mando, all is ritual observance. So, too, this same evocation of ritual notates Maas' Nattie's reiteration of his death, when dressed all in black astride his fiery steed he rides through the spaces of the hills.

> And every year he bought a big piece of black cloth from town and cut
> and sew himself a suit with a waistcoat. 'Im say is 'im suit to bury in. An'
> every year when 'im didn't dead, 'im bring out the suit at Christmas and
> get on him big ol' horse named "Hell-Dynamite-Lightning-and-Thunder"
> and ride through the district. (38)

It is from Maas' Nattie that Ivan learns the oral history of African peoples,
not as enshrined in folk tales, but as depicted in the lived history of Black
men and women.

> But by evening he would be sitting on Maas' Nattie's knee listening to
> his stories about Cudjo the Maroon warrior and Ma Nannie his sister who
> was a witch and a warrior too, and about the great Marcus Garvey who
> was "the black man savior" and who was born not forty miles away. (38)

Clearly, then, Thelwell is celebrating the sense of freedom, the gift of
space, with which Blue Bay, the Jamaican hillside, is blessed. Man, beast,
bird, all seem to ordain through movement this quality of freedom, the
element of space. Even the precision and the gliding movement of the
predator bird, as it streaks down to kill, is painted in broad, sweeping
strokes; it is not simply a word painting but rather a graphic illustration, a
vivid lesson to Ivan of the tragic consequences of uncontrolled fear—the
result of the parakeet's leaving its flock.

> The hawk, moving with arrogant grace, made three powerful, unhurried
> wing strokes, then locked his wings and went into a dive so fast and steep
> it appeared that he must crash into the hillside. At the last second the
> parakeet cut sharply, looking slow and awkward. The hawk veered,
> extended talons hammering the smaller bird. (41–42)

Thelwell heightens his representation of reality in Blue Bay, making action
and phenomena take on dramatic, at times heroic, dimensions.

In this representation, not only is the African presence actualized but its
continuum is established, its mythos celebrated. In these hills the earth, the
river and the sea abound with plenty; the rich earth, rich through careful
husbandry, is linked together in communality.

> The hillsides had been alive with activity . . . .
>   . . . food trees dense with leaves and hidden fruit—the purple leaved
> star apple, regal breadfruit, mango, pear, ackee, jackfruit . . . (13, 15)

All is shared participation. The land for planting is cleared in unison.
Through example and by teaching, the young learn the language of the
earth, the rhythms of the sea.

Ivan was drunk with sensation . . . watching . . . the richly colored and
strangely shaped fish that Maas' Burt sorted, identifying each kind,
explaining their value, habits, and how they should be handled. (23)

Through this and many of the teachings of the elders—Maas' Nattie, Miss
'Mando—Ivan is initiated into manhood, taught self-reliance, generosity, life.
Traditional wisdom is handed down through a rich orality, an integrative
tradition in which the bounty of the hills is shared.

> The old man picked up an ear of corn and said . . . . "What you see
> to eat, eat. What you see to drink, drink. Is nutten much, but whatsoever
> you see, you welcome to." (47)

It is here that Ivan becomes a free self-reliant spirit. In the embrace of the
valley, under Miss 'Mando's stern but loving tutelage and Maas' Nettie's
exemplary guidance, Ivan roams, a free spirit through the hills, enjoying the
valley's peace, its luxuriance, garnering the bounty of its rivers.

> In the deep water beneath these cliffs he dived for the big grandfather
> *janga* that filled his hands, wriggling powerfully and attacking with their
> claws. Soon his pail was almost full and he lay down on the raft and
> allowed the slow current to carry him. (62–63)

With the same lyrical brush stroke, Thelwell paints the figure of Mirriam,
with whom Ivan has his first mating.

> Mirriam lay, her face in shadow, its clean angles gleaming like soft velvet
> and her golden maroon eyes glowing with dull fire. (67)

But this idyllic scene is rudely shattered by an alien and foreign urban voice
and lifestyle.

> They lay intertwined, very still for a long time, the breeze cool on
> their hot damp bodies. Then Ivan sat up and turned on the radio.
> Mirriam was crying as she leapt up and shouted, "Turn the damn
> somethin' off, Ivan—you mean say even at a time like dis—?" She
> became inarticulate with rage. (67)

The radio, now shattering this moment of pure love between Ivan and
Mirriam, is what destroyed the harmonious affectionate relationship between
grandmother and grandson, contributing to, indeed hastening, Miss 'Mando's
death. The intimation of change with the ensuing falling apart of things is
sounded in the very opening notes of the novel: "But now Miss 'Mando
listened to the echoes of her holler die away into silence" (14). Later, with
Miss 'Mando's death, with these dying echoes, the passing of an era is
actualized and celebrated by Thelwell in large liturgical and ritualistic

evocations. The preparations for the wake are as lavish as the hills were bountiful, as distinctive as were Miss 'Mando's husbandry and Maas' Nettie's generosity. Miss 'Mando's dying marks the passage of a certain folk quality, the falling apart of an oral indigenous tradition, the loss of a hill spirit and presence.

Under the conjurings of the hard hands of the master drummer of the hills, Miss 'Mando's spirit is summoned to utter the last word to predict Ivan's downfall. Symbolically, the harder they come, the harder they fall.

> But Izaac just peered at him nearsightedly and began to weep, pounding his head with his hands in the timeless female gesture of distress.
>
> "'Aaiee! Mi pickney, mi pickney. Mi pickney. Fire an' gunshat. Gunshat and bloodshed. Bloodshed and gunshat, waiee oh." . . .
>
> Then the voice, again cold and without emotion: "Behold dat dreamer cometh . . . let us take an' slay 'im . . . an' den we shall see . . . what shall become of his dreams." (97)

Among the tremulous notes of her frail Garvey brethren, her age-mates, Miss 'Mando's body is laid to rest in the hills. In the dirge and lament of the equally frail Maas Nattie, Miss Mando's love affair with him is given the promise of another life, of an eternity.

> Finally he spoke. "So, me dear, you gone, eh? . . . But don't fret 'bout nutten. We soon meet again . . . . Res' easy. Res' easy—everyt'ing goin' be jus' as you did want it—in the propah way—like in you grandfather time, jus' as Ah promise you . . . ." Gently, gently he touched the face. (74)

From the initial peace and communality of the hills, Ivan hurtles in the belly of a smoke-belching bus into the labryinth and vortex of Kingston. Here, indeed, begins Ivan's movement away from certainty, away from home. And it won't be until later, as he lies dying in the cave, womb center of his island, that he will symbolically go back home.

With artistic assurance and consummate skill, Thelwell sculpts in motion a dervish-like figure, the Indian bush driver coolie man, as he propels his bantering, quarreling cargo, among whom is Ivan, across the Jamaican countryside into the teeming city.

> He was a study in motion. He didn't sit on the seat so much as brace himself against the edge, in a kind of splendid tension between his body and the instruments. . . . The right hand flashed between the busy gearshift, his mouth with the ever present cigarette, and the horn, while his feet danced between brake, clutch, and accelerator as he geared up and down on the hilly, twisting, narrow road. (108–109)

Here the author romps through all the piquant, rowdy folk flavor and language so characteristic of Caribbean, in this instance Jamaican, bus riders.

> "All Ah say," the man said pedantically, "is dat dem *mus'* ha' *manners*
> . . . . English people ha'manners," he sniffed.
> "G'way," the woman jeered, "you face favor manners. Is English man
> you love, eh? . . . Look 'pon you too, a talk 'bout manners, you teeth tusk
> like fe hog." (106).

From the very beginning of Ivan's transition to the city, his assumed pose becomes a liability.

> With his new clothes and the little stingy-brimmed straw hat he had
> bought to give him what he hoped was a look of urban sophistication, he
> didn't want his nervousness to betray him. . . .
> "Bus comin?"
> "Me no see nutten."
> "Is wha' do dis big head boy, eh?" demanded a fat lady in an irritable
> voice, "Him must be t'ink say him pay more fare dan everybody else?"
> (104)

The speed of the bus hurtling toward Kingston, the dramatic stylizing, the assumed posing of coolie man, are but harbingers of the whirling speed, the theater of movement that confronts Ivan in the city.

> Behind the banner in disciplined ranks, dread and matted locks framing
> their faces, in prideful oblivion to their surroundings, came the band
> chanting in unison:
> *RAS TA FAR iie* . . .
> *Let the POWAH* . . .
> *from ZION fall on I* . . .
> The rest being lost, as they swept out of sight and earshot as suddenly
> as they had appeared. (122)

From the very first, Ivan not only unwittingly encounters a conflict situation but senses the upbeat pulsings of the city, experiences its rhythmical throbbing, perceives all of the kaleidoscopic energy of its surging movement.

> Ivan was surrounded simultaneously by the din of the crowd and
> pounding bass rhythms from the sound system of a music shop across the
> street. He could see the bobbing heads of teenagers dancing in front of
> the store, and for a moment he felt as if the entire street was pulsing and
> rocking with an energy that ebbed and flowed with the music's insistent
> beat. (124)

This maelstrom of a city—every shifting configuration, every changing mood and inner vitality, eddying grouping and stratified classism, all of its random vibrant living—is captured by Thelwell with a deft and stylized craftsmanship. Into this arena, Ivan is catapulted through a series of dazzling new impressions, of happenings, of jolting experiences, of dramatic episodes. Here Ivan's movement away from the communality of the hills pushes him into another special configuration, into a new materiality.

Quickly, and perhaps because of his attempted swagger, Ivan's Blue Bay possessions and heirlooms are filched, a symbolic divesting of the things that linked him to that past. Then again, in a poignantly presented scene but one lacking in true pathos, Ivan meets and quickly exits from the oppressive presence of his mother, a victim of city living.

> He surveyed the room to avoid looking at her. It seemed small, stifling hot, and crowded. Not a place to live, it was a place to sleep or to die. (136)

In rapid succession, under the tutelage of Jose, the cool, debonair, city-wise, slickster, Ivan excitedly experiences three facets of city reality that shape his later actions and career. He is turned on by the speed, power, and drama generated by a new motorbike.

> One hand holding his hat, the other clutching the seat, Ivan peered over Jose's shoulder into a blinding glare of headlights, enthralled by the heady sensation of speed. . . . Wind whipped into his eyes, stinging them with particles of dust and soot, so that the world was seen through a blur of speed and a veil of tears. (142)

Ivan enters the world of the movies, with all its make-believe dazzle and dramatic romantic heroics of gun play.

> Then the orgy of destruction was over. *"Ayah. Django tek no prisoners."*
> A long shot of a single standing figure and a hillside strewn with corpses. The audience danced and howled in gleeful transport long after the screen went dark. Ivan sat without the power to rise. (149)

The world of the movies, which has so profoundly shaped and contoured the actions and attitudes of so many Caribbean youth, has a profound effect on Ivan's perceptions of reality, his subsequent pose, his behavior.

> Ivan's nod became a barely perceptible inclination of the chin; his smile a frosty, understated tensing and relaxing of the muscles of the face. . . .
> The new persona worked well. (196)

The third affective reality encountered by Ivan on his first night is that of nightclub life with all of its robust vitality, its color, its swagger, its music and excitement, its pimping and bravado, its code of ethics.

> "First you must check out de man dem. Certainly Jah. You mus' check out de man dem. Dat is where trouble deh. You see dat slim guy over dereso? Is a badman dat. Dem call 'im Needle. You no wan' mess wid any daughtah dat him ground wid. Remember dat—Needle." (152)

This collaging of spectacle, this montage of the spectacular, soon undergoes a rapid transformation, the montage of a dream, a deferment. His initial and dramatic entry into Kingston, with all of its whirling newness and excitement, soon alters, and there follows a period of drift, of decline. The seemingly unending relentless hunger, aloneness, and fatigued drudgery are the attendant conditions of being down and out in Kingston. Clearly Ivan's attempts at surviving in the city provide Thelwell ample scope to underscore, almost to the point of caricature, the politicized nepotism of labor, the arrogant unconcern, the crass snobbery and affluence, of the privileged, the specter of color, class, caste. When Ivan goes searching for a job he experiences at first hand the crassness of the trade unionist boss.

> "How you mean you can do it? You ever do it yet?" He was shouting. "Ah say leave de place. Leff' de place, man. We need experienced people here. Don't bother waste my time. Next." (168)

Again looking for work, Ivan trespasses on the suburban domain of a privileged woman of leisure and experiences an equally brutish rejection. Even though he adopts a cringing and demeaning attitude, he is met by an ill-concealed lack of civility, even hostility.

> He clears his throat diffidently. She starts up and nearly spills her nail polish on the gleaming tiles of the verandah.
> "Excuse, mam . . . Good day, mam?"
> "What you doing here?" Her voice is not perfect. . . .
> "Ah looking work, mam." . . . He is intimidated by the opulence of the house and the conspicuously elegant grounds. He tries to smile.
> "How did you get in here?" (171)

The third principal structural formulation of *The Harder They Come* evinces other examples of that venality, corruption, and arrogance that Thelwell ascribes to the Jamaican ruling class, in this instance, those responsible for upholding morality, the very ethics of the system: preacher, judge, jailers, police officers, and superintendents. Ivan encounters them as he moves upward from being down and out in Kingston, as he arcs toward his rendezvous with his destined name, Rhygin. At this juncture, Ivan begins to lead two lives: one by day under the rigid vigilance of the preacher; the other, the life of the movies and the freewheeling nighttime camaraderie of youthful Kingston gangs. Here, too, Thelwell explores the nature and affective, somewhat pernicious, influence of external foreign influences on the attitudes of the youth gangs, of the police, and of the church of Father Ramsey.

From the very beginning of his sojourn within Preacher Ramsey's church, misunderstanding tinges the relationship between Preacher and Ivan; indeed, Ivan becomes somewhat suspect in the preacher's eyes. But, again, from the very beginning, Elsa, one of Preacher Ramsey's most devout and beloved wards, seems to be attracted to Ivan.

These two different responses to Ivan's presence heighten and eventually lead to an ever-deepening conflict situation. The preacher objects with righteous indignation, to Ivan's worldly behavior.

> "Are you going to let the Lord come back and find you doing this? Eh? Eh?"
>
> "Doing what, sah?"
>
> "Doing what? Boogie-woogieing and shaking up yourself in my yard."
>
> "Nothing no name boogie-woogie again, y'know Preacha. Dat done long time."
>
> "I don't care. I don't care what you call it, it's the devil's work, y'hear. The devil's work and I don't want it in my yard." (220)

This incipient conflict not only deepens, but flares into a raw and visceral hostility when Ivan begins trespassing on forbidden territory, the virginal devout Elsa, the preacher's prize lamb. When the deepening relationship between the still devout yet ever-ripening Elsa and the swaggering Ivan manifests itself in an unforbidden daylong jaunt on Ivan's carefully built-up cycle, all hell breaks loose. Ivan is dismissed from the compound and Elsa excoriated by the preacher, whose covert, venal, and vengeful character is maddened by his hidden passion and lust for Elsa.

> He fell to his knees on the cold concrete and prayed aloud. In a voice that shook and cracked and quivered and roared he prayed over the sobbing girl. . . .
>
> Her knees were on fire. Her legs trembled. Her head swam. And still he went on preaching until his voice was a whisper, a hoarse cracking whisper. (236)

The figure of the preacher, though one-dimensional, is so passionately intense, so wrathful, that it takes on all the configurations of an avenging

Old Testament preacher. Indeed, the curse he intones for Elsa is reminiscent of the curse Miss 'Mando invoked for Ivan.

> "Dust to dust, ashes to ashes. Let the dead bury the dead." . . .
> *"Lawd Jesus Chris' Almighty God!"* A woman broke the silence in an involuntary outburst of fear and disbelief. "Oh me God," she whimpered, "him preachin' her death." (265)

Many of the characters moving through the novel *The Harder They Come* are etched in bold relief, in their own unique pose and swagger, seeming to become stylized, dramatic forms whose actions mimic all the heroics of the screen. And their mimicry of the foreign is near perfect, their adopting of its drama near total.

> "Aye, Color Blue?"
> "Dem call me Rhygin."
> They faced each other under the streetlight. Shoulders hunched, thumbs hooked into his belt with elbows straight, Ivan squinted through the smoke at Bogart and the semicircle.
> "Well—Rhygin den. Good show?"
> "Truly."
> Suddenly Bogart bent over wheezing for breath. A fit of hollow, consumptive and explosive coughs rattled in his chest. He . . . was thrown to one knee by the vehemence of the fit. . . . Then he stood, gasping uneven gusts of air into his tortured chest, with an open rachet knife dangling ever so casually from his hand. The expression on his face was one of pure malevolence.
> "Oowee!" Ivan shouted, laughing with delight and unfeigned admiration. "Doc Holliday to raas!" (197)

All the idiosyncracies of the many gang members roaming the Kingston streets are given a heroic stamp that negates the actual poverty of circumstances in which they live. Thus playacting becomes an essential ingredient, feeding and nurturing what is indeed a condition of deprivation. This melodrama, this theatricality, colors the attitudes and underscores the figural representation of the police superintendent, Ray, who controls the drug trade.

> Then a spotlight flashed on and revealed a figure standing on the wall *above* the screen. A slender, young black man in military khakis was silhouetted against the sky.
> *"Ah say,"* he announced into the surprised silence, *"show done!"* He wore a Sam Browne belt and a pistol in a clasped holster at his waist and he had a swagger stick tucked casually under his arm. (215)

No less flashy, no less melodramatic, are the proportions in which Jose and Ivan are cut as they interact and confront one another, as Ivan runs toward his rendezvous with Rhygin. Ivan not only confronts the authority of Jose, the pusher, but encounters the corrupt and controlling power of the law in the figure of the superintendent and of the music industry in that of Hilton.

In a series of explosive, often melodramatic scenes, the action of the novel zooms toward its climax and Ivan toward his personhood in the name Rhygin. For his rightful defense of his bicycle against Preacher Ramsey's seedy bully, handyman Longa, whom he stabs repeatedly, Ivan is sardonically sentenced to a brutal whipping with the cat o' nine tails. The subsequent delirium is perhaps but a prelude to the headiness of his swift, seemingly inevitable journeying to his assumption of presence. In the vice of the corrupt and brutal Hilton, Ivan's giddy dreams of stardom go crashing down.

> Him t'ief de record, dat hurt, but it no kill. . . . Kill me record, might as cheap 'im kill me too. But Ivan wasn't even angry, there was only shock and bitterness starting in his chest that left him numb and unfeeling—at first. (297)

Ivan's excitement, his exhilaration at his record, is but momentary, and leads him ironically into drug trafficking and happily into a meeting and compassionate relationship with Ras Pedro, a poignantly sensitive, deeply righteous and religious Rastafarian figure.

> Across the table, as if at a distance, the tangled pillars of hair framed the dread-man's face . . . . Suddenly Ivan's recent blows and present problem seemed less urgent, in fact almost comic . . . . He seemed, Ivan thought dreamily, to have the entire Bible in his head, and to take a peculiar comfort in its doleful verse which he kept intoning to himself with a hypnotic monotony. (300)

Clearly the passing of the chalice is still, for Ras Pedro, a deeply ritualistic act. It has not for him become a socialized habit on which thousands depend and from which an illicit subcultural economy springs. It still sets him apart from the economic subculture on which so many of the poor and dispossessed depend for survival, which is controlled, both from the outside by U.S. antidrug agents and from the inside by higher-up police brass. The image Thelwell presents of the latter, their brutality, their cruel, sadistic methods of coercion stands in sharp contrast to the figure of Ras Pedro, his religious sensitivity, his stoicism, his deep morality.

In spite of the redemptive figure of Ras Pedro, the society depicted by Thelwell is one undergoing swift, dislocating changes, rapid social upheavals, with a new quality of violence. The mock heroics of the earlier gangs have, in the lament of Bogart, undergone a radical, worsening change.

> It was true and Ivan must have seen it too but the change had been so gradual that he hadn't been conscious of it. (204)

> Something was happening. That was clear. . . . But it was just beginning, just beginning . . . where it would end? (206)

Astride his motorbike, returning to his home, where Ivan was nurtured, Ivan realizes that the countryside, too, has undergone radical change, notably that the land where Miss Mando stood has become overgrown with wild vegetation, her grave lies hidden under thick and untended undergrowth. He finds the landscape scarred and polluted, its poetry lost through the presence of white foreigners.

> The door opened and two more apparitions emerged. *"Bumbo,"* Ivan muttered, snatching off his glasses. *"Bumbo.* You mean to say dem have 'merican nyaman?" Because that was all they could be, white Dreadlocks. . . .
> . . . Ivan knew that he had before him, in the presence of these barefoot, naked, raggedy, insect-bitten and none too clean-looking apparitions, the only white Dreadlocks in the whole world. (322)

Dispossessed, as it were, of his city dreams of becoming a great musician, and disinherited of his past, indeed fragmented from his former reality, Ivan begins his final movement to his dying.

> He felt rootless and adrift in a world without rules or boundaries. "Ivanhoe Martin, you no come from nowhe'," he told himself bitterly, and knew the pain of losing something important. . . . "'E dat increaset' knowledge, increaset' sorrow." As Ras Pedro would say.
> Instead of the joyous and triumphant homecoming of the mind, he had learned, abruptly and with no preparation, that he had no home to come to. (323)

He becomes a gunslinger. The thrill of learning to use guns and the feeling of excitement that possessing them gives him help to fill the void and become substitutes for his lost roots.

> Ivan went into the canefields and . . . . practiced until his ammunition and his excitement were spent . . . . felt as though something had been replaced. Not restored, for what was gone could not be restored, but there was something in its place. (326)

And as an archetypal hero who challenges the ethics of the oppressors, the drug dealers, agents, he blasts his way out of ambush after ambush. In a sensual melodramatic episode, Ivan's will to power attains a startling climax.

> The door across the hall was kicked open. The blast of handguns was deafening in the confined space.
>
> Naked and gleaming like a newborn baby, his turgid penis standing out woman-slick and reeking of carnality, a pistol in either hand, Rhygin stepped out the door and truly into legend.
>
> The three bunched in the door went down with the first burst, their wild fire adding to the confusion. Rhygin didn't think, feel, or see. He leapt the railing, landing on the stairs behind the back-ups. His guns kept barking. There was nothing but noise, shouts, and confusion and he was running through a backdoor. (348)

Now, indeed, Rhygin has assumed presence, has become an indigenous legend, a folk hero.

A different, more formal kind of role-playing is used by Earl Lovelace in *The Dragon Can't Dance.* As the revels of Carnival come to an end, the head of the mask, the dragon, which has danced so proudly, which has danced the warrior dance, lies discarded by its dragon dancer, Aldrick. Symbolically the head has gotten too heavy for him and, now powerless, it lies apart, void of its function, its role. The costumes, which also imbued the masqueraders with power, these also are being discarded; the masqueraders, stripped of their masks, face a new reality, that of Ash Wednesday.

> Suddenly the head of the dragon on his neck weighed a ton, and he unhooked the head and rested it on the ground beside him and wiped his face with a handkerchief and watched the Carnival ending; masqueraders, so splendidly dressed earlier in the day, moving across the streets leaving a trail of bits and pieces of their costumes, dragging their swords and spears and banners, going home now, leaving it now. And he thought, Aldrick thought: "You know, tomorrow is no Carnival." (Lovelace, *The Dragon Can't Dance,* 125)

At this point of Earl Lovelace's novel, *The Dragon Can't Dance,* Aldrick, the central character, is made to confront the reality of his existential self, to question the validity and the essentiality of the dragon dance. He will no longer dance the Dragon, and on this last occasion, the warrior who has been refused by the Slave Girl limps home befuddled and alone.

Then he began to walk; each aching step, alone; a strange new torturing
pain and sweetness in his soul, a kind of crazy new caring and respect for
the girl and a kind of warrior's pride in himself that he had chosen her,
Sylvia, in that very instant, to be his woman. (128)

It is at his height of aloneness that Aldrick moves from being a carnival
character, the Dragon; moves, too, from simply playing that role, to confront
his own presence, to search for his own being, to come to grips with the
woman spirit of the hills, Sylvia. Sylvia's vitality, her womanhood, not only
asserts itself but forces Aldrick to confront his mere role-playing life.

"No, mister!" she said, "I have my man!"

"You have your . . . your man?" he mumbled, and he felt a numbness
close over him. "You have your man?" And, looming up beside her in a
white sailorsuit was Guy: Guy, his grabbing hand closing around her bare
waist as she moved close to him. He wanted to laugh, to ease himself of
his embarrassment, but his muscles didn't work. He couldn't laugh . . . .
He stood not so much stubborn as seized, until he was all alone behind
the band. (128)

Indeed, this confrontation between Aldrick and Sylvia and his growing
realization of his need for her become central to the action of the novel,
which pendulates between the carnivalesque identification, with its role
playing, its essential masking of the surrounding social reality, and the
coming to grips with that reality with its attendant searching for selfhood.
For Earl Lovelace in *The Dragon Can't Dance* explores the meaning and
nature of responsibility, the existential dimension of being, of person. On
Ash Wednesday, the day after the Carnival and a ritual time of atonement
and questioning, Aldrick asks himself a fundamental question, stumbles on
a new way of seeing, achieves a new vision, realizes he has been "living in
the world of the dragon."

All his life he had managed in such ways to disconnect himself from
things which he couldn't escape and which threatened to define him in
a way in which he didn't want to be defined, and go on untouched,
untouched by things that should have touched him, hurt him, burned
him. . . . And he said to himself in anguish: "I have to learn to feel."
(131)

Indeed, the ending of the Carnival on the night before Ash Wednesday
becomes a demarcation point between the two modalities: one, the role-
playing; the other the assumption by the various characters of their own
innerness, the externalization of attitude and behavior, evinced by the role-
playing. The masqueraders—the Queen, the Slave Girl, the Dragon, and the

Bad John—undergo an essential change. The Queen comes to grips with her position on the stage where the novel is set, a yard in Alice Street. The Slave Girl initially assumes her role as dependent and slave but, in that very dependency, achieves her own liberation. The Dragon becomes not simply a nonparticipant actor, a mask, but, beheaded, as it were, stumbles toward a personhood. The Bad John continues to play the role of warrior, later a revolutionary, but he, too, realizes the futility of his role-playing. So that the band of masqueraders, which left with exuberance, vitality and excitement, now returns, limping slowly back, its rhythms muffled, its members depleted by the Bad John's inability to accept a change in the social order of the steelband.

> The music was a bit raggedy, because not all the steelbandsmen were playing. . . . all the shouting and talking was at an end—it was just a quietness and this sweet, tired, slow strumming. (126)

This slow movement of going home climaxes the novel's first movement, the whole building up toward Carnival, the assumption of carnival characters by the masqueraders, the music of the steel band and of the calypso: cultural transformative agents belying the poverty, the outer reality of the hill, marking the inner reality of its inhabitants.

In a lyrically dramatic prologue, Earl Lovelace paints the setting for the novel, the larger outer reality, Calvary Hill. Indeed, Calvary Hill, more particularly a single street in Calvary Hill, Alice Street, becomes a stage upon which the characters, the individual masks, are introduced sequentially; upon which their roles unfold, crisscross, and open out; their entanglements, a series of plots and subplots whose actions are constructs for character formulations. Clearly Lovelace imbues the hill and its rich culture with heroic qualities, ritualizing poverty, celebrating an innate rebel quality of its dwellers.

The hill, in the prologue, is invested with the vital presence, is enshrined with a kind of holy poverty. Its inhabitants, men and women, are captured in all the exhilaration of unfettered movement of vital living, with

> the songs that announce in this season the new rhythms for people to walk in, rhythms that climb over the red dirt and stone, break-away rhythms that laugh through the groans of these sights, these smells, that swim through the bones of these enduring people so that they shout: Life! They cry: Hurrah! They drink a rum and say: Fuck it! They walk with a tall hot beauty between the garbage and dog shit, proclaiming life, exulting in the bare bones of their person and their skin. (13)

The children, too, participate in this choreography of dance, chorus its rhythms, swishing their skirt tails, moving their waists, laughing, their laughter scattering like shells into the hard flesh of the hill. Dance! (13)

And the men of this hill, by celebrating it in music and steel, give it an authenticity, lend to it an aura of religiosity, indeed seem to make it "a cathedral," an altar on which to celebrate their mass.

Small wonder, then, that in the yard at Alice Street, Carnival and its coming bring about a transformation in the character and in the daily lives of all its inhabitants; one by one as if leading them onto a carnival stage, Earl Lovelace introduces them. The Queen of the band, Cleothilda, who has assumed her queenhood as if by right:

> Her being queen was not really a masquerade at all, but the annual affirming of a genuine queenship that she accepted as hers by virtue of her poise and beauty, something acknowledged even by her enemies, something that was not identical with her mulattohood, but certainly impossible without it. And now assuming the mantle of her queenship, she would be all laughter and excitement. (18–19)

Paradoxically, however, during Carnival this woman, who treats the other inhabitants of the yard with critical aloofness and disdain throughout the year, acts as if she were truly a part of the yard, its queen. But when she indeed assumes the role of Queen, she awakens a feeling of pity from Olive, the washer woman who slaves to support her seven children. Olive sees through Cleothilda's fragile arrogance, her assumed aristocracy. Cleothilda, the aging busybody, the yard's gossip, at Carnival time takes on the mantle of generosity, assumes a queenliness counter to her true nature. From her grandeur she parades this acquired costume, and like everyone else, moves to the beat of the music of the hill. She transforms her gallery into a stage, which she mounts:

> Now she would come out on her verandah and stand below her potted flowers, her thin legs in shorts, her wrinkled knees showing her years more truthfully than her face. . . .
> "You hear rhythm, Miss Olive? You hear song? Carnival!" she would cry out. "Bachanal! Trinidad! All o' we is one." (19)

Of Cleothilda's past all we know is that as a young woman she was an attractive cream-skinned contestant placing high in a white-dominated beauty contest, and was also a lively, coquettish and appealing dancer. Now a middle-aged woman, she relives her past, continually flaunting it, trying to recapture that aura of the prima donna who once completely captivated and made Philo, the young Calypsonian, her eternal suitor.

"This woman, Cleothilda, been in my blood for years . . . . I see this woman, Cleothilda Alvarez, on stage in the Queens' Park Savannah with the pick of the Carnival queens . . . . I decide that I want this woman for my own . . . . And she don't know if I living. And nothing I do I could get she out my mind." (156)

How he slowly gains access to the Queen's boudoir and mounts her throne is but one of the many subplots eagerly followed by the yard community, which somewhat maliciously hopes that Philo will cut Cleo down to size.

No such malice clouds the hope and dream that the women of the hill hold out for Sylvia.

The women, the older women who had eyes, who had felt the burnings of this living, would watch her sweeping along . . . that bold swinging openness that narrowed men's eyes . . . would want to wish a magic guard over her so that she would not be trampled by this hill. (26)

Sylvia, Cleo's character foil, her contrasting image, has no need to play the princess. Sylvia is distinct, a unique spirit, she is royalty, and so need not play princess: "You is a princess already. . . . Play a slave girl (34)." They wish to preserve her from the lot, from that fate Earl Lovelace insists is the only future, the only inheritance, awaiting young women from the hills, from areas such as Calvary Hill. And although through her natural grace, the choreographed rightness, the sensuous freedom of her young, ripe body, she awakens men's desires, makes them crave her, Sylvia, when fondled by various men of the hill, "[watches], felt, the . . . performance as if she wasn't there"; she remains "the virgin fucked but untouched" (25). Indeed, the author imbues her with an essential freedom, a quality of resistance, making of her a spirit force so vital that it abides in the midst of oppressive poverty, of deprivation. Sylvia possesses

a quality that had chosen her out with that sense of poetry by which oases rise up in deserts and the most delicate flowers select dunghills for their blooming. (30)

Indeed, Lovelace turns Sylvia into a concept who, though able to resist— even triumph over—the harsh external social reality of the hill, yet succumbs to the spirit of a cultural force, Carnival, which overlays and transmutes that social harshness. Through the dynamic process, the author makes the princess play the role of slave and sell her body for its livery.

She bargains with her body language for her slave costume, contracting for it with the lascivious older man, the rent collector, who lusts after her.

She stood there, one leg drawn back a little behind the other, keeping still the tension in the cloth of her dress, her lower lip tucked into her mouth . . . listening to his whispered offer and wanting cartwheeling about her head, holding her immodest pose, savouring with an innocent delight the fact of her woman-ness. (28)

Just at that point of fulfilling her contract, of paying her pound of flesh, she encounters Aldrick, Aldrick whose world has been encompassed by his dragon mask and whose life reality has been embodied by it; who though not oblivious of her, has never thought of her as a woman. Sylvia's touch penetrates the dragon's underbelly, stirring and awakening feelings that have lain masked and dormant.

> At her words she pressed against the window, flattening herself against the wall so that her head was just below Aldrick's chin, and her scent filled his nostrils, and a few strands of her hair brushed against his cheeks. He didn't move . . . .
> She straightened herself. He was choking. She was all inside him now. (34)

Sylvia's innocent proposal of marriage to Aldrick contributes to his unmasking, making him come face to face with his quickening emotions. He is unable to sidestep his growing attraction to her, can neither hide behind the dragon mask nor conceal his true feelings with a jest, "refusing even to think of her meaning, far more comment on it . . . knowing that for his manness sake the smile nor the joke wouldn't do" (43).

Thus begins Aldrick's movement away from the role-playing his dragon costume has offered him. The journey from that accidental touch to a realization of his feelings is the trajectory, becomes the novelistic contouring, of his character. Aldrick's world of the Dragon has shielded him from the drabness and degradation of Calvary Hill, allowing him to live in a detached world of his own making, one steeped in heroics. He invests his costume with all the features of his lineage, breathing into it, as it were, the spirit and lives of his ancestors, his grandfather, his father, his mother. Indeed, the Dragon seems to be the replication of his heritage and inheritance, which lends historical dimension to his yearly creation, the making of his dragon. Through the Dragon he not only celebrates his very soul but, as it were, collages the continuity of his line.

> Aldrick worked slowly, deliberately; and every thread he sewed, every scale he put on the body of the dragon, was a thought, a gesture, an adventure, a name that celebrated some part of his journey to and his surviving upon this hill. (36)

Indeed, Aldrick's creating of the dragon allows Lovelace to trace and develop his protagonist's genealogy, to fill out, to give density to, his characterization. Thus we are told about Aldrick's grandfather's stubborn will to hold on to a dream,

> holding on then to the five acres of mountain and stone that had exhausted its substance, if it ever had any . . . as if the land, that mountain and stone land, held some promise. (37)

We learn, too, about the pathos and unfulfilled intentions of his father, who came to the city seeking his fortune. The gift of his father to his children was not fortune but the gift of self, the "sense of miracle and manness, this surviving on nothing and standing up to be counted as somebody" (41). Aldrick embroiders his mother's soft patience and generous waiting for him despite his unfulfilled dreams: "Just go as you going. Don't promise anything" (40), she tells him.

The Dragon, then, takes on a quality of heraldry; the act of creating it becomes a ritual. Here Aldrick is high priest, and the admiring little boy becomes an acolyte.

> The little boy of ten who came from somewhere in the neighbourhood of Alice Street . . . stood at the door and gazed in at the dragon costume Aldrick was then making . . . maintaining that attitude of reverence throughout, as if he were in the presence of holiness . . . . So the boy was here again this year. And, working now, he seemed to divine exactly which tool or piece of material Aldrick needed for his work, and he handed it to him with a ceremonial solemnity as if he, the boy, were an acolyte, and Aldrick the priest. (35)

Not only does the little boy participate in the making of this costume but later on, like Sylvia, he becomes a catalyst for change in Aldrick's way of seeing. For indeed, Aldrick, though aware of the boy's presence, has never truly seen him, has never taken the trouble to find out his name or from where he came. Thus, when stubbornly the little boy refuses to return to his home, Aldrick is suddenly confronted with that immediate reality of finding out the little boy's identity, later of taking him to his home. Here Aldrick must confront the boy's father and, more importantly, participate in an immediate and real life situation. The inadequacy with which Aldrick responded to Sylvia's symbolic and innocent proposal of marriage is registered once again in his manner of confronting the boy's "Bad John" father, Fisheye. In both situations, Aldrick attempts to cover up this inadequacy through jest, which instead only makes him aware of the nature of his own inability, or unwillingness, to confront his immediate social and personal circumstance. His joking with Fisheye seems empty and false, and he gets "confused by his shame now that Fisheye had refused to play the game" (72). Aldrick again realizes that he has lived only for his dragon and that he has not really seen the people who live around him, nor really taken in his surroundings.

The third incident that helps to bring about the alteration of Aldrick's way of seeing is the meeting with the East Indian, Pariag. Aldrick realizes that though the East Indian lived in the same yard, not far from him, he has never really seen him.

> And it was only afterwards, when he was inside and lying on his bed, thinking of the day's events, the boy, Basil, Fisheye, and Sylvia crowding his brain, that his mind ran on Pariag, and he thought: "Shit! I never try to talk to him in the two years either." (76)

Lovelace makes Aldrick the pivotal point, the radial center of the staging of *The Dragon Can't Dance*. It is Aldrick who offers Lovelace an opportunity to introduce both Fisheye and Pariag, to bring them into the action, to lead them onto the stage, for the novel is structured along dramatic lines; each character is brought on in sequence, which leads to each one's depiction and the delineation of his or her past circumstances. Each protagonist becomes a representation of a particular cultural or social reality. Thus Fisheye, the exemplar of a Bad John, seems to represent the initial spirit of warriorhood, of the steel bandsmen, and becomes the mirror in which the changing social history of the steel bands refracts and is reflected. Pariag represents the condition of the East Indian who has migrated from the country, fleeing the unending cycle of plantation servitude in search of a larger world.

Like so many of Lovelace's characters, both Fisheye and Pariag are characters who migrate from the country in search of a fortune, but who, in its pursuit, are made to confront their own reality, to explore the nature of their relationships to others, to attempt to apprehend their own existential responsibility. Initially, Fisheye comes to the city not so much confident of his strength but more so savoring it. Not unlike Sylvia, he, too, initially exudes a certain pure physicality unaffected by his surroundings. He exults in his strength, celebrating it through work. How Fisheye finally channels his strength—how he becomes first the Bad John, then the warrior, and ultimately the rebel—structures his characterization, contours his actions. In the same way that Lovelace makes the hill heroic, makes Aldrick, in the creating of his dragon, heroic, so, too, by imbuing Fisheye with an unyielding spirit of rebellion, he gives him the distinctiveness of a warrior. To Lovelace, Fisheye represents all the vital and continuous spirit of rebellion present in those who have triumphed over oppression. Fisheye is represented as possessing an essential warrior quality, which marked the beginnings, the early years of the steel band's movements.

Two peaks on the same rebelling Hill, had been for years locked in a war that they themselves must have created out of their own need to cultivate and uphold that spirit of rebellion and warriorhood .... In fact, to Fisheye, their warring had become the celebration and consecration of a greater brotherhood. (58–59)

Thus, through his initial characterization of Aldrick and of Fisheye, Lovelace articulates his notion of the warrior, establishing, thereby, a historical linkage, an unbroken continuum with an African resistance and presence.

A ritual, heralding the masqueraders' coming . . . goes back centuries for its beginnings, back across the Middle Passage . . . back to Africa when Maskers were sacred and revered . . . linking the villagers to their ancestors, their Gods . . . Aldrick Prospect, with only the memory burning in his blood . . . . had a desire, a mission, to let them see their beauty, to uphold the unending rebellion they waged. (120–121)

Fisheye's youthful physicality, that raw, clean strength with which he came from Moruga, he initially channels into hard work. But soon that very strength makes him restless. Like so many youthful characters in Caribbean life and literature, Fisheye, influenced by the movies, begins to mimic its tough men.

He began to develop a crawl, a way of walking that was kinda dragging and slow, in which his knees barely bent, his feet were kept close and his legs spread apart to give the appearance of being bow-legged from riding a horse .... but, his readiness was its own warning, and he went, almost a spectacle, unmolested through the streets, nobody wanting to tackle him. (51)

The lines between fantasy and reality fade. Fisheye's role-playing not only gives him an identifiable badge and presence but finds fertile soil for its celebration in the gang warfare between rival steel bands. Later Fisheye views with deepening suspicion and resentment the sponsorship of steel bands by large businesses and its corollary, the growing participation of colored and whites. He views this not only as a cooptation but indeed a corruption of that spirit of warriorhood which gave its root power, its vital essence, to the steelbands,

steelbands whose very names—Merry Boys, Dixie Land, Star Land, Happy Boys, held no salute nor acknowledgement of the fire, the blood, the heat of the early days of the movement. (63)

Fisheye's unswerving belief in warriorhood fuels his resistance to that cooptation by the privileged, and his resentment of any who would make peace with those of the sponsoring class or adopt and exhibit their social mores. Initially Fisheye's resistance assumes two forms. One is disruptive violence aimed at reviving a climate of steel-band rivalry and warfare.

> He began to fight again. Sponsors did not like violence in bands. Indeed, one of the conditions of sponsorship was no misbehaving in the band.
> . . . Suddenly he was a warrior again, and in the midst of the peace, the decency of the steelbands, the well-behaved emasculated warriors, Calvary Hill, because of Fisheye, had a bad name. (69–70)

Then in his isolation, having been touched by the euphoria that swept through Trinidad and Tobago during the early years of PNM (People's National Movement), he tries to instill in the steelbandsmen the notion of power derived from an organized togetherness.

> This was the thing that the steelband might have become. . . . the strength of his arms, would lift their arms to break down these shanty towns . . . and build something clean, something tall. (65)

Later surrounded by a small gang of sycophants, Fisheye dissipates his warrior energy by street-corner harassment of the Calvary Hill people, whose mere working seemed to him surrender.

Aldrick drifts along with this gang, spinelessly refusing to take on Fisheye or to assert his own beliefs. He remains silent in the face of Fisheye's uncompromising and brutal rejection of Philo's show of friendship and togetherness. To be sure, Philo achieved his success and fame when he turned away from singing political calypsos with a message, a warrior content, and began to offer to the public a steady diet of suggestively sexy ballads. With his success he became a capricious consumer, a high-spender. But even though the author seems bent on building a case against Philo in order to justify the warriors' brutish rejection, Fisheye's calculated insult and Aldrick's conniving silence are negative expressions of their initial warriorhood.

Philo's need to belong, to be identified with something, and his basic aloneness are similar to Pariag's. Both the calypsonian, with his overt success, and Pariag, the moderately successful shop owner, are essentially lonely men. Indeed, the theme of aloneness, with its attendant exploration into the meaning and the place of existential self in a changing societal polity becomes a dominant chord, a recurrent motif, sounding throughout the representation of character in *The Dragon Can't Dance*.

Pariag's shop gives him the visibility that he has craved and whose acquisition he has so pathetically sought. Fleeing the seemingly oppressive communal ties and a generational cycle of indenture and drudgery, Pariag has come to Calvary Hill with its predominantly creole presence. There with his shy young bride he lives in anonymity, friendlessness, at times missing the all-fours camaraderie of his country friends; he remains a partnerless observer, an outsider. At random occasions, through nicknames, he loses that anonymity, becoming "channa boy," "Bottles," "Crazy Indian." But always he walks alone in the midst of a crowd, wanting to, but seemingly unable to, cross the threshold, move across the cultural divide.

A new bicycle affords him a euphoric visibility but awakens in the Alice Street people a deep, endemic racial hostility fanned by Cleothilda's jealous and stereotypic accusations.

> "That is why I never trust them," Miss Cleothilda was saying. "They too sly and secretive. You could never know what going on with them. Turn, just turn your head, and they knife you in the back." (103)

The wanton and malicious destruction of the cycle evinces, but too late, gestures of friendly acceptance from his yard neighbors, who deplore the senseless act.

Later on, Pariag ponders on the part he may have unwittingly played in shaping his own outsideness, his essential displacement. In a lyrical statement, Pariag laments his not having joined his music to the new music of fire and steel, regrets not adding his harmony to the music of the others. Indeed, he has not shared his life with them, he has remained anonymous.

> . . . I wish I did walk with a flute or a sitar, and walk in right there in the middle of the steelband yard where they was . . . chiselling out new notes. New notes. I wish I woulda go in there where they was making their life anew in fire. (210)

In a similar vein, Philo, alienated and displaced from his new surroundings in Diego Martin, chafes against its replicated monotony, ponders on the ironic nature of success and on the question of belonging.

> He felt upon him a strange, draining tiredness, and he felt old and alone. He thought of himself as the only live soul in a pretty, well laid out cemetery. . . . Or, was he also dead? (220)

This tone of introspection, this element of self-scrutiny shapes the content of the last Ash Wednesday segment of the novel so that ultimately its action is presented and takes form through dialogue. The characterization becomes analysis, the questioning about one's role, one's responsibility, in that search for self-realization, for selfhood.

While in jail for an unplanned minor act of rebellion, agented by Fisheye and gratuitously entered into by Aldrick, the former warrior and the Dragon discuss their relationship to the external political reality and ponder on the nature of their essences. Aldrick asserts:

> "They want to tell us that we can't be free unless we beat them, that we can't be men unless we win, that we don't have no claim to anything because we lose to them. You see, they want us to make winning a condition for freedom. I mean they want to make it appear that because we didn't have no plan, and because we didn't win that we don't have no right to be free, that we don't have no right to be people." (185)

And finally Aldrick asks himself what was the role, what indeed was the function of his dragon dance.

> "All we could do is a dragon dance; all we could do is to threaten power, to show off power we have but don't know how to organize, how to use." (186)

Paradoxically, only when he stops his dragon dance will the Dragon begin truly to dance, to live. Thus the image symbol of the Dragon undergoes a fundamental change. The Dragon becomes a man who finally confesses love.

> "Now I know I ain't a dragon. . . . Funny, eh? Years. And now I know I is more than just to play a masquerade once a year for two days, to live for two days," he said. "It have life for us to live, girl. Life." (198)

> "I wanted to say I love you," he said. "I wanted to shout it for everybody to hear."
> "Why you didn't do it? 'Fraid?"
> "Yes. But I ain't afraid now." (197)

By taking off his assumed costume, by divesting himself of his maskery, Aldrick arrives at selfhood. Sylvia, too, sheds herself of her carnival Slave Girl costume and unmasks her hill woman spirit. The Dragon is no longer dragon; the Slave Girl is no longer slave. They enter a new space together of love and freedom.

It is not costumes and masks but material possessions that Avey Johnson must shed in Paule Marshall's *Praisesong for the Widow*. In a half-twilight world in which shafts of sun and quiet shadows interplay, Avey Johnson's ritual return into presence begins. She has moved from the harsh, blinding sunlight into a quiet space of a shrine and sanctuary. It is here in this shrine and temple that *Praisesong for the Widow* begins its final intoning, its drummed and rhythmical orchestration. For Marshall in this novel, through an unending series of polyrhythms, drums out and orchestrates a praisesong whose ever-shifting and linked melodies resonate with and intone an African presence, assuring continuity and flow and essentiality, and ordaining symbolic return to the source and center. This symbolic return, though seemingly inexplicable—"All I knew was that I wanted to go home . . ." (171)—lies at the center of the praisesong, which is intoned with a majestic inevitability by Marshall. Avey Johnson, who has gone away from the cultural matrix and heart-pull of the African presence, goes home. Without knowing why, she is drawn into the sanctuary and temple over which presides the African elder spirit: A hand will lead her home.

> But gradually, in the midst of the vertigo, she became aware of the cool dark current of air that had met her at the door. She felt it come to rest, like a soothing hand on her head, and it remained there, gently drawing away the heat and slowing down both her pulse and the whirling ring of harsh light behind her closed eyes. Finally, under its calming touch, the dizziness subsided enough for her to raise up and look around her. (Marshall, *Praisesong for the Widow*, 158–159)

And thus begins the cleansing, the release from the harshness, from the numbing vertigo, of the "going away" of the Middle Passage: the laying on of hands, the *Lave Tête*. It is the elder of the tribe, of the nation, of the race, through whom all the scarification lines of continuity have gathered their force and strength. It is he, Lebert Joseph, who takes Avey Johnson by the hand and leads her on. Avey Johnson has been weakened by her crossing and her passage from Tatem, South Carolina, to Halsey Street in Brooklyn, to White Plains in Westchester, New York. And now the gnome-like spirit-figure of Lebert Joseph begins the negation of the triangularity of the Middle Passage and orchestrates, through a powerful countermovement, her return to self and presence.

Paule Marshall ascribes to Lebert Joseph, whose hand performs the miracle of return, all the spirit-wisdom, all the enshrined ritualistic energy and power, all the consecrated energy and fire of that eldership. Marshall endows him with the spirit-force of an African presence. He is representation and replication, seer and medicine man. He is mask, "the lines etched over his face like the scarification marks of a thousand tribes" (161). He is elder who has undergone trial by fire and who has passed into the realms and spaces of the ancestor.

> He was one of those old people who give the impression of having undergone a lifetime trial by fire which they somehow managed to turn to their own good in the end; using the fire to burn away everything in them that could possibly decay, everything mortal. (161)

He is continuity and endurance, "the indestructible will: old people who have the essentials to go on forever" (161).

Clearly, then, Lebert Joseph, who himself has achieved presence, can lend his energy and wisdom to assure the attaining to presence by someone of the tribe who is undergoing her own trial by fire. For Avey Johnson, whose material personality has been denuded, who at the point of her encounter with Lebert Joseph sees her life as an empty void in the yawning chasm, is rescued from this void, this chasm, through the spirit-wisdom of the seer-man, whose foresight and foreknowledge divine Avey Johnson's anguished journeying.

> It didn't matter that she could not go on. Because the man already knew of the Gethsemane she had undergone last night, knew about it in the same detailed and anguished way as Avey Johnson, although she had not spoken a word. His penetrating look said as much. It marked him as someone who possessed ways of seeing that went beyond mere sight and ways of knowing that outstripped ordinary intelligence (*Li gain connaissance*) and thus no need for words. (172)

This anguished journeying is the larger structural formulation, the essential thematic construct, of *Praisesong for the Widow*. It provides the framework within which the character of Avey Johnson pendulates, swinging between acquired personality and oral presence; moving from a youthful assurance located within the folk wisdom of Aunt Cuney through a vital throbbing early togetherness with her husband, Jay; she descends into the depths of a heightened materialistic personality and the overaccumulation of material resources in the movement away from Tatem to Westchester, and then into an anguished groping from the depths, a circular spiraling upward into presence. Avey Johnson's journeying, then, becomes the divestment of the excess acquired matter with its consequent loss of spirituality of her personality and her struggle toward an investiture into presence.

At the high point of her first meeting with Lebert Joseph, he simply feels and senses her anguished journeying—the main theme and motif of the novel, the going away and the going home—

> with a look like a laser beam. He used it now to examine her again, this time seeing her half-combed hair, the damp wrinkled dress and the self crouched like a bewildered child behind the vacant, tear-filled eyes. He saw how far she had come since leaving the ship and the distance she had yet to go. (172)

Already the external acquired trappings have clearly been shed, and the external acquired personality has been shrunken—the wrinkled dress, the crouched self—and now as medicine man he begins the cleansing of the inner body, of the soul, of the spirit. All is ritual gesture and offertory. All is ritual acceptance.

Without a word but with the knowing and compassion in his eyes, he
held the glass out to Avey Johnson across the table. . . .
    . . . She was holding the glass cupped between her hands. (173–174)

And thus begins the ritual cleansing, the essential revitalization and regeneration.

She almost instantly felt that first swallow of the drink soothe her parched
throat and begin to circle her stomach like a ring of cool wet fire. Eagerly
she raised her glass to her lips again. . . .
    . . . Before she had finished half the glass, it had reached out to her
dulled nerves, rousing and at the same time soothing them; and it was
even causing the pall over her mind to lift again. (174)

These sensations of dryness and barrenness—"parched throat," "dry river
bed," the feelings of "dulled nerves" and "pall over her mind"—are the
resultant conditions from that process of going away, a process whose
destructive elements have pushed Avey Johnson into a yawning void: "She
sensed the yawning hole down which her life of the past thirty years had
vanished by the time it was over" (172).

The movement from this depersonalized condition into the attainment
of a new presence structures Avey Johnson's characterization as it pendulates
between these two states of being. Paule Marshall, in depicting the fierce
struggle of Avey Johnson's movement into presence, incorporates into the
polity of the novel the orality of the Southern Black person of Aunt Cuney;
all the immediate ritual and spiritual formulations of African-American music
and song and religion; all the ritual of African continuity in the Grenada-
Carriacou ecology—these are all endowed with a mythic, metaphoric
reference and vital force. It is when these vital African elements become
referential energy sources that Avey Johnson's life and character take on
qualitative strength and an enduring possibility—that is, the going home.
Conversely, Avey Johnson's character swings downward into the chasm and
void into a loss of personality where there is no affective perception of self.
When she attempts to negate these vital forces, these African continuities
resident in the orality of Tatem, the lived folk reality of African-American
music and religion, the political and social struggle of Black peoples and her
African linkages, she becomes depersonalized. Paule Marshall affords to
these linkages an effective and abiding restorative strength and qualifying
energy.

Avey Johnson's husband, Jay Johnson, when energized by these linkages,
despite his lack of material resources, moves with all the quiet exciting
assurance that derives from those linkages. Conversely, when he forgets his
roots, his vital linkages, and accepts the materialistic personality of corporate

America, Jay Johnson becomes Jerome Johnson, a pallid, schizoid, devitalized effigy of his former self. Even as Jerome Johnson assumes a mask that hides him and denies him a presence, Avey Johnson's movement is ultimately a counter one: the shedding of the vitiating, devitalizing accumulative personality; the attendant emptying and shedding of that personality; and the refilling of a voided self with a ritual African presence.

Through repeated flashbacks, Marshall realigns linear space and time into a linked contrapuntal but spiraling temporality, thereby imbuing the narrative structure with a to-and-fro motion and a metaphoric elasticity, a holistic and dramatic tension. The series of recurrent dreams and hallucinations, which are the essential modalities for Avey Johnson's characterization, provides the means by which her personality is fragmented and her presence assumed. Thus, *Praisesong for the Widow* becomes an essential statement and is an exact formulation of the need to arrive at presence through a fragmentation of an oppressive personality with its ensuing changes and a shaping of a new self through continuous and dynamic transformation.

Carefully and with novelistic certainty, Marshall orchestrates the fragmentation of Avey Johnson's personality and her assumption, through a transformative vision, of presence. In this process, all forms and shapes, accessories and elements are imbued with a referential and symbolic quality. From the very beginning of the novel, the notion of the crossing, the ship, underscore the contrasting modes with which the journeying of African peoples has been qualified. Installed in a luxury liner with her costly and stylish luggage, Avey Johnson already is presented as the epitome of one who has made it in the American-dream syndrome. Her unplanned departure from the shining luxury liner is the beginning of a departure from that syndrome, an opting out of it. Centuries earlier, as enshrined in the orality of her Great-aunt Cuney's tale, the early slave arrivals, the Ibos, also opted out, refusing to participate in their own debilitating enslavement, which would have been the cost of making it. They went back across the waters, brought away from their ritual certainty but going home before that ritual certainty could be damaged, before the need for the anguished fragmentation of their personality, before that presence could be tarnished.

Clearly a technique that underscores the constructs of *Praisesong for the Widow*, metaphoric correspondences and symbolic cross-references, gives an essentiality to every action, gesture and statement, providing a strength and power to her webbing of her Anancy tale. The big ol' slave ship is transformed into the Bianca Pride. Avey Johnson's luggage, acquired at such expense of will and spirit, becomes like the chains that bound the Ibos, fettering them. The Ibos walked away, realizing how burdensome the new chains would become. Through their own ascribed foresight and prevision, they visualized the mutations attendant on the acquiring of that luggage and fled—chains and all. Unlike the Ibos, however, when Avey Johnson leaves the Bianca Pride and arrives on the shores of Grenada, she is unable to carry that luggage and seems trapped by her accessories.

Through a process of linked correspondence, by injecting an elastic continuum into African history, Lebert Joseph, the gnome-like elder who leads Avey Johnson home, still retains that prescience, that prevision, ascribed to the Ibos in Aunt Cuney's great-grandmother's folk tale. The Ibos were said to be able to "see in more ways than one . . . can tell 'bout things happened long before they was born and things to come long after they's dead" (37). Lebert Joseph is represented similarly:

> There was no thought or image, no hidden turn of her mind he did not have access to . . . . he saw and understood them all from the look he bent on her. (171)

Clearly the Ibos would have foreseen the loss Avey Johnson suffers wandering in strange places and the attendant filth by which she is burdened in those wanderings. Similarly, Lebert Joseph sees the clogging derived from that filth and the need to release the clogged body and soul.

Thus it is that even as Paule Marshall establishes Tatem in South Carolina as the radial and focal source of the many correspondences and the replicative process, indeed as the initial and finite source of return, she makes of Carriacou the native land of symbolic return. Avey Johnson's journeys, then, take her from the source through a searing passage into her native land. The source is Tatem, and its aural spirit and elder, the retainer of folk wisdom, Great-aunt Cuney, is the catalyst that begins the extrication of Avey Johnson from the materiality she has gathered in her passage. It is when Avey Johnson—imprisoned in the luxury of the Bianca Pride, secure in her financial holdings and possessions—it is when she dreams of Great-aunt Cuney that the process of return to the native land begins. In her dream, Avey Johnson violently resists her Great-aunt Cuney's call to come home, to forfeit the luxury, the holdings, the hypermateriality, and to touch again the source of soul energy. In a powerfully delineated and dramatically intense confrontation, Marshall underscores the cultural conflict latent in the African-American existential condition. Avey Johnson wonders as she resists her Aunt Cuney's call.

> What was wrong with her? Couldn't she see she was no longer the child in scratchy wool stockings . . . . No longer the Avey (or Avatara as she insisted on calling her) she had laid claim to for a month each summer from the time she was seven. Before she was seven! Before she had been born even! (42)

Now Avey Johnson has become a woman of means enveloped in her fineries, in a "new spring suit she had just put on to wear to the annual luncheon at the Statler given by Jerome Johnson's lodge" (40).

The struggle here is between the soul of Avatara and Avey Johnson, the wife of Jerome Johnson. This Avey Johnson attempts to avert her face, "hoping, that when she looked back, she would find that the old woman had given up and gone on the walk alone" (41). She not only rejects the summons, the coaxings from the ancestor figure, exemplar of folk wisdom, the carrier of folk history, but also resists the call to return to the source, resisting the cultural pull of the African-American church and spirituality.

> But not only was the tall figure still there when she looked around again, the coaxing had become more impassioned. Her body straining forward as though to bridge the distance between them, she was pleading with her now to join her, silently exhorting her, transformed into a preacher in a Holiness church imploring the sinners and backsliders to come forward to the mercy seat. *"Come/O will you come . . . ?"* (41–42)

The cultural conflict that ensues between Avey Johnson and the ancestor figure, Great-aunt Cuney, is not simply a "silent tug-of-war" between two equal forces. It is one fraught with all the intense problematic possibilities attendant on the African-American's search for roots, for source. Avey Johnson's resistance is momentarily weakened by an instinctive recalling of folk teachings and the ensuing call by the teacher of that folk wisdom that she remember those teachings.

> The eyes held none of her rage . . . In them was reflected also the mute plea: *"Come/Won't you come."* (44)

Marshall invests the metaphoric source, Tatem and its elders, with an ecology of continuing resistance and an abiding struggle to retain their essential rootedness, their essential freedom; all the personages that Great-aunt Cuney meets on her way to the symbolic place where the Ibos landed, all of these people who become recognizable symbols in the memory of Avatara, have resisted conquest. There are "Doctor" Benitha Grant, "with samples of the herbs she used to treat the sick and ailing" (35), Pharo Harris and his wife Miss Celia, "with all the rusted washtubs . . . from the years she had taken in washing . . . all the broken plows, pitchforks, hoes and the like from his sharecropping days" (35), and Mr. Golla Mack, "seated in monumental stillness on his tumbled down porch" (36).

Even as Marshall establishes Tatem as the source of continuity and of potential flow, so too she establishes the Bianca Pride, the epitome of excessive luxury, the replica of the slave ship, as the space in which blockage to that flow and an interruption of natural folk and body rhythms take place. Not only does Avey Johnson suffer a "mysterious clogged and swollen feeling which differed in intensity and came and went at will," but the ship, too, seems to have incorporated it.

> When she got out of bed . . . she thought she felt the liner rolling and pitching ever so slightly around her, as if it too had fallen victim to the same strange malaise. (52)

Both the struggle with her great-aunt, which was actualized by a dream, and the strange sensation attendant on the parfait she had eaten, become in Marshall's narrative formulation not simply catalyst for Avey Johnson's departure from the liner but indeed the dualistic and antithetical polarities between which pendulate her change and transformation: the source and the passage. Symbolically, Avey Johnson is unable to see her own reflection, that is, to perceive her true self or locate her inner being.

> She easily recognized them both in the distant mirror. But for a long confused moment Avey Johnson could not place the woman in beige crêpe de Chine and pearls seated with them. (48)

> Other times the same stylishly dressed matron surprised her from the dingy windows of the train to and from work. She confronted her in the plate glass exteriors of stores and restaurants . . . . One morning she even accosted Avey Johnson in her bathroom mirror as she raised up from washing her face. (49)

So Avey Johnson's attempt to find a silent place in the midst of the excessive luxury represented by the decorations and furnishings on the Bianca Pride signifies a headlong flight from an unrecognizable self. During the flight a macabre transposition of form takes place.

> And before she could think to act, her eyes played another of their frightening tricks. In a swift, subliminal flash, all the man's wrinkled sun-baked skin fell away, his thinned-out flesh disappeared, and the only thing to be seen on the deck chair was a skeleton in a pair of skimpy red-and-white striped trunks and a blue visored cap. (59)

All this culminates in her frantic self-propulsion away from the replica of the slave ship, the Bianca Pride, with its cargo of surfeited travelers trapped, as it were, in their own hypermateriality. Clearly this leaving the vessel is representative of a larger divestiture. As in the first movement of the novel, "Runagate," so too in the second, "Sleeper's Wake," Paule Marshall establishes a dualism in her formulation of character and action, a dualism that arches between the poles of cultural identification coupled with nonexcessive material prerequisites, and a deculturization into an ecology of accumulation and acquisition of matter. In the second movement, Avey Johnson is slowly divested of the external trappings reflective of her acquisition of excessive materiality.

On the wharf while waiting for a taxi to the plane to take her back to the White Plains house, Avey Johnson attempts to surround herself with her expensive and fashionable luggage but finds it an encumbrance more than a protection. The carefully planned clothing with accessories of gloves and girdles under the tropical heat and sun becomes more a liability than aesthetic and attractive stylish fittings. With all the luggage, all the stylish accessories, Avey Johnson attempts to separate herself from the island presence. Slowly, however, the island celebrants, through their own way of seeing, strip her of her external attributes and seem to dress her in their own garb. They see in her a kinship—a recognizable body motion, a physique similar to theirs. She seems so much one of them that

> But from the way they were acting she could have been simply one of them there on the wharf. Some in passing even gave her a quizzical look along with their smiles, as if questioning why she was standing in the one spot and not moving with them toward the boats. (69)

Clearly the process of reidentification and recognition has begun.

Paule Marshall ascribes a sense of family to those going home, of communality to their movement, to their ingathering. But the metaphoric island condition, even as it divests Avey Johnson, seems to entrap her. She balks at being included in the sense of communality that binds the celebrants together. She is appalled at being taken for the exact twin of someone. She reacts to and rejects the touch of both the old woman and the young baby and attempts to surround herself with her acquired artifacts.

Marshall endows the taxi driver, who eventually takes Avey Johnson away from the thronging communality of the celebrants, with an ambiguity exhibiting both the attributes of the going away and those of the going home. Both his hands and his body seem to have in them an essential Africanness, which is masked by the dark sunglasses that he sports.

> His stride as he swiftly approached her seemed designed to cover an entire continent in a day, and there was a reddish, burnt ocher cast to the blackness of his face and his swinging arms. He might have stepped off the pages of the expensive photography book with the word "Masai" on its cover which Marion kept in her living room. (73)

Even as Avey Johnson is unable to comprehend the language of the people, the patois to which they have reverted as they prepare for their going home to Carriacou, the taxi driver, too, is unable to comprehend this reversion by the celebrants to their own identifiable and known symbols. It is not surprising that this taxi driver is unable to identify and accept his fiancée's cultural rootings. It is he who deposits Avey Johnson at a complex of luxury hotels, thereby repositing her to her "awayness."

Marshall, using a cyclical structure, places Avey Johnson, having left the luxury of the Bianca Pride, in a complex of gaudy luxury hotels which stand in sharp contrast to the vegetation and ecology of the Grenadian landscape. Once again her entry into this unnatural locus of luxury, which obscures and dwarfs the natural light of the hills, occasions another dream sequence—the climax of the neurotic seizures begun on the Bianca Pride—a frightening, hallucinatory experience that brings her to her knees, a simpering supplicant. As with the dream and the parfait on the Bianca Pride, Avey Johnson's hallucination or dream on the balcony of the luxury hotel swings between a cultural space inhabited by the souls of Black folk, the Halsey Street of the first years of her marriage with Jay Johnson, and the deculturalized motion and harsh strivings that would take Avey and Jerome Johnson into the excessive acquisitive materialism of their White Plains living.

In Halsey Street, the younger Jay Johnson, before his masking time and his shrouding into Jerome Johnson, is energized by the music and poetry of the African American. The ritual of dance and song and poetry in which he and Avey Johnson and the two young childen nest, is a cocooning African source of strength and renewal, a protection against the external threats to Jay's Black manhood, against his long hours of unrequited labor in a white commercial ethos.

> The change that came over him from the moment he stepped in the door! His first act after greeting her was to turn up the volume on the phonograph . . . . he would lower his tall frame into the armchair, lean his head back, close his eyes, and let Coleman Hawkins, The Count, Lester Young (old Prez himself), The Duke—along with the singers he loved: Mr. B., Lady Day, Lil Green, Ella—work their magic, their special mojo on him. Until gradually, under their ministrations, the fatigue and strain of the long day spent doing the two jobs—his and his boss's—would ease from his face, and his body as he sat up in the chair and stretched would look as if it belonged to him again. (94)

He is sustained, energized, and revitalized by listening to the blues records, the folk inheritance from his father. Marshall makes her narrative resonate with all the inner vibrations of the music and poetry of African Americans sculpturing Avey Johnson in liquid dance motion and freedom, carving the bodies of Avey and Jay in all the earth flow and water movement of an African mythos, as in their mobile love-making.

He would lie within her like a man who has suddenly found himself inside a temple of some kind, and hangs back, overcome by the magnificence of the place, and sensing around him the invisible forms of the deities who reside there: Erzulie . . . Yemoja . . . Oya . . . Jay might have felt himself surrounded by a pantheon of the most ancient deities who made their temple the tunneled darkness of his wife's flesh. (127)

During her dream on the hotel balcony, Avey Johnson, and indeed perhaps Paule Marshall, mourn Jay's loss of that vitalistic flow and energy; his loss of a sense of his own cultural roots as he attempts to climb into the American corporate structure; his holding down a series of three to four jobs while studying for his examinations; his loss of a sense of self, his assumption of a new, cold, sterile mass and personality. Avey's grief is for the man who self-destructed as he pursued his dream of matter, as he entered into the corporate dehumanizing ethos, punishing and flagellating himself:

> "When you come this color, it's uphill all the way," he would say, striking the back of one dark hand with the other—hard, punishing little blows that took his anger out on himself . . . . until finally the confusion, contradiction and rage of it all sent the blood flooding his brain one night as he slept in the bed next to hers. (134–135)

The intensity of Avey Johnson's grief and violent spasms mirror and match and equal all the deep, self-inflicted violence that eventually destroyed her husband; now the personality she assumed also self-destructs. The ultimate fragmentation of the personality ensues. A new birth, a new entry into presence, begins.

> Her mind, like her pocketbook outside, had been emptied of the contents of the past thirty years during the night, so that she had awakened with it like a slate that had been wiped clean, a *tabula rasa* upon which a whole new history could be written. (151)

The ritual return takes her back to her earliest infancy. Space and time merge, the past cohering with the present.

In a series of violent neurotic spasms on the balcony of the luxury hotel, Avey Johnson divests herself of her well-chosen stylish accessories, gloves, hat, pocketbook.

> Avey Johnson shucked the gloves off her hands with such violence the fingers turned inside out. The hat . . . found itself being hurled into the nether darkness of a corner. (144)

But here, too, on the balcony, the sharply contrasting memories of her life with her husband rip and tear at her very being: where, for instance, had they slipped away from "those small rites, an ethos they held in common . . . to join them to the vast unknown lineage that had made their being possible" (137). When did Jay Johnson become Jerome, and when did she, Avatar, become Avey Johnson? What made Jay into that mask, "a stranger's cold face laughing in Mephistophelian glee behind his in the coffin" (135)? On the balcony for the first time she weeps for the loss of Jay, mourning inconsolably for "not his death so much, but his life" (134).

The smell of curdling milk, of baby powder, her changing from girdle to diaper—once again she is a toddler, uncertain of her new limbs, her new life. The beginning of her voyaging into presence takes place on a "wide flawless apron of sand" (153), unmarked by footprints. She leaves behind the glitter of the hotels, which slowly and symbolically disintegrate, becoming "for all their solid concrete, stone and glass, as insubstantial as mirages" (154). Here Marshall celebrates the beauty of the landscape, imbuing it with naturalness that reduces and destroys the power of symbolic matter. The sea, the hills, the morning, become a vital space, regenerative in their authenticity.

> With a child's curiosity and awe Avey Johnson surveyed the familiar elements which made up the still-life of the beach—sand, sea, trees and overarching sky—as if she were seeing their like for the first time. (154)

All is new wonder, all a new freedom, and she begins her exploration of embryonic forms again, exploring the inner mystery of things.

> She was unaware of the blazing sun, so absorbed did she become in the small marine life and non-life to be found near the water. The sandcrabs scuttling in and out of their holes, the shells and coral scattered about, the occasional sandpiper goosestepping quickly out of the way as a wave broke. (155)

Now, heedless of time and not bound by space, she moves along the sands into the dunes, welcomed from her wanderings by the voices of children who are still in tune with their own vital space, still living within their natural rhythms, still free. They are the first figures she meets and through their freedom, through their unbounded, unencumbered spirit, Avey Johnson begins a reconnecting, her new contacting.

Traversing symbolic space, she enters the shrine space and is received by the hand of the elder griot, Lebert Joseph, who later, as it were, in a linked continuum, reposits Avey Johnson into the hands of those African mother women, keepers of the faith, votive attendants of the altar of the shrine-repository of the African presence.

> And the moment she saw them sitting there in their long somber dresses, their black hands folded in their laps and their filmy eyes overseeing everything on deck, she experienced a shock of recognition. (193)

In their kind embrace, on the bosom of the serene waters of the Caribbean sea, Avey purges herself of all the excess, the waste matter she has accumulated in her crossing, living, and wandering on other shores. In a series of spasms with a violence matching perhaps the damage consequent on her previous acquiring of matter, Avey is made to divest herself of the waste matter. Time and time again she undergoes the watery baptism, the expunging. Purged and, as it were, in the filth of the holds of a slave ship, but now a mourning ground, Avey is relinked to the whispering souls of her folk. Alone in the deckhouse,

> she had the impression as her mind flickered on briefly of other bodies lying crowded in with her in the hot, airless dark. A multitude it felt like lay packed around her in the filth and stench of themselves, just as she was. Their moans, rising and falling with each rise and plunge of the schooner, enlarged upon the one filling her head. (209)

Avey is going home. Home to these new Caribbean shores, so different from the apartment on Halsey Street or the Westchester house. Home here is a clean, unadorned libated space, with its "room in the rosewater glow of the lamp . . . sparsely furnished" (215). In this sanctuary, rich with the harvests of the earth and adorned with a pure altar piece, are two ritual representations,

> a lighted candle in a holder and, next to it on a plate, a roasted ear of corn fresh from the harvest. An embroidered runner—a starched, immaculate white—had been placed under them for the occasion. (213)

Avey Johnson undergoes her period of ritual traveling during which there is an emptying of her former life with a "yawning hole where her life had once been" (214). She is washed and cleansed by Rosalie Parvay, the shepherd woman, daughter of the elder, Lebert Joseph, and by her acolyte.

> She discovered Rosalie Parvay, the bath finished at last, gently rubbing her back with a lime-scented oil from a bottle the maid was holding. (221)

All during this ritual cleaning, Rosalie Parvay chants Avey's return to the flock, to the fold, the reawakening of wonder, the soothing of the spirit.

> Her lips began to move, and the silence was broken by what sounded like a plainsong or a chant—a long string of half-spoken, half-sung words in Patois. It was a curious, scarcely audible singsong. (220)

Indeed there is a balm in "Gilead." Later, the true balming, the powerful laying on of hands, ungirdles Avey's loins. Under the ceaseless kneading of Rosalie Parvay's hands, and through the urgency of their summons, a vital contacting occurs, restoring circulation and flow to a dammed-up, unused radial center, to the "remotest corners of her body" (224).

Now at last the final ceremony, the intoning of the praisesong for the widow, takes place in the deep, dark, Caribbean night. At a crossroads in the hills, Avey, accompanied by her shepherd sister, meets the ageless spirit form, Lebert Joseph:

> The crippled figure up ahead shifted to his good leg, pulled his body as far upright as it would go (throwing off at least a thousand years as he did), and was hurrying forward with his brisk limp to take her arm. (233)

As he unlatches and opens the gate and then with great ceremony ushers Avey Johnson through it, he is once again the ageless, misshapen creature she thought she saw on the road below. It is he who leads her into the yard where are gathered all the nations, all the elders, where the African spirit presence, Ogun, calls to offer his greetings.

Avey's return to the source, to the native land, is drummed out on the libated drum heads. The spirit songs chorus that commingling of sorrow and joy, the anguish and the vital empowerment wherein coheres that ecstatic history of African peoples. In a clear strong voice, Marshall articulates all the visceral spirit quality enshrining the history of the sorrow songs.

> And the single, dark, plangent note this produced, like that from the deep bowing of a cello, sounded like the distillation of a thousand sorrow songs . . . . The note was a lamentation that could hardly have come from the rum keg of a drum. Its source had to be the heart, the bruised still-bleeding innermost chamber of the collective heart. (244–245)

And slowly Avey Johnson, there in the Caribbean, entering the ordained circle of the nation dance, consecrates the memory of Tatem, of her Great-aunt Cuney, and of the old folk who kept vigil over their root dance. Indeed, after the beg-pardon, Avey treads the earth of return, her feet lifting but always touching that earth.

> Not once did the soles of her feet leave the ground . . . . her feet held to the restrained glide-and-stamp, the rhythmic trudge, the Carriacou Tramp, the shuffle designed to stay the course of history. Avey Johnson . . . in the company of these strangers who had become one and the same with people in Tatem. (250)

Now truly she is one with those who have never forgotten their roots and free at last, becomes.

Until suddenly Lebert Joseph did something. . . . He had remained at her side all along, watching her dance with the smile that was at once triumphant and fatherly, and dancing himself, the slow measured tramp. But as her arms went up . . . his smile faded. . . . His eyes probing deep . . . . His oversized hands went out, bringing out to a halt for a moment the slow-moving tide around them. . . .

To her utter bewilderment others in the crowd of aged dancers, taking their cue from him also, began doing the same. One after another of the men and women trudging past, who were her senior by years, would pause as they reached her. . . . Then, singing, they would continue on their way. (250–251)

And what is of the world
is of ours
to draw on
to build from
and no one has the patrimony
of the power of the world
we are not artifacts
of mastodons
and never must be
we must root ourselves
within the singing blue mists
of our mountains
indigenizing
all our waters
we must flow within the amber crystals
of our dreams
we must sing
beholden to the singing
of our lands
our rivers

beholden to our flowing dreams
beholden not to mastodons
and finding our way
to cross the rivers
we must find
that ultimate geology
within the mist of blue
within the hills of Mona
and find our dreams
within ourselves
together
and

to the sea
will flow
eight rivers
pure and free
and our children
sommersault
into their dreams

Wilfred Cartey, *Embryos,* 42–43

GLOSSARY

Bacra. White person, colonist; or a white native of lowly origins; also, octoroon.

Break buisse. Cut classes; run away from school.

Buse. To abuse; to curse out roundly.

Coasting lime. Hanging out and talking good-naturedly.

Courida. Thick underbrush in marshy area of Guyana.

Dougla Girl. A girl of mixed East Indian and African parents.

Dungle. Large slum area of West Kingston, Jamaica, that is home to some Rastas and many members of the underclass.

Fatigue. Pinpoint and exaggerate some quality in a person and tease them about it at length.

Fête. Party, dance, make merry.

Griot. In traditional West African culture, oral historian who recites from memory, with musical accompaniment, the history of a clan or group. He frequently also serves as the conscience of the group.

Houngan. A priest/holy man who conducts the rites in the *tonelle;* an intercessor between the living and the dead.

Janga. Brown river shrimp.

Kling-kling. A bird also called the tinkling grackle; a sound imitative of that bird's cry.

Labaria. Tropical rain forest snake.

Loup-garou. Werewolf-like creature; evil spirits in Trinidad and Tobago and other West Indian islands.

Mauvaise langue. To bad-mouth.

Ngoma. Ceremonial dance.

Obeah. West Indian form of African magic and witchcraft; the use of herbs, spiritualism, and the occult to heal, to cure, or to harm.

Osnaburg. Thick coarse cloth such as is used to clothe prisoners; formerly given to slaves as work clothes.

Panga. A short spear.

Picong. Tease humorously, cleverly, wittily; Trinidadian teasing and poking fun.

Pocomania. Cult mixing revivalism with ancestral spirit possession.

Saga boy. Someone who loves fine clothes, who loves women, and who often lives off them.

Shake church. Participative religious services, some of whose practitioners may achieve states of possession; shouters, shaker Baptists.

Soucoyant. Vampire-like creature; evil spirits in Trinidad and Tobago and
    other West Indian islands; "blood-sucker."

Springe. Trap.

Tonelle. Ritual space through which spirits are summoned and through which
    they may enter a larger ritual space; where a healing or confession takes
    place, presided over by a *Houngan.*

Wanderobo. A large bow.

BIBLIOGRAPHY

Anthony, Michael. *The Games Were Coming*. London: Andre Deutsch, 1963.
———. *Green Days by the River*. London: Andre Deutsch, 1965.
———. *The Year in San Fernando*. London: Andre Deutsch, 1965.
Barrett, Lindsay. *Song for Mumu: A Novel*. London: Longmans Green and Company Ltd., 1967.
Carew, Jan. *Black Midas*. London: Longman, 1970.
———. *The Wild Coast*. London: Secker and Warburg, 1958.
Clarke, Austin C. *Amongst Thistle and Thorns*. London: Heinemann, 1965.
———. *The Meeting Point: A Novel*. London: William Heinemann, Ltd., 1967.
Dathorne, O. R. *The Scholar-Man*. London: Cassell and Co. Ltd., 1964.
Dawes, Neville. *The Last Enchantment*. London: Macgibbon and Kee, 1960.
Guy, Rosa. *The Friends*. New York: Holt, Reinhart and Winston, 1973.
Harris, Wilson. *The Far Journey of Oudin*. London: Faber and Faber, 1961.
———. *The Guyana Quartet*. London: Faber and Faber, 1985.
———. *Palace of the Peacock*. London: Faber and Faber, 1960.
———. *The Whole Armour*. London: Faber and Faber, 1962.
Hearne, John. *The Autumn Equinox*. London: Faber and Faber, 1959.
———. *The Faces of Love*. London: Faber and Faber, 1957.
———. *Land of the Living*. London: Faber and Faber, 1961.
———. *Stranger at the Gate*. London: Faber and Faber, 1956.
———. *Voices under the Window*. London: Faber and Faber, 1955.
Hodge, Merle. *Crick Crack, Monkey*. London: Andre Deutsch, Ltd., 1970.
Jones, Marion Patrick. *Pan Beat*. Port of Spain, Trinidad: Columbus Publishers, Ltd., 1967.
Lamming, George. *The Emigrants*. London: Michael Joseph, 1954.
———. *In the Castle of My Skin*. London: Longman Group, 1970.
———. *Of Age and Innocence*. London: Allison and Busby, 1981.
———. *The Pleasures of Exile*. London: Michael Joseph, 1960.
———. *Season of Adventure*. London: Michael Joseph, 1960.
———. *Water with Berries*. London: Longman Group, Ltd., 1971.
Lovelace, Earl. *The Dragon Can't Dance*. Washington, D.C.: Three Continents Press, 1979.
———. *While Gods Are Falling*. London: Collins, 1965.
Mais, Roger. *The Three Novels of Roger Mais: The Hills Were Joyful Together, 1953; Brother Man, 1954; Black Lightning, 1955*. London: J. Cape, Ltd., 1966.
Marshall, Paule. *Brown Girl, Brownstones*. Chatham, N.J.: Chatham Bookseller, 1972.

————. *Praisesong for the Widow*. New York: G. P. Putnam's Sons, 1983.

McDonald, Ian. *The Humming-Bird Tree*. London: Heinemann, 1969.

Mittelholzer, Edgar. *Children of Kaywana, A Novel*. New York: John Day Company, 1952.

————. *The Harrowing of Hubertus*. London: Hogarth Press, 1950.

————. *Kaywana Blood*. London: Secker and Warburg, 1960.

————. *The Life and Death of Sylvia*. New York: The John Day Company, 1954.

————. *A Morning at the Office*. London: Hogarth Press, 1950.

————. *My Bones and My Flute*. London: Secker and Warburg, 1955.

————. *Of Trees and the Sea*. London: Secker and Warburg, 1956.

————. *Shadows Move Among Them*. Philadelphia: Lippincott, 1951.

————. *The Weather Family*. London: Secker and Warburg, 1959.

Naipaul, V. S. *A House for Mr. Biswas*. London: Andre Deutsch, 1961.

————. *Miguel Street*. New York: Vanguard Press, 1960.

————. *The Mimic Men*. New York: The MacMillan Company, 1967.

————. *The Mystic Masseur*. London: Andre Deutsch, 1957.

————. *The Suffrage of Elvira*. London: Andre Deutsch, 1958.

Patterson, H. Orlando. *The Children of Sisyphus*. London: New Authors, Ltd., 1964.

Reid, V. S. *The Leopard*. New York: Viking, 1958.

————. *New Day*. London: Heinemann, 1949.

Salkey, Andrew. *Escape to an Autumn Pavement*. London: Hutchison, 1960.

————. *A Quality of Violence*. London: New Beacon Books, 1978.

Selvon, Samuel. *A Brighter Sun: A Novel*. New York: Viking, 1953.

————. *The Housing Lark*. London: MacGibbon and Kee, 1965.

————. *An Island is a World*. London: MacGibbon and Kee, 1965.

————. *The Lonely Londoners*. London: A. Wingate, 1956.

————. *Turn Again Tiger*. London: MacGibbon and Kee, 1958.

————. *Ways of Sunlight*. New York: St. Martin's Press, 1957.

Stewart, John. *Last Cool Days*. London: Andre Deutsch, 1971.

St. Omer, Garth. *Another Place, Another Time*. London: Faber and Faber, 1968.

————. *The Lights on the Hill*. London: Faber and Faber, 1968.

————. *Nor Any Country*. London: Faber and Faber, 1969.

————. *A Room on the Hill*. London: Faber and Faber, 1968.

Thelwell, Michael. *The Harder They Come*. New York: Grove Press, Inc., 1980.

Williams, Denis. *Other Leopards*. London: New Authors, 1963.

INDEX

[This index lists all literary works by title and author. For convenient cross reference, the author's name is given in parentheses after the title, and works by each author are listed at the end of the author entry.]

Abortion, 214, 215, 227, 229, 251, 282. *See also* Pregnancy

Africa: call of ancestry, 56, 118, 154, 308, 436–437; characters from, 251–52, 258; history of, 81, 301, 303, 304–5, 309; and slavery, 23, 25; as source of culture, 71, 79, 292, 307, 467, 473; and spirit world, 24, 158, 471, 475, 481, 483; as symbol, 173, 302, 361, 434–35, 449; travel to, xv, 246, 300, 302, 306. *See also The Leopard; Other Leopards; The Scholar-Man*

Amongst Thistles and Thorns (Clarke): compared to other works, 155, 156, 161, 164, 165, 167, 169, 176; discussed, 155–60; quotations from, 155–60. *See also* Education; Rural life; Violence

Anancy tales, 280

Animals: characters linked to, 10, 16–17, 55, 324, 327, 365, 419, 424, 426–27, 445, 446; and landscape, 6, 51, 152, 415–16, 422; symbolic use of, 56, 120, 419–20, 424, 432–33, 438–39, 449. *See also* Dogs; Landscape

Another Place, Another Time (St. Omer): compared to other works, 225; discussed, 224–28; quotations from, 224–28. *See also* Education; Family life; Rape

Anthony, Michael: characterization in, 195, 205; landscape in, 115; sociopolitical issues in, 116, 193, 204. *See also* Works by: *The Games Were*

Coming; Green Days by the River; The Year in San Fernando

Artists, 386, 394–95, 408

The Autumn Equinox (Hearne): compared to other works, 361, 365; discussed, 356, 357, 366, 369, 370; quotations from, 357, 361, 363–64, 365, 369, 370. *See also* Animals; Landscape; Social action

Baptism, 75, 122; and identity, 301–2, 306, 308–10, 482. *See also* Religion; Water

Barbados: characters from, 282, 295, 297; landscape of, 59–60; life in, 155, 284–85, 299. *See also Amongst Thistles and Thorns; Of Trees and the Sea*

Barrett, Lindsay: landscape in, 122; sociopolitical issues in, 120; writing style of, 79, 118. *See also* Works by: *Song for Mumu: A Novel*

The Black Jacobins, 244–45

Black Lightning (Mais): compared to other works, 128–29, 134, 139–41, 143–47; discussed, 128, 134–36, 139; quotations from, 134, 139, 140, 141, 144, 145, 146, 147, 149. *See also* Loneliness; Suicide; Thunderstorm

Black men: as athletes, 201–2, 204, 231; madness of, 120, 341, 343; protests of, 27–28, 179, 342; as religious figures, 131, 146, 307, 471–73, 475, 481, 483; as servants, 47, 370, 445; as source of wisdom,

wives, 215, 282. *See also* Miscegenation, with white women; white men

The Whole Armour (Harris): compared to other works, 419, 427; discussed, 419–27; quotations from, 419–27. *See also* Animals; Death; Miscegenation

The Wild Coast (Carew): compared to other works, 53, 84; discussed, 54–58; quotations from, 55, 56–57, 58, 71–72, 81–82. *See also* Africa; Landscape; Rural life; Slavery

Williams, Denis: See *Other Leopards*

Writers: depictions of, 162–63, 349; qualities of, xiv, xv, 238–39, 241–42, 246, 274–75

The Year in San Fernando (Anthony): compared to other works, 192, 193; discussed, 192–96; quotations from, 193–95. *See also* Class system; Family life; Travel

Wilfred Cartey is a Martin Luther King Jr. Distinguished Professor at the Department of Black Studies, City College, City University of New York, where he has taught since 1973. Born and raised in Trinidad, Cartey has lived both on the island and in the United States since winning a Fulbright scholarship in 1955. In 1962, he suffered blindness as the result of airplane pressure destabilization, yet continued to teach and write. The esteemed poet and scholar now has eleven books of poetry and five volumes of literary criticism to his credit, including *The West Indies: Islands in the Sun* (T. Nelson & Sons), *Palaver: A Critical Anthology of African Literature* (T. Nelson & Sons), and the highly acclaimed *Whispers from the Continent: Literature of Contemporary Black Africa* (Random House).

During his long and illustrious career, Cartey has been a professor of comparative literature at Columbia University, a Distinguished Professor at Brooklyn College, a visiting scholar at a number of universities worldwide— including the University of California at Berkeley, Howard University, the University of Puerto Rico, and the University of Ghana—and a popular lecturer and contributor to numerous seminars and journals. The recipient of many awards (including election into the prestigious Black Academy of Arts and Letters), he was most recently honored by the African Heritage Studies Association for his outstanding scholarly contributions. Wilfred Cartey resides in New York City, where he teaches and edits *Cimarrón: Journal of Caribbean Culture*.

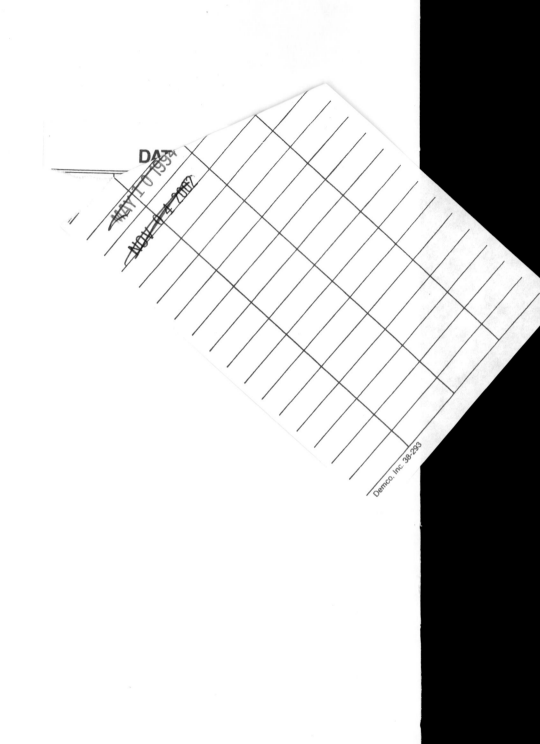